# Hiking Idaho

## HELP US KEEP THIS GUIDE UP TO DATE

Every effort has been made by the authors and editors to make this guide as accurate and useful as possible. However, many things can change after a guide is published—trails are rerouted, regulations change, techniques evolve, facilities come under new management, and so on.

We would appreciate hearing from you concerning your experiences with this guide and how you feel it could be improved and kept up to date. While we may not be able to respond to all comments and suggestions, we'll take them to heart, and we'll also make certain to share them with the authors. Please send your comments and suggestions to the following address:

Globe Pequot Press
Reader Response/Editorial Department
PO Box 480
Guilford, CT 06437

Or you may e-mail us at: editorial@GlobePequot.com

**Thanks for your input, and happy trails!**

# Hiking Idaho

A Guide to the Area's Greatest Hiking Adventures

Third Edition

**Ralph and Jackie J. Maughan and Luke Kratz**

FALCON GUIDES

GUILFORD, CONNECTICUT
HELENA, MONTANA

AN IMPRINT OF GLOBE PEQUOT PRESS

FALCONGUIDES®



Maps by Design Maps Inc.
Library of Congress Cataloging-in-Publication Data
Kratz, Luke, 1974
Maughan, Ralph, 1945-
Hiking Idaho / by Ralph Maughan & Jackie Johnson Maughan.—2nd ed.
p. cm.—(A Falcon guide)
ISBN 0-7627-1113-2
1. Hiking—Idaho—Guidebooks. 2. Idaho—Guidebooks. I. Maughan, Jackie Johnson, 1948- II. Title. III. Series.
GV199.42.I2 M38 2001
917.9604'34—dc21 2001040247
ISBN 978-0-7627-7087-8

Printed in the United States of America
10 9 8 7 6 5 4 3 2 1

This book is dedicated to all family and friends who throughout the years have taught generations respect and gratitude for the wild and scenic places we know in Idaho.

In memory of H.W.W. "Blue Moose" Johnson (1918–77), outfitter and guide, Frank Church–River of No Return Wilderness. Thanks, Dad, for helping us love these wild places of the heart and of the landscape.

Little by little we push back
Free flowing river and wilderness tract,
Winnow the color from the blue
And starve upon the residue.

What is the use in tears and laughter?
The root of the thing is what we're after.
But fallen trees will spill their fruit
And worms and darkness keep the root.

Fallen days stagnate with silt,
But cardboard castles must be built.
And so while we industrialize
A bird outwits us twice as wise.

There's no sweet repose or spiritual wine
From concrete monsters with juice on the line.
And a push-button world will never light
Joy by day or stars by night.

H.W.W. "Blue Moose" Johnson

# Acknowledgments

This is to acknowledge those who contributed to this new edition of *Hiking Idaho* with hikes, rehikes, trail descriptions, and photographs: Ric Bailey, Phil Blomquist, Don Crawford, Katie Fite, Gwen Gerber, Josh Keeley, Anne Kratz, Catherine Kratz, John Kratz, Lawrence Kratz, Mary Kratz, Mark Leininger, John McCarthy, Lee Mercer, Chris Murphy, Jamie Dewey, Cecile Perez, and Lindsey Tucker.

# Contents

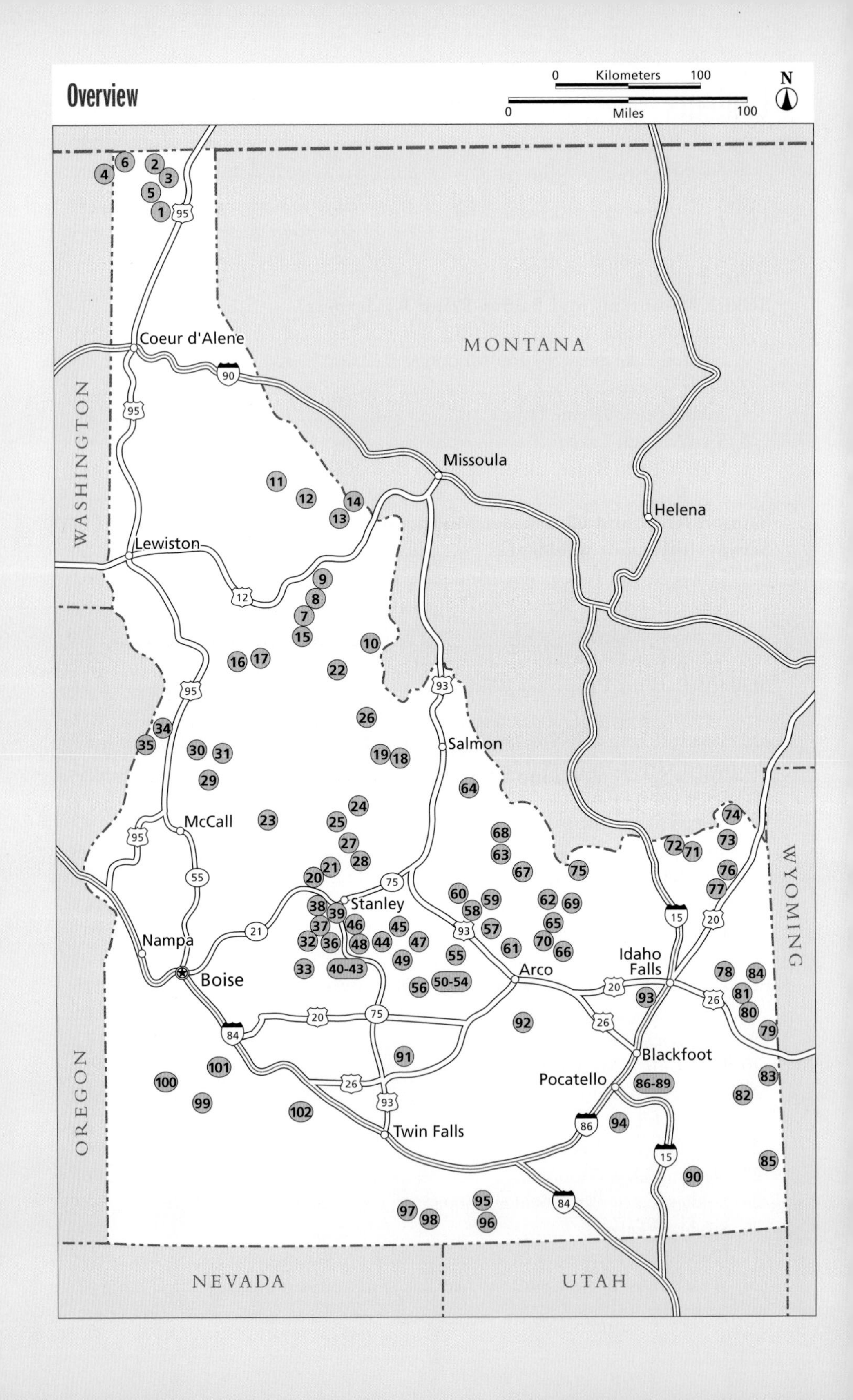
Overview
0 Kilometers 100
0 Miles 100
N
MONTANA
WASHINGTON
OREGON
NEVADA
UTAH
WYOMING
Coeur d'Alene
Missoula
Helena
Lewiston
Salmon
McCall
Stanley
Nampa
Boise
Arco
Idaho Falls
Blackfoot
Pocatello
Twin Falls
95
90
12
93
55
75
21
20
84
26
15
86
1
2
3
4
5
6
7
8
9
10
11
12
13
14
15
16
17
18
19
20
21
22
23
24
25
26
27
28
29
30
31
32
33
34
35
36
37
38
39
40-43
44
45
46
47
48
49
50-54
55
56
57
58
59
60
61
62
63
64
65
66
67
68
69
70
71
72
73
74
75
76
77
78
79
80
81
82
83
84
85
86-89
90
91
92
93
94
95
96
97
98
99
100
101
102

*The East Fork of the Wood River trail #50 begins in rugged terrain at over 8,000 feet.*
PHOTO BY LUKE KRATZ

# INTRODUCTION

### Welcome!

Idaho is one the most diverse states for hiking and exploring new landscapes. It is truly a gem, where you can find places to get away and explore without paying exorbitant amounts for guides, lodging, or transportation. There is great variety in the landscape as well as in creating excursions that work for your time and abilities.

*This book has two simple goals:*

1. To provide supplementary information to hikers as to the locations of various trails throughout the state and general descriptions of the hikes.
2. To introduce people to the diverse natural settings found in Idaho so they may enjoy, respect, and help protect these areas for future generations.

## Idaho's Backcountry

As citizens of a beautiful green planet, we must act as stewards to use the land appropriately but preserve natural places for the flora and fauna we share the earth with well into the distant future. In a fast-paced world of exponentially growing technology and pressures, it is also a relief to know that wild places of healing and recuperation still exist.

Idaho has more undeveloped backcountry than any other state except Alaska. The percentage of accessible and inhabitable scenic country that remains roadless and untamed by humans within its borders could be among the highest anywhere in the planet. Recreational use of wilderness areas has been increasing through the years and in some places has doubled or even quadrupled. While recreational use such as hiking poses less of a threat than development, there are still measures all visitors should take. It is becoming ever more crucial that users touch the land only lightly.

The wilderness is available to the public to share and will be further preserved if we all follow some general guidelines.

**Litter:** Pack out what you packed in. All items, including perishables such as toilet paper and sanitary napkins, should be either burned or carried out. Human waste should be buried deep in the humus layer of the soil, and latrines should be located at least 200 feet away from watercourses.

**Backcountry camping:** Most backpacking trails have many places available for camping that have been previously used. If at all possible, camp below timberline at least 200 feet from a lake or stream and at least 100 feet away from the trail. This is to ensure less impact on the area and a more enjoyable experience for campers.

**Fires:** Make sure all aluminum or cooking debris is packed out of fire rings. Save campfires for campsites with existing fire rings. Make sure a fire is completely out before you rest or leave the site.

**Cleaning:** Do all cleaning of dishes, clothes, and so on with soap (including "biodegradable" soap) away from water sources such as lakes, rivers, springs, streams, or creeks. Dispose of the dirty water away from the water source.

**Off-trail hiking:** Stay on the trail and avoid "shortcuts" through switchbacks; these contribute to erosion and damage plant growth. When you're hiking off-trail use good judgment to avoid disturbing fragile areas, especially in pristine alpine country where natural vegetation is fragile.

## History of Wilderness

Once all the earth was wild, but now only fragments of its four billion years of history before humankind are left, some protected in the National Wilderness Preservation System, more in national parks and monuments, and much protected informally by the continual struggle of folks who love the land and fight off recurring attempts to damage it.

In 1964, after years of political struggle, the US Congress recognized the value of pristine undeveloped land and passed the Wilderness Act. The act empowers Congress to protect select parts of roadless public lands. It allows for permanently setting aside exceptional undeveloped public lands. The designation of undeveloped public land as wilderness prohibits the use of recreational motorized vehicles, construction of roads and buildings, logging, and most mining activity within its boundaries. It does not exclude livestock grazing that was in place before the wilderness designation. Pack animals, hunting, fishing, camping, and hiking are encouraged by the Wilderness Act. Wilderness designation is a very powerful tool for protecting pristine public lands. Unfortunately, it is a form of protection that is increasingly difficult to achieve because Congress has become more and more anti-wilderness since the late 1980s.

As of 2000 about 3,900,000 acres (6,100 square miles) of wild public land in Idaho have been permanently protected as part of the National Wilderness Preservation System. There are five designated wilderness areas that are all, or partially, in Idaho: the Selway-Bitterroot, the Frank Church–River of No Return, the Sawtooth, Hells Canyon, Gospel Hump, and Craters of the Moon National Monument Wilderness. The Salmo-Priest Wilderness adjoins roadless land in Idaho, but the legal wilderness is in Washington state.

Most of Idaho's roadless country has no strong legal protection. Each year hundreds of square miles of this "de facto" wilderness falls to the ax and bulldozer. The pace of wilderness destruction accelerated when Congress passed the "timber salvage rider" in 1996. Called the worst piece of public lands legislation ever to become law by prominent columnist Jessica Matthews, this law suspended all environmental protections governing logging on national forest lands. Conservation groups referred to it as "Logging Without Laws."

The justification given by the supporters of the law was the emergency need to "salvage" the wood in dead and dying forests. The reality of this law is that *salvage* is defined in such a way that most of the logging taking place is of perfectly healthy, large green trees. Most sales of burned and dead trees have no bidders. It is estimated that the law will cost American taxpayers about $1 billion because revenues received don't come close to the costs of administering the salvage sales.

In Idaho this law was used to destroy several hundred thousand acres of roadless land. The most severely affected national forests were the Boise and the Payette, but national forests throughout the United States felt the sting of this legislation. After the bill expired in 1997, the Clinton administration set about to prevent further damage by reducing the timber cut in the national forests, and in 2000 President Clinton took steps to protect all remaining roadless national forest land, not as wilderness but at least without any new permanent roads. Whether this effort prevails still depends on future politics.

In all about ten million acres of de facto wilderness still exists on your public lands in Idaho. For years most Idaho conservationists advocated a compromise that would protect about four million acres of this as designated wilderness. Despite many congressional attempts, no more wilderness has been designated in Idaho since 1980, when the Frank Church–River of No Return Wilderness was established.

Many wilderness supporters have come to believe that in Idaho compromise has yielded no benefits. As a result, in the last several years, most of the major groups favoring wilderness have come to advocate that all land still wild in Idaho be kept that way.

The immediate prospects for change in Idaho appear dim. The League of Conservation Voters yearly rates Idaho's congressional delegation as among the worst in the country. Several of Idaho's congressional members are supporting legislation to give management of America's public land in Idaho to the Idaho State Land Board or to the timber corporations.

Cherish your trips into Idaho's backcountry. This opportunity could disappear. That any of Idaho is left is entirely the result of a time when Idaho public officials, both Republicans and Democrats, cherished protecting the outdoors; of the constant efforts of local and national conservation groups; and of an environmentally friendly administration in Washington from 1993 to 2000.

—Ralph Maughan and Jackie Johnson Maughan, 2001

In more recent years we have developed the technology to view the world from satellite images and see how limited the space on the planet is. Protection of wilderness is a growing concern, with many philosophies on how and why to preserve certain areas. Many people are still of the mind-set that the earth is for the taking and its enjoyment is at its own expense. Growing trends toward using off-road machinery and developing lands for housing and business encroach upon truly natural settings. We need to find ways to gently persuade others how important true wilderness is. Become educated about what is truly best for people and the environment. If there are imminent threats to places sacred to you, then please email representatives or organizations your concerns to make your voice heard. Check out the conservation organizations that have been listed in appendix A of this book and get involved today!

Several areas in the Owyhee desert have become protected wildernesses. Currently two potential national monuments are under review. The long awaited Boulder/White Cloud national monument and Caldera national monument which encompasses over 700,000 acres Island Park area would have potential to become protected. If enough voices are heard these land can be kept wild for many generations.

The hiker believes in minimal impact to the earth. As you lightly tread along trails into wild places full of life and adventure, it is my hope that you find a sense of peace and gratitude for the opportunity to fully connect with natural surroundings.

—Luke Kratz, 2014

## Type of Hike

Suggested hikes in this book have been split into the following categories:

**Day hike:** This is best for short excursions, due to lack of either water or suitable camping sites.

**Backpack:** Best for backpacking, with one or more nights in the backcountry. Many of the overnight hikes can be done as day hikes if you have the time and stamina.

**Loop:** Starts and finishes at the same trailhead with no (or very little) retracing of your steps. Sometimes the definition of a *loop* is stretched to include creative shapes (like a figure eight or a lollipop), and sometimes the hike requires a short walk on a dirt road to get you back to the trailhead.

**Out-and-back:** A hike that travels the same route coming and going. The route back will feel different, with new sights and vantage points.

**Shuttle:** A point-to-point trip that requires two vehicles (one at each end of the trail) or a prearranged pickup at a designated time and place. One effective way to manage the logistical difficulties of shuttles is to arrange for a second party to start at the other end of the trail. The two parties then rendezvous at a predetermined time and place along the trail, trade keys, and meet later.

**Options:** Also available on many of the hikes for further travel and exploration of nearby areas as long as you have the ambition and knowledge of the area.

## Distance

Measuring trail distances is an inexact science. In this edition most distances have been taken from map measurements and from in-the-field estimates. Most trail signs in the backcountry do not include distances, and when they do you can bet they are just someone's best guess. Policy in many wilderness areas has become to minimize the number of signs and the information they give.

Some of the distances are based on "as the crow flies" rather than actual hiking mileage. As GPS units become more common and technically advanced, exact distances will become available.

Keep in mind that distance is often less important than difficulty. A steep 2-mile climb on rocky tread can take longer than a 5-mile stroll through a gentle river valley. It may be helpful to note that most hikers average about 2 miles an hour on relatively level ground.

## Approximate Hiking Time

Again, these are estimates and do not account for stops and off-trail exploration. Some hike times are measured in hours while others, including backpacking expeditions, are measured in days. They don't include the time it takes to reach the trailhead. Hiking times should give you a general idea of how to plan for your trip.

## Difficulty

Difficulty ratings are inherently flawed: What's easy for you might be difficult for someone else. Still, such ratings serve as a general guide and give an approximation of a hike's challenge. Remember that ratings are not the final word, and that the most important factor is to be honest about your own fitness level when planning your trip. In this guidebook difficulty ratings consider both how long and how strenuous a hike is. Here are general guidelines for the ratings:

**Easy:** Suitable for any hiker—young or old. Expect no serious elevation gain, hazards, or navigation problems.

**Moderate:** Suitable for hikers who have at least some experience and an average fitness level. Likely includes some elevation change and may have places where the trail is faint.

**Strenuous:** Suitable only for experienced hikers with above-average fitness levels. May feature hazardous trail sections, navigation difficulties, and serious elevation change.

## Best Season

This heading tells you the best months of the year to venture out on the given trail. Many trails have only a short window of "hiking season" due to spring runoff and fall hunting season. If you're hiking during any other times of the year, please take the necessary precautions.

## Trail Surface

Nearly all of the trails in this guide have normal trail surfaces of dirt with rock gravel or stones found along or in the trail. Good footwear is a must for any trail. This is one of those you-get-what-you pay-for situations: Good boots and careful hiking does avoid blisters and ankle sprains, which can sadly lead to months or more without hiking.

## Land Status

This indicates the name of the agency or organization managing the land where the trail is located. Most of the trails are on USDA Forest Service land or lands governed by the Bureau of Land Management.

More information on national forests of Idaho can be found at www.fs.usda.gov.

## Canine Compatibility

Dogs can be great hiking companions and enjoy the outdoors as well as hikers. However, our furry friends can also wreak havoc on the land, native critters, and other hikers. Because of this most land agencies insist that pets be under control or leashed; they are not allowed in designated wilderness areas. The headings used are: **Voice control, On Leash,** or **No dogs allowed.**

## Fees and Permits

These may vary from year to year. Most recently a permit was not needed for trails in the Sawtooth National Recreation Area, but that could change. In some wilderness areas a permit is required, but that is usually available upon entrance into the wilderness. Fees for backcountry permits and campground parking are also needed in some areas. If in doubt, check in with the nearest forest service ranger station.

## Maps

The maps in this book serve as a general guide to get you started. It is always better to have more maps of the area in addition to consulting with the forest service about it. Remember, trail conditions can change on a dime.

**Forest service maps:** The forest service has maps of all of the national forests, and over time these maps have become more detailed and more accurate. Nevertheless, they are usually not sufficient for a hike that is the slightest bit complicated. Most wilderness areas have their own forest service maps for purchase, and a number of private groups have available for purchase maps of selected wilderness or prime backcountry areas.

**USGS maps:** Usually the very best maps are the topographic quadrangles of the United States Geological Survey. They come in a number of degrees of detail, but we recommend the most detailed, the 1:24,000, 7.5-minute scale. In past editions of this guide, some parts of Idaho lacked 7.5-minute USGS quadrangles. Hikers had to use the less detailed 15-minute topos. Now all of Idaho is mapped to the 7.5-minute scale. However, don't count on these maps being completely accurate. They are revised on a ten- to thirty-year schedule, so recent changes in trails, roads, fires, timbering, rivers, and lakes may not appear.

Maps can be purchased at outdoor specialty stores in Idaho cities and most of the tourist towns near the hike locations. Maps are also available from many sources on the Internet, including the USGS site (www.usgs.gov) and www.trails.idaho.gov.

## Trail Contact

This is the contact information for the given trail's land governing agency. The people here are quite willing to assist, provide updates on the trails, and answer any questions you may have.

Some websites that may help include:

**USDA Forest Service:** www.fs.usda.gov

**Bureau of Land Management in Idaho:** www.blm.gov/id

**Other sites:**

trails.idaho.gov

wilderness.net

## Natural History and Geography of Idaho

Idaho has a more diverse natural topography within its borders than most places. It has oceans of basalt-covered lava flows and semi-arid deserts, fertile rolling hills, temperate rain forests, and perhaps a greater percentage of land area covered by many types of mountains than any other state. It hosts the deepest canyon on the continent as well as the highest sand dunes. It also has the most wild waterways and natural hot springs in the lower forty-eight. Altitude ranges from 700 feet to well over 12,000 feet.

**Topography and mountain ranges:** When you drive across the state of Idaho, it seems like a relatively flat agricultural land dotted with cities and towns. This is because most people in Idaho live along or near the Snake River Plain, from the Boise area to Idaho Falls. Even northern Idaho cities are far from the vast wilderness areas. What people rarely see is the miles and miles of mountainous country that cover the state.

In eastern Idaho near Wyoming are mountain ranges termed the Middle Rocky Mountains. The various long strips of mountain ranges in the south are part of the Basin and Range physiographic province, a vast area that covers all of Nevada and part of Utah and Arizona. Southwest Idaho is part of the Columbia Plateau. Most of Idaho north of the Snake River Plain consists of the Northern Rocky Mountains, including the Great Divide along the border with Montana. You could walk from the Boise Front all the way to Canada or along the divide and be in mountains all the way!

Idaho has wet and dry areas and everything in between. Storms from the Pacific water the western slopes and especially the north, where large trees grow and temperate rain forest ecology is present. As the storms head eastward, less moisture is sucked out and the mountains on the eastern side of the state—some of the highest in Idaho—are semi-arid. Idaho's narrow southern ranges may appear to be dry at their base, but their upper elevations form small "sky islands" that are quite moist and lush. The Middle Rocky Mountains receive intermediate amounts of moisture and are especially prone to summer thunderstorms.

**Geology: Summary of the Geologic Provinces of Idaho**

**1. Idaho Batholith:** The Idaho Batholith comprises two main lobes in central Idaho. The Atlanta lobe, named after the historic mining town in the heart of the Sawtooth Mountains, forms the large expanse in south-central Idaho. The Bitterroot lobe in north-central Idaho is named after the dividing range between Idaho and Montana. These lobes underlie much of the Sawtooth and Salmon-Bitterroot, and portions of the Frank Church–River of No Return Wildernesses. The smaller lobe exposed in the panhandle is called the Kaniksu Batholith. The Idaho Batholith represents the period in Idaho's geologic history, between 110 and 60 million years ago (Late Cretaceous), when great melts were created deep in the earth's crust during the collision of exotic terranes to the west. Millions of years of uplift, erosion, and faulting (still active in Sawtooth Valley) have led to their present-day exposure.

**2. Belt Supergroup:** This 9-mile-thick package of rock, exposed from British Columbia (known as the Purcell Supergroup) to Montana and Idaho, is quite enigmatic. Its immense thickness, large aerial expanse, and immaculately preserved sedimentary features remain a puzzle for geologists. The Belt Supergroup preserves a depositional history of a long-lived shallow lake or sea between about 1.5 and 1.4 billion years ago, well before the emergence of plants or animals and quite a bit before North America rifted from Australia, Antarctica, or Siberia. These strata formed as environments such as beaches, shoals, mudflats, and lake bottoms were superpositioned by progressive deposition and burial over geologic time. Originally made up of sandstone, siltstone, and mudstone, these innumerable layers are now metamorphosed to quartzite, schist, and slate.

**3. Columbia River Plateau:** The Columbia River Plateau is a geologic and physiographic province spanning much of eastern Washington and Oregon and portions of western Idaho. In west-central Idaho the plateau rises to elevations of over 4,000 feet and is exposed along the Snake River. It is underlain by package of flood basalt 0.6 to 1.2 miles thick that, between seventeen and fourteen million years ago, literally flooded the earth's surface, erupting from volcanic vents and rifts. This occurred around the same time that the Owyhee Volcanic Field came into being to the southwest (sixteen million years ago), when the southwestern arm of the Snake River Plain began forming. Current studies suggest that the eruption of voluminous amounts of basalt of the Columbia River Group was the result of impingement of the Yellowstone hot spot beneath the North American tectonic plate. This hot spot is hypothesized to have originated at least 125 miles and possibly as deep as 375 miles in the earth's mantle, risen by thermal buoyancy, and finally erupted onto the surface.

**4. Accreted Terrane:** The relatively small exposure of accreted terrane is well exposed in Hells Canyon along the Snake River at Idaho's border with Oregon and Washington. As an exotic terrane, this body of rock formed somewhere in the proto–Pacific Ocean about 370 to 250 million years ago as a volcanic island arc, much like Japanese archipelago and the Aleutian Islands. In the Cretaceous, the tectonic plate carrying this chain of volcanoes collided with the North American Plate in the Middle Cretaceous around 120 to 100 million years ago. The exposed rock has the namesake of the mountains they make up, the Seven Devils Mountains in west-central Idaho.

**5. Challis Volcanic Field:** Between fifty-two and forty-five million years ago, a series of explosive eruptions formed the Challis Volcanic Field. A large expanse of central Idaho is underlain by these rocks, including much of the Salmon-Challis National Forest and the Frank Church–River of No Return Wilderness. In contrast with the slow-moving molasses-like flood basalts that effusively covered the Snake River Plain and the Columbia Plateau, these volcanic rocks were violently explosive due to their differing chemical composition. Similarly, as they erupted, the source magma chamber in the earth's crust was emptied. Current research suggests that the Challis magmatic episode resulted from a series of tectonic events that led to tectonic and magmatic instability. First, the dense oceanic Farallon Plate (once at the bottom of the Pacific Ocean) was subducted beneath the more buoyant North American Plate. The wet oceanic slab lent its water to the surrounding mantle, thus causing the ingredients to produce large volumes of magma beneath central Idaho, which then rose through the planet's crust and eventually erupted.

**6. Snake River Plain:** The astounding geologic history of the Yellowstone hot spot is still very apparent when you view the Snake River Plain. From a plane or on a physical map, you can observe the clear track of lowlands and plains that runs across southern Idaho leading westward right into Yellowstone National Park. Using the essential words of James Hutton, founder of geology, that "the present is the key to the past," geologists have observed that the Yellowstone volcanic caldera is just the most recent in a long series of calderas that go as far back as sixteen million years and as far east as the Oregon-Idaho-Nevada junction. The Snake River Plain is essentially the blazed path formed as the North American Plate traveled southwest over the fixed Yellowstone hot spot. Geologists have confirmed the relative movement of the plate by demonstrating a northeast-younging age-progression of calderas on the Snake River Plain.

**7. Basin and Range:** The Basin and Range, a prominent physiographic and geologic province of the southwest United States, stretches from the Mojave Desert to its northeastern corner here in Idaho. As you drive east or west across it, you'll notice the typical pattern of range, basin, range, and so on. It has formed much like the stretch marks on a rubber band as you pull slowly to its full extent and has led to the modern topography we see at the earth's surface. Active crustal extension has occurred over the last fifteen million years and continues along many active faults like the Sawtooth fault near Stanley, Idaho, and the Wasatch fault in Utah. We have this tectonic activity to thank for the spectacular mountain ranges from the Bear River Range to the south to the Lost River Range. The location of the Basin and Range is also accompanied by an older geologic province called the Idaho-Utah-Wyoming fold-and-thrust belt. This curved mountain belt is best seen on a physical map near the Idaho-Wyoming border, where large, relatively thin sheets of rock were thrust eastward as much as 37 miles. This deformation was the result of collision of accreted terranes to the west.

**8. Owyhee Plateau:** The origin and history of the Owyhee Plateau is much like the Snake River Plain with the exception that it never subsided.

### Summary of the Geologic History of Idaho

In short, the geologic history of Idaho begins with accreting terranes between 2.5 and 1.7 billion years ago in several mountain-building events in the Early Proterozoic era. Deposition and erosion continued routinely over geologic time until to the piecemeal North American (or Laurentian) continent was formed. At the time when the Purcell-Belt Supergroup was being deposited, North America was still connected to another landmass. Geologists suggest that Australia, Antarctica, or Siberia was positioned just to the west of Idaho. Several billion years passed before this "supercontinent" began to rift around 700 million years ago in the Late Proterozoic era. North America finally began drifting away from its western counterpart by 600 million years ago. What followed was similar to the present-day Atlantic coast, a passive margin, where up to 7.5 miles of sediments were accumulated along the continent margin in to the proto–Pacific Ocean. This stage of passive deposition lasted until about 300 million years ago and saw the dawning of complex life in the ocean and finally the invasion of land by plants and animals.

Millions of years passed in Idaho before the proto-Pacific began subducting beneath the North American Plate in the Mesozoic era. Between 110 and 60 million years ago, the Idaho Batholith formed deep in the earth's crust, followed by accretion of the Seven Devils Group and thrusting of tectonic sheets in the Idaho-Utah-Wyoming fold-and-thrust belt. During this crustal compression, the subducted oceanic slabs were finding their way into the earth's mantle beneath Idaho. When the speed of subduction slowed, the Farallon Plate became unstable and it roll backward into a steeper angle, resulting in extension and magmatism at the surface manifested as the Challis magmatic episode around fifty-two to forty-five million years ago in the Cenozoic era. Since then, crustal extension has taken many forms and has occurred in at least two phases. The modern Basin and Range extensional faulting began around twelve million years ago and seemed to have been aided by volcanism along the Snake River Plain and the migration of the Yellowstone hot spot.

The times from the Late Miocene (fifteen million years ago) to the present have been dominated by rift basin development, subsequent deposition, and sporadic volcanism. Relationships among faulting, erosion, climate, and volcanism have resulted in a very complex history. Ten million years ago the Yellowstone hot spot was just north of Pocatello, causing all streams to flow south. When the Snake River Plain subsided, the streams changed their course back to north. After the ice age, glacial meltwater had created the enormous glacial Lake Bonneville, which eventually rose to the elevation of Red Rock Pass near Downey, Idaho. There it breached an earthen dam and cataclysmically flooded the Snake River Plain drainage, carrying large boulders from there all the way to Hagarman Falls.

—Josh Keeley

**Suggested non-technical reading:** *Roadside Geology of Idaho,* by David D. Alt and Donald W. Hyndman; *Etched in Stone: The Geology of City of Rocks National Reserve and Castle Rocks State Park, Idaho,* by Kevin R. Pogue; *Rocks, Rails and Trails,* by Paul Karl Link and E. Chilton Phoenix; *Geology of the Pacific Northwest,* by William N. Orr and Elizabeth L. Orr; *Basin and Range,* by John McPhee; *Northwest Exposures,* by David Alt and Donald W. Hyndman.

Geologic Provinces of Idaho: Modified from Digital Geology of Idaho at geology.isu.edu.

**Forests:** Over 40 percent of Idaho is forested. Climate, latitude, and elevation all impact soils of the various woodlands. The forest types are most easily understood when broken down into the different ecological life zones where certain tree species thrive.

**Lower Sonoran Zone:** In lower elevations much of Idaho's land is either sagebrush deserts or prairies of tall or short grasses. Cottonwood trees dominate the lowland forests alongside rivers.

**Upper Sonoran Zone:** This is where the expanses of the Great Basin Desert give way to sporadic forests of junipers and occasional pinyon and limber pines. These areas are quite dry and found primarily in southern Idaho and in the Snake River Plain at elevations of 5,000 to 7,000 feet.

**Transition Zone:** Here there is a transition from arid to lush mountain country normally at 5,500 to 8,000 feet. In Idaho, the western slopes are usually dominated by forests of ponderosa pine; the east are Douglas fir. Aspen groves begin here as well.

**Canadian Zone:** Also known as the Montane Zone, this area receives more yearly precipitation and snowfall. These forests usually begin at around 7,000 feet, but are at much lower elevations in the north, where they become the temperate rain forests of the Pacific Northwest. These north Idaho forests are full of western red cedar, Douglas fir, white pine, hemlock, and larch trees. In most parts of the state, however, this zone is defined by forests of Douglas fir, lodgepole pine, and Engelmann spruce. In the Middle Rockies groves of quaking aspen thrive in these forests due to the moisture and fertile sedimentary rock. This also contributes to the abundance of many varieties of wildflowers in this zone.

*The largest of all deer, the moose commonly found in Idaho's backcountry.*
PHOTO BY ANNE KRATZ

**Hudsonian Zone:** In most parts of the state, this is where the forest begins thinning at upper elevations around 8,000 to 9,000 feet. Whitebark pines, subalpine firs, and subalpine spruce are introduced, with occasional groves of lodgepoles and Engelmann spruce. The trees become smaller, and the winters are harsher.

**Wildlife:** The wildlife of Idaho still consists of all the large North American animals before the settlements by Euro-Americans except the great bison herds. Idaho has populations of rare animals such as the grizzly bear, desert bighorn, and a small herd of woodland caribou. Idaho is also stronghold for the threatened lynx and the rare wolverine. Wolves were reintroduced to the state in 1995. More common predators include black bear, badger, bobcat, coyote, fox, and the rarely seen mountain lion.

Idaho has large herds of elk and both mule and white-tailed deer. Moose populations are growing while bighorn sheep, pronghorn antelope, and mountain goats have stable numbers in most of their range.

Unfortunately the salmon and the steelhead trout runs have been decimated by the dams on the lower Snake River in Washington State. Sturgeon, too, have been damaged by dams. The fish could make a comeback with continued efforts from environmental protection agencies.

**Landownership:** Perhaps the best thing about Idaho geography is that the American people own 62 percent of it, more than any state except Utah and Nevada. The national forests and Bureau of Land Management (BLM) lands in Idaho are part of America's heritage. They belong to all of us, and with eternal vigilance, monitoring, and fighting off threats, the politicians and special interests will not take them.

## Forest Fires

In August 1910 forest fires swept over three million acres of northern Idaho and northwestern Montana. On August 20 and 21 alone, in the "Big Blowup," several million acres burned, along with dozens of towns, and eighty-seven people died. Rain and snow on August 23 halted the firestorm, but this event left its impact on the forest and on forest policy for at least seventy-five years.

Even today, in some parts of remote Idaho mountains, there are vast meadows but few large trees. We describe several hikes in the "Great Burn" proposed wilderness. The great fire also launched the forest service on an extensive crusade to stamp out all forest fires.

As firefighting technology improved, the annual acreage of forest fires declined precipitously, but most of Idaho's forestland is forest that has been subject to natural burns every 20 to 30 years, depending on the type of trees. As years pass with no fires, small trees grow up under the big trees, forming a fuel ladder in which the forest giants are more likely to ignite in a fire.

In some parts of Idaho, the problem of too much fire suppression was complicated by bad logging practices, especially in ponderosa pine country, which originally consisted of scattered large ponderosa (yellow) pine with an understory of grass and small bushes beneath the fire-resistant boles of the great yellow pine. "Park-like" is how early timers described the area, but the yellow pine was a prize for timber interests. The biggest—and hence most fire-resistant—trees were cut, and the gentle ground fires were suppressed. The result was not harmless natural ground fires every twenty to thirty years, but hot fires in the dense coniferous forest that grew up where the ponderosa had been cut.

Beginning in the late 1970s, the forest service began to experiment with allowing some naturally ignited fires to burn in remote areas. Fires were also deliberately set in a few places during the spring, when fires burn light and tend not to spread. This may have been too little and too late, however.

In 1980 giant fires burned in the Frank Church–River of No Return Wilderness and also the Italian Peaks, and in the dry years since, many large fires have burned both inside and outside Idaho wilderness areas. In particular the years 1988, 1989, 1992, and 1994 saw many large forest fires; but the summer of 2000 almost became another 1910. Including range fires, in the summer of 2000 almost 1.3 million acres of land inside Idaho burned.

In 2000 there were major fires in every part of the state except the Selkirk Mountains rain forest of the extreme northwestern part of the panhandle. The largest fires were in central Idaho. Hundreds of thousands of acres burned in the Frank Church–River of No Return Wilderness and the roaded forest to its east and west. The largest single blaze was the 217,000-acre Clear Creek Fire, which included the lower portion of the Big Horn Crags in the wilderness area, but mostly burned developed forestland to the east.

Other large fires included the Burgdorf Fire northeast of McCall, the Trail Creek Fire just southwest of the Sawtooth Wilderness, and scores of others in the range of 1,000 to 20,000 acres. In 2012 the Mustang Complex fire burned over 350,000 acres north of Salmon.

These fires burned hot enough in some places to sterilize the soil. Such areas take a long time to recover. However, most fire areas saw a medium to light burn, with many patches of unburned area inside the perimeters of the fires. Left alone, burned areas that were not disturbed with heavy firefighting machinery will recover. We have little concern about the burns inside the Frank Church and the Selway-Bitterroot Wildernesses, which were by default at least not aggressively fought.

For the fires in which heavy machinery was used to build fire lines, or which were salvage-logged, recovery is more problematic. Machinery disturbs the blackened, but intact, ground. This accelerates runoff and, worse, grinds in the seeds of exotic weeds, such as spotted knapweed, that have invaded central Idaho. The legacy of the fires of 2000 may be not meadows and a slow return to forest, but rather, in disturbed lands, permanent gigantic patches of weeds that are not native to Idaho and are useless to wildlife.

Over the years many of the hikes described have burned, including some since 2000 when the last edition of this book was published. We have rehiked most of these trails to update the descriptions.

Hiking in burns has previously been an unusual experience, but it is becoming more common. Depending on the time of day, the light, and your mood, burns can be either beautiful or ugly and depressing. Fortunately, total burns do not usually extend over great distances, so you will find many unburned patches of trees. Meadows respond very nicely after burns. Fires often produce brilliant floral displays of lupine, fireweed, and aster for a few years. Morel mushrooms are also abundant for a year or two after a burn. Patchy burns can benefit wildlife.

You should be very cautious camping or hiking inside a burn because the dead trees—the snags—tend to fall, especially in windy conditions when the ground is wet, such as in a windy May or June. Burned lodgepole pine forests are the most dangerous because these trees have shallow roots. While three-quarters of a burned forest of subalpine fir may be standing fifty years after the fire, within a decade about 50 to 75 percent of burned lodgepole will have fallen.

## Pine Beetles

Pine beetles infect forests by eating the wood beneath the bark and killing the tree. This is also reason for cautious hiking in predominantly pine forests. They are currently in decline and have infected less than 750,000 acres of Idaho forests.

## Leave No Trace

### Leave No Trace Principles

- Leave with everything you brought in.
- Leave no sign of your visit.
- Leave the landscape as you found it.

Most of us know better than to litter—in or out of the backcountry. Be sure you leave nothing, regardless of how small it is, along the trail or at your campsite. This means you should pack out everything, including orange peels, flip tops, cigarette butts, and gum wrappers. Also, pick up any trash that others leave behind.

Follow the main trail. Avoid cutting switchbacks and walking on vegetation beside the trail. Don't pick up "souvenirs," such as rocks, antlers, and wildflowers. The next person wants to see them, too, and collecting such souvenirs violates many regulations.

Avoid making loud noises on the trail (unless you are in bear country) or in camp. Be courteous. Remember, sound travels easily in the backcountry, especially across water.

Carry a lightweight trowel to bury human waste 6 to 8 inches deep at least 200 feet from any water source. Pack out used toilet paper.

Go without a campfire. Carry a stove for cooking and a flashlight, candle lantern, or headlamp for light. For emergencies, learn how to build a no-trace fire.

Camp in obviously used sites when they are available. Otherwise, camp and cook on durable surfaces, such as bedrock, sand, gravel bars, and bare ground.

Leave no trace—and put your ear to the ground and listen carefully. Thousands of people coming behind you are thanking you for your courtesy and good sense.

Details on applying Leave No Trace principles to specific outdoor activities can be found in the FalconGuide *Leave No Trace*. Visit your local bookstore or call Globe Pequot Press at (800) 243-0495 to order a copy.

## Make It a Safe Trip

The Boy Scouts of America have been guided for decades by what is perhaps the single best piece of safety advice—Be prepared! For starters, this means carrying survival and first-aid materials, proper clothing, a compass, and a topographic map—and knowing how to use them. Perhaps the second-best piece of safety advice is to tell somebody where you're going and when you plan to return. Pilots must file flight plans before every trip, and anybody venturing into a blank spot on the map should do the same. File your "flight plan" with a friend or relative before taking off.

Close behind your flight plan and being prepared with proper equipment is physical conditioning. Not only does being fit make wilderness travel more fun, it makes it safer. Here are a few more tips:

- Check the weather forecast. Be careful not to get caught at high altitude during a bad storm or along a stream in a flash flood. Watch cloud formations closely so you don't get stranded on a ridgeline during a lightning storm. Avoid traveling during prolonged periods of cold weather.

- Avoid traveling alone in the wilderness; keep your party together.
- Don't exhaust yourself or other members of your party by traveling too far or too fast. Let the slowest person set the pace.
- Study basic survival and first aid before leaving home.
- Before you leave for the trailhead, find out as much as you can about the route, especially its potential hazards.
- Don't wait until you're confused to look at your maps. Follow them as you go along, so you have a continual fix on your location. Identify prominent landmarks and take care to notice how their images change as you progress along the trail.
- If you get lost, don't panic. Sit down and relax for a few minutes while you carefully check your topo map and take a compass reading. Then plan your next move. It's often smart to retrace your steps until you find familiar ground, even if you think it might lengthen your trip. Lots of people get temporarily lost in the wilderness and survive—usually by calmly and rationally dealing with the situation.
- Stay clear of all wild animals.
- Take a first-aid kit that includes, at a minimum, a sewing needle, a snakebite kit, aspirin (or other painkiller), antibacterial ointment, antiseptic swabs, butterfly bandages, adhesive tape, adhesive strips, gauze pads, two triangular bandages, two inflatable splints, moleskin or Second Skin for blisters, 3-inch gauze, a CPR shield, rubber gloves, and lightweight first-aid instructions.
- Take a survival kit that includes, at a minimum, a compass, a whistle, matches in a waterproof container, a cigarette lighter, a candle, a signal mirror, a flashlight, fire starter, aluminum foil, water purification tablets, a space blanket or large trash bag, and a flare.
- Lastly, don't forget that knowledge is the best defense against unexpected hazards. Read up on the latest in wilderness safety information in the FalconGuide *Wild Country Companion.*

## Should I Drink the Water?

There are few backpacking pleasures that can top a cool drink from a high-country lake or stream. Unfortunately, that cool sip from a cold mountain stream may be hazardous to your health.

The most common problem is wild strains of the intestinal bacteria *E. coli,* which is teeming in areas heavily used by humans or grazing animals. The most serious problem is the protozoan *Giardia lamblia.* The best measure to avoid both is the purchase of a water filter. These are available from mountaineering supply companies such as REI (Recreational Equipment, Inc.), and increasingly from sporting goods stores. They range in cost from $40 to $100 and are worth the investment if you like to hike. If not, the second best option is to purchase water purification tablets, in which the active ingredient is iodine, from a pharmacy or outdoor equipment store. Make sure to check the expiration date on the bottle.

*E. coli* will manifest in a few hours and is characterized by stomach pain and diarrhea. Giardiasis is caused by ingestion of the dormant cyst form of a protozoan. These cysts can survive, even in cold streams (40 degrees Fahrenheit), for up to three months and can be spread by domestic livestock, wild animals, and humans. Onset can occur from within several days to six weeks.

Professional medical treatment is required. Since it is beyond the scope of this book to advise on how to treat these various other medical problems, we strongly suggest you purchase either *Medicine for the Backcountry* or *Wilderness Medicine: Beyond First Aid,* published by Globe Pequot Press.

A final note—some backcountry water is drinkable without treatment. Use caution. Is the area very remote? Freely flowing springs that lack seepage areas above or around their margins are the best bet for a safe backcountry drink. If you decide to try it, remember you do so at your own risk.

## Be Mountain Lion Alert

Most of Idaho's backcountry is mountain lion territory. These big cats are found even along trails abutting cities like Boise or Pocatello.

Though many people consider themselves lucky indeed to see a mountain lion in the wild, the big cats—nature's perfect predator—are potentially dangerous. Attacks on humans are extremely rare, but it's wise to educate yourself before heading into mountain lion habitat.

### Safety guidelines for traveling in mountain lion country

To stay as safe as possible when hiking in mountain lion country, follow this advice.

1. Travel with a friend or group and stay together.
2. Don't let small children wander away by themselves.
3. Don't let pets run unleashed.
4. Avoid hiking at dawn and dusk—the times mountain lions are most active.
5. Know how to behave if you encounter a mountain lion.

### What to do if you encounter a mountain lion

In the vast majority of mountain lion encounters, these animals exhibit avoidance, indifference, or curiosity that doesn't result in human injury. They see you much more often than you see them. It is natural to be alarmed if you have an encounter of any kind. However, try to keep your cool and consider the following:

- Recognize threatening mountain lion behavior. A few cues may help you gauge the risk of attack. If a mountain lion is more than 50 yards away and directs its attention to you, it may be only curious. This situation represents only a slight risk for adults but a more serious risk for unaccompanied children. At this point, you should move away, while keeping the animal in your peripheral vision. Also, look for rocks, sticks, or something to use as a weapon, just in case.

If a mountain lion is crouched and staring at you less than 50 yards away, it may be assessing the chances of a successful attack. If this behavior continues, the risk of attack may be high.

- Do not approach a mountain lion. Give the animal the opportunity to move on. Slowly back away, but maintain eye contact if close. Mountain lions are not known to attack humans to defend their young or a kill, but they have been reported to "charge" in rare instances and may want to stay in the area. It's best to choose another route or time to hike through the area.
- Do not run from a mountain lion. Running may stimulate the mountain lion's predatory response.
- Make noise. If you encounter a mountain lion, be vocal; talk or yell loudly and regularly. Try not to panic. Shout to make others in the area aware of the situation.
- Maintain eye contact. Eye contact presents a challenge to the mountain lion, showing you are aware of its presence. Eye contact also helps you know where it is. However, if the behavior of the mountain lion is not threatening (if the animal is, for example, grooming itself or periodically looking away), maintain visual contact through your peripheral vision and move away.
- Appear larger than you are. Raise your arms above your head and make steady waving motions. Raise your jacket or another object above your head. Do not bend over, since this will make you appear smaller and more prey-like.
- If you are with small children, pick them up. Bring children close to you, maintain eye contact with the mountain lion, and pull the children up without bending over. If you are with other children or adults, band together.
- Defend yourself and others. If attacked, fight back. Try to remain standing. Do not feign death. Pick up a branch or rock; pull out a knife, pepper spray, or other deterrent. Individuals have fended off mountain lions with rocks, tree limbs, and even cameras. Keep in mind this is a last effort, and defending pets is not recommended.
- Respect any warning signs posted by agencies.
- Teach others in your group how to behave in case of a mountain lion encounter.
- Report encounters. Record your location and the details of any encounter and notify the nearest landowner or land management agency. The land management agency (federal, state, or county) may want to visit the site and, if appropriate, post education or warning signs. Fish and wildlife agencies should also be notified because they record and track such encounters.

- If physical injury occurs, it is important to leave the area and not disturb the site of attack. Mountain lions that have attacked people must be killed, and an undisturbed site is critical for effectively locating the dangerous mountain lion.
- See the FalconGuide *Mountain Lion Alert* for more details and tips for safe outdoor recreation in mountain lion country.

## Be Bear Aware

Bears inhabit most of Idaho's mountains and some of the lower country as well. While the vast majority of Idaho bears are black bears, a few grizzly bears wander the panhandle near the Washington–British Columbia border. A significant number of grizzlies also live in a small area near Yellowstone National Park.

The first step of any hike in bear country is an attitude adjustment. Being prepared for bears means not only having the right equipment, such as pepper spray, but also having the right information. Bears rarely attack humans, but they don't like to be surprised, and a female can be very defensive when she has cubs.

The greatest danger from bears occurs if you handle your food improperly. If a bear eats your food, and destroys your equipment in doing so, your trip is ruined. If you are deep in the wilderness, your life may be at risk as a result. Moreover, letting a bear get human food rapidly conditions it to seek human food in the future. The slogan "A fed bear is a dead bear" is often true. Think of following proper bear etiquette as protecting the bears as much as protecting yourself.

### Camping in bear country

The presence of food, cooking, and garbage can attract a bear into camp. Plus, you are in bear country at night, when bears are usually most active.

A few basic practices greatly minimize the chance of a bad encounter. To be as safe as possible, store everything that has any food smell. Ziplock bags are perfect for reducing food smell, and they help keep food from spilling on your pack, clothing, or other gear. Before going to bed change into other clothes for sleeping and hang clothes with food smells with the food and garbage. If you take the soiled clothes into the tent, you aren't separating your sleeping area from food smells. Try to keep food odors off your pack, but if you fail, put the food bag inside and hang the pack.

Finalize your food storage plans before it gets dark. Not only is it difficult to store food after darkness falls, but it's easier to forget some juicy morsel on the ground. Store food in airtight, sturdy, waterproof bags to prevent odors from circulating throughout the forest. You can purchase dry bags at most outdoor specialty stores, but you can get by with a trash compactor bag. Don't use regular garbage bags—they can break too easily.

See the diagrams for ways to hang a bear bag. If you have two bags to hang, divide your food into two equal sacks. Use a stone to toss the end of a piece of nylon cord over the limb well out from the trunk, then tie half your food to the end. Pull the

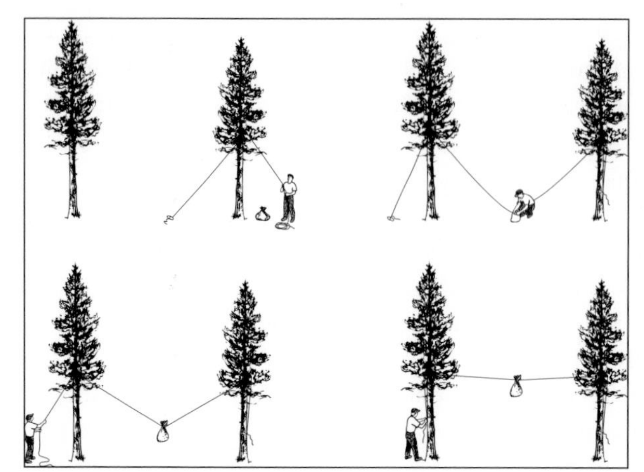

*Hanging food and garbage between two trees*

*Hanging food and garbage over a tree branch*

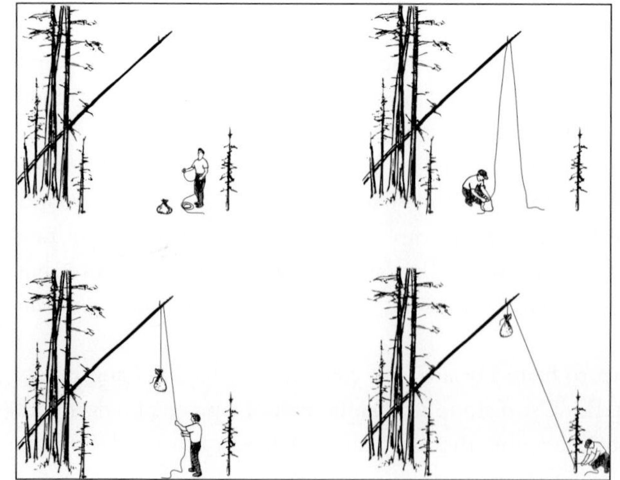

*Hanging food and garbage over a leaning tree*

food up to the limb, then tie your remaining food sack onto the cord as high as you can reach. Stuff the excess cord into the food sack and use a stick to push the second sack several feet higher than your head. The first sack will act as a counterweight and descend a few feet, but it should remain at least as high as the second sack. In the morning, use a stick to pull down one of the sacks.

Avoid smelly foods and consciously reduce the number of dishes you use. (You should pack out all food scraps.) By consuming everything on your plate as well as paying careful attention to storage, you will make your backpacking culinary experience not only more enjoyable and hassle-free but also more bearproof.

Read Globe Pequot Press's *Bear Aware,* by Bill Schneider, for complete information on camping in bear country.

## Remember Rattlesnakes

Rattlesnakes are present in much of the lower country in Idaho. This is especially true of the rugged, low-elevation canyons in the central part of the state.

Rattlesnakes strike humans only out of self-defense, when they're startled or otherwise afraid. The solution, of course, is to avoid scaring them. Look where you place your feet and hands when hiking in rattlesnake country, and carry a walking stick.

If you do encounter a rattlesnake, slowly back away and give it a chance to move away. Almost invariably, it will seize the opportunity and slither off. If it doesn't, simply give the snake a wide berth and leave well enough alone. Do not throw rocks or sticks at it.

If you're bitten by a rattlesnake, don't panic. Rattlesnake bites are rarely fatal to healthy adults. Use a snakebite kit immediately to extract as much of the venom as possible. (It may actually be a "dry bite," in which no venom is delivered; the snake intended only to frighten you.) Do not run or otherwise speed up your circulation, since that increases the spread of the venom in your bloodstream. Keep the bite site lower than your heart to decrease the spread of venom. Seek medical attention as soon as possible.

| Trail Finder: (authors' suggestions) | | | | | | | | | |
|---|---|---|---|---|---|---|---|---|---|
| North Idaho<br>Major Accesses: Coeur d'Alene, Grangeville, Moscow, Sandpoint, Bonners Ferry, Lewiston, Missoula MT | Day Hike | Backpack | Fun for the Family | Wilderness | Time to Climb | Scenery | Lakes | Wildflowers | Wildlife |
| 1. Harrison Lake | ● | | | | ● | ● | ● | ● | ● |
| 2. Hidden Lake and Red Top Mountain | ● | | ● | | | | ● | ● | ● |
| 3. Long Canyon | | ● | | | | ● | | ● | ● |
| 4. Salmo-Priest Divide Loop | | ● | | ● | | | | ● | ● |
| 5. Two Mouths Lakes | ● | ● | | | | | ● | ● | ● |
| 6. Upper Priest River | ● | ● | ● | | | ● | | ● | ● |
| 7. Lower Selway River | | ● | ● | ● | | | | | |
| 8. Selway Crags via Big Fog and Legend Lakes | | ● | | ● | ● | ● | ● | ● | |
| 9. Seven Lakes Loop | | ● | | ● | | ● | ● | ● | ● |
| 10. White Cap Creek | | ● | | ● | | ● | ● | ● | ● |
| 11 Larkins Lake | | ● | | | | ● | ● | ● | ● |
| 12. Pete Ott Lake and Vicinity | | ● | | | | ● | ● | ● | |
| 13. Goat Lake | | ● | | | | ● | ● | ● | ● |
| 14. Steep Lakes Loop | | ● | | | | ● | ● | ● | |
| 15. Meadow Creek | | ● | | | | ● | | ● | |
| 16. Hanover Ridge | | ● | | ● | | ● | ● | ● | ● |
| 17. Oregon Butte | | ● | | ● | ● | ● | ● | ● | |

| West Central Idaho<br>Major Accesses: Boise, Challis, Riggins, Stanley, Sun Valley, McCall, New Meadows, Cascade, Nampa, Weiser | Day Hike | Backpack | Fun for the Family | Wilderness | Time to Climb | Scenery | Lakes | Wildflowers | Wildlife |
|---|---|---|---|---|---|---|---|---|---|
| 18. Bighorn Crags: Reflection Lake | | ● | | ● | | ● | ● | | |
| 19. Bighorn Crags: Ship Island Lake | ● | ● | | ● | ● | ● | ● | | ● |
| 20. Blue Bunch Mountain | ● | | | ● | ● | ● | | ● | |
| 21. Cape Horn Mountain | ● | | | ● | ● | ● | | ● | |
| 22. Sheep Hill | | ● | | ● | ● | | | | |
| 23. Shell Rock and Rainbow Lakes | ● | | ● | ● | | ● | ● | | |
| 24. Sleeping Deer Mountain | | ● | | ● | ● | ● | ● | | |
| 25. Soldier Lakes–Patrol Ridge Loop | | ● | | ● | | ● | ● | | |
| 26. Stoddard Lake | | ● | | ● | | ● | ● | | |
| 27. Upper Vanity Lakes | ● | | | ● | | ● | ● | ● | |
| 28. West Yankee Fork–Crimson Lake | | ● | | ● | | ● | ● | | ● |
| 29. Box Lake | ● | ● | | | | ● | ● | ● | |
| 30. Lava Lakes | | ● | | | | ● | ● | ● | |
| 31. Loon Lake Loop and Beyond | | ● | | | | ● | ● | ● | |
| 32. Jennie Lake | ● | ● | | | | | ● | ● | |
| 33. Rainbow Lakes | ● | ● | ● | | | ● | ● | ● | ● |
| 34. Rapid River | | ● | | ● | | | | | |
| 35. Seven Devils Loop | | ● | | ● | ● | ● | ● | | ● |

| | Day Hike | Backpack | Fun for the Family | Wilderness | Time to Climb | Scenery | Lakes | Wildflowers | Wildlife |
|---|---|---|---|---|---|---|---|---|---|
| 36. Alpine Creek | | • | | • | | • | • | • | • |
| 37. Bench Lakes | • | • | • | • | | • | • | | |
| 38. Iron Creek to Sawtooth Lake | • | • | • | • | | • | • | | |
| 39. Stanley Lake Trail | • | • | • | | | • | • | | |
| 40. Toxaway–Pettit Loop | | • | | • | | • | • | | |
| 41. Baker Lake | • | • | • | | | • | • | • | |
| 42. Prairie Creek Loop | • | • | | | | • | • | • | |
| 43. West Fork of Prairie Creek | • | • | | | | • | | • | |
| **East Central Idaho<br>Major Accesses: Challis, Sun Valley, Leadore, Mackay, Salmon, Arco, Stanley** | | | | | | | | | |
| 44. North Fork of the Big Wood River | | • | | | | • | | | • |
| 45. Boulder Chain Lakes | | • | | | | • | • | • | |
| 46. Boundary Creek | | • | | | | • | • | • | • |
| 47. East Pass Creek | | • | | | | • | | • | • |
| 48. Fourth of July Creek to Born Lakes | • | • | | | | • | • | | • |
| 49. High Ridge Trail | | • | | | • | • | | | |
| 50. East Fork of the Big Wood River | | • | | | | • | | | |
| 51. Fall Creek | | • | | | • | | • | | |
| 52. Left Fork of Fall Creek | | • | | | | | | | • |
| 53. Right Fork of Fall Creek | | • | | | • | • | • | | |

| | Day Hike | Backpack | Fun for the Family | Wilderness | Time to Climb | Scenery | Lakes | Wildflowers | Wildlife |
|---|---|---|---|---|---|---|---|---|---|
| 54. Hyndman Creek | | ● | | | ● | ● | | | |
| 55. Iron Bog Lake | ● | ● | ● | | | ● | ● | | |
| 56. Summit Creek | | ● | | | | ● | | ● | |
| 57. Bear Creek Lake | ● | ● | ● | | ● | ● | ● | | |
| 58. Leatherman Pass | ● | ● | | | ● | ● | | | |
| 59. Merriam Lake | | ● | | | | ● | ● | | |
| 60. Mount Borah | ● | | | | ● | ● | | | |
| 61. Ramshorn Canyon | ● | | | | | | | | |
| 62. Bell Mountain Canyon Loop | ● | ● | | | | ● | | | ● |
| 63. Big Creek–Big Timber | | ● | | | | ● | ● | ● | |
| 64. Buck and Bear Valley Lakes | | ● | | | | | ● | ● | ● |
| 65. Bunting Canyon | ● | | | | | | | | |
| 66. Middle Canyon | ● | | | | ● | | | | |
| 67. Mill Creek Lake | ● | ● | | | | | ● | | |
| 68. Nez Perce Lake | ● | | | | | | ● | | |
| 69. Rocky Canyon | | ● | | | | ● | | | |
| 70. South Creek | ● | | ● | | | | | | ● |

| East Idaho Major Accesses: Blackfoot, Driggs, Dubois, Idaho Falls, Pocatello, Ashton, Alpine WY, Jackson WY, Soda Springs, Montpelier, West Yellowstone MT, Logan UT | Day Hike | Backpack | Fun for the Family | Wilderness | Time to Climb | Scenery | Lakes | Wildflowers | Wildlife |
|---|---|---|---|---|---|---|---|---|---|
| 71. Aldous/Hancock Lakes | • | | • | | | • | • | | • |
| 72. Salamander Lake Loop | • | | • | | | • | • | • | |
| 73. Sawtell Peak–Rock Creek Basin | • | • | | | | • | | • | • |
| 74. Targhee Creek | • | • | | | • | • | • | • | • |
| 75. Webber Creek | | • | | | | • | • | • | • |
| 76. Box Canyon to Big Burns | • | | • | | | | | | • |
| 77. Coffee Pot Rapids | • | | • | | | | | | • |
| 78. Black Canyon | • | | • | | • | | | • | |
| 79. Big Elk Creek | | • | | | | • | | • | • |
| 80. Little Elk Creek | | • | | | | • | | • | • |
| 81. Palisades Creek | • | • | • | | | • | • | | • |
| 82. South Fork of Tin Cup Creek to Lau Creek | • | • | | | | | | | • |
| 83. Trail Creek | • | • | | | | | | • | • |
| 84. Waterfall Canyon | | • | | | | • | | | |
| 85. Giraffe Creek | • | | | | | | | • | • |
| 86. Corral Creek | • | | • | | | | | • | |
| 87. Gibson Mountain Loop | • | | • | | • | • | | • | |

<table>
<tr><td>88. Scout Mountain–East Fork of Mink Creek</td><td>●</td><td></td><td>●</td><td></td><td>●</td><td>●</td><td>●</td><td>●</td><td></td></tr>
<tr><td>89. West Fork Mink Creek</td><td>●</td><td></td><td>●</td><td></td><td></td><td></td><td></td><td>●</td><td></td></tr>
<tr><td>90. Worm Creek</td><td>●</td><td>●</td><td></td><td></td><td></td><td></td><td></td><td>●</td><td>●</td></tr>
<tr><th>South Idaho & Miscellaneous<br>Major Accesses: Boise, Gooding, Idaho Falls, Kuna, Carey, American Falls, Malad, Burley, Twin Falls, Mountain Home, Salt Lake City UT, Elko NV</th><th>Day Hike</th><th>Backpack</th><th>Fun for the Family</th><th>Wilderness</th><th>Time to Climb</th><th>Scenery</th><th>Lakes</th><th>Wildflowers</th><th>Wildlife</th></tr>
<tr><td>91. Gooding City of Rocks</td><td>●</td><td></td><td>●</td><td></td><td>●</td><td></td><td></td><td></td><td></td></tr>
<tr><td>92. Echo Crater</td><td>●</td><td></td><td>●</td><td>●</td><td></td><td></td><td></td><td>●</td><td></td></tr>
<tr><td>93. 20 Mile Rock</td><td>●</td><td></td><td>●</td><td></td><td>●</td><td></td><td></td><td>●</td><td></td></tr>
<tr><td>94. Deep Creek Crest</td><td>●</td><td></td><td></td><td></td><td>●</td><td>●</td><td></td><td>●</td><td></td></tr>
<tr><td>95. Independence Lakes</td><td></td><td>●</td><td></td><td></td><td>●</td><td>●</td><td>●</td><td></td><td></td></tr>
<tr><td>96. Silent City of Rocks</td><td>●</td><td></td><td>●</td><td></td><td>●</td><td></td><td></td><td></td><td></td></tr>
<tr><td>97. Eagle Loop</td><td>●</td><td>●</td><td></td><td></td><td></td><td></td><td></td><td>●</td><td></td></tr>
<tr><td>98. Third Fork Rock Creek–Wahlstrom Hollow Loop</td><td></td><td>●</td><td></td><td></td><td></td><td></td><td></td><td>●</td><td></td></tr>
<tr><td>99. Big Jacks Creek</td><td>●</td><td></td><td></td><td>●</td><td></td><td></td><td></td><td></td><td>●</td></tr>
<tr><td>100. Shoofly Overlook</td><td>●</td><td></td><td></td><td>●</td><td></td><td></td><td></td><td></td><td>●</td></tr>
<tr><td>101. Bruneau Dunes State Park</td><td>●</td><td></td><td>●</td><td></td><td>●</td><td></td><td>●</td><td></td><td></td></tr>
<tr><td>102. Malad Gorge State Park</td><td>●</td><td></td><td>●</td><td></td><td></td><td></td><td></td><td></td><td></td></tr>
</table>

## Map Legend

| | |
|---|---|
| Interstate Highway | Bridge |
| U.S. Highway | Building/Point of Interest |
| State Highway | Campground |
| County/Forest Road | Cave |
| Local Road | Cliff |
| Unpaved Road | Dam |
| Featured Trail | Mountain/Peak |
| Trail | Parking |
| Paved Trail/Bike Path | Pass/Gap |
| State Line | Peak/Summit |
| Ditch/Scarp | Picnic Area |
| Small River or Creek | Ranger Station |
| Intermittent Stream | Rapids |
| Marsh/Swamp | Rocks |
| Body of Water | Scenic View/Viewpoint |
| Dunes | Spring |
| National Forest/Park | Town |
| National Wilderness Area | Trailhead |
| State/County Park | Visitor/Information Center |
| | Waterfall |

85
76
28
2658
1

# Selkirk Mountains and Salmo-Priest Wilderness

In the far northwest corner of Idaho and in northeast Washington rises one of the major mountain ranges of the Northern Rockies—the Selkirks. They are largely the product of the huge Kaniksu Batholith, emplaced, then uplifted and eroded into a rugged, glaciated, 250-mile-long range stretching northward deep into British Columbia. Here they differentiate into many subranges, and then they finally merge with the Monashee Range to become the Cariboo Mountains.

This "big tree" country is nurtured by heavy annual rain and snowfall. The result is a mix of huge western red cedar, Douglas fir, white pine, and spruce, usually covered by a healthy growth of moss and lichen. This is rain forest, both in Idaho and in interior British Columbia, and although the forest has been heavily logged, some very special places remain intact. Even in the logged areas, the glaciated crest of the range provides cirques with undeveloped mountain lakes, horns and pyramidal peaks of hard granite, and some big trees in places too rough to have been timbered.

The lichen of the lower-elevation, unlogged rain forest provides a major source of food for the only band of woodland caribou remaining in the United States. Not to be confused with the barren ground caribou, the rare woodland caribou struggles to hang on, with about thirty-five animals roaming the international border. Another rare inhabitant of the Selkirks is the grizzly bear. About thirty of the great bears wander the southern section of the Selkirks, the area between northwest Idaho and Nelson, British Columbia. The great bear is rarely seen, but the smaller black bear is abundant. Many of the walks in these mountains are along trails where most of the trailside forest understory consists of August bear food—berries, including currant, snowberry, serviceberry, gooseberry, thimbleberry, elderberry, and especially huckleberry.

This section describes six hikes in the Selkirks—three in the lower-elevation rain forest and three in the Selkirk Crest area.

The bulk of the lower-elevation rain forest in the American Selkirks is concentrated around the South Salmo River of northeast Washington and the Upper Priest River nearby in Idaho, and in Long Canyon just northwest of Bonners Ferry, Idaho.

*Beautiful high country of the Selkirks.* Photo by John Kratz

The 39,976-acre Salmo-Priest Wilderness was created by the Washington Wilderness Act of 1984 after a long battle. The Upper Priest River in Idaho was supposed to follow the Salmo into wilderness classification in separate legislation, but Idaho's political establishment became intensely anti-environment, and the Upper Priest was never added. So, ironically, the Salmo-Priest Wilderness contains no Priest. The Upper Priest area is, however, managed by the USDA Forest Service just as though it were designated wilderness; but lacking congressional protection, its administrative protection could blow away with shifting political winds.

Idaho conservationists have also labored to protect as wilderness the crest of the Selkirks and Long Canyon, the only major mountain canyon in the Idaho Selkirks that has not been logged at all. Both the crest zone and Long Canyon are presently being protected by the administrative power of the forest service. This protection, too, is subject to change if politics so dictate.

—Ralph Maughan

# 1 Harrison Lake

Harrison Lake is notably one of the largest lakes in the Selkirk Crest of Idaho. Scenic Harrison Peak and granite walls dominate its edges.

**Start:** 15 miles west of Bonners Ferry
**Type of hike:** Day hike or backpack; out-and-back
**Distance:** 8 miles round-trip
**Approximate hiking time:** 5–6 hours
**Difficulty:** Moderate
**Best season:** July–September
**Trail surface:** Dirt to rocky
**Land status:** Idaho Panhandle National Forests
**Canine compatibility:** On leash
**Fees and Permits:** None
**Maps:** Roman Nose and The Wigwams USGS quadrangles; Idaho Panhandle National Forests–Kaniksu National Forest map
**Trail contacts:** Sandpoint Ranger District, (208) 263-5111; Bonners Ferry Ranger District, (208) 267-5561, www.fs.usda.gov/ipnf
**Special considerations:** Huckleberries line the trail for about 3 miles. They ripen in August, so watch for bears.

**Finding the trailhead:** Begin from downtown Bonners Ferry, which is just off US 95. Drive toward the Kootenai River and find Riverside Street; follow Riverside Street west, out of town, to the Kootenai Wildlife Refuge. Pass the refuge headquarters, which sits near the mouth of Myrtle Creek, at about 5 miles. Continue past the headquarters 1.5 miles on paved road until you reach the gravel road up Myrtle Creek. The Myrtle Creek road is at an oblique angle to the paved road, and the sign is hard to see.

Drive up and into big and deep Myrtle Creek Canyon on this road, FR 663. Watch for logging trucks. The road is narrow in places, and the drop into Myrtle Creek is a long way down. Stay on this main road as it approaches the head of the canyon. After about 10.5 miles, you pass the side road to Myrtle Lake; the main road is renumbered FR 633A. From here it is 2 miles to the Two Mouths Trailhead. FR 633A begins to make a semicircle around the scenic head of the canyon, reaching and passing the Two Mouths Trailhead, where the number of the road changes to FR 661. Continue on FR 661 for 1.5 miles to FR 2409 to your right. Follow FR 2409 1.5 miles to its abrupt end. GPS: N48 42.25' / W116 37.32'

**Parking and trailhead facilities:** The dead-end road has room for about three vehicles. The trailhead is undeveloped and in partial shade.

## The Hike

The trail is well marked and signed: HARRISON LAKE 4, TRAIL NO. 6. It is well maintained and immediately leads up a nicely re-vegetated logging road. Parts of the trail are wet as you quickly reach and cross the double outlet stream from inaccessible Brooks Lake high above.

The straight and easy trail goes for 0.8 mile to a good bridge over the uppermost headwaters of Myrtle Creek. At the bridge the trail makes a right angle and crosses a corduroy path over a bog. After 0.2 mile the gentle trail abruptly ends. This is where the logging road ended. The trail now makes another right angle (back to the south)

*Looking down on Harrison Lake.* PHOTO BY JOHN KRATZ

and begins a moderately steep climb toward the Myrtle Creek–Pack River Divide. It passes almost continuously through huckleberry, currant, gooseberry, serviceberry, elderberry, and mountain sumac. It also passes under some large spruce trees. Openings give some good views to the north of the Selkirk Crest near Myrtle Creek.

It is a 950-foot climb to the divide. The grade is fairly easy via two long and several short switchbacks. As you reach the divide, the trail climbs gently a bit more and then drops, climbs again, and drops to the junction with Trail 217. This trail comes up out of the Pack River drainage, climbing steeply to meet Trail 6. Examine the trail junction carefully because it is much less obvious on the return trip, and you, like me, could end up a ways down the Pack River before the error is noticed.

About 0.5 mile prior to the junction with Trail 217, you begin to cross scenic slabs of granite. The route across the rock is well cairned.

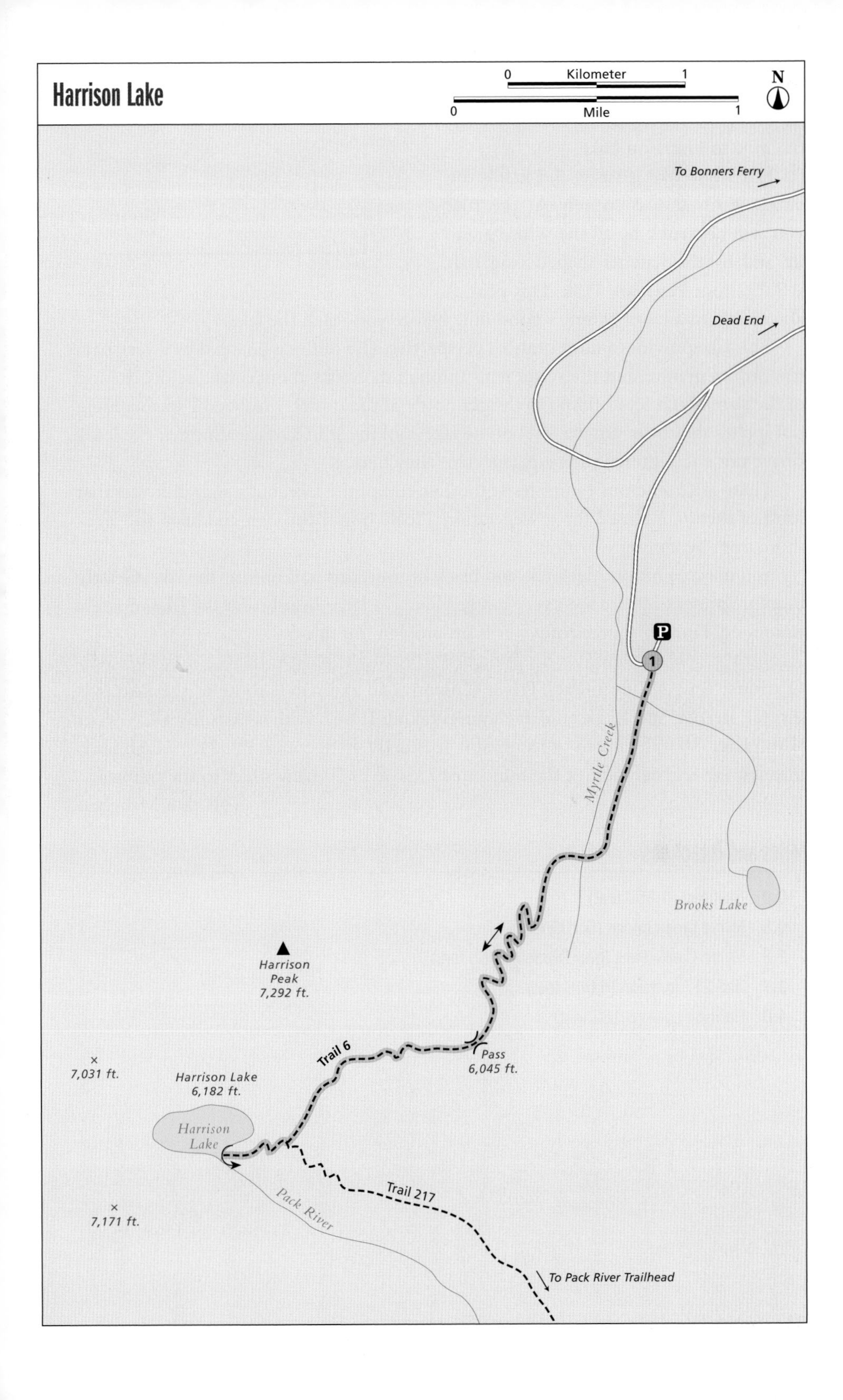
Harrison Lake
0
Kilometer
1
0
Mile
1
N
To Bonners Ferry
Dead End
P
1
Myrtle Creek
Brooks Lake
Harrison
Peak
7,292 ft.
Pass
6,045 ft.
Trail 6
7,031 ft.
Harrison Lake
6,182 ft.
Harrison
Lake
Trail 217
Pack River
7,171 ft.
To Pack River Trailhead

Past the trail junction, the trail climbs up moderately steep granite slabs the last 0.3 mile to Harrison Lake.

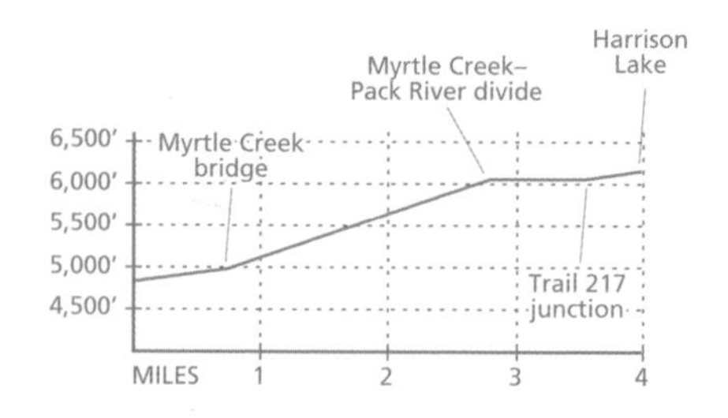


Harrison Lake is large, and it fills the cirque basin almost entirely. At the lake you will be struck by all the white granite and by the hatchet-shaped crag that is 7,292-foot Harrison Peak. This peak is also visible to a lesser extent a good mile before you reach the lake.

This lake provides a most unusual perspective. The outlet is guarded by a very narrow slab of granite, and the water runs through its cracks about 5 feet below the top of the slab. When I was filling my water bottle at the outlet, I realized I was standing just inches above the surface level of the lake, looking at its surface almost at eye level. I have not encountered such a perspective elsewhere.

There are numerous campsites at the east end of the lake, but a sign indicates that most of them are closed for re-vegetation. Please honor the sign and keep the lakeshore from becoming worn out.

You may see moose, deer, elk, and black bear on this trail or near the lake. Grizzly bears are present but are seen very rarely. There is a large bear box at the lake to safely store food. Finding sources of water is no problem on this trail.

**Options:** Trail 217 from Pack River Canyon is an alternative route to the lake. It is shorter, steeper, and less scenic. It requires taking ID 47, which exits from US 95 at Walsh Lake, 10 miles north of Sandpoint, Idaho. ID 47 becomes FR 213, which leads through the regeneration of the Sundance Fire of 1967 many miles to the trailhead.

—Ralph Maughan

## Miles and Directions

**0.0** Trailhead (4,850 feet)

**0.8** Myrtle Creek bridge (5,100 feet)

**2.8** Myrtle Creek-Pack River Divide (6,060 feet)

**3.7** Trail 217 junction (6,040 feet)

**4.0** Harrison Lake (6,182 feet)

# 2 Hidden Lake and Red Top Mountain

Here is a short hike to a large Selkirk Mountain lake. Note the fine views of the Selkirk Crest from Red Top Mountain.

**Start:** 15 miles northwest of Bonners Ferry
**Type of hike:** Day hike; out-and-back
**Distance:** 6.4 miles round-trip
**Approximate hiking time:** 2–3 hours
**Difficulty:** Moderate
**Best season:** Late August–mid-September
**Trail surface:** Dirt to rocky
**Land status:** Idaho Panhandle National Forests–Kaniksu National Forest
**Canine compatibility:** On leash. Dogs not recommended because of bear activity and heavy use of the trail
**Fees and permits:** None
**Maps:** Grass Mountain and Shorty Peak USGS quadrangles
**Trail contact:** Bonners Ferry Ranger District, (208) 267-5561
**Special considerations:** Huckleberries line the trail. They ripen in August, so watch for bears. Motorized vehicles are not allowed.

**Finding the trailhead:** From Bonners Ferry, drive north on US 95. You soon come to the junction with ID 1, which leads north to Canada. Take ID 1. One mile down ID 1, turn left onto the paved side road. This road leads downhill to the floor of the Kootenai Valley and a road junction. Turn left and cross over the Kootenai River; then continue west directly toward the Selkirk Mountains front. The canyon you are looking into is Fisher Creek. At the base of the mountains is the paved Westside Road. You reach it at a T intersection. Turn right onto Westside Road. A sign indicates that your destination, Smith Creek Road, is 9 miles.

At Smith Creek Crossing the paved road continues. In another mile it swings around and climbs into Smith Creek Canyon. Don't continue north on the gravel Boundary Creek Road, which soon ends. This road has been closed because of continued concern over its potential for erosion.

Smith Creek is typical Selkirk Canyon—forested, big, deep, and long. The road is paved for 6 miles up Smith Creek before it turns to gravel. After the end of the pavement, continue 3 more miles on this road (FR 281), but then keep to the left and take FR 665, which leads up Cow Creek. After 2 more miles take FR 2545 up Beaver Creek, a canyon that has been burned and logged, and which I found overgrazed by cattle in the few places there is grass. It is 3 miles to the end and the trailhead. GPS: N48 53.62' / W116 45.64'

**Parking and trailhead facilities:** The undeveloped trailhead has room for about four vehicles. There's only scant shade in a regenerating burn.

## The Hike

Though this hike is possible from about late June through mid-October, taking it in late summer is best because of the beautiful foliage colors and lack of insects.

The obvious trail begins as a gentle walk through the regenerating burn with the trees about 10 to 20 feet high. Soon the trail begins 350 feet of gentle switchbacks up the cirque wall through second growth with many trailside huckleberries. There

*A clearing along the trail to Hidden Lake.* PHOTO BY LUKE KRATZ

are some good views of Beaver Creek Canyon through openings in the trees. Finally the trail enters an unlogged forest of medium to small subalpine fir and spruce. From here it climbs little in the last 0.3 mile to Hidden Lake.

The lake is approximately circular with the dominant feature being the shoulder of Joe Peak, which is pleasant but not especially impressive from the lake. The lake has abundant trout and huckleberry bushes under the forested shore.

The trail splits just before reaching the lake. The right trail leads to the lakeshore and ends. The left trail, Trail 102, also leads to the lakeshore but continues around to the left (east), crossing outlet streams in two places. It comes to a large campsite and a possible point of confusion. The correct trail to the divide leaves the campsite on the left as you face uphill.

From here the trail climbs 0.6 mile and 320 feet to a forested pass on the ridgetop and a junction with Trail 21 (see Options below). Go left, still on Trail 102. The trail

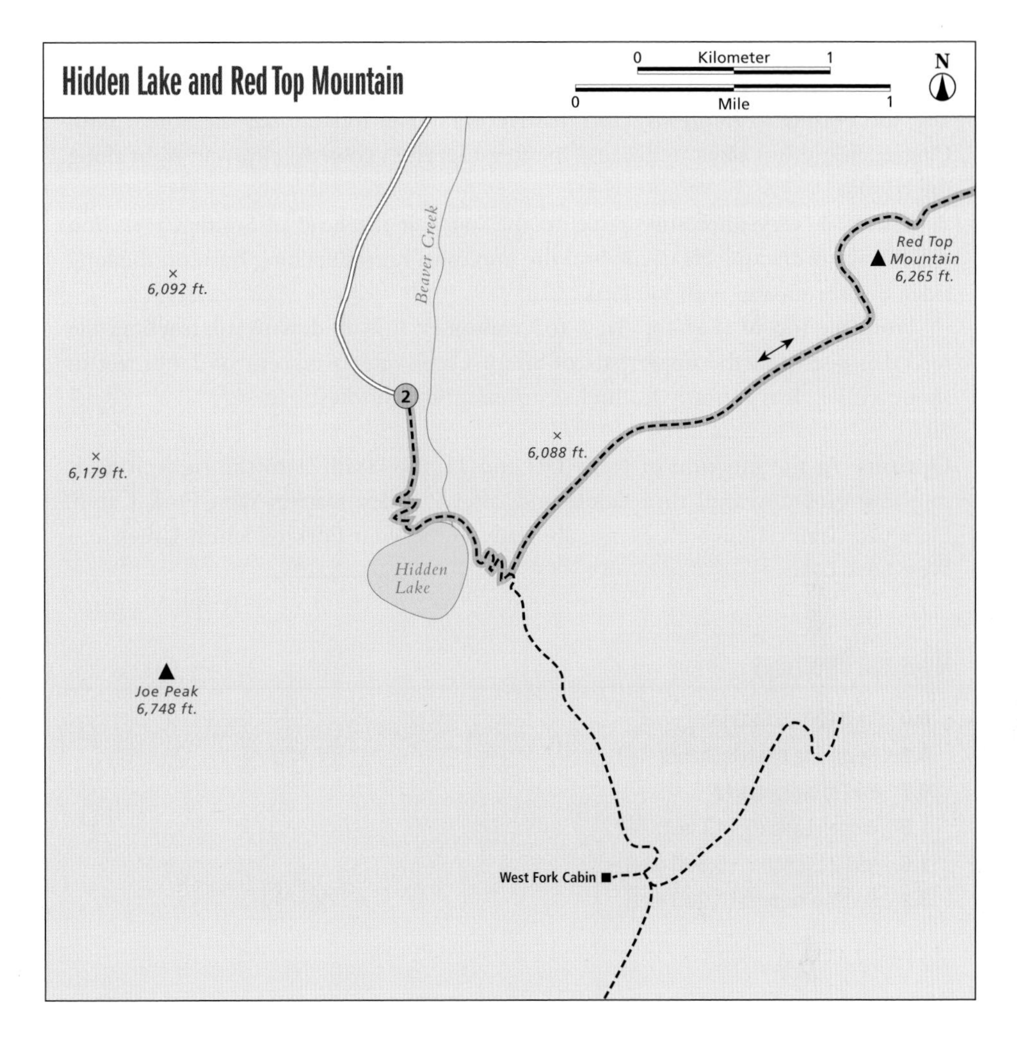


leads through forest, staying on the right side of the ridge. You'll have occasional views of the impressive Selkirk Peaks in the area through the trees. Even during the driest season, count on one spring (not shown on the map) that begins just above the trail and runs across it. The trail's tread was faint, but easy to follow and well cleared, in the year 2000.

Gradually the trail attains the ridgetop, then sinks below it but gains it again. It slowly emerges from the timber into the regenerating burn. Through the short trees you can see Red Top Mountain, so named not because of the rock (which is gray granite), but because of the bright red of the huckleberry bushes in September.

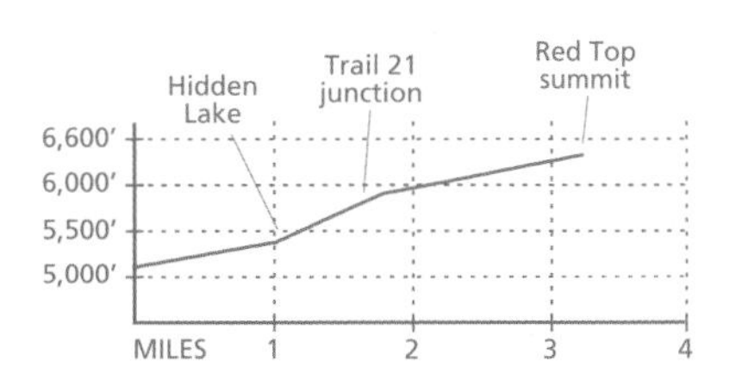

On the bare summit you have a fine view in all directions. In fact there was once a fire tower on the mountain, but it lies burned, probably by the forest fire. From Red Top, Joe Peak is an impressive and massive mountain. You can see the border with Canada clearly. It is obvious because the forest service allowed a clear-cut right along the border.

There are very impressive peaks to the south at the head of Smith Creek. You can also see distracting clear-cuts and the impressively regenerating burn on the long ridge that terminates with Joe Peak.

From the top of Red Top, Trail 102 continues. It is all downward, reaching the road that goes into the upper part of Smith Creek after a descent of 2,400 feet in about 3 miles. It is a mostly featureless descent through forest.

**Options:** At the junction of Trails 102 and 21, take Trail 21 to the right. It leads southeastward downhill to a saddle and, after 2 miles, reaches West Fork Cabin. Here take Trail 347, which eventually leads to the West Fork of Smith Creek and West Fork Lake.

—Ralph Maughan

## Miles and Directions

**0.0** Trailhead (5,020 feet)
**0.1** Beginning of switchbacks
**0.7** End of switchbacks
**1.0** Hidden Lake (5,443 feet)
**1.6** Trail 21 junction (5,800 feet)
**3.2** Red Top summit (6,265 feet)

# 3 Long Canyon

Long Canyon is a splendid example of a northern climax rain forest. Opportunities arise for wildlife viewing, mushroom hunting, and fishing. It is a magnificent ridge walk.

**Start:** Approximately 10 miles northwest of Bonners Ferry
**Type of hike:** Multiday backpack; near loop.
**Distance:** 30 miles
**Approximate hiking time:** 5–6 days
**Difficulty:** Strenuous due to sometimes tough stream crossings, a ridge walk, and a steep descent with faint spots and long gaps between water sources
**Best season:** July–October (depending on snow)
**Trail surface:** Normal dirt and rocks
**Land status:** Idaho Panhandle National Forests
**Canine compatibility:** On leash
**Fees and permits:** None
**Maps:** Smith Peak, Pyramid Peak, Smith Falls, and Shorty Peak USGS quadrangles; Kaniksu National Forest–Idaho Panhandle National Forests map
**Trail contact:** Bonners Ferry Ranger District, (208) 267-5561, www.fs.usda.gov/idahopanhandle
**Special considerations:** Since this area is popular, exceptional, and fragile, please keep parties small, select entry days of light use, and use backpacking stoves instead of fires. The three crossings of Long Canyon Creek are difficult during high water. Conditions in the rain forest portion are often very wet, but there is no reliable water on the steep climb the first 5 miles and no water on the last 5 miles down Parker Ridge. You will need a shuttle if you exit at Parker Creek.

**Finding the trailhead:** From Bonners Ferry, drive north on US 95. You soon come to the junction with ID 1, which leads north to Canada. Take ID 1. One mile down ID 1, turn left onto the paved side road. This road leads downhill to the floor of the Kootenai Valley and a road junction. Turn left and cross over the Kootenai River; then continue west directly toward the Selkirk Mountains front. The canyon you are looking into is Fisher Creek. At the base of the mountains is the paved Westside Road. You reach it at a T intersection. Turn right onto Westside Road. At about 3.7 miles the road crosses Parker Creek (which is the return route for the loop); just north of the creek is Parker Creek Trail (Trail 14). About 2.8 miles farther north is Long Canyon Creek, and 0.5 mile past the road crossing of the creek is a sign and a side road that leads to the Long Canyon Trailhead. GPS: N48 57.34' / W116 32.72'
**Parking and trailhead facilities:** Parker Creek has no trailhead, just room for about two vehicles on the side of the road. The Long Canyon Trailhead has parking for about eight vehicles and includes a horse loading ramp. Both Parker Creek and Long Canyon Creek Trailheads are in partial shade.

## The Hike

This area is one of the last two unlogged drainages of the American Selkirk Mountains. Parker Canyon, which lies next to it, is the other. The other drainages still have high recreation values, especially near the crest of the range, but they have been partially or completely logged. This prime area consists mainly of hemlock, western

red cedar, white pine, and larch in the middle third. The upper third and ridges are covered with Engelmann spruce and subalpine fir. Wildlife abounds. A few grizzlies and woodland caribou still live in the area. The Selkirk Mountains is the only place that the woodland caribou, an endangered species, still exists in the United States. (See the Selkirk Mountains and Salmo-Priest Wilderness overview earlier.) Mushroom hunting in this rain forest, particularly in September, is good. Two of the three highest mountains in northern Idaho flank Long Canyon: Smith Peak at 7,653 feet and Parker Peak at 7,670 feet. The drainage holds four large lakes.

Long Canyon proper covers about 20,000 acres. Whether or not to log this virgin old-growth timber was debated for years. Many have sought to protect Long Canyon and designate it as part of the Selkirk Crest Wilderness. The proposal takes in not only Long and Parker Canyons but also the rugged crest area of glacier-polished granite peaks, subalpine lakes, and ridges. But Long Canyon supplies irreplaceable old-growth forest for wildlife, the only such forest in northern Idaho for primitive recreation, and a natural forest by which to gauge success in managing other forests. For the present, the attitude of the forest service has changed toward managing this area for primitive backcountry recreation with no thought of timber. But because the area hasn't been designated wilderness by Congress, all this could change with a bad president or bad Congress.

The good, reconstructed Trail 16 runs most of the length of the narrow Long Canyon of Canyon Creek. It entails a 2,800-foot elevation gain to the junction with Smith Lake Fork and a 5,200-foot elevation gain total to Pyramid Pass. The steepness of this entry is the very reason this canyon hasn't been logged, although Myrtle and Smith Creeks also have steep entrances and roads were blasted up into them. Long Canyon Creek itself is difficult to reach until some 5 miles in. As a result water sources require bushwhacks.

From the trailhead, the path winds through the timber. Then it switchbacks 600 feet to the ridge between Smith Creek to the north and Long Canyon Creek to the south. After a gentle 0.5 mile, the trail approaches Long Canyon Creek and makes a 90-degree turn up into that canyon but does not descend into it for a long way. The first 3 miles are through forest, with the trail staying a good 400 to 600 feet above the creek and climbing up the canyon. Next, the trail continues above the creek and goes through a mostly rocky section of slate, still climbing.

*The trailhead at Long Canyon.* PHOTO BY CATHY KRATZ

The lower section's slate eventually yields to granite, signaling a gentler grade, and eventually the trail and the creek meet. The ponderosa pine, aspen, and cottonwood will have disappeared when you reach the first crossing of Long Canyon Creek just past the 6-mile mark, where you enter the rain forest. This magnificent forest, about 0.5 mile wide, now continues for 7 miles. Apparently forest fires have always stopped here due to the wetness. Experience has shown that clothing can't be dried, no matter how warm the weather. But then, that's why the mushrooms are so abundant. Despite major rehabilitation efforts by various volunteer groups, this lowest creek crossing can be tricky even late in the season, and the water is always cold.

In 1.5 miles the trail crosses the creek again. This, too, can be difficult. There is one more crossing at about 9 miles. At about mile 11, you reach a very large open area near Smith Lake Creek. The creek tumbles down numerous small waterfalls and flows into Long Canyon Creek at the only real flat in the valley bottom.

Slightly more than 1.5 miles upstream, the hemlock-cedar forest begins to play out in the higher altitude (over 4,000 feet) and gives way to spruce and fir. In late

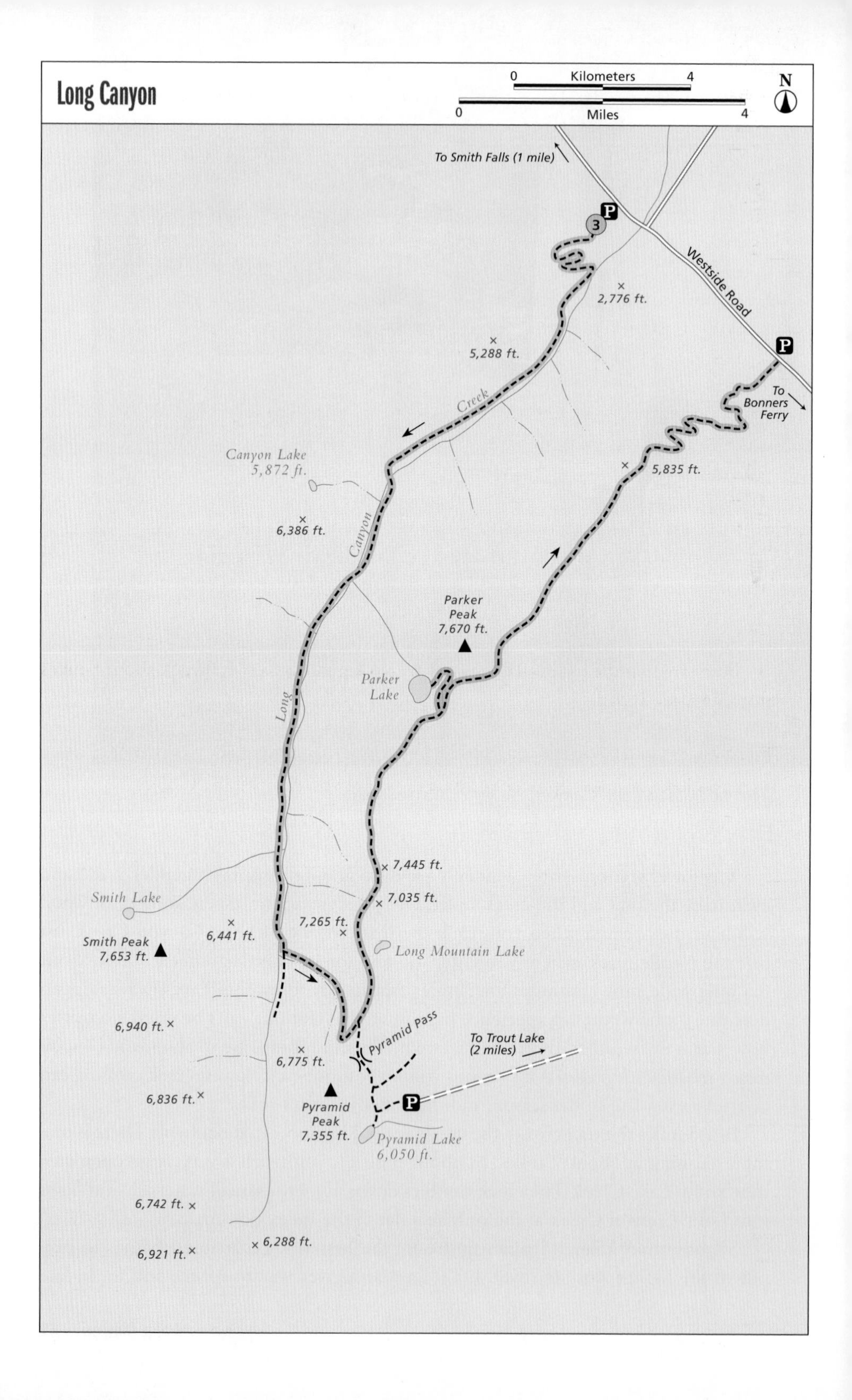

Long Canyon
0 Kilometers 4
0 Miles 4
N
To Smith Falls (1 mile)
3
P
Westside Road
2,776 ft.
5,288 ft.
P
To Bonners Ferry
Creek
Canyon Lake
5,872 ft.
5,835 ft.
6,386 ft.
Canyon
Parker Peak
7,670 ft.
Parker Lake
Long
7,445 ft.
7,035 ft.
Smith Lake
7,265 ft.
6,441 ft.
Smith Peak
7,653 ft.
Long Mountain Lake
Pyramid Pass
6,940 ft.
To Trout Lake
(2 miles)
6,775 ft.
6,836 ft.
P
Pyramid Peak
7,355 ft.
Pyramid Lake
6,050 ft.
6,742 ft.
6,288 ft.
6,921 ft.

summer, huckleberries, present on most of the trail, often bear abundant fruit. Here, Trail 16 fades out. The upper third of Long Canyon no longer has a maintained trail.

Where Trail 16 fades, Trail 7 fords the creek and leaves Long Canyon to climb steeply (especially at first) toward Pyramid Pass. From here it is 2,400 feet in 4 miles to the pass—but 0.5 mile below the pass, begin the second half of the loop by taking Trail 221, which climbs northeast to the ridgetop and soon breaks out into the open on Long Mountain. There are several lakes below the ridge on Long Mountain. From Long Mountain, with one exception, the trail stays on the ridgeline all the way back to Westside Road. There are fine views but no water the last 5 miles.

Just before you reach big Parker Peak, a side trail leaves to the left (the north) and drops 500 feet down to Parker Lake, where the trail ends.

An exception to staying on the ridgeline is found at Parker Peak. Here the trail keeps to the east and drops down, passing about 600 to 1,100 feet below the peak, which is 7,670 feet high, making it the highest peak in the American Selkirks. It has a tremendous north wall, but there is no good view of it from the trail. Fortunately a spur trail leaves and climbs Parker Peak for a tremendous view.

Past Parker Peak, the trail is fairly uneventful, with the big exception of the final descent to Westside Road, which is a very steep, knee-jarring descent of 3,200 feet on top of and along the very rugged wall of Parker Creek! As of the summer of 2000, this trail had received maintenance, and the descent was in pretty good condition.

Be aware that the last available water is a spring just off a switchback about 5 miles from Westside Road.

**Options:** Continue to Pyramid Pass (7,080 feet) and over it to reach Ball Lake or Pyramid Lake. A road approaches this area where you can park a shuttle.

## Miles and Directions

**0.0** Canyon Creek Trail 16 (1,820 feet)

**0.5** Top of Smith Creek–Long Canyon Creek toe (2,700 feet)

**0.8** Right-angle turn into Long Canyon (2,600 feet)

**6.0** First stream crossing; enter rain forest (3,800 feet)

**7.5** Second stream crossing (4,000 feet)

**11.0** Meadow at mouth of Smith Lake Creek (4,400 feet)

**14.5** Trail 221 junction (6,400 feet)

**16.0** Trail high point on Long Mountain (7,200 feet)

**17.5** Trail just below Peak 7,445 (7,390 feet)

**20.0** Parker Lake side trail (6,850 feet)

**21.5** Trail immediately below Parker Peak (6,400 feet)

**22.5** Trail regains the ridgeline (6,600 feet)

**25.0** Beginning of major descent (5,700 feet)

**30.0** Westside Road (1,805 feet)

# 4 Salmo-Priest Divide Loop

Along the northern Washington and Idaho border there are still mountains with vast old-growth rain forests. This is the wild homeland of the endangered mountain caribou, the Canada lynx, and the grizzly bear.

**Start:** Extreme northeastern Washington and northwestern Idaho; 90 miles north-by-northeast of Spokane, Washington
**Type of hike:** Backpack loop
**Distance:** 16.1 miles
**Approximate hiking time:** 3-4 days
**Difficulty:** Moderately strenuous
**Best season:** Mid-July–late September
**Trail surface:** Normal dirt and rocks
**Land status:** Salmo-Priest Wilderness Area; Colville National Forest (in Washington State); Idaho Panhandle National Forest
**Canine compatibility:** On leash. Not allowed in wilderness
**Fees and permits:** None
**Maps:** Continental Mountain, Salmo Mountain USGS quadrangles. The forest service's Salmo-Priest Wilderness map is the most accurate
**Trail contact:** Sullivan Lake Ranger District, (509) 446-7500
**Special considerations:** Early-season hikers face a difficult ford of the South Salmo River. Late-season hikers face difficulty finding water beyond the headwaters of the South Salmo River. Watch for black bears and a possible grizzly during berry season (August).

**Finding the trailhead:** Drive north on WA 31 to Metaline Falls, Washington. Then take WA 6 toward the Canadian border, but after just 1.5 miles turn right onto Pend Oreille County Road 9345. This road is paved to scenic Sullivan Lake, but just before Sullivan Lake, at 5.5 miles from WA 6, turn left onto FR 22. This road is paved for about 0.5 mile, then becomes a good gravel road up Sullivan Creek. The trailhead is now about 18 miles away. Continue on FR 22 until you reach FR 2220. (FR 22 turns right here and climbs out of the canyon at this plainly evident junction. It leads to the upper Priest River area and also to Granite Creek.) Continue now on FR 2220 to the end of the gentle part of Sullivan Creek. The road makes a sweeping turn of about 90 degrees, just beyond Gypsy Meadows, and climbs steeply up Deemer Creek to Salmo Pass. Turn right at the pass and continue a short distance to the trailhead. While the road is steep in places, it is good gravel all the way. GPS: N48 57.33' / W117 4.85'
**Parking and trailhead facilities:** The trailhead has room for about ten vehicles. The two ends of the trail loop leave from the trailhead about 50 yards from each other. The pleasant trailhead has an outhouse, a small spring, a loading ramp, and partial shade.

## The Hike

Going clockwise, take well-marked Trail 506 down toward the South Salmo River. You drop immediately and follow well-constructed switchbacks down through an increasingly beautiful old-growth forest to the river. There are plenty of springs and small creeks. You wind down among huge Douglas fir, white pine, and western red cedar. Some are more than 1,000 years old. The understory consists of many kind of berries, devil's claw, ferns, carpets of moss, and many more species. The high-elevation beginning of this trail may cross deep snow under the trees in early to mid-July.

The drop to the river is 3.5 miles and a descent of almost 2,000 feet. The stream is clear, beautiful, and fairly large. There once was a bridge, but it washed out, and there are no immediate plans to build a new one. Fords in July can be difficult, although you may find some fallen giants nearby that can serve as a bridge. Be mindful that these big logs are treacherous in wet weather or when kept wet by spray from the river.

Across the river, the trail heads upstream. After 1.2 miles you cross Crutch Creek, and the trail begins to climb above the river. Late in the season or during a dry season, Crutch Creek is the only reliable water source until you reach the very head of the river.

You cross into Idaho and leave the Salmo-Priest Wilderness 0.8 mile past Crutch Creek. Maybe someday Idaho will have an environmentally friendly congressional delegation that will add the upper Priest River drainage of this roadless area to the Salmo-Priest Wilderness, so that it actually includes the Priest.

The climb up the river gradually steepens as you reach its headwaters under 7,572-foot Snowy Top Mountain. Finally the trail switchbacks to a beautiful saddle—Snowy Top Pass—between Snowy Top just to the north and Little Snowy Top to the south. Lots of folks climb Snowy Top. On top you get a view of the Selkirk Mountains in Idaho, Washington, and British Columbia, the latter just 0.25 mile to the north. You can see the international border clearing. It will take you two or three extra hours to climb the peak and then return to the trail.

At the pass, the trail (now numbered 512) turns south. You are on the Salmo-Priest River Divide, also called the Shedroof Divide, as you move farther south. Views are into the old-growth forest of the upper Priest River and the Selkirk Crest to the east. Distant clear-cuts are almost always visible where there's a view, bringing the realization that this country was saved in just the nick of time. The Idaho portion remains not permanently protected.

Once over the Snowy Top Pass saddle, the trail traverses a steep slope under Little Snowy Top Mountain. Just 0.4 mile past Little Snowy Top, Trail 349 exits to the left, taking a tremendous plunge of 70 switchbacks, 4.5 miles, and 3,400 feet to the upper Priest River. I did not check out this trail, although I did meet the founder of the Pacific Northwest Trail, of which this trail is a part, who said it is well constructed.

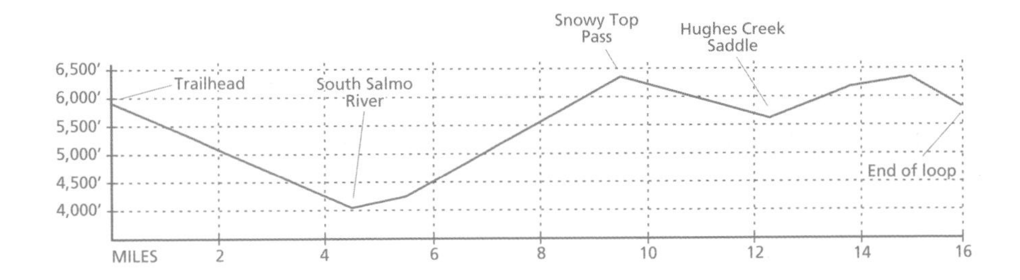

*Two Mouth Lakes at dawn.* PHOTO BY RALPH MAUGHAN

The Salmo-Priest loop trail continues its scenic course just on the Priest River side of the divide until it drops to a saddle at the head of Hughes Creek. If there are snowdrifts, you will probably find some water to drink along the divide, and occasionally there are seeps and small springs for a while after snowmelt.

As you descend the 600 feet to Hughes Saddle, you get some good views of Shedroof Mountain and understand why it has that name. Hughes Creek was partially logged, that is obvious, but the forest service has since followed a much more environmentally friendly management course for the lengthy drainage.

The trail climbs from the saddle until it crosses under steep, unnamed Peak 6,682. During this section you cross back into Washington and into the designated wilderness. Here, under the steepest mountain slope, you are likely to find a spring or two that runs most of the year. If snow patches remain, this stretch may be somewhat difficult due to steepness.

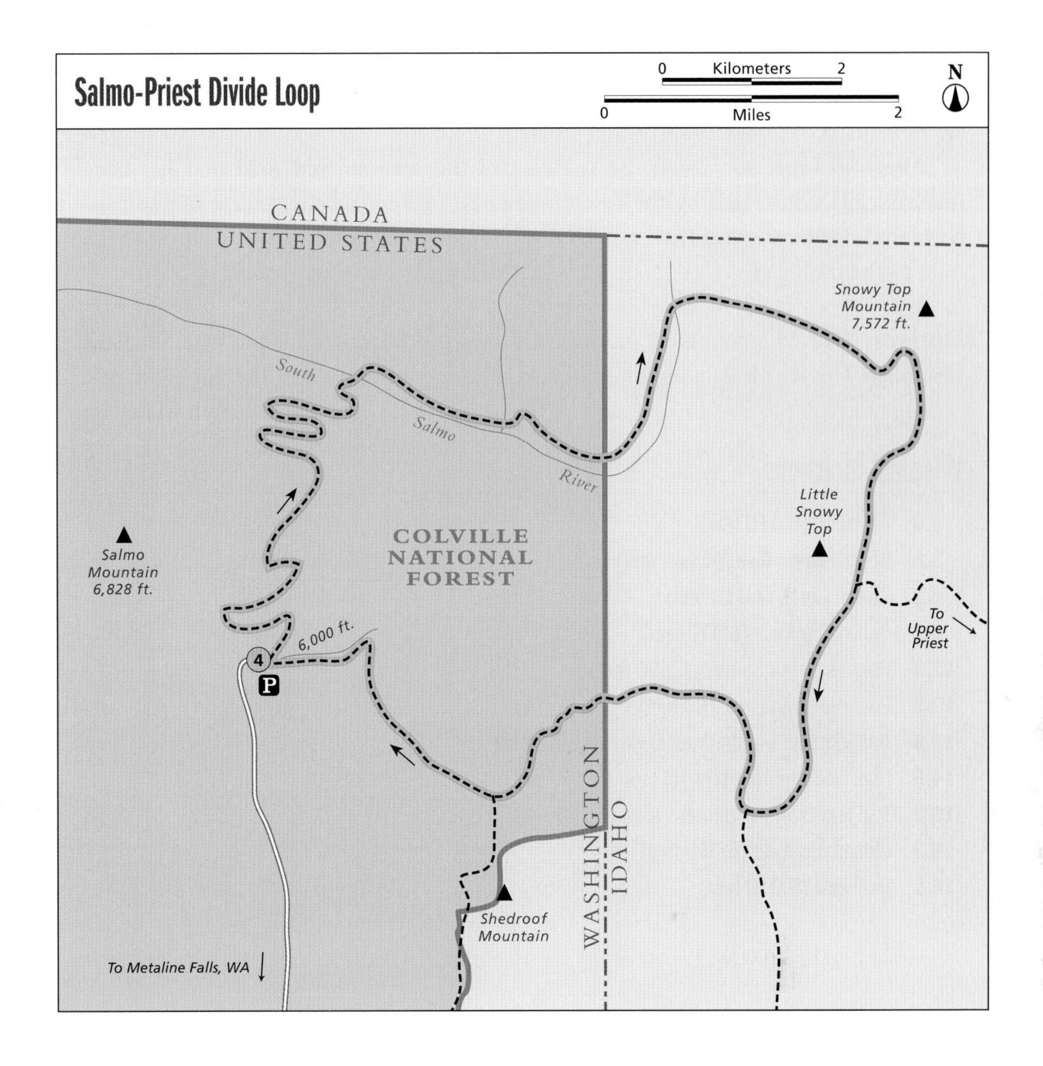


About 2.5 miles from the saddle is the top of the Shedroof Divide and a trail junction. Take Trail 535 back to the trailhead. Trail numbers are no longer marked in the wilderness area, but the direction sign is clear. The trail climbs about 200 feet and reaches some of the highest elevations of the trip. The first part of the last leg is just outside the wilderness area. There are good views of the head of Sullivan Creek and the mountains beyond to the south, and there is a clear-cut right at the base of Shedroof Mountain. It has filled in well, but the origin of the young trees is obvious. Perhaps in twenty years it will look like a regenerated burn. The trail passes through some pleasant meadows just below the ridgetop, then goes into an unremarkable forest and crosses the ridge back into the wilderness area. Once you are into the wilderness area, you drop 120 feet in 0.3 mile and again leave the wilderness, soon coming to a closed road that is reverting to the wild. There are good views from this road of

the scenic peaks forming the north side of the South Salmo River Canyon. The tops of these mountains, since the international boundary runs horizontally across them, are in Canada.

After 0.5 mile, you reach the last part of the hike, an old road that has been mechanically obliterated by the forest service to prevent motor vehicle use and has been replaced by a good trail stabilized by boulders on both sides. It is another 0.3 mile to the trailhead.

**Options:** Trail 512 continues southward down the Shedroof Divide past Shedroof Mountain. This is a pleasant down-and-back, although water is scarce after the snowmelt.

—Ralph Maughan

## Miles and Directions

**0.0** Trailhead (5,910 feet)
**3.5** South Salmo River (4,040 feet)
**4.7** Crutch Creek (4,310 feet)
**9.7** Snowy Top Pass (6,410 feet)
**12.3** Hughes Creek Saddle (5,590 feet)
**13.5** Possible springs (6,200 feet)
**13.8** Trail junction on Shedroof Divide (6,300 feet)
**14.8** High point on return leg of loop (6,400 feet)
**15.2** Trail leaves the wilderness area (6,120 feet)
**15.3** Closed old road (6,080 feet)
**16.1** Trailhead (5,910 feet)

# 5 Two Mouths Lakes

These are two beautiful lakes set in granite, right on top of the Selkirk Crest.

**Start:** 15 miles west of Bonners Ferry
**Type of hike:** Long day hike or overnight; out-and-back
**Distance:** 8 miles round-trip
**Approximate hiking time:** At least 3 hours
**Difficulty:** Moderate
**Best season:** July–September
**Trail surface:** Normal dirt and rocks
**Land status:** Idaho Panhandle National Forests
**Canine compatibility:** On leash
**Fees and permits:** None
**Maps:** Roman Nose and The Wigwams USGS quadrangles; Idaho Panhandle National Forests–Kaniksu National Forest map
**Trail contact:** Bonners Ferry Ranger District, (208) 267-5561, www.fs.usda.gov/idahopandandle
**Special considerations:** Huckleberries line the trail. They ripen in August, so watch for bears.

**Finding the trailhead:** Begin from downtown Bonners Ferry, which is just off US 95. Drive toward the Kootenai River and find Riverside Street; follow Riverside Street west, out of town, to the Kootenai Wildlife Refuge. Pass the refuge headquarters, which sits near the mouth of Myrtle Creek, at about 5 miles. Continue past the headquarters 1.5 miles on paved road until you reach the gravel road up Myrtle Creek. The Myrtle Creek road is at an oblique angle to the paved road, and the sign is hard to see.

Drive up and into big and deep Myrtle Creek Canyon on this road, FR 663. Watch for logging trucks. The road is narrow in places, and the drop into Myrtle Creek is a long way down. Stay on this main road as it approaches the head of the canyon. After about 10.5 miles, you pass the side road to Myrtle Lake; the main road is renumbered FR 633A. From here it is 2 miles to the Two Mouths Trailhead. GPS: N48 43.21' / W116 37.51'
**Parking and trailhead facilities:** The undeveloped trailhead has room for about eight vehicles by the roadside. There is no shade, but there is a good view of a hulking granite dome just to the south.

## The Hike

The trail is well marked, and you are likely to find a cluster of vehicles at the trailhead, underscoring that you are at the right place.

The trail (Trail 268) is a rapidly overgrowing logging road for about the first 1.5 miles. You begin hiking gradually uphill to the north, but you soon enter Peak Creek. The trail makes a right angle and starts up Peak Creek. Soon the trail splits, and a decaying, closed logging road goes to the right and crosses Peak Creek. Stay on the trail to the left.

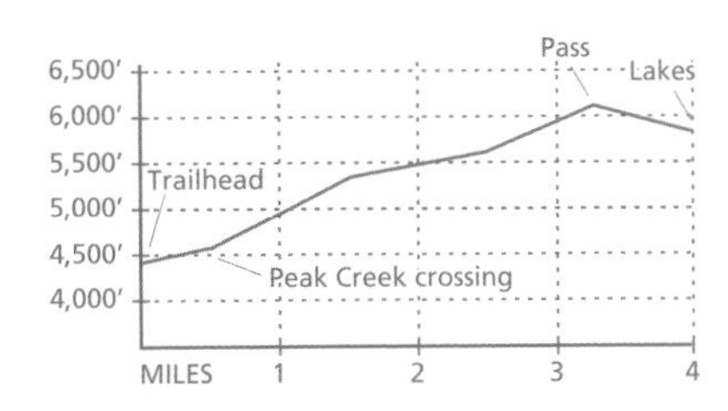


The trail contours back and forth up the mountainside until it drops into the next drainage to the south, Slide Creek.

*Two Mouth Lakes at dawn.* PHOTO BY RALPH MAUGHAN

Just before dropping into Slide Creek, the old road ends. The trail climbs slowly in this increasingly damp canyon. Soon Slide Creek is not far below the trail. The forest is damp, and there are some very big conifers, even including a few giant white pines.

The damp upper part of Slide Creek is very well maintained. Perhaps 0.5 mile of corduroy plank has been built to protect the vast areas of seeps the trail crosses.

There is a large granite dome to the south. Its top is Point 6,168. *The Wigwams* topo map shows the trail crossing Slide Creek and passing across the steepest part of the dome. Were this so, it would be one of the most amazing trails in the world. Of course, the map is wrong. The trail climbs to near the very top of Slide Creek and then makes a half circle to climb steeply up the much gentler back side of the dome to a pass above Two Mouths Lakes. If you have difficulty on this trail, it will be in early season. It is a north-facing slope in a very wet and snowy mountain range. Before July, take an ice ax.

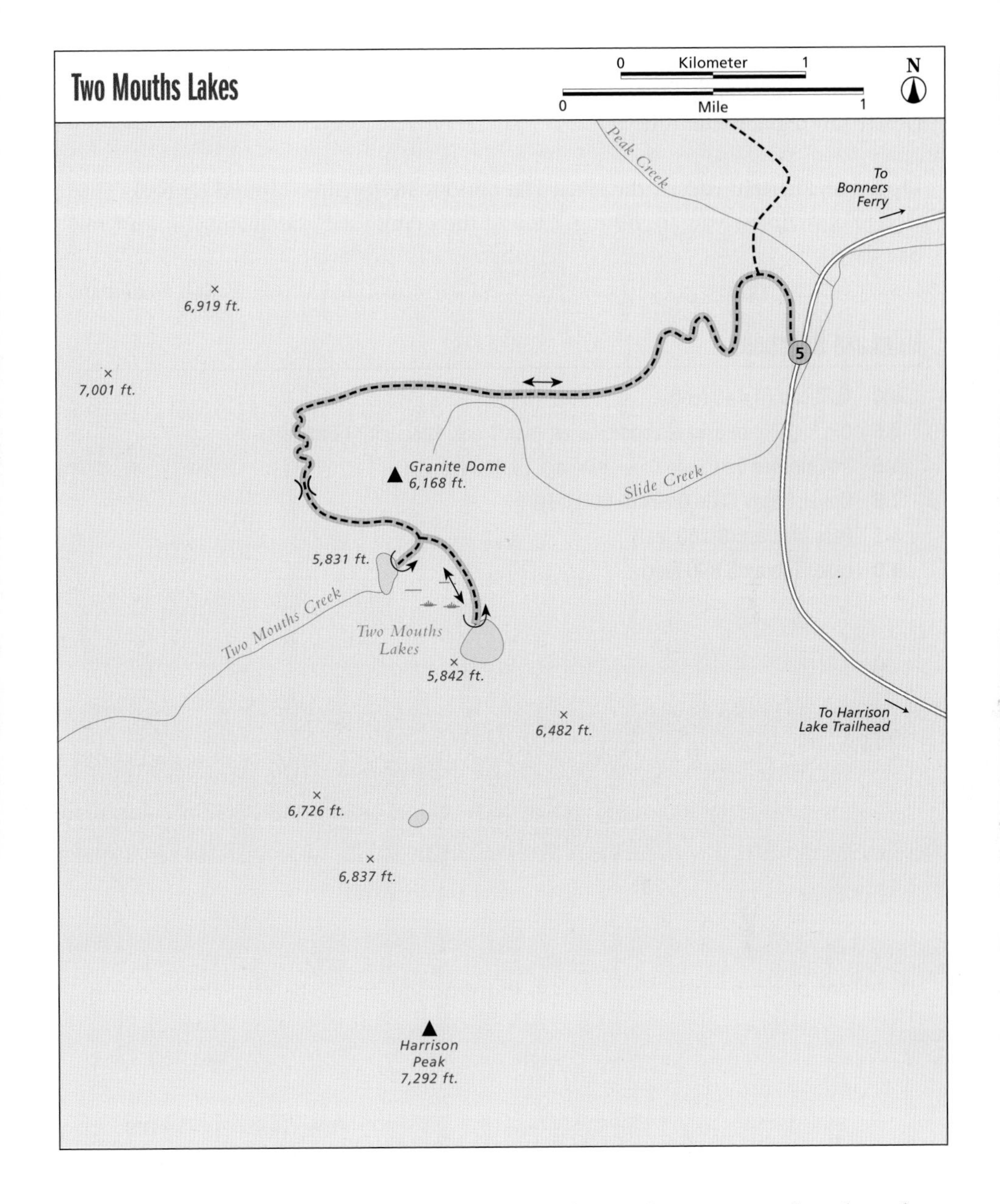


At the pass, which is the Selkirk Crest, you have a fine view north and northwest to the unnamed glaciated peaks around the head of Slide Creek. The highest is Peak 7,001.

From the pass the trail drops down toward Two Mouths Lakes. It soon splits, with the left fork leading to the east lake and the right fork to the west lake. The lakes are about 0.3 mile apart. The east lake is 5 feet higher in elevation than the west. Springs emerge below the granite wall that encases the east lake, and a gentle spring-fed creek meanders lazily through meadow, bog, and granite outcrops to the west lake. The area is relentlessly granite slickrock except for the meadows. It seems as if every peak were chiseled by a giant sculptor.

**Options:** The trail ends at the lakes. The options are to climb around on peaks and take photos, unless you are fishing. I found the granite slabs fascinating (at least for one day).

—Ralph Maughan

## Miles and Directions

- **0.0** Trailhead (4,440 feet)
- **0.5** Old logging road leaves and crosses Peak Creek; keep left (4,600 feet)
- **1.5** Trail crosses into Slide Creek drainage (5,350 feet)
- **2.5** Upper, boggy Slide Creek (5,600 feet)
- **3.2** Pass on crest (6,160 feet)
- **4.0** Lakes (about 5,840 feet)

# 6 Upper Priest River

Experience low-elevation, old-growth interior rain forest, full of giant cedars. There are also occasional sightings of endangered mountain caribou and grizzly bears.

**Start:** Extreme northwestern Idaho; 110 miles northeast of Spokane, Washington; 100 miles north of Coeur d'Alene, Idaho
**Type of hike:** Day hike or overnight backpack; out-and-back or shuttle
**Distance:** 13 miles round-trip, although most people don't complete the hike to American Falls from the Trail 308 trailhead
**Approximate hiking time:** 5 hours–2 days
**Difficulty:** Easy, except for the short Trail 28, which is moderate due to a steep descent and climb back up
**Best season:** Mid-June–October
**Trail surface:** Normal dirt and rocks
**Land status:** Idaho Panhandle National Forests
**Canine compatibility:** On leash
**Fees and permits:** None
**Maps:** Continental Mountain USGS quadrangle; Idaho Panhandle National Forests–Kaniksu National Forest map
**Trail contact:** Priest Lake Ranger District, (208) 443-2512, www.fs.usda.gov/ipnf/priestlake
**Special considerations:** None

**Finding the trailhead:** The trailhead is easy to find, but it is a long drive. Begin in Priest River, Idaho, and take ID 57 north 36 miles to Nordman. ID 57 ends here, but a paved road continues for about 2 miles, then turns to good gravel and becomes FR 302. Follow this pleasant road 10 miles up Granite Creek into Washington and Granite Pass. At the pass is a three-way junction. Take the road in the middle, FR 1013, down Muskegon Creek. This good road descends into Idaho. The road crosses the valley of the upper Priest River and Priest River to reach the roadside trailhead for Trail 308 (about 12 miles from Granite Pass). You have gone too far if the road begins to climb up a switchback.

The trail is hikable quite early and until late in the season. Closure is usually due to snow at Granite Pass. GPS: N48 53.88' / W116 58.01'

**Parking and trailhead facilities:** The undeveloped roadside trailhead has room for about eight vehicles. Very tall trees provide shade most of the day.

## The Hike

The trail proceeds immediately into the forest a few yards south of the trailhead and instantly enters a rare Idaho rain forest. Huge Douglas fir and even larger western

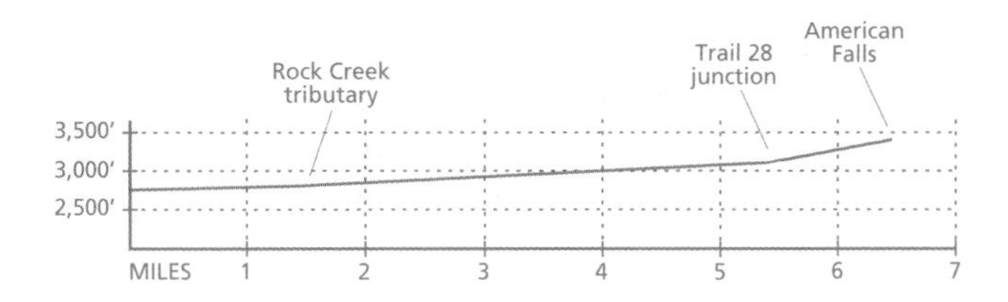

*Upper Priest or "American Falls" near the Canadian Border.* PHOTO BY LUKE KRATZ

red cedar tower well over 100 feet above. The trail is nearly flat as it rambles under the towering conifers through ferns; the big, maple-leaf-like but thorny devil's club; salmonberries; and usually millions of fruiting fungi.

There is little change of elevation or canopy as you walk up the deep, but broad-bottomed, canyon. Most people go part of the way and turn around. If you continue, you eventually reach a junction with Trail 28 and climb into a gorge near the international boundary where American Falls, also called Upper Priest Falls, tumbles through a gorge between the shoulder of Snowy Top and Kaniksu Mountain.

**Options:** Most people who come to the falls take the shorter route provided by Trail 28, which begins near the end of FR 1013. This is the continuation of the road that

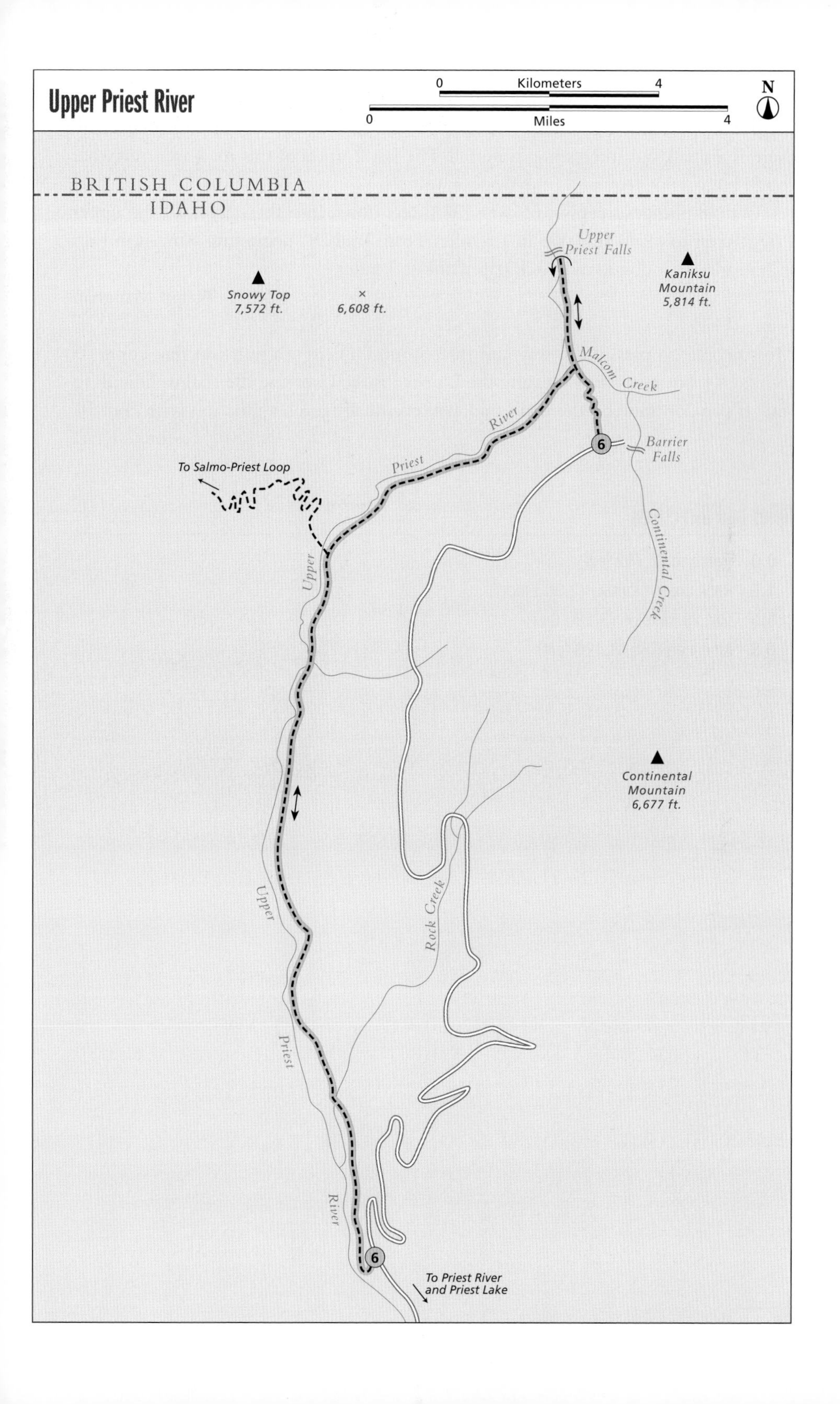

Upper Priest River
0
Kilometers
4
0
Miles
4
N
BRITISH COLUMBIA
IDAHO
Upper
Priest Falls
Kaniksu
Mountain
5,814 ft.
Snowy Top
7,572 ft.
6,608 ft.
Malcom
Creek
River
Barrier
Falls
Priest
To Salmo-Priest Loop
Continental Creek
Upper
Continental
Mountain
6,677 ft.
Upper
Rock Creek
Priest
River
To Priest River
and Priest Lake

leads to and past the trailhead for Trail 308. The road switchbacks part of the way up massive Continental Mountain and in 12 miles ends at Continental Creek, where there is a small, but interesting, waterfall. The last 2 miles of this road are somewhat rough but do not require a four-by-four vehicle.

Trail 28 plunges steeply just over 1,000 feet down into the canyon of the upper Priest River to reach Trail 308 in 1.5 miles. From Trail 28's beginning, American Falls is 2.5 miles, so a down-and-back trip is about 5 miles.

—Ralph Maughan

Most people go part of the way and turn around. There is a junction that connects to hike #4, but it involves crossing the Upper Priest River and the trail is difficult to find. If you continue on the main trail, you eventually reach a junction with Trail 28.

—Luke Kratz

## Miles and Directions

**0.0** Trailhead (2,762 feet)

**1.5** Rock Creek tributary (2,805 feet)

**5.5** Trail 28 junction (3,180 feet)

**6.5** American Falls (3,420 feet)

# Salmon River and Clearwater Mountains

If you can imagine a continuous mass of mountain ridges and canyons 300 miles long and more than 100 miles wide, you can picture the Salmon River and the Clearwater Mountains. This continuous mass makes up most of central and north-central Idaho and the bulk of what is considered the Northern Rocky Mountains in Idaho.

Here, three great wilderness areas have been designated: the Frank Church–River of No Return, the Selway-Bitterroot, and the Gospel Hump. More wilderness still should be designated.

This continuous, rugged stretch of ridges has largely precluded human habitation and development and has cut northern Idaho off from southern Idaho, both economically and socially. Historically, mining and, later, timbering, mostly fueled by taxpayer subsidies, have led to some human habitation in the Salmon River–Clearwater Mountains.

The mountain front that rises immediately north of Boise to where the main stem of the Salmon River cuts directly through the central Idaho mountains from east to west is generally called the Salmon River Mountains. The western boundary is the North Fork of the Payette River; the eastern boundary is the Salmon River as it courses between Challis and Salmon City.

North of the Salmon River Canyon across central Idaho, these mountains are called the Clearwater Mountains, although there is no clear geological distinction. This huge mountain fastness is primarily made of granite-like igneous rocks formed out of one of the largest batholiths in the world—the Idaho Batholith. A batholith is an enormous intrusion of molten rock that pushes toward the earth's surface but cools and crystallizes before it reaches the surface as lava. It is then gradually exposed by uplifting, weather, and water.

Geologists subdivide the Idaho Batholith into a southern and a northern section. The southern is the Atlanta Batholith; the northern, the Bitterroot Batholith. Most

*Mountains of the wild Salmo-Priest area.* Photo by Luke Kratz

people think batholithic rock is all granite. In fact, only some of it is. Whether an igneous crystalline rock is granite depends on its percentage composition of various minerals. Many of these rocks lack the composition of granite. We use the term *granite-like* for these abundant crystalline rocks, such as quartz monzonite and granidiorite.

Finally, much of the eastern part of the Salmon River Mountains consists of huge piles of volcanic rock from ancient tremendous eruptions. These rocks, the Challis Volcanics, are often very colorful. They consist of rhyolite and andesite, but no basalt. These eruptions buried part of the Atlanta lobe of the Idaho Batholith and injected thousands of dikes into the batholith. We find that the color and variety of rock forms in east-central Idaho make some of the most picturesque mountains of the state.

Portions of the Salmon River and Clearwater Mountain masses are broken into subranges and have earned their own names due to their distinctive elevation, scenery, or historic factors. We use some of these distinctions and organize many Salmon

River Mountain hikes by subrange. Examples of these subranges include the Boise Mountains, Trinity Mountain, the Lick Creek Mountains, the Gospels, the Bighorn Crags, and the Selway Crags.

The lower elevations of the Salmon River and Clearwater Mountains are accessible as early as April since the canyon bottoms are as low as 1,500 feet. The peaks reach to 10,000 feet. Strangely, the highest portions of these mountains surround the deep canyons of the Middle, South Fork, and main Salmon River. This is due to isostasy, wherein the removal by erosion of the mountain mass that once filled these enormous, 5,000-foot-deep canyons actually caused the adjacent land to rise.

The number of hiking and backpacking trails in this 30,000-square-mile region is immense. This book represents only a portion of these trails.

While the geology of the Salmon River and Clearwater Mountains is very similar, the climate is not. It becomes increasingly damp as you move from the Boise Front to the heart of the Frank Church–River of No Return Wilderness, and wetter still as you climb north into the Clearwater River drainage. These mountains are, as a result, not one big mass of very similar scenery.

All of the major wildlife species of the Northern Rockies inhabit these mountains, except the grizzly bear. This includes even rare mammals such as lynx and wolverine. Plans are afoot to restore the grizzly to its rightful place in central Idaho, but there is much resistance. The newly restored wolf population is doing well here and spreading in all directions. Hopefully, the salmon and steelhead runs that have become little more than museum tokens will be restored to the time when central Idaho streams ran red with spawning salmon.

—Ralph Maughan

# Selway-Bitterroot Wilderness

The northern third of the great wild country of central Idaho is largely contained within the 1.4-million-acre Selway-Bitterroot Wilderness.

Geologically similar to much of the River of No Return Wilderness country to the south, the Selway-Bitterroot sits atop the huge granitic bulge of the Idaho Batholith. This northern portion is often referred to as the Bitterroot Batholith. Its rocky bones jut to the surface in the form of the Selway Crags in the wilderness's northwest corner and the towering Bitterroot Range to the east on the Idaho-Montana border as well as all of the lesser ridges.

Essentially all of the Selway-Bitterroot is steep country of ridges and canyons. The canyons center on the Selway River (a unit of the National Wild and Scenic Rivers

*Selway River.* Photo by John Kratz

System) and its many tributaries, such as Moose Creek. Much of the wilderness is heavily forested, but nevertheless most of the area is natural fire country. It was partly burned by the great fires of 1910 and 2000.

Efforts by the timber industry and the forest service to dismember the old Selway-Bitterroot Primitive Area when it was administratively reclassified as a wilderness area in the early 1960s gave impetus to the efforts of conservationists nationwide to establish the National Wilderness Preservation System. These efforts were successful in 1964 when Congress passed the Wilderness Act, providing for permanent protection of designated wildernesses by US statute instead of by bureaucratic discretion.

The success of the Wilderness Act and of the classification of the Frank Church–River of No Return Wilderness in 1980, which restored wilderness protection to much of the area ripped out of the Selway-Bitterroot Primitive Area by the forest service in 1963, means that the Selway River today runs clear and clean. The sandy soils derived from the granitic batholith, which run like sugar when logging and road building strip them of their protective cover of vegetation, are secure in this wilderness area. Chief among the areas restored is the north side of Magruder Corridor on the Selway-Bitterroot's south side.

The same protection was not obtained for the Lochsa Face on the north side of the wilderness. The Lochsa River, another famed stream in the National Wild and Scenic Rivers System, is today threatened by logging on its steep slopes, much of it carried out by means of subsidies that make it artificially attractive to cut timber but end up costing more than the trees are worth—a process that some people call "welfare logging."

It will be interesting to watch the regeneration of those portions burned by the wildfires of 2000. Because fire is natural and normal in the area, full regeneration should be expected, but noxious weeds have invaded the lower canyons over the last twenty years, especially spotted knapweed, the tall, many-headed pink flower that blooms in August. This weed from across the oceans could forestall recovery of this great wilderness as it chokes out everything else. The specter of global warming pretends that future fires may not be natural.

—Ralph Maughan

# 7 Lower Selway River

This is a beautiful wilderness river in a deep forested canyon. There is early- and late-season access as well as routes to many loop backpacking trips.

**Start:** 132 road miles east of Lewiston in the Selway-Bitterroot Wilderness
**Type of hike:** Day hike or backpack; out-and-back, with loop side-trip options
**Distance:** 12 miles round-trip described here, although many loops of great distance can be started from this trail
**Approximate hiking time:** 4–5 hours
**Difficulty:** Moderately easy. Most of the options are strenuous
**Best season:** July–September
**Trail surface:** Normal rocks and dirt
**Land status:** Selway-Bitterroot Wilderness; Nez Perce National Forest
**Canine compatibility:** On leash. Not allowed in wilderness
**Fees and permits:** None
**Maps:** Fog Mountain and Selway Falls USGS quadrangles; Selway-Bitterroot Wilderness map; Nez Perce National Forest map
**Trail contact:** Moose Creek Ranger District, (208) 926-4258, www.fs.usda.gov/nezperce

**Finding the trailhead:** From Lewiston, drive east on US 12 for 114 miles up the Clearwater River to Lowell, Idaho. Here, the Lochsa and Selway Rivers meld their waters to form the Middle Fork of the Clearwater River. All three rivers are units in the National Wild and Scenic Rivers System. From Lowell cross the river and continue right (east) onto Selway River Road (FR 223).

It is about 18 miles to the trailhead. This road is paved for 7 miles to O'Hara Creek and then turns to gravel. It is usually passable throughout the hiking season, except occasionally during the peak of spring snowmelt (late May to mid-June), when the river may flood its banks and the road in places. Stay on the main road, always with the river on your right. You'll pass scenic Selway Falls and continue along the river for a mile or so to the road's end at Race Creek Campground. GPS: N46 2.65' / W115 17.01'

**Parking and trailhead facilities:** Parking for twenty to thirty vehicles. Three developed sites, pit toilets, but no running water. (For information about other Selway River campgrounds, see Hike 15, Meadow Creek.)

## The Hike

Due to its low elevation, this is one of the earliest accessible trails in northern Idaho. It begins at 1,780 feet elevation at the upstream end of the lower parking area, where you will see the trail register. The trail (Trail 4) heads upstream (east) along the north side of the Selway. It sparkles with mica on sunny days as it winds along the river

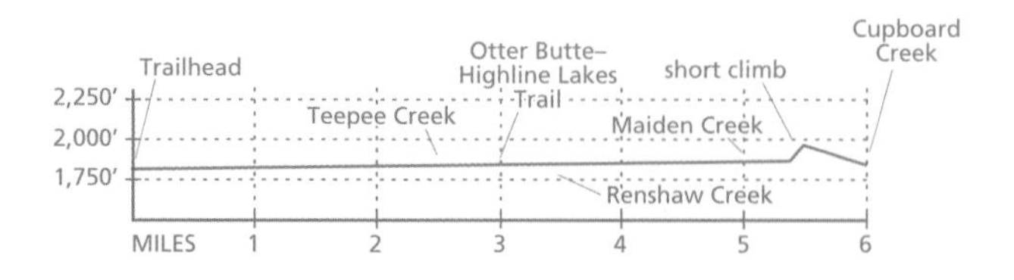

through a canyon cutting through decomposing Idaho Batholith granite. The first level 1.5 miles is outside the wilderness area, but the forest service has banned trail bikes in this area so it is wilderness in fact, even if not by law.

You'll see the sign marking the wilderness boundary shortly after you cross Packer Creek at about mile 1.5. This and other creeks flow steeply down from Fog Mountain (6,538 feet) to the Selway (1,785 feet). They roar with icy clear snowmelt during May and June, but they can be easily crossed on appropriately placed logs. Although the Selway also runs bank-full in spring, it nevertheless runs clear because it drains more than a million acres of pristine Selway-Bitterroot Wilderness. Alas, the fishing doesn't get really good until the water begins to recede (in some years, late July). All along the trail are nice rest stops under big cedars or on the numerous sand beaches. This trail is perfect for leisurely weekend family hikes, but watch small children closely since the trail traverses ledges and cliffs that drop abruptly to the river.

About 2.5 miles in, you cross Teepee Creek; 0.5 mile farther you meet Otter Butte–Highline Lakes Trail. Continue on the main river trail through mixed ponderosa pine, western red cedar, and Douglas fir to reach Renshaw Creek at 3.5 miles. The forest here is young and vigorous, especially on the north-facing slopes across the river. Young conifers have replaced a forest scorched by the tremendous fire of 1910, which swept over three million acres of northern Idaho in a matter of days. Numerous picturesque snags still stand as reminders of the great fire.

There are several nice, heavily used campsites at Renshaw Creek, and this is where you will lose most day hikers. From here the trail climbs about 100 feet in a mile and then stays high for a while. There are great views up and down the canyon, with occasional upstream glimpses of snowcapped mountain ridges. At about 6 miles, you'll reach Cupboard Creek, a beach, and roaring rapids with a big drop. Cupboard Creek is a good goal for hikers out for a weekend trip.

The Selway River itself is a very important stream for fish. Chinook salmon and steelhead trout spawn in the river and its tributaries. It also has abundant rainbow, brook, cutthroat, and bull trout (the latter is on the threatened species list, as is this run of salmon). Wildlife in the area include deer, elk, moose, black bear, beaver, river otter, and an occasional wolf.

**Options:** Otter Butte–Highline Lakes Trail: If you wish to take this trail, you must make a difficult (impossible in spring) ford of the river. Once across, you climb a steep 3.3 miles and 4,300 feet from the river level to Otter Butte (6,088 feet). Then the trail climbs Highline Ridge to the crest of Mink Mountain (7,260 feet) and drops down into the cirque basin of the two Highline Lakes. It is a strenuous hike but rewarding for those interested in panoramic views and mountain lakes less crowded than those of the Selway Crags farther north. The Highline Lakes can also be reached, without such an extreme climb, from a trailhead at Indian Hill (6,810 feet).

Big Fog Saddle Trail: From Cupboard Creek, an unsigned side trail (Trail 710, not on the topographic quadrangle) takes off from the river trail and climbs about

4,100 feet from river level (at approximately 1,800 feet) to Big Fog Saddle (at 5,900 feet) and the terminus of Fog Mountain Road, from which many hikers enter the Selway Crags.

For hikers interested in an extended trip into the Selway country, the river trail continues upstream, and there are side trails to take you into the high country. Your choices are limited only by your imagination (or stamina, if you choose to hike up out of the canyon). On the river trail, you can walk upstream all the way to the Magruder Road's crossing of the Selway and then into the river's headwaters, which are inside the 2.4-million-acre Frank Church–River of No Return Wilderness.

A challenging one-way loop trip involving the lower Selway trail starts at Big Fog Saddle (see Hike 8, Selway Crags via Big Fog and Legend Lakes, for directions) and loops through the Selway Crags via the Cove Lakes, Jesse Pass, and the South Three Links Lakes. It then drops down to the Selway River via Three Links Creek Trail. From here it is 15 miles downstream to the trailhead at Race Creek. The total distance is more than 30 miles with lots of ups and downs. A week is needed to really enjoy the country. Logistics will require two vehicles, one to get you to Big Fog Saddle and one waiting at Race Creek Campground when you finish the hike.

—Don L. Crawford

## Miles and Directions

**0.0** Trailhead (1,780 feet)

**1.5** Wilderness boundary (1,800 feet)

**2.5** Teepee Creek (1,800 feet)

**3.0** Otter Butte–Highline Lakes Trail (requires ford) (1,800 feet)

**3.5** Renshaw Creek (1,800 feet)

**5.0** Maiden Creek (1,830 feet)

**5.5** Top of short climb (1,934 feet)

**6.0** Cupboard Creek (1,830 feet)

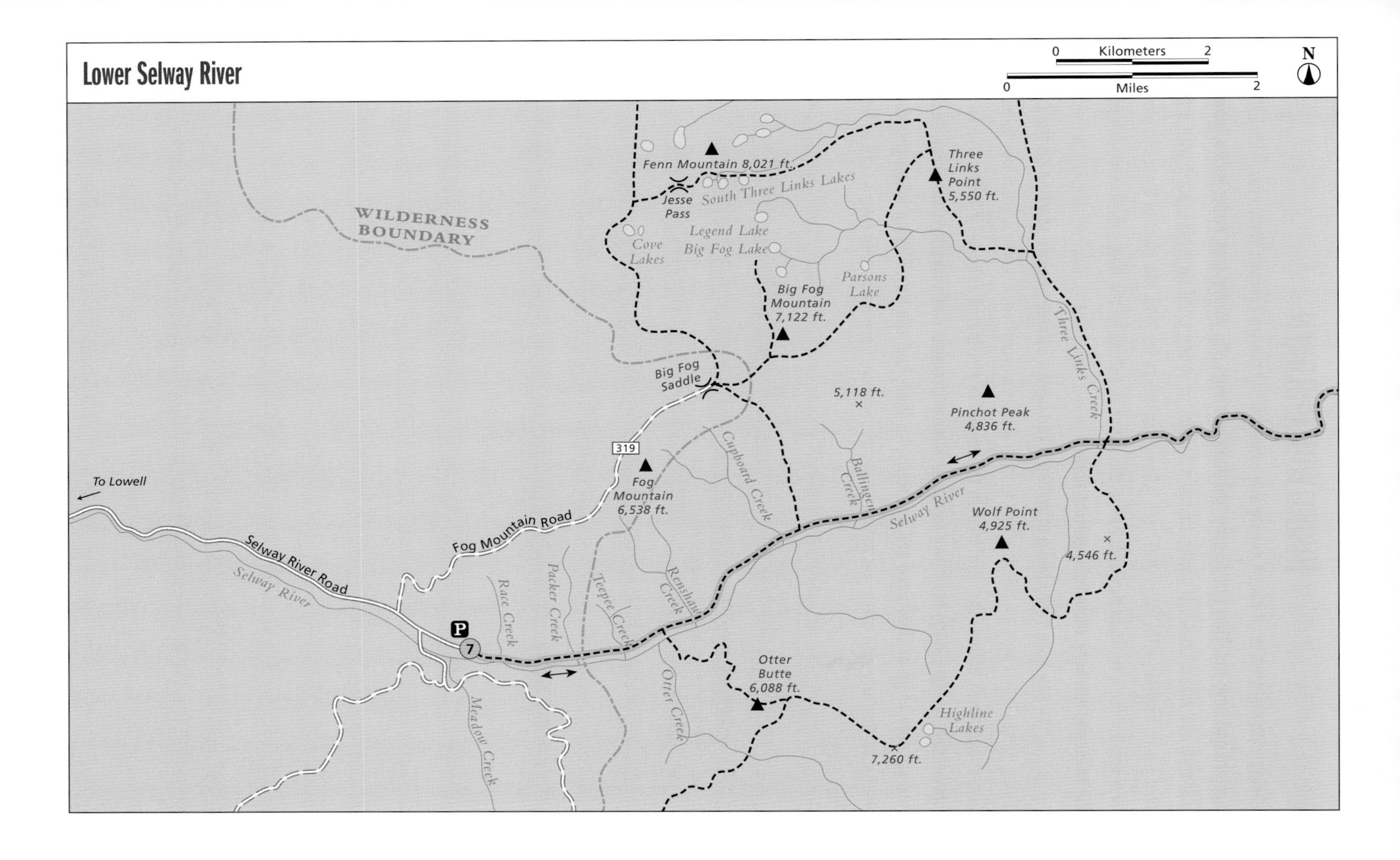
Lower Selway River
0 Kilometers 2
0 Miles 2
N
WILDERNESS BOUNDARY
Fenn Mountain 8,021 ft.
Jesse Pass
South Three Links Lakes
Cove Lakes
Legend Lake
Big Fog Lake
Three Links Point 5,550 ft.
Parsons Lake
Big Fog Mountain 7,122 ft.
Big Fog Saddle
5,118 ft.
Pinchot Peak 4,836 ft.
Three Links Creek
319
Fog Mountain 6,538 ft.
Cupboard Creek
Ballingen Creek
Selway River
Wolf Point 4,925 ft.
4,546 ft.
To Lowell
Fog Mountain Road
Selway River Road
Selway River
Race Creek
Packer Creek
Teepee Creek
Renshaw Creek
Otter Creek
Meadow Creek
P
7
Otter Butte 6,088 ft.
Highline Lakes
7,260 ft.

# HIKING WITH CHILDREN

Hiking with children is all about seeing and experiencing nature through their eyes. Kids like to explore and have fun. They like to stop and point out bugs and plants, look under rocks, jump in puddles, and throw sticks. If you're taking a toddler or young child on a hike, start with a trail that you're familiar with. Trails that have interesting things for kids, like piles of leaves to play in or a small stream to wade through during the summer, will make the hike much more enjoyable for them and will keep them from getting bored.

You can keep your child's attention if you have a strategy before starting on the trail. Using games is not only an effective way to keep a child's attention, it's also a great way to teach him or her about nature. Quiz children on the names of plants and animals. If your children are old enough, let them carry their own daypacks filled with treats and a favorite (small) toy. So that you are sure to go at their pace and not yours, let them lead the way. Playing follow the leader works particularly well when you have a group of children. Have each child take a turn at being the leader.

# 8 Selway Crags via Big Fog and Legend Lakes

The crags' entrance up Big Fog Mountain provides access to ridgeline hiking in the Selway-Bitterroot Wilderness to lightly used alpine lakes. Much of the trail traverses old burns with picturesque snags and panoramic views.

**Start:** 146 road miles east of Lewiston
**Type of hike:** Backpack out and back with options for loops
**Distance:** 8.6 miles round-trip
**Approximate hiking time:** 2–3 days
**Difficulty:** Strenuous due to elevation gain and loss and cross-country navigation
**Best season:** July–mid-October
**Trail surface:** Normal dirt and rocks
**Land status:** Selway-Bitterroot Wilderness; Nez Perce National Forest.
**Maps:** Fog Mountain and Fenn Mountain USGS quadrangles; Selway-Bitterroot Wilderness map; Nez Perce National Forest map
**Canine compatibility:** Not allowed
**Fees and permits:** None
**Trail contact:** Moose Creek Ranger District, (208) 926-4258
**Special considerations:** Snow keeps Fog Mountain Road closed before and after July and October. Access to Legend and Big Fog Lakes is cross-country and requires navigational skills.

**Finding the trailhead:** From Lewiston drive east on US 12 for 114 miles to Lowell. From Lowell, continue right (east) onto Selway River Road (FR 223).

Follow Selway River Road upstream for about 17 miles. Just short of Selway Falls and directly after the Gedney Creek crossing, you will come to Fog Mountain Road (FR 319), which meets Selway River Road from the left (north). Take Fog Mountain Road. If you miss this turn, you'll come to the end of the river road after another mile, at Race Creek Campground.

Fog Mountain Road ends at Big Fog Saddle after a drive of about 14 miles with a steep climb of 4,100 feet! A sign at the bottom warns that it's steep, narrow, and winding. Indeed, Fog Mountain Road is extremely steep and loaded with rocks that can kiss an oil pan or burn out an automatic transmission. GPS: N46 6.83' / W115 12.24'

**Parking and trailhead facilities:** At Big Fog Saddle you'll find ample parking but few good campsites. This undeveloped site is heavily used despite the difficult access.

## The Hike

The Selway Crags are large in area, containing numerous alpine lakes hidden within deep cirques and surrounded by jagged peaks. The hiker who takes the trail described here avoids the crowds, which tend to congregate at just a few of the lakes, and finds real solitude among the crags. Big Fog Lake and Legend Lake lie in a beautiful basin to the south of the main peaks. They are reached by a strenuous hike across the top of Big Fog Mountain (7,122 feet). From this trail, the panorama of the Selway-Bitterroot Wilderness unfolds to the north, south, and east as far as the eye can see.

Three trailheads are located at Big Fog Saddle. The far left trail drops down to the northwest to cross Canteen Creek. It then climbs 6 miles to the Cove Lakes. This is one of the most popular trails in the entire wilderness. The far right trail heads east and contours the south side of Big Fog Mountain, passes Parsons Lake, and then joins the Three Links Lakes. These lakes lie directly below Fenn Mountain (8,021 feet) in the heart of the crags.

The center trail (Trail 343) heads northeast up and over Big Fog Mountain and then follows a high ridge north into the south side of the crags. This is the trail to take. Reconnoiter the trailhead choices carefully before starting out. The first time I hiked in the crags, I headed for the Cove Lakes (like almost everyone else), took the wrong trail by mistake, and ended up at Legend Lake (with no regrets).

Fog Mountain Trail is the only one that starts out with a stiff climb. It initially switchbacks from the 5,920-foot level to 6,880 feet in a distance of 1 mile. Most of this area was once burned, and there are many snags. Once atop the ridge, you'll have an easier time as the trail climbs more gently to a high point at 6,920 feet. This is a good spot to rest and have lunch as you look northward across the glacier-carved canyon of Canteen Creek to its sheer white-and-gray rock headwall rising abruptly more than 1,500 feet to peaks as high as 7,623 feet.

The trail continues northeast along the ridgeline and skirts the south side of Big Fog Mountain (7,122 feet). This is wide-open country, where cross-country travel is easy and trails tend to disappear. From Big Fog Mountain, you're mostly on your own. Don't continue eastward on the main trail, for it will drop down in a distance of 2 miles to a point (6,312 feet) above Parsons Lake. Instead, now 1.5 miles into the journey, turn to your left at Big Fog Mountain and onto Trail 363 to follow the sharp ridgeline north. The trail is generally good, but from this point on you may find yourself on animal trails that abruptly fade away to nothing. These "goat" trails are numerous and easy to take by mistake. You cannot go wrong, however, since the ridge drops off sharply on both the east and west. The ridgelines are beautiful in early September when the abundant buckwheat turns a golden brown.

This narrow ridgeline separates the Canteen Creek drainage (west) from that of Three Links Creek (east). Big Fog Lake and Legend Lake lie in cirques that form the headwaters of the West Fork of Three Links Creek. You'll drop from the 7,000-foot level to a windy saddle (6,795 feet) about 0.8 mile north of Big Fog Mountain. From here you look directly down on a small, unnamed lake to your right (east). Continue to contour northward along the 6,800-foot line (refer to your topo), and after passing through a rocky, marshy area with crags above you to the left, you'll see Big Fog Lake well below you to the east. The entire lake is visible from above. It is often frequented by moose. Indeed, I have had the luck of seeing moose every time I've hiked in the crags.

Access to Big Fog Lake is easiest by continuing on to Legend Lake and then approaching Big Fog from the north. Still on the trail, continue north. The Selway Crags are visible to the northeast, especially the sharp ridge separating the cirque

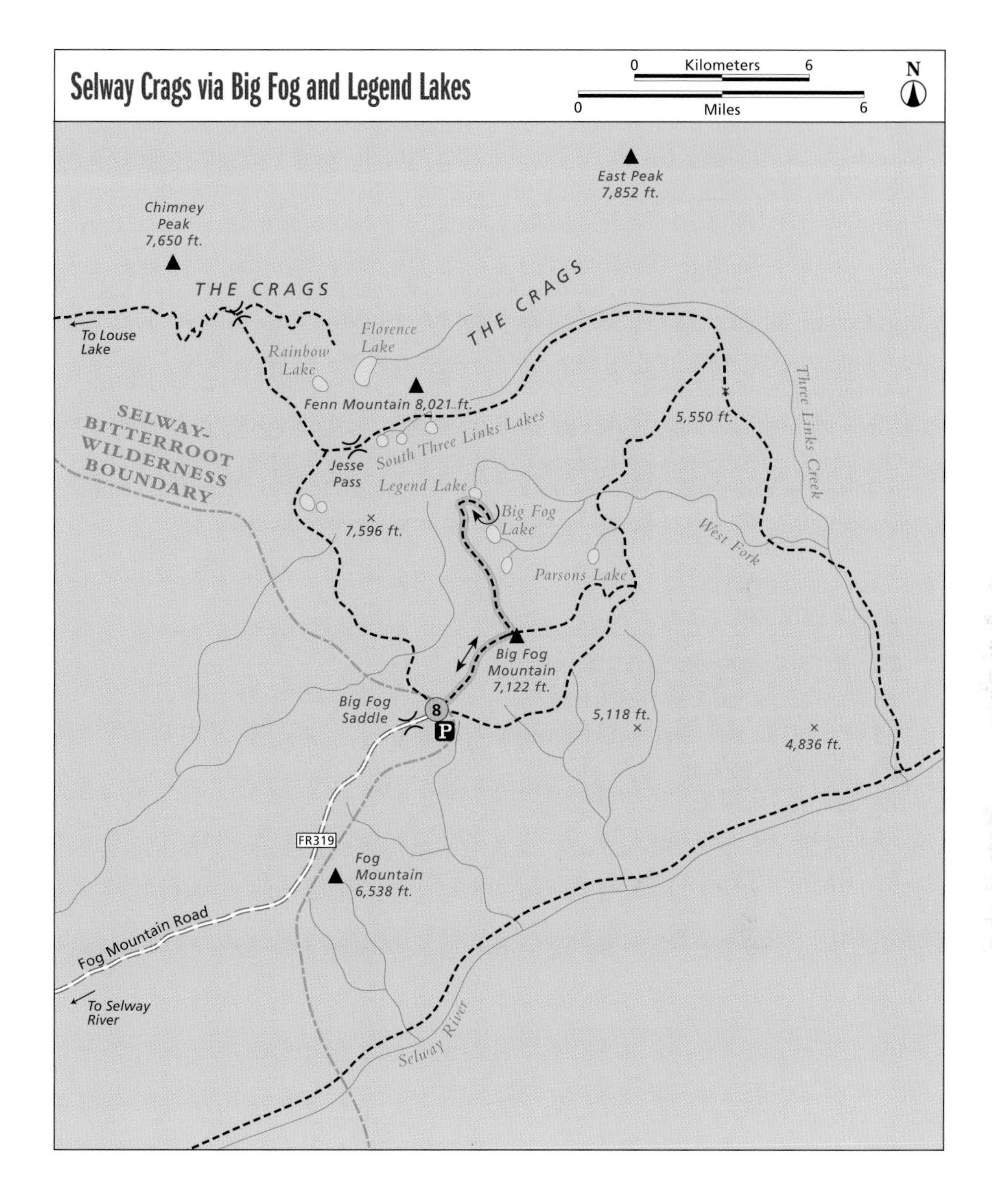


of Legend Lake on the south from that of the South Three Links Lakes on the north. As you continue northward and approach this massive wall of sheer rock and talus, there is but faint sign of any trail. At mile 3.5 you'll reach Point 7,315 and the end of the trail shown on your maps. Here you drop down from the east side of Point 7,315 for 500 feet and 0.3 mile cross-country to reach the deep, blue waters of Legend Lake (6,800 feet). There is a small, but nice, campsite at the west end of the lake.

No trail leads from Legend Lake to Big Fog Lake, so start downhill from the east side of Legend, then turn south to skirt above the cliffs, and then aim for Point 6,464 (shown on your topo) to drop easily down to the north side of Big Fog. No campsites are evident, but there is a flat spot above the lake on the northeast side (near Point 6,464). This is a fragile site; make it a fireless camp if you choose to stay the night. Photographers will like this spot, especially in the early-morning hours on clear days.

**Options:** There is no simple loop through the crags via Big Fog and Legend Lakes that does not require some backtracking. From Big Fog Mountain, you can continue east and connect with South Three Links Lakes Trail via forest service Trail 693. From the upper of these three lakes (6,780 feet), you can climb by trail over Jesse Pass (7,200 feet) and then drop down to the Cove Lakes (6,320 feet). Cove Lakes Trail then provides a route back to Big Fog Saddle. This is a strenuous loop with many ups and downs. But in reality, there are no hikes in the rugged Selway Crags that can be considered easy. All, however, can be considered infinitely worthwhile.

—Don L. Crawford

## Miles and Directions

**0.0** Big Fog Saddle trailhead (5,920 feet)

**1.0** Big Fog Mountain ridge (6,880 feet)

**1.5** Trail 363 junction below Big Fog Mountain (7,000 feet)

**2.3** Saddle (6,795 feet)

**3.5** Point (7,315 feet)

**3.8** Legend Lake (6,800 feet)

**4.3** Big Fog Lake (6,464 feet)

# 9 Seven Lakes Loop

The Seven Lakes Loop is an extensive adventure to several lush and rocky lake basins in the rarely visited northern portion of the Selway Crags with a stopover at Stanley Hot Springs on the way.

**Start:** Trailhead parking area at Wilderness Gateway, milepost 122 on US 12; 120 miles east of Lewiston, Idaho, and 100 miles west of Missoula, Montana
**Type of hike:** Multiday backpack; lollipop hike
**Distance:** 22.9 miles
**Approximate hiking time:** 20 hours in 3–4 days of hiking
**Difficulty:** Strenuous due to length
**Best season:** After high-water season due to ford crossing at Boulder Creek; July–October
**Trail surface:** Normal dirt and rock
**Land status:** Selway-Bitterroot Wilderness; Clearwater National Forest
**Canine compatibility:** Not allowed
**Fees and permits:** None
**Maps:** Huckleberry Butte and Greenside Butte USGS quads
**Trail contact:** Lochsa Ranger District, (208) 926-4275, www.fs.usda.gov/nezperceclearwater
**Special considerations:** Due to the ford crossing of Boulder Creek at mile 4.5, this hike is not possible during high water (May, June). However, you can take Lochsa Peak Trail (Trail 220), which leaves from southern end of the same wilderness gateway. This alternative route is a 23-mile out-and-back hike and does not pass Stanley Hot Springs.

**Finding the trailhead:** From Lewiston up the Clearwater River on US 12 drive approximately 120 miles until you reach the Wilderness Gateway Campground at milepost 122. From Missoula, Montana, take US 12 100 miles to cross the bridge over Boulder Creek, and access the Boulder Creek Trail (Trail 211) on the east side of the stream. GPS: N45 20.16' / W115 18.76'

## The Hike

The Selway Crags are a small group of rugged mountains between the Lochsa River to the north and the Selway River to the south in the western portion of the Selway-Bitterroot Wilderness. Most backpackers visit the more popular lakes in the central Selway Crags area farther south; the trails there are accessed from steep and rough roads leaving the Selway River. This hike is a strenuous yet rewarding alternative if you'd like to experience the crags' ruggedness and isolation but don't want to drive for hours on unmaintained four-by-four forest roads to get to the trailhead. This hike's trailhead is easily reached from US 12.

The Selway Crags' abrupt elevation gains create varying life zones ranging from wet cedar forests to high, subalpine forests and peaks; plant and wildlife diversity here is high. The Seven Lakes area of the crags is composed of several small lake basins of subalpine forest and meadows surrounded by rocky buttes. This route provides opportunities for exploring ten or more lakes and the ridges surrounding their basins, including summiting 7,362-foot Stanley Butte. Backpackers also have a good chance at observing wildlife and catching fish in the lakes and streams. As an even greater incentive for completing the difficult route, you can reward yourself with a relaxing soak at Stanley Hot Springs on the way in and out of the Seven Lakes area.

The hike begins near the mouth of Boulder Creek at a low 2,019 feet in elevation. The Lochsa River Canyon here is dominated by moist forests of cedar, white pine, and ponderosa pine with a fern understory. The trail starts to climb immediately and skirts the hillside above the south side of the creek. After the first 0.5 mile the trail begins to pass through open forests of birch, maple, scattered conifers, and dense ferns. For the next couple of miles, the trail gives scenic vistas of the Lochsa River and Lochsa Peak behind you, along with thickly forested peaks ahead. After 2.7 miles you pass a sign marking the entrance to the Selway-Bitterroot Wilderness. At just over 4 miles, you reach an open hillside with gorgeous views and a marked junction with the Rock Lake Creek Trail (Trail 2210). You want to veer right on this trail and start heading down the hill toward the rushing sound of Boulder Creek. *Do not attempt to ford the creek during high water.* The Seven Lakes can be accessed from an alternative route (Lochsa Peak Trail, or Trail 220, from Wilderness Gateway) during dangerous spring runoff. While this is a fairly easy ford to make during low-water season, always exercise extreme caution. I prefer the help of a walking stick collected from the forest; I also take along a pair of sandals or old tennis shoes so I can keep my hiking boots dry.

After fording Boulder Creek, you reach a nice campsite that might be a good option for the first night. Half a mile up the trail you encounter the magical Stanley Hot Springs, situated in an open glade in dense cedar forest. This is the last point on the route where you might find other hikers. Most backpackers prefer to spend the first night at one of the many campsites in the vicinity and save the remaining 5 miles of climbing to the lake basins for the second day. This also gives you more time to relax in the hot springs and fish the Huckleberry and Boulder Creeks. When I arrived at about 2 p.m. in early July, the pools were just beginning to get shaded by trees. Since Stanley Hot Springs sees relatively high use, be sure to practice low-impact techniques while camping in the area.

From Stanley Hot Springs, Rock Lake Trail continues south through thick forests—it's possible to lose the trail here due to the many spur trails leading to campsites. To avoid this, veer left shortly after you leave the springs area, following the trail south and up the hillside. After 0.5 mile the trail reaches the junction with Greenside Butte Trail (Trail 222). I met three trail maintenance workers there who were clearing the trails and were very surprised and glad to see another hiker. They told me they rarely encounter hikers in the area, and horse parties only once every ten days or so.

At this junction, bear left and follow the Greenside Butte Trail for a couple miles of steep climbing. Here the elevation changes abruptly from 4,000 to nearly 6,000 feet and you can observe the forest transform from lower cedar forest, to Douglas fir forest, and finally to the lodgepole pine forest at the ridgeline of Greenside Butte. A mile and a half past the junction, the trail crosses a tributary of Rock Lake Creek in a gorgeous meadow; this is a good spot to take a break and get water. Three miles after the junction, you reach the ridge south of Greenside Butte, and the trail now follows

*Looking north towards Greenside Butte.* PHOT BY JOHN KRATZ

a gentler grade. Gorgeous views of the Surprise Creek drainage to the east and the Central Crags area to the south begin to open up. For the next mile you are treated to an easy ridge walk. There is spectacular scenery to enjoy, including a view of Rock Lake through the trees, 500 feet below you. The trail now begins a gradual descent into the Seven Lakes basin. Four miles after the junction with Greenside Butte Trail, you reach a signed junction with Lochsa Peak Trail (Trail 220). Veer left at the junction and hike 0.5 mile east to reach campsites at the Seven Lakes. This a great place to camp on your first or second night of the trek. For a quick survey of the vicinity, climb the enormous granite boulder between the two main Seven Lakes. From here you can see the Seven Lakes on both sides of you, the ridge west of Stanley Butte to the southeast, and Surprise Creek drainage to the south.

Before traveling west to the next lake basin, I highly recommend making the 3-mile round-trip day hike to the top of Stanley Butte. Trail 220 provides access to the peak itself. Just follow this trail southeast out of camp, climbing along open ridges with patches of spruce, whitebark pine, and lodgepole pine forest. From the top of Stanley Butte, you can see a full panorama of the Selway-Bitterroot Wilderness. The Bitterroot Mountains form a crest in the eastern horizon while the giants of the central crags—Fenn Mountain, East Peak, and Chimney Peak—all loom above lake basins and canyons a few miles to the south.

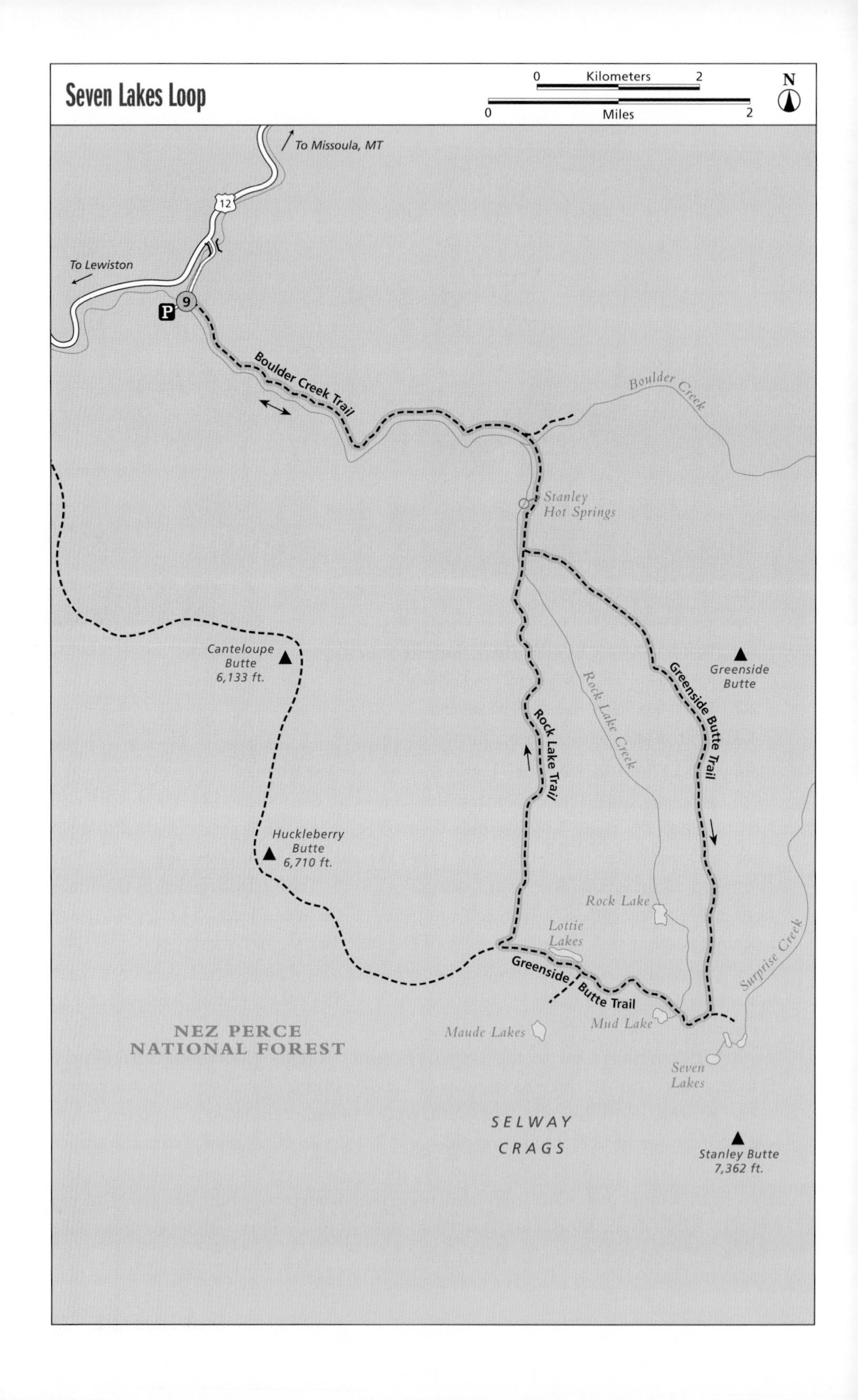
Seven Lakes Loop
0 Kilometers 2
0 Miles 2
N
To Missoula, MT
12
To Lewiston
9
P
Boulder Creek Trail
Boulder Creek
Stanley Hot Springs
Canteloupe Butte 6,133 ft.
Greenside Butte
Rock Lake Creek
Greenside Butte Trail
Rock Lake Trail
Huckleberry Butte 6,710 ft.
Rock Lake
Lottie Lakes
Surprise Creek
Greenside Butte Trail
Mud Lake
Maude Lakes
NEZ PERCE NATIONAL FOREST
Seven Lakes
SELWAY CRAGS
Stanley Butte 7,362 ft.

On the next day of the hike, retrace your steps 0.5 mile to the junction with Greenside Butte Trail 222. This time, continue west on Trail 220 to reach other lakes in the vicinity. You have your choice of making camp at a number of lakes along this trail. First, you will reach Mud Lake, about a mile past the Seven Lakes. At 1.5 miles you reach a rocky opening in the forest with incredible views of the Lottie Lakes in the green valley below. Continue downhill another mile from this ridge to the Lottie Lakes, passing close by East Maude Lake on the way. You will find a good campsite between Upper and Lower Lottie Lake. The scenery is beautiful in this area; while somewhat less rocky than Seven Lakes, the vegetation is more lush. If you choose to explore or fish the nearby Maude Lakes, there is a trail heading south from the campsite between the Lottie Lakes.

The final portion of the route returns to Stanley Hot Springs via Rock Creek Trail (Trail 2210). Head west on Trail 220 for less than a mile to reach the junction with Rock Creek Trail. Bear right on this trail and climb for 0.5 mile or so before descending for 4 miles into Huckleberry Creek and the familiar Stanley Hot Springs. Follow the trail past the hot springs, ford Boulder Creek again, and return to the trailhead on the same Boulder Creek Trail (Trail 211) that you came in on.

## Miles and Directions

**0.0** Trailhead parking area, Wilderness Gateway

**0.3** Inception of trail at Boulder Creek Trailhead

**2.7** Trail enters Selway-Bitterroot Wilderness

**4.3** Junction with Trail 2210; bear right

**4.5** Trail fords Boulder Creek

**4.6** Good campsite at Boulder Creek

**5.0** Stanley Hot Springs

**5.5** Junction with Trail 222; bear left

**8.2** Overlook near top of Greenside Butte

**9.5** Trail 220

**10.0** Bridge over Surprise Creek

**10.5** Trail backtracks to junction with Trail 220; bear left

**11.0** Rock Lake Creek

**11.4** Overlook with views of Lottie Lakes below

**11.9** East Maude Lake

**12.5** Campsite between Upper and Lower Lottie Lakes

**13.3** Junction with Trail 2210; bear right

**17.3** Junction with Trail 222; continue forward on 2210

**17.9** Stanley Hot Springs

**18.4** Boulder Creek

**22.6** Wilderness Gateway

**22.9.** Trailhead parking area

# 10 White Cap Creek

If you really want to get away from it all this is the hike for you. It is quite a long hike into deep, deep wilderness with lakes and amazing scenery.

**Start:** 65 miles west of Darby, Montana. White Cap Creek drains from the west slope of the Bitterroot Mountains in the Selway-Bitterroot Wilderness
**Type of hike:** Multiday backpack; out-and-back, although loops of more than a week can be done using this trail as part of the loop
**Distance:** 45 miles round-trip
**Approximate hiking time:** 6–7 days plus
**Difficulty:** Once the snowmelt has receded, moderately strenuous
**Best season:** August
**Trail surface:** Normal dirt and rock
**Land status:** Selway-Bitterroot Wilderness; Bitterroot National Forest
**Canine compatibility:** Not allowed
**Fees and permits:** None
**Maps:** Burnt Strip Mountain, Mt. George, Mt. Paloma, and Tin Cup Lake USGS quadrangles
**Trail contact:** Bitterroot National Forest, (406) 363-7100
**Special considerations:** Bring wading shoes. Rattlesnakes are present in the lower part of White Cap Creek. Black bears are common. Make sure you hang your food: You don't want a bear to eat your rations when you are 25 miles from the trailhead.

**Finding the Trailhead:** To reach the trail head you must access the Magruder Corridor Road which meanders over 100 miles from Conner, Montana, on the east to Red River Ranger Station near Elk City. The Montana access leaves US 93 at Conner, where you turn west up the West Fork of the Bitterroot River on paved Road 473. After 13 miles on Road 473, you come to a junction on the right leading 18 paved miles to Nez Perce Pass to cross the Bitterroot Divide. A high-standard gravel road leads 15 miles from the pass to the Magruder Crossing bridge over the Selway River, a popular boat-launch site. From here it becomes one lane, although with a good rock base. It climbs 3,000 feet and 12 miles to skirt Salmon Mountain.

From the west side out of Grangeville, take ID 13 west 9 miles to ID 14 on the right (south). From here, it is 31 miles to Elk City. Before Elk City, turn right onto paved FR 222 and continue 13 miles to Red River Ranger Station. Half a mile south of the station is a large sign warning of the hazards of driving the Montana Road (FR 468). Turn left. This trailhead starts at Paradise Ranger Station, set in the mouth of White Cap Creek. It is a 12-mile drive down the Selway River after you turn north off the Magruder Corridor Road.

Much of the area near the road corridor (FR 468) in Montana burned in the big fires of 2000. The fire only burned in a few places right along the roadside. GPS: N45 52.05' / W114 43.8'
**Parking and trailhead facilities:** There is ample parking, a 12-unit campground, loading ramps, and a latrine.

## The Hike

Depending on the number of days you've allotted, your destination can be Cooper Flat, Patzy Ann Falls, the Triple Lakes, or White Cap Lakes, the farthest of which is White Cap Lakes, about 27 miles from the trailhead.

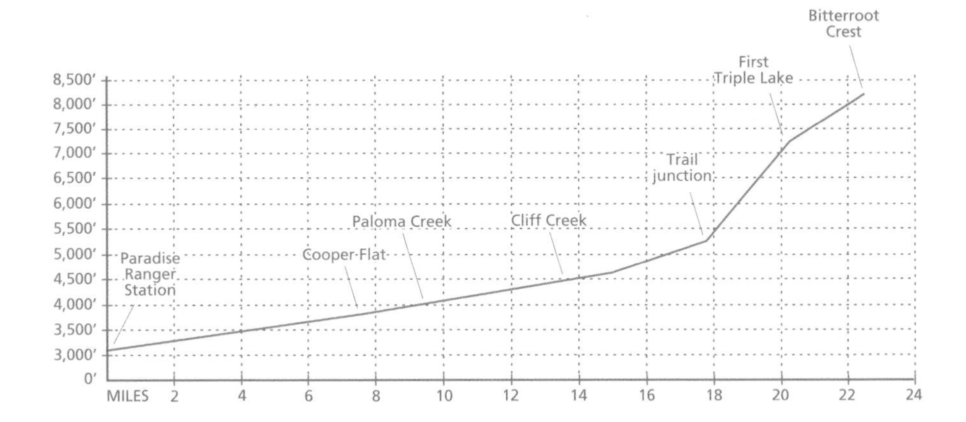


A major forest fire burned the south side of White Cap Creek some years ago, and its impact is still quite evident. An area about 3 to 4 miles up White Cap Creek near and on Mt. Paloma Trail burned in the fires of 2000.

The entire Selway-Bitterroot Wilderness is under a natural fire plan that allows naturally caused fires to burn themselves out when conditions are not extreme. In years like 2000, when conditions are extreme and there are multitudes of fires everywhere, fighting fires inside the wilderness area is the last priority regardless of what a fire management plan says. Aside from these burns, this country is heavily forested.

The trail (Trail 24) begins just past the ranger station near an outfitter's camp, following the river up what is at first a fairly narrow canyon and staying on the north of the creek. You don't have to ford White Cap Creek, but you need wading shoes for some of the tributaries. This is a big creek. It could be named the White Cap River.

The trail is well maintained to Patzy Ann Falls, but in the early season you can expect to cross winter deadfall. In the lower elevations you might see rattlesnakes on the trail. Black bears are common; keep a clean camp and hang your food bag.

Cooper Flat, about 7 miles from the trailhead, takes a day to reach. There is an old forest service cabin here, but it isn't open to public use. Here White Cap Creek is joined by a major tributary, Canyon Creek. A major trail crosses White Cap Creek here on a bridge, providing access to Cooper Flat. The trail heads up the narrow, timbered mouth of Canyon Creek. This narrow mouth is deceptive, however, because Canyon Creek widens considerably after 1.5 miles. This is a potential side hike.

The second day you may want to hike to Cliff Creek, 7 miles farther. The canyon has a nice broad bottom for about a mile near the confluence of Cliff Creek. In June, however, both Paloma Creek (2.5 miles past Canyon Creek) and Cliff Creek are high with runoff, and crossing may be dangerous. It is not unusual during spring melt for White Cap Creek to rise more than a foot by midafternoon. The trail to Cliff Creek is good except for early-season deadfall and avalanche debris in bad avalanche years: Broken timber, rocks, and mud may form a short, miserable jungle over the trail.

On day three your options double, for after 4 miles you reach a trail junction near fabulous Patzy Ann Falls. You can either climb 3.5 miles and 2,000 feet to Triple Lakes or continue up White Cap Creek on the fainter Trail 701 to end at the White Cap Lakes. (It's 4 miles from the beginning of Trail 701 to the largest of these lakes, at 6,910 feet.) This trail is not shown on the 1991 Tin Cup Lake USGS quadrangle.

Triple Lakes have excellent fishing. The trail leads to the middle lake (the lower one to the west is well off the trail). The highest lake requires about 0.25 mile of easy off-trail hiking. You'll find much alpine larch, which grows in Idaho only along the Bitterroot Divide. From the lakes, the trail snakes over the Bitterroot Divide into Montana and down to large (and popular) Tin Cup Lake.

To get to White Cap Creek Lakes, at the head of White Cap Creek, follow the lower route across Triple Lakes Creek below Patzy Ann Falls. The trail might have much deadfall and many detours made by animals and hunters. Keep your eye on the aged tree blazes. Do not cross White Cap Creek. Stay on the east side for 4.5 miles, passing through huge trees in a subalpine environment with the ground cover consisting largely of huckleberries, which means bears in August.

At this point you ford White Cap Creek. You are 0.5 mile from, and several hundred feet below, the lakes. The broad ford is shallow and easy even early in the season. After a bit more forest, the trail slants steeply upward through a meadow below a rock outcrop to lead to the outlet stream. A short travel upstream takes you to White Cap Lakes. There are a couple of lightly used campsites on the northeast side of the largest lake. Once you've reached your destination, take pride in your accomplishment. Very few make it to this area.

Fishing in the large, relatively low-elevation lake is outstanding and worth the 27 miles. California golden trout were first stocked here in 1973. You should plan on at least three days to reach the lake from the trailhead and three days to hike out. Of course, you'll probably want a few extra days to explore the area.

**Options:** The major option is described above—hiking to the head of White Cap Creek and the large White Cap Lakes. You can cross the Bitterroot Crest and hike out Tin Cup Creek just above Darby, Montana. This is a very long shuttle.

Trail 46/45, not ground checked, appears to provide a side loop of about 9 miles, going over Vance Point (6,823 feet) and coming down Fall Creek to White Cap Creek. Another side trail goes up the ridge between Lookout Creek and Cedar Creek to Cedar Saddle and down the ridge between Cedar Creek and Barefoot Creek to White Cap Creek. From Cedar Saddle, you can also follow the trail to Mount Paloma before returning to White Cap Creek.

Longer loops are possible. The stretch of wilderness seems to be endless.

—Philip Blomquist with Erik Fisher

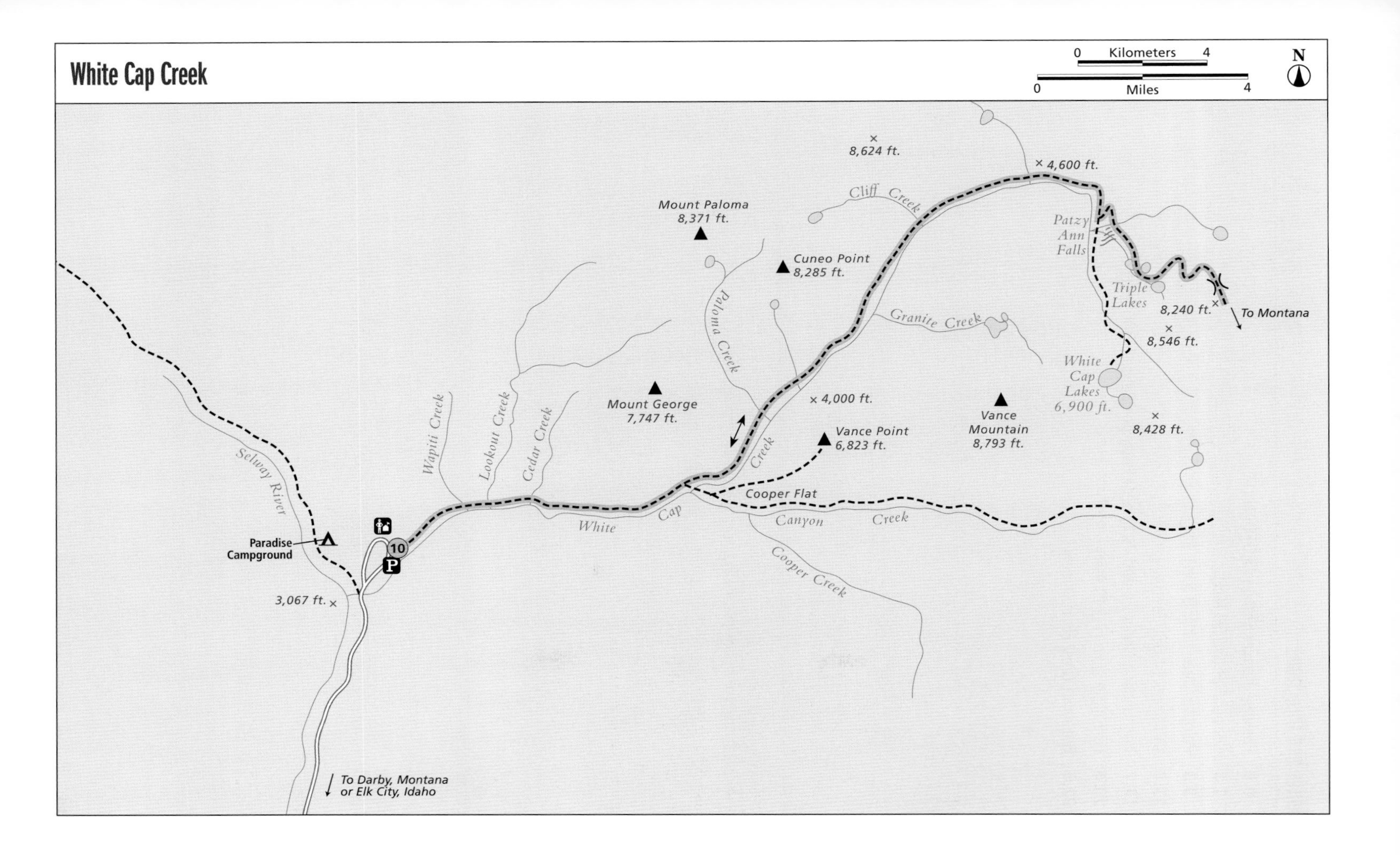
White Cap Creek
0 Kilometers 4
0 Miles 4
N
8,624 ft.
4,600 ft.
Mount Paloma
8,371 ft.
Cliff Creek
Cuneo Point
8,285 ft.
Paloma Creek
Granite Creek
Patzy
Ann
Falls
Triple
Lakes
8,240 ft.
To Montana
8,546 ft.
White
Cap
Lakes
6,900 ft.
8,428 ft.
Mount George
7,747 ft.
4,000 ft.
Vance Point
6,823 ft.
Vance
Mountain
8,793 ft.
Wapiti Creek
Lookout Creek
Cedar Creek
Selway River
Creek
Cooper Flat
White
Cap
Canyon
Creek
Cooper Creek
Paradise
Campground
10
P
3,067 ft.
To Darby, Montana
or Elk City, Idaho

## Miles and Directions

**0.0** Paradise Ranger Station (3,070 feet)

**7.3** Cooper Flat (3,750 feet)

**9.3** Paloma Creek (3,950 feet)

**13.8** Cliff Creek (4,550 feet)

**17.7** Trail junction (Trails 24 and 701) near Patzy Ann Falls (5,300 feet)

**20.4** First Triple Lake (7,240 feet)

**22.5** Bitterroot Crest (8,190 feet)

# Mallard-Larkins Proposed Wilderness

The large Mallard-Larkins Roadless Area of more than 300,000 acres lies astride the long ridge dividing the St. Joe and Clearwater River Valleys. Crossing the low-grade Fly Hill Road, the area extends eastward to the Montana border.

The idea of protecting this area as designated wilderness originated with Lewiston forester and sawmill designer Morton Brigham, who began visiting the region as early as 1938. In a 1973 article in *Living Wilderness,* Brigham shared his vision with a broader public, and the magnificent area has been included in every serious Idaho wilderness debate since then.

Idaho conservation and hunting and fishing groups now propose the establishment of a 265,000-acre wilderness. It would include the high lakes near Mallard Peak (see Hike 11, Larkins Lake), the deep valleys of Buck and Foehl Creeks, and that of the Little North Fork of the Clearwater River. On the south, the Elizabeth Lakes would be included, as would the stunning subalpine scenery around Five Lakes Butte.

The wildest part of the wilderness lies to the east, in Chamberlain and Vanderbilt Creeks. Here, in a huge valley with the Bitterroot Range as an eastern border, you can find deer, elk, moose, certainly wolves, and perhaps even an occasional grizzly bear. Few trails enter this eastern section.

Fly Hill, Smith Ridge, and Surveyor Ridge Roads all provide good access to the Mallard-Larkins, even into the higher elevations. Several outfitters make their living in the area and they, along with hunters and fishers, have been among its best friends.

Wilderness boundaries for Mallard-Larkins, as proposed by both the forest service and various Idaho politicians, have been uniformly poor, often running on straight lines across cliffs. The boundary proposed by both Idaho and national conservation groups follows roads and valleys in an attempt to be both identifiable and ecologically sound. Strenuous legal efforts have, so far anyway, fended off the numerous logging road intrusions planned by the forest service and private companies.

In the 1983 congressional examination of Idaho wilderness, the Mallard-Larkins received more public support for wilderness classification than any other area. Despite that, government agencies and many Idaho politicians still wage an unrelenting war against the area.

The Mallard-Larkins Pioneer Area is a scenic, but small, bit of country and the only portion of the Mallard-Larkins with any official protection. It comprises about 20,000 acres and was actually created to forestall wilderness designation. The forest service instead used its administrative authority to create the pioneer area.

The pioneer area was aptly described as "a castle, a fortress surrounded by a sea of bad policy," by Charles Pezeshki in his 1998 book *Wild to the Last: Environmental Conflict in the Clearwater Country.* Pezeshki is among many who have complained about the overharvesting of timber from the Clearwater National Forest and the adjacent state trust lands in the Floodwood State Forest. Then there is the industrial deforestation practiced on private "checkerboard" lands, entire sections of forest given to the railroad company in 1864 and now mostly owned by Plum Creek, a company spun off from the Burlington Northern Railroad. For more information, see *Railroads and Clearcuts: Legacy of Congress's 1864 Northern Railroad Grant,* by Derrick Jensen and George Draffan. For information about how to help protect the rest of the Mallard-Larkins and not just the high country in the Pioneer Area, contact The Lands Council.

—Ralph and Jackie Maughan and Dennis Baird

# 11 Larkins Lake

Late-summer hiking is available to this high mountain lake country with cutthroat trout fishing and a chance to see mountain goats, moose, elk, deer, and an occasional black bear.

**Start:** About 80 miles northeast of Lewiston and 30 miles northeast of Pierce
**Type of hike:** Backpack; out-and-back
**Distance:** 6.75 miles one way
**Approximate hiking time:** 2–4 days
**Difficulty:** Moderately strenuous due to elevation gain
**Best season:** Mid-July–mid-October
**Trail surface:** Normal dirt and rock
**Land status:** Clearwater National Forest
**Canine compatibility:** On leash
**Fees and permits:** None
**Maps:** Buzzard Roost and Mallard Peak USGS quadrangles; Clearwater National Forest map
**Trail contact:** North Fork Ranger District, (208) 476-3775
**Special considerations:** No water along the trail. Mosquitoes can be voracious at Larkins Lake. Wildlife, including mountain goats, deer, and elk, but especially the goats, are reported to have become so tame at this popular spot that they can be a hazard. Food should be hung high enough that an elk perched on its hind feet cannot reach it.

**Finding the trailhead:** From Lewiston, drive 48 miles east on US 12 to Greer. Turn left onto ID 11, where the Greer grade travels 9 steep and winding miles out of the canyon to emerge on the Weippe Prairie. You'll pass through Weippe at mile 57, then Pierce at mile 66, and finally Headquarters at mile 86. This is where ID 11 and the pavement end. Just north of Headquarters, take a right and drive 4 miles down the good, dirt FR 246. You'll come to a fork where you'll go left onto FR 251. This road continues for 10 miles as it drops into the East Fork of Beaver Creek to meet FR 247. Continue on Forest 247 for 7 miles as it follows Beaver Creek to the North Fork of the Clearwater. From Headquarters, you will have traveled 21 miles, and although this drive is long, it's quite scenic.

Cross the river and turn left. (A right turn leads 0.25 mile to the Aquarius Campground.) In 1 mile you'll come to Isabella Creek, where you turn right (north) onto dirt FR 700. Stay left on steep and winding FR 700 (Smith Ridge) for 9 miles, where you'll reach the trailhead and Trail 240. GPS: N46 54.41' / W115 40.71'

**Parking and trailhead facilities:** The trailhead includes a hitching post on the left and latrines and forest service trail mileage signs on the right.

## The Hike

The good Trail 240 climbs almost 1,200 feet in 2 miles as it winds through white pine, Douglas fir, and grand fir forest to cross into the Mallard-Larkins Pioneer Area. Ferns line the lower levels, giving way to colorful wildflowers, huckleberry bushes, and at higher altitudes bear grass. One mile in, you'll pass a trail on the right (south), but you'll continue east as you near Grassy Point. Here the trail swings north to

*Big cedar groves at the trailhead up Isabelle Creek.* Photo by Luke Kratz

climb onto Goat Ridge. On top is a side trail leading right (south) to Grassy Point.

Continue north for another 0.5 mile to the Goat Ridge Benchmark, where you'll stay right and continue on Trail 240. In another 0.5 mile you'll pass the cutoff (Trail 96) to Elmer Creek on the right (east). Here's a good place to view Mallard Peak to the east.

The trail continues up and down along Goat Ridge to skirt the south reach of Larkins Peak at Benchmark 6,391. Here a side trail to the left (north) climbs Larkins Peak (6,661 feet). Larkins Peak in its upper reaches has subalpine fir, Douglas fir, and thickets of alder. From the top, 3,000 feet below and to the north, is the Little North Fork of the Clearwater. Back at the junction and on the trail again, you can peer 700 feet down to Larkins Lake, a clear, cold, inviting gem.

Now comes the descent. Going north-northeast, in 1 mile and 100 feet you'll come to another junction; turn left (north) and drop on Trail 108 another 400 feet

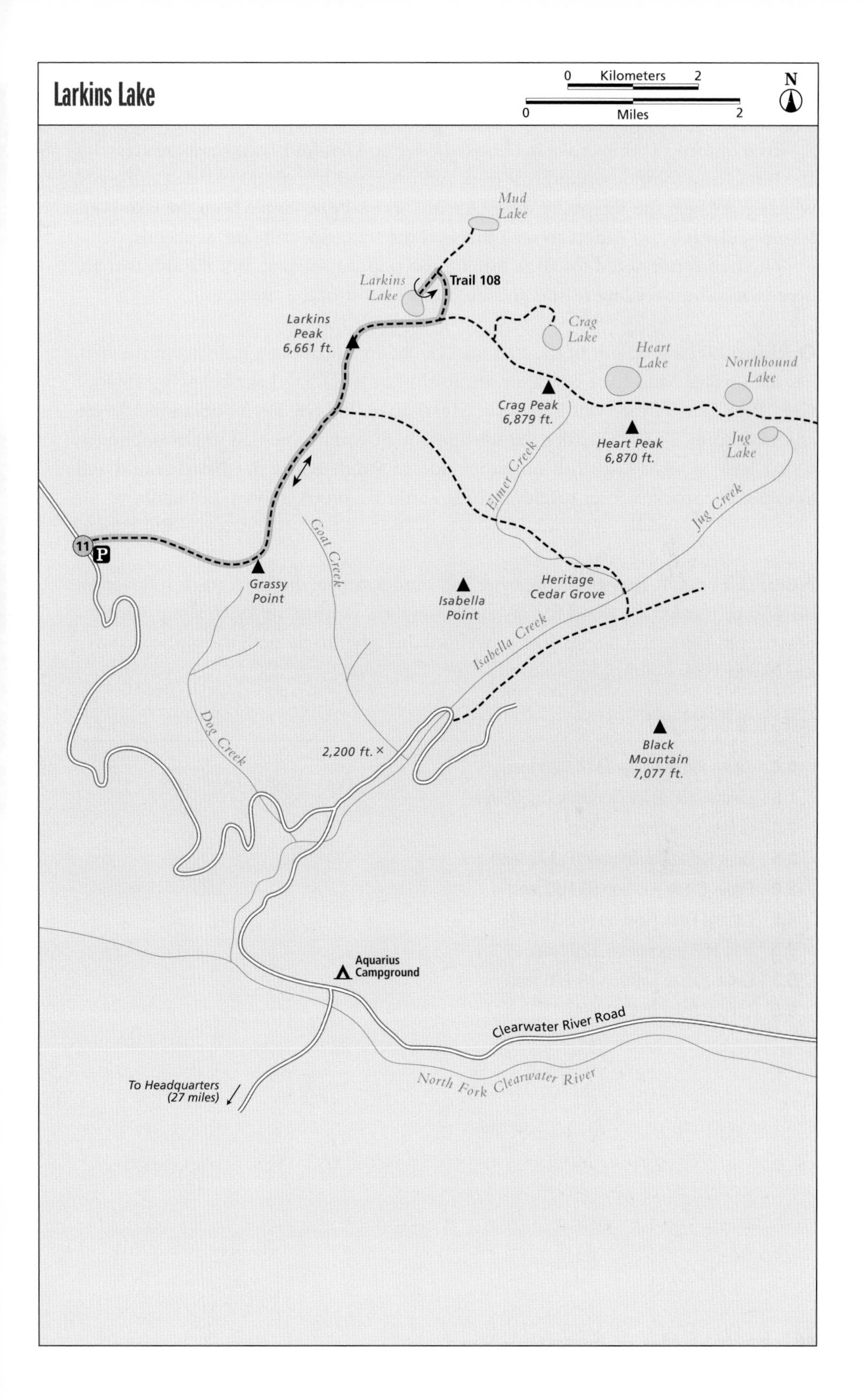
Larkins Lake
0 Kilometers 2
0 Miles 2
N
Mud Lake
Larkins Lake
Trail 108
Larkins Peak 6,661 ft.
Crag Lake
Heart Lake
Northbound Lake
Crag Peak 6,879 ft.
Heart Peak 6,870 ft.
Jug Lake
Elmer Creek
Jug Creek
11
P
Goat Creek
Grassy Point
Isabella Point
Heritage Cedar Grove
Isabella Creek
Dog Creek
2,200 ft.
Black Mountain 7,077 ft.
Aquarius Campground
Clearwater River Road
North Fork Clearwater River
To Headquarters (27 miles)

and 0.75 mile to a four-way junction. Take the extreme left (south) trail to arrive at Larkins Lake in less than 0.5 mile with a descent of 200 feet.

Oval in shape, Larkins Lake is 12 acres in size and has four large camping areas. It's also home base for moose, cutthroat trout (which greedily grab at a dry fly), and goats, which graze near the top of the steep face of Larkins Peak, visible from the lakeshore. It's a popular hike, so expect to see others on the trail, especially on weekends.

The lake is not noted for large fish; it's too popular for that. But the fish that are here have a short feeding season and are hungry most of the time.

**Options:** Nearby, up out of the Larkins Lake basin and about a mile down the trail, lies the smaller Mud Lake to the north. To the east sits Crag Lake below 6,879-foot Crag Peak, and farther still is 40-acre Heart Lake, known for its occasional larger cutthroat trout. These lakes dot the subalpine high country nestled in glacial cirques. Other lakes stocked with fish on either side of Smith Ridge are Northbound and Skyland. The stocked trout species include cutthroat, brook, brown, and rainbow.

—Bill Francis

**Note:** Bill Francis, newspaper reporter and outdoorsman, died in a truck rollover on his way to receive an award for his environmental writing. In 1999, along with his best friends Gene and Jennie Winter, we took his ashes to fly with the goshawks over the North Fork country he so loved.

## Miles and Directions

- **0.0** Smith Ridge Trailhead (4,920 feet)
- **1.0** Salmon Ridge Trail junction (5,388 feet)
- **2.0** Grassy Point Trail junction
- **2.5** Goat Ridge Benchmark (6,372 feet)
- **3.0** Elmer Creek junction (6,160 feet)
- **4.5** Larkins Peak junction (6,391 feet)
- **5.5** Trail 108 junction (6,120 feet)
- **6.3** Larkins Lake junction (5,720 feet)
- **6.8** Larkins Lake (5,600 feet)

# 12 Pete Ott Lake and Vicinity

Scenic lakes dot the southeast corner of the Mallard-Larkins Proposed Wilderness with some distant views of the vast "ocean" of the Clearwater Mountains.

**Start:** About 85 miles east of Lewiston deep in the Clearwater Mountains
**Type of hike:** Out-and-back day hike or base camp
**Distance:** 5 miles round-trip to Pete Ott Lake
**Approximate hiking time:** 2 hours
**Difficulty:** Moderately easy
**Best season:** Late July–mid-September
**Trail surface:** Normal dirt and rock
**Land status:** Clearwater National Forest
**Canine compatibility:** On leash
**Fees and permits:** None
**Map:** Elizabeth Mountain USGS quadrangle
**Trail contact:** North Fork Ranger District, (208) 476-4541
**Special considerations:** The access road requires a four-wheel-drive vehicle.

**Finding the trailhead:** It's a long drive to the trailhead, so it is best to do this hike if you are already way up the North Fork of the Clearwater, or if you want to do some exploration beyond Pete Ott Lake itself.

From Lewiston, drive 48 miles east on US 12 to Greer. Turn left onto ID 11, where the Greer grade travels 9 steep and winding miles out of the canyon to emerge on the Weippe Prairie. You'll pass through Weippe at mile 57. At mile 68, you reach a junction with ID 11 and French Mountain Road (FR 250). This is just south of the small town of Pierce. Turn onto French Mountain Road. This road climbs through low mountains and then descends Orogrande Creek to the North Fork of the Clearwater River. This is 29 miles from the turnoff of ID 11. Cross the North Fork bridge, turn right (still FR 250), and drive upstream along the North Fork.

Now drive about 15 miles to Cold Springs Road (FR 711), then turn left up gravel FR 711. If you arrive at Kelly Forks, you have gone 3 miles too far up the North Fork.

When you are 1.7 miles up FR 711, turn right onto FR 5295, which begins a steep and long climb up to a high saddle between Flat Mountain and Cold Springs Peak. There is a maze of old logging roads, but most are gated. Stay on FR 5295 until you reach FR 5297. Follow FR 5297 until you reach FR 5297A, which makes the final climb to the ridgetop. Signs should help if these road numbers change. This is 7.4 miles and 3,000 feet above the turnoff from FR 711. GPS: N46 45.75' / W115 18.15'

**Parking and trailhead facilities:** There is room to park about six vehicles at the undeveloped trailhead, which has partial shade. An old road continues to the right toward Flat Mountain, but it is abandoned to soon become a trail and then just a game track. You want to take the obvious trail that goes to the left (approximately north), Trail 176.

## The Hike

Trail 176 is a fairly gentle trail for ATVs that leads toward Cold Springs Peak, a high point on Pot Mountain Ridge, in the Mallard-Larkins Roadless Area.

*Views near trailhead of Pete OH trail.* PHOTO BY LUKE KRATZ

The trail passes above Ring Lake, which is barely visible below. Then it passes behind Point 6,310. Just beyond this point the trail to Pete Ott Lake, Ice Lake, and the Elizabeth Lakes (Trail 445) leaves to the right and heads steeply downslope to the northeast. When we visited in 1999, we found Trail 176 blocked by a large blowdown just before the junction of Trail 445. The side trail was easy to miss. Trail 445 is closed to ATVs but not motorcycles. Contact the North Fork Ranger District if you see marauding ATVs on the trail.

After 0.3 mile from the junction and a descent of 300 feet, an unmarked trail descends to Ice Lake, a small lake in a small cirque set against a big northeast-facing cliff. Due to its location, Ice Lake has ice well into June.

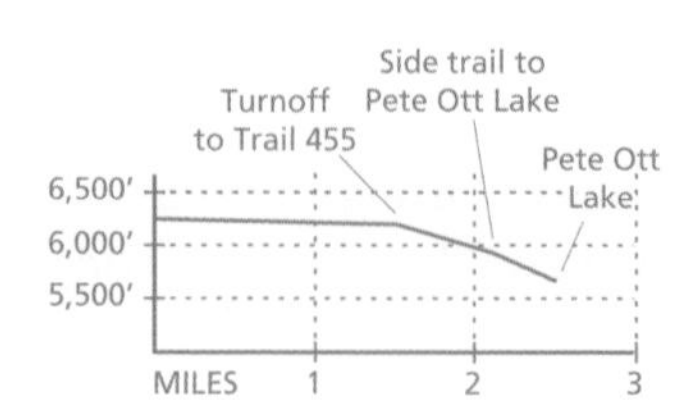

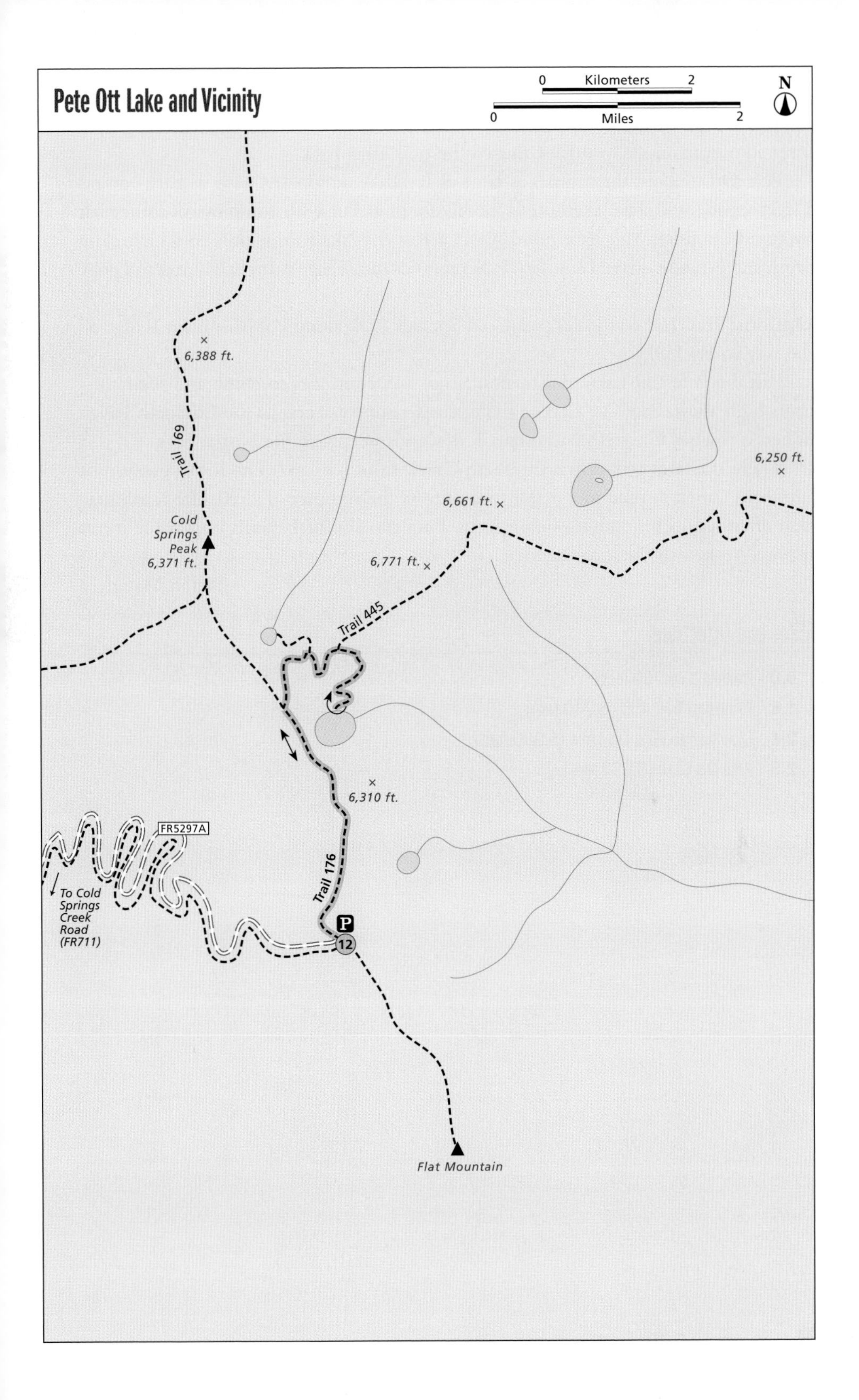

Pete Ott Lake and Vicinity
0
Kilometers
2
0
Miles
2
N
6,388 ft.
Trail 169
Cold
Springs
Peak
6,371 ft.
6,661 ft.
6,250 ft.
6,771 ft.
Trail 445
6,310 ft.
FR5297A
To Cold
Springs
Creek
Road
(FR711)
Trail 176
P
12
Flat Mountain

Another 0.3 mile brings you to the unmarked trail to Pete Ott Lake. It leaves to the right and heads downhill 200 feet to the lake. If you find yourself climbing up a forested mountainside, you have missed the trail. Turn back.

Pete Ott is about three times as large as Ice Lake. It, too, sits with its back toward a steep cirque wall. The lakeshore is heavily forested, but with a number of somewhat overused campsites. You have good views across the lake to the cliffs to which cling brush and pyramid-shaped conifers. In September this foliage turns bright red and gold.

**Options:** Trail 169 continues past Cold Springs Peak along Pot Mountain Ridge all the way to Fly Hill.

Past the Pete Ott Lake trail turnout, Trail 445 continues to climb and then contours high above Pete Ott Creek, giving cross-country access to the Elizabeth Lakes. When it reaches Elizabeth Mountain, it descends steeply to the North Fork.

There is a faint trail down Elizabeth Creek from Ice Lake. The lower portion of Elizabeth Creek burned in a major forest fire in the summer of 2000. Fire rehabilitation often results in old trails being recut. Fires can also make trails impassable if not recut. Check with the forest service.

—Ralph Maughan

## Miles and Directions

**0.0** Trailhead (6,260 feet)

**1.5** Turnoff to Trail 455 (6,240 feet)

**2.1** Side trail to Pete Ott Lake (5,960 feet)

**2.5** Pete Ott Lake (5,680 feet)

# Proposed Great Burn Wilderness

The Great Burn was the result of the intense fires of 1910 on the Idaho-Montana border. Now a century or so later, much of the Bitterroot Divide here still lacks good commercial stands of timber. The Great Burn Wilderness would protect the area permanently. It is stunningly beautiful country, with many meadows brimming with wildlife, including two or three wolf packs and a possible reinhabitation area for grizzly bears, not to mention the huge elk herds.

Geologically, the Bitterroot Divide may be considered a prominent subrange of the vast Clearwater Mountains. It reaches its greatest height in the Selway-Bitterroot Wilderness just to the south of the Great Burn—south of US 12.

Fortunately, the forest service has recommended much of the Great Burn area for wilderness designation. Unfortunately, however, it hasn't recommended enough. The Kelly Creek drainage to the north and northeast has mostly been left out of the wilderness proposal, along with Cayuse Creek, a major tributary of Kelly Creek. The trees have grown back in these drainages to a greater extent, and both of these nationally famous trout streams are threatened by logging and road-building plans.

—Ralph Maughan

*The Great Burns area at the Goat Lake trailhead.* Photo by John Kratz

# 13 Goat Lake

Goat Lake is a cirque mountain lake in the proposed Great Burn Wilderness of Idaho and Montana, set amidst 7,000- to 8,000-foot peaks and numerous trail connections to other lakes and the Bitterroot Divide. There are good views into the 100,000-acre proposed Weitas Creek Wilderness.

**Start:** 55 miles southwest of Missoula, Montana, and 165 miles northeast of Lewiston, Idaho
**Type of hike:** Backpack; out-and-back
**Distance:** 11 miles round-trip
**Approximate hiking time:** 5–6 hours over 1–3 days
**Difficulty:** Moderate
**Best season:** Mid-July–mid-September
**Trail surface:** Normal dirt and rock
**Land status:** Clearwater National Forest
**Canine compatibility:** On leash
**Fees and permits:** None
**Maps:** Rhodes Peak USGS quadrangle; Clearwater National Forest map
**Trail contact:** North Fork Ranger District, (208) 476-4541
**Special considerations:** The 28-mile dirt road to the Goat Lake Trailhead is passable in passenger cars with good tires but, depending upon snowpack and weather, may have snow at higher elevations. The last 0.5 mile after the turnoff to the trailhead requires four-wheel-drive and high-clearance vehicles. Traveling such a distance on this scenic but long gravel-and-dirt road takes about four or five hours.

**Finding the trailhead:** From Missoula drive south to Lolo, Montana, and turn right (west) onto US 12. From here it is 45 miles west to Parachute Hill Road (FR 569), just before the turnoff to Lochsa Lodge and the Powell Ranger Station.

From Lewiston, drive east on US 12 for 164 miles to Parachute Hill Road, just after the turnoff to Lochsa Lodge and the Powell Ranger Station.

Parachute Hill Road is to the north, and a sign at the beginning gives distances to Rock Point (7 miles), Papoose Saddle (8 miles), and Cayuse Junction (19 miles). The road climbs for more than 3,500 feet to Papoose Saddle, drops into Cayuse Creek Canyon, and then climbs again to Blacklead Mountain.

Drive north up Parachute Hill Road for 2.7 miles to a three-way fork. Take the middle fork (FR 569) and continue 1.7 miles to another fork. Keep left. Another 1.6 miles farther is the signed Powell Junction. This is the end of FR 569. Proceed on FR 500 (the Lewis and Clark Trail) for another mile to Papoose Saddle. Continue straight ahead, and after 11.5 miles you arrive at Cayuse Junction. The stretch of road you have just traveled follows the approximate route of the Lolo Indian Trail used by Lewis and Clark to cross the Idaho mountains in 1805 and 1806.

At Cayuse Junction, turn right onto FR 581. A sign here gives mileage to Blacklead Mountain; from here it is 8.2 miles to the unsigned turnoff (right) to Blacklead Mountain. It is another rocky, rutted, narrow, and steep 0.5 mile to the first of two trailheads.

If you have a two-wheel-drive vehicle, park about 0.25 mile before the summit of Blacklead Mountain and walk the jeep road to the final trailhead. This walk of about 0.75 mile crosses over Blacklead Mountain. You will enjoy beautiful views all the way.

If you have a four-wheel-drive vehicle, drive over Blacklead Mountain to the small trailhead 240 feet down and about 0.5 mile north. It is located on a saddle where the Deer Creek Trail (Trail 513) takes off to the north. GPS: N46 38.39' / W114 51.08'
**Parking and trailhead facilities:** Undeveloped site in the sun.

## The Hike

The trail to Goat Lake starts from the parking area at the end of a jeep track that leads over Blacklead Mountain. The summit offers an outstanding view of the proposed Great Burn Wilderness of the Bitterroot Divide. To the northeast is the divide, the heart of the wilderness. To the north and northwest is the Kelly Creek drainage. To the south is Cayuse Creek, and due west is the Bighorn-Weitas Roadless Area.

From the end of the jeep trail, the Deer Creek Trail (Trail 513) takes off to the north. Look instead for the unsigned Trail 508 on the right (east), which drops 280 feet in several switchbacks to pass an old mine digging and a grave (a pile of stones with a worn wooden marker). This side ridge is untimbered, and the valley below is pocketed with fir, pine, and small meadows.

After dropping about 0.5 mile, you'll come to a small, cold, clear spring that flows right out of the mountain to form Billy Rhodes Creek. After the spring, the trail drops less steeply. The next 0.25 mile is easy to follow but can't be seen from the ridge above as it passes through a bear grass meadow and patches of lodgepole pine and alpine fir.

Shortly after the trail levels out at about 6,650 feet, it splits. Go left. The right fork goes to Silver Creek and ultimately Cayuse Creek. The trail levels as it contours around the ridge for about 2 miles to cross the two small streams. These flow out of two impressive cirques (which the topo shows as lakeless). Numerous rock outcroppings begin to appear on the ridge above.

Here you come out onto a wide open stretch of ridge. To the southeast is a view across Silver Creek to Williams Peak (7,501 feet), a gray slab dominating the skyline. On the eastern horizon is Rhodes Peak (7,930 feet). Goat Lake still can't be seen because it is hidden by its own cirque wall, which juts in front of the trail.

The lake comes into view as you round the southern end of the cirque wall. Surrounded by the 180-degree wall that rises abruptly to 1,000 feet above, this beautiful lake makes you automatically reach for your fishing rod. However, the northeast, outlet side of the lake, although marshy, makes for an especially nice view of the lake and its wall.

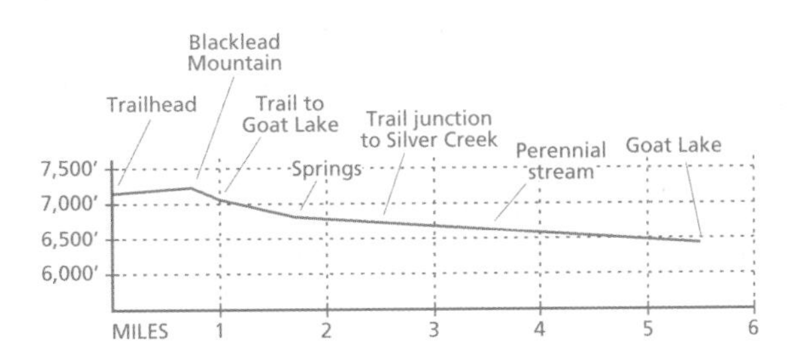


An extra attraction for hikers is the number of trail connections to other lakes, to Cayuse Creek, and to the

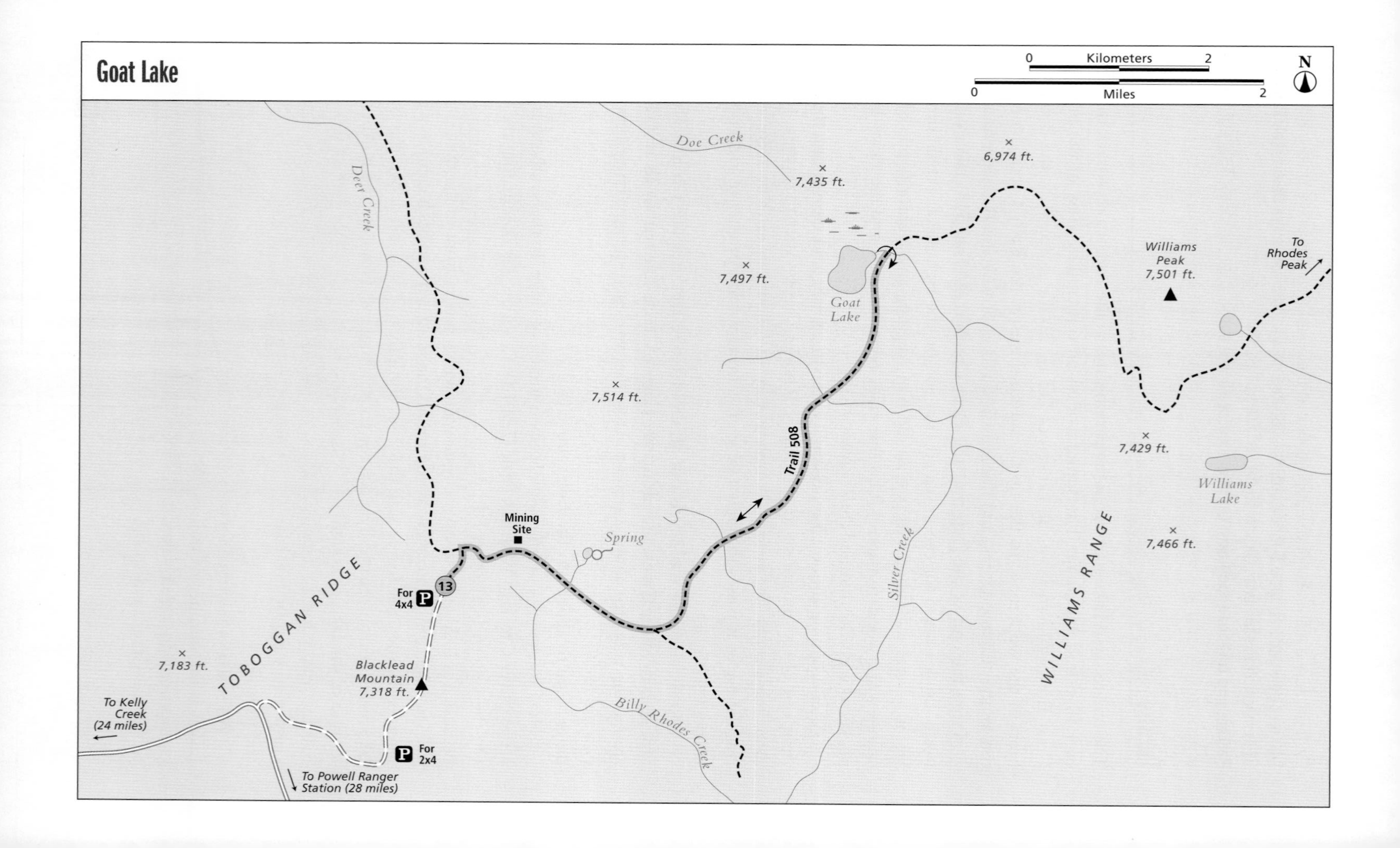
Goat Lake
0 Kilometers 2
0 Miles 2
N
Doe Creek
Deer Creek
6,974 ft.
7,435 ft.
7,497 ft.
7,514 ft.
Goat Lake
Williams Peak 7,501 ft.
To Rhodes Peak
Trail 508
7,429 ft.
Williams Lake
7,466 ft.
WILLIAMS RANGE
Silver Creek
Mining Site
Spring
13
For 4x4
TOBOGGAN RIDGE
7,183 ft.
Blacklead Mountain 7,318 ft.
Billy Rhodes Creek
To Kelly Creek (24 miles)
For 2x4
To Powell Ranger Station (28 miles)

Bitterroot Divide. A good extension from Goat Lake is the trail over Williams Peak (7,501 feet) and down to Williams Lake (7,005 feet). This trail ultimately reaches the divide via Rhodes Peak.

The return to the trailhead from Goat Lake is leisurely and mostly level, except for the last steep climb back to the top of Blacklead Mountain. From the top, you can look northeastward back across the proposed Great Burn Wilderness as you plan your next hike into this remote and magnificent region.

—Don L. Crawford

## Miles and Directions

**0.0** Two-wheel-drive vehicle parking (7,100 feet)

**0.3** Summit Blacklead Mountain (7,318 feet)

**0.8** Four-wheel-drive vehicle parking and trail to Goat Lake (7,060 feet)

**1.2** Springs (6,780 feet)

**1.5** Trail junction to Silver Creek (6,780 feet)

**3.5** Second perennial stream

**5.5** Goat Lake (6,492 feet)

# 14 Steep Lakes Loop

Along the Idaho-Montana border lies a beautiful ridgeline hike.

**Start:** In the Clearwater National Forest, northeast of Kelly Creek. Approximately 150 miles east of Lewiston, Idaho, or 60 miles west of Missoula, Montana
**Type of hike:** Multiday backpack. Requires a short shuttle unless you are willing to walk roads for 4 miles to make it a loop
**Distance:** 18 miles (not counting the 4 miles of road)
**Approximate hiking time:** 4–5 days
**Difficulty:** Moderately strenuous
**Best season:** August
**Trail surface:** Normal dirt and rock
**Land status:** Clearwater National Forest
**Canine compatibility:** On leash
**Fees and permits:** None
**Maps:** Bruin Hill and Straight Peak USGS quadrangles
**Trail contact:** North Fork Ranger District, (208) 476-4541
**Special considerations:** The greatest difficulty on this trip is that each night you have to climb down off the Bitterroot Divide to camp. In many places, that requires a steep descent. There are some campsites on or near the ridgeline. Lightning danger exists on the divide.

**Finding the trailhead:** Access to the trailhead is possible in a number of ways. The best route is from Superior, Montana, west over Hoodoo Pass (paved FR 250), then downstream along Long Creek to its junction with Lake Creek. Both streams are tributaries of the North Fork. Proceed up Lake Creek on FR 295 about 7 miles to a barrier. The barrier is near the mouth of Siam Creek.

Much longer back-road access is available from Idaho. Due to the distance and complexity, it is not described here. GPS: N46 50.77' / W114 59.18'

**Parking and trailhead facilities:** There is a small parking area. The trailhead is undeveloped.

## The Hike

The proposed Great Burn Wilderness is located in the northern part of the Bitterroot Mountain system. This large expanse of backcountry encompasses land in both Idaho and Montana.

The present-day environment of the region was shaped by the Great Idaho Fire of 1910 (hence the name Great Burn). This catastrophic event burned three million acres in northern Idaho in just a few days and destroyed a number of early towns. Major fires continued in the area until 1919. As a result, a century after the fires much of the area proposed for wilderness is still quite open. The lack of big trees has kept the timber companies at bay.

The Steep Lakes cirque is nestled at the headwaters of the North Fork of the Clearwater River. This lake basin, aptly named for its precipitous position below the ridge separating Idaho and Montana, is seldom visited. The only way to reach these lakes is on foot or by horse via Boundary Trail. The best month is probably August, although thunderstorms are most common then, and this hike is on an exposed ridge.

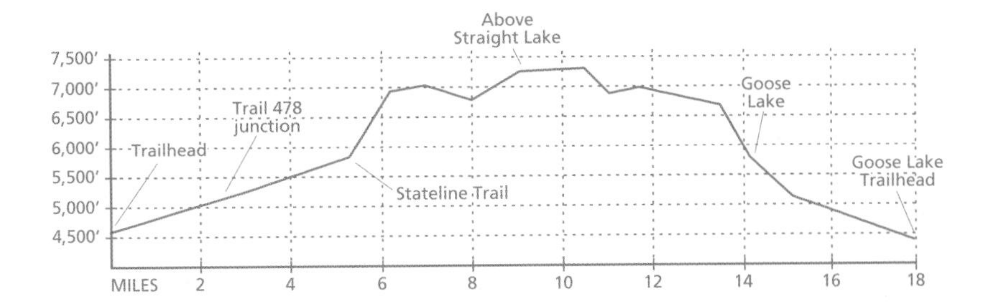


Early July finds snowdrifts. In September the foliage on the ridge turns a beautiful red and gold, but by mid-September the air is getting cold.

This 18-mile near loop begins by following the closed logging road at the barrier just below Lake Creek's tributary, Siam Creek. From the trailhead, it is 5 miles to large Fish Lake. The old road track has turned into a broad trail (Trail 419). Unfortunately, at present, dirt bikes and ATVs are allowed to travel to the lake. This is the source of numerous complaints, but wilderness designation would prevent this situation. The hike begins in a narrow canyon, which broadens as you ascend. Two miles below Fish Lake, you meet Trail 478 coming from the south. At this junction the trail becomes Trail 478, and you also begin a moderately steep climb of 600 feet in 2 miles to Fish Lake.

Special fishing regulations delay the opening day for Fish Lake and Steep Lakes until August 1 to protect the spawning of west slope cutthroat in Fish Lake and the California golden trout in Steep Lakes. Because of the regulations, the fishing is quite good. However, if you prize solitude and quiet, do not walk to Fish Lake on August 1!

You reach Stateline Trail (Trail 738) just beyond Fish Lake, which is barely inside Idaho. Motorized travel is prohibited on this trail, which follows the Bitterroot Divide closely. This trail actually begins quite a way to the south—a few miles north of Lolo Pass where US 12 crosses into Idaho—and it follows the state line for more than 45 miles to Hoodoo Pass.

The view from the trail is excellent into both states. Some twenty lakes are scattered along it on both sides of the divide. Elk, moose, and deer abound in the area, making it a popular hunting destination in the fall. The area has been claimed by several wolf packs in recent years. It is possible to see a pack of as many as fifteen wolves in the area.

The section of Stateline Trail from Fish Lake northward to Goose Lake is not busy. The route is moderately difficult in places as the trail disappears on some of the more rocky and open parts of the ridgeline. Finding the route is no great problem, however, because the ridgeline is the only logical route of travel. Most of the lakes below on either side of the ridge are reached only with off-trail hiking. There is no water on top of the Bitterroot Divide, except for temporary snowmelt.

Before you reach the Steep Lakes, you pass the Siamese Lakes and Straight Lake, which are in Montana. The upper Siamese Lake is an excellent overnight camping choice after a first night at Fish Lake. Fishing for cutthroat trout is excellent here.

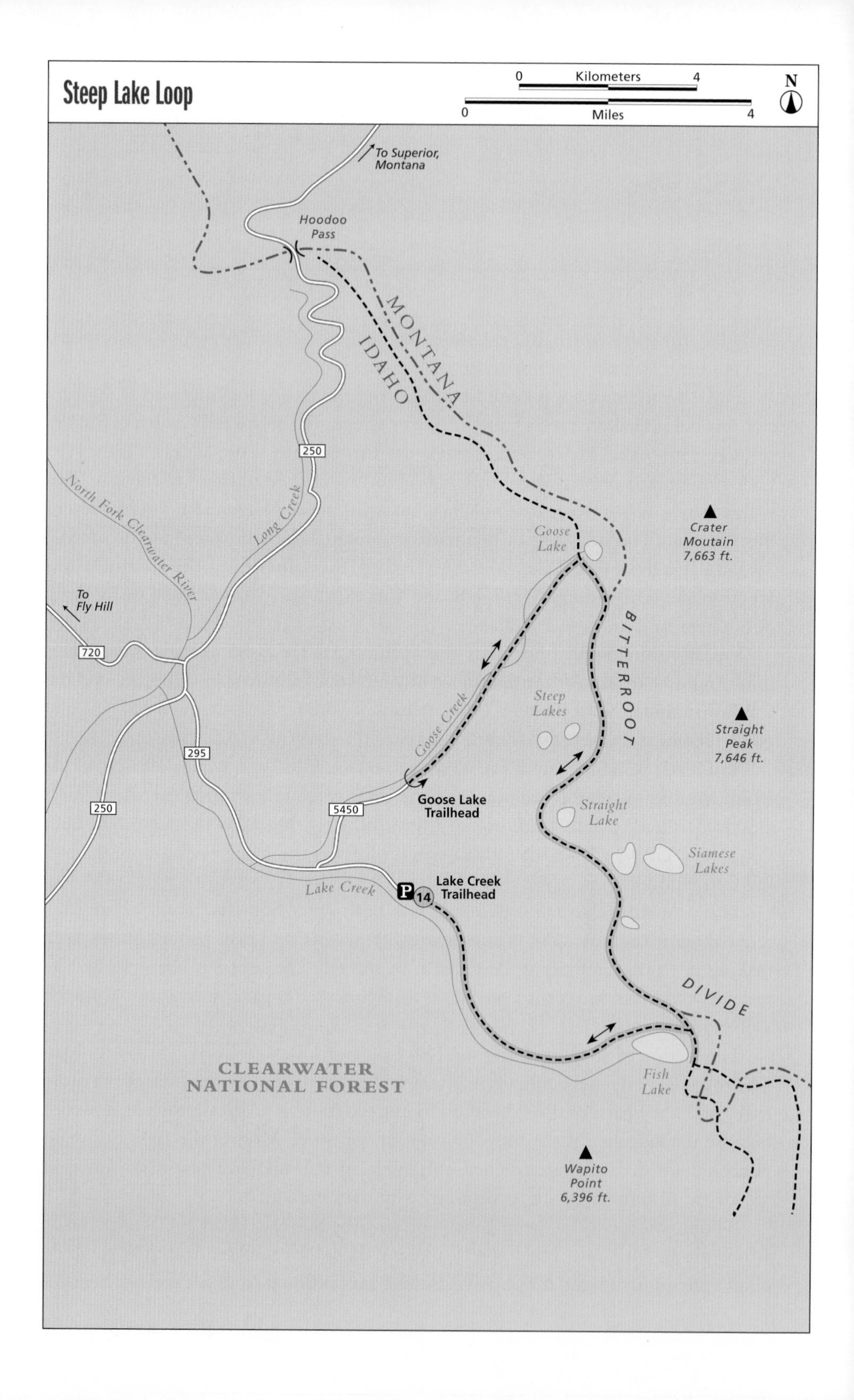

Steep Lake Loop
0
Kilometers
4
0
Miles
4
N
To Superior, Montana
Hoodoo Pass
MONTANA
IDAHO
250
North Fork Clearwater River
Long Creek
Goose Lake
Crater Moutain 7,663 ft.
To Fly Hill
720
BITTERROOT
Steep Lakes
Straight Peak 7,646 ft.
Goose Creek
295
250
5450
Goose Lake Trailhead
Straight Lake
Siamese Lakes
Lake Creek
14
Lake Creek Trailhead
DIVIDE
CLEARWATER NATIONAL FOREST
Fish Lake
Wapito Point 6,396 ft.

The country near Steep Lakes is appropriately named and has probably the best view of the hike. Straight Peak, on the Montana side, is a sight to behold from Boundary Trail, and the Steep Lakes Cirque has to be one of the most sublime locations in Idaho. The Steep Lakes are deep and dark blue, set among rugged cliffs. The lower Steep Lake supports a naturally reproducing population of California golden trout. The limit here for this rare fish is two. Carefully release all others so that once again the flash of crimson and gold may strike your dry fly.

From Steep Lakes, Stateline Trail continues 4 miles to the Goose Lake basin. The trail leaves the Bitterroot Divide and follows a ridge down, 1.2 miles from Goose Lake. This small, shallow, fishless lake is a watering hole for moose and elk. It is marshy around the lake. A sign at the trail junction here should steer you down Goose Creek Trail (Trail 414). It's about 4 miles down this well-maintained and easy-to-follow trail to the Goose Creek Trailhead. The first 2 miles descend gently through open country. Just before you cross Steep Creek, the grade increases considerably. Goose Creek Trail is closed to motor vehicles. From the trailhead, it is a road walk of about 4 miles back to your vehicle in Lake Creek. You may be able to thumb a ride.

—Phil Blomquist; revised by Ralph Maughan

## Miles and Directions

**0.0** Trailhead (4,600 feet)
**3.0** Junction with Trail 478; begin steep climb to Fish Lake (5,258 feet)
**5.0** Fish Lake (5,890 feet)
**5.2** Beginning of Stateline Trail (5,940 feet)
**5.4** Mount the Bitterroot Divide into Montana (6,108 feet)
**6.5** On point above cirque lake (6,985)
**7.3** On point above second cirque lake (7,021 feet)
**8.1** Saddle above the Siamese Lakes (6,870 feet)
**9.1** High point above Straight Lake (7,322 feet)
**10.2** Highest point of hike (7,350 feet)
**11.2** Lowest of the Steep Lakes is due west under you (6,920 feet)
**11.8** On point above unnamed Montana lake (7,000 feet)
**12.9** Trail passes just below Point 6,746 (6,710 feet)
**14.2** Goose Lake (5,763 feet)
**15.2** Goose Lake Trail crosses Steep Creek Crossing (5,100 feet)
**18.0** Goose Lake Trailhead (4,450 feet)

# Meadow Creek

The Meadow Creek Roadless Area abuts the western side of the Selway-Bitterroot Wilderness but is not part of the designated wilderness. Conservationists lobbied hard to have the Meadow Creek roadless area, particularly its east side, added to the Selway-Bitterroot Wilderness in 1980, when Idaho senator Frank Church was guiding the River of No Return Wilderness bill through Congress. While Senator Church ultimately did agree to make some significant additions along the southern edge of the Selway-Bitterroot (along the Magruder Corridor), he was never convinced to add Meadow Creek. For political reasons, most likely timber interests in nearby Elk City, Idaho, Senator Church ignored the pleadings of conservationists, even though he understood the need to preserve this pristine, but fragile, area.

The Burnt Backbone logging project was planned for the early 1990s in the Horse Creek drainage of lower Meadow Creek. It was shelved and has not resurfaced, but these things tend to never go away. In general, timber interests have always coveted the upper reaches of the drainage, in particular the west side where there is more timber. Nevertheless, the Meadow Creek drainage is still largely roadless, and the Nez Perce National Forest plan for the area is to leave it mostly as is, at least for a while.

A new threat to solitude and wilderness qualities comes from increased use by off-road vehicles, including ATVs. A motorized route to accommodate ATVs and motorcycles is proposed in upper Meadow Creek. The first 3 miles in the lower portion are presently open to motorcycles and bicycles.

We encourage the forest service, rather than go ahead with plans for motorized development, to instead recognize the beauty and importance of Meadow Creek as de facto wilderness. Better yet, perhaps someday we will see this magnificent area added to the Selway-Bitterroot Wilderness.

—Don L. Crawford and Jackie Jackson Maughan

# 15 Meadow Creek

This is the second most heavily used trail in this vicinity of the Selway River—and for good reason. It's a shady hike along fern-covered, stone wall formations beside sizable Meadow Creek.

**Start:** 130 miles east of Lewiston
**Type of hike:** Day hike or backpack; out-and-back. First portion makes a good family hike.
**Distance:** 14 miles one way
**Approximate hiking time:** 1 hour to several days
**Difficulty:** Easy for first 3 miles, difficult for 1.5 miles, then moderate
**Best season:** Early April–November
**Trail surface:** Normal dirt and rock
**Land status:** Nez Perce National Forest
**Canine compatibility:** On leash
**Fees and permits:** The Meadow Creek Guard Station, available by reservation from May 1 to September 15, is 15 miles up the trail. Also available for reserved rental is the Lookout Butte fire tower, 20 miles downriver from the Meadow Creek Trailhead.
**Maps:** Selway Falls, Anderson Butte, Vermilion Peak, and Sable Hill USGS quadrangles; Nez Perce National Forest map
**Trail contact:** Moose Creek Ranger District, (208) 926-4258
**Special considerations:** Rainbow and cutthroat trout inhabit these waters, but be aware that protected chinook salmon and steelhead birth and spawn along the Selway tributaries; check Idaho Fish and Game regulations. The first 3 miles are open to motorcycles and bicycles.

**Finding the trailhead:** From Lewiston, drive east on US 12 for 114 miles to Lowell, where the Lochsa and Selway Rivers join to form the Clearwater (Three Forks). Cross the bridge and continue east on Selway River Road (FR 223) for 19 miles to Slims Campground and the trailhead.

The road is paved for the first 6 miles to O'Hara Creek Bridge. From there it is gravel for 11 miles to Selway Falls, a magnificent sight, especially in the spring. At dusk, ospreys fish here and all along the river. Cross the Selway on the one-lane bridge just above the Selway Falls Guard Station, and begin following Meadow Creek for 2 miles along a narrow, but good, dirt road. Just before Slims Campground, side roads take off to Elk City and the active Indian Hill fire lookout. GPS: N46 01.72' / W115 17.37'

**Parking and trailhead facilities:** There are eleven campgrounds strung along the Selway River, but only the large O'Hara (thirty-two sites) has water. Slims and Selway Falls are closest to the trailhead. Both have outhouses and sites for two and seven parties, respectively. Park at Slims Campground, and find the trailhead at the south (upstream) end of the area.

## The Hike

The trail begins at 1,800 feet and continues with virtually no change in elevation for the first 3 miles. The canyon of Meadow Creek is narrower than that of the Selway and has a tree canopy, which provides a welcome retreat from the heat in these low-elevation canyons. Ferns and lichen-covered rock walls add to the coolness. Mica glitters in the mostly dirt surface of the trail.

*Rapid waters of Meadow Creek.* Photo by Lindsey Tucker

Meadow Creek quietly rushes over boulders and logjams or pools in the shade of old-growth cedars. While the bank is mostly rocky, there are some pockets of sand. The trail offers opportunities to slip over to the creek's edge to rest or fish. My experience is that in the lower 3 miles you can catch a rainbow or cutthroat about every other cast, but most are small (3 to 6 inches). Still, occasionally you catch a bigger one (10 to 12 inches) here.

A little over a mile up the trail, you will encounter bridged Squirrel Creek, the first of many streams that empty into Meadow Creek. Rabbit Creek follows 0.5 mile later and is narrow enough to step over.

Little Creek marks the end of the easy part of the trail. The forest map shows a trail to Horse Point on the west side of Meadow Creek here, but it doesn't really exist anymore. Just on the other side of Little Creek bridge, a ramble through the brush to Meadow Creek's edge is worthwhile. Horse Creek tumbles out of the steep west wall of the canyon into beautiful, deep pools. You can stand on boulders and look straight down into clear water 10 to 20 feet deep. Looking upstream, you will see the canyon narrow into a trailless gorge of cliffs and whitewater.

The next stretch of trail brings 0.5 mile of switchbacks, not indicated on the USGS map, which ascend from Little Creek along the steep hillside to an elevation

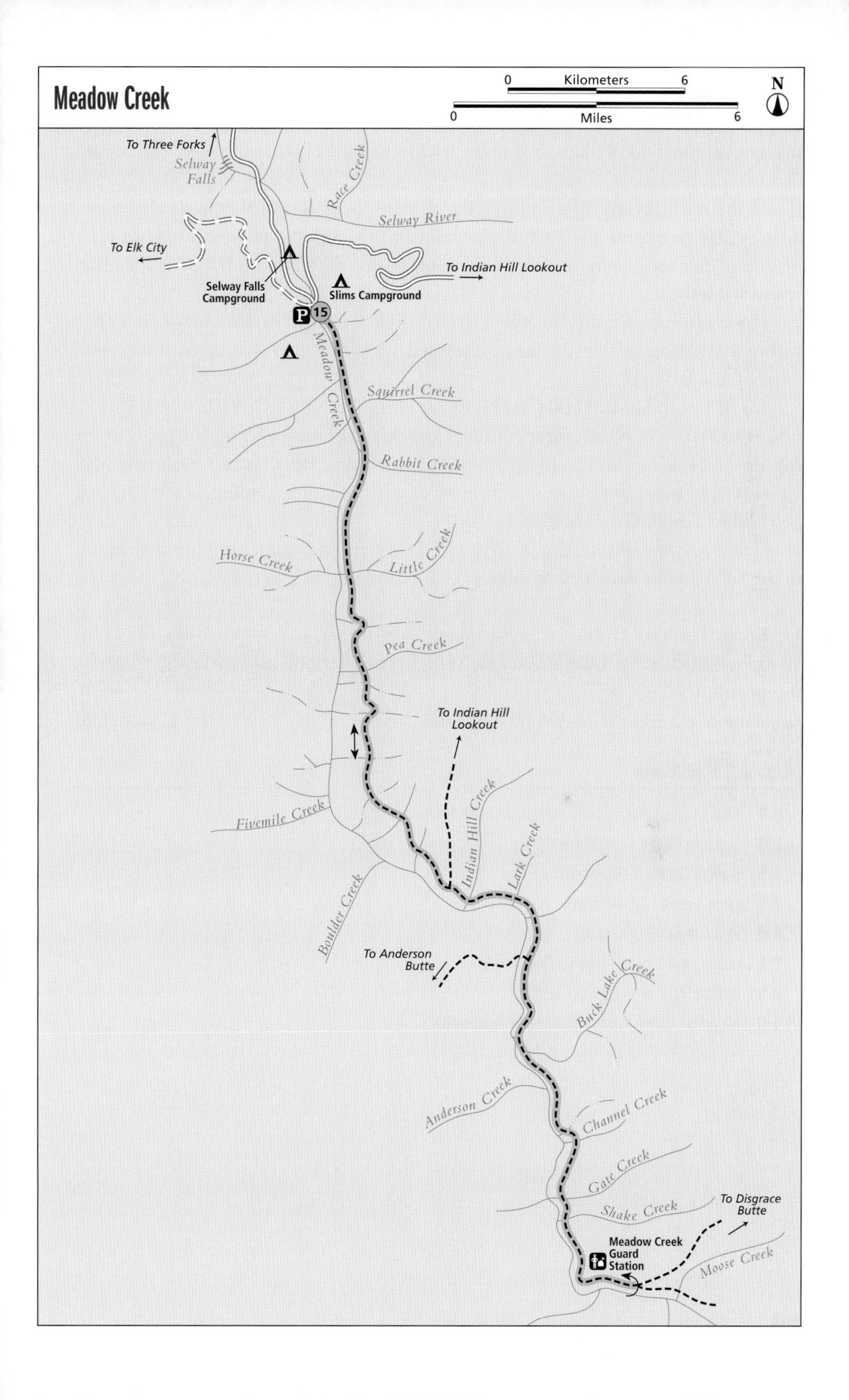
Meadow Creek
0 Kilometers 6
0 Miles 6
N
To Three Forks
Selway Falls
Race Creek
Selway River
To Elk City
To Indian Hill Lookout
Selway Falls Campground
Slims Campground
15
Meadow Creek
Squirrel Creek
Rabbit Creek
Horse Creek
Little Creek
Pea Creek
To Indian Hill Lookout
Fivemile Creek
Indian Hill Creek
Lark Creek
Boulder Creek
To Anderson Butte
Buck Lake Creek
Anderson Creek
Channel Creek
Gate Creek
Shake Creek
To Disgrace Butte
Meadow Creek Guard Station
Moose Creek

almost 1,000 feet higher. The trail then stays at this level for about 3 miles before dropping back down to Meadow Creek. Pea Creek, the only one indicated as permanent on the USGS maps, is a mere trickle in July. This trickle veils the mouth of a cave.

As the trail traverses the hillside, the timber opens up on this fairly dry, west-facing ridge to expose the vast timber stands to the south and west. This is a view of one of the most remote, fragile sections of this de facto, undesignated, central Idaho wilderness.

The trail drops quickly to where Indian Hill Creek joins Meadow Creek. Just before the bottom is the junction on the left with Trail 603 leading to Indian Hill lookout at 6,810 feet.

A mile beyond Indian Hill Creek and just beyond the Lark Creek bridge is a junction with Trail 608, which fords Meadow Creek and climbs west to Anderson Butte. Meadow Creek Trail continues 6 more miles, crossing Buck Lake Creek, Channel Creek, Gate Creek, and Snake Creek, none of which requires fording, before arriving at Meadow Creek Guard Station.

Meadow Creek Recreation Trail can be a peaceful excursion until hunting season in the fall, when it becomes very busy.

**Options:** The trail to Indian Hill lookout (6,810 feet) is a 3,000-foot climb. This 13-mile round-trip requires a shuttle vehicle at either end and makes an interesting possibility.

—Don L. Crawford

## Miles and Directions

**0.0** Slims Campground and Meadow Creek trailhead (1,800 feet)
**1.0** Squirrel Creek (1,880 feet)
**1.5** Rabbit Creek (1,960 feet)
**2.5** Little Creek (2,040 feet)
**4.5** Pea Creek (3,000 feet)
**7.8** Indian Hill lookout trail (3,000 feet)
**8.0** Indian Hill Creek (2,600 feet)
**14.0** Meadow Creek Guard Station (3,000 feet)

# Gospel Hump Wilderness

Born of controversy and compromise, the 206,053-acre Gospel Hump Wilderness is one of Idaho's most wild and least visited places. It was established by Congress in 1978 after several years of legal and political battles. Lengthy negotiations between conservation and development interests preceded introduction of legislation. The final settlement, enacted by Congress as part of the Endangered American Wilderness Act (PL 95-237), not only established the wilderness but also allocated roadless land along the South Fork of the Clearwater River to timber development. Still other roadless land was the subject of wildlife and fishery studies completed in 1982, and the 1983 Nez Perce Forest Plan made final decisions on the uses of the "study" lands. Neither the final wilderness boundary nor the final allocation of lands for development pleased all the interested parties, and for years environmental protesters have tried to stop the Cove-Mallard timber sale to the area's east. Nevertheless, creation of a Gospel Hump Wilderness by Congress had been most unlikely, and when the unexpected opportunity appeared, environmentalists at the time made the necessary compromises. Had this not been so, there would be no Gospel Hump Wilderness today and the Cove-Mallard sale would have been cut anyway (and probably much more).

Elevations within the wilderness range from 1,970 feet at the Wind River Pack Bridge on the Salmon River to 8,940 feet at the summit of Buffalo Hump, a lovely and quite dramatic mountain. Vegetation types along the Salmon River breaks (southern) portion of the wilderness consist chiefly of grass and large-diameter ponderosa pine. The old wagon road (now a trail) leading east from the Gospels toward Buffalo Hump serves as a hydrologic divide for the wilderness. To the north, streams flow into the South Fork of the Clearwater in deep, but often wide, valleys. Lovely meadows predominate here, with fir species and lodgepole pine the most common type of trees found. Brush is thicker on this side as well, due to higher rainfall. Precipitation on the Salmon River side is as low as 18 inches a year but reaches 60 inches farther north.

This climatic variation also affects visitor use. The Wind River (southwest side) and trails associated with it are often snow-free by March, yet trails on the north side leading into the Ten and Twenty Mile Creeks country off the Sourdough Road don't open up until late June or July. The high country around Wildhorse Lake on the east edge of the wilderness is the last to open, although increased mining activity in the Buffalo Hump mining district, which was excluded from the wilderness, could mean earlier plowing some years.

The wilderness is rich in both fish and wildlife. Both resident and anadromous fish can be found in some streams, and most of the numerous lakes in the wilderness have fish as well. Several of the north-side drainages are especially popular with moose, and there is evidence of elk migration back and forth across the wilderness, with large wintering populations found on the Salmon River side. Both goats and sheep are fairly common on the canyon breaks, especially in Crooked Creek. Cougars are common, black bears uncommon, and there is occasional wolf use on the

*A clearing on the bumpy road to Jumbo Camp.* PHOTO BY LUKE KRATZ

east side of the wilderness. The large deer and elk populations make hunter camps a common autumn sight.

The road system leading to Gospel Hump trailheads is generally well kept and well marked. On the southwest side of the wilderness, the Salmon River road to Wind River is a charming drive in itself. On the northeast side, equally charming is the road from Crooked Creek up to Wildhorse Lake, where the trail to North Pole Mountain begins. On the west side, the Gospels Road is by far the most lovely vehicle access route to the wilderness, offering dramatic views south into Wind River and across the Salmon River into the adjacent Frank Church–River of No Return Wilderness. On the north side, ID 14 follows the South Fork of the Clearwater River on what is known both as Sourdough Road and the Southern Nez Perce Trail and is the key route accessing this edge of the wilderness.

Trails within the wilderness range from well kept to not maintained at all. As a result, the Gospel Hump Wilderness offers a superb chance to escape crowds and yet still enjoy fine stream or lakeside camping, hunting, and fishing. The rough country southwest of Buffalo Hump is by far the least visited part of the wilderness, but spring hikers in the Wind River and Crooked Creek country can also expect no crowds.

A 1983 management plan and subsequent documents offer guidance to the forest service on how to manage the wilderness and would make interesting reading for visitors as well. The plan also outlines several threats to the wilderness, including mineral exploration and development (chiefly for gold) among those parts of the wilderness that border the mining district exclusion, and development of a major resort on private land within the wilderness at lovely, historic Shepp Ranch.

—Dennis Baird

# 16 Hanover Ridge

There are good views of the Gospels, Seven Devils, and Buffalo Hump in prime elk and cougar habitat.

**Start:** 45 miles southeast of Grangeville in the Gospel Hump Wilderness
**Type of hike:** Day hike; out-and-back
**Distance:** 4 miles one way
**Approximate hiking time:** 3–4 hours
**Difficulty:** Moderate
**Best season:** July–August
**Trail surface:** Normal dirt and rock
**Land status:**, Gospel Hump Wilderness; Nez Perce National Forest
**Canine compatibility:** Not allowed
**Fees and permits:** None
**Maps:** Hanover Mountain USGS quadrangle; Gospel Hump Wilderness map
**Trail contacts:** Slate Creek Ranger Station; Salmon River Ranger District, (208) 839-2211
**Special considerations:** Gospels Road, although very scenic, is also very steep on the approach to Gospel Peak, heavily washboarded, and traction-poor because of loose gravel. While passenger-vehicle access is possible, four-wheel drive is strongly recommended.

The Gospel Hump Wilderness map is the most recent and shows primary and secondary trails not recorded on the USGS or Nez Perce National Forest maps.

**Finding the trailhead:** From Grangeville, drive south on the winding, paved CR 221, which becomes FR 221. After 32 miles, turn left (east) onto FR 444, which is the well-marked entryway to the west side of the wilderness. A sign warns that this is a steep mountain road not recommended for trailers. Plenty of horse parties do pull trailers on this road—but none without large engines and four-wheel drive.

After 6 miles you'll top the range and encounter Gospel Hill (8,121 feet) and Gospel Peak (8,345 feet). Another 5 miles brings you to the signed turnoff on the right (south) to Slate Lake and the trailhead. You'll travel another 2.3 miles down a road that is rocky and narrow in places but accessible to sedans with good tires and patient drivers. GPS: N45 35.74' / W115 55.48'
**Parking and trailhead facilities:** Large, undeveloped site with no facilities, characteristic of most of this side of the Gospel Hump. Well-maintained pit toilet is located at the top of the road, and there are many informal campsites along the main Gospels Road.

## The Hike

The trail throughout this hike is well maintained until you reach the cutoff to climb Hanover Mountain. The trail follows an old road for about a mile to climb through forest and grouse habitat to Umbrella Butte meadow. Umbrella Butte meadow is a lovely example of a healthy, ungrazed mountain riparian area, and the ranger district has been

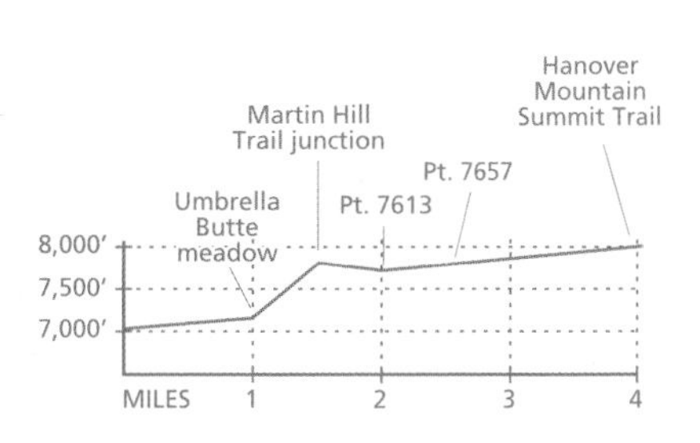

*Lakes around the high Gospels.* PHOTO BY LUKE KRATZ

vigilant in keeping it and the Wind River meadows free of cows. Umbrella Butte is a photographic feature in itself, with large granite slabs backdropping a meadow of long grasses, sedges, and purple harebells.

From here the climb becomes more pronounced as you travel through forest to reach the ridge. Once on the ridge, you are generally in forest except for a couple of places where you must hike a bit off the trail for the views. Be sure to look back for a good view of Gospel Peak and Gospel Hill. Off to the east, you can see Square Mountain and the lookout on top, plus, farther east, the Buffalo Hump (8,938 feet). You can also look west into Hanover Creek and see the Seven Devils beyond. To your south, once you approach Hanover Mountain (7,966 feet) and reach the highest unforested point before the switchbacks, you can see the Wind River drainage as it slopes toward the Salmon River.

Hanover Mountain summit itself is somewhat of a grunt through forest with views generally no better than what is available at the bottom.

Among fauna seen on this side of the Gospel Hump are red-tailed hawks, calliope hummers, red-breasted nuthatches, yellow-rumped warblers, flickers, juncos, moose, elk, deer, and three-striped chipmunks.

**Options:** Try Wind River Meadows Trail for elk and Slate Lake Trail for birds, including goshawks.

Moores Lake Trail is a popular 4-mile round-trip hiking destination as it drops steeply through forest to the lake's inlet.

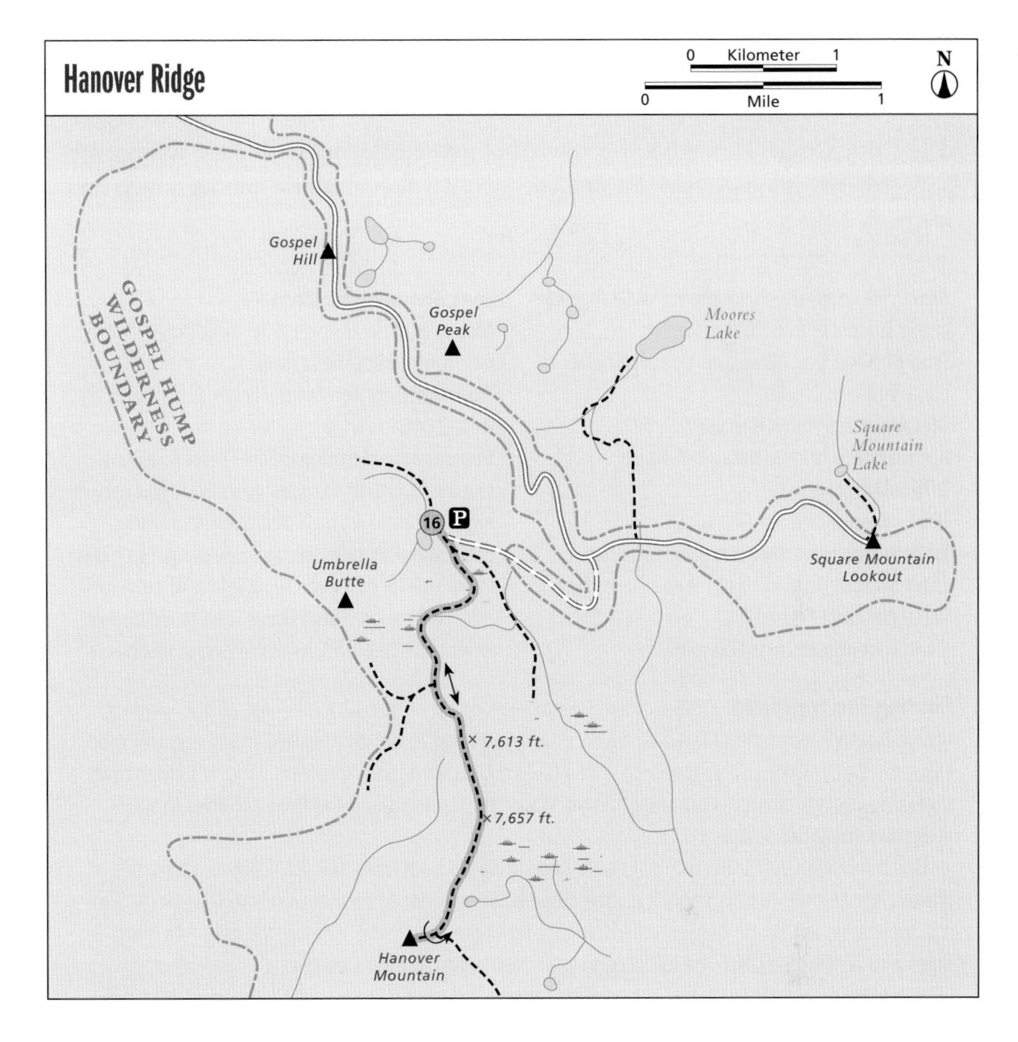


The drive to Square Mountain fire lookout will give good views of the Buffalo Hump and Jumbo Canyon. The lookout is being restored to its original specifications, but since the water is far below, one has to wonder how it was hauled up to the lookout.

—Jackie Johnson Maughan

## Miles and Directions

**0.0** Hanover Mountain Trailhead (7,000 feet)
**1.0** Umbrella Butte meadow (7,200 feet)
**1.5** Marten Hill Trail junction (7,680 feet)
**2.0** Point 7,613 (7,420 feet)
**2.5** Point 7,657
**4.0** Hanover Mountain summit trail (7,800 feet)

# 17 Oregon Butte

The classic Gospel Hump hike is known for profuse wildflowers, solitude, fishing, and a spectacular vista of Salmon River Canyon. It is a also a historic mining district and has glory holes.

**Start:** 50 linear miles southeast of Grangeville in the Gospel Hump Wilderness
**Type of hike:** Day hikes and possible backpack; out-and-back
**Distance:** 3.5 miles one way
**Approximate hiking time:** 3–4 hours
**Difficulty:** Moderate
**Best season:** Mid-July–August
**TrailsSurface:** Normal dirt and rock
**Land status:** Gospel Hump Wilderness; Nez Perce National Forest
**Canine compatibility:** Not allowed
**Fees and permits:** None
**Maps:** Buffalo Hump USGS quadrangle; Gospel Hump Wilderness map
**Trail contact:** Red River Ranger District, (208) 842-2245
**Special considerations:** Past Orogrande Summit, this is one of the worst roads in Idaho and requires patience, high clearance, four-wheel drive, and a rig that can take a beating. Two hikes in the vicinity that don't require four-wheel drive are Fish Lake and Wild Horse Lake to North Pole Mountain. (See Options at the end of this hike.)

**Finding the trailhead:** From Grangeville, take paved ID 14 for 42 miles east up the winding, scenic South Fork of the Clearwater River to Crooked River Road. On this well-marked gravel road, cross the South Fork and proceed 13 miles toward Orogrande, a turn-of-the-century mining town that is now just a cluster of summer homes. Watch for moose along the Crooked River in the overgrown mine tailings ponds.

One mile past Orogrande, turn right onto Orogrande Summit Road (FR 233). This is where the gravel ends, but the road is good. It climbs steadily through dense conifer woods to Orogrande Summit, the watershed divide between the Salmon and Clearwater Rivers. On top, the right fork leads 2 miles into Wild Horse Lake. The left goes to your destination, Jumbo Canyon.

Just past this intersection, the road deteriorates as it descends into Lake Creek. The next 3 miles are negotiable by truck, but tough for a sedan because of large rocks. Don't try to get past the summit in a car unless you are an experienced mountain driver and don't mind beating up your vehicle.

Half a mile past Lake Creek Campground, the road is passable to four-wheel-drive vehicles only. This 3-mile section is badly washed; water flows over it even in the summer. In several places it climbs steep ledges of bedrock that are challenging even with four-wheel drive. The road tops out near Hump Lake (7,850 feet) at a spectacular view of the Buffalo Hump plus a much-improved road. A right turn here is a 0.5-mile side trip to the lake at the base of the Buffalo Hump.

Continuing another 2.5 miles brings you to a private airstrip on the old Calendar Mine property. Past the turnoff to the airstrip, the road drops gradually into the headwaters of Jumbo Creek and, in about 1.8 miles, the trailhead at the end of the road near Jumbo Mine. GPS: N45 33.55' / W115 41.25'

**Parking and trailhead facilities:** Large, undeveloped site. No potable water or improvements. Orogrande Summit Campground (five sites) is the closest campground. Wild Horse Lake Campground (four sites) is just past Orogrande Summit and is a 2-mile side trip. Both have pit toilets but no potable water.

## The Hike

The Gospel Hump area, just north of where the Salmon River runs through the maze of the Salmon River Mountains, is characterized by pronounced glacial features on the north and east side of the ridges and by fairly gentle south and west slopes.

The trails typically wander along the more gentle slopes through subalpine fir, whitebark pine, and Engelmann spruce combined with numerous open parks and meadows. The meadows are wet most of the year and display many kinds of wildflowers, such as alpine heather, shooting star, pinks, and lupine.

Mountain goats and a few bighorn sheep inhabit the heights, while mule deer and elk are common on the lower slopes. Moose migrate from lake to lake and are particularly common in Jumbo Canyon. The eastern part of the Gospel Hump is the country most likely to be visited by the wolves reintroduced into central Idaho in 1995–96.

Oregon Butte lies about 7 miles southeast of one of the most unusual features of the Gospel Hump Wilderness, the Buffalo Hump. This granite exfoliated dome is named for its east–west profile, which resembles a buffalo.

The trail to Oregon Butte lookout and Oregon Butte Lake begins in a wet meadow in the headwaters of Jumbo Creek. After a boggy creek crossing, it switchbacks steeply for 0.25 mile to a low saddle between Jumbo Creek and the East Fork of Sheep Creek. Here you'll find a seemingly confusing system of trails and shortcuts. The trail to the right (Trail 201) leads into the East Fork of Sheep Creek. Stay left; this will put you on Trail 202.

About 0.25 mile past the junction, on the right, is a trail into the Brandon Lakes. The Brandon Lakes lie in two adjacent east-facing cirques on Quartzite Ridge. Both of the lakes' basins were burned over in 1969 in the Elk Creek Fire, which caused evacuation of Oregon Butte lookout. Quartzite Ridge is very rugged and supports a small population of mountain goats.

The trail now climbs slowly, staying on the ridge between Sheep Creek and Jumbo Canyon, and in another 0.25 mile on the left, an easy-to-follow fisher's trail leads down from a broad saddle into Deer Lake.

From here the trail climbs moderately for 1 mile to the Teepee Flats Saddle. Keeping to the right at the intersection will put you on the trail that switchbacks to Oregon Butte lookout for a superb view of Salmon River Canyon and the Wallowa Mountains in Oregon. This lookout is one of the few wilderness lookouts still staffed every season. First established as a tent camp in the 1920s, it is on the National Historic Lookout Register.

This part of the Gospel Hump Wilderness remains little used. The summer Mary-Ann, coauthor of this hike, did fire watch on Oregon Butte lookout, she learned the meaning of solitude and loved it.

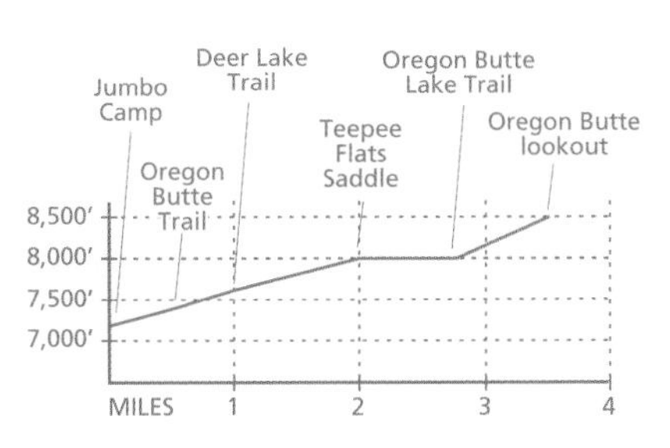

**Options:** Teepee Flats is a possible base for hikes into Round, Oregon Butte, and Fawn Lakes. About 200 yards before the trail levels off above Teepee Flats, a rather indistinct fisher's trail goes to Round Lake. It follows a small perennial stream down into a cirque, crosses the stream to avoid a bog, then drops through dense old-growth spruce to Round Lake. The lake is hard to find if you lose the trail but has excellent angling for big fish.

About 0.5 mile past Teepee Flats, a trail on the left side drops fairly rapidly into the West Fork of Crooked Creek. Another 0.5 mile or so down the West Fork Trail, a distinct fisher's route leaves the main trail and continues to Oregon Butte Lake. This lake is rarely fished and even less frequently stocked. It has a few large fish, which are hard to catch. However, the lake is highly scenic, and the hike is well worth it.

Another trail follows Drumlumen Ridge out to Fawn Lake. The first 0.5 mile crosses a meadow and is indistinct. However, it is easy to find once it leaves the meadow if you stay on top of Drumlumen Ridge. The fishing at Fawn Lake is not as productive as at other lakes in the vicinity, but the area often has moose.

If you have a little extra time and are interested in old mines, the Jumbo Mine is a half-hour hike from the trailhead at Jumbo Canyon. To find the mine, follow Jumbo Canyon Trail (Trail 230) down a steep granite slope to where it reaches the valley floor. On the way down this hill, you can see the mine buildings on your left and to the north. Cross Jumbo Creek on the trail, and shortly thereafter you will see old mine tailings near the trail. Follow them uphill less than 0.25 mile from the trail, and you will come upon the old mine and mill buildings. Heavy machinery for processing is still evident at the mill site. How could such equipment possibly have been brought in with no road the last 0.5 mile? One old-timer in Grangeville explained that the machinery was skidded in from Grangeville in the middle of the winter over an old trail that followed the Clearwater–Salmon Rivers Divide. An elaborate winch-and-pulley system was devised to get the machinery down the cliffs in Jumbo Creek.

If you are interested in a short day hike into Shining Lake, which is slow fishing for big fish, follow these directions. The junction for the trail into Shining Lake (Trail 228) is about 0.5 mile past the junction for Oregon Butte Trail. The trail is hard to find, but if you lose it, remember that the lake is about the same elevation as the saddle. It lies in an indistinct glacial cirque 1 mile due north of the saddle. It has a perennial outlet stream, and if all else fails you can follow the outlet up to the lake.

Fish Lake: Orogrande USGS quadrangle. Just after topping Orogrande Summit, you'll descend 1.75 miles to the Fish Lake Trailhead. If you find the descent too rough, you can park at the summit. From the trailhead it's 2 miles to the lake, a excellent place to look for moose.

Wild Horse Lake to North Pole Mountain: North Pole USGS quadrangle. This trail climbs 1,500 feet in 2 miles along the eastern spur to the summit of this dramatic peak.

—Dan and MaryAnn Green

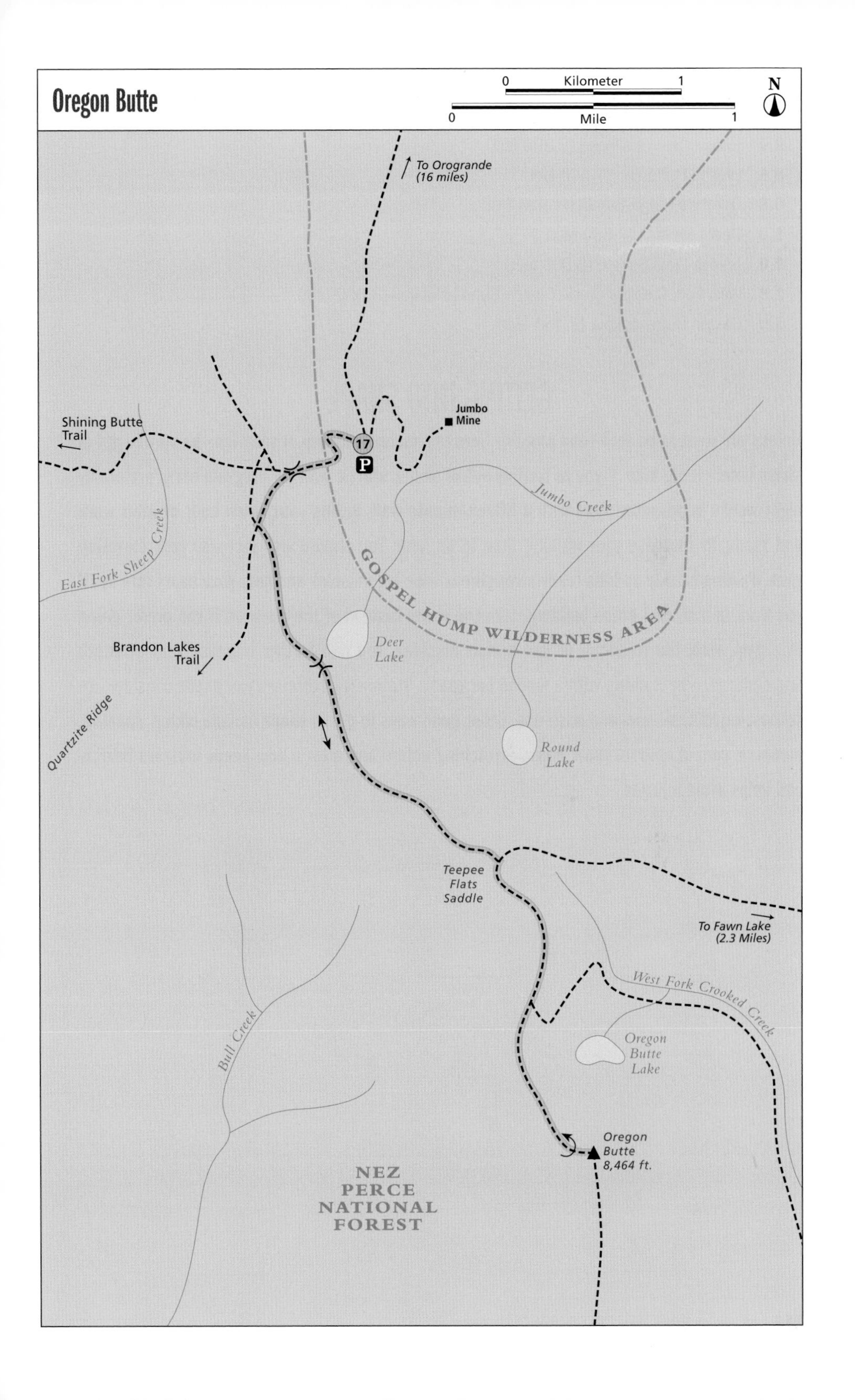
Oregon Butte
0 Kilometer 1
0 Mile 1
N
To Orogrande (16 miles)
Jumbo Mine
Shining Butte Trail
17
P
Jumbo Creek
East Fork Sheep Creek
GOSPEL HUMP WILDERNESS AREA
Deer Lake
Brandon Lakes Trail
Quartzite Ridge
Round Lake
Teepee Flats Saddle
To Fawn Lake (2.3 Miles)
West Fork Crooked Creek
Oregon Butte Lake
Bull Creek
Oregon Butte 8,464 ft.
NEZ PERCE NATIONAL FOREST

## Miles and Directions

**0.0** Jumbo Camp trailhead (7,200 feet)

**0.5** Oregon Butte Trail (7,440 feet)

**0.8** Quartzite Ridge–Brandon Lakes Trail

**1.0** Deer Lake Trail (7,680 feet)

**2.0** Teepee Flats Saddle (8,000 feet)

**2.8** West Fork Crooked Creek–Oregon Butte Lake Trail (8,000 feet)

**3.5** Oregon Butte lookout (8,464 feet)

## GETTING INTO SHAPE

**Unless you want to be sore—and possibly have to shorten your trip or vacation—be sure to get in shape before a big hike. If you're terribly out of shape, start a walking program early, preferably eight weeks in advance. Start with a fifteen-minute walk during your lunch hour or after work and gradually increase your walking time to an hour. You should also increase your elevation gain. Walking briskly up hills really strengthens your leg muscles and gets your heart rate up. If you work in a storied office building, take the stairs instead of the elevator. If you prefer going to a gym, walk the treadmill or use a stair machine. You can further increase your strength and endurance by walking with a loaded backpack. Stationary exercises you might consider are squats, leg lifts, sit-ups, and push-ups. Other good ways to get in shape include biking, running, aerobics, and, of course, short hikes. Stretching before and after a hike keeps muscles flexible and helps avoid injuries.**

# Frank Church-River of No Return Wilderness

The story of how the River of No Return Wilderness came to be is not quite as romantic as its name. But it's sure to arouse passion and nostalgia in the hearts of the many who put their minds, mouths, and money into this labor of love. Although many concessions were made, this was a victory to which every major environmental group contributed. It was the last wilderness area established by Congress in Idaho. Since then, brown Idaho politicians have created a generation of wilderness drought.

At 2.4 million acres this is the largest wilderness area in the lower forty-eight states. Its birth as official wilderness in 1980 was breathtaking in that several decades of effort could have been lost. The Central Idaho Wilderness Act was passed in August 1980. In November 1980 the act's most important sponsor, Senator Frank Church, lost his bid for reelection. A scant three months' delay in passage could have sunk the whole ship.

Several years later, after Church's death, the name "River of No Return Wilderness" was modified by Congress with Church's name added. The name of Frank Church, a man of great achievement in American history, on the wilderness area may be remembered when other deeds have been forgotten.

The River of No Return is the Salmon River, declared unnavigable by explorers Lewis and Clark back in about 1804. It remains that way except for recreational navigation: It provides some of the best whitewater boating in the world.

The wilderness itself comprises the former Idaho and Salmon River Breaks Primitive Areas and adjacent wildlands previously unprotected. The need to protect the wildlands of central Idaho was recognized way back in 1931 when, on its own initiative, the forest service established the Idaho Primitive Area. This administratively protected area included a million acres of rugged Salmon River Mountains out of an area of wild country four times that size existing in one vast mountain fastness.

A "primitive area" was a temporary classification, however, and in the late 1930s the forest service began to study and reclassify the various primitive areas around the nation into the permanent status of wilderness area. Unfortunately, rather than keeping a bit of America wild forever, the reclassification often turned out to be a method of stripping an area of all potential merchantable timber and "protecting" the rest—the rocks. "We will allow no logging above timberline," assured one regional forester.

Conservationists began to seek a more reliable form of protecting the wild country than the old method of administrative decree. Although many forest service leaders were strong proponents of wilderness, conservationists realized that something stronger was needed—something that would be difficult to rescind. The answer was to pass a law guaranteeing some lands by US statute permanently as wilderness.

For many years, the battle to create a National Wilderness System was fought in Congress. Progress was slow, but in 1964 a federal bill creating the National Wilderness Preservation System was signed into law. Senator Church was a co-sponsor and a leading supporter of the Wilderness Act.

*Wild gentions.* PHOTO BY JOSH KEELEY

In 1963, the year just before the Wilderness Act, the forest service had, by administrative fiat, reclassified much of the 1.8-million Selway-Bitterroot Primitive Area, just north of Idaho Primitive Area. While the resulting 1.2-million-acre Selway-Bitterroot Wilderness was the largest in the nation at the time, hundreds of thousands of acres of forest, canyon, and mountain meadow had first been torn out of the primitive area, including Elk Summit, the Magruder Corridor, and Meadow Creek. Twenty years later Congress made the Magruder Corridor part of the Selway-Bitterroot Wilderness, and conservationists still battle to keep Elk Summit and Meadow Creek (see Hike 15) off the chopping block.

Conservationists redoubled their efforts after passage of the Wilderness Act. The National Wilderness Preservation System at first included only those areas already classified as "wilderness" by the forest service. However, additions could be made. The remaining unreclassified primitive areas were to be studied for wilderness classification over a ten-year period. Recommendations for their future were to be made to Congress. Among the areas in Idaho, this review included the Idaho and Salmon River Breaks Primitive Areas.

In 1972 the 200,000-acre Sawtooth Primitive Area was successfully reclassified as the Sawtooth Wilderness, but the great Idaho Primitive Area and its neighbor, the Salmon River Breaks Primitive Area, totaling 1.4 million acres, were saved for last.

In 1974 the forest service began to solicit public opinion to determine the future of these areas. Options ranged from protecting the entire 1.4 million acres of the two primitive areas down to protecting nothing at all. Losing any part of the official primitive areas seemed, in the words of one Idaho conservationist, like choosing which of your children would live and which would die.

But the future of the paper primitive areas wasn't the only worry. These areas were surrounded by another million acres of orphan wildland that had been protected only by their inhospitality to development. Environmentalists had a brainstorm, one that would save both. All the existing wildlands in central Idaho, those with pedigree and those without, should be protected.

This idea was embodied in the 2.4-million-acre River of No Return Wilderness bill. The bill was drawn up and presented in public meetings. From one end of the state to the other, in public hearing halls packed to the rafters and hot with debate and histrionics, the contenders made their case—the 500,000-acre "roadless recreation area" proposed by the Boise-Cascade Corporation versus the 2.4-million-acre bill for a River of No Return Wilderness, along with the middle-of-the-road forest service option of 1.4 million acres. Environmentalists turned the tide. When the results were in, the 2.4 million acres were overwhelmingly endorsed by the citizens of Idaho. Finally then, in 1980, this public support convinced enough politicians so that almost all of the 2.4 million acres (more than 3,500 square miles) became formally protected wilderness.

The individual victories in the bill's passage were many. Among lands now protected, in addition to the former primitive areas, were the headwaters of Camas Creek and Warm Springs Creek. The airy upper reaches of Loon Creek were included as a detached portion of the wilderness. Sulphur Creek and Elk Creek, important spawning streams for salmon and nurseries for elk, were saved from below-cost logging. Marsh Creek and lower Bear Valley Creek were included, making the headwaters of the Middle Fork of the Salmon sacrosanct from off-road vehicles and other internal combustion intrusions. Poker and Ayer Meadows, slated for noisy auto campground futures, were instead kept for the elk and sandhill crane. The entire watershed of the Middle Fork, both inside the wilderness and out, was withdrawn from dredge mining.

Bitter compromises were made, too. The lower portion of the Bighorn Crags and the Panther Creek breaks were made part of the wilderness, but cobalt mining was declared the dominant use. This came after a Canadian mining company, in a fit of altruism no doubt, mounted a public relations campaign highlighting the risk that the United States would run out of this "strategic" mineral. Subsequent to this concession, the foreign firm lobbied for a government subsidy to make cobalt mining profitable. To date, no mining has taken place.

Small miners were allowed to continue their low-value diggings in Big Creek, the Middle Fork's main tributary. Mining was allowed on Thunder Mountain adjacent to the west boundary of the wilderness. Since that time, several bad spills of mining waste have found their way into adjacent wilderness streams.

With the exception of the subdued topography of Elk Creek on the south end of the wilderness and the vast plateau called Chamberlain Basin, the Frank Church–River of No Return Wilderness is a sea with waves of one steep mountain ridge after another. The major canyons of the Middle Fork and main Salmon twist through the mountains, in places almost 7,000 feet deep! This is deeper than the Grand Canyon.

Long ago, a vast body of molten rock pushed up under central Idaho. It never reached the surface as lava. Instead, it cooled and crystallized into a complex of granite-like rocks—a batholith. Millions of years later this batholith was exposed to the elements, carved by wind, water, thawing and freezing, and glaciers into mountains and canyons. The rocks of the Idaho Batholith, one of the world's largest such igneous intrusions, underlie much of central Idaho, including much of the Frank Church–River of No Return Wilderness. When roads are blasted into its mountains, the soft, coarse-grained rock washes into the rivers, choking them with sand.

Most environmentally aware citizens are familiar with the Idaho Batholith. What is not so well known is that most of the southeastern part of the wilderness, as well as Big Creek, is instead a pile of volcanic rock, part of the vast Challis Volcanic Field. These mountains, too, are fragile with erosion after disturbance. Here the result is cloudy water as devastating to fish as the clear, but sand-clogged, streams from disturbed batholithic soils.

The undisturbed mountains and canyons of the wilderness are rich in wildlife, including elk, bighorn sheep, mountain goats, mule and whitetail deer, cougar, black bear, and moose. Lynx, fisher, and wolverines exist in smaller numbers. The reintroduction of the wolf to central Idaho in 1995 and 1996 restored a top predator. The only missing large animal is the grizzly bear. As this edition goes to press, a furious battle is being waged over restoration of the grizzly to its Idaho home. The abundance of wildlife is due not to the area's fertility as much as to its untouched nature, especially the deep canyons that provide rare undisturbed winter range for wild animals.

# 18 Bighorn Crags: Reflection Lake

This part of the Bighorn Crags hosts beautiful fishing lakes amid rugged scenery. There are fewer visitors than at the northern end of the Bighorn Crags.

**Start:** 35 linear miles west of Salmon, Idaho, in the Frank Church–River of No Return Wilderness
**Type of hike:** Backpack; out-and-back
**Total distance:** 26 miles round-trip from Crags Campground
**Approximate hiking time:** At least 4 days
**Difficulty:** Moderate from the junction with Ship Island Lake Trail, 6.5 miles from Crags Campground
**Best season:** August
**Trail surface:** Normal dirt and rock
**Land status:** Frank Church Wilderness; Salmon-Challis National Forest
**Canine compatibility:** Not allowed
**Fees and permits:** None
**Maps:** Hoodoo Meadows and Mt. McGuire USGS quadrangles
**Trail contact:** Salmon-Cobalt Ranger District, (208) 756-5200
**Special considerations:** As with the hike to Ship Island Lake (Hike 19), the access roads and probably part of this trail burned in the Clear Creek Fire of 2000. Check with the forest service for current information on rehabilitation of the access roads and trails. The area remained closed to recreational entry through the end of 2000. Check with the forest service for current information on rehabilitation of the access roads and trails. There is no reliable water for the first 4.7 miles.

**Finding the trailhead:** There are two possible routes to reach the Bighorn Crags Campground and trailhead. From Salmon, drive 5 miles south on US 93 to the signed Williams Creek Road (FR 021) on the right (west). This good 12-mile road climbs over the Salmon River Range for about 3,000 feet to the junction with Panther Creek Road (FR 055). At the junction turn left (south) and drive 10.5 miles up Panther Creek until you reach Porphyry Creek Road.

From Challis, drive 9 miles north on US 93 to the signed Morgan Creek Road turnoff. Turn left and follow Morgan Creek Road for 19.6 miles (pavement, then good gravel) to Morgan Creek Summit, where the road becomes Panther Creek Road. From Morgan Creek Summit, drive north down Panther Creek for 14 miles to the signed turnoff at Porphyry Creek.

Porphyry Creek Road (FR 112) is graded and climbs 2,000 feet in 6 miles to a four-way junction. Take FR 113 to the right (north), and continue 8 miles to FR 114, which leads to Crags Campground in 2.5 more miles. You will have climbed another 800 feet and passed, on the right, the turnoff to FR 167. (Once the road has climbed out of Porphyry Creek, it keeps near an 8,500-foot ridgetop just 300 feet outside the wilderness boundary. The Blackbird Mountain USGS quad is useful for identifying sites from this impressive, sometimes white-knuckle road.) GPS: N45 6.25' / W114 31.47'
**Parking and trailhead facilities:** Crags Campground is a large, developed fee site. There is a nearby stream, but don't count on potable water.

## The Hike

Of the two Bighorn Crags hikes in this book, this is the less popular—though equally beautiful—traverse to the southwestern portion of the crags.

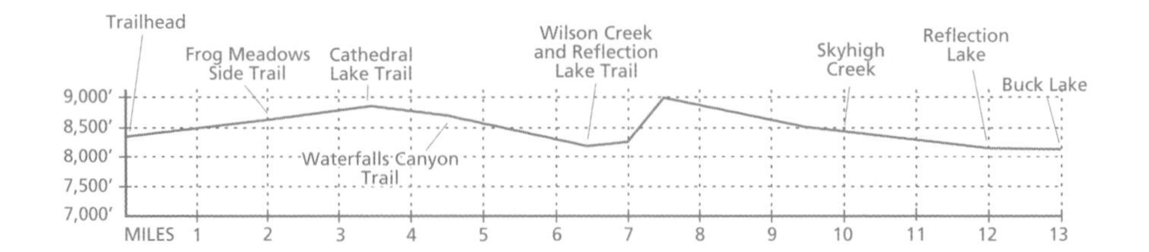


As with the trail to Ship Island, begin at Crags Campground near Golden Trout Lake and climb the ridgeline, passing by Cathedral Rock and continuing to the junction with the Clear Creek and Waterfall Trails at 4.5 miles. On this trip, however, unlike the hike to Ship Island Lake, continue to the left to Welcome Lake at the trail junction at 7.0 miles.

At 6.5 miles from the trailhead, you come to a trail junction. The path to the right leads up into a tight cirque basin that shelters Harbor and Wilson Lakes and over Fishfin Ridge and down to Birdbill and Gentian Lakes (see Hike 19). You should go left, following the sign to Welcome Lake. Welcome Lake is surrounded by peaks more than 9,500 feet high. This shallow, but beautiful, lake basin is filled with lush grass and marsh. It has plenty of campsites but is usually devoid of fish due to winterkill. Mosquitoes can be a real threat here in the early summer, so be prepared to fend them off with repellent. As you approach Welcome Lake, a trail junction marks the way to Reflection Lake. This trail does not appear on USGS quadrangles.

The trail switchbacks six times in 0.5 mile up the steep ridge to the southeast to climb to an elevation of 9,000 feet. Follow the ridge to drop down a moderate grade. The trail takes three long switchbacks down, totaling nearly 3 miles in length. The mammoth basin below to the west is a beautiful timbered margin along the celebrated Bighorn Crags ridgeline. Eight lakes dot the nappy pine quilt of trees—Skyhigh, Turquoise, Echo, Reflection, Twin Cove, Fawn, Doe, and Buck. The area is also alive with wildlife, primarily deer, elk, goats, and bighorn sheep.

At mile 10 cross Skyhigh Creek, just below Skyhigh Lake. Descend, and gently switchback through the basin. Cross another small creek and follow the trail uphill to Reflection Lake at 12 miles.

You may be able to get into this country by mid-July. It remains open until about mid-September. August is probably the best time.

**Options:** Reflection Lake is a good base camp. It contains numerous cutthroat and rainbow trout. The trail continues for another mile to Buck Lake and nearby Doe and Fawn Lakes. You can reach more lakes via cross-country ridge travel.

—Philip Blomquist

# Bighorn Crags: Reflection Lake

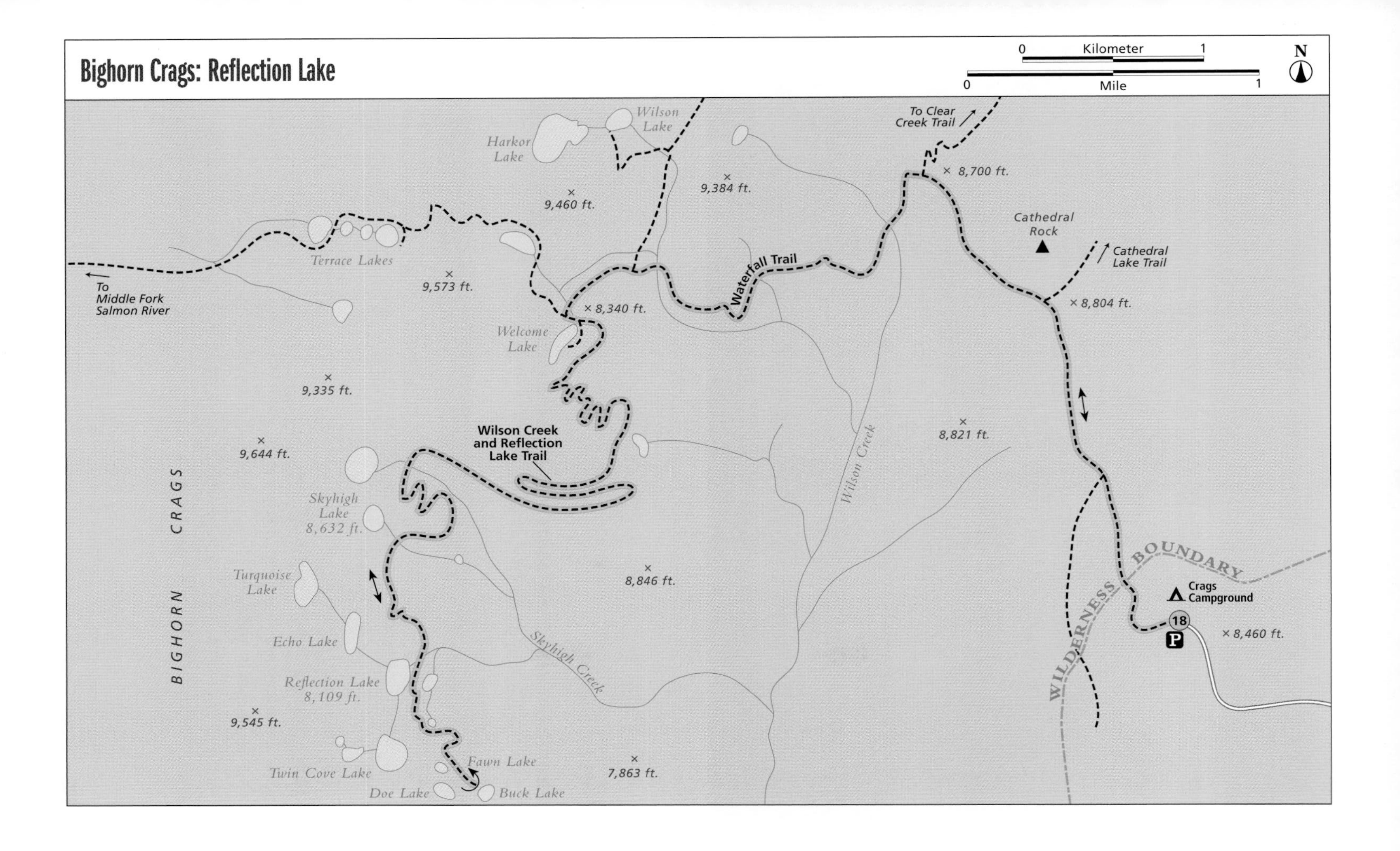

*View from the pass above Welcome Lake.* PHOTO BY LUKE KRATZ

## Miles and Directions

**0.0** Crags Campground trailhead (8,400 feet)
**2.0** Frog Meadows side trail (8,667 feet)
**3.5** Cathedral Lake cutoff (8,800 feet)
**4.5** Waterfalls Canyon Trail (8,720 feet)
**4.7** Stream (8,200 feet)
**6.5** Wilson Creek and Reflection Lake Trail (8,200 feet)
**7.0** Welcome Lake (8,332 feet)
**7.5** Pass (9,000 feet)
**10.0** Crossing of Skyhigh Creek (8,500 feet)
**12.0** Reflection Lake base camp (8,109 feet)
**13.0** Buck Lake (8,100 feet)

# 19 Bighorn Crags: Ship Island Lake

This is one of the most spectacular areas in the Frank Church–River of No Return Wilderness. Witness stunning views of Ship Island Lake and the breaks country of the Middle Fork of the Salmon River with spires, knobs, and the huge monoliths of rugged granite mountains. Many lakes have good fishing. The north and west sides of the Bighorn Crags are especially noted for bighorn sheep.

**Start:** 35 linear miles west of Salmon, Idaho, in the Frank Church–River of No Return Wilderness
**Type of hike:** Backpack; loop to Harbor Lake
**Distance:** From Crags Campground it is 15 miles round-trip to Harbor Lake and 22 miles round-trip to Ship Island Lake
**Approximate hiking time:** 4 hours to Harbor Lake, 3 or more nights
**Difficulty:** Moderate from the junction with Ship Island Lake Trail, 6.5 miles from Crags Campground
**Best season:** August
**Trail surface:** Normal dirt and rock
**Land status:** Frank Church Wilderness; Salmon-Challis National Forest
**Canine compatibility:** Not allowed
**Fees and permits:** None
**Maps:** Hoodoo Meadows and Mt. McGuire USGS quadrangle; Frank Church–River of No Return Wilderness North Half forest map
**Trail contact:** Salmon-Cobalt Ranger District, (208) 756-5200
**Special considerations:** Be prepared for foul weather, including snow in August. Neither the USGS quads nor the forest maps show updated versions of many trails in the Bighorn Crags. Do not attempt Fishfin Pass until you're sure it's clear of horse traffic.

When I hiked the trail in 2012, I noticed that the access roads have been slightly reworked due to the Clear Creek Fire of 2000. Check with the forest service for current information on rehabilitation of the access roads and trails. There is no reliable water for the first 4.7 miles.

**Finding the trailhead:** There are two possible routes to reach the Bighorn Crags Campground and trailhead. From Salmon, drive 5 miles south on US 93 to the signed Williams Creek Road (FR 021) on the right (west). This good 12-mile road climbs over the Salmon River Range for about 3,000 feet to the junction with Panther Creek Road (FR 055). At the junction turn left (south) and drive 10.5 miles up Panther Creek until you reach Porphyry Creek Road.

From Challis, drive 9 miles north on US 93 to the signed Morgan Creek Road turnoff. Turn left and follow Morgan Creek Road for 19.6 miles (pavement, then good gravel) to Morgan Creek Summit, where the road becomes Panther Creek Road. From Morgan Creek Summit, drive north down Panther Creek for 14 miles to the signed turnoff at Porphyry Creek.

Porphyry Creek Road (FR 112) is graded and climbs 2,000 feet in 6 miles to a four-way junction. Take FR 113 to the right (north), and continue 8 miles to FR 114, which leads to Crags Campground in 2.5 more miles. You will have climbed another 800 feet and passed, on the right, the turnoff to FR 167. (Once the road has climbed out of Porphyry Creek, it keeps near an 8,500-foot ridgetop just 300 feet outside the wilderness boundary. The Blackbird Mountain USGS quad is useful for identifying sites from this impressive, sometimes white-knuckle road.) GPS: N45 6.25' / W114 31.47'
**Parking and trailhead facilities:** Crags Campground is a large, developed fee site. There is a nearby stream, but don't count on potable water.

## The Hike

Milton's words in *Paradise Lost* best describe this popular hiking and horse-packing area: "Heaven's high towers." It is a must for those who enjoy major excursions.

The hike to Ship Island Lake can be very demanding, depending on which route you take. If thunderstorms threaten, it's better to take Waterfalls Canyon Trail rather than the ridge route (see Options for instructions). The trail described here begins by climbing 500 feet along the ridge overlooking the basin of Golden Trout Lake, where cutthroat have displaced the California goldens. The climb continues for just under a mile and 500 feet, then descends to a junction at the 2-mile point. From this ridgeline, you can see in the distant south the 9,045-foot granite Sugarloaf monolith.

The trail to the left (south) leads to Frog Meadows and Yellowjacket Lake. The trail on the right (northeast) is a horse route. Take the trail in the middle (northwest).

Now you climb again 250 feet to the ridgeline. Below, on the left, is the deep Wilson Creek drainage. In the distance ahead is the Crags divide. At 3.5 miles, you reach the base of another monolith called Cathedral Rock. Here a sign reads CATHEDRAL LAKE and points to the right. The lake is reached by a 0.3-mile route and offers an excellent view of Cathedral Rock and fishing for rainbow and cutthroat trout. Continuing on the main trail, begin a mile-long contour along the top of Wilson Creek Canyon. After this contour, 4.5 miles from the trailhead, you reach the junction of Waterfalls Canyon Trail on the left.

Waterfalls Canyon Trail descends in a long grade to Wilson Canyon. In 0.25 mile you come to the first and biggest stream. Although the map shows a second perennial stream in another 0.5 mile, this stream was almost dry in mid-August in a year of normal precipitation.

The trail continues for 1.75 miles west through forest, then turns north to head up Wilson Canyon. The fork here, at the 6.5-mile point, leads left (west) to Welcome and Heart Lakes (see Hike 18, Reflection Lake). The USGS map is off a bit here, but just take the right fork and go north up to the headwaters of Wilson Creek. The trail gains about 400 feet in elevation as it tracks along the canyon rim about 100 feet above the creek (unlike the map, which shows it in the creek bottom). Follow the trail through this high alpine forest, where it gets lost a little way north of Peak 9,460. The trail, once found, is broad and obvious, leading to Wilson and Harbor Lakes. Here, the USGS quad is seriously wrong. It puts the trail in the canyon bottom and crossing below the outlet of Wilson Lake. (There is a 120-foot waterfall at the outlet, a lovely meadow, and a headwall of spires

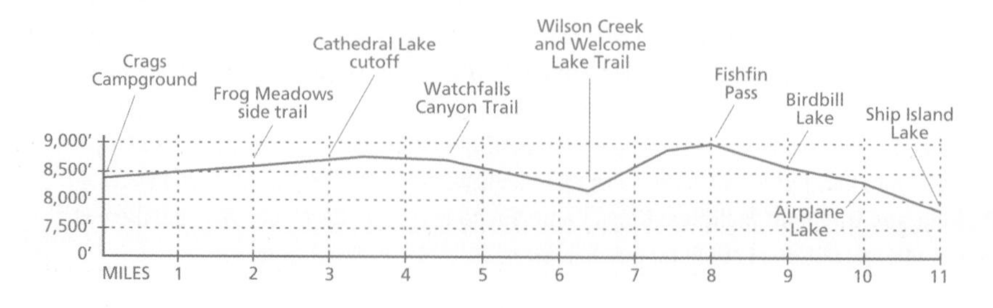

*Harbor and Wilson lakes from crags trail.* Photo by Josh Keeley

and crags.) But this won't get you to Fishfin Pass without a struggle. Instead, stick to Harbor Lake Trail, which will take you up to the pass.

The trail down Fishfin is along a vertical cliff and quite narrow. It spirals down about 280 feet on the right side of the canyon, then crosses to the left side. We could smell the carcass of a horse that had fallen from the pass. There is not enough room on Fishfin for hikers and equestrians to pass safely. At the bottom, you cross to the other side of the canyon, just above the creek, and gain about 80 feet to contour along the trail cut in the rock. From the pass, you can look down into Mirrow Lake but cannot see Gentian and Birdbill Lakes until you round the bend and rise again to drop down the rocky saddle into these lakes. They have small rainbow trout.

Near Gentian Lake you'll find an outhouse and a hitching post. The campsites in this high lake basin are heavily used, and this site is a major trail intersection. The northern route, recommended for horse traffic, comes in here.

After Gentian Lake it is a climb of 160 feet on a low, slow horse trail and a traverse over the ridge into the huge Ship Island basin. At the top of the ridge, you can see both Airplane Lake and Ship Island Lake as well as the massive granite cliffs backdropping the latter. It's about 2.5 miles to the eastern shore of Ship Island Lake and a 1,000-foot drop from the pass. The trail in places is very eroded, exposing bare bones of rocks. The descent, outside of the 400 feet to Airplane Lake, is in heavy forest. (Horse traffic is not allowed beyond Airplane Lake.) Both lakes offer fishing for rainbow and cutthroat trout. From Airplane Lake, you can cut cross-country to Shoban and Sheepeater Lakes. It's 0.25 mile and a 200-foot climb to Shoban and another 0.5 mile and 250-foot climb to Sheepeater. Both have fishing.

The view at Ship Island Lake itself will take your breath away for a couple of months. The basin holding the lake is large and beautiful, hemmed in by rugged

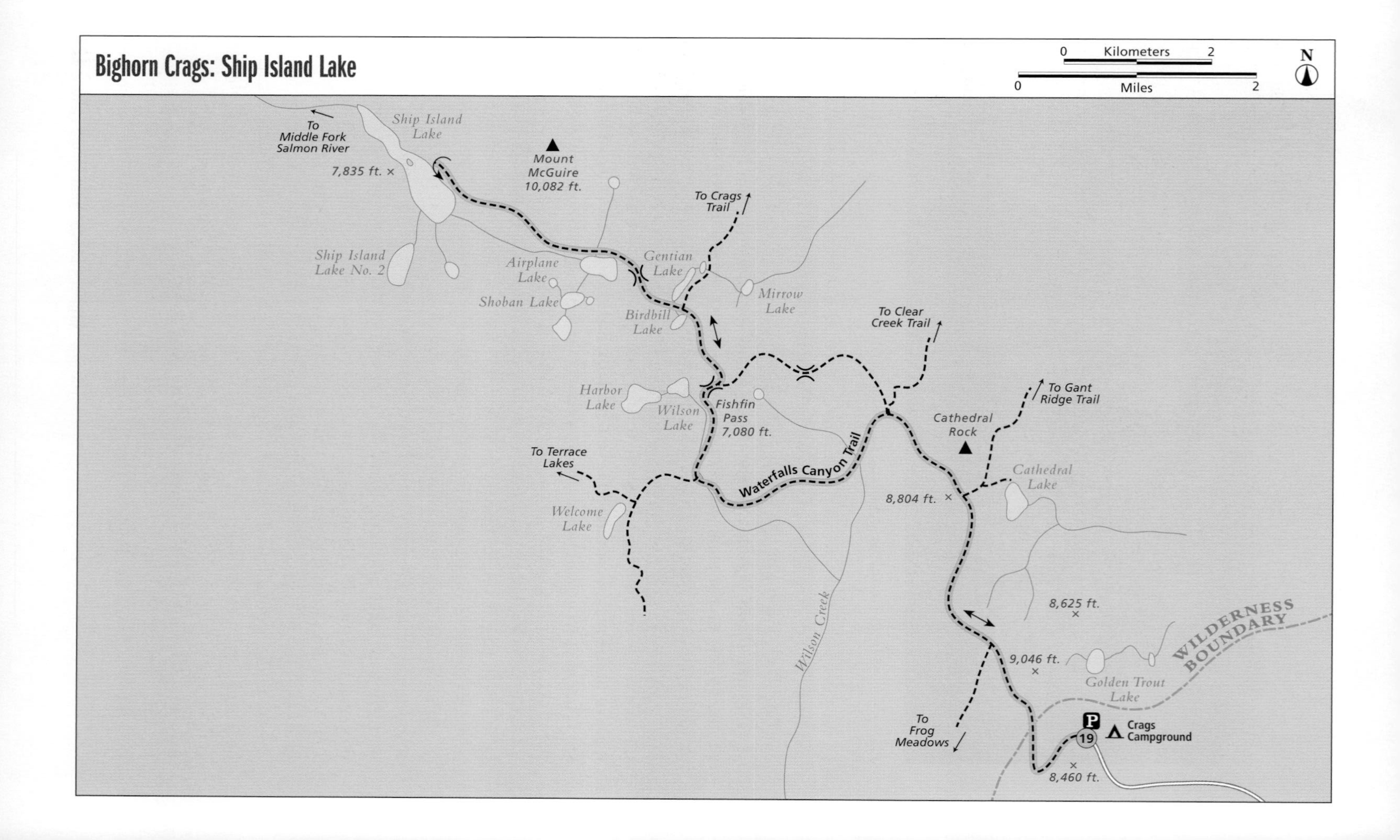
Bighorn Crags: Ship Island Lake
0 Kilometers 2
0 Miles 2
N
To Middle Fork Salmon River
Ship Island Lake
7,835 ft.
Mount McGuire 10,082 ft.
Ship Island Lake No. 2
Airplane Lake
Shoban Lake
Gentian Lake
Birdbill Lake
To Crags Trail
Mirrow Lake
To Clear Creek Trail
Harbor Lake
Wilson Lake
Fishfin Pass 7,080 ft.
To Gant Ridge Trail
Cathedral Rock
To Terrace Lakes
Welcome Lake
Waterfalls Canyon Trail
Cathedral Lake
8,804 ft.
Wilson Creek
8,625 ft.
9,046 ft.
Golden Trout Lake
WILDERNESS BOUNDARY
To Frog Meadows
Crags Campground
19
8,460 ft.

ridges of nearly 10,000 feet. You can hike down and around the east side of Ship Island Lake to its outlet. All told, it is about 1 mile to the lake outlet. The trail is at times faint, not maintained. The going is somewhat slow due to a huge amount of deadfall, the faintness of the trail, and the crossing of a boulder field.

The country on the right of the outlet is very rugged, and the trail, such as it is, through the smooth sheets of granite is marked by only an occasional cairn. Stay to the right side on the rocks up here while you drop some in elevation to round the bend to the view down Ship Island Creek Canyon. At the outlet of the lake, immense granite spires line the canyon walls, and here Ship Island Creek begins to tumble down a steep, trailless canyon. It drops 4,500 feet in 5 miles to the Middle Fork of the Salmon River. Few have ever descended this canyon.

**Options:** To take the ridge trail from the Waterfalls Canyon Trail junction, continue for a short distance past the junction and a climb of 120 feet. You will see Clear Creek Trail on the right. Clear Creek is the large, pristine drainage to the northeast, heavily fought over by the timber industry before it was included in the Frank Church–River of No Return Wilderness. Ironically, the Clear Creek Fire began in this general area. The fire burned 216,000 acres. First detected July 10, 2000, it was finally declared 100 percent contained on October 14. The 216,000 acres is hardly a total burn. Only 10 percent was judged to have been a severe burn. Many parts suffered ground fires only, and many areas inside its perimeter did not burn at all. Nevertheless, it was a humongous fire.

Pass this trail by unless you want to investigate. Instead, take the trail that continues climbing along the ridgeline. It is not on the Mt. McGuire topographic quadrangle or the Salmon National Forest map, but it is shown on the Frank Church–River of No Return forest map. Following this trail, climb up and around a granite knob of over 9,200 feet; then drop to a small saddle. From here you traverse over to Fishfin Pass. Do not take this demanding route if thunderstorms threaten. If you take this route, it is about 6 miles before you reach the first water.

—Jackie Johnson Maughan and Phil Blomquist

## Miles and Directions

**0.0** Crags Campground trailhead (8,400 feet)
**2.0** Frog Meadows side trail (8,667 feet)
**3.5** Cathedral Lake cutoff (8,800 feet)
**4.5** Waterfalls Canyon Trail (8,720 feet)
**4.7** Stream (8,200 feet)
**6.5** Wilson Creek and Welcome Lake Trail (8,200 feet)
**7.5** Wilson Lake (8,920 feet)
**8.0** Fishfin Pass (9,000 feet)
**9.0** Birdbill Lake (8,680 feet)
**10.0** Airplane Lake (8,402 feet)
**11.0** Ship Island Lake (7,835 feet)

# 20 Blue Bunch Mountain

Atop Blue Bunch are grandiose views of Bruce, Ayers, and Poker Meadows and, at the end of the hike, of the Middle Fork of the Salmon River.

**Start:** 50 miles north-northwest of Stanley.
**Type of hike:** Day hike or overnight; out-and-back
**Distance:** 8 miles round-trip
**Approximate hiking time:** 3–4 hours
**Difficulty:** Moderately difficult day hike; moderate overnighter
**Best season:** Mid-July–August
**Trail surface:** Normal rock and dirt
**Land status:** Frank Church Wilderness; Boise National Forest
**Canine compatibility:** On leash until wilderness boundary where not allowed
**Fees and permits:** None
**Maps:** Blue Bunch Mountain USGS quadrangle; Boise National Forest map; Frank Church–River of No Return Wilderness South Half forest map
**Trail contact:** Lowman Ranger District, (208) 259-3361
**Special considerations:** Water is not abundant on the mountain after snowmelt, so take advantage of the few springs. Depending on the year, you may be able to complete the hike by the latter part of June. Snow usually comes in October.

**Finding the trailhead:** From ID 21, turn onto the well-marked gravel road a few miles east of Banner Summit that climbs to Cape Horn Summit and then descends Bruce Meadow and points beyond. This road is all-weather gravel and maintained, but it is also badly washboarded due to heavy recreational traffic for the Middle Fork of the Salmon River put-in at Dagger Falls. Be very alert for buses and vehicles towing trailers.

Follow this road for about 12 miles until the sign and the side road for Fir Creek Campground. If you break out of the timber into Bruce Meadows, you have gone too far. Drive down the side road, but stay to the left at the fork—that is, don't take the road into Fir Creek Campground. The correct road ends right at Bear Valley Creek, where there is a good pack bridge over the stream. The wilderness boundary is immediately on the other side of this bridge. The trailhead is situated at the start of Bear Valley Creek Canyon (upstream lie miles of meadows). GPS: N44 25.65' / W115 17.64'
**Parking and trailhead facilities:** Room for about eight vehicles, fewer if large horse trailers are present; horse unloading ramp; and Frank Church–River of No Return Wilderness information sign.

## The Hike

Blue Bunch and nearby Cape Horn Mountain stand at the headwaters of the Middle Fork of the Salmon River, which begins at the confluence of Bear Valley Creek and Marsh Creek. The hike to the summit ridge of Blue Bunch Mountain gives a splendid view of the Dagger Falls portion of the great Middle Fork Canyon; the expansive Poker, Bruce, and Ayers Meadows and meandering Bear Valley Creek to the west; the rugged mountains of the Soldier-Langer Lakes area to the east; and Cape Horn Mountain to the south.

The trail to the top of Blue Bunch is not difficult, but it does involve a moderately paced climb of 2,000 feet. Once on the ridgetop, at 2.5 miles, the trail rolls up and down gently for 1.5 more miles to the highest point on the mountain. The hike can be done fairly easily in a day by those who are in moderately good shape. The mountain has many rolling uplands on its east slope where you can find places to camp. You don't have to complete the entire hike to enjoy it. A walk just halfway up the mountain is splendid.

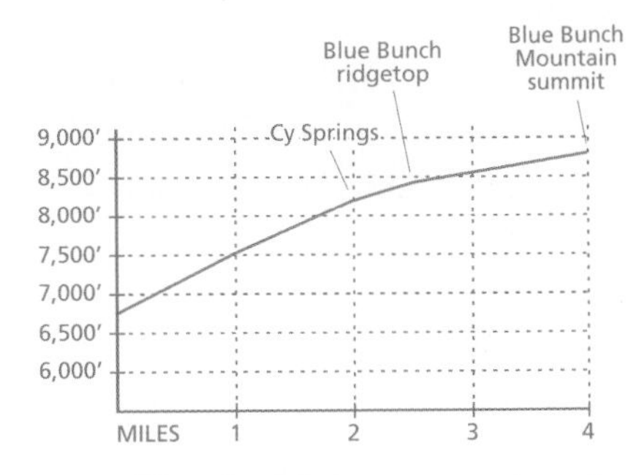


After crossing the pack bridge over Bear Valley Creek, turn left. The trail on the right leads down Bear Valley Creek. It's beautiful, but there are several fords of this small river, difficult wades even in mid-August.

After turning left, walk upstream just briefly. The trail then makes a right-angle turn and begins to climb the mountain. It is steep at first but levels out, only to steepen and level repeatedly. You soon reach occasional burned trees from the Deadwood Fire of 1987, but most trees remain green.

As you near the top of the ridge, you reach Cy Springs, a good water source. The trail becomes faint near the springs, but just climb to the top of the ridge and you will find it again. Walking the ridgetop trail is fairly easy, though you should keep an eye out for gathering thunderstorms.

From the ridge, the view to the immediate east is over green, undulating cirque basins with a few small ponds, then farther east across the partially hidden canyon of the Middle Fork of the Salmon. These basins are a good place to spot elk. You also have a view of Cape Horn Mountain to the south and the Bruce Meadows area to the southwest. Continue until the trail reaches the north end of the ridge for a fine view across the Dagger Falls area and down Middle Fork Canyon. To the west are those wonderful, wildlife-rich areas: Ayers and Poker Meadows.

The location of the wilderness boundary on the banks of Bear Valley Creek and the inclusion of the meadows and Blue Bunch Mountain were a great environmental victory. The forest service had recommended putting the wilderness boundary about 10 miles to the north and developing the Bear Valley area and Poker and Ayers Meadows as "staging areas" for recreationists heading for Dagger Falls and the Middle Fork. Idaho environmentalists wanted to include Blue Bunch Mountain, Cape Horn Mountain, and the Bear Valley Mountain area to the west (then called the Sulphur Creek Roadless Area) in the proposed River of No Return Wilderness, but even they had given up the lush meadow area in between as lost.

In the summer of 1980, I was sitting in Washington, DC, with Andy Weissener, then the majority counsel to the House Subcommittee on Public Lands, helping draw the boundaries for the River of No Return Wilderness. Together we drew into the wilderness about 500,000 additional acres on the south and southeast sides of the

*On the crest of Blue Bunch Mountain in the Frank Church Wilderness.*
PHOTO BY RALPH MAUGHAN

old Idaho Primitive Area; environmentalists felt that preservation of these acres was important. Andy asked me, "Why Blue Bunch Mountain but not the meadows below it?" I said there was no reason except the forest service would go nuts. He took a red pen and placed these two large, wildlife-rich meadows inside the wilderness, putting the boundary down the middle of Bear Valley Creek for a number of miles and only 50 feet on either side of the lengthy road leading to Dagger Falls.

The additions, including the meadows, quickly gained the approval of Representative John Seiberling, the subcommittee chair, and of Idaho's Senator Frank Church, who only asked us to delete 25,000 acres of proposed additions in the Furnace–Camas Creek area near Challis. This was so the entire River of No Return Wilderness package would be 2.24 million acres and thus could not be rounded off to 2.3 million acres (the size of the Idaho environmentalists' proposal). In delicious irony, official recalculation of the size of the Frank Church–River of No Return Wilderness years later revealed its actual size to be almost 2.4 million acres.

Today signs along Dagger Falls Road inform visitors about the late Senator Frank Church and note that they are privileged to drive through a "wilderness corridor" flanking the road all the way from the Bear Valley Creek crossing to Dagger Falls. One is led to think the forest service originated the idea.

Wolves were reintroduced to Idaho in 1995 and 1996. The area around Bear Valley west of this trail has experienced the highest density of wolves in the state, and the habitat for all wild animals in the area has improved.

**Options:** If you are prepared to wade, you can walk from the trailhead down the lower canyon of Bear Valley Creek to the confluence with Marsh Creek at Big Hole—the beginning of the Middle Fork of the Salmon.

—Ralph Maughan

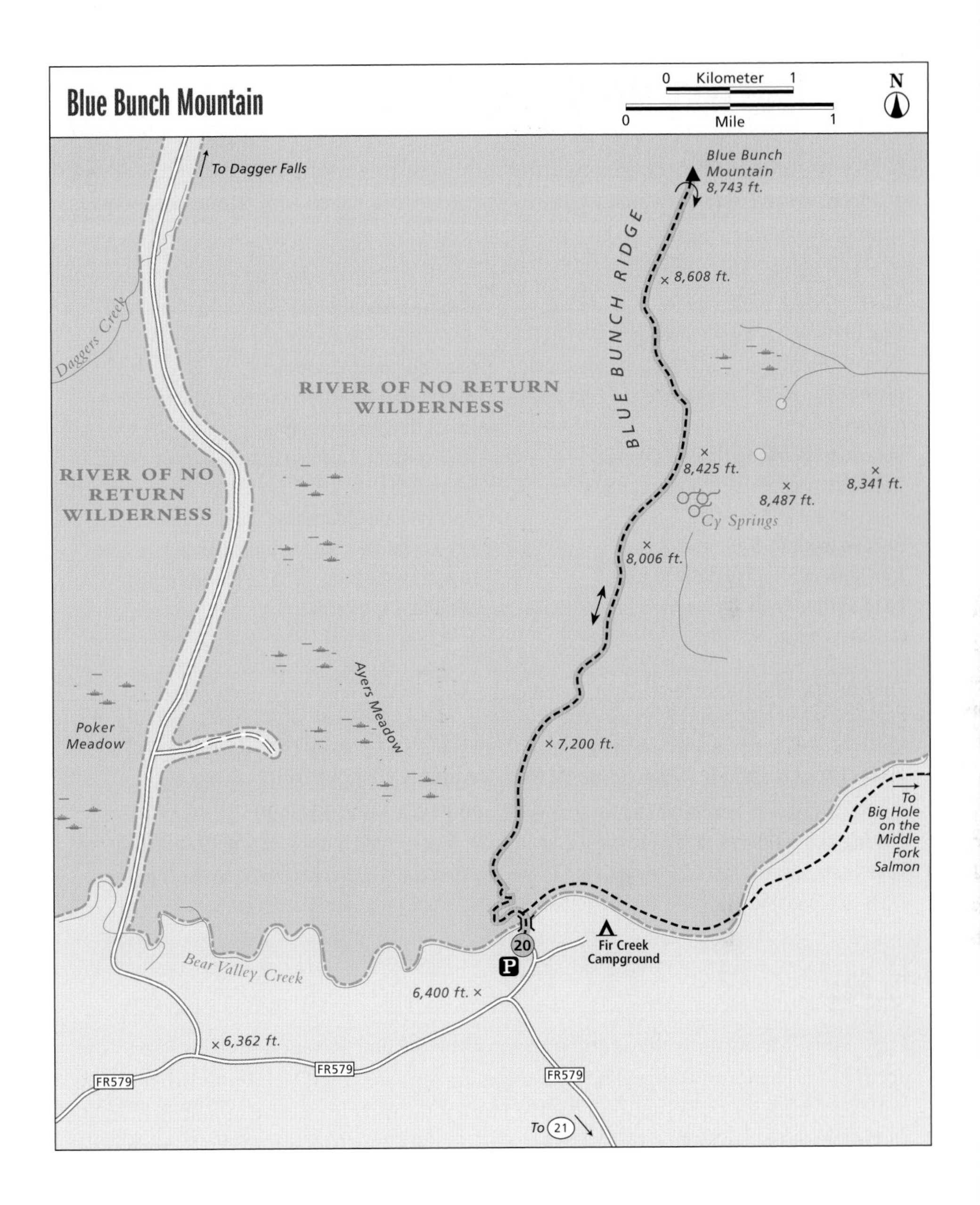


## Miles and Directions

**0.0** Trailhead (6,360 feet)

**2.0** Cy Springs vicinity (8,200 feet)

**2.5** Blue Bunch ridgetop (8,426 feet)

**4.0** Blue Bunch Mountain summit (8,743 feet)

# 21 Cape Horn Mountain

A hike to panoramic vistas showing the southwest part of the Frank Church–River of No Return Wilderness and a view of the crest of the Sawtooth Mountains—from an unusual vantage point.

**Start:** 45 miles north-northwest of Stanley.
**Type of hike:** Day hike or overnight; out-and-back. Overnight camp would be in Lola Creek.
**Distance:** 7 miles round-trip to the Lola Creek overlook
**Approximate hiking time:** 3–5 hours
**Difficulty:** Moderately strenuous due to the steep ascent and descent
**Best season:** Mid-July–mid-August
**Trail surface:** Normal dirt and rock
**Land status:** Frank Church Wilderness; Boise National Forest
**Canine compatibility:** Not allowed in within wilderness boundaries
**Fees and permits:** None
**Maps:** Blue Bunch Mountain and Cape Horn Lakes USGS quadrangles
**Trail contact:** Lowman Ranger District, (208) 392-6681
**Special considerations:** There is water in a stream not far from the trailhead, but be sure to carry enough to climb to the top of the mountain and back.

**Finding the trailhead:** From ID 21, turn onto the well-marked gravel road a few miles east of Banner Summit that climbs to Cape Horn Summit and park on the left (southwest) side of the road. This road is all-weather gravel and maintained, but it is also badly washboarded due to heavy recreational traffic for the Middle Fork of the Salmon River put-in at Dagger Falls. Be very alert for buses and vehicles towing trailers. GPS: N44 21.85' / W115 16.12'
**Parking and trailhead facilities:** The trailhead is an undeveloped parking spot under trees right at Cape Horn Summit. Trail 024 leaves both to the southwest and to the northeast across the road. Cross the road and begin the section of Trail 024 that climbs up Cape Horn Mountain.

## The Hike

Cape Horn Mountain is the southernmost of the Salmon River Mountains just to the north of the Sawtooth Range. The two ranges are separated by ID 21. From Bruce, Ayers, or Poker Meadows, many-summited Cape Horn is the most impressive mountain in sight, and most people probably think it is part of the Frank Church–River of No Return Wilderness. In fact, it's just south of the Frank. Efforts to add it back in 1980 failed because it was alleged that an old sheep driveway up Lola Creek on the east side of the mountain would conflict with wilderness designation. Despite its omission from the wilderness, Cape Horn Mountain has remained in a wild, undeveloped condition.

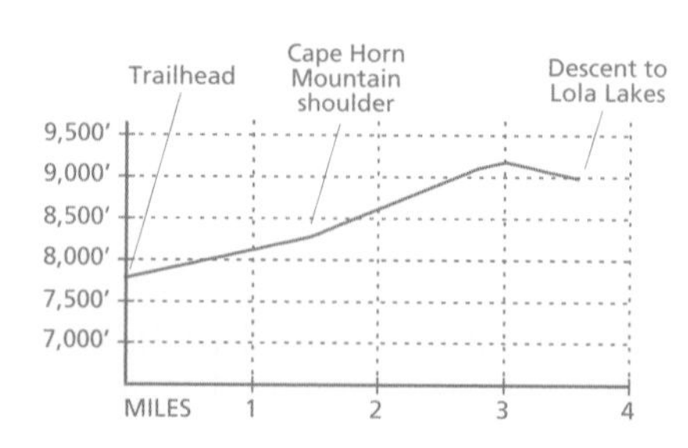

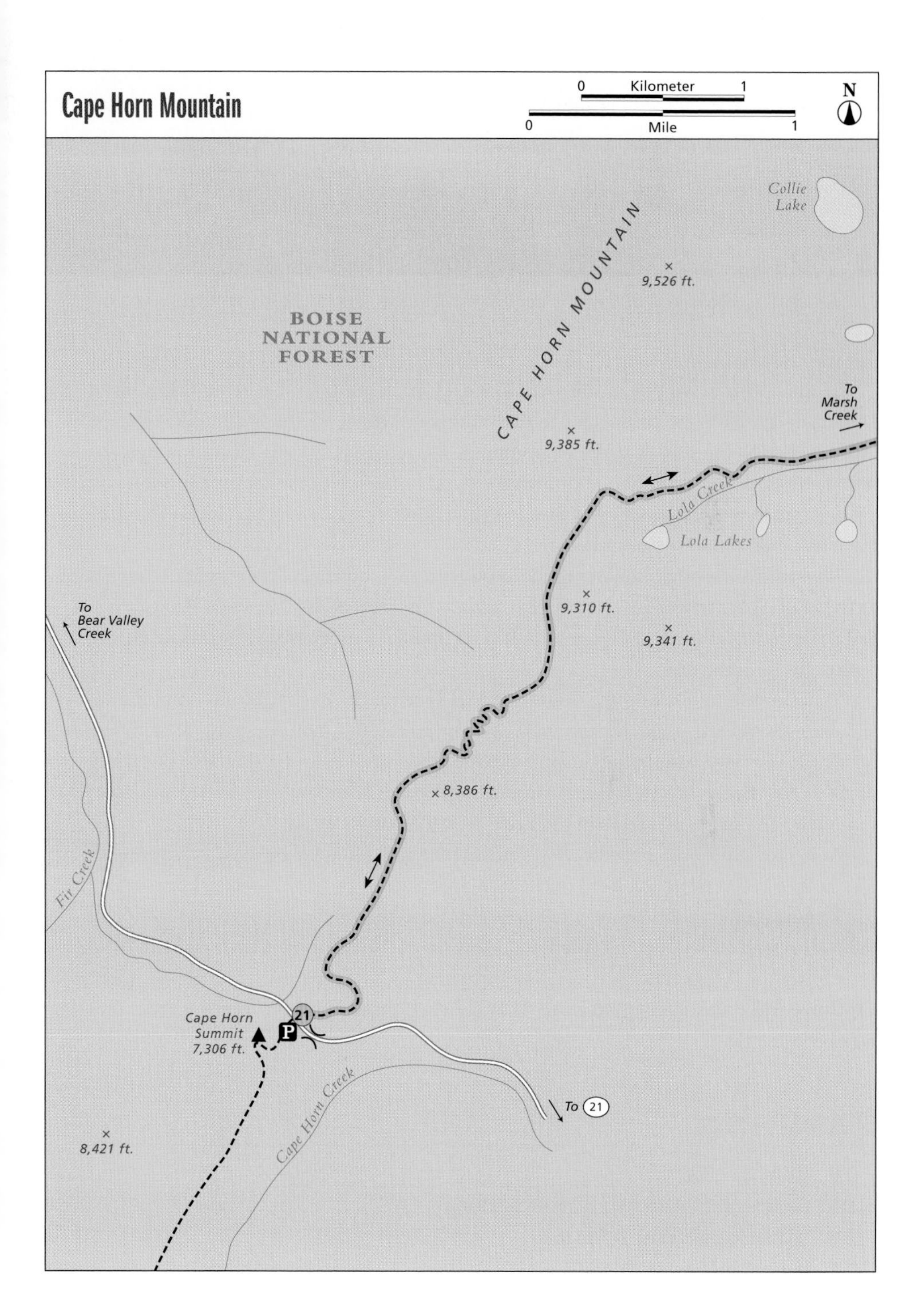
Cape Horn Mountain
0 Kilometer 1
0 Mile 1
N
Collie Lake
CAPE HORN MOUNTAIN
9,526 ft.
BOISE NATIONAL FOREST
To Marsh Creek
9,385 ft.
Lola Creek
Lola Lakes
9,310 ft.
9,341 ft.
To Bear Valley Creek
8,386 ft.
Fir Creek
21
P
Cape Horn Summit 7,306 ft.
Cape Horn Creek
To 21
8,421 ft.

*Down Lola Creek from trail on top of Cape Horn Mountain.* PHOTO BY RALPH MAUGHAN

In the 1990s a wildfire swept over Cape Horn Summit and part of Cape Horn Mountain as well as the mountains to the southwest, which are the headwaters of Cape Horn Creek. Some may find the beginning of the trail ugly, but the climb through the burned forest is not continuous, nor does it extend to the top of the mountain. Soon you are in green forest with wildflower meadows and good views down Cape Horn Creek to the north end of the Sawtooth Range.

The trail reaches the shoulder of the mountain after 1.5 miles. It is another 1.3 miles to the crest. Some may want to stop here, admire the view of the Sawtooth Range's jagged peaks to the south, and then return. It is an unusual perspective. Most people see the Sawtooths from the east.

You can continue along the crest. The trail is relatively level. It avoids climbing up and over the several peaks on the crest. As you follow the trail along the crest to the northeast, you have wonderful views of the meadows in or near the southern boundary of the Frank: Bruce Meadow, Ayers Meadow, and Poker Meadow. You also see the lower mountains and many meadows of the Elk Creek lobe of the Frank.

At 3.5 miles the trail drops steeply over the crest and down Lola Creek, a canyon with four lakes and several ponds. I did not visit them.

Visitors on the mountain may see deer, elk, black bear, and perhaps wolves, although the wolves tend to frequent the meadows below the mountain more than they roam on it.

**Options:** Hike down Lola Creek to Lola Creek Campground on Marsh Creek. This requires a shuttle.

—Ralph Maughan

## Miles and Directions

**0.0** Trailhead (7,306 feet)

**1.5** Shoulder of Cape Horn Mountain (8,386 feet)

**2.8** On the mountain crest (9,100 feet)

**3.0** High point of hike (9,200 feet)

**3.5** Trail begins descent to Lola Lakes (9,080 feet)

# 22 Sheep Hill

Sheep Hill boasts mountain lakes and fishing with overviews of the Frank Church–River of No Return and Selway-Bitterroot Wildernesses.

**Start:** 80 road miles southeast of Grangeville, Idaho, and 72 road miles west of Conner, Montana, on the northern rim of the Frank Church.
**Type of hike:** Backpack
**Distance:** 10.5 miles one way
**Approximate hiking time:** 3–4 days
**Difficulty:** Moderately strenuous because of elevation loss and gain from climbing into and out of lake basins
**Best season:** Mid-July–mid-September
**Trail surface:** Normal dirt and rock
**Land status:** Frank Church Wilderness; Nez Perce National Forest
**Canine compatibility:** Not allowed in within wilderness boundaries
**Fees and permits:** None
**Maps:** Sheep Hill, Spread Creek Point, and Sabe Mountain USGS quadrangles; Frank Church–River of No Return Wilderness North Half forest map; Nez Perce National Forest map
**Trail contact:** Elk City Ranger Station, Red River Ranger District, (208) 926-4258
**Special considerations:** Check fire and weather conditions. This high-elevation road is sometimes impassable into July and even August, and snow comes early in the fall. Chains and four-wheel drive may be needed. The road is rough, mountainous, and winding, with few places to pass other vehicles. It is not recommended for trailers and is definitely not accessible to RVs. Top off your gas tank.

**Finding the trailhead:** Road access is over the Magruder Corridor, also known as the Montana Road. It connects Red River Ranger Station on the west with Conner, Montana, on the east in a primitive, one-lane, 101-mile-long road. All major points along the road are well marked, perhaps as a preventive measure against years of conservationists' attempts to close it. If this closure had come to pass, the Selway-Bitterroot Wilderness and River of No Return Wilderness would have been joined in a continuous wilderness of mind-boggling size: over 3.5 million acres.

The Montana access leaves US 93 at Conner, where you turn west up the West Fork of the Bitterroot River on paved Road 473. The route crosses two major rivers and two mountain ranges before reaching the trailhead. After 13 miles on Road 473, you come to a junction on the right leading 18 paved miles to Nez Perce Pass to cross the Bitterroot Divide. A high-standard gravel road leads 15 miles from the pass to the Magruder Crossing bridge over the Selway River, a popular boat-launch site. From here it becomes one lane, although with a good rock base. It climbs 3,000 feet and 12 miles to skirt Salmon Mountain. Now it is 14 miles to the Dry Saddle Trailhead. An outstanding view of the Bitterroot Divide and deep forest are the redeeming qualities of this 72-mile passage.

From the west side out of Grangeville, take ID 13 west 9 miles to ID 14 on the right (south). From here, it is 31 miles to Elk City. Before Elk City, turn right onto paved FR 222 and continue 13 miles to Red River Ranger Station. Half a mile south of the station is a large sign warning of the hazards of driving the Montana Road (FR 468). Turn left. The road climbs steadily up the Salmon River–South Fork Divide to Mountain Meadows for a total of 7 miles. This area was scheduled for a controversial timber sale that would have destroyed prime elk summer range and caused untold damage to the pristine watershed of Meadow Creek, the largest tributary of the Selway River. This sale was dropped due to an administrative appeal led by the Idaho Environmental Council.

From Mountain Meadows, the road gradually drops into the headwaters of Bargamin Creek, passing Granite Springs and Poet Creek Campgrounds to arrive in 20.5 miles at the Dry Saddle Trailhead. You will have traveled a total of 80 miles from Grangeville. GPS: N45 40.63' / W114 59.62'

**Parking and trailhead facilities:** The large, gravel Dry Saddle Trailhead has horse loading and a pit toilet, but no water. Developed campgrounds west of the trailhead are Poet Creek (6 miles), four sites, pit toilets, no water; Granite Springs (11 miles), four sites, pit toilet, potable water. Developed sites to the east are Magruder Crossing Campground (22 miles), four sites, pit toilet, no potable water; and Deep Creek Campground (27 miles), three sites, pit toilet, no potable water.

## The Hike

This was the last place in the lower forty-eight states to be mapped by the US Geological Survey, and good topo maps only became available in 1979. An up-and-down ridgeline hike positions you to drop into the fourteen lakes nestled below. Drops into the lakes are between 300 to 700 feet. Old and new fires have left their marks as part of the ecology of this region.

Spruce, subalpine fir, and whitebark pine cover most of the ridges, and none of the trail is above timberline. Wildlife, wildflowers, mountain lakes, and high-rent vistas make this trip worth the long road access. Bighorn sheep, black bear, elk, deer, and golden-mantled ground squirrels are common. Wolves do inhabit the area but are seen only occasionally. In mid-July and early August, the open ridges are covered with wildflowers, including bear grass, mountain pinks, penstemon, lupine, Indian paintbrush, heath, and shooting stars.

The main trail (Forest 575) follows the divide between Bargamin Creek and Sabe Creek to the junction to Sheep Hill lookout on the right or Bear Point on the left. The grades are not steep, but the trail is heavily used by pack stock in the hunting season. It is very well defined, and all intersections are signed.

Beginning with a slow drop into a saddle overlooking the Trilby Lakes, the first mile goes through timber. Trilby Lakes is a popular, although not especially good, fishing day hike, so expect to see other people.

At the Trilby Lakes junction, the trail climbs a moderate 350 feet to Spread Creek Point. Just before the final pitch, an unmarked fishing trail into Spread Point Lake meets the main trail at a high saddle. Spread Point Lake, a large lake, lies on the west side of the ridge. Several meadows at its outlet provide good big-game conditions.

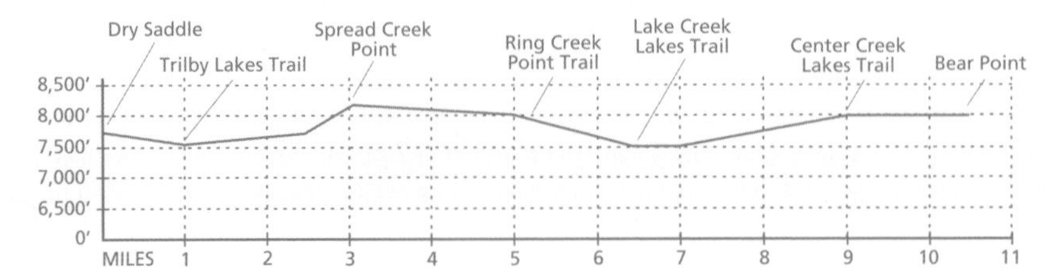

*The Trilby Lakes.* PHOTO BY LUKE KRATZ

From Spread Creek Point on, the trail rises into the open and becomes more scenic. Spread Creek Point, once a fire lookout, provides a good 360-degree view of the surrounding country.

From Spread Creek Point, the trail stays on top of the divide for about a mile to where the main ridge meets a spur coming up from Sabe Creek. Here, two side trails leave the ridge. Ring Creek Point Trail leads down into Sabe Creek, 5,000 vertical feet below the ridge, and into some beautiful country that rarely sees anybody. The other is a trail for fishers that climbs down toward Saddle Lake and peters out.

At the Ring Creek Point Trail junction, the main trail begins its descent into Lake Creek Lakes. This drop is the longest on the hike but is well graded. Carefully observe the location of the three lakes on your way down if you plan to visit them, since they're in thick forest with no connecting trails. At the bottom of this grade is a sign marking a fishing trail that leads 0.25 mile down to the upper lake.

Lake Creek Lakes are heavily used, and you can expect to meet other parties. The upper lake generally produces the largest fish, while the lower lake, which has good natural reproduction, is the easiest from which to catch them.

At the Lake Creek junction, the main trail climbs 300 feet to a low saddle dividing Lake Creek from Rattlesnake Creek. Don't let the name throw you; all the rattlesnakes

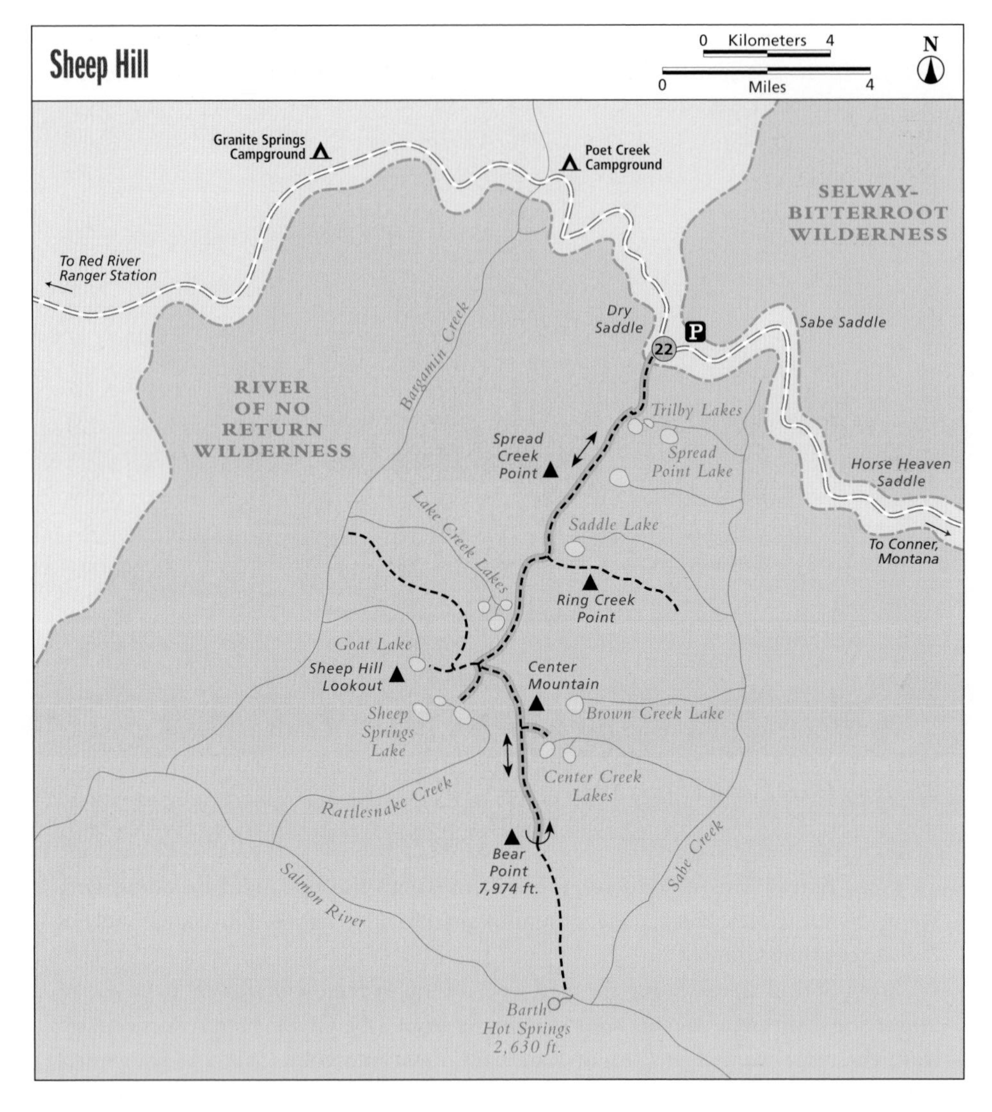


are at Rattlesnake Creek's lower elevations. At the saddle you'll meet trails leading to three destinations: Bear Point to the left, Sheep Hill to the right, and Rattlesnake Lake in the middle.

Bear Point Trail climbs through open parks and clumps of whitebark pine to a saddle overlooking Ring Creek. Just past the saddle is a sign marking a fishing trail to Brown Creek Lake. This trail is faint and hard to follow in places. It continues around the face of Center Mountain, then generally follows the inlet down to the lake.

About 0.5 mile past the Brown Creek Lake sign, a well-marked trail leads down to the Center Creek Lakes. These lakes are also hard to find, but you can improve your odds by walking an extra couple hundred yards out Bear Point Ridge to where you can see them both.

After the Center Creek Lakes trail junction, it is another 1.5 miles to Bear Point. Bear Point offers a spectacular view of the Salmon River, 5,300 feet below. The area around Bear Point burned to sterile earth in 1989. As mentioned, wildfires are natural to this country, and so are bears. You may encounter both. Part of Center Creek burned in the big fire year of 2000.

**Options:** Back at the three-way fork above and south of the Lake Creek Lakes, the right fork heads toward Sheep Hill. It climbs gradually along a ridge for 320 feet and 0.9 mile to 8,000-foot Deadman's Saddle, where it meets a side trail dropping into Bargamin Creek. From Deadman's Saddle climb another 400 feet and 0.75 mile to the active Sheep Hill lookout. Near the lookout is a spring sometimes frequented by bighorn sheep. From this lookout you can see four small lakes surrounding Sheep Hill. All have fish, but they aren't as productive as some of the larger lakes. A good trail leads from the lookout down to Sheep Springs Lake, but the route into Goat Lake does not have a trail.

To access Rattlesnake Lake from the three forks, take the middle fork. It starts out as a very well-worn track that drops 0.5 mile directly into an outfitter's camp. From here the unmaintained trail becomes very faint. You'll have to pay close attention to blazes cut into the trees. It contours along an east-facing slope to end with a 150-foot drop to the lake. Be cautious not to lose your elevation as you walk along the east-facing slope. If you do, you'll drop down into Rattlesnake Creek and end up headed toward the Salmon River. Once you get to Rattlesnake Lake, you may wish to explore Upper Rattlesnake Lake. To do so, follow the inlet on the northwest side of lower Rattlesnake for about 0.5 mile.

—H. W. W. "Blue Moose" Johnson

## Miles and Directions

**0.0** Dry Saddle Trailhead (7,720 feet)
**1.0** Trilby Lakes Trail (7,560 feet)
**2.5** Spread Point Lake Trail (7,720 feet)
**3.0** Spread Creek Point (8,190 feet)
**5.0** Saddle Lake fishing trail (8,000 feet)
**5.2** Ring Creek Point Trail (8,000 feet)
**6.5** Lake Creek Lakes Trail (7,560 feet)
**7.0** Sheep Hill Lookout Trail (7,520 feet)
**9.0** Center Creek Lakes Trail (8,000 feet)
**10.5** Bear Point (7,974 feet)

# 23 Shell Rock and Rainbow Lakes

There are two very picturesque subalpine lakes in the Salmon River Mountains. The hike makes an excellent jumping-off point for climbing Log Mountain (9,179 feet) and Shell Rock Peak (8,574 feet). Possible off-trail adventures are available to access pristine, wild, hidden meadows, or treks on the Idaho Centennial Trail.

**Start:** About 35 miles northeast of Cascade.
**Type of hike:** Day hike or base camp; out-and-back
**Distance:** 5 miles round-trip to Rainbow Lake; 9 miles round-trip from trailhead to Rainbow Lake, then to Shell Rock Lake (with a short backtrack)
**Approximate hiking time:** 2–5 hours
**Difficulty:** Moderate
**Best season:** Late June–late September
**Trail surface:** Normal dirt and rock
**Land status:** Frank Church Wilderness; Boise National Forest
**Canine compatibility:** Not allowed in within wilderness boundaries
**Fees and permits:** None
**Maps:** Log Mountain USGS quadrangle; Boise National Forest map
**Trail contact:** Cascade Ranger District, (208) 382-4271
**Special considerations:** High-clearance (preferably four-wheel-drive) vehicle needed for last 5 miles.

**Finding the trailhead:** From Cascade, drive 1 mile north on ID 55 and turn right (east) on Warm Lake Road. At 26 miles, pass the turnoff to Warm Lake. Continue east. At 35 miles, the road becomes dirt. At 35.5 miles, turn left onto signed FR 413 leading north to Yellow Pine. Drive 15 miles north on this well-maintained gravel road. Between Coffee and Halfway Creeks (just south of Halfway Station), turn left on signed FR 410. Take this road through burned and salvage-logged forest 11 miles to its end at the trailhead in a broad saddle. This mostly good logging road has several water bars and ruts in the last 5 miles, requiring a four-wheel-drive or at least a high-clearance vehicle. GPS: N44 48.84' / W115 33.57'
**Parking and trailhead facilities:** The trailhead has horse-unloading ramps but no water or toilets.

## The Hike

Pretty Rainbow Lake is an excellent introduction for children and beginning backpackers to Idaho's backcountry. Shell Rock Lake is a scenic and peaceful gem. Moose, elk, and black bear can be observed in the area. Shell Rock and Rainbow Lakes are located in an unnamed range dividing the South Fork of the Salmon River from Johnson Creek. This range is situated in the relatively unknown and unprotected Caton Lake Roadless Area. Both Rainbow and Shell Rock Lakes are ringed by lush, but fragile, sedge meadows full of wildflowers as well as forests of subalpine fir, large old-growth Engelmann spruce, and lodgepole pine.

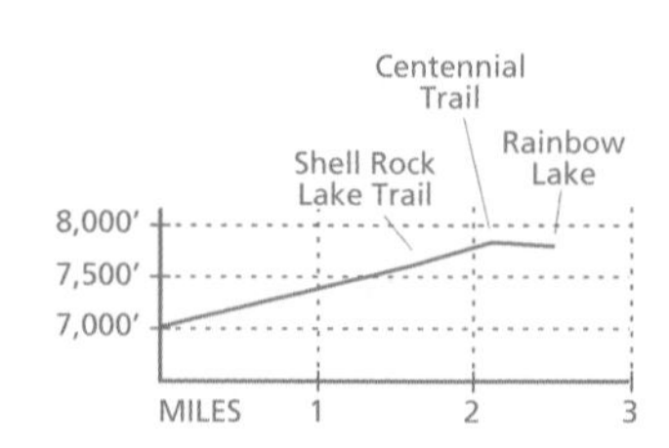

*Rainbow Lake.* Photo by Luke Kratz

During my summer 2000 visit, I saw elk, a moose cow and her calf, and a black bear, all while watching the impressive plumes of smoke rising ominously from wildfires in the Frank Church–River of No Return Wilderness to the east.

Massive logging and road building during the 1980s and additional postfire salvage logging in the mid-1990s on this part of the Boise National Forest scarred the lower slopes and carved into this roadless country. Current access is on a logging road allowing you to clearly see the results of this mismanagement of our national forests—large de-vegetated log landings and eroding skid roads.

From the trailhead, follow Forest Trail 094 toward Rainbow Lake. Although the first mile of this hike is through disappointing salvage-logged burned forest, it gives you a perspective on both the impacts of salvage logging (note the lack of large-diameter snags, the homes of many bird and mammal species) and the quick recovery of diverse vegetation after fires, even with human abuse.

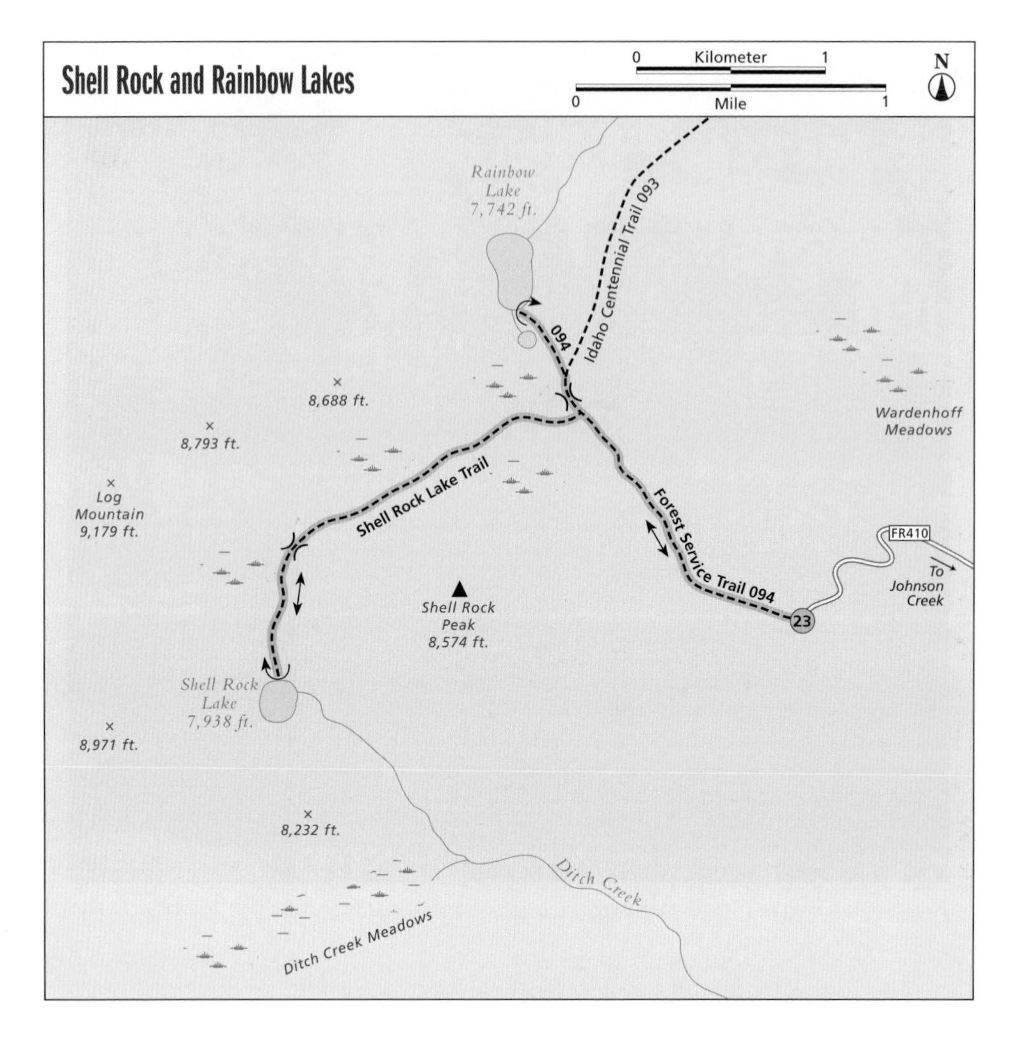


The first 0.3 mile follows an old logging skid road toward a drainage. At 0.4 mile, look for a major trail leading uphill to the northwest marked with sign indicating that it is Rainbow Lake Trail (titled the "Ditch Creek" trail on the Log Mountain quadrangle). After 1.2 miles of hiking on this maintained trail, you will approach a low saddle in a subalpine fir forest. Rising to the west is the rugged slope of Shell Rock Peak. Look for an unmarked but obvious trail heading to the west just before the saddle. This is the trail to Shell Rock Lake.

To reach Rainbow Lake, continue straight on your original trail. At 2.2 miles you will see another major trail leaving to the north marked IDAHO CENTENNIAL TRAIL (Forest Trail 093). This trail could be the start of an extensive trek into Idaho's wild roadless country. But keep straight ahead for now. In a short distance you will come to a quaint pond and lush, wet meadow. Approach quietly and look for moose. The trail will then gently descend for 0.3 mile until you reach Rainbow Lake at 2.5 miles.

Rainbow Lake is a fine destination for children and beginning hikers or a peaceful lunch stop for those continuing to Shell Rock Lake.

**Options:** To reach Shell Rock Lake, backtrack 0.6 mile to the unmarked trail heading from the forested saddle to the west. Follow this trail through the forest as it climbs steeply onto a bench on the north side of Shell Rock Peak. If you miss this trail at the saddle, or lose it, do not head down the drainage away from Rainbow Lake. Set your sight on the bench, and hike up through the forest until you meet the obvious trail heading southwest up it. Atop the bench, the trail will progress for 1 mile up this gently sloping platform while paralleling, and occasionally crossing, a drainage filled with meadows and islands of conifers, huckleberries, and Labrador tea shrubs. Watch for elk in this area. This trail is less often maintained and occasionally faint across meadows, so go slowly and search for the main trail—it always reappears.

At 4.2 miles from the trailhead, you will reach a low saddle immediately to the west of Shell Rock Peak. Although you cannot see Shell Rock Lake through the thick lodgepole pine forest here, you are getting close. To the west is the steep and rocky slope of the massive flat-topped Log Mountain.

At the saddle is a path heading into the trees, but don't take it. Instead follow the main trail as it steeply descends south into the Shell Rock Lake basin. It drops through a small meadow in 0.25 mile and then takes you through the forest a short distance until you reach Shell Rock Lake at 4.5 miles.

Shell Rock Lake receives little use from recreationists despite its beauty. It is surrounded by sedge carpet with taller beaked sedge and floating bur reed lining the shoreline. On a still day the rugged granite ridges of this cirque are reflected in its waters.

Rainbow and Shell Rock Lakes provide excellent access for climbing Log Mountain and the aptly named Shell Rock Peak (which looks like a clamshell with its wide end stuck in the earth).

Near the lakes, adventurous hikers can discover vast, pristine wet meadows with sinuous streams and grazing elk. A rugged descent along the outlet of Shell Rock Lake will lead to Ditch Creek Meadows while an off-trail descent from Idaho Centennial Trail near Rainbow Lake takes you to Wardenhoff Meadows. These meadows occupy large, hanging, glaciated troughs and offer true solitude in a wild roadless area.

—Chris Murphy

## Miles and Directions

**0.0** Trailhead (7,000 feet)

**1.6** Side trail to Shell Rock Lake (7,600 feet)

**2.2** Low saddle Idaho Centennial Trail junction (7,840 feet)

**2.5** Rainbow Lake (7,742 feet)

# 24 Sleeping Deer Mountain

In this high mountain wilderness, you'll find lovely scenery and decent fishing in small, subalpine cirque lakes. There is a long but very scenic and inspiring road trip to the trailhead.

**Start:** At the end of a long improved dirt road deep in the Frank Church–River of No Return Wilderness about 39 road miles from Challis
**Type of hike:** Backpack; out-and-back
**Distance:** 5.5 miles one way
**Approximate hiking time:** 1–2 days
**Difficulty:** Moderately easy to Cache Creek Lakes, except in the early summer. Moderate to (the more distant) West Fork Lakes
**Best season:** Mid-July–mid-September
**Trail surface:** Normal dirt and rock
**Land status:** Frank Church Wilderness; Salmon-Challis National Forest
**Canine compatibility:** Not allowed
**Fees and permits:** None
**Maps:** Sleeping Deer Mountain USGS quadrangle; Frank Church–River of No Return Wilderness South Half forest map; Middle Fork, Yankee Fork, Challis, and Lost River Ranger Districts/Challis National Forest map
**Trail contact:** Challis Ranger District, (208) 879-4100
**Special considerations:** Access road is suitable for trucks, marginal for sedans, and unsuitable for RVs and horse trailers. Check weather and fire conditions.

**Finding the trailhead:** This access road—perched on a wilderness ridgetop for 18 miles—is as impressive as the hike. The boundary of the Frank Church–River of No Return Wilderness is just 300 feet away on either side, and all drains into the Middle Fork of the Salmon River. The road is improved dirt for a total of 28 miles to the Sleeping Deer Trailhead.

In Challis turn right (north) from Main Street onto the Challis Creek county road. Follow this paved road through farmland in lower Challis Creek Canyon for 8 miles. It eventually becomes gravel. Soon thereafter, take a right onto the improved dirt Bear Creek Road (FR 086). The road passes through some recreational homesites, then climbs 3,200 feet and 9 miles to a pass at 9,190 feet elevation between the cone-shaped Twin Peaks, which rise to well over 10,000 feet. There is an active fire lookout on the southern peak.

From the pass, the road follows a ridgeline to the trailhead. You pass a number of trailheads that lead down into the wilderness canyons 3,000 to 5,000 feet below. There are also a number of primitive campsites along the road (no water).

From Twin Peaks, it is 3.5 miles to Spider Creek. The road has been improved to Spider Creek helispot for firefighting deployment but is still a 15-mile-per-hour drive. The last 15 miles beyond the helispot have a number of rocky spots but do not require four-wheel drive. At times the road is paint-scratching narrow, and you must back up anywhere from several hundred feet to 0.5 mile if you encounter another vehicle. GPS: N44 45.21' / W114 40.78'

**Parking and trailhead facilities:** The trailhead, located at the end of the road and perched on a ridgetop high above Rock Lakes at 9,300 feet, has room for about four vehicles. In the unlikely event that it is full, you must go back 0.5 mile. There is a hillside outhouse with a view but no water.

## The Hike

This is a strikingly beautiful area—exciting, rugged, and not heavily used. Sleeping Deer (9,881 feet) is one of the highest mountains in the wilderness and the highest in this area.

One of the great victories of the political fight to establish the River of No Return Wilderness was to include not just the area from Sleeping Deer Mountain westward to the Middle Fork of the Salmon River but also all of the canyons to the east of this striking mountain. The forest service felt this addition was "just too much wilderness." However, this area of more than 500,000 acres to the east and south of the old Idaho Primitive Area was just as wild as the primitive area itself and did indeed become part of the River of No Return Wilderness.

Like many routes in the Salmon River Mountains, this one goes up and down, up and down, from pass to basin, from basin to pass. In all, you'll cross four passes, two of which are notable: Sleeping Deer and Woodtick. None of these pulls is long. In fact, the trailhead is the highest elevation of the trip.

From the trailhead, the trail immediately swings around a ridgetop and contours high above Cabin Creek to Sleeping Deer Pass just southeast of beautiful Sleeping Deer Mountain. The views, framed by contorted whitebark pine, are outstanding. At the pass, a trail fork to the left takes you quickly thousands of feet down into Cabin Creek. Straight ahead a trail climbs to the Sleeping Deer fire lookout, still used in emergencies.

Take the trail to the right, which descends in seven switchbacks to the cirque just below Sleeping Deer Mountain at the head of Pole Creek. This descent is fairly easy except early in the summer, when snow makes it dangerous.

At the bottom of the switchbacks is an intersection; the trail to the right leads down Pole Creek Canyon. Stay to the left. The trail traverses the rocky head of Pole Creek basin (directly below the cliffs of Sleeping Deer Mountain) to the easy pass between Pole and Cache Creeks. This section from the trailhead to the top of Cache Creek gets a lot of weather because it's high and exposed. It is dangerous during lightning storms. In addition to keeping an eye on the weather, however, look for bighorn sheep.

From the divide, you descend 400 feet on a rocky, eroded trail to the first of the four trail-accessible Cache Creek Lakes. Near the lake's inlet on the right side is a pretty little spring. Despite its beauty, in July it might be mosquito-ridden because it is flanked by an extensive wet meadow. Several big horse camps are also situated in this area. Although we saw little wildlife here in late

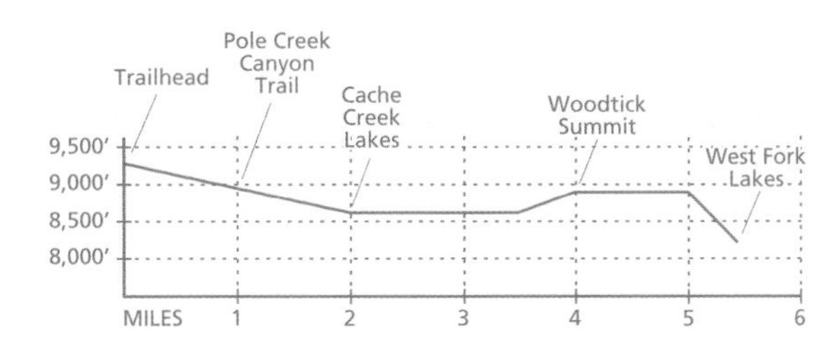

*Sleeping Deer Mountain.* Photo by Josh Keeley

August, we did see and hear many pikas and marmots as well as a lot of grouse in the wooded areas. The grouse whortleberries (the smallest of the blackberries) were ripe. We also found the fishing here good for brook trout (6 to 12 inches).

The trail drops down past the cabin and continues north. Losing little elevation, it passes three more lakes. They lie about 100 feet below on a shelf above dramatic Cache Creek Canyon. The second lake is the largest. The third one loses much of its water by midsummer and so contains no fish. The fourth lake is within the burned area of the 1988 Battle Axe Fire. There are six more Cache Creek Lakes scattered about the area. Access to them is cross-country.

Just past the third lake, you enter the Battle Axe burn. Here you must look carefully for the trail junction on the right, which takes you to Woodtick Summit. If you find yourself descending to the lake, you've missed the junction. You can spot the correct trail up on the flank of Woodtick ahead.

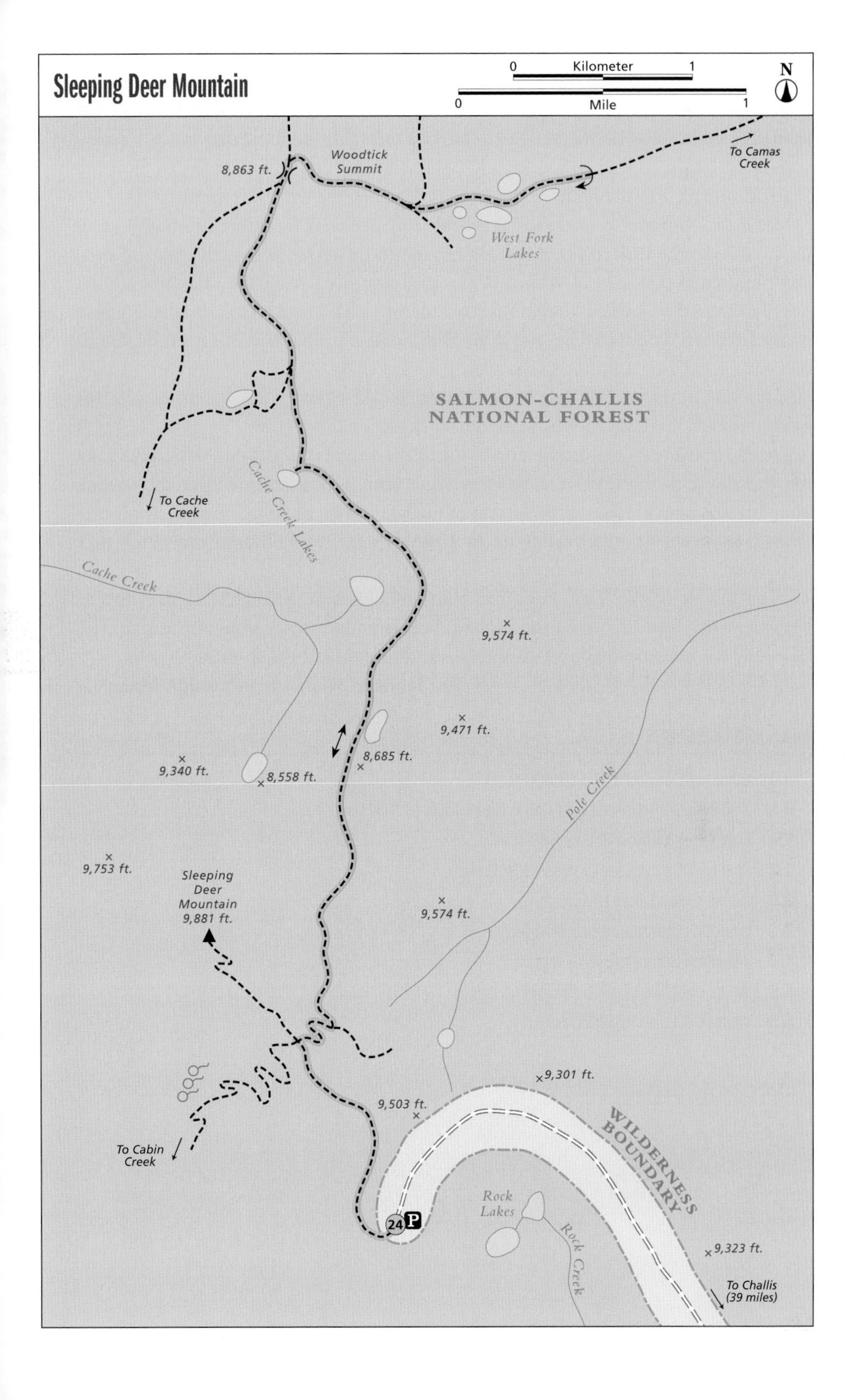

Sleeping Deer Mountain
0 Kilometer 1
0 Mile 1
N
Woodtick Summit
8,863 ft.
To Camas Creek
West Fork Lakes
SALMON-CHALLIS NATIONAL FOREST
To Cache Creek
Cache Creek Lakes
Cache Creek
9,574 ft.
9,471 ft.
8,685 ft.
9,340 ft.
8,558 ft.
Pole Creek
9,753 ft.
Sleeping Deer Mountain 9,881 ft.
9,574 ft.
9,301 ft.
9,503 ft.
WILDERNESS BOUNDARY
To Cabin Creek
Rock Lakes
24
P
Rock Creek
9,323 ft.
To Challis (39 miles)

From the junction, the trail climbs over a corner of Peak 9,488 to Woodtick Summit at 8,863 feet. The elevation gain is only about 300 feet. This entire portion of the route lies within the Battle Axe burn. The area near the trail burned twice in forty years, so it ought to remain a generally open slope providing fine views of Sleeping Deer Mountain and the basin at the head of Cache Creek.

Woodtick Summit is not notable for the presence of ticks. At the summit is a trail junction. Take the fork to the right, which descends two steep switchbacks and then contours across the head of Woodtick Creek. From here you have fine views down heavily forested Woodtick Creek. After a mile or so, this rocky trail leads to a grassy divide between Woodtick Creek and the West Fork of Camas Creek. From the divide, you get a good view of three of the West Fork Lakes. At the trail junction on the pass, take the one in the middle that descends into the West Fork. The descent of 500 feet is steep, and the trail is at times worn and rocky.

At the bottom, you're on the north side of the largest of the West Fork Lakes. Take the right fork of the trail here, and continue until you've crossed over the stream, which is the inlet. We found this largest of the lakes to be the only one to have fish—a few large trout we were unable to catch. We saw plentiful elk sign and much pika activity as well as a bighorn sheep.

The lowest of the West Fork Lakes has increased considerably in size due to beavers, which have dammed the outlet. Their large lodge is visible in the lake. The lakeshore has an eerie quality—swamped, dead timber and marsh grass.

—Jackie Johnson Maughan and Ralph Maughan

## Miles and Directions

**0.0** Sleeping Deer Trailhead (9,300 feet)

**0.8** Sleeping Deer lookout and Cabin Creek Trails (9,300 feet)

**1.0** Pole Creek Canyon Trail (8,880 feet)

**1.3** Pole and Cache Creeks Pass (8,960 feet)

**2.0** Cache Creek Lakes (8,635 feet)

**3.5** Woodtick Summit Trail (8,600 feet)

**4.0** Woodtick Summit (8,863 feet)

**5.0** West Fork Lakes Trail (8,600 feet)

**5.5** West Fork Lakes (8,295 feet)

# 25 Soldier Lakes-Patrol Ridge Loop

This is a nostalgic hike known for good fishing in numerous subalpine lakes and breathtaking views into the Middle Fork of the Salmon River Canyon and distant peaks in the Frank Church–River of No Return Wilderness.

**Start:** 42 road miles north of Stanley
**Type of hike:** Backpacking loop
**Distance:** 16 miles
**Approximate hiking time:** 3-4 days
**Difficulty:** Moderately easy to Soldier Lakes. Doing the entire loop is moderately strenuous
**Best season:** July-mid-September
**Trail surface:** Normal dirt and rock
**Land status:** Frank Church Wilderness; Salmon-Challis National Forest
**Canine compatibility:** Not allowed within wilderness
**Fees and permits:** None
**Maps:** Soldier Creek and Big Soldier Mountain USGS quadrangles; Frank Church–River of No Return Wilderness South Half forest map; Middle Fork, Challis, Yankee Fork, and Lost River Ranger Districts/Challis National Forest map
**Trail contact:** Challis Ranger District, (208) 879-4100
**Special considerations:** Patrol Ridge is a long stretch exposed to lightning.

**Finding the trailhead:** Drive northwest from Stanley on ID 21 for 18.6 miles, and turn left (north) onto the gravel road. Then turn right again almost immediately onto another gravel road. From here it is 21 miles to the trailhead at Josephus Lake. This road quickly crosses Marsh Creek, and 100 yards past the bridge there is yet another fork. Stay to the left and follow this road over Vanity Summit. The gravel road is wide and in good condition until the climb to Vanity Summit. As you begin the ascent, it turns to large (rocky) gravel but remains two lanes wide. The right side of the road burned in 1999 all the way to Vanity Summit (elevation 7,813 feet).

Descend from Vanity Summit on a graded dirt road that stays high above the creek. The road has one and a half lanes, as well as many tight (often blind) curves; it's steep but at least not very rocky. About 16 miles from ID 21, you reach the junction with Float Creek Road and the road down Rapid River. Stay left and follow the graded Float Creek dirt road on a 5-mile, 1,100-foot climb to Josephus Lake. All of these junctions are well signed. GPS: N44 33.01' / W115 8.56'

**Parking and trailhead facilities:** Scenic Josephus Lake is actually two lakes separated by a short stream. It is heavily used by fishers. There is room for about five vehicles at this well-shaded trailhead.

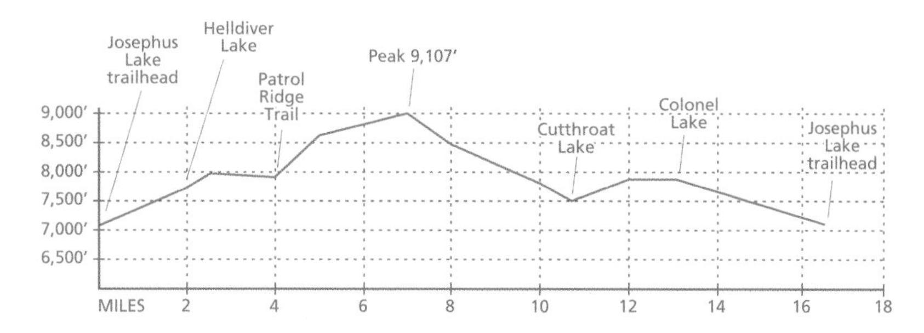

## The Hike

This hike covers a popular area of lake and high ridge country in the southern part of the Frank Church–River of No Return Wilderness. It ranges from forest to approximately the alpine zone at 9,000 feet. The trail begins at 7,100 feet at Josephus Lake in Float Creek and passes by, or near, more than a dozen lakes and goes along a high ridge with tremendous views as it traces a rough horseshoe shape. Most of the lakes are fishable for cutthroat trout.

The lakes are in two groups: Soldier Lakes and Cutthroat Lakes. Both lie in large basins beneath the long Patrol Ridge, which sports numerous rugged, but short, peaks. The ridge is unnamed on most maps. The more popular and perhaps the more scenic of the two groups of lakes is the Soldier Lakes, nestled beneath Patrol Ridge at the headwaters of Soldier Creek. Each of the Soldier Lakes is named after a military rank. The Cutthroat Lakes are generally unnamed (except one large one named Cutthroat Lake). They lie under Patrol Ridge at the head of Muskeg Creek.

The north side of Patrol Ridge, which overlooks the lakes, is precipitous. Its opposite side is steep but smooth, plunging several thousand feet into the Middle Fork of the Salmon River Canyon. The trail on the ridge keeps close to the top and offers outstanding views of both sides.

The trail leaves from the heavily timbered trailhead just above lower Josephus Lake, but it soon breaks out into the open at the marshy and very scenic upper end of Josephus Lake. Here, you can see not only the lake but a number of rocky peaks just to its south and southeast, including Mount Mills.

After this short stretch with a view, the trail heads into deep forest and quickly reaches the Frank Church Wilderness boundary. You'll then climb steadily through forest and a few openings to reach pretty Helldiver Lake after 2 miles. There are a few springs along the trail to Helldiver Lake early in the summer. Mushroom Springs, about a mile from the trailhead, usually flows all summer. Float Creek remains far below the trail.

Past Helldiver Lake, a climb of 400 feet in 0.5 mile puts you on a pass between Float Creek and the Soldier Creek drainage. Climbing 30 yards up the north slope from the pass will give you a fine view. This pass also marks the spot where Greyhound Ridge joins Patrol Ridge.

The trail drops steeply, but briefly, down from the pass and past a pond to a trail junction. At the junction, follow Soldier Lakes Trail to the left. The trail soon breaks into the open as it begins to cross the head of Soldier Creek Canyon, whose thickly timbered bottom spreads below. After less than a mile, drop down to the first of the Soldier Lakes: First Lieutenant. Immediately after that comes Colonel Lake and a trail junction. Right goes to others of the Soldier Lakes and to the Cutthroat Lakes. Left goes to more Soldier Lakes and then to the top of Patrol Ridge, the route described here. Most people end their trip near this junction.

On Patrol Ridge Trail, you quickly come to a pretty blue-green lake called The General. From The General, an unmarked trail climbs briefly to the biggest of the lakes,

*Major Lakes at the foot of Patrol Ridge.* PHOTO BY RALPH MAUGHAN

The Captain. The main trail circles The General, then circles a lake with no fish called The Major, after which it begins a steep 400-foot ascent to the top of Patrol Ridge.

Once you are on the ridge, views are few at first and the trail is quite narrow, but both conditions soon improve, and after 0.5 mile the trail follows the very top of the ridge, offering dramatic views of the Soldier Lakes below and down toward the Middle Fork in the opposite direction. In July the ridge is covered with flowers between the scenic clumps of whitebark pine.

As the trail follows the ridge, it gradually climbs, offering views of the Cutthroat Lakes below and finally (to the south) the headwaters of the Middle Fork where

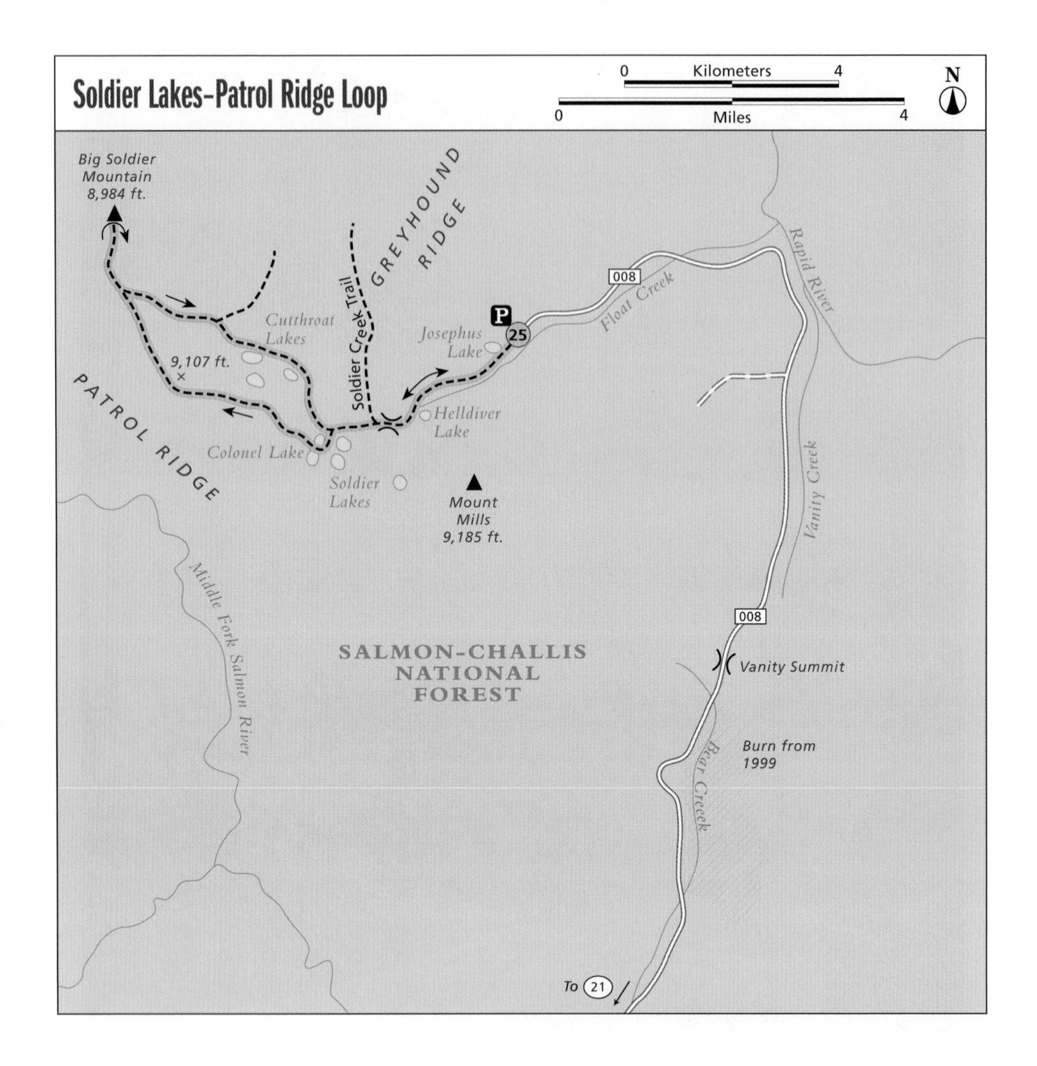


Marsh Creek and Bear Valley Creek run together. You see not just the canyon but the actual river. You also see the results of the huge Deadwood Fire of 1987.

The trail reaches its highest point (about 9,000 feet) as it bends northward and traverses under Peak 9,107. Here, as you cross the head of Lincoln Creek (which bears a lake far below), the trail grows quite narrow, with a very steep slope down into Lincoln Creek. It is not so treacherous, however, as to prevent its use by horses (which, prudently, should be walked).

Soon there comes a saddle that may appear to be the one on the map showing the loop trail dropping eastward off Patrol Ridge back to the Soldier Lakes. This is not the case. The correct saddle is 0.25 mile farther north. This saddle is broader than the first (wrong) one. There may or may not be a sign marking Muskeg Creek Trail, but the track is obvious if you walk to the edge of the saddle-top meadow.

The trail leaves the saddle to contour directly under the cliffs of Patrol Ridge. For about a mile, as it contours around the head of a tributary of Muskeg Creek, it is rocky, narrow, and somewhat difficult. Soon, however, it begins to ramble through forest and meadow as it approaches the Cutthroat Lakes. For the last mile before reaching Cutthroat Lake, it descends 900 feet.

Cutthroat Lake is at the base of Peak 8,996 on Patrol Ridge. A small cascade tumbles into the lake on its west side. At a junction 0.5 mile above Cutthroat Lake, a fork leaves to the left down Muskeg Creek, Soldier Creek, and eventually the Middle Fork of the Salmon River.

From this junction to Colonel Lake, the trail you follow is called Cutthroat Trail. It generally climbs, sometimes steeply, and fails to go close to most of the Cutthroat Lakes. About 2 miles past Cutthroat Lake, the trail drops into the Soldier Creek drainage and passes two beautiful and large Soldier Lakes—Staff Sargeant Lake and Sargeant Lake. Soon thereafter, you complete the loop at the junction at Colonel Lake.

**Options:** From the Patrol Ridge pass, which connects with Muskeg Trail, you will probably want to make a side trip along the ridge to its terminus at Big Soldier Mountain. This is a 3-mile round-trip to Big Soldier lookout, which is used for emergency fire detection. Here you have views of all of the southern part of the Frank Church. You can't see the actual Middle Fork from the lookout. However, you can see it on your way to the lookout as well as glimpsing the Dagger Falls boat put-in on the river.

—Ralph Maughan and Jackie Johnson Maughan

## Miles and Directions

**0.0** Josephus Lake trailhead (7,100 feet)
**2.0** Helldiver Lake (7,720 feet)
**2.5** Float Creek and Soldier Creek Pass (8,088 feet)
**3.0** Soldier Lakes Trail (7,020 feet)
**4.0** Patrol Ridge Trail (7,900 feet)
**5.0** Patrol Ridge (8,600 feet)
**7.0** Peak 9,107 (9,000 feet)
**8.0** Muskeg Trail (8,520 feet)
**10.0** Cutthroat Trail (7,880 feet)
**10.7** Cutthroat Lake (7,560 feet)
**12.0** Staff Sergeant Lake (7,960 feet)
**12.8** Colonel Lake (7,900 feet)
**16.5** Josephus Lake trailhead (7,100 feet)

# 26 Stoddard Lake

Here we have spectacular vistas of the Middle Fork of the Salmon River's Impassable Canyon and the Bighorn Crags. It is a challenging yet rewarding trip into remote parts of the Frank Church–River of No Return Wilderness.

**Start:** 40 miles northwest of Salmon 7 miles from the end of the Salmon River Road, and just beyond the mouth of the Middle Fork of the Salmon River
**Type of hike:** Backpack; out-and-back
**Distance:** 11.25 miles one way
**Approximate hiking time:** 4–5 days
**Difficulty:** Very strenuous
**Best season:** Mid-July–early September
**Trail surface:** Normal dirt and rock
**Land status:** Frank Church Wilderness; Salmon-Challis National Forest
**Canine compatibility:** Not allowed
**Fees and permits:** None
**Maps:** Butts Creek Point, Cottonwood Butte, and Long Tom Mountain USGS quadrangles; Frank Church–River of No Return Wilderness North Half forest map is preferable to the Salmon National Forest map.
**Trail contact:** North Fork Ranger District, (208) 865-2700
**Special considerations:** Climb of 5,400 feet in one day. Stoddard Lake is no weekend hike. Trip needs to be planned according to scarce water sources. Route-finding skills required.

Although it is situated on the edge of the Chamberlain Basin—a gentle 300,000-acre plateau in the middle of the giant, 2.4-million-acre Frank Church–River of No Return Wilderness—getting here is a physical challenge. You begin by climbing out of one of the world's deepest canyons. The trailhead is at the Stoddard Pack Bridge, 3,000 feet in elevation. It climbs to no less than 8,800 feet, and most of the climb (more than a mile in altitude change) is immediate.

**Finding the trailhead:** Drive about 11 miles north from Salmon on US 93 to North Fork. Leave the highway and follow the paved Salmon River Road left (west) to Shoup for some 19 miles as it follows the winding path of the Salmon River. From here, the road becomes gravel to continue for another 21 miles to the mouth of the Middle Fork of the Salmon River. Just beyond this is the Middle Fork Trailhead and in another 0.5 mile the trailhead at Stoddard Pack Bridge. GPS: N45 17.96' / W114 35.72'
**Parking and trailhead facilities:** Parking and trailhead only. One mile back, at the Middle Fork Trailhead, are toilets and horse loading but no developed overnight camping sites. Ebenezer Bar Campground, 6 miles back, is a developed overnight site. Bring your own water since sources at campgrounds are not reliable.

## The Hike

Here, where the Middle Fork flows out of the Impassable Canyon into the Main Fork of the Salmon, there used to be a sign that read YONDER LIES THE IDAHO WILDERNESS. Fortunately, one of the major battles for Idaho wilderness was won here in 1980, so although the sign no longer exists, the wilderness does.

Parts of this trail have been reconstructed recently, and some of the bad sections have been improved. On the other hand, substantial forest fires have burned areas near the trail.

The pack bridge is 0.5 mile downstream on the Main Fork of the Salmon River from the confluence of the Middle Fork. Cross the bridge, carrying plenty of drinking water. The trail immediately begins climbing up the face of the Salmon River Canyon. In 12 switchbacks, you climb from the river's elevation of 3,000 feet to 4,613 feet. At this point you round a ridge and continue climbing in the company of excellent views of Middle Fork Canyon, with the river chewing its way ever deeper into the bedrock of the Idaho Batholith.

The trail is now above the breaks of the Middle Fork Canyon, and you continue to climb but less steeply. At an altitude of 5,800 feet, you reach a saddle where the trail crosses a small, grassy park. Here is an excellent stop for a rest, with a very photogenic view of both the canyon and the Bighorn Crags on its opposite side.

Color Creek is 4 miles from the trailhead and 6,414 feet in elevation. Just 0.25 mile past Color Creek, watch for the cutoff trail leading to the right to Nolan Mountain. Take this cutoff trail; it is unmarked but fairly easy to find. Here you depart from the well-built Stoddard Trail, leaving it to wander along the side of the Middle Fork's canyon. (Stoddard Trail does lead to Stoddard Lake, but it's a two-day horse ride.)

Now on the trail to Nolan Mountain, you'll have to switchback steeply uphill. As you near the top (a climb of about 1,000 feet from Color Creek), the trail worsens and deadfall may be a problem. At various times Nolan Mountain becomes prominent on the skyline, and before too long you are on top of the mountain next to what's left of the lookout tower (four steel corner brackets).

Fire damage has taken out the trail downhill to a spring. The spring is used for a campsite by hunters in the fall and is a good place to rest.

From the spring, the trail runs along the top of the ridgeline. However, its path deteriorates and is easily lost in the deadfall. This is no great matter, however, since you are on a high ridge with only one way to go: west toward the 9,000-foot Twin

Peak massif. Soon you'll find the trail again; however, just as it seems to improve, it ends. It ends just as the topographic map shows—at a magnificent saddle that certainly looks like the bighorn sheep country it is. The best, and really the only, way to go is onto the saddle and straight up the mountain. It is not a technical climb, but you'll have to contend with loose rocks.

Once you get to the top of the first point of the Twin Peak massif (9,108 feet), descend to the saddle between it and ascend to the second point (9,258 feet).

The top of the second and highest point is really interesting, and you can get a feel for how large sections of the mountain slough off over time and ultimately fall. There is also a large cairn on top, which is home to about a gazillion little flies.

From here descend due west 0.25 mile and 400 feet to an outfitter trail (not shown on maps), which leads south to a camp on the southwest edge of Stoddard Lake and to good cutthroat fishing. It is another mile, and 700 feet of switchbacking, to the lake.

From Stoddard Lake, trails lead deep into the primal wilderness to Papoose Lake, Cottonwood Lake, Basin Lake, Black Lake, and the vastness of Chamberlain Basin.

**Options:** To fish the two larger lakes in the South Fork of Kitchen Creek, follow the outfitter trail northeast for about 2 miles and 500 feet of elevation gain. The trail then switchbacks downhill steeply to join the upper lake near its outlet on the northeast side. Camping is not recommended because of deadfall and a lack of level spots.

You can follow Stoddard Trail to make a loop back to the trailhead, but count on at least two hard days. You will also need the Aggipah Mountain and Papoose Peak USGS quads. If you are tempted to take any other route back to the Main Salmon River other than the one that crosses the Stoddard Pack Bridge, remember that you'll have to swim across this major river to get back to Salmon River Trail. There are no other bridges within hiking distance.

If you decide to do this loop, a trail leads due west from Stoddard Lake to Stoddard Trail. This trail is somewhat hard to find, but it makes the steep climb (750 feet in 0.25 mile) easier.

A water source and a good stopping place are located where the North Fork of Stoddard Creek joins Stoddard Creek. Make certain to stock up on water here. There are two small, human-made places by Reese Creek to pitch a tent. Make sure to replenish water here also. The rest of the terrain is too steep for camping.

—Philip Blomquist and Mark Leininger

◀ *Bridge to Stoddard Lake Trail.* PHOTO BY LUKE KRATZ

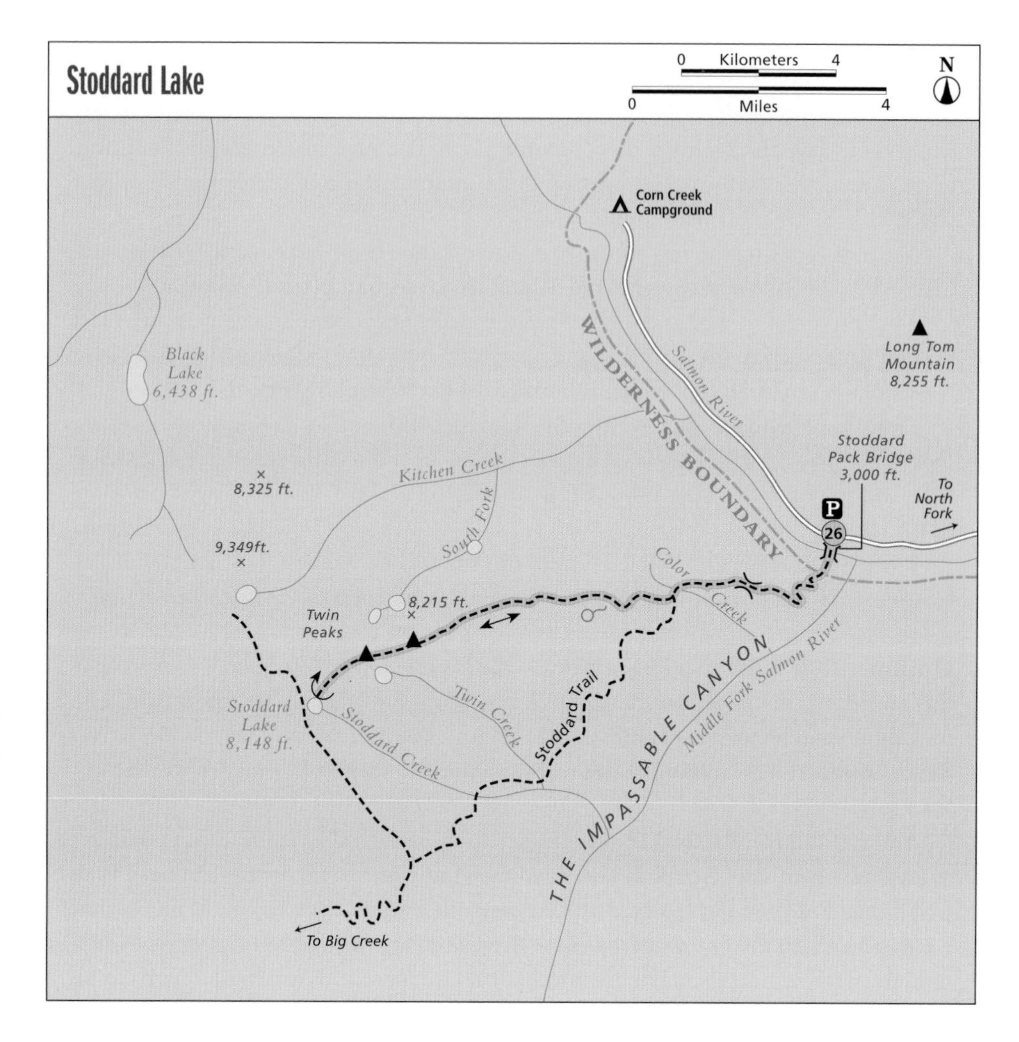


## Miles and Directions

**0.0** Trailhead and Stoddard Pack Bridge (3,000 feet)

**3.0** Saddle (5,800 feet)

**4.0** Color Creek (6,414 feet)

**4.3** Nolan Mountain junction (6,800 feet)

**5.8** Nolan Mountain lookout site (8,215 feet)

**6.0** Spring (8,000 feet)

**8.0** Saddle before Twin Peak and end of trail (8,400 feet)

**10.0** Twin Peak (9,258 feet)

**10.3** Outfitter trail to Stoddard Lake (8,800 feet)

**11.3** Stoddard Lake (8,148 feet)

# 27 Upper Vanity Lakes

Four easily reached but trailless subalpine lakes are nestled in the Frank Church–River of No Return Wilderness.

**Start:** On top of Vanity Summit, 20 linear miles north of Stanley
**Type of hike:** Day hike; out-and-back
**Distance:** 2.2 miles round-trip
**Approximate hiking time:** 1–2 hours
**Difficulty:** Easy to moderate cross-country (there are faint trails)
**Best season:** July–September
**Trail surface:** Dirt and grass (cross-country)
**Land status:** Frank Church Wilderness; Salmon-Challis National Forest
**Canine compatibility:** Not allowed
**Fees and permits:** None
**Map:** Langer Peak USGS quadrangle
**Trail contact:** Challis Ranger District, (208) 879-4100
**Special considerations:** None, unless you need a trail. The Bear Creek side of the ridge burned in 1999. Be careful if you enter it. Standing burned snags fall easily in a new burn.

**Finding the trailhead:** Drive northwest from Stanley on ID 21 for 18.6 miles, and turn left (north) onto the gravel road. Then turn right again almost immediately onto another gravel road. From here it is 21 miles to the trailhead at Josephus Lake. This road quickly crosses Marsh Creek, and 100 yards past the bridge there is yet another fork. Stay to the left and follow this road to Vanity Summit. The gravel road is wide and in good condition until the climb to Vanity Summit. As you begin the ascent, it turns to large (rocky) gravel but remains two lanes wide. The right side of the road burned in 1999 all the way to Vanity Summit (elevation 7,813 feet). GPS: N44 28.99' / W115 05.23'
**Parking and trailhead facilities:** There is a pullout with room for about three vehicles. The site is undeveloped.

## The Hike

No marked trails lead to any of the twelve lakes draining into Vanity Creek. The four lakes described here are the closest to the road and the easiest to get to, yet because they are trailless, they still get little use. Although short, this hike should not be undertaken without the Langer Peak USGS quadrangle plus knowledge and possession of a compass.

It is about 1 mile round-trip, with minimal elevation gain, to the first of the Upper Vanity Lakes. Begin hiking going east-by-southeast on the broad ridge from Vanity Summit. In fact, you can follow the edge of the 1999 burn line, which has made it easier. As you do this, you enter the Frank Church Wilderness, but the boundary is not marked. In 0.25 mile you reach a small but pretty meadow. It has a small creek that flows much of the summer. The creek may be dry at first, but the bed is obvious.

Follow the creek to the first lake, which is the largest. There is a faint human/game trail. The going is not difficult. Then follow the creek to the second lake, which

*One of the prestine Vanity Lakes.* PHOTO BY LUKE KRATZ

is really a pair of very close lakes. The topographic quadrangle shows just one lake, which is incorrect. The two lakes are separated by a 30-foot-high ridge, which the map does not show. There may be a trickle of water from this third lake down to the second, but you cannot miss the lake because it is just over this tiny ridge.

Each lake is a different color. I found the third lake to be blue-green. The second was very transparent, but with an aqua cast where deepest. The first lake was conifer green. The color probably changes by season and by year. There is a good view to the west of the rugged Langer Peak–Langer Lakes country to the west of Vanity Summit.

The area also has a nice fourth lake, which you reach by climbing to the south from the south side of the second lake. It is about 0.3 mile and a 200-foot climb to this lake. Hiking to the last lake would be rated as moderate.

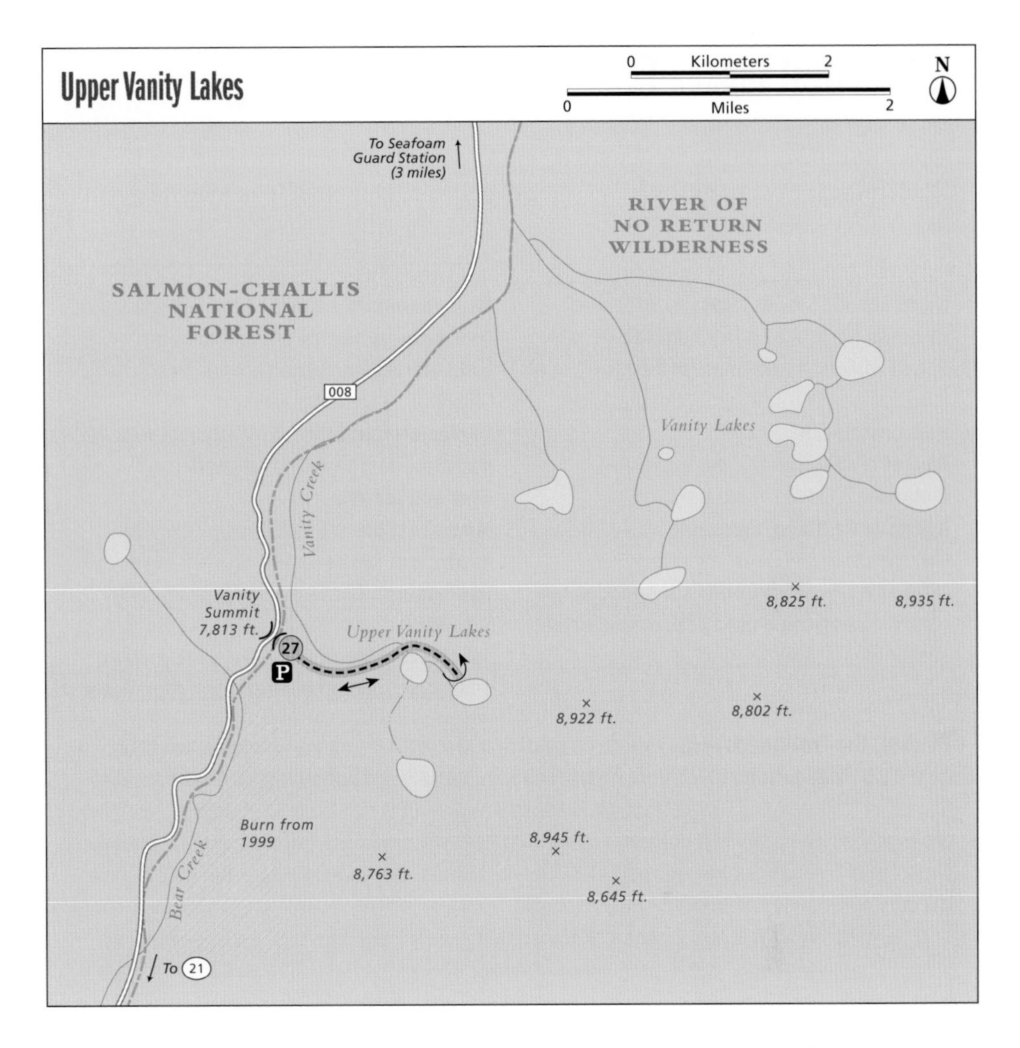


**Options:** You can scramble up the ridge behind the lakes, although this is not easy. You can walk along the ridge or cross over it for fine views in all directions.

—Ralph Maughan

## Miles and Directions

**0.0** Trailhead at Vanity Summit (7,813 feet)

**0.3** Meadow stream (7,840 feet)

**0.5** First lake (7,960 feet)

**0.8** Second and third lakes (8,030 and 8,040 feet)

**1.1** Fourth lake (8,205 feet)

# 28 West Yankee Fork–Crimson Lake

Crimson Lake is one of the finest lakes in the Frank Church–River of No Return Wilderness. It has a rugged setting, colorful peaks, and big trout. The long hike to the lake itself is worth it.

**Start:** About 15 miles northeast of Stanley. The lakes are in the Frank Church–River of No Return Wilderness, but most of the hike is in a roadless area that was left out of the wilderness designation.
**Type of hike:** Backpack; out-and-back
**Distance:** 20 miles round-trip
**Approximate hiking time:** At least 7 hours to Crimson Lake; 3–4 days
**Difficulty:** The West Yankee Fork is moderately easy. The climb to Crimson Lake is moderately strenuous.
**Best season:** Mid-July though mid-September
**Trail surface:** Normal dirt and rock
**Land status:** Frank Church Wilderness; Salmon-Challis National Forest
**Canine compatibility:** On leash until wilderness boundary where not allowed
**Fees and permits:** None
**Maps:** East Basin Creek, Knapp Lakes, Mt. Jordan, and Sunbeam USGS quadrangles
**Trail contact:** Challis Ranger District, (208) 879-4100
**Special considerations:** Take wading shoes. Bring rope to hang your food away from bears.

**Finding the trailhead:** Drive 13 miles east of Stanley on ID 75; or, from the other direction, drive 41.5 miles west on ID 75 from its junction with US 93 just south of Challis. In either case, turn off at Sunbeam to head northward up the Yankee Fork of the Salmon River on a narrow, paved two-lane road. The pavement ends in 3 miles just about where you will see the burn of the Rankin Creek forest fire. It dates from August 2000. The fire burned west-to-east across the road but did not burn out your destination.

Drive north on what is now a good gravel road that goes through the ruins left by gold dredge mining some fifty to seventy-five years ago. The Yankee Fork of the Salmon River Canyon is quite wide through here.

Turn left onto a dirt road (FR 074) at the ghost town of Bonanza, a cluster of log cabins 7.5 miles north of Sunbeam. A sign here indicates that your destination, West Fork Trail, is 1 mile. It also says Bonanza G.S. 0.1; Bonanza Cemetery 0.5; Boot Hill (Cemetery) 1.3. Pass by the forest service guard station and follow the road at the fork that says cemetery or Boot Hill Cemetery. Avoid the road that goes to West Fork Campground. Follow the road downhill about a mile to the trailhead in an old clear-cut. The road continues down the hill to a gravel pit, but this part is usually gated. GPS: N44 23.23' / W114 44.69'
**Parking and trailhead facilities:** The partially shaded trailhead has a loading ramp and a latrine as well as room for about ten vehicles. The trail is the gated road. Follow it downhill to your right. The hike is open to trail machines for 6 miles, but I have not found their numbers oppressive.

## The Hike

I first wondered about this area when I was in the Sawtooth Range, weary of the streams of people passing by on the trail. I noticed that across the Stanley Basin and to the northeast a clump of jagged peaks rose that looked a lot like the Sawtooths and, I thought, seemed a lot less crowded. These peaks didn't seem to have a name, and I couldn't find anyone who had been there. But during the public hearings on the River of No Return Wilderness, people began referring to them as the Tango Peaks since many of them cluster about the head of Tango Creek.

Years later, now familiar with the area, along with many others, I helped push the headwaters of Loon Creek and Tango Creek into the wilderness classification. Included in this addition were the Crimson Lake and the Knapp Lakes basins, even though they do not drain directly into the Middle Fork of the Salmon River (which was the official justification for including the headwaters of Loon and Tango Creeks in the wilderness). The colorful Crimson Lake area, however, contained mineralized rock. I hope I helped stop a nasty mine there, similar to the Grouse Creek Mine in nearby Jordan Creek, which destroyed a mountain and produced gold for about one year before shutting down for good.

The old road/trail leads down toward the canyon, but avoid an ATV trail that soon leaves to the left. Rather than reaching the canyon bottom, the trail you are on soon comes to a gravel pit. Cross the pit; West Fork Trail (Trail 155) leaves on the other (west) side. The trail quickly climbs 300 feet up the mountainside to avoid a short gorge that constricts the West Fork. After the top of the climb, the trail quickly drops down to the floor of West Fork Canyon, which, by south-central Idaho standards, is quite lush. After the climb and descent of the first mile, the trail is easy all the way to the confluence of Cabin Creek, about 3 more miles. As soon as you descend to the West Fork of Yankee Creek, you'll find many small meadows among the conifers. The grade of the trail is essentially flat. If you camp in this canyon, you may find it to be amazingly cold in midsummer. I have seen it freeze hard on a day when in the afternoon the temperature was over 80 degrees. The canyon seems to collect cold air in its bottom.

You quickly come to the Deadwood Creek Trail junction. Deadwood Creek Trail leaves to the left, fords the West Fork, and goes up into Deadwood Creek, which burned in the Rankin Creek forest fire. Next comes the trail up Lightning Creek. West Fork Trail passes by an impressive volcanic rock face and swings up into the mouth of Lightning Creek Canyon; Lightning Creek Trail (Trail 156) leaves to the right. Then West Fork Trail crosses Lightning Creek with a bridge for better crossing.

West Fork Trail continues upstream for 2 more miles, passing through forest and willow thicket and occasional meadows that give views of pink-colored Red Mountain ahead. The willows look like a good place to meet a bear, and they are. There are lots of black bears in this country.

Turn right at Cabin Creek Trail and head up Cabin Creek (alternatively, a hike to the head of the West Fork is certainly pleasant as well). You are now on Trail 156. The trail up Cabin Creek soon crosses the creek to its west side and heads up a linear meadow. About 0.75 mile from the start of Cabin Creek Trail, the path may disappear under avalanche debris (it depends on the year and how recent maintenance

*Majestic Crimson Lake.* PHOTO BY LUKE KRATZ

has occurred). Cross to the east side of the creek here, where you'll pick up the trail again. As you continue up the canyon, each open area gives you a closer view of the rugged gray mountain at what appears to be the head of Cabin Creek. Actually, Cabin Creek bends to the west and then to the south to where it begins at Crimson Lake. The gray mountain is really a wall of the canyon. As you reach its base, avoid any side trails that leave to the left.

Staying on the right, cross the stream (the "north fork" of Cabin Creek) and begin to climb. At the west edge of the bend in the big switchback, Crimson Lake Trail leads to the left. The main trail (Trail 113) continues to the right, climbing 1,400 feet to drop into Pioneer Creek in the Frank Church Wilderness. Climb instead, to the left, up Cabin Creek on the rough Crimson Lake Trail (Trail 202, which isn't shown on the USGS quadrangle). Soon you'll hear the creek crashing below you in a gorge. A short step off the trail gives a good view of the gorge, of the north side of Red Mountain, and down Cabin Creek.

The trail continues in a rocky fashion, crossing over slides and through sparse forest with fine views of the rugged and increasingly colorful mountains. Soon you pass into the River of No Return Wilderness and drop down to Cabin Creek, cross a

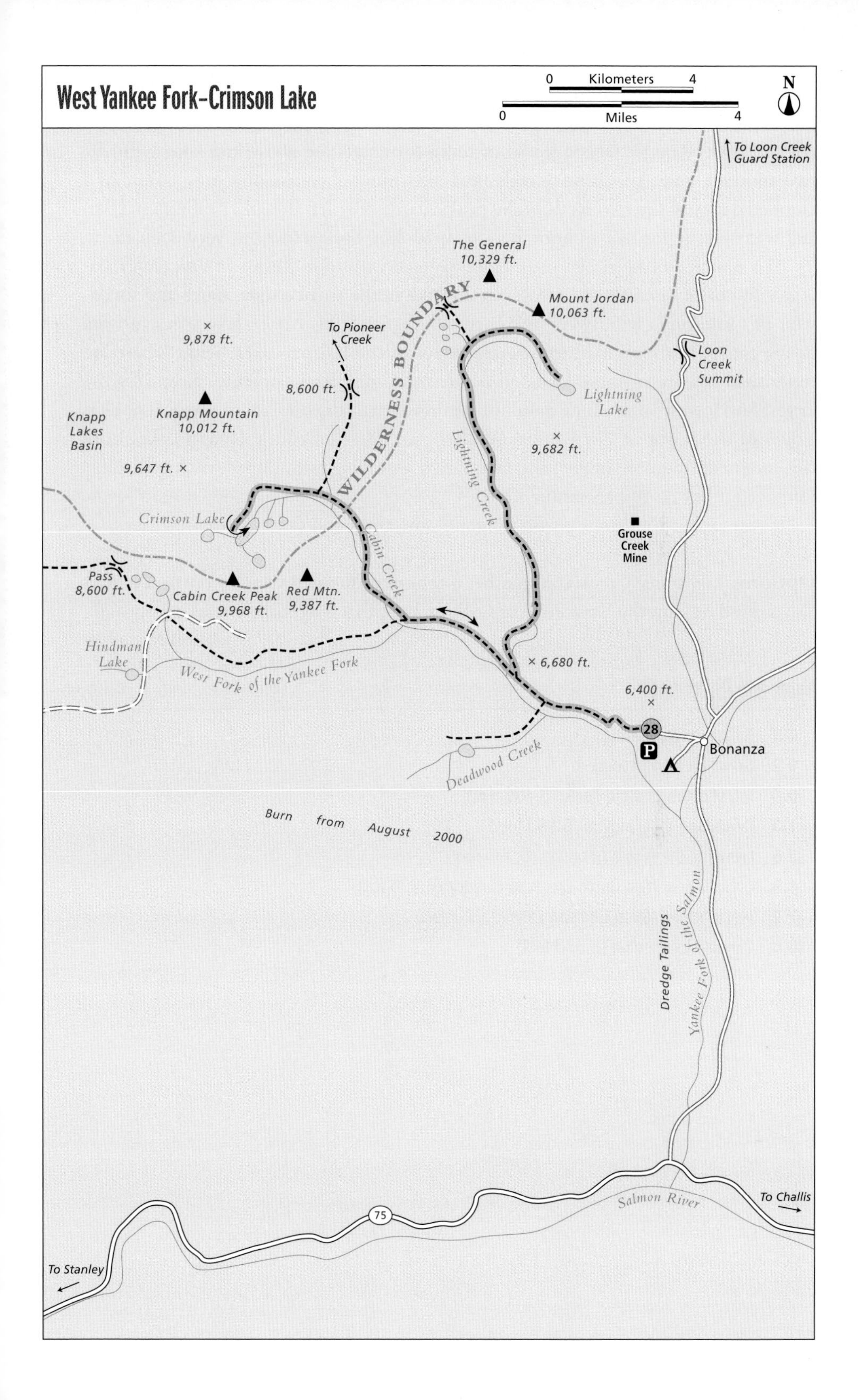
West Yankee Fork–Crimson Lake
0 Kilometers 4
0 Miles 4
N
To Loon Creek Guard Station
The General 10,329 ft.
Mount Jordan 10,063 ft.
WILDERNESS BOUNDARY
To Pioneer Creek
9,878 ft.
8,600 ft.
Loon Creek Summit
Lightning Lake
Knapp Mountain 10,012 ft.
Knapp Lakes Basin
9,647 ft.
9,682 ft.
Lightning Creek
Crimson Lake
Cabin Creek
Grouse Creek Mine
Pass 8,600 ft.
Cabin Creek Peak 9,968 ft.
Red Mtn. 9,387 ft.
Hindman Lake
West Fork of the Yankee Fork
6,680 ft.
6,400 ft.
28
P
Bonanza
Deadwood Creek
Burn from August 2000
Dredge Tailings
Yankee Fork of the Salmon
Salmon River
75
To Challis
To Stanley

tributary, and labor the last 0.3 mile and 600 feet up to Crimson Lake. This lake, large, deep, and full of cutthroat trout (some of them quite large), rests on top of crimson-colored rock. Rough, jagged peaks of reddish orange rise above the lake, with the two-toothed spires of Cabin Creek Peak providing a contrasting gray color. As I climbed between the two teeth of the peak, a large billy left the other mountain goats and watched me for half an hour, his legs straddling the narrow, but very deep, crack.

The unnamed lake at elevation 8,565 feet, above and southeast of Crimson Lake, is also full of large cutthroat. However, the lake in the small cirque above and southwest of Crimson is windswept and barren. Still, from this barren lake you can walk to the top of the mountain for a grand view of the Knapp Lakes below. There are more than twenty of these lakes, all barren and completely pristine except for the largest and lowest lake, which is full of rainbow trout. Beyond are the typical endless ridges of the River of No Return Wilderness. A descent to the Knapp Lakes from this mountain requires an exciting ride down a moving talus slope—rock glissading. I enjoyed it but do not recommend it.

If you camp in the area, please dismantle fire rings and don't create new ones.

**Options:** Lightning Creek trail has been removed due to excessive burns. There is also a good trail up the West Fork of Cabin Creek that eventually meets a jeep trail.

—Ralph Maughan

## Miles and Directions

**0.0** Trailhead (6,580 feet)
**0.2** Gravel pit (6,450 feet)
**0.6** Top of climb to avoid gorge (6,750 feet)
**1.3** Deadwood Trail junction (6,480 feet)
**2.5** Lightning Creek ford or bridge (6,550 feet)
**4.8** Cabin Creek–West Cabin Creek confluence (6,690 feet)
**7.2** Trail junction; left to Crimson Lake (7,220 feet)
**10.0** Crimson Lake outlet (8,330 feet)

# Lick Creek Mountains

The Lick Creek Mountains are a big subrange of the vast Salmon River Mountains. The canyon of the South Fork of the Salmon River is generally regarded as the east side of the Lick Creek Mountains. Long Valley, which contains the towns of McCall and Cascade, is the western boundary.

Their mostly granitic rock has been intensely carved by ice age glaciers into a variety of scenic peaks and cirque basins filled with subalpine or alpine lakes.

About 150,000 acres of this area burned in fire the summer of 1994 and more again in the summer of 2000. Vast areas of these mountains now have regenerating forests. Hikers should understand the dangers (such as falling snags) and the joys (wildflowers) of walking through burns with the standing dead trees and new forests.

A large portion of the Lick Creek Mountains is roadless, perhaps 200,000 acres. Idaho conservationists have for years sought wilderness protection for this area, but without success.

—Ralph Maughan

*Granite cliffs are common in the Lick Creek Mountains.* Photo by Luke Kratz

# 29 Box Lake

Lovely granite mountains and a large subalpine lake radiate within burned areas and new growth.

**Start:** 13 road miles northeast of McCall
**Type of hike:** Day hike or overnight backpack; out-and-back with an option of a longer hike requiring a shuttle
**Distance:** 8 miles round-trip
**Approximate hiking time:** 4–5 hours
**Difficulty:** Moderate due to elevation gain of 1,860 feet in 3 miles, followed by a 350-foot descent to Box Lake
**Best season:** August–mid-September
**Trail surface:** Normal dirt and rock
**Land status:** Payette National Forest
**Canine compatibility:** On leash
**Fees and permits:** None
**Maps:** Box Lake and Fitsum Summit USGS quadrangles; McCall and Krassel Ranger Districts, Payette National Forest map
**Trail contact:** McCall/Krassel Ranger District, (208) 634-0400 (McCall); (208) 634-0600 (Krassel)
**Special considerations:** Wading shoes needed in June and July.

**Finding the trailhead:** Where ID 55 reaches Payette Lake from the south, it makes an abrupt left turn. This is downtown McCall, where you'll part with ID 55. Make a right turn here, and take Park Street to Davis Street to the signed Lick Creek Road (FR 48). The road is paved for 3 miles as it travels along the north shore of Little Payette Lake. The road gradually turns north into Lake Fork Canyon. Broken pavement, which contains some impressive holes, continues for about 3 more miles. At the end of the pavement, you are fully in Lake Fork Canyon. The road is all-weather gravel, one and a half to two lanes wide, but it is also rough and busy. The canyon is very scenic. Thirteen miles from the beginning of the signed road back in McCall, you reach the Black Lee Trailhead. GPS: N44 59.35' / W115 57.25'
**Parking and trailhead facilities:** Black Lee Trailhead is mostly in the shade under big conifers. It has an outhouse and room for five or six vehicles. A sign at the trailhead reads Box Lake 4.

## The Hike

This hike provides a good introduction to the Lick Creek Mountains, which form part of the westernmost portion of the massive Idaho Batholith. Glaciers once filled the valleys in the Box Lake area during the Pleistocene (ice age) era and left many tarns (glacial lakes) when they receded. These mountains are also characterized by steep river breaks with shallow soils. Much more recently (1994), a large portion of the Lick Creek Mountains burned in the hot Blackwell Fire. The fire burned part of this trail, including Box Lake itself. The area is still

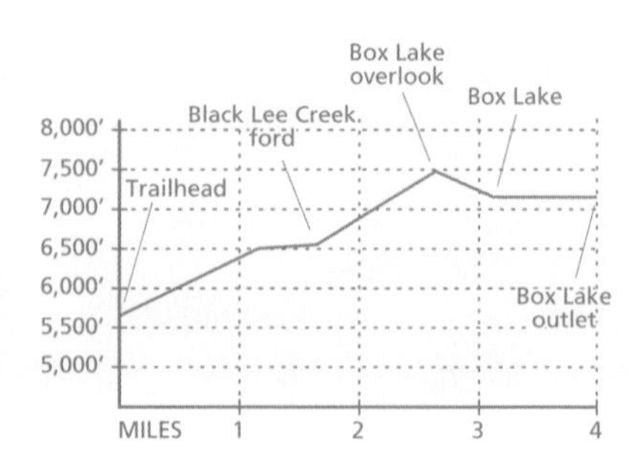

*Box Lake post-burns.* PHOTO BY LUKE KRATZ

scenic, and the fire recovery is underway, even in the areas where the fire was so hot it sterilized the soil.

Box Lake is one of the largest in the Lick Creek Mountains—about a mile long and a third of a mile wide. You can reach it most years by late June, but you will slog through some snow and the fords might be difficult. August is best, with many wildflowers. September has beautiful foliage, and the biting flies and mosquitoes have disappeared by then.

The trail (Trail 110) heads northwest from the trailhead and immediately begins to climb steeply on switchbacks up a steep slope into the canyon of Black Lee Creek. This steep section is in the shade of large Douglas fir and Engelmann spruce. Black Lee Creek tumbles to your left not far below the trail. The trail then levels out a bit, enters the burn, and meanders through several meadows after a ford of Black Lee Creek. Here you'll find yellow columbine, red Indian paintbrush, blue penstemon, yellow composites, and much bear grass, which blooms mid-July through mid-August. Before reaching the summit, the trail crosses Black Lee Creek three more times.

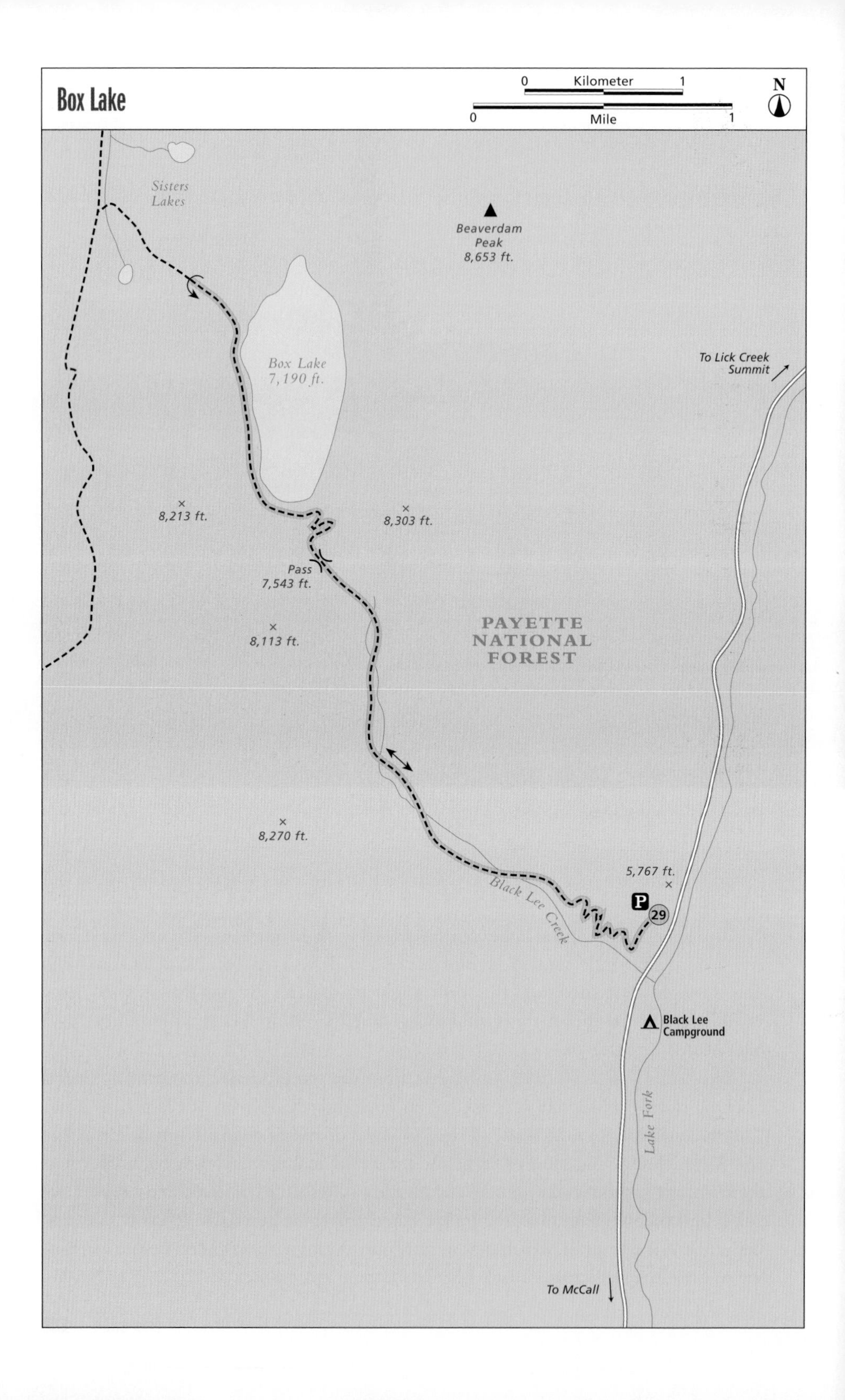
Box Lake
0
Kilometer
1
0
Mile
1
N
Sisters Lakes
Beaverdam Peak 8,653 ft.
Box Lake 7,190 ft.
To Lick Creek Summit
8,213 ft.
8,303 ft.
Pass 7,543 ft.
8,113 ft.
PAYETTE NATIONAL FOREST
8,270 ft.
5,767 ft.
P
29
Black Lee Creek
Black Lee Campground
Lake Fork
To McCall

The rest of the way to the summit, the trail passes in and out of the burn several times. The burn has opened up the views of the impressive walls and peaks of granitic rock. The trail climbs steeply in places, and this part of the climb is usually in the sun.

The trail was well cleared, but because the burned snags will be falling for some time, trail maintenance crews will have to cut the trail frequently to keep it in good condition.

The summit is gentle and broad with very nice meadows through which course the rivulets that become Black Lee Creek. At the very end of the summit area, you come abruptly to a steep overlook of Box Lake. There are also good views of the granite ridges around you. The fire burned especially hot right here near the overlook.

The trail descends from the overlook 350 feet to the lake, switchbacking down first to the right and then to the left (west) side of the lake. It follows the west side of the lake to its broad outlet area. Although the trail is close to the lake, getting to the shore is not easy because it is lined with boulders. The outlet area, where Box Lake Creek begins, is marshy, but there is a beach as well as an old dam, which has raised the lake slightly from its natural level.

Upon your return to the trailhead, be sure to stop near the top of the first set of switchbacks on the trail and look southward down the classic U-shaped valley of the North Fork of Lake Fork Creek. To the right is Slick Rock, an 800-foot-high vertical slab of granite. From here, looking down this canyon that now has a road in it, you can imagine how truly wild this country once was.

**Options:** Beyond Box Lake, a backpacking trip can continue past the marshy Sisters Lakes to Crestline Trail (Trail 109). Here, you can proceed north-northwest to marshy Heart Lake (2 miles), Brush Lake (2.7 miles), or Pearl Lake (4.5 miles). This is all in the burned, but scenic glaciated granite, country. You could extend the hike farther west to the junction with Wagon Creek Road (7 miles) or 5 miles along the road in the Pearl Creek drainage. This should bring you out at the North Fork of the Payette River. You'll need the Granite Lake USGS quadrangle to route this part of the hike, plus a shuttle vehicle since you'll come out at a different trailhead. Unfortunately, Trail 109 is open to ATVs, reducing the quality of what could otherwise be a hike of statewide importance.

—Jerry Dixon and Ralph Maughan

## Miles and Directions

**0.0** Black Lee Trailhead (5,680 feet)

**1.2** End of steep climb (6,480 feet)

**1.6** First ford of Black Lee Creek (6,550 feet)

**2.7** Box Lake overlook (7,543 feet)

**3.2** Box Lake (7,190 feet)

**4.0** Box Lake outlet (7,190 feet)

# 30 Lava Lakes

This trail offers spectacular scenery and solitude, the sublime Lava Ridge, and chances to see wildlife.

**Start:** 25 linear miles north of McCall in the Salmon River Mountains
**Type of hike:** Day hike or base camp; out-and-back
**Distance:** 8.4 miles round-trip
**Approximate hiking time:** 4–5 hours
**Difficulty:** Moderate
**Best season:** Mid-July–mid-September
**Trail surface:** Normal dirt and rock
**Land status:** Payette National Forest
**Canine compatibility:** On leash
**Fees and permits:** None
**Maps:** Hazard Lake, Hershey Point, and Patrick Butte USGS quadrangles; Weiser, Council, and New Meadows Ranger District–Payette National Forest map
**Trail contact:** New Meadows Ranger District, (208) 347-0300
**Special considerations:** The topographic quadrangles are badly out of date and show almost none of the roads or trails in the right places.

**Finding the trailhead:** From McCall, drive 6 miles west on ID 55, and turn right on the paved road to Brundage Mountain ski resort, FR 257. At 3 miles, bear left at the turnoff to the resort, and continue north on FR 257, which quickly becomes a good, but sometimes washboarded, dirt road. At 6 miles bear left at a Y junction and continue north on FR 257. The road parallels the long shores of Goose Lake and continues climbing. You pass Hard Creek Guard Station at 19 miles and Hazard Lake Campground at 22 miles before reaching the road's end and turnout at the Clayburn Trailhead at 26 miles. GPS: N45 10.61' / W116 10.72'
**Parking and trailhead facilities:** The Clayburn Trailhead has a latrine and space to park many cars. Camping (fee) is available at Hazard Lake Campground, 4 miles back down Goose Lake Road.

## The Hike

This is a beautiful hike that takes you up and over the incredible ramparts of Lava Ridge in the Patrick Butte–French Creek unprotected roadless area. Timber companies have been chipping away at this roadless area for years, with the compliance of the Idaho congressional delegation and the USDA Forest Service. The abundant old growth that this area contains makes it highly coveted by extractive interests.

This hike can be done as a day hike or a backpacking trip. You could spend several days exploring this magnificent area.

From the trailhead, descend 100 yards to a signed junction indicating that Trail 505 heads (right) east. The main trail, Trail 347, is a closed road that has become popular with off-road vehicle enthusiasts. It continues straight (north).

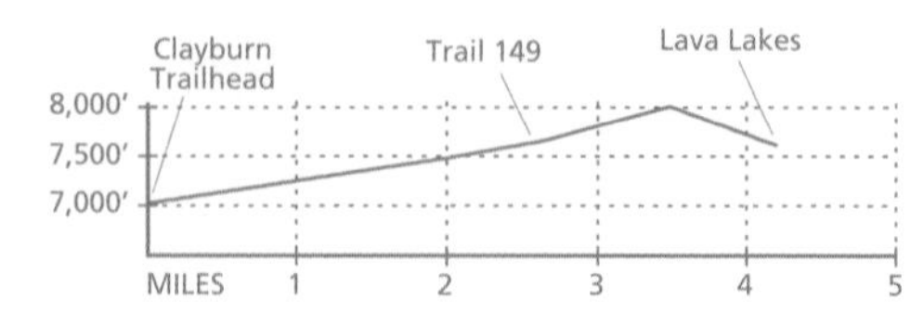

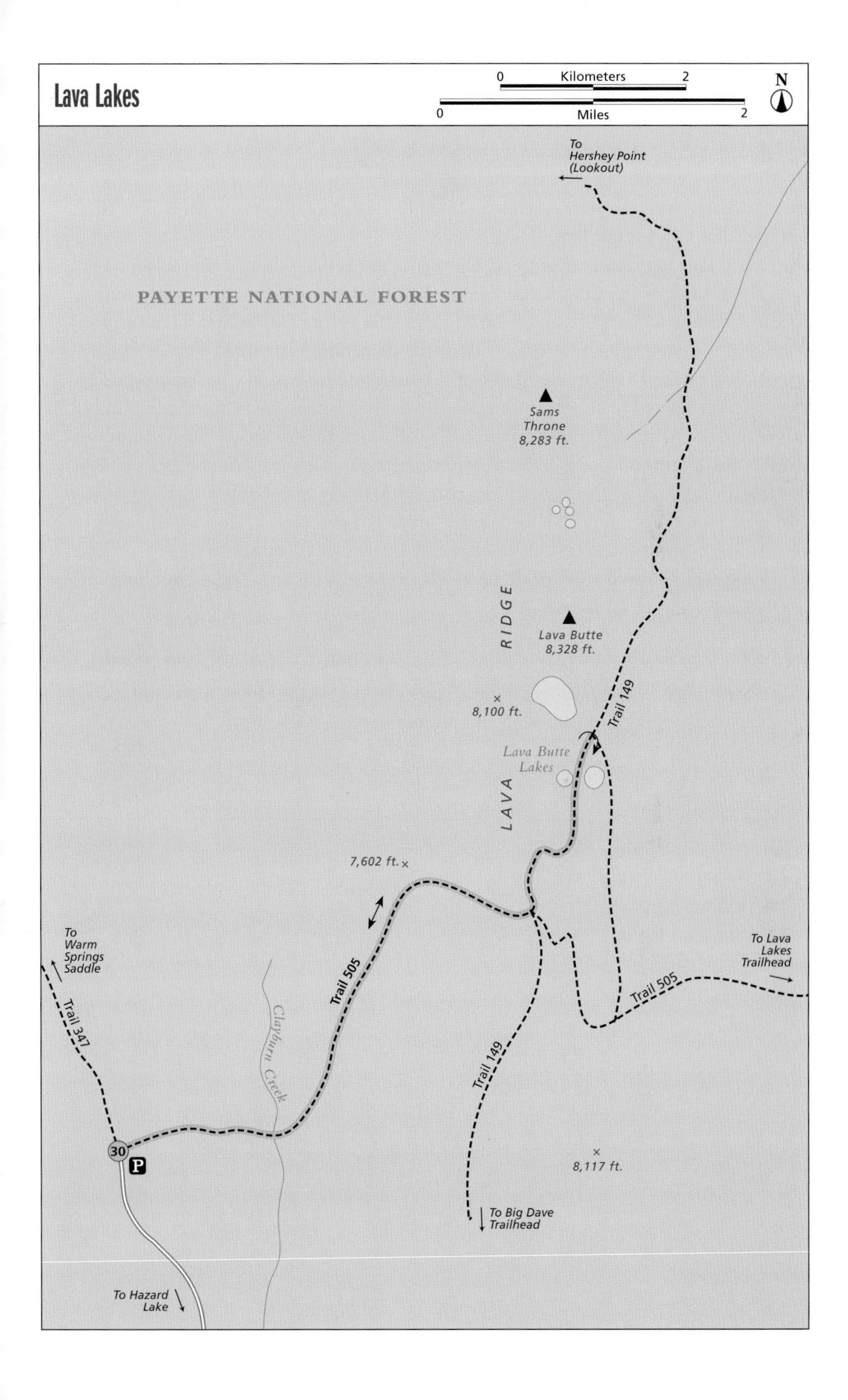

Lava Lakes
0
Kilometers
2
0
Miles
2
N
To
Hershey Point
(Lookout)
PAYETTE NATIONAL FOREST
Sams
Throne
8,283 ft.
RIDGE
Lava Butte
8,328 ft.
8,100 ft.
Trail 149
Lava Butte
Lakes
LAVA
7,602 ft.
To
Warm
Springs
Saddle
Trail 347
Clayburn Creek
Trail 505
Trail 149
To Lava
Lakes
Trailhead
Trail 505
30
P
8,117 ft.
To Big Dave
Trailhead
To Hazard
Lake

The trail starts to climb immediately. It is faint and difficult to follow, at times going through open meadows. If you lose it, just head east to Clayburn Creek. You can pick the trail up again where it crosses the creek.

Once you reach the creek, the trail climbs in earnest to Lava Ridge and the junction with Trail 149, which it reaches at 2.7 miles. Trail 149 traverses Lava Ridge. Turn left here and follow Trail 149.

Lava Ridge is a unique feature. It represents an overlap of Columbia River basalt with the granitic rock of the Idaho Batholith. Lava Ridge itself is aesthetically similar to the limestone Scapegoat massif or Chinese Wall of the Bob Marshall country in Montana. It is an imposing feature, continually demanding attention.

On top of Lava Ridge, the views of the surrounding country are incredible. To the west, the Seven Devils tower magnificently above Rapid River, the Little Salmon River, and the Salmon River, while massive Patrick Butte dominates the foreground. To the north, beyond the Salmon River, is the Gospel Hump country. To the east are the great peaks in the Secesh unprotected roadless area, highest in the Payette National Forest. So much of this country remains unprotected. Continued support for roadless area preservation will be necessary to save what you see from destruction.

From here, the trail soon descends to the eastern side of the ridge, reaching the lovely Lava Lakes at 4.2 miles.

**Options:** From the Lava Lakes, you can explore the lofty heights of Lava Ridge. Lava Butte, Sams Throne, and Hershey Point all provide spectacular views. You could spend a couple of days gazing at some big and remote mountain country.

—Lee Mercer

## Miles and Directions

**0.0** Clayburn Trailhead (7,000 feet)

**2.7** Junction with Trail 149 (7,600 feet)

**3.4** Trail high point (7,980 feet)

**4.2** Lava Lakes (about 7,600 feet)

# 31 Loon Lake Loop and Beyond

Explore two scenic canyons and a large, productive lake.

**Start:** 25 miles northeast of McCall
**Type of hike:** Day hike or backpacking loop. It is a long day hike
**Distance:** 10 miles
**Approximate hiking time:** 7-plus hours
**Difficulty:** Moderate
**Best season:** Early September
**Trail surface:** Normal dirt and rock
**Land status:** Payette National Forest
**Canine compatibility:** On leash
**Fees and permits:** None
**Maps:** Loon Lake and Victor Peak USGS quadrangles
**Trail contact:** McCall Ranger District, (208) 634-0400

**Finding the trailhead:** To approach Loon Lake from McCall, turn north at McCall onto Warren Wagon Road (FR 22), and drive toward Burgdorf. This "wagon road" is a paved highway for 31 miles north of McCall over Secesh Summit and down to the Burgdorf junction. Much of the route passes through the giant Blackwell Burn of 1994.

Stay to the right at the Burgdorf junction. You immediately find the edge of the huge Burgdorf Burn from the summer of 2000 on your left and the Secesh River on your right. Follow the pretty Secesh River 7 miles to Chinook Campground Road. Drive 1.5 miles down this road to its end. GPS: N45 12.76' / W115 48.53'

**Parking and trailhead facilities:** The trailhead is at the very end of the campground, that is, as far down the canyon as you can drive. You'll find a latrine and bulletin board next to the trailhead. Horse-loading ramps are farther back up the road. The trailhead is in partial shade.

## The Hike

It is February 1943. A four-engine bomber on a routine flight from Nevada to Idaho's Mountain Home airbase is lost in the snow above the rugged peaks of the Salmon River Mountains. Searching for a radio beam coming out of Oregon, the pilot sees he will soon run out of gas, and he starts to nose the plane down. Through the swirling clouds, jagged glacier-carved peaks reach up, locked in winter's grip. Surely landing the bomber in the rugged terrain is impossible. The pilot is not even sure where he is—somewhere over central Idaho in the dead of winter.

Suddenly the canyon opens up and, miraculously, a field 0.5 mile in diameter lies below. It is surrounded by an expanse of trees, and mountains loom at one end. The pilot edges the bomber around and makes a once-only-and-forever approach with the wheels

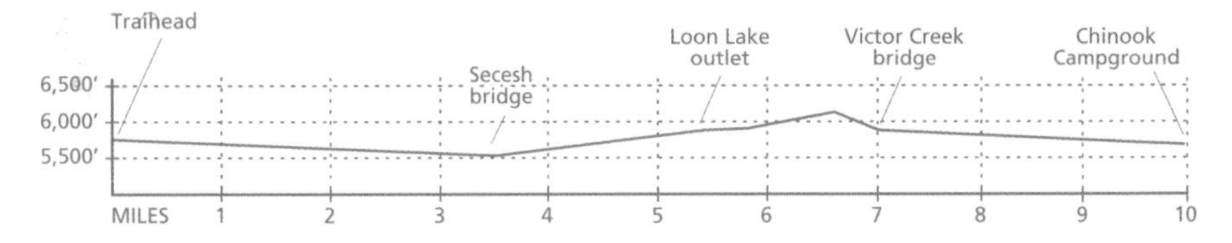

*Loon Creek, several miles above Loon Lake.* PHOTO BY RALPH MAUGHAN

up. The lumbering plane drops into the opening and skids across the field—a frozen lake. It slides into the lodgepole pine on the far side, tearing off the wings. The fuselage careens through the trees and stops. One aviator suffers a broken leg; no one is killed.

How the aviators escaped from these mountains in winter with no winter gear, snowshoes, food, or information on their position has become a local legend. That they got out, after several of them walked overland for days without snowshoes across mountain passes buried 12 feet deep in snow, attests to their determination and courage.

The patch of snow that appeared out of the mountain vastness and saved their lives is Loon Lake. The wreckage can still be seen near the lake, although for about 60 years hikers have carved their names in it and carried off souvenirs like a band of ants.

The trail to Loon Lake is usually done as a loop. In the past, however, the big question was whether you could ford the Secesh River, because it was not bridged at Chinook Campground, and because it's a river, not a creek. Finally, in the fall of 2000, the forest service built a pack bridge over the Secesh in order to protect the Chinook salmon that spawn in and near this very location.

The name Secesh has an interesting origin. During the Civil War, when Warren (12 miles to the east) was one of the largest towns in what was to become Idaho, the people in the area were deeply divided in their loyalties. The town of Warren physically divided itself. Part called itself Washington, and part belonged to the secessionists. Some of the Rebels moved to the river, which became known as the Secessionist River, or Secesh. Some of these sentiments still haunt Idaho today, with its many political leaders owing their offices to constant bashing of the federal government and suggestions that Idaho would do best if there were no national forests or other public lands.

This hike can be done from late June through September, but early September is best. Secesh Canyon is cooler, the bugs are gone, and the understory of huckleberry and many other plants turns a bright red and yellow. The quaking aspen leaves turn to gold.

The hike is described in a clockwise direction, but either way is fine. From the trailhead, take Trail 080, bypassing the new pack bridge and following the wide trail down the Secesh River. The trail is pretty from the start as you follow the clear water through a small-diameter forest in a shallow canyon. The canyon changes, however. It deepens, and the tree diameter grows, as does the size of the river. The trail does not remain wide, soon narrowing to about 2 feet. It is in good condition, composed of granite-derived sand, and does not get muddy. While not entirely flat, it could be rated as easy. You cross one major tributary on the way—Alex Creek—which is bridged.

At 3.5 miles you reach a big bridge over the Secesh. While Trail 080 does continue down the river, cross the bridge onto Trail 084, and you quickly reach the confluence of the Secesh with Loon Creek. The trail climbs steeply up Loon Creek, switchbacking about 150 feet in elevation. Then it climbs 150 more feet on a more gentle ascent. This places you on the broad shelf that holds Loon Lake and the marsh and meadow around it.

You soon pass an abandoned trail leaving to the left. Avoid it unless you like thrashing through lumpy deep grass. Continue to the right, cross a small stream, and you quickly reach a junction of Trail 084 and Trail 081. The right fork, Trail 081, is the one you will take to return to Chinook Campground. Stay to the left and cross the meadow. In 0.25 mile, you reach another trail junction. Left (Trail 081) takes you quickly to Loon Lake's outlet (Loon Creek) to the south shore and also continues many miles to the south to Split Creek and beyond. Right (Trail 084) takes you around the north side of the lake and up into rugged Loon Creek Canyon.

Loon Lake is marshy around much of its margin, and there is no access from the north shore, although the right-hand trail does eventually reach the west shore (the inlet), where there is access.

Loon Lake sits right on the south edge of the great Blackwell Burn. The north-shore trail is in many places the burn boundary (probably because backfires were set from its edge). You walk around the north side of the lake with few views except burned forest on your right and green on your left.

At the head of the lake, the trail splits. The wider tread is to the left and leads to the lake inlet area. If you want to continue up Loon Creek Canyon, stay to the right.

The right fork goes upcanyon through generally unburned forest at a level, easy grade and reaches a boggy but scenic meadow after 0.7 mile. Loon Creek meanders gently below the trail through tall grass. Beavers have ponded parts of the stream here.

The trail now begins to climb up and down, keeping tightly to the right side of the canyon. You cross numerous wet places, but the trail is easy to follow. Finally you break out into a large avalanche area with fine views of the increasingly rugged peaks.

The trail crosses the avalanche, passes though a patch of forest, and comes to a very pretty riparian meadow. Then it goes back through the forest and another avalanche run. Soon after, the trail drops and crosses Loon Creek, which is not an easy ford until late summer. Large logs cross the creek, but they are mostly high above the creek and

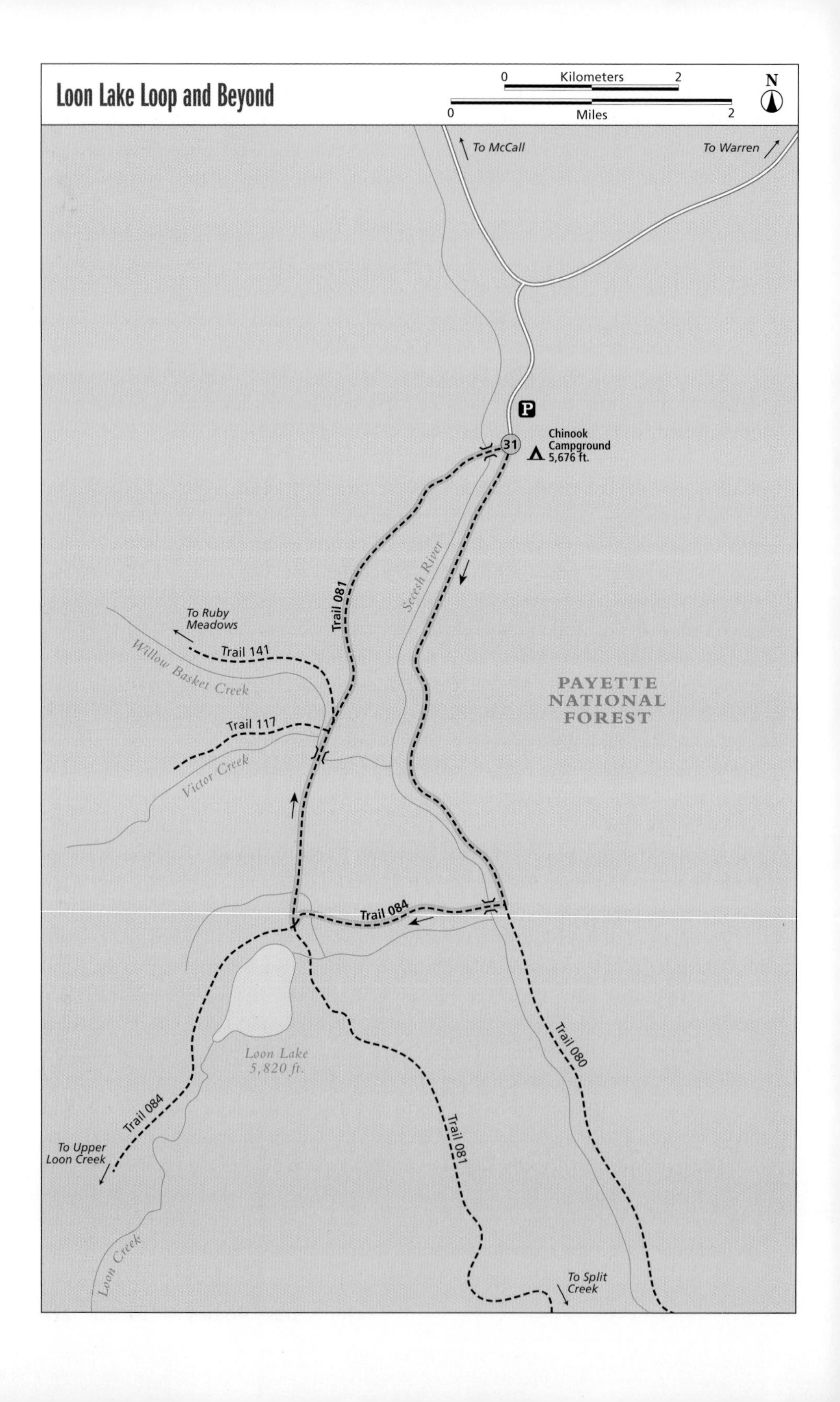
Loon Lake Loop and Beyond
0
Kilometers
2
0
Miles
2
N
To McCall
To Warren
P
31
Chinook
Campground
5,676 ft.
Seesh River
Trail 081
To Ruby
Meadows
Trail 141
Willow Basket Creek
PAYETTE
NATIONAL
FOREST
Trail 117
Victor Creek
Trail 084
Loon Lake
5,820 ft.
Trail 080
Trail 084
To Upper
Loon Creek
Trail 081
Loon Creek
To Split
Creek

tilt and appear very dangerous to use. The trail continues, although it is faint to the top of the canyon and down to a trailhead at Foolhen Meadows, on the road just east of Lick Creek Summit. The crossing described above is the only ford between Loon Lake and the top of the canyon. I stopped at the creek crossing.

If you want to explore the streamside zone just downcanyon, you will find it to be very beautiful with bedrock-bottomed pools, small waterfalls, and lazy meadow stretches. Be warned, however, that it is very treacherous near the creek. Many springs near the creek flow into it by means of very narrow and very deep slots in the sod. You could easily be walking in the grass and huckleberry riparian zone and suddenly step into an almost invisible spring that is 5 or 6 feet deep!

The return half of the loop begins at the trail junction described previously. This trail is wide because it is the preferred route for horse parties.

The trail climbs into a mostly burned forest of small-diameter lodgepole pine. The snags are beginning to fall, so be cautious. Then you come to unburned forest, then more burned forest, and so on. Finally you wind steeply downhill to a good bridge over Victor Creek. Just over the bridge is a junction of three trails. Take the rightmost trail, which has a sign that reads CHINOOK CAMPGROUND 3 MILES.

The middle trail goes up Willow Basket Creek. The leftmost trail, which is not as easy to see but is a good trail, crosses the mouth of Willow Basket Creek and goes up Victor Creek.

Keeping right, you climb 200 feet and drop into a shallow, willow-filled drainage. The trail climbs out and then contours high above the Secesh, which is out of sight. You drop quickly 300 feet down to the Secesh. Once you reach the river, walk briefly alongside and then across the new bridge to the trailhead.

**Options:** The major option is the side hike from the loop into upper Loon Creek, described previously.

You can also follow Trail 081 south to Split Creek, then take Trail 082 up North Fork Lick Creek Canyon to Trail 084 and back to Loon Lake for a really grand loop.

Victor Creek Trail 117 is a very long point-to-point trail that leads to the North Fork of the Payette. Willow Basket Creek Trail 141 leads to a primitive road after 2 miles at Ruby Meadows.

—Jerry Dixon; rehiked by Ralph Maughan

## Miles and Directions

**0.0** Chinook Campground Trailhead (5,676 feet)

**3.5** Secesh Bridge at mouth of Loon Creek (5,504 feet)

**5.5** Loon Lake outlet (5,820 feet)

**5.8** Beginning of loop back (5,825 feet)

**6.6** High point between Loon Lake and Victor Creek (6,050 feet)

**7.0** Victor Creek bridge (5,820 feet)

**10.0** Chinook Campground (5,676 feet)

# Boise Mountains

The Boise Mountains are located north and east of Boise and cover a vast area south of the Salmon River Mountains. These mountains are more great examples of the Idaho Batholith granite and its history of uplifting and carving through faulting and waterways.

The area is heavily forested and receives more rainfall than most of the central Idaho ranges. Most of the evergreen forests are mixes of ponderosa pine, grand fir, Douglas fir, Engelmann spruce, lodgepole pine, and subalpine fir. The mountains contain large numbers of big-game species, including mule deer, elk, and black bear.

The 2,612,000-acre Boise National Forest manages much of the land in the Boise Mountains as well as the Salmon River Ranges in Idaho. The district offices are located at Emmett, Garden Valley (Emmett RD), Boise (Mountain Home RD), Mountain Home, Lowman, Idaho City, and Cascade, Idaho. Contact the forest service for many more hiking opportunities that are available within hours of the Boise area.

*Anderson Ranch Reservoir in the Boise Mountains.* Photo by John Kratz

# 32 Jennie Lake

Jennie Lake is a beautiful mountain lake nestled in the Boise mountains.

**Start:** 27 miles southeast of Lowman, 69 miles northeast of Boise
**Type of hike:** Day hike or backpack; out-and-back
**Distance:** 9 miles round-trip
**Approximate hiking time:** 3–4 hours
**Difficulty:** Moderate
**Best season:** July–September
**Trail surface:** Normal dirt and rocks
**Land status:** Boise National Forest
**Canine compatibility:** Voice command
**Fees and permits:** None
**Maps:** Jackson Peak and Bear River USGS quadrangles, Boise National Forest map
**Trail contact:** Lowman Ranger District, (208) 259-3361

**Finding the trailhead:** Take ID 21 east from Boise for 55 miles, past Idaho City. Fourteen miles before you reach Lowman, turn right onto the well-marked FR 384. Stay on this good gravel road for 6.2 miles until it forks. Take the left fork, FR 348, for 7.6 miles before reaching the .1 mile turnoff to the well-marked Jennie Lake Trailhead. GPS: N43 59.49' / W115 27.09'

## The Hike

This is a great opportunity for residents of a large growing urban area of Boise to visit a pristine lake. Due to its proximity (a little over an hour) to such a populated area this trail is quite popular and special consideration to preserve this delicate area should be considered.

The trail begins by following Bear Creek upstream. It gently climbs, skirting flowery hillsides and meadows and thick fir forests typical of the Boise mountains. It is well suited for any hiking ability and there are plenty of resting spots near the creek. After 3 miles the trees slightly thin out and the trail moves away from the creek to more open sage and meadow terrain. Nice views of colorful forest pockets along the slopes can be enjoyed with the changing seasons. The trail then veers south and climbs toward the lake.

Jennie Lake is nestled among nice granite outcroppings at the foot of Wolf mountain. There are plenty of places to set up camp. Please do not form new campfire rings. The lake area serves as a nice jumping off point for cross-country exploring and scrambling opportunities.

**Options:** The Crooked River Trail is a popular hike near FR 384's turnoff from ID 21. Farther along FR 348 is the Bear River Trail and eventually the North Fork of the Boise River Trail, which both provide extended backcountry experiences. Boise National Forest has numerous named and unnamed trails along the sides of the forest roads. Always look for the nonmotorized signs!

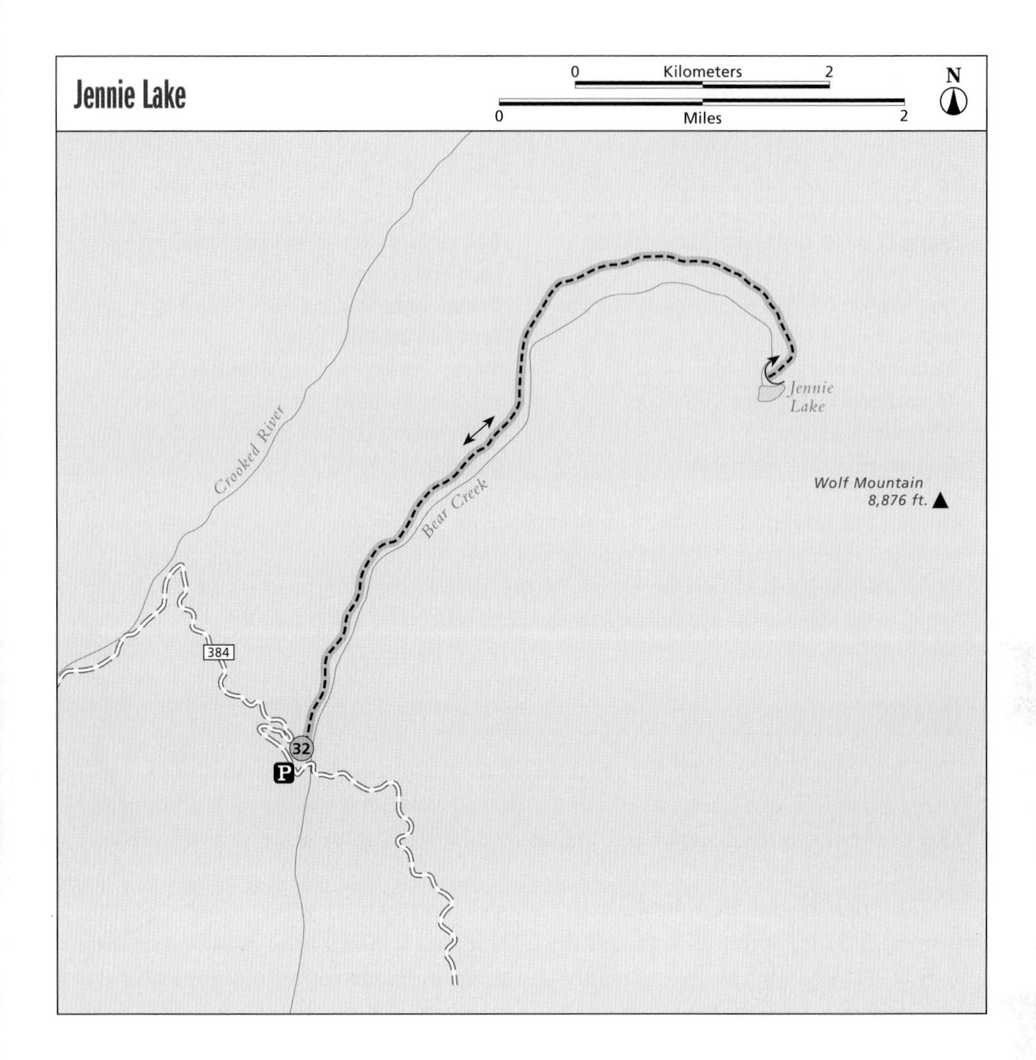


## Miles and Directions

**0.0** Trailhead (5,943 ft)

**3.2** Trail curves westward

**4.2** Trail begins final ascent

**4.5** Jennie Lake

# Trinity Mountains

The Trinity "Alps" are a small but scenic subrange of the Boise Mountains that rise just west of Anderson Ranch Reservoir on the South Fork of the Boise River. The subrange harbors about 20 scenic subalpine lakes. Trinity Mountain is also the name of the high point in the range. At 9,451 feet, it seems a bit higher because on top sits one of Idaho's most picturesque fire tower lookouts.

Most of the big lakes in the range are accessible by truck and even sedan if driven carefully. Big Trinity, Little Trinity, Big Roaring, and Little Roaring Lakes all have busy campgrounds because they are set in very scenic locations just north of Trinity Mountain itself.

A number of trails climb the flanks of the Trinity Mountains, but the most popular by far is the one we describe here, Rainbow Lakes Trail, which takes you on a nonmotorized route to a ring of subalpine lakes in a big cirque on the east side of Trinity Mountain.

—Ralph Maughan

*Widflowers along slopes in the Boise Range.* PHOTO BY LUKE KRATZ

# 33 Rainbow Lakes

The basin has beautiful scenery, including nine fishable lakes close together.

**Start:** About 50 linear miles north of Mountain Home
**Type of hike:** Day hike or backpack; out-and-back
**Distance:** 4.5 miles (one way) to the most remote lake—Hideaway Lake
**Approximate hiking time:** 4 hours to several days
**Difficulty:** Moderate due to elevation gain and loss
**Best season:** July and August
**Trail surface:** Normal dirt and rock
**Land status:** Boise National Forest
**Canine compatibility:** Voice command though leash recommended
**Fees and permits:** None
**Maps:** Little Trinity Lake and Trinity Mountain USGS quadrangles; Boise National Forest map.
**Trail contact:** Mountain Home Ranger District, (208) 587-7961
**Special considerations:** The drive is long and, at Anderson Ranch Reservoir, somewhat hazardous.

**Finding the trailhead:** It is a long drive to Trinity Mountain. From I-84 at Mountain Home, turn northeast onto US 20 and follow it 20 miles up into the mountains to the signed turnoff to Anderson Ranch Reservoir Dam. This road is paved for 3.5 miles, until it descends into the canyon of the South Fork of the Boise to Anderson Ranch Dam. It is a steep 2-mile descent to the dam (washboard road), but you cross the dam on a paved road. Across the dam at the road fork, turn right and follow the gravel road (FR 113) 8.5 somewhat treacherous miles to Fall Creek. The road winds above the reservoir the entire distance. There are many blind curves and no guardrails. Many folks drive big RVs on the road, so be very careful.

At Fall Creek, turn left onto FR 123 up Fall Creek. From here, it is 19 miles on gravel and dirt to Big Trinity Lake. FR 123 is gravel and follows Fall Creek for 5 miles to a junction where FR 123 ends. Here at the junction, take FR 129. In 2 more miles there is another junction. Turn right. Now the road gets steeper, narrower, and rougher, but it can be negotiated by a small sedan.

The road eventually climbs out of Fall Creek. Most problematic is the switchback ascent across the face of Peak 9,037. Snowslides from the winter sometimes block the pass here until mid- or even late July. Views are dramatic as you reach the pass at 8,500 feet. Especially intriguing is nearby Trinity Mountain. At 9,451 feet, it is the highest mountain in the area. On its top is a fire tower, one of the highest in Idaho. This mountain will dominate your view for most of the hike.

From the pass, descend to a number of pretty lakes with motorized campgrounds. It is 2 miles from the pass to the campground and trailhead at Big Trinity Lake. The main road continues on, eventually leading to Featherville, an alternative but longer route to the Trinity Mountain area. GPS: N43 37.50' / W115 25.52'

**Parking and trailhead facilities:** The well-developed parking lot on the east side of Big Trinity Lake has an outhouse and room for about twenty vehicles but no potable water.

*Green Island Divide.* PHOTO BY LUKE KRATZ

## The Hike

Rainbow Lakes Trail is well signed and obvious as it leaves southward from the trailhead. It is open to foot traffic only—no horses or mountain bikes. There is no forage or room at the lakes for horses.

The trail climbs moderately up a mostly open slope with great views to the northwest of unnamed lesser peaks in the Trinity Mountain area. Wildflowers are exceptional from July to mid-August, with mountain sorrel especially prominent. The trail levels out and then makes a steep final climb to the divide into the Rainbow Lakes basin. From the divide, you immediately see Trinity Mountain and Green Island Lake 450 feet below.

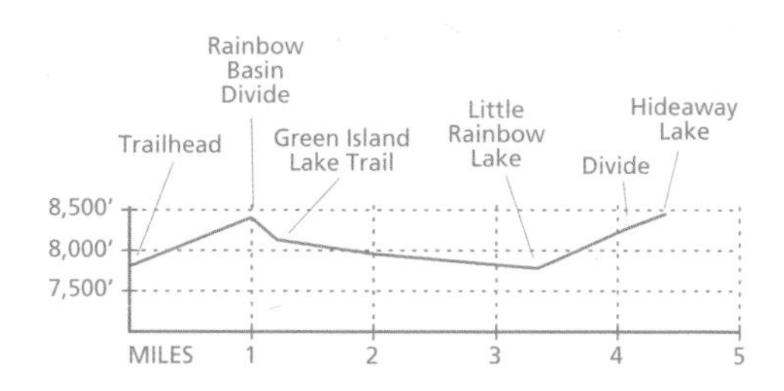

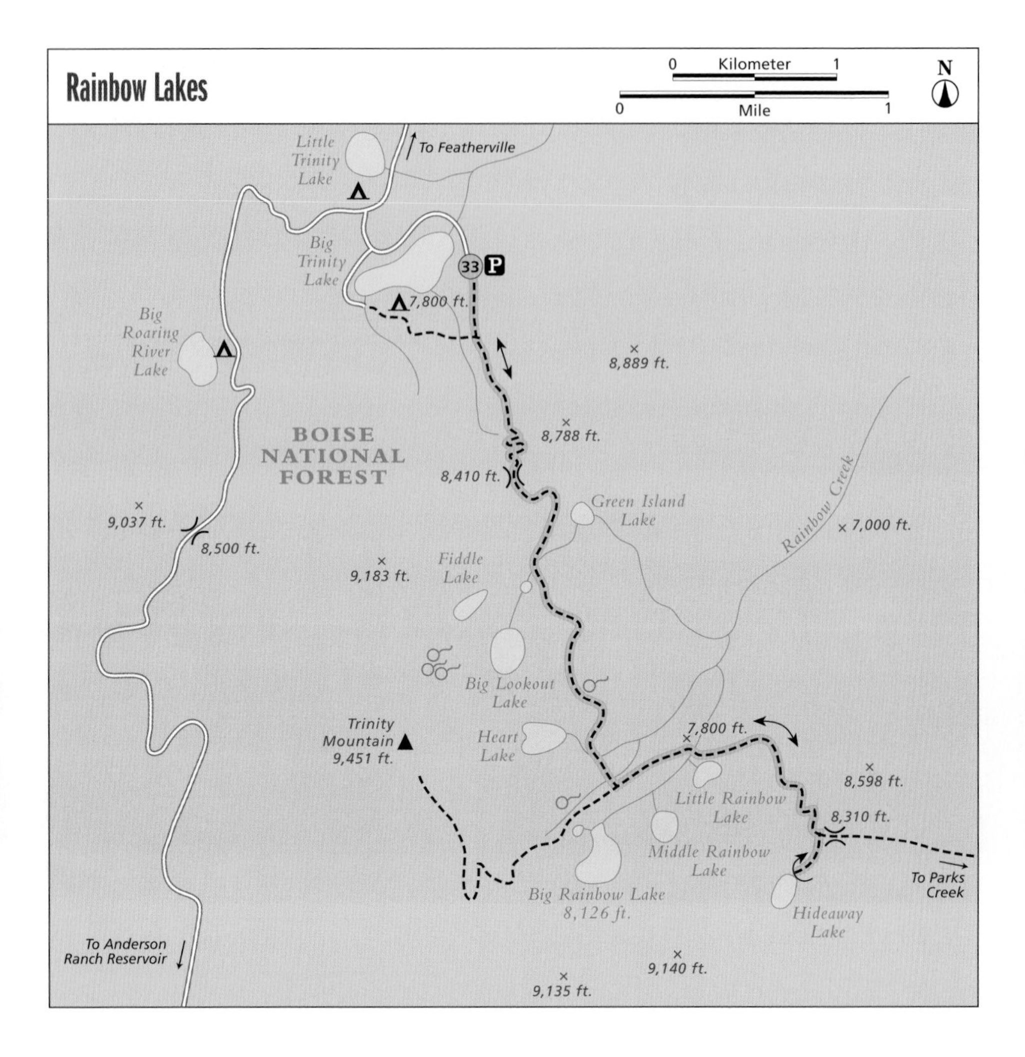


The trail switchbacks down into the basin and soon reaches the side trail leading down to Green Island Lake. This is the first of many such trails to the lakes. Except for this one, all are short climbs up to the lakes. The main trail passes directly by only one lake—Little Rainbow. The shortest side trail is to Little Lookout Lake.

Every lake is scenic, and all have small rainbow and brook trout, except Hideaway, which has far fewer, but bigger, rainbow trout.

A sign marks every side trail to every lake with an estimate of the distance to that lake. All creeks have good log bridges. The main trail is well maintained to Little Rainbow Lake, after which the quality of tread and frequency of maintenance decline.

After passing Little Rainbow Lake and then two ponds, which are not on the topo quad, the trail fades but is quite easy to find. Soon you climb steeply to the divide between the Rainbow Lakes basin and Parks Creek. One steep section harbors a snow patch well into July.

At the divide, a faint trail proceeds down the left side of meadowy Parks Creek. The trail to Hideaway, on the other hand, is more obvious and climbs steeply right up the ridge to the south (topped by Peak 8,916). Follow this steep trail for about 0.2 mile; it then swerves just to the right of the ridge and leads into the basin that holds Hideaway Lake. There is an unmapped pond just below Hideaway and a creek between the two.

**Options:** The side trail to Big Rainbow Lake (8,126 feet) continues past the lake and on to Trinity Mountain, where it joins the road to the lookout at 9,300 feet elevation.

—Ralph Maughan

## Miles and Directions

**0.0** Trailhead (7,790 feet)

**1.0** Rainbow Basin Divide (8,410 feet)

**1.3** Green Island Lake Trail (8,150 feet)

**3.5** Little Rainbow Lake; basin low point (7,790 feet)

**4.2** Rainbow Basin and Parks Creek Divide (8,340 feet)

**4.5** Hideaway Lake (8,420 feet)

# Hells Canyon

Many claim that Hells Canyon is the deepest gorge on earth. Some hold that it is "merely" the deepest gorge in North America. However, relief and exposure are only one aspect of the precarious balance of Hells Canyon and the surrounding glacier-carved canyon country that reaches west to Oregon and Washington's Blue Mountains and east to Idaho's Little Salmon River Valley: In terms of geologic, botanic, scenic, ecological, and historical significance, the Hells Canyon country is a story unto itself.

The Hells Canyon ecosystem rests at the geographic heart of the vast Columbia River basin. It is literally the hub of the wheel in terms of the large wildland and ecosystem complexes in the Pacific Northwest. Its wildlands are a veritable conduit for genetic interchange, including the migration of large mammals, throughout the region.

In the era before full occupation by settlers (a mere 125 years ago), the Hells Canyon environs were home to the Joseph band of the Nez Perce tribe, led in its latter years by the renowned Chief Joseph. In modern times, the native civilization is not to be found in Hells Canyon. (The Nez Perce tribe was driven out in 1877 by the US Cavalry in one of the saddest chapters in Native American history.) Yet artifacts and homesites remain. The Hells Canyon country is identified as one of the most significant archaeological sites in the American West. Part of the area is designated as a National Archaeological Sensitivity Area.

The canyon bottom is a furnace of inversion-induced heat in summer: lower in elevation, warmer, and climatically isolated from the cold, snow-mantled upland regions. At the floor of Hells Canyon, 100 miles of the Snake River is still free flowing, 67 of which are designated under the National Wild and Scenic Rivers Act. This section of river represents the largest watercourse still in a predominantly wilderness condition in the lower forty-eight states. Including the adjoining Wallowa Mountains in Oregon, well over a million acres of roadless land remain, about half of which is designated wilderness. Most of these protective classifications are a result of the 1975 Hells Canyon National Recreation Area Act, which established the 652,000-acre Hells Canyon National Recreation Area (HCNRA) in recognition of the need to protect the unique and irreplaceable values of Hells Canyon.

Wildlife is diverse and abundant, mainly due to the diversity of vegetation and climate in a relatively concentrated area and also because of the predominantly wild character of the landscape. In addition to supporting one of the two largest elk herds in North America, this is the habitat of a healthy predator population: a wide variety of hawks and other birds of prey, including ospreys and bald and golden eagles, which winter in the depths of the canyon. Peregrine falcons have been reestablished on the canyon's west rim. Relatively large numbers of predatory mammals exist, including black bears, cougars, martens, and fishers. There have even been sightings of grizzly bears in the Lord Flat area on the Oregon side. (These were thought to have been extinct in Oregon for more than fifty years.) In recent years wolves may have crossed from Idaho into Oregon by way of Hells Canyon.

Endangered salmon and steelhead, greatly diminished from historic levels, retain a precarious hold despite interference from numerous downstream impoundments and habitat degradation from logging and livestock grazing. Good potential for increased anadromous fish runs exists, provided the habitat is maintained. In addition, prehistoric giant white sturgeon also inhabit the Snake River. A variety of other rare or infrequent species, such as the great gray owl, bighorn sheep, and Franklin's grouse, find a haven in Hells Canyon.

Despite the bounty, grace, and unique features of Hells Canyon, the rush to consume and develop it has been almost overwhelming. The latter-day struggles that have taken place over the fate of these lands have been nearly as hard fought and bitter as the wars between the Nez Perce and the US Cavalry. The initial controversies began in the late 1950s and raged over the "use" and "ownership" of the Hells Canyon country. Conservationists, recreationists, and Native Americans engaged the hydro and resort developers and timber companies in administrative and legal skirmishes.

The timber companies covet the old-growth ponderosa pine, while the hydro developers had varying visions of huge dams that would have flooded the remainder of the free-flowing Snake. The proposed sites of these dams are still in evidence via painted inscriptions imposed high on the canyon walls. They remain as a reminder to those who were involved in the initial controversies of the narrowly avoided doom, which culminated with the passage of the Hells Canyon National Recreation Area Act.

The act protected 67 miles of the Snake River and 26 miles of the Rapid River from dams as well as designated 194,000 acres of wilderness. It also set restrictions on developmental activities among goals aimed at protecting and maintaining the myriad natural phenomena within the 652,000-acre HCNRA. Yet while the victory of 1975 was tremendous, the controversy is far from over. The forest service, entrusted with management of the HCNRA, has instead instigated enthusiastic programs of timber extraction, motorized recreation, and livestock grazing within the HCNRA, ignoring the stewardship obligation of the HCNRA Act.

These timbering, livestock, and motorization priorities in the HCNRA have completely overshadowed the pursuit of legislatively mandated goals for protection of fish, wildlife, wilderness, scenic, and unique ecological values. Logging and road-building projects in the HCNRA are concentrated in the most critical strongholds of ecological integrity.

Unfortunately, the prospect looms of having to "reprotect" what was presumed protected when the HCNRA Act was passed. Current management practices in the HCNRA have inspired litigation and calls for new legislation. Discussion of legislative proposals is proceeding. Chief among alternative proposals is the application of National Park and Preserve status, an option that could more fully protect the area and still allow traditional activities such as hunting to continue. This option would entrust management of the Hells Canyon ecosystem to the national park service instead of to the forest service.

The Hells Canyon Preservation Council (HCPC), formed in 1965 to preserve the qualities that define the deepest gorge on earth and its surrounding terrain, continues the effort to keep Hells Canyon intact. For additional information regarding Hells Canyon, or to become part of this nonprofit organization, please contact the HCPC. (See Appendix A.)

—Ric Bailey, executive director, Hells Canyon Preservation Council

# 34 Rapid River

This is a deep, dramatic canyon with a crystal-clear stream. It is hikable for three seasons of the year. Rapid River is a unit of the National Wild and Scenic Rivers System.

**Start:** 29 road miles north of New Meadows and 4 road miles south of Riggins
**Type of hike:** Day hike to long backpack; out-and-back, unless you do a long backpack. Long backpacking loops are possible
**Distance:** From 1 or 2 miles to 40 miles
**Approximate hiking time:** 1 hour to several days
**Difficulty:** Easy to strenuous
**Best season:** May and September for the first 10 miles of the canyon
**Trail surface:** Normal dirt and rock
**Land status:** Hells Canyon National Recreation Area; Nez Perce National Forest
**Canine compatibility:** Not allowed in wilderness area
**Fees and permits:** None
**Maps:** Heavens Gate Lake USGS quadrangle for the day hike. He Devil, Old Timer Mountain, Polluck Mountain, and Purgatory Saddle USGS quadrangles for longer trips
**Trail contact:** Hells Canyon National Recreation Area, (208) 628-3916, www.fs.usda.gov/wallawallawhitman; Salmon River Ranger District Slate Creek Ranger Station (208) 839-2211
**Special considerations:** Watch out for poison ivy and rattlesnakes in the lower canyon.

This canyon is hikable, at least in its lower portion, from mid-March to mid-November. However, due to its low elevation, it can be a furnace in the summer. A hike during a dry winter also seems possible. However, the presence of ice in the shadows would make slipping and tumbling over a cliff very possible. The orientation of the canyon makes for very little direct sunlight in winter.

There are no places to camp until you reach the West Fork and go up it a little way. The main fork widens near Rattlesnake Creek, about 5.5 miles in.

The crossings are bridged for a long way upriver, but they do wash out. Check with the Slate Creek Ranger District for current bridge and other trail information.

**Finding the trailhead:** Drive north from New Meadows on US 95 for 29 miles, or south from Riggins on the same highway for 4 miles. Turn onto the paved road to the Rapid River fish hatchery. The hatchery, owned by the Idaho Power Company, is 3 miles up the river, at the end of the road. GPS: N45 21.14' / W116 23.92'
**Parking and trailhead facilities:** Park at the top of the loop road into the fish hatchery. There is room on the shoulder of the road for about four vehicles in the sun, which is very hot in the summer.

## The Hike

This is a three-season paradise. In the spring everything is green, and there are many wildflowers on slopes that will become brown in the summer heat. In mid-September the foliage begins to turn in this mixed deciduous-conifer forest.

You can walk approximately 11 miles (with little elevation gain or loss) along the main fork of the Rapid River without getting your feet wet, because bridges have been thoughtfully placed everywhere the trail crosses the river. The trail is closed to motor vehicles, too, although some of the side trails far up the canyon are open to machines.

The trail climbs about 200 feet up the right side of the canyon from the fish hatchery road instead of leading directly up the canyon along the streamside. After about 0.75 mile the trail drops down to the stream. This canyon is very scenic from the start, so even a short hike is worthwhile. Most people only go up the canyon for a couple of miles, but you can easily spend a week on a big backpacking loop if you care to.

Within the first mile, the trail enters a strikingly narrow canyon. If you hike this area in the spring, look to the high cliffs for white-throated swifts. These swallow-size birds with white gorgets (throats) are such adept aviators that their habitat is listed as "open sky." Swifts are known to mate in flight. If you look intently, you can see their acrobatics high in the blue, cloud-brushed skies.

At about 1.5 miles the trail crosses the Rapid River. Another 1.5 miles after the crossing, you'll enter a unique area, for here there grows a tree called the Pacific yew. The yew is a special evergreen because its trunk is red and smooth and divides into thick auxiliary branches more like a proper maple or sycamore than an evergreen. This yew provides great shade with its thick, dark green foliage. The Pacific yew is decidedly out of its normal seaboard range here in Idaho; this grove marks the farthest place east it has managed to call home.

One mile farther upstream, the trail again crosses the river. Just 0.5 mile past here, the trail forks to the West Fork of Rapid River. The West Fork is also part of the Wild and Scenic Rivers System. This trail leads you in about 3 miles to a ranch. Go another 5 miles or so, and you will come to the toe of the Seven Devils Peaks and the Idaho side of the Hells Canyon Wilderness.

About 1.5 miles upstream of the West Fork confluence, the canyon widens. Side streams are frequent throughout the hike and become more numerous the farther upstream you go.

By continuing up the main fork of Rapid River, you'll find two trails (Dutch Oven Creek and Wyant Creek) that exit to the west in the next 3 miles past the West Fork. After these trails (which may or may not be maintained), the main trail crosses the Rapid River near Castle Creek and then doubles back to the west side of Copper Creek. There are bridges at these crossings.

As you walk along the Rapid River in the springtime, keep your eyes open for herds of wintering deer and elk. During the spring, these herds have often been seen

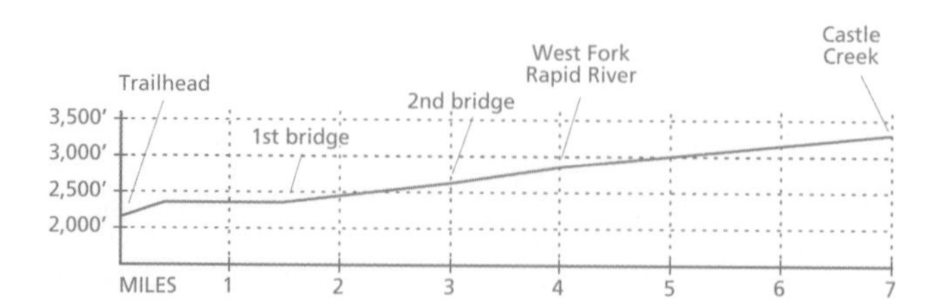

*Rapid River.* PHOTO BY LUKE KRATZ

above the main trail on the high grassy slopes. In the winter and spring, when confined to the canyon, the animals are highly susceptible to disturbance. Make a special effort not to bother them.

The trail stays on the west side of the Rapid River for 2 more miles to where it parallels Paradise Cabin. Here it crosses the river again. You have about 1.5 miles of trail left before you hit Frypan Creek, which flows down into the canyon from the east. At this point, it is necessary either to ford the Rapid River or to do a 1.5-mile cross-country hike on high ground. The ford can be difficult in high-water season.

There are many loop routes you can do once you get about 2 miles and more beyond the ford. One such loop goes to the source of the Rapid River and back along North Star Trail. Another climbs toward the Seven Devils following the Black Lake Fork of the Rapid River.

The Rapid River Wild and Scenic River Corridor, including the West and Main Forks, is 26.8 miles long and 0.5 mile wide. It was designated as Wild and Scenic as

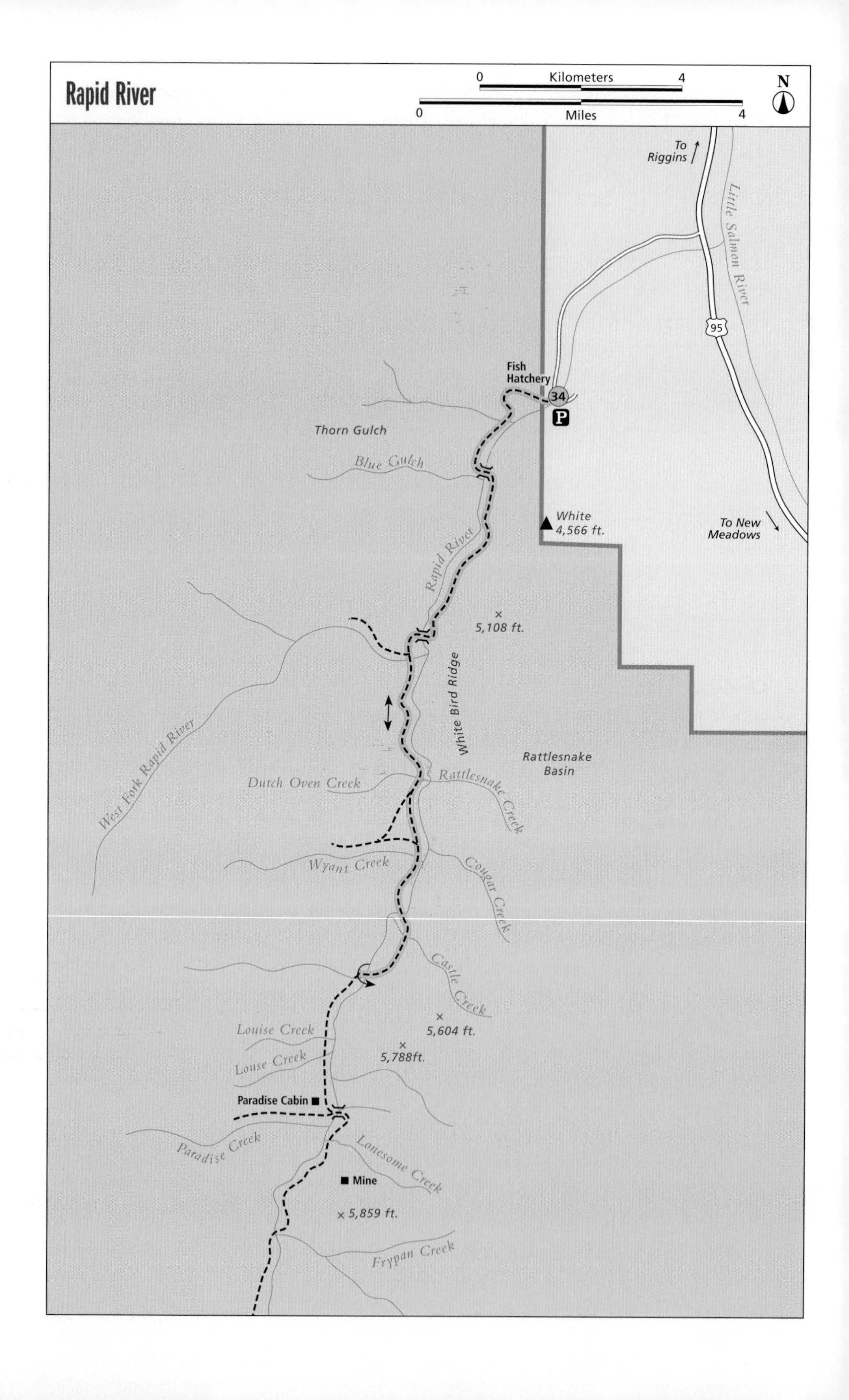
Rapid River
0
Kilometers
4
0
Miles
4
N
To Riggins
Little Salmon River
95
Fish Hatchery
34
P
Thorn Gulch
Blue Gulch
White 4,566 ft.
To New Meadows
Rapid River
5,108 ft.
White Bird Ridge
West Fork Rapid River
Rattlesnake Basin
Dutch Oven Creek
Rattlesnake Creek
Wyant Creek
Cougar Creek
Castle Creek
5,604 ft.
Louise Creek
5,788ft.
Louse Creek
Paradise Cabin
Paradise Creek
Lonesome Creek
Mine
5,859 ft.
Frypan Creek

part of the congressional legislation that created the Hells Canyon National Recreation Area (HCNRA) in 1975. However, the land surrounding the corridor was not officially protected. Logging remains a threat.

The canyon is still wild enough to have been at least eyed by the forest service for inclusion as wilderness in the HCNRA. The Rapid River flows into the Little Salmon River to its east to mix waters with the main Salmon and eventually the Snake River. The fish hatchery near its mouth is a good indication that dams do ruin fish runs. Construction of Idaho Power's Brownlee, Oxbow, and Hells Canyon Dams on the Snake River in the 1950s and 1960s exterminated the salmon runs in the upper Snake River. To make amends and undo the destruction, Idaho Power was required to work with the Idaho Department of Fish and Game to build the hatchery to restock the world-famous chinook salmon run. The Rapid River's Wild and Scenic status was granted partially to protect this hatchery.

Although some tourist manuals claim that the hatchery is a success, all of the wild salmon runs in Idaho today are listed as threatened or endangered. This is mostly due to the four dams on the Lower Snake River in Washington State that were built after the Hells Canyon Dam.

When I first visited this canyon in 1992, it was the clearest stream I had ever seen. I rehiked part of the trail in September 2000. The stream was very clear, but it didn't seem quite as transparent.

**Options:** There are many options, although none come early in the hike. Many people go up the West Fork of the Rapid River. There are many side trails as you continue up the main fork. By combining them, you can hike up into the Hells Canyon Wilderness using part of Seven Devils Loop (see Hike 35, Seven Devils Loop) and then descending the West Fork of the Rapid River. This is a loop of perhaps 40 miles with a tremendous elevation gain and loss. Needless to say, it is very strenuous.

—Jerry Dixon; rehiked by Ralph Maughan

## Miles and Directions

**0.0** Trailhead (2,190 feet)

**0.5** Trail enters canyon on cliffs above the river (2,400 feet)

**1.5** First bridge (2,360 feet)

**3.0** Second bridge (2,640 feet)

**4.0** West Fork of Rapid River (2,710 feet)

**7.0** Castle Creek (3,380 feet)

# 35 Seven Devils Loop

Circumnavigate the rugged and well-named Seven Devils Mountains. This 25-mile-plus loop offers magnificent views into Hells Canyon with some thirty lakes and abundant wildlife.

**Start:** 17 miles west (and far above) Riggins, in the Hells Canyon Wilderness
**Type of hike:** Backpack loop
**Distance:** 29 miles round-trip. This includes side mileage to Dry Diggins fire lookout and Echo, Baldy, and Lower Cannon Lakes.
**Approximate hiking time:** 4–7 days plus
**Difficulty:** Strenuous
**Best season:** Mid-July–mid-September
**Trail surface:** Normal dirt and rock
**Land status:** Hells Canyon National Recreation Area and wilderness
**Canine compatibility:** Not allowed within wilderness
**Fees and permits:** None
**Maps:** He Devil and Heavens Gate USGS quadrangles; Hells Canyon National Recreation Area map
**Trail contact:** Hells Canyon National Recreation Area, (208) 628-3916, www.fs.usda.gov/wallawallawhitman
**Special considerations:** Lots of elevation gain and loss. To camp by a lake usually means a 400-foot, 1-mile climb off the main trail.

**Finding the trailhead:** The access road climbs 5,400 feet in 17 miles. From US 95 just south of Riggins, take the signed FR 517 on the right (west), which leads to the Seven Devils. This road is oiled to control dust for 5 miles to the national forest boundary. At the boundary, it becomes a gravel road, but the last 7 miles are rough, with much embedded rock. It requires high clearance but not four-wheel drive. It is not an acceptable road for trailers or RVs. GPS: N45 20.96' / W116 30.75'
**Parking and trailhead facilities:** The trailhead is located at Windy Saddle Campground, but Seven Devils Campground (0.5 mile farther) is nicer and has more cover; there are ten units at Seven Devils and five at Windy Saddle. No water.

## The Hike

This is an excellent loop hike because each day offers fine views and each night a lake to camp by. The terrain is rugged with a good deal of elevation loss and gain.

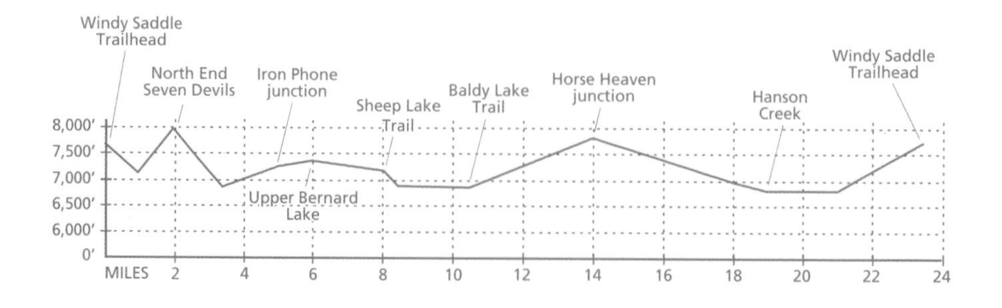

*The Seven Devils Mountains.* PHOTO BY LUKE KRATZ

The Seven Devils create their own weather as storms sweep off Lord Flat on the Oregon side of Hells Canyon and recirculate over these pinnacled mountains. The west side is where one encounters the fiercest weather, including hailstorms.

Hells Canyon is visible from points on the west side of the range. It is approximately 8,000 feet deep, measuring from the top of the Seven Devils to the canyon bottom. The Hells Canyon National Recreation Area Act established the 223,000-acre Hells Canyon Wilderness. Although inclusion of the Seven Devils proper in the wilderness was never contested, privately owned domestic sheep grazing on federal land here have passed a fatal disease on to wild bighorn sheep. On the Oregon side, the beautiful Lord Flat, visible during much of this hike, is still under threat from logging and road building.

There is scarring from forest fires that have burned in the past on or near the loop, most extensively near the head of the Rapid River.

I recommend doing the loop counterclockwise, saving the easiest part (Lower Cannon Lake to the trailhead) for last and taking the toughest part (Windy Saddle to Bernard Lakes) first.

The trail starts by dropping 480 feet through forest into the East Fork of the Sheep Creek Valley. It then climbs 1,000 feet to cross the northern spur of the Seven Devils range. Here you can look back and see the Heavens Gate lookout at 8,407 feet. As the trail skirts west and then south, it drops 1,300 feet to a log crossing at the West Fork of Sheep Creek. In this section, the Devils Tooth monolith dominates the weird and wild-looking terrain. The trail goes west, contouring the head of the West Fork for approximately 1 mile, then climbs yet again for 400 feet to Iron Phone junction. So far you have covered 5 miles but climbed some 1,200 feet.

Portions of the old downed telephone line still lie abandoned near the four-way Iron Phone junction. Most people take Sheep Lake Trail on the extreme left, which leads into the heart of the Seven Devils and to a cluster of six lakes. Sheep Lake Trail also forks in 0.5 mile to lead on the right (west) to Hibbs Cow Camp, where you'll pick up the continuation of the loop described here.

However, to see Hells Canyon from Dry Diggins fire lookout, continue straight ahead on the trail to the Bernard Lakes. It is a little over a mile, and 300 feet in elevation gain, to the second of the Bernard Lakes. Just past this lake is a lily-covered pond. Here, keep to the right in a confusing and unsigned web of trails. This will lead you up 500 feet and another 0.25 mile to the lookout. The Snake River and Hells Canyon lie 6,500 feet below in a sloping descent through forest and old burns. You may also see mountain goats.

Back down on the main trail, continue to your right (south) for a little over a mile through open then sparsely wooded country. Do not take the trail on the left, which leads to Sheep Lake. Instead, continue for 0.3 mile to the signed Potato Hill and Little Granite Creek Trails above Hibbs Cow Camp. Stay to the left, which will put you on Potato Hill Trail and eventually the trail leading to Echo Lake. This part is confusing, but stay to the left and you'll be okay. The basic idea is to hug the toe of the range and not wander too far downhill into Little Granite Creek.

From the Dry Diggins lookout junction to the turnoff to Echo Lake is 2 miles. Little Granite Creek and others in Hells Canyon have seen massive forest fires in recent years. This forested lake is about 300 feet above and a rocky 0.5 mile from the main trail. Its rocky cirque basin is headed by the He Devil, at 9,393 feet the highest in the range.

Back on the main trail, it is about 1.5 miles to the cutoff trail to Baldy Lake. The trail drops 160 feet west through forest, then contours generally south to cross the southernmost fork of Little Granite Creek. It is a steep (500-foot), 1-mile climb to Baldy Lake, one of the more heavily used sites. Baldy Lake itself is splendid. Here you are able to see the He Devil, Mount Belial, the Devils Throne, and the Twin Imps. This country might remind you of the "Night on Bald Mountain" segment of Disney's classic *Fantasia*.

From this point to the Cannon Lakes, the trail is not heavily used. It is about 4.5 miles and 1,280 feet of elevation gain to the southern end of the range and the Horse Heaven junction. This is probably the most outstanding section of the loop because of the eagle's view as you head due south above timberline for almost the entire trek.

Once past Horse Heaven, you begin a slow, easy downhill walk. After you turn north, you're on Boise Trail. The aspect of the land changes dramatically as you descend into old-growth forest, and this looks like the good black bear habitat that it is. While there are many lakes on this side of the range, we found trails to only one. Although the USGS quad shows a trail to Dog Lake, we could not find it. It is another 7.5 miles to Hanson Creek. There is one trail (about 1 mile before Hanson Creek) that leads down to the Rapid River. Stay to the left, but consider the Rapid River hike as a possible, even larger loop for those who just can't get enough wild country.

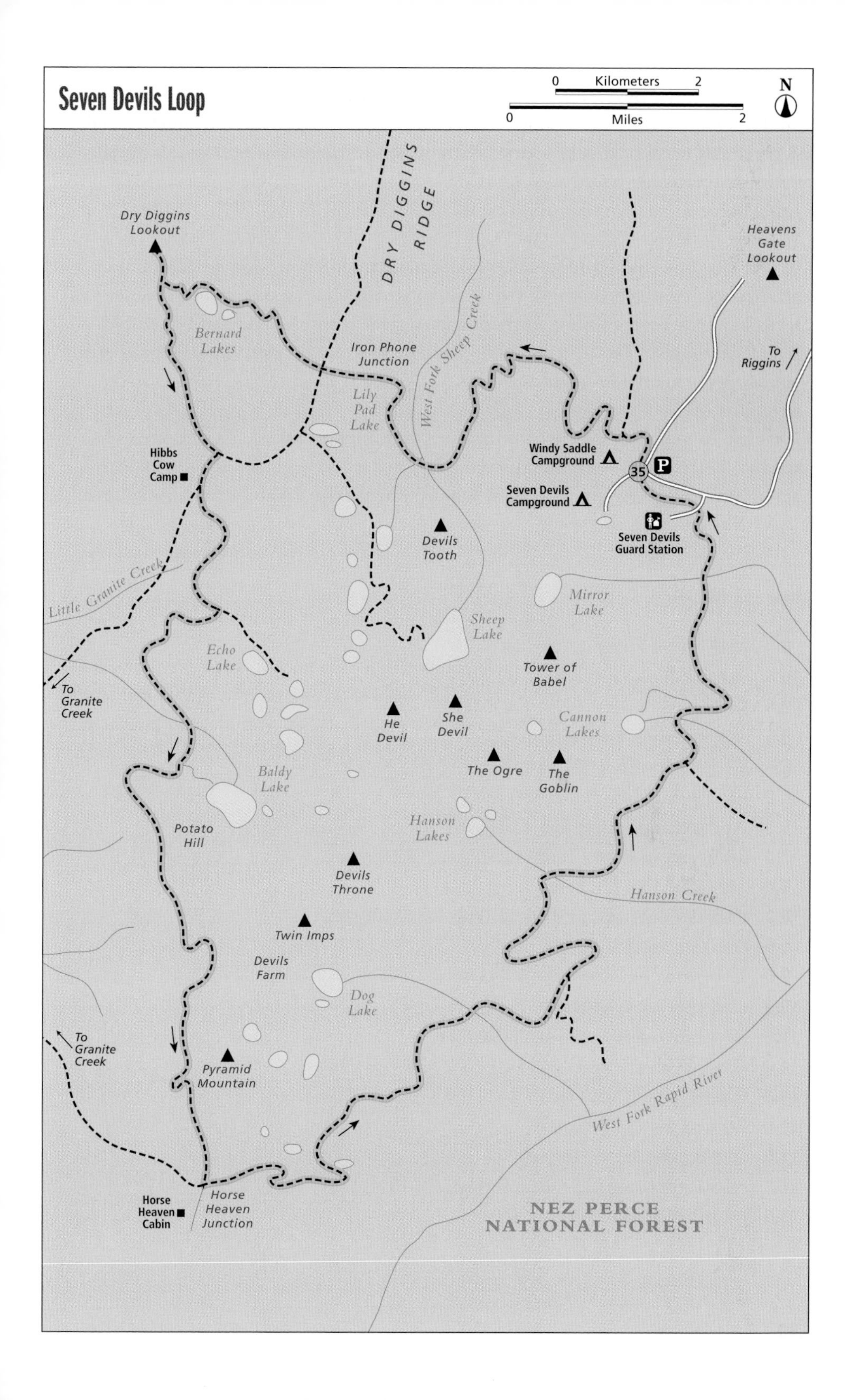
Seven Devils Loop
0 Kilometers 2
0 Miles 2
N
Dry Diggins Lookout
DRY DIGGINS RIDGE
Heavens Gate Lookout
Bernard Lakes
Iron Phone Junction
West Fork Sheep Creek
To Riggins
Lily Pad Lake
Hibbs Cow Camp
Windy Saddle Campground
35
P
Seven Devils Campground
Seven Devils Guard Station
Devils Tooth
Little Granite Creek
Mirror Lake
Sheep Lake
Echo Lake
Tower of Babel
To Granite Creek
He Devil
She Devil
Cannon Lakes
The Ogre
The Goblin
Baldy Lake
Potato Hill
Hanson Lakes
Devils Throne
Hanson Creek
Twin Imps
Devils Farm
Dog Lake
To Granite Creek
Pyramid Mountain
West Fork Rapid River
Horse Heaven Cabin
Horse Heaven Junction
NEZ PERCE NATIONAL FOREST

Hanson Creek itself is not remarkable. The land is slumping and full of deadfall, and the creek is difficult to access. It is another easy 2 miles of contour through forest cover and occasional deep woods to the Cannon Lakes. The trail to this popular area leaves on the left (west) and climbs 240 feet in less than a mile to Lower Cannon Lake. The peaks surrounding the Cannon Lakes are the Goblin, the She Devil, and the Tower of Babel.

The hike from the Cannon Lakes to the trailhead is 2.5 miles, in good condition, and rises about 240 feet. For more than a decade, much of the trail work in the Seven Devils has been accomplished through annual service trips conducted by the Sierra Club. If you would like to participate in these adventures, contact the Sierra Club Outing Department. (See Appendix A.)

**Options:** To get a full view of this country, you might want to take Heaven's Gate Road to the Heaven's Gate fire lookout. The road is nicely graded for the first two-thirds but then is rocky, almost requiring four-wheel drive. From the end of the road, it is a 0.25-mile walk to the top.

—Jackie Johnson Maughan

## Miles and Directions

**0.0** Windy Saddle Trailhead (7,600 feet)
**0.8** East Fork Sheep Creek Trail (7,200 feet)
**2.0** Northern end of Seven Devils (8,000 feet)
**3.5** West Fork Sheep Creek (6,900 feet)
**5.0** Iron Phone junction (7,310 feet)
**6.0** Upper Bernard Lake (7,400 feet)
**6.5** Dry Diggins Fire Lookout Trail (7,560 feet)
**7.0** Dry Diggins fire lookout (1 mile round-trip) (7,828 feet)
**8.0** Sheep Lake Trail (7,310 feet)
**8.2** Hibbs Cow Camp and Little Granite Creek Trail (7,400 feet)
**8.5** Echo Lake Trail (6,920 feet)
**9.0** Echo Lake (1 mile round-trip) (7,243 feet)
**10.5** Baldy Lake Trail (6,880 feet)
**11.5** Baldy Lake (2 miles round-trip) (7,200 feet)
**14.0** Horse Heaven junction (7,840 feet)
**18.0** Rapid River Trail (7,014 feet)
**19.0** Hanson Creek (6,800 feet)
**21.0** Cannon Lakes Trail (6,800 feet)
**21.8** Lower Cannon Lake (1.5 miles round-trip) (7,320 feet)
**23.5** Return to trailhead

# Sawtooth Mountains

Perhaps the most famous mountains in Idaho, the Sawtooth Range rises abruptly on the west side of the beautiful and spacious Sawtooth Valley and nearby Stanley Basin. Near the southern end of the Sawtooth Valley, the Sawtooths give way to the Smoky Mountains, which then extend southward all the way to the Snake River Plain.

The core of the Sawtooth Range is composed of beautiful pink granite, which originated as a molten intrusion—a pluton—into the already emplaced igneous formation called the Idaho Batholith, which covers most of central Idaho. Unlike the mostly gray granitic rock of the Idaho Batholith, the Sawtooth Batholith is noted for its pink or even apricot color, the result of the high concentration of potassium feldspar (a granitic mineral) in the rock. The hard pink granite, sculpted into walls, peaks, and spires by ice age glaciers, is a mecca for climbers. Parts of this range indeed resemble sawteeth.

The 216,000-acre Sawtooth Wilderness protects the core of the Sawtooth Mountains and is Idaho's best-known designated wilderness area. Use of the east side of this fairyland of rock is heavy. The western side is relatively uncrowded, and the vast unprotected roadless country that adjoins it is virtually unused.

The entire wilderness is well served with good trails. Access to the trailheads is easy on the east side of the wilderness, which has all-weather gravel or paved roads with mostly well-developed trailheads. The west side, however, involves longer drives, mostly on dirt or gravel roads.

Anglers will discover more than 300 stunning alpine and subalpine lakes, 60 or so of which support fisheries. The most common game fish is the brook trout. Unfortunately, many of these brook trout populations consist only of small fish due to overpopulation and the inherent low productivity of these high, granite, rock-bound lakes.

Wildlife is varied, with most of the Rocky Mountain game species represented except grizzly bears. The Sawtooth Range is a stronghold for wolverines. Despite all the variety, however, the density of wildlife is low. The growing Idaho wolf population has found the White Cloud Mountains on the east side of the Sawtooth Valley more to its liking.

At the base of the Sawtooth Mountains are a number of large moraine-dammed lakes. Alturas, Pettit, Redfish, and Stanley Lake are the largest. Redfish Lake was named for the color of the tens of thousands of salmon returning to spawn in the lake and

*The jagged edge scenery of the Sawtooths.* PHOTO BY ANNE KRATZ

die. Sadly, dams on the Columbia River and the Snake River in Washington State have caused the extinction of many salmon runs, almost including the Snake River sockeye, which spawn in these lakes and adjacent creeks. The grimmest year was 1989, when just one sockeye salmon returned to Redfish Lake. (He was nicknamed "Lonesome Larry.") Since then, a very expensive effort to save the Snake River sockeye run from extinction has slowly resulted in a partial restoration of the run. Between 1991 and 1999, sixteen wild and seven hatchery-produced adults returned to Idaho. In the fall of 2000, 257 hatchery-produced adults had returned—making it the best sockeye return for Idaho since 1977. The run won't be considered recovered until more than 2,000 fish a year return. 2010 and 2011 had good runs of over 1500, but declined in 2012 and are still not self-sustaining.

Adjacent to the Sawtooth Wilderness west, northwest, and south is 320,000 acres of unprotected de facto wilderness. Outdoor lovers want to add it to the Sawtooth Wilderness, increasing the size of the protected country to 536,000 acres. This would be one of America's biggest wildernesses. A considerable portion of this country to the west and southwest (including part of the existing Sawtooth Wilderness) burned in the Rabbit Creek Fire of 1994, and more burned in the Trail Creek Fire of 2000. There is no timber resource left to cut, and due to the low growth rate of trees in these mountain lands, there never was one unless the logging was fueled by taxpayer subsidies.

The Sawtooth Wilderness is part of the larger Sawtooth National Recreation Area (SNRA), which also gives protection to the pastoral beauty of the Sawtooth Valley and the Stanley Basin. The act of Congress that created the SNRA in 1972 also gives limited protection to the wild character of the White Cloud and Boulder mountain ranges, which lie on the SNRA's east and southeast sides. In recent years, however, the SNRA has suffered from lack of funding. One result is a charge to hike at almost all trailheads. You can purchase a pass for several days or, for just a bit more, for the entire season.

—Ralph Maughan

# 36 Alpine Creek

This is a short hike that takes you to outstanding Sawtooth mountain scenery and cross-country access to many alpine lakes.

**Start:** 40 miles north of Ketchum in the extreme southern end of the Sawtooth Wilderness
**Type of hike:** Day hike; out-and-back, with opportunities for vast backcountry scrambling
**Distance:** 6 miles round-trip
**Approximate hiking time:** 2–3 hours
**Difficulty:** Moderately easy
**Best season:** July–September
**Trail surface:** Normal dirt and rock
**Land status:** Sawtooth Wilderness; Sawtooth National Recreation Area
**Canine compatibility:** Dogs must be leashed until after Labor Day.
**Fees and permits:** Depends on the year. Check with the forest service. Some years require a Sawtooth National Recreation Area (SNRA) trailhead fee. In addition, a free wilderness permit (available at the trailhead) is needed. Parties of eight or more must get a wilderness permit from the SNRA headquarters or the Stanley office of the SNRA.
**Maps:** Snowyside Peak USGS quadrangle; Fairfield and Ketchum Ranger Districts and Sawtooth National Recreation Area–Sawtooth National Forest map
**Trail contact:** Sawtooth National Recreation Area, (208) 774-3000
**Special considerations:** No campfires allowed in the Alpine Creek drainage.

**Finding the trailhead:** From Ketchum, take ID 75 about 40 miles north to Alturas Lake Road. Or drive 21 miles south from Stanley on ID 75 to the turnoff for the road. The paved Alturas Lake Road takes you to large Alturas Lake after passing through 3 miles of meadow and forest. The pavement ends shortly after you reach the southwest side of this moraine lake (5 miles from ID 75). You arrive at Alpine Creek after 1.5 miles on the gravel road, which becomes fairly rough just before the trailhead. GPS: N43 53.88' / W114 54.22'
**Parking and trailhead facilities:** The trailhead has room for about ten vehicles in the shade and has a Sawtooth Wilderness information bulletin board. The trailhead also serves as the beginning of Alturas Creek Trail.

## The Hike

Here is a delightful, short trail into the Sawtooths The scenery is exquisite, although there are no lakes by the trailside. The trail is 3 miles long and not very steep, climbing only 500 feet, but it takes you a good distance into the jagged Sawtooth Mountains.

This is a good trail that leads uphill from the trailhead. You soon come to a registration box to obtain a Sawtooth Wilderness pass.

The trail at first wanders nearly level through a pine and fir forest. The going is very easy for 0.2 mile, until you begin a 300-foot climb to a shelf. From the shelf, you climb with ease around a granite knob (7,400 feet) and are immediately rewarded with a fine view of Alpine Creek's glaciated canyon, with rugged light gray peaks (9,000 feet plus) of the Sawtooth crest rising all along this wilderness hike. It's less

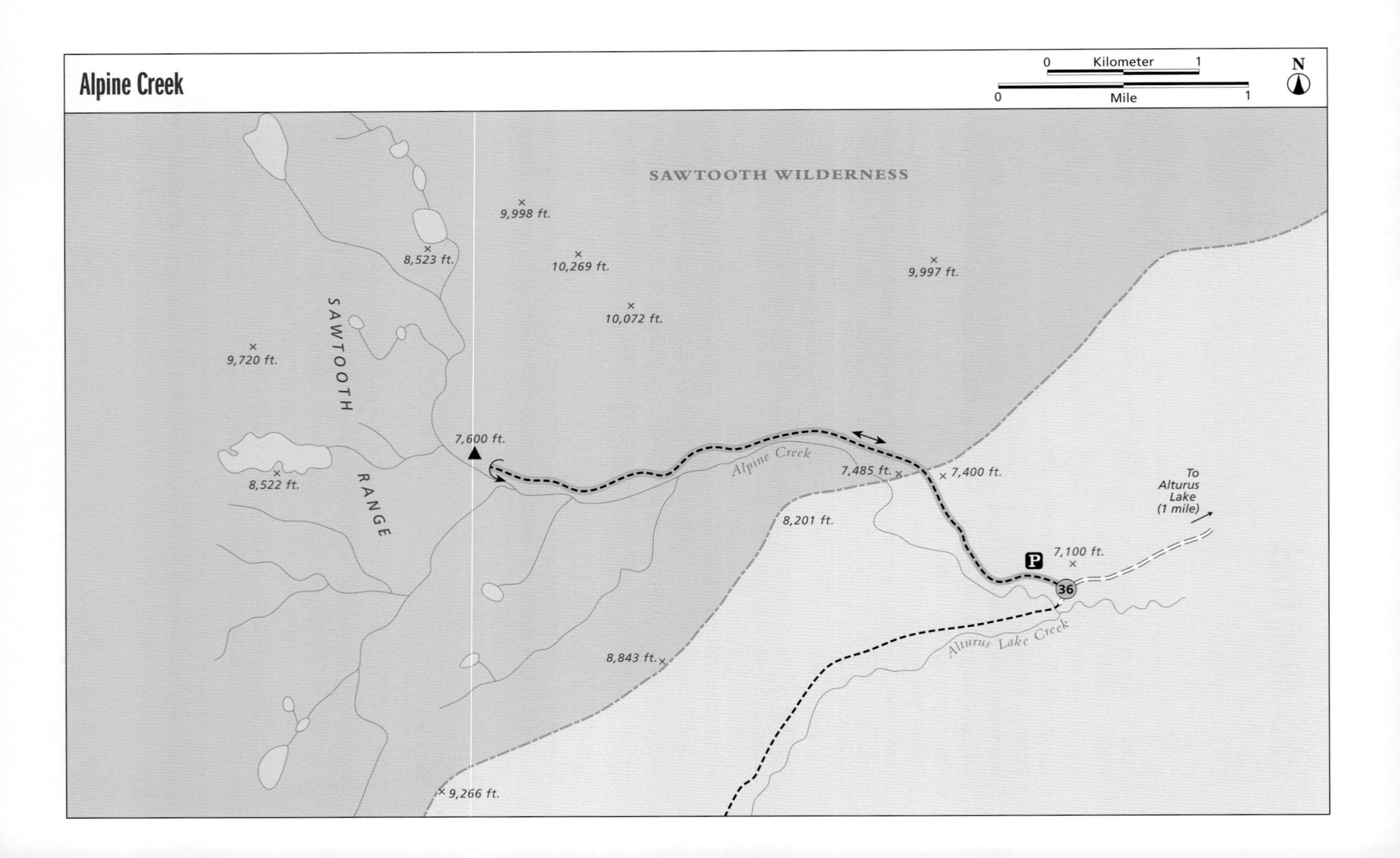
Alpine Creek
0
Kilometer
1
0
Mile
1
N
SAWTOOTH WILDERNESS
9,998 ft.
8,523 ft.
10,269 ft.
9,997 ft.
10,072 ft.
9,720 ft.
SAWTOOTH
RANGE
7,600 ft.
8,522 ft.
Alpine Creek
7,485 ft.
7,400 ft.
To
Alturus
Lake
(1 mile)
8,201 ft.
7,100 ft.
36
8,843 ft.
Alturus Lake Creek
9,266 ft.

than mile to this viewpoint entrance to the Alpine Creek Valley. For some, this viewpoint could mark the destination of the hike.

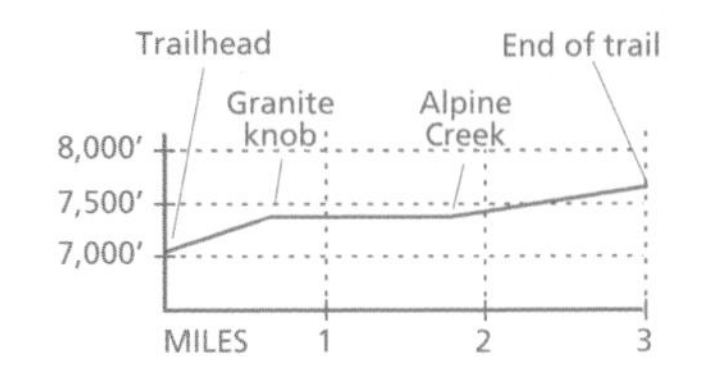


From here, the trail drops into some forest and quickly emerges again onto an open slope (kept that way by avalanches) of grass, wildflowers, and sagebrush. The trail wanders again into the forest and emerges in a large avalanche run near Alpine Creek.

In 1.75 miles the trail reaches the bank of Alpine Creek. It then climbs gradually through more timber and openings. If you lose the track, just keep to the slope where the going is relatively easy instead of getting down onto the often-wet valley floor.

Finally, about 3 miles from your vehicle, the trail ends beside the creek in a deep and boggy forest. Just beyond here, the valley ends. Three hanging tributaries lie above the main valley, each sheltering numerous trailless lakes. This portion of the wilderness is being managed to keep it in a trailless condition.

Most people who continue head for the largest lake (8,522 feet). There is a fishing route that you can follow for the 0.6 mile (and 900-foot climb) to this 0.5-mile-long lake. Many people hike up into this trailless area so, in fact, the routes are fairly clearly defined.

About forty-five lakes or ponds are situated in the headwaters of Alpine Creek. The larger lakes contain brook trout, but as with so many of the lakes in the Sawtooths, the trout are mostly small due to overpopulation and infertile waters.

**Options:** From the Alpine Creek Trailhead, you can also hike up Alturas Creek. This hike follows a former road that has been turned into a good trail. It is much different from the Alpine Creek hike in both length and environment, traveling through a large stream valley marking the boundary between the Sawtooth Mountains and the Smoky Mountains.

—Ralph Maughan

## Miles and Directions

**0.0** Trailhead (7,040 feet)

**0.7** Granite knob and viewpoint (7,400 feet)

**1.7** Trail descends to the bank of Alpine Creek (7,350 feet)

**3.0** End of the official trail (7,600 feet)

# 37 Bench Lakes

This is a beautiful ridgeline walk above Redfish Lake leading to five-plus lakes nestled below Mount Heyburn.

**Start:** Redfish Lake area 5 miles south of Stanley
**Type of hike:** Day hike or backpack; out-and-back
**Distance:** 4 miles to first lake
**Approximate hiking time:** 5–7 hours
**Difficulty:** Easy to moderate
**Best season:** Summer, fall
**Trail surface:** Sand along ridge to dirt and rock
**Land status:** Sawtooth Wilderness; Sawtooth National Recreation Area
**Canine compatibility:** Not allowed in wilderness.
**Fees and permits:** Depends on the year. Check with the forest service. Some years require a Sawtooth National Recreation Area (SNRA) trailhead fee. In addition, a free wilderness permit (available at the trailhead) is needed. Parties of eight or more must get a wilderness permit from the SNRA headquarters or the Stanley office of the SNRA.
**Maps:** Mt. Cramer and Stanley USGS quadrangles; Sawtooth National Recreation Area–Sawtooth National Forest map
**Trail contact:** Sawtooth National Recreation Area–Stanley Office, (208) 774-3000

**Finding the trailhead:** On ID 75 at 4.1 miles south of Stanley, turn at the sign for Redfish Lake. Follow this road until another sign indicates REDFISH TRAILHEAD. If you hit the lodge, you've gone too far. GPS: N44 8.84' / W114 55.19'
**Parking and trailhead facilities:** The parking lot generally fills up by midday with occasional overflow.

## The Hike

Park at the Redfish Trailhead and follow the path across the road to where the Fishhook Creek Trail begins. At 0.6 mile there is a junction with the Bench Lakes Trail. Turn left here and follow the trail across a bridge over Fishhook Creek. The trail winds up the ridge over Redfish Lake until it finally maintains a straight path parallel to the lake. This stretch is an enjoyable walk. On the right (west) are views of Sawtooth peaks: Mount Heyburn, Horstmann Peak, and the Grand Mogul. On the left (east) overlooking the deep blue Redfish Lake are views of Castle Peak and the White Clouds.

After nearly 2.5 miles you reach another junction with the Bench Lakes Trail. Head right here into the Sawtooth Wilderness, where you must obtain a permit. Begin the climb up the gentle switchbacks to the first lake. The waters are pristine with a more intimate view of the Sawtooth Peaks than normally encountered. The second lake is a mere stroll from the first. The third lake takes a little more time—the trail diminishes and you must follow its outflow. There is also a good-size fourth lake that can be reached by hiking 0.5 mile cross-country from the third. A fifth lake is

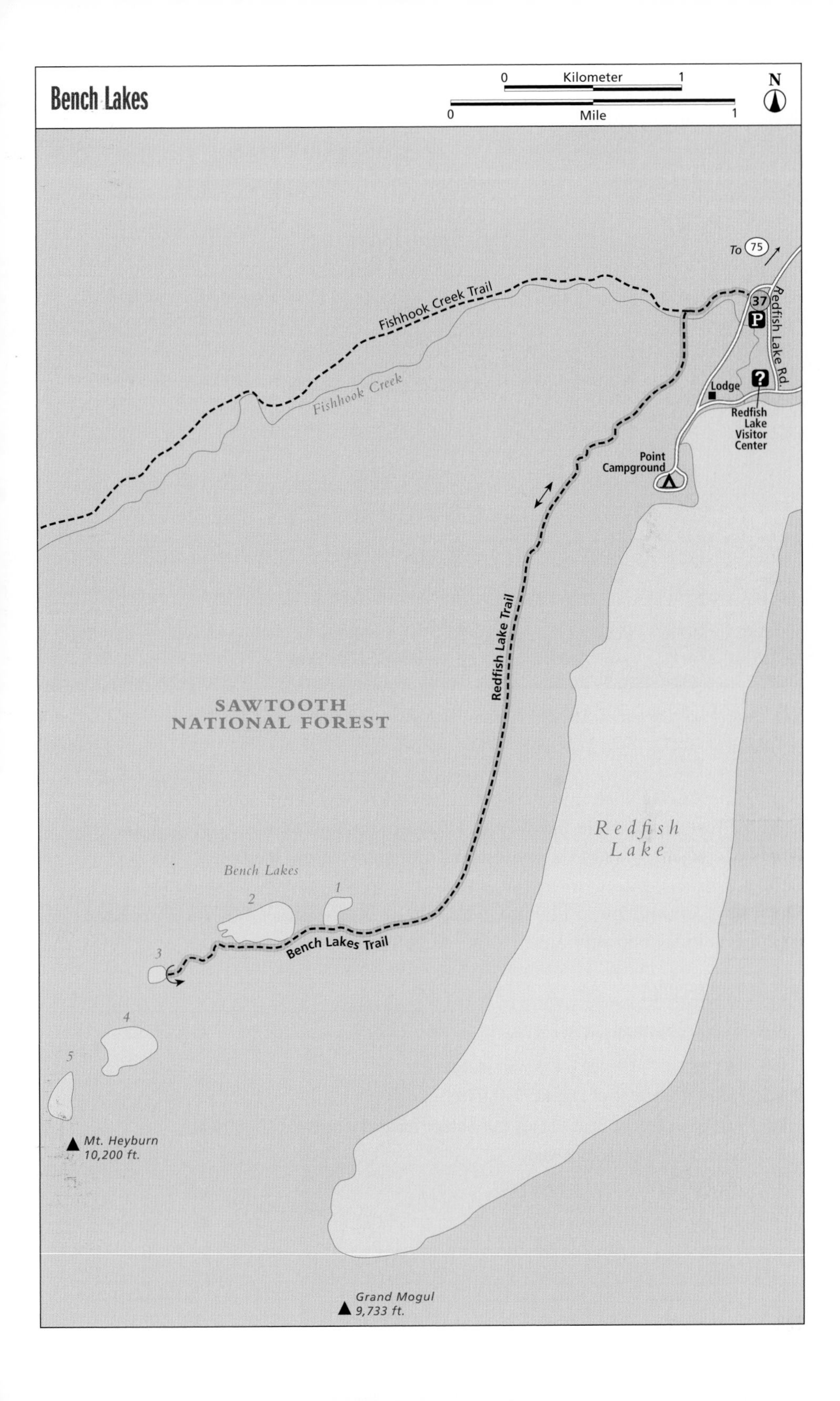

Bench Lakes
0 Kilometer 1
0 Mile 1
N
To 75
37
Redfish Lake Rd.
Fishhook Creek Trail
Fishhook Creek
Lodge
Redfish Lake Visitor Center
Point Campground
Redfish Lake Trail
SAWTOOTH NATIONAL FOREST
Redfish Lake
Bench Lakes
1
2
3
4
5
Bench Lakes Trail
Mt. Heyburn 10,200 ft.
Grand Mogul 9,733 ft.

*The First Bench Lake with Mt. Heyburn in the background.* PHOTO BY LUKE KRATZ

even farther, tucked high in the crags; this may take some climbing to access. These all lie at the base of the castle-like Mount Heyburn; this and McGown, Regan, and the Grand Mogul are some of the most scenic mountains in the state.

**Options:** Continue on Fishhook Creek Trail or Redfish Inlet Trail for more back-country multiday opportunities.

## Miles and Directions

**0.0** Redfish Lake Trailhead (6,600 feet)
**0.6** Turn right at the Bench Lakes trail junction
**1.1** Ridgeline above Redfish Lake (7,100 feet)
**3.5** Turn left at second Bench Lakes trail junction towards mountains (7,500 feet)
**3.7** Sawtooth Wilderness boundary
**4.0** The third Bench Lake (7,800) feet)

# 38 Iron Creek to Sawtooth Lake

Scenic Sawtooth Lake is the biggest lake inside the Sawtooth Mountains and makes for one of the most photographic backcountry scenes in Idaho.

**Start:** 6 miles west of Stanley
**Type of hike:** Long day hike or overnight backpack; out-and-back, but with many opportunities for extended hikes beyond Sawtooth Lake requiring a shuttle
**Distance:** 10 miles round-trip
**Approximate hiking time:** 4–5 hours
**Difficulty:** Moderate due to the climb
**Best season:** Late July–August
**Trail surface:** Normal dirt and rock
**Land status:** Sawtooth Wilderness
**Canine compatibility:** Not allowed in wilderness
**Fees and permits:** Depends on the year. Check with the forest service. Some years require a Sawtooth National Recreation Area (SNRA) trailhead fee. In addition, a free wilderness permit (available at the trailhead) is needed. Parties of eight or more must get a wilderness permit from the SNRA headquarters or the Stanley office of the SNRA.
**Maps:** Stanley Lake USGS quadrangle; Fairfield and Ketchum Ranger Districts and Sawtooth National Recreation Area–Sawtooth National Forest map
**Trail contact:** Sawtooth National Recreation Area Headquarters, (208) 774-3000
**Special considerations:** Campfires are not permitted. Weather at Sawtooth Lake can be harsh. The winds can really gather force as they whip across this 160-acre lake. Camping at the lake does environmental damage, so camp below or beyond Sawtooth Lake. Until after Labor Day, all dogs must be leashed.

**Finding the trailhead:** From Stanley, follow ID 21 northwestward, out of town, 2.6 miles to the Iron Creek Road turnoff. Drive 3.2 miles on this all-weather gravel, but often badly washboarded, road to the Iron Creek Transfer Camp. Here there is plenty of room to park, but expect to see many other vehicles because this is a popular hike. The trailhead also gives access to Alpine Way Trail. GPS: N44 11.92' / W115 0.85'
**Parking and trailhead facilities:** The trailhead is large with room for perhaps twenty vehicles. It has partial shade, a bulletin board, and a restroom.

## The Hike

Entire generations of photographers have packed their 35mm, 2.25-inch, and bulky view cameras with tripods the 4 miles, and 1,700 feet in elevation, to Sawtooth Lake, the largest alpine lake in the Sawtooth Mountains. Photographs of Sawtooth Lake reflecting 10,190-foot Mount Regan (usually taken from among the whitebark pine on the lake's northern end) have graced hundreds of calendars from that of the Sierra Club to the local feed-and-seed store.

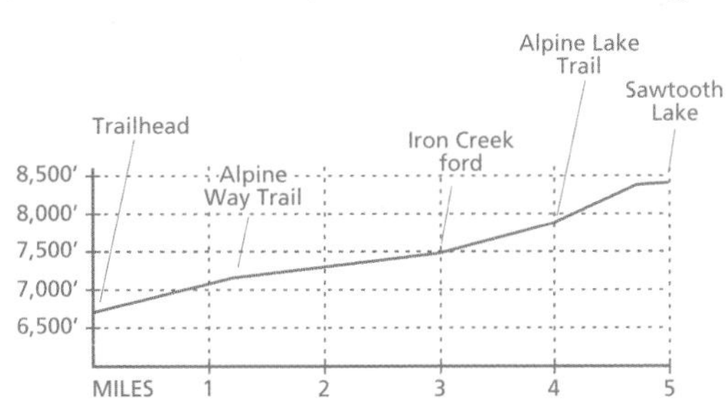

*Sawtooth (the largest lake in the SWA) and Mt. Regan.* PHOTO BY RALPH MAUGHAN

You can make the hike up and back in a day, camp overnight, or make this part of a much longer backpacking trip. Start by following the well-built trail for about a mile through a lodgepole-pine-covered flat to the Sawtooth Wilderness boundary. A short distance past the boundary, you meet Alpine Way Trail. Follow this trail to the right. Soon you cross a willowy meadow providing good views of the Sawtooth Mountains. In about 0.5 mile the trail to Sawtooth Lake leaves Alpine Way Trail at a right angle on the left. It heads away from the creek, makes a few switchbacks under large Douglas fir trees, and then climbs steadily until reaching a lovely subalpine avalanche meadow with a ford (until August) of Iron Creek. Just beyond the crossing the trail climbs steeply up a forested mountainside.

A side trail leading to Alpine Lake is reached at a ridgetop after a climb of about 300 feet in 0.5 mile. This trail to Alpine Lake is a bit hard to see, but the lake can be reached by walking cross-country should you miss it.

Alpine Lake is not an alpine lake. Subalpine fir surround it on three sides, framing the view of massive Alpine Peak on its south.

Continue now upward, switchbacking up the rising ridge that parallels Alpine Lake more than 100 feet below. It's a fine view from here. The grade flattens as you approach Sawtooth Lake, and you pass by a pond.

Your first view of Sawtooth Lake is the classic one. The trail forks here near the point overlooking the lake. The left fork heads over the crest of the range southward, and the right fork climbs to McGown Pass and the high-altitude McGown Lakes. All of this is magnificent country.

**Options:** One mile past your first view of Sawtooth Lake, you reach McGown Lake after an additional 400-foot climb. From here, you can continue down into Stanley Lake Creek and out at Stanley Lake for a long shuttle.

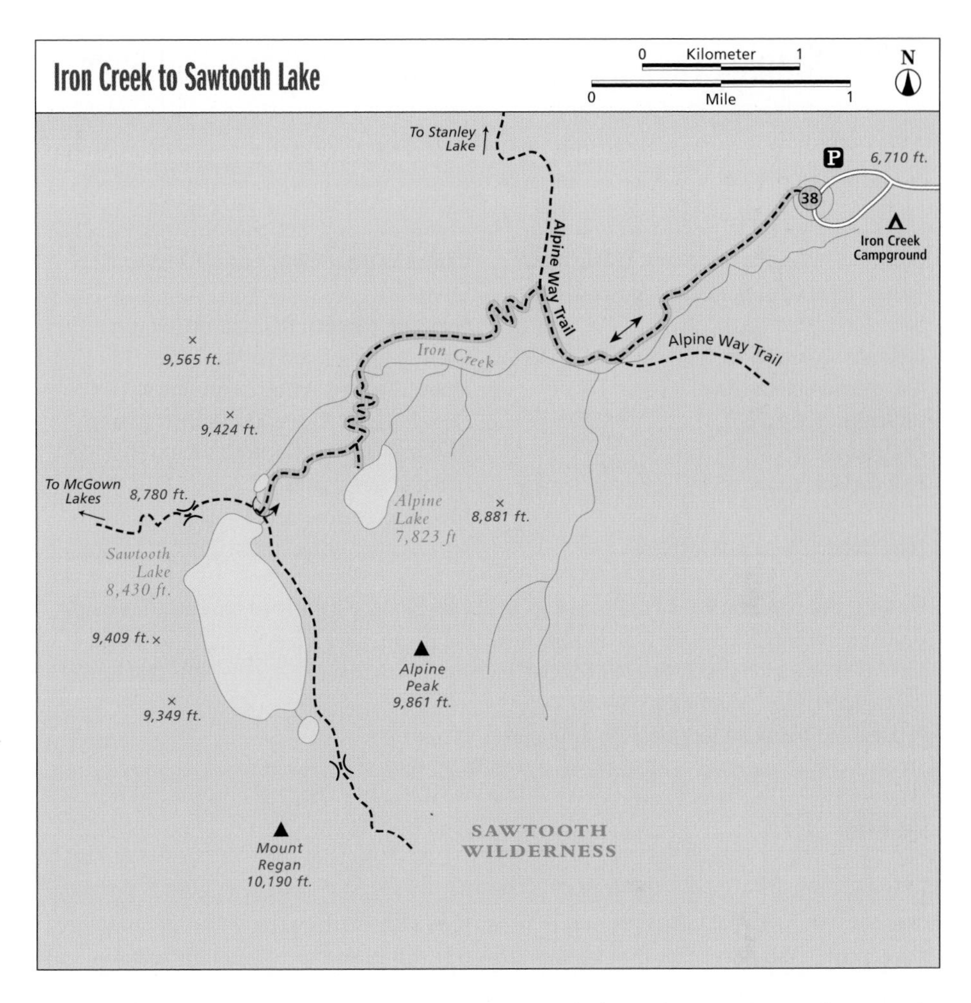


Another option is to follow the trail southward along the east shore of Sawtooth Lake. Just beyond Sawtooth Lake is another lake, right at the crest of the range. Beyond the crest, you head gently downhill, past three more lakes, until the trail drops steeply into the North Fork of Baron Creek. This leads eventually out of the wilderness on the west side of the Sawtooths at Grandjean, another long shuttle hike.

—Ralph Maughan

## Miles and Directions

**0.0** Iron Creek Trailhead (6,710 feet)
**1.2** Alpine Way Trail (7,200 feet)
**3.0** Iron Creek ford (7,490 feet)
**4.0** Alpine Lake side trail (7,823 feet)
**4.8** Pond just before Sawtooth Lake (8,410 feet)
**5.0** Sawtooth Lake (8,430 feet)

# 39 Stanley Lake Trail to Lady Face and Bridal Veil Falls

This trail offers gorgeous Sawtooth scenery and two very distinct waterfalls. Hikers of all ages and abilities will enjoy the trip.

**Start:** 3.5 miles from the Stanley Lake turnoff
**Type of hike:** Day hike or backpack; out-and-back
**Distance:** 6.4 miles round-trip
**Approximate hiking time:** 4 hours
**Difficulty:** Moderate
**Best seasons:** Summer, fall
**Trail surface:** Gravel at the beginning, turning to dirt and rock
**Land status:** Sawtooth Wilderness
**Canine compatibility:** Dogs on leash July 1-Labor Day
**Fees and permits:** Depends on the year. Check with the forest service.
**Maps:** Stanley Lake USGS quadrangle; Fairfield and Ketchum Ranger Districts and Sawtooth National Recreation Area-Sawtooth National Forest map
**Trail contact:** Sawtooth National Recreation Area-Stanley Ranger Office, (208) 774-3000

**Finding the trailhead:** Take ID 21 north past Stanley or south if coming from Boise/Lowman. 4 miles north of Stanley is the Stanley Lake road. Take this road for 3.5 miles that leads to the popular campground celebrating the amazing scenery and clean air. Follow the signs that lead to the trailhead. GPS: N43 14.83' / W115 3.95
**Parking and trailhead facilities:** Plenty of parking is available.

## The Hike

Leaving the parking area, the trail cuts though the forest and follows a road that borders the Stanley Lake Campground. This very quickly leads to the well-signed Stanley Lake Trail (Trail 640). The trail spends a lot of time meandering though willows and mountain meadows with the looming spires of Mount McGown ever present at different angles. Mosquitoes are common and can spoil the experience, so use what works best to repel the little critters!

There is a junction with the Alpine Way Trail after 1 mile. Stay on the Stanley Lake Trail as it enters the lodgepole forest and starts ascending. The first waterfalls and rapids are Lady Face; a short side traverse can get you glimpses of the raging waters of Stanley Lake Creek spilling down narrow rock walls. Farther along the trail—over 2 miles from the trailhead—comes a crossing of Stanley Creek itself. After another 1.5 miles you'll reach the second waterfall turnoff, to the right this time. In contrast with Lady Face, Bridal Veil Falls is above you. Depending on the time of year, white rapids may be toppling down the beautiful ridge like ringlets of a bride's hair. There are places to camp in this area, but a permit maybe required as it borders the Sawtooth Wilderness.

**Options:** At Bridal Veil, you can bushwhack to the falls up the mountain to access Hanson Lakes. You can also continue on the Stanley Lake Trail. A little over a mile

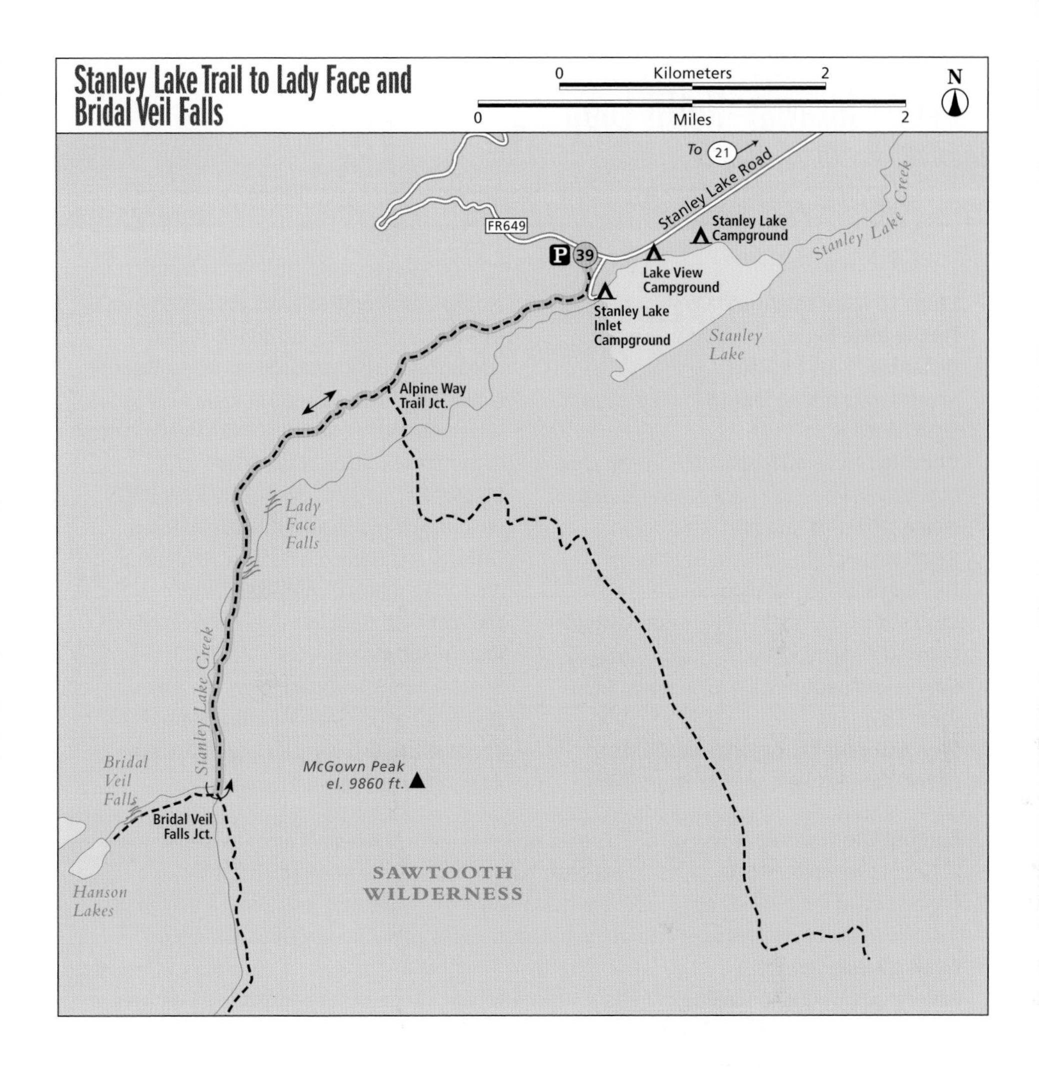


past Bridal Veil is a junction to the Bench Creek trail which heads north and west to Elk flats. Another 2 miles beyond this junction on the Stanley Lake trail you reach a junction to Observation peak trail to the right and into the Sawtooth Wilderness on the left. Heading left gives you an opportunity to reach Sawtooth Lake (Hike 38) and taking the Alpine Way trail north to form a loop.

## Miles and Directions

- **0.0** Trailhead at Stanley Lake Campground (6,520 feet)
- **1.0** Intersection with Alpine Way Trail
- **1.7** Side trail on the right to Lady Veil Falls
- **2.1** Ford of Stanley Lake Creek
- **3.2** Side trail on the right to views of Bridal Veil Falls and camping spots

# 40 Toxaway-Pettit Loop

This is a classic backpacking trip in the Sawtooth Mountains. There are alpine lakes, waterfalls, and some of the most jagged of the Sawtooths.

**Start:** 15 miles south of Stanley
**Type of hike:** Backpack loop
**Distance:** About 18 miles
**Approximate hiking time:** 3–5 days, depending on options
**Difficulty:** Moderately strenuous due to elevation gain and possible early-season snowfield crossing (mid- to late July)
**Best season:** Late July–mid-September
**Trail surface:** Normal dirt and rock
**Land status:** Sawtooth Wilderness; Sawtooth National Recreation Area
**Canine compatibility:** Dogs on leash July 1–Labor Day
**Fees and permits:** Depends on the year. Check with the forest service. Some years require a Sawtooth National Recreation Area (SNRA) trailhead fee. In addition, a free wilderness permit (available at the trailhead) is needed. Parties of eight or more must get a wilderness permit from the SNRA headquarters or the Stanley office of the SNRA.
**Maps:** Mt. Everly and Snowyside Peak USGS quadrangles; Fairfield and Ketchum Ranger Districts and Sawtooth National Recreation Area–Sawtooth National Forest map
**Trail contact:** Sawtooth National Recreation Area Headquarters, (208) 727-5000
**Special considerations:** Snow can make Snowyside Pass, Sand Mountain Pass, and Imogene Divide tricky until late July or even August. Campfires not allowed.

**Finding the trailhead:** Turn off ID 75 about 45 miles north of Ketchum onto the signed road to Pettit Lake. Follow this much-used, but often badly washboarded, road about 2 miles to a T intersection at Pettit Lake's outlet. Take the road to the right. At the next fork, turn left and go about 0.5 mile to the obvious parking area at the trailhead. Signs guide the way. GPS: N43 59.05' / W114 52.33'
**Parking and trailhead facilities:** This is a major trailhead with room for perhaps thirty vehicles at the well-developed, gravel parking lot, which is mostly in the shade of lodgepole pine. The trailhead has a nice restroom and a bulletin board.

## The Hike

The 18-mile loop begins and ends at Pettit Lake, a large moraine lake on the valley floor. The loop encounters all the features that have made the Sawtooths famous: toothed peaks, glacial boulders, large and small mountain lakes, avalanche runs, talus slides, granite cliffs, mountain meadows, waterfalls, cascading streams, and dense stands of lodgepole pine

A brief walk down the trail brings you to the junction with the trail that goes up Pettit Lake Creek (straight ahead) and the trail leading up into Yellow Belly Creek (to the right). It's best to take the right fork and climb over into Yellow Belly Creek, making Pettit Lake Creek the last leg of the hike. The prospect of climbing over the

550-foot-high moraine between the two drainages is more inviting on the first day, when you're fresh, than on your last.

At the trail junction, begin the switchbacking ascent of the moraine amid grass, sage, and flowers. The dark blue waters of Pettit Lake sparkle behind you. After about 0.3 mile you'll reach the edge of the forest. Giant, weathered, outlying Douglas firs quickly give way to dense lodgepole thickets as you continue to climb. You'll have to find some other inspiration besides anticipation of the view to egg you on: There is no view at the top. From the top, switchback down into the canyon of Yellow Belly Creek, continuing through lodgepole forest. You arrive at the bottom of the canyon 2.7 miles from your vehicle and join the trail that comes up Yellow Belly Creek. Just a few yards down this trail is McDonald Lake, a somewhat marshy lake with a burn on its south side from a 1981 fire. Larger Yellow Belly Lake, another 0.5 mile down-canyon, has a burn from a 1982 fire.

Continuing on the main trail, head up the canyon, walking almost on the level through more lodgepole forest. After about a mile you climb a short hill and then cross Yellow Belly Creek.

Just 0.2 mile past the stream crossing, you begin the 600-foot climb to Farley Lake. After 0.75 mile the trail goes past a small, thundering waterfall on Yellow Belly Creek. Then, in another 0.5 mile, you cross through a grassy scrub timber basin through which the creek cascades. Soon you're at Farley Lake (about 1.75 miles from the start of the climb). This pretty lake is full of brook trout, a very common fish in the Sawtooths.

For the next 1.5 miles, the trail climbs moderately, but erratically, through small meadows and scrub timber and past large boulders and rock slabs.

At 6.5 miles from the trailhead, you come to a junction. The trail to the right leads to Edith Lake, then over a 9,200-foot pass and down to lovely Imogene Lake, which rests in the Hellroaring Creek drainage. Stay on the trail to the left. Soon you'll pass an elongated pond at an elevation of 8,165 feet. Continue past this and a smaller pond, then past small Bowknot Lake. One mile and about 150 feet above the junction with Edith Lake Trail, you finally reach big, beautiful Toxaway Lake. Gorgeous peaks rise above the lake at the head of the canyon.

The lake itself is a mile long, making it one of the biggest in the Sawtooth Mountains. You'll generally find good fishing in Toxaway for brook trout of up to a foot—pretty large for Sawtooth brookies.

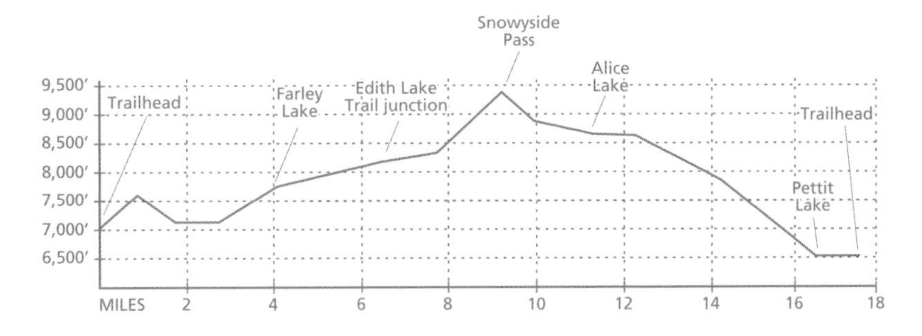

*Elegant Sawtooth backcountry.* Photo by Josh Kelley

On the north side of the lake is a trail that climbs over Sand Mountain Pass, providing access to Vernon, Edna, and Virginia Lakes (all on the other side of the Sawtooth crest) at the headwaters of the South Fork of the Payette River. The trail over Sand Mountain is also an alternative route to Edith Lake and then down into the Hellroaring drainage to Imogene Lake.

To reach your goal, Twin and Alice Lakes in the Pettit Lake Creek drainage, continue around Toxaway Lake. The trail has been completely rebuilt since the Snowyside USGS quadrangle was published in 1964, so the map is incorrect. You can't get lost, however.

It's a 1,000-foot climb and about 1.5 miles from Toxaway to Snowyside Pass (9,390 feet). The trail rounds big Toxaway Lake and climbs up into a steep canyon that harbors three small lakes. The scenery is absolutely sublime as you switchback to the pass. Note that snow often remains here on the northeast-facing slope of 10,651-foot Snowyside Peak until late July.

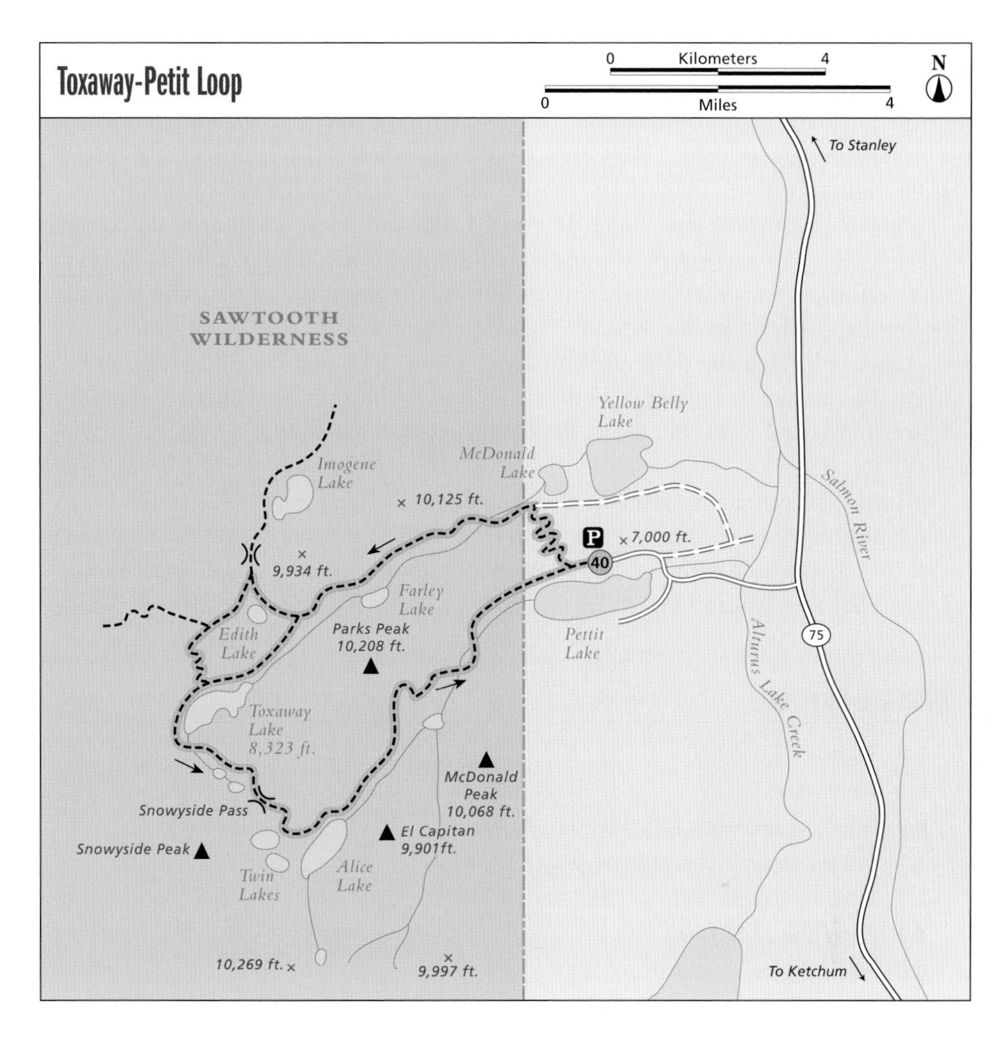


From the notch at the pass, start down into the Pettit Lake Creek drainage by following the trail that is lodged into the wide part of a steep wall. Right below, 500 feet down, is the upper of the Twin Lakes. The trail loops around the north side of the cirque and descends to the Twin Lakes, two sapphire pools situated just below timberline in a wonderful pink cirque basin. Rugged peaks rise all around these fish-filled lakes, which are separated by only a narrow rock band.

From Twin Lakes, head east over a saddle and switchback down to Alice Lake, another large lake, fully the size of the Twin Lakes together. Alice is a scintillating blue, bejeweled with small rock islands and surrounded by subalpine fir struggling through the granite. El Capitan thrusts up on the lake's east side, looking somewhat similar to its namesake in Yosemite National Park. The serrated crest of the Sawtooth Range forms the skyline to the south and southwest and shows why these mountains are called the Sawtooths.

Past Alice Lake, heading down Pettit Lake Creek, walk on the level past two small lakes, then begin a moderate descent through open forest to a creek ford 0.5 mile below the last of the two small lakes. Descend now at a steeper angle for 0.3 mile to a bridged crossing of Pettit Lake Creek. Continue to descend, switchbacking at times, as the right (northwest) wall of the canyon becomes very rugged and convoluted.

After 2 miles you'll pass under the rugged cliffs and reach the floor of the lower canyon. Here the atmosphere is moister, and the trail can be muddy after a summer thundershower. You cross the creek twice, but you can probably get across on logjams or foot logs without having to wade. There is a lush flat at the inlet of Pettit Lake.

Once you reach the shore of Pettit Lake, follow the trail for another mile on its north side, passing in and out of timber. Here you can take a classic photo of the lake waters and 10,068-foot McDonald Peak rising to the southwest.

**Options:** You can climb over Imogene Divide (9,270 feet) into Hellroaring Creek and visit Imogene Lake. Or you can climb over Sand Mountain Pass (9,400 feet) and visit the lakes in the South Fork of the Payette headwaters: Vernon, Edna, and Virginia Lakes. They are all beautiful.

—Ralph Maughan

## Miles and Directions

- **0.0** Trailhead (7,000 feet)
- **0.1** Trail junction
- **0.9** Pettit Lake and Yellow Belly Divide (7,570 feet)
- **1.7** Trail junction in bottom of Yellow Belly (7,100 feet)
- **2.7** Yellow Belly Creek crossing (7,190 feet)
- **4.2** Farley Lake (7,750 feet)
- **6.5** Edith Lake Trail junction (8,200 feet)
- **7.8** Trail junction to Sand Mountain Pass at Toxaway Lake (8,380 feet)
- **9.3** Snowyside Pass (9,390 feet)
- **10.0** The first Twin Lake (8,854 feet)
- **11.2** Alice Lake (8,600 feet)
- **12.2** Pettit Lake Creek crossing (8,580 feet)
- **14.2** Pass under rugged cliff (7,800)
- **16.4** West shore, inlet of Pettit Lake (7,000 feet)
- **18.0** Trailhead (7,000 feet)

# Smoky Mountains

The fabulous Sawtooth Mountains blend into another mountain range at their southern end—a complicated and rugged mass known as the Smoky Mountains. While not as jagged as the Sawtooths, the Smokies cover a larger area, and they are just as tall. More than 300,000 acres of them are roadless de facto wilderness. The Smokies are high and rough, and they have lengthy canyons, subalpine lakes, and fewer visitors than the more famous Sawtooths. Most of the users approach the Smokies from ID 75 and head for the closer lake basins.

The area's administration is split among the Sawtooth National Recreation Area (SNRA), the Sawtooth National Forest, and the Boise National Forest. Most of the visits are to the westernmost side of the SNRA or just beyond its western edge, such as Baker Lake and Prairie Creek.

This eastern part of the Smokies is a beautiful and complex mixture of volcanic rocks, quartzite, sandstone, limestone, and conglomerate. The western, more isolated portion is built of the generally gray, intrusive quartz monzonite, grandiorite, and quartz diorite of the vast Idaho Batholith. The Smokies seem to merge imperceptibly into the Salmon River Mountains on their west side. Their southern flank looks out over the Camas Prairie near Fairfield.

Wildlife in the Smokies is typical of the wild reaches of central Idaho, meaning most of the large animals found in the Northern Rockies are present, save only the grizzly bear. Idaho seems to be the wolverine state, and like the Sawtooths to the north, the Smokies have wolverines. They also have at least one wolf pack as of the year 2000—the Big Smoky Pack. One of the largest mountain goat herds in the state also plies their slopes.

We have included three hikes in the area. Two are well-known hikes, and one is not.

—Ralph Maughan

*Norton Lake in the Smokies.* PHOTO BY LUKE KRATZ

# 41 Baker Lake

Beautiful Baker Lake is a short, easy hike in Idaho's Smoky Mountains.

**Start:** 25 road miles northwest of Ketchum
**Type of hike:** Day hike; out-and-back
**Distance:** 2.6 miles round-trip
**Approximate hiking time:** 1 hour
**Difficulty:** Moderately easy (steep but short)
**Best season:** July–September
**Trail surface:** Normal dirt and rock
**Land status:** Sawtooth National Recreation Area.
**Canine compatibility:** Dogs on leash July 1–Labor Day
**Fees and permits:** Depending on the year, a Sawtooth National Recreation Area trailhead fee may be required. Check with the forest service.
**Maps:** Baker Peak USGS quadrangle; Fairfield and Ketchum Ranger Districts and Sawtooth National Recreation Area–Sawtooth National Forest map
**Trail contact:** Sawtooth National Recreation Area Headquarters, (208) 727-5000

**Finding the trailhead:** Follow ID 75 northward from Ketchum and into the Sawtooth National Recreation Area (SNRA) for 15.5 miles. Turn left onto the gravel Baker Creek Road. This road is usually in good condition. It's a pleasant drive of 9.5 miles to its end, where the trailhead is located. GPS: N43 41.42' / W114 39.29'
**Parking and trailhead facilities:** This is a very nice, large, reconstructed trailhead with a latrine. An earthen berm provides for horse loading, and a sign indicates that trailhead fees paid for the reconstruction.

## The Hike

Baker Lake sits just beneath the crest of the Smoky Mountains. Small but rugged Peak 10,099 forms part of the Smoky Mountain crest just behind the lake.

It's a fairly easy hike to the lake. The trail is obvious all the way as it climbs, quite steeply, through flower-filled meadows to the lake in just 1.3 miles. Total elevation gain is about 900 feet.

The trail is closed to motor vehicles, and a sign says so at the beginning of the trail. A few yards past the trailhead, an unnamed tributary of Baker Creek flows over the trail, requiring a wade in June. Beyond this point, the trail is easy and obvious. Until recently there were several large eroded shortcuts in addition to the trail here, but in the year 2000 trees were felled over the shortcuts. Let's hope the scars heal quickly.

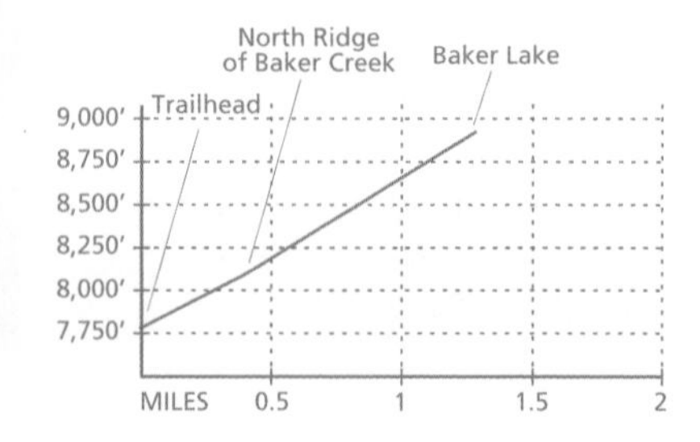


You walk through meadow with some sagebrush and pass under a few large Douglas fir. Then you begin to ascend steeply. The trail quickly climbs to, and generally stays near, the ridge between Baker Creek and its

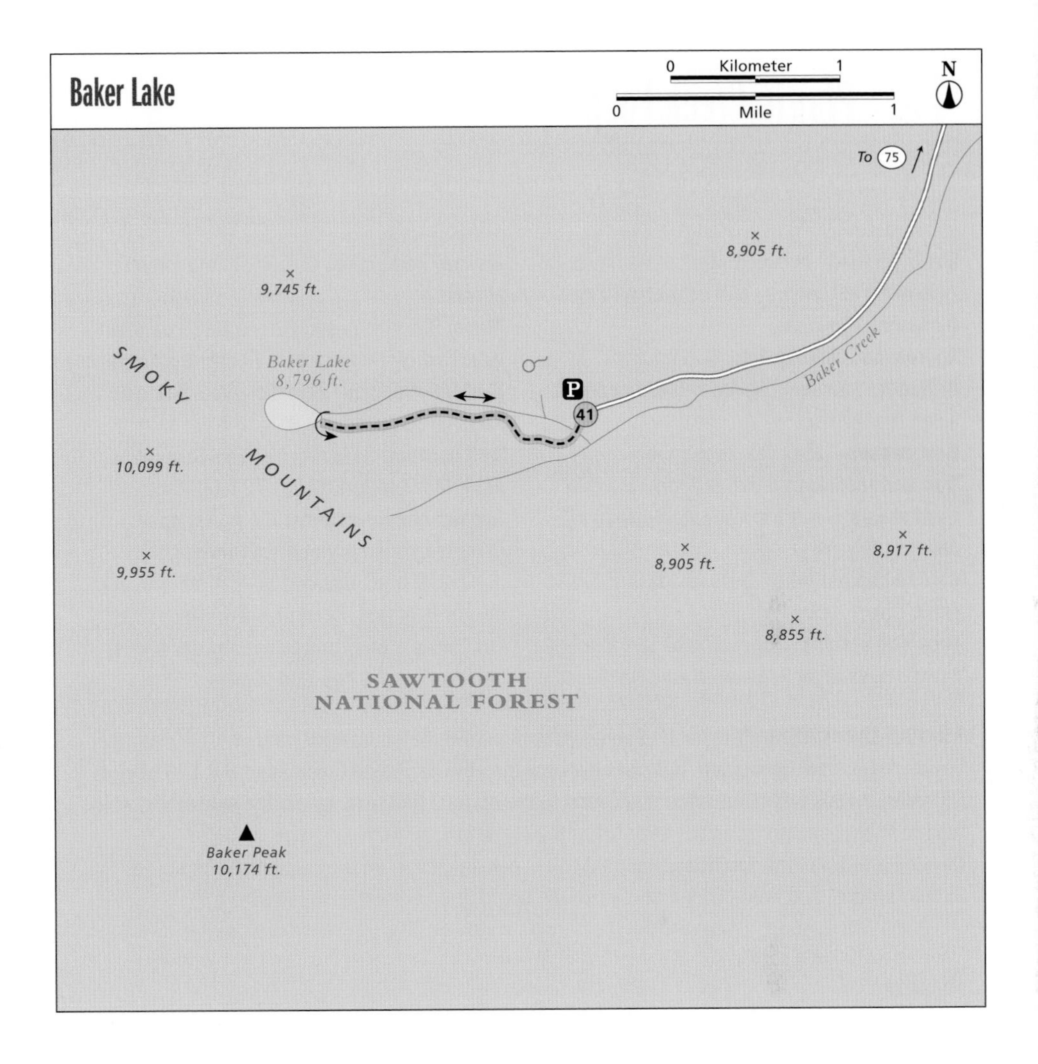


tributary canyon, which holds Baker Lake. On my hike this portion of the trailside was colored with the bright blue of small penstemon all the way to the lake.

Fishing at Baker Lake is catch-and-release using artificial lures only. I didn't fish, but the lake appeared full of 7- to 12-inch trout.

—Ralph Maughan

## Miles and Directions

**0.0** Trailhead (7,880 feet)

**0.3** Onto north ridge of Baker Creek (8,120 feet)

**1.3** Baker Lake (8,796 feet)

# 42 Prairie Creek Loop

The Prairie Creek Loop accesses scenic mountains and several subalpine lakes.

**Start:** 25 road miles northwest of Ketchum
**Type of hike:** Long day hike or overnight loop
**Distance:** 10 miles
**Approximate hiking time:** 6–8 hours
**Difficulty:** Strenuous as a day hike; moderate as an overnighter
**Best season:** Late June–September
**Trail surface:** Normal dirt and rock
**Land status:** Sawtooth National Recreation Area
**Canine compatibility:** Dogs on leash July 1–Labor Day
**Fees and permits:** Depending on the year, a Sawtooth National Recreation Area trailhead fee may be needed. Check with the forest service.
**Maps:** Baker Peak and Galena USGS quadrangles; Fairfield and Ketchum Ranger Districts and Sawtooth National Recreation Area–Sawtooth National Forest map
**Trail contact:** Sawtooth National Recreation Area Headquarters, (208) 727-5000
**Special considerations:** The trail is open to motorcycles but not ATVs. However, the number of trail machines is relatively low, and my guess is that social pressure keeps them out. This is a busy trail with many day hikers, backpackers, horses, and joggers.

**Finding the trailhead:** Drive 18.9 miles from downtown Ketchum northward on ID 75 into the Sawtooth National Recreation Area. Turn left onto the obvious Prairie Creek Road (FR 179). Drive 2.6 miles up this well-used, often dusty road to the obvious trailhead. Ignore the side roads, which lead to informal camping areas. GPS: N43 48.23' / W114 38.60'
**Parking and trailhead facilities:** The trailhead is constructed in an oval, with room for ten to fifteen vehicles, and has a latrine and a bulletin board. The trailhead is in full sun.

## The Hike

Trail 133, the Prairie Lakes Trail, leaves the trailhead as an obvious wide path. You immediately come to the West Fork of Prairie Creek flowing across the trail, which requires an easy wade until late summer. It could be difficult at the peak of snowmelt in mid-June. Across the creek, the wide trail continues, leading you into forest.

The trail climbs briefly, about an 80-foot gain, up, into, and across a rocky area. After a mile, you come to the first of several meadows. Small tributaries flow across

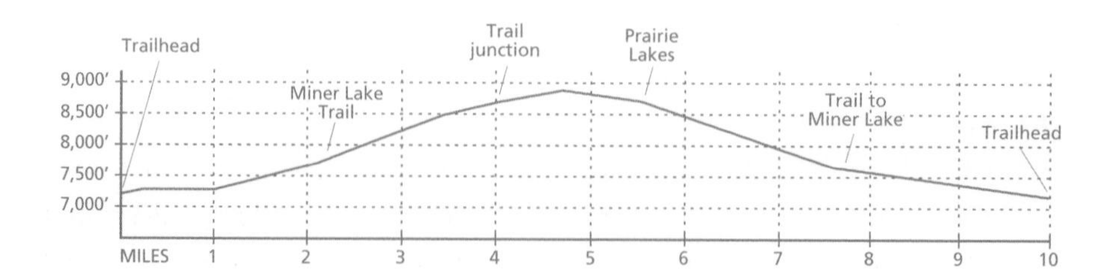

*The crystal clear water and lush vegation of Prairie Creek.* PHOTO BY LUKE KRATZ

the creek and down into the meadow. Here is a fine view of the Smoky Mountains on both sides of the trail and upcanyon, where the rugged face of Peak 9,892 dominates.

Another mile and another large meadow bring you to the junction with the trail that climbs to Miner Lake. If you are doing the loop in a clockwise fashion, take the left trail junction here. The trail to Miner Lake drops down and crosses Prairie Creek. I found several logs crossing the creek, but on a rainy day they would be very slippery.

Assuming you go to Miner Lake first, the trail immediately begins to climb up toward the Miner Lake cirque once you cross the creek. It is about a 1,000-foot climb to the lake, and the trail is steep and somewhat eroded as it climbs through uninteresting, dry lodgepole pine forest. However, there are a few nice views northward across Prairie Creek to the series of 9,500-foot-plus peaks that form the north and northwest wall of Prairie Creek Canyon.

After climbing about 400 feet in 0.75 mile, you come a rest spot where the trail seems to flatten. You may believe you are almost into the cirque, but this is not the case. The trail soon climbs another 400 feet before it crosses Miner Creek at the bottom of the cirque.

You soon are walking up a lovely flower-filled avalanche meadow with a fine view of Norton Peak (10,336 feet) dominating the view. After passing through several small stands of timber, you come to a trail junction at the creek, which leaves to the

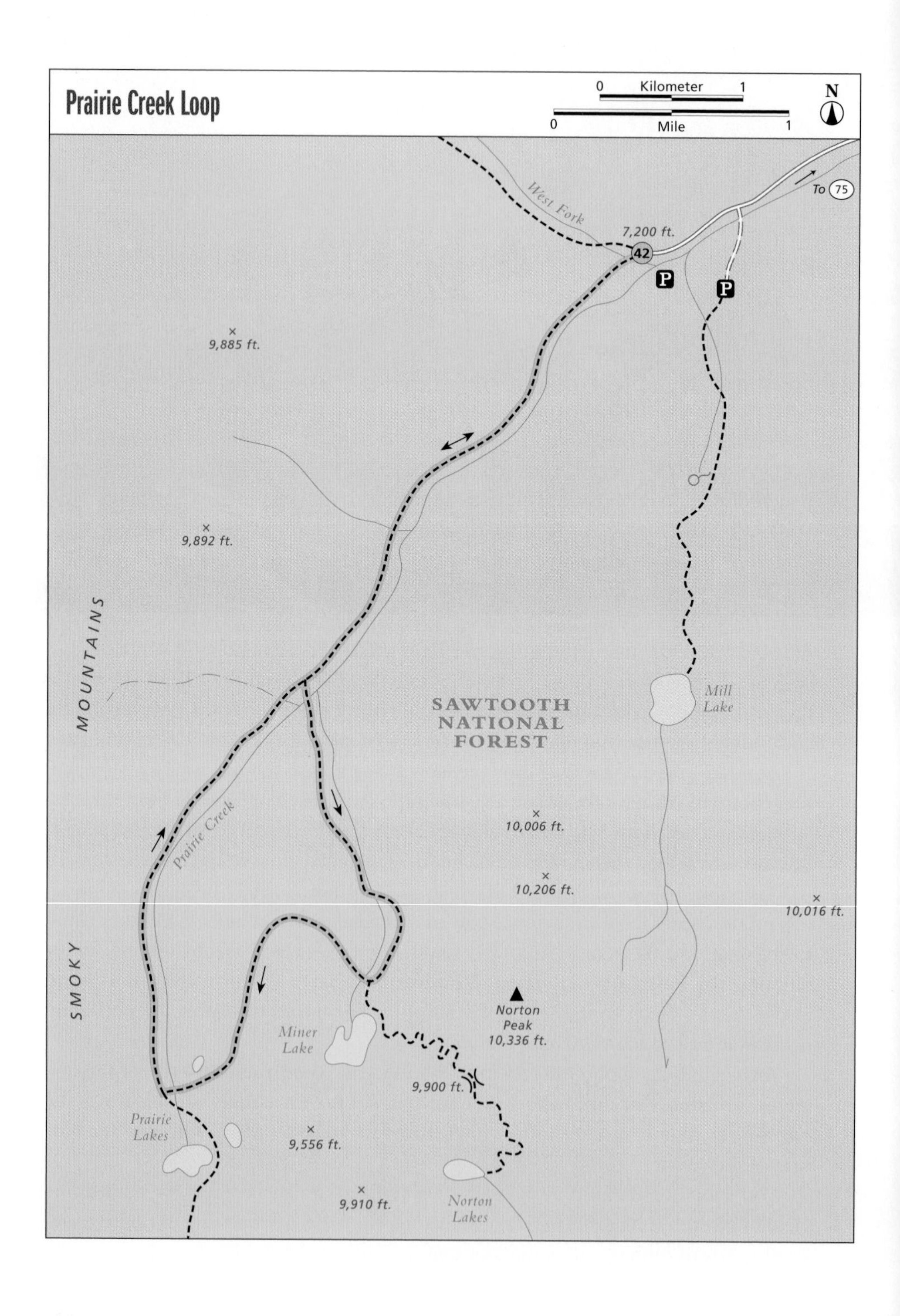
Prairie Creek Loop
0 Kilometer 1
0 Mile 1
N
West Fork
7,200 ft.
42
To 75
9,885 ft.
9,892 ft.
MOUNTAINS
SMOKY
SAWTOOTH
NATIONAL
FOREST
Mill
Lake
Prairie Creek
10,006 ft.
10,206 ft.
10,016 ft.
Norton
Peak
10,336 ft.
Miner
Lake
9,900 ft.
Prairie
Lakes
9,556 ft.
9,910 ft.
Norton
Lakes

right at an oblique angle. This is the trail you want to take, but first you will want to see Prairie Lake, which is just 0.2 mile ahead. At 8,770 feet, it pretty much fills the top of the cirque. It's a large, shallow lake with much driftwood, intricately carved by water, wind, rain, and snow. The quadrangle shows an ephemeral lake or marsh above Prairie Lake. It is difficult to reach, but it is not an ephemeral pond. Rather, it is a year-round small lake. Neither lake seems to have fish, and the warm water of Prairie Lake invites a swim, but be aware that it contains leeches.

Back at the trail junction, you immediately cross Miner Creek. The trail is not on the quadrangle, but it is easy to follow. It climbs a bit and circles the end of the prominent, but narrow, ridge that forms the west side of the Miner Lake cirque. After making a 180-degree turn from north to south, the trail is easy going and comes upon the easternmost group of the Prairie Lakes. The trail passes just below them and soon joins Prairie Lake Trail in the forest, just above the largest of the Prairie Lakes at 8,720 feet. There are five Prairie Lakes, and all are shallow.

After you have explored the Prairie Lakes area, follow the trail downcanyon. It is an easy walk with a nice sandy tread in many places. You pass through a number of small meadows and are soon back to the trail junction to Miner Lake, completing the loop. It is 2 miles back to the trailhead from here.

**Options:** You can climb a trail from Miner Lake to the high pass (9,900 feet) on the shoulder of Norton Peak and then drop down to the Norton Lakes on the south side of the pass. Follow the trail from Miner Lake to its east side. The trail soon begins to switchback, twenty-five times, as it climbs the 1,100 feet from the lake to the pass. It has been well cleared, but any avalanche could change that. From the pass, it is not hard to climb to the summit of Norton Peak, which provides an even better view than that from the pass, especially of the lovely, meadow-laced cirque at the head of Mill Creek, above Mill Lake. Unfortunately, a descent into this canyon looks very difficult.

From the pass, the trail descends steeply to the two Norton Lakes. The upper lake is at 9,107 feet, and the nearby lower lake is at 8,947 feet.

—Ralph Maughan

## Miles and Directions

**0.0** Trailhead (7,200 feet)
**0.3** Rocky area (7,300 feet)
**1.0** First big meadow (7,350 feet)
**2.2** Miner Lake Trail (7,680 feet)
**3.5** Bottom of Miner Lake cirque (8,540 feet)
**4.1** Trail junction just below Miner Lake (8,760 feet)
**4.7** Trail crosses the north end of Miner Lake; west-side cirque ridge (8,840 feet)
**5.5** Prairie Lakes (8,701 feet)
**7.8** Trail to Miner Lake (7,680 feet)
**10.0** Trailhead (7,200 feet)

# 43 West Fork of Prairie Creek

The short West Fork trail follows a meadowy creek that sinks into a rockslide and emerges at the bottom.

**Start:** 25 road miles northwest of Ketchum at the Prairie Lakes Trailhead
**Type of hike:** Day hike; out-and-back, with option to climb, mostly cross-country, to the head of the canyon (which would be a long day hike or an overnighter)
**Distance:** 3.6 miles round-trip
**Approximate hiking time:** 1–2 hours for day hike
**Difficulty:** Moderately easy
**Best season:** July–September
**Trail surface:** Normal dirt and rock
**Land status:** Sawtooth National Forest
**Canine compatibility:** On leash
**Fees and permits:** None
**Maps:** Galena USGS quadrangle; Fairfield and Ketchum Ranger Districts and Sawtooth National Recreation Area–Sawtooth National Forest map
**Trail contact:** Fairfield Ranger District, (208) 764-3202; Ketchum Ranger District, (208) 622-5371
**Special considerations:** The creek crossing can be a bit difficult for those with little experience crossing streams.

**Finding the trailhead:** Drive 18.9 miles from downtown Ketchum northward on ID 75 into the Sawtooth National Recreation Area. Turn left onto the obvious Prairie Creek Road (FR 179). Drive 2.6 miles up this well-used, often dusty road to the obvious trailhead. Ignore the side roads, which lead to informal camping areas. GPS: N43 48.23' / W114 38.60
**Parking and trailhead facilities:** The trailhead is constructed in an oval, with room for ten to fifteen vehicles, and has a latrine and a bulletin board. The trailhead is in full sun.

## The Hike

The scenic Prairie Lakes Trail (Trail 133) described in Hike 42, Prairie Creek Loop, is a busy, widely worn path with many hikers, horses, and some motorbikes. West Prairie Trail (Trail 134) leaves from the same trailhead but does not get even a tenth as much use. It can serve as a quiet and short alternative.

The trail leaves from the trailhead, leading northwest in the mouth of West Prairie Creek. You quickly come to this creek, a splashing, full-size brook that emerges from a huge cone of scree just upstream. The scree is the beginning of a large landslide that sprawls down from the craggy peaks on the canyon's right (east) side.

The trail crosses the creek just below the spring (be careful here, since the creek bottom is uneven and the stones slippery). Cross it here, nevertheless, and avoid the treacherous scree slope just above the spring. On the other side of the creek, which is lined with

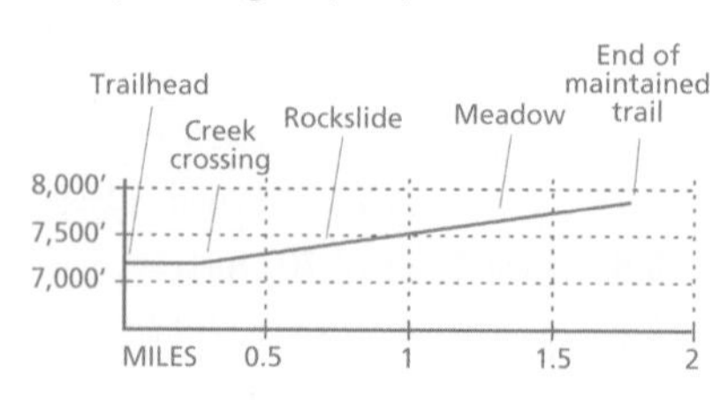

*Along the West Fork of Prairie Creek.* PHOTO BY LUKE KRATZ

bluebells and monkey flowers in midsummer, the trail leads up the canyon under forest but with the scree slide and barren peaks of well over 9,000 feet visible to the right. The rockslide is gray with a lot of rose-shaded pieces.

Within 0.25 mile, the forest thins, then disappears alongside the trail due to the relentless action of many winter snowslides. You emerge into an open canyon filled with flowers, rockslides, conifer seedlings, and the very few huge Douglas fir that have managed to avoid the avalanches.

The trail climbs steadily up the rockslide along an easy, unshaded route. You soon find that the creek has reappeared, flowing slightly below the trail over the rocks, promoting the growth of willows and numerous wildflowers. Soon, however, it disappears again. You gain the top of the slide 0.75 mile from its beginning and after an ascent of 300 feet in elevation (480 feet from the trailhead).

At the top of the slide, you emerge into totally different surroundings—a flat-bottomed, verdant canyon. The trail angles to the extreme left of the grassy and willow-filled meadow ahead. The track is faint now because the grass grows fast enough to erase the depressions left by boots and horse hooves. If you walk out into the meadow, you will find the creek meandering slowly along.

**Options:** The trail soon ends, but you can continue up the canyon. The grade is gentle at first, but you will be scrambling on game trails that are also used by a few people in the middle reaches of the canyon and are not especially scenic because you are in a forest. The grade eventfully lessens, and the canyon sweeps to the south in a semicircle. You can walk along a shelf from the southernmost part of the canyon's

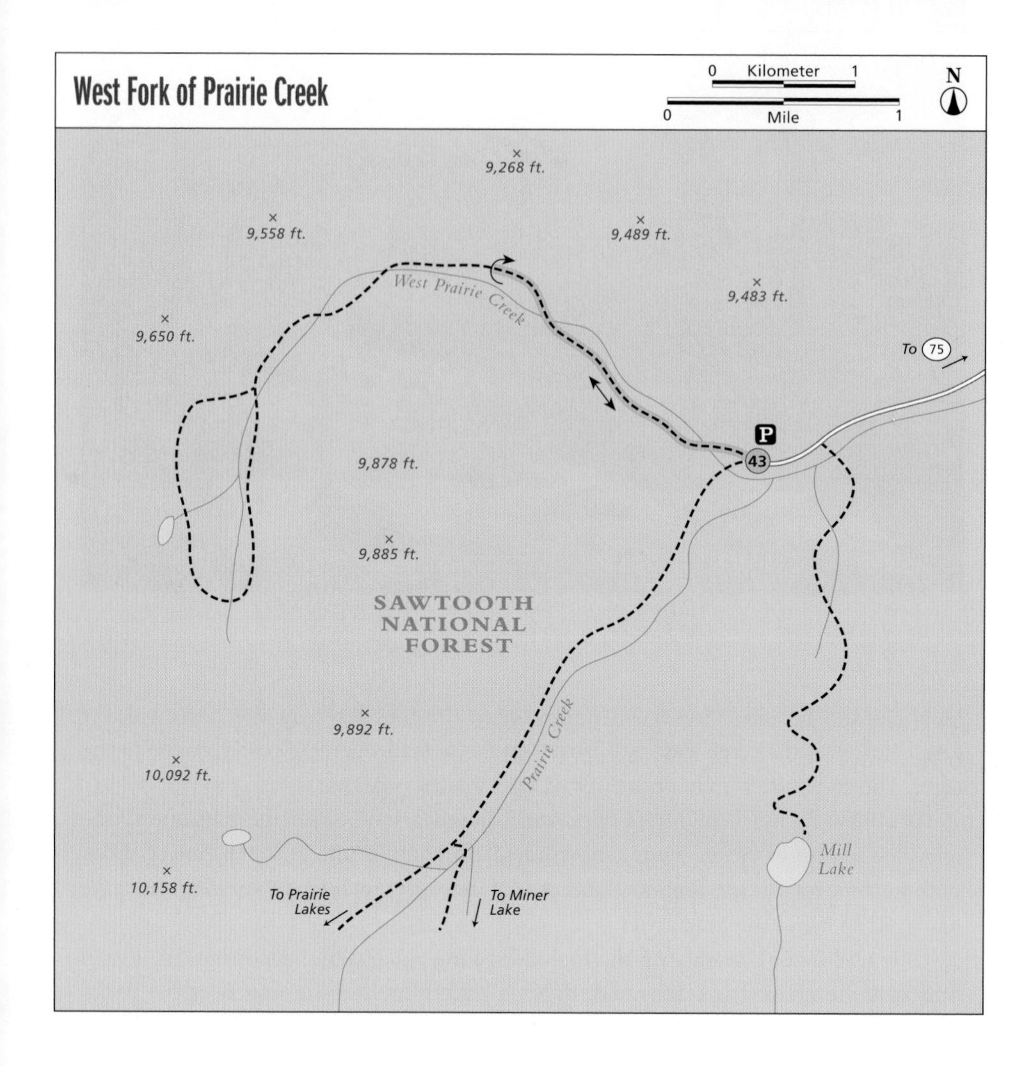


head northward and then northeastward for quite a way. The map shows a small lake and a few ponds, but these are shallow and transient. The beauty is in the alpine wildflowers, burbling springs, and fine views of the Boulder and White Cloud Mountains to the east and northeast.

—Ralph Maughan

## Miles and Directions

**0.0** Trailhead (7,200 feet)
**0.2** Creek crossing (7,280 feet)
**0.6** Onto rockslide (7,390 feet)
**1.3** Onto verdant meadow (7,680 feet)
**1.8** End of maintained trail (7,800 feet)

# Boulder and White Cloud Mountains

Salmon River Mountains is a nonspecific name applied to a 30,000-square-mile maze of high ridges and deep canyons in central Idaho. On the edges of this mountain fastness radiate other mountains, identifiable as separate ranges.

One such string of mountains, consisting of hundreds of 10,000- to 11,000-foot peaks, runs southward from the Salmon River Mountains to form the east side of the Sawtooth Valley; then it humps farther south past Ketchum, Hailey, and Bellevue to end in the basalt of the Snake River Plain.

Although this is one continuous mountain range, over the years the string has been broken into three separate groups in people's minds. On the north, against the Salmon River Canyon and Salmon River Mountains, they are known as the White Clouds.

This was originally a local name, limited to just one magnificent ridge of high, often white, peaks. Today all mountains between Salmon River Canyon on the north, Germainia and Pole Creek on the south, and the East Fork of the Salmon River to the east bear this name.

The next mountains in this string are not pearls but boulders. The Boulder Mountains are perhaps the least known and visited of the three mountain groups, especially their eastern flank, which is beginning to take on the name Herd Peak Highlands.

Finally, the southernmost and highest group is the Pioneer Mountains. In average elevation, they are the second highest range in the Gem State. One peak, Hyndman Peak, just tops 12,000 feet.

The Boulders, it is generally agreed, end at Trail Creek Gorge. Here, the Pioneers more than take up the slack of the colorful Boulders with their glistening gray peaks, speckled tarns, and gorges thundering with cascades. See the separate overview regarding the Pioneer Mountains later in this book.

The White Clouds became celebrities in the late 1960s when a group of hikers found then-lonesome Willow Lake, the first of the Boulder Chain Lakes, under siege. The waters of the lake were normally perfectly clear, reflecting the rainbow colors of

*Boulder and White Cloud Mountains from the East Fork area.* PHOTO BY ANNE KRATZ

a nearby peak. But the hikers found the waters full of "mud" from a driller's bit. One side of the lake had been stripped bare of trees to make room for mining exploration. One of Idaho's most famous conservation battles ensued. Before the dust would settle, there would be a new conservation-minded governor (Cecil Andrus) in the statehouse, with a whole new outlook and the political clout to back it. The legacy of Andrus, and his allies Frank Church and John Evans, lasted an entire generation before it devolved to the present group of anti-environmental politicians.

When the hikers protested the destruction, the now-famous retort was, "Don't worry, when we're done there won't be a lake. Hell, there won't even be a mountain!" The mountain they were referring to was none other than Castle Peak—at 11,810 feet the highest by far of the White Clouds, ruler of the range. This giant is now one of the best-known mountains in Idaho. Back then, however, Castle Peak was pretty obscure despite its exciting, towering beauty. It just didn't tower over any highways—or even dirt roads, for that matter.

Dedicated Idaho conservationists and the public were not convinced by talk of temporary jobs from the proposed mine or of the "critical" need for molybdenum in the economy—a metal that is now in extreme surplus.

Persistence led to creation of the Sawtooth National Recreation Area (SNRA) in 1972. This not only withdrew the White Clouds, most of the Boulders, and the

Sawtooth Mountains from the filing of further mining claims but also provided the means to clean up the subdivisions sprouting like mushrooms in a cowpie in Sawtooth Valley. It also reclassified the old Sawtooth Primitive Area into the new, larger and better Sawtooth Wilderness.

Ironically, while the White Clouds heralded the victory for many other successful battles, they themselves still lack wilderness designation today. The White Clouds are not protected wilderness despite the best efforts of the Idaho Conservation League and the Boulder–White Clouds Council. ATVs rip through too many high meadows, and bands of sheep beat some places to dust while threatening the native wildlife, such as the wolves that have recently re-inhabited these mountains.

The White Clouds have many subalpine and alpine lakes. These see the most use, while the lower mountains to the north and west are where you will find the most solitude.

The Boulder Mountains rise in full view of ID 75 in the SNRA, but this face is too steep for much hiking. The good hiking portion requires a longer drive to the backside (northeast) of these mountains. The southwestern flank of the Boulders fronts the Ketchum–Sun Valley area, and they get a lot of use—usually by cheerful, fit, environmentally conscious, and well-educated folks. The comparatively lakeless Boulders offer rugged cliffs, booming waterfalls, and colorful rock.

Both ranges have much wildlife—elk, deer, mountain goats, pronghorn antelope, black bear, mountain lion, bighorn sheep, one or two wolf packs, and, of course, coyotes.

The White Clouds and part of the Boulders are a congressionally mandated Wilderness Study Area of about 200,000 acres. Idaho conservationists propose a 500,000-acre White Clouds–Boulder Wilderness. This is one of the largest remaining legally unprotected roadless areas in the United States. Idaho is lucky to have it, but the state's present congressional delegation doesn't see it that way. This delegation, financed by every moneyed special interest group in the alphabet (from AMAX to Zinc), thinks that the wilds of Idaho are a mote in the eye of humanity. But the decision is up to all American citizens. Will we prevail?

—Ralph Maughan

Even with deadlock in the congress to preserve this area there is still a push to form the 571,276 acre Boulder-White Cloud National Monument. This would have to be an effort based on a coalition of many different Idaho groups with a unified goal to see ecological and economical benefits from preserving such an area. While it may not completely restrict grazing and off-road vehicles as a wilderness area would, this plan would provide a single management for the entire area and balanced access for users of the backcountry. National monument status would also allow consistent coordination of protecting the wilderness character of the area and generate national interest and support of keeping this area unchanged. Please contact the Idaho Conservation League and voice your support and opinions!

-Luke Kratz, 2014

# 44 North Fork of the Big Wood River

This hike climbs from forest to rock. There are numerous wildflowers, springs, cascades, and avalanche runs, which open the forest for views of the rugged scenery.

**Start:** 13 miles north of Ketchum in the Sawtooth National Recreation Area (SNRA) at the headwaters of the North Fork of the Big Wood River
**Type of hike:** Day hike or overnight backpack; out-and-back
**Distance:** 5.3 miles to Ibex Pass, but most people stop before the 4-mile mark
**Approximate hiking time:** 1–2 days
**Difficulty:** Easy to the bend in the canyon (2 miles); moderate above the bend due to increasingly faint trail and steeper grade; strenuous from the head of the canyon to Ibex Pass due to elevation gain and some route finding
**Best season:** Late June–September to the head of the canyon; mid- to late summer to Ibex Pass, depending on snowline
**Trail surface:** Normal dirt and rock
**Land status:** Sawtooth National Recreation Area
**Canine compatibility:** Dogs on leash July 1–Labor Day
**Fees and permits:** None
**Maps:** Amber Lakes, Galena Peak, and Ryan Peak USGS quadrangles; Fairfield and Ketchum Ranger Districts–Sawtooth National Forest map
**Trail contact:** Sawtooth National Recreation Area Headquarters, (208) 727-5000
**Special considerations:** You may have to cross numerous snow cones at avalanche runouts into midsummer after heavy winters.

**Finding the trailhead:** From downtown Ketchum, drive north on ID 75 into the SNRA. Just past the entrance sign where the highway crosses the Big Wood River, take the road to the right that leads to, and past, the SNRA headquarters. At the headquarters, you can get plenty of information about hiking and other features of the SNRA. The building is set right in the mouth of the North Fork Canyon, 8.2 miles from downtown Ketchum.

Continue on the dirt road for 5.1 miles up North Fork Canyon, passing Murdock Creek and the East Fork (of the North Fork) tributary canyons. The road is paved, then oiled, then gravel, and finally dirt. GPS: N43 51.20' / W114 26.18'

**Parking and trailhead facilities:** The partially shaded trailhead, with parking room for seven or eight vehicles, is located at the end of the road. There is a trail register at the beginning of the trail and a sign announcing NO MOTOR VEHICLES ALLOWED. This is also the trailhead for the West Fork of the North Fork Trail.

## The Hike

The obvious trail climbs up the hillside from the trailhead. After gaining about 50 feet in elevation, it turns and leads into deep forest. Surprisingly, after 0.3 mile you break out into the open to cross the first of many avalanche chutes.

There is a fine view here as well as a ford that is difficult until midsummer. Equestrians take this ford, but the hiking trail has been rebuilt to avoid it and is located on a cutbank on the right side of the river. It is narrow and slopes outward, requiring care. Unless maintained, it will eventually slough off, so it might be prudent to carry wading shoes just in case.

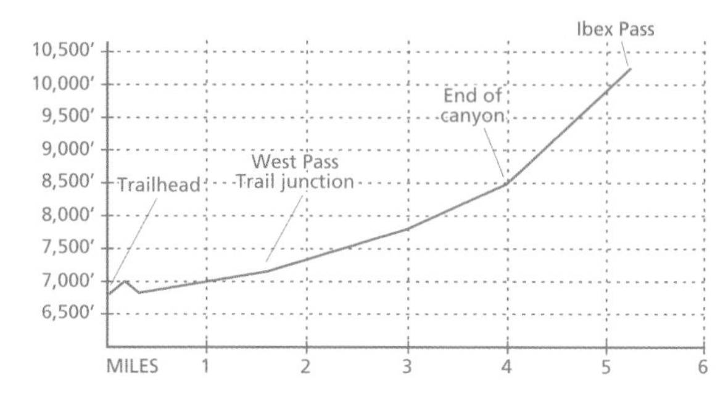


From the narrow traverse, the trail passes in and out of forest but generally remains in the open. The clearings are due to the megatons of snow that thunder down the walls of the canyon in the winter. Between the trailhead and the upcanyon junction with the trail to West Pass at 1.7 miles, you cross eight major avalanche chutes. In years after heavy winters, these avalanche runouts will have snow until mid-July. After snowmelt, they blaze with wildflowers, and these meadows provide fine views of the craggy, rugged, and tall Boulder Mountains. Kent Peak, at 11,664 feet, lies just to the right of the canyon's big bend.

The hiking continues at an easy pace until you see a steep side canyon ahead to the right, where a waterfall leaps. West Pass Trail climbs up this canyon, ascending 2,900 feet in just 2 miles to West Pass, then descending into West Pass Creek. To find the start of this trail, keep on the main trail after sighting the falls and side canyon until you cross a meadow. West Pass Trail leaves on the far side of this meadow. It's a faint track until you reach the trees on the meadow's northeast side; then it becomes obvious. Cairns may or may not be present to help guide you to the trees. Most recently, a sign indicated the trail.

After this trail junction, the main trail bends gradually to match the canyon's north-to-west right-angle turn. From here on, you climb moderately as the canyon's grade increases. At the same time, the trail becomes less distinct. You may even lose it briefly as you walk through the lush, tall wildflowers. Fear not—it is always easy to relocate. Note also that the tall wildflowers also contain some stinging nettle. I would not recommend hiking in shorts.

One and a quarter miles past the bend, the canyon's grade decreases, and there are flat spots and springs. A moderate, but steepening, climb then begins until you reach the end of the canyon at about 4 miles. Most folks stop here, but you can follow a faint trail that may have cairns to rugged Ibex Pass at 10,250 feet. This is a strenuous route that requires route-finding ability, especially the first 0.5 mile beyond the end of the trail.

It's a little difficult to find the pass on the topographic maps because it lies exactly where the Ryan Peak and Galena Peak quads intersect.

As the route becomes more alpine, you cross several headwater rivulets and rise ever upward. Toward the top, as you pass timberline, you should find a distinct path up through the talus. Ibex Pass itself is abrupt; the trail goes right down the other side to Ibex Creek. From the pass, there is a fine view of the White Cloud Mountains, including the rarely seen southern face of famous Castle Peak. You can see the trail

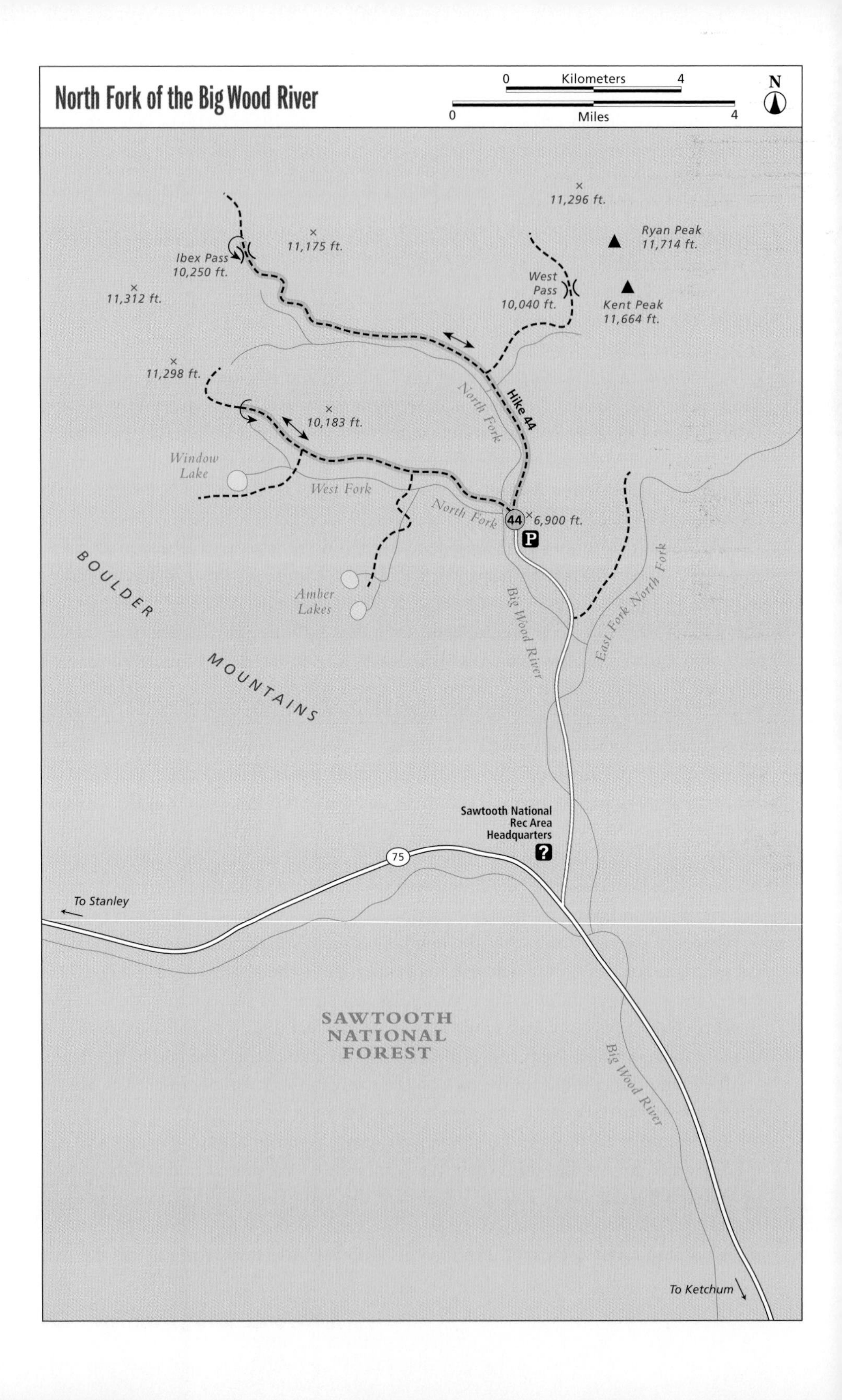
North Fork of the Big Wood River
0
Kilometers
4
0
Miles
4
N
11,296 ft.
Ryan Peak
11,714 ft.
11,175 ft.
Ibex Pass
10,250 ft.
11,312 ft.
West
Pass
10,040 ft.
Kent Peak
11,664 ft.
11,298 ft.
North Fork
Hike 44
10,183 ft.
Window
Lake
West Fork
North Fork
44
6,900 ft.
P
BOULDER
MOUNTAINS
Amber
Lakes
Big Wood River
East Fork North Fork
Sawtooth National
Rec Area
Headquarters
?
75
To Stanley
SAWTOOTH
NATIONAL
FOREST
Big Wood River
To Ketchum

*Lush meadows along the North Fork of the Big Wood River.* PHOTO BY LUKE KRATZ

descend Ibex Creek on the other side, but the trail has not been recut for years and has much deadfall.

**Options:** West Pass Trail takes you across the crest at just over 10,000 feet, adjacent to the Boulder Mountain giants Kent Peak (11,664 feet) and Ryan Peak (11,714 feet). The view north into the East Fork of the Salmon country is exceptional. It is 6.3 miles from the trailhead to West Pass.

You can also scramble over the southwest wall at the end of North Fork Canyon into the West Fork of the North Fork and make it a loop trip. But these options are strenuous; the latter also requires route-finding ability.

—Ralph Maughan

## Miles and Directions

**0.0** Trailhead (6,840 feet)

**0.3** Horse party ford

**0.4** Horse party reford

**1.7** West Pass Trail junction (7,200 feet)

**3.0** Canyon bottom flattens (7,800 feet)

**4.0** Approximate end of the canyon (8,500 feet)

**5.3** Ibex Pass (10,250 feet)

# 45 Boulder Chain Lakes

Hike to a string of lakes with many small rainbow trout and access many other lake basins. This is a well-used and absolutely beautiful trail.

**Start:** In the White Cloud Mountains of the Sawtooth National Recreation Area (SNRA) about 35 miles southwest of Challis
**Type of hike:** Backpack; out-and-back
**Distance:** 10 miles one way
**Approximate hiking time:** 3–5 days
**Difficulty:** Moderate
**Best season:** Mid-July–August
**Trail surface:** Normal dirt and rock
**Land status:** Sawtooth National Recreation Area
**Canine compatibility:** Dogs on leash July 1–Labor Day
**Fees and permits:** None
**Maps:** Boulder Chain Lakes and Livingston Creek USGS quadrangles; Fairfield and Ketchum Ranger Districts and Sawtooth National Recreation Area–Sawtooth National Forest map
**Trail contact:** Ketchum Ranger District, (208) 622-5371; Sawtooth National Recreation Area Headquarters, (208) 727-5000
**Special considerations:** High altitude with variable snowpack

**Finding the trailhead:** From Challis, take US 93 south to its junction with ID 75 on the right. Follow ID 75 about 16 miles south to where it bends right (west) to lead to Clayton. Before reaching Clayton, turn left (south) onto the signed and paved East Fork of the Salmon Road. It is 17 miles (the last 3 are gravel) until the turnoff on the right (west) to the dirt Livingston Mill Road (FR 667). Another 5 miles brings you to the trailhead. GPS: N44 07.85' / W114 30.80'
**Parking and trailhead facilities:** In most years and in most vehicles, you won't be able to drive clear to the trailhead but will have to stop 0.25 mile before. A site crowded with many vehicles is not uncommon.

## The Hike

This hike will confirm everything you may have heard about the beauty of the White Clouds and Castle Peak. It has just about every lure for the outdoorsperson: deep, cool forests, mountain springs, lakes to fish or swim, mountains to climb, and a conservation battle to get you out of your armchair. (See the Boulder and White Cloud Mountains overview.)

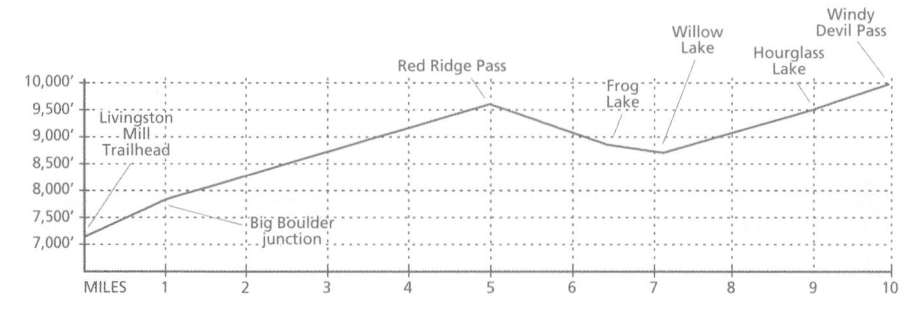

*Two of the lakes in the Boulder Chain.* PHOTO BY LUKE KRATZ

Although this area gets heavy use, you lose about half the traffic early on when the trail forks to the Big Boulder Lakes. You lose another half after Frog Lake because trail machines are not allowed into the Boulder Chain Lakes.

The first 0.5 mile of the trail is an old jeep road that ascends Big Boulder Creek Canyon. After the road disappears in a slide, you'll pass briefly through a lodgepole pine and spruce forest. The trail is good throughout, and you should have no navigation problems. After the section of forest, you'll come out into a willow flat. Here you cross a bridge over Big Boulder Creek. Shortly thereafter, the trail forks. The right fork leads to the Big Boulder Lakes.

The left fork, the one you follow, immediately leaves Big Boulder Creek and begins the long climb to Red Ridge, which involves about 4 miles and a gain of 1,900 feet of altitude. The trail was rebuilt to accommodate horse and off-road vehicle traffic; therefore, it has many more switchbacks than appear on the topographic quad. After you've climbed about a quarter of the way to Red Ridge, you'll encounter one good heart-stopper view out over Big Boulder Creek's timber, its meadow, and the high peaks that rein it all in. Shortly after this view is a side trail on the left (south) leading to Little Redfish Lake.

Now you're stuck with the rest of the long pull to the top of Red Ridge. You make slow progress but then finally reach the pass. Big Boulder Creek lies behind you, creating a magnificent view. Below Railroad Ridge to the northwest, not quite in sight, is Livingston Mill. On the other side of the pass, Castle Peak rises ahead, framed by the ridge's wind-lashed whitebark pine. Below are the two Frog Lakes in a meadow of marsh grass.

The trail descends toward the Frog Lakes in seven long switchbacks. We tried fishing here, but the only things jumping were the frogs. From Frog Lakes, you can see the northeast face of Castle Peak and, in front of it, Merriam Peak (10,920 feet). Dr. John Merriam was an economist who was extremely influential in saving the White Clouds and establishing the SNRA. Upon his death in a hypothermia-drowning accident, Merriam Peak was named after him.

You'll leave Frog Lakes as the trail turns in a westerly direction to traverse a sagebrush hill. An excellent view accompanies you as you walk along into the Little Boulder Creek drainage below.

The hike from Frog Lakes on is pure joy. After a brief trek through sagebrush, you'll enter forest and lake country. The trail crosses the outlet of Willow Lake, where the forest has mostly reclaimed itself after the debacle that first aroused concern for this area. (See the Boulder and White Cloud Mountains overview.) Just past the lake outlet is a trail junction. Take the right fork; the left leads down into the Little Boulder Creek drainage.

After Willow Lake the trail climbs steadily from lake to lake, each one jumping with little trout. Once you turn south to skirt the edge of Hourglass Lake, the country becomes more alpine. The next lake up is Lake 9,643. To the south, you'll see a boulder slope that you ascend to get to Windy Devil Pass. From the lake, it looks more difficult than it is. Once you start up the trail, it's easy and obviously marked.

The pass welcomes you with a great view. A few hundred yards beyond the pass is a wonderful view of Serrate Ridge as it merges with Castle Peak. The nameless peak on the east side of the pass is Peak 10,296.

**Options:** Little Boulder Creek access to the Boulder Chain Lakes is about a mile shorter than from Livingston Mill but less pleasant. The first 2 miles climb 1,000 feet through sagebrush. However, there are excellent, classic views of Castle Peak on this route. To access the route, continue 3 miles past Livingston Mill Road. There is no room to park at the trailhead, so you must walk the last 0.3 mile. This route is open to motorcycles until it meets Boulder Chain Lakes Trail.

If you want close-up views of Castle Peak, a traverse can be done with a shuttle (long) or by two parties exchanging vehicle keys after meeting in the middle.

From the west, the Sawtooth Valley side, you enter via a 12-mile drive on Pole Creek Road to the Germainia Creek Trailhead. The last 4 miles are rough and may

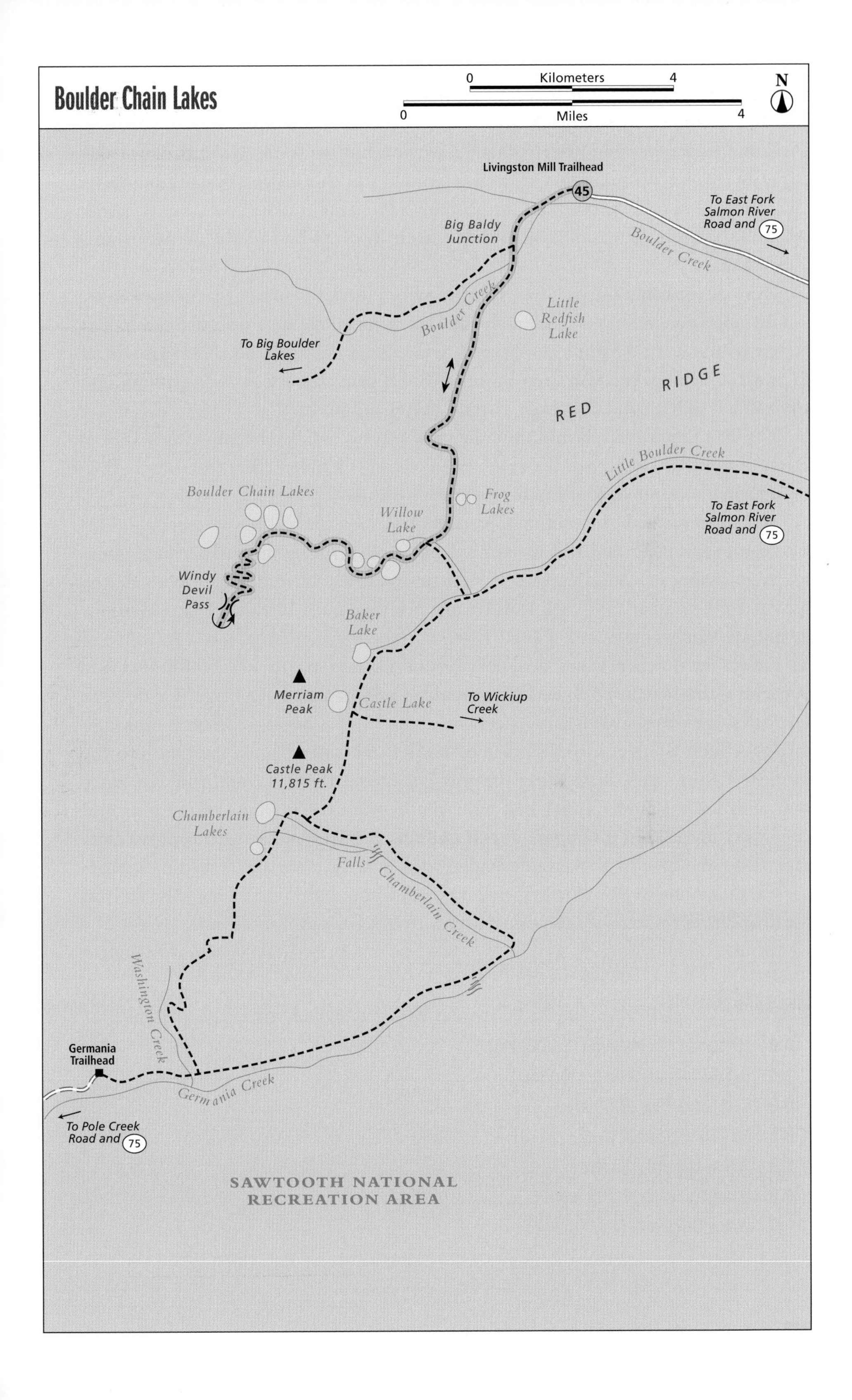
Boulder Chain Lakes
0
Kilometers
4
0
Miles
4
N
Livingston Mill Trailhead
45
To East Fork
Salmon River
Road and 75
Big Baldy
Junction
Boulder Creek
Little
Redfish
Lake
To Big Boulder
Lakes
Boulder Creek
RED RIDGE
Little Boulder Creek
Boulder Chain Lakes
Frog
Lakes
Willow
Lake
To East Fork
Salmon River
Road and 75
Windy
Devil
Pass
Baker
Lake
Merriam
Peak
Castle Lake
To Wickiup
Creek
Castle Peak
11,815 ft.
Chamberlain
Lakes
Falls
Chamberlain Creek
Washington Creek
Germania
Trailhead
Germania Creek
To Pole Creek
Road and 75
SAWTOOTH NATIONAL
RECREATION AREA

require four-wheel drive if the road is muddy and the stream is high. Germainia Creek Trail is open to trail machines.

From the trailhead and Germainia Creek, you can get to the Chamberlain Lakes either by taking Washington Creek Trail (easier and shorter) or by continuing up Germainia Creek for 5 miles to Chamberlain Lakes Trail (marked by a cairn). About 0.5 mile before this junction, not visible from the trail but audible, is Germainia Creek Falls.

From the east side, Germainia Creek Trail from the East Fork of the Salmon River to Chamberlain Creek is a moderately difficult, 5-mile hike on a well-defined trail. It begins with a steep 0.5-mile climb up to wide meadows that gradually narrow over the next 1.5 miles. You will then be treated to a panoramic view of a willow- and aspen-filled valley, framed by high, rugged ridges and peaks.

The trail then descends into the valley and intersects Chamberlain Creek Trail in about 3 miles. You will cross the creek twice about 0.5 mile before this intersection. Be prepared to remove your boots for these crossings.

The junction with the trail up Chamberlain Creek to the lakes is steep (a 2,000-foot climb) and little used. It is marked by only a cairn. Along the trail itself are places where it disappears. Good navigation skills are required. In its upper reaches are the spectacular Chamberlain Creek Falls (visible from the trail). They are your reward for taking the harder route.

From Chamberlain Lakes, you skirt around Castle Peak to a 10,000-foot divide between Chamberlain Basin and the Boulder Creek drainage. The trail (Castle Peak Divide) is a bit rocky, with fairly steep switchbacks. It is another 2.5 miles through forest to Little Boulder Creek Trail and another mile after that to the trail into the Boulder Chain Lakes. Navigating the part between Baker Lake and the trail junction with Little Boulder Creek can be tricky because you're down in the trees and encounter myriad old mining roads and trails. As you work your way northeast for a mile along the base of Slickenslide Ridge, look and listen for the well-used motorcycle trail coming in from Little Boulder Creek to the right (east). This will take you north and over Slickenslide to connect with Boulder Chain Lakes Trail.

—Jackie Johnson Maughan

## Miles and Directions

**0.0** Livingston Mill Trailhead (7,200 feet)

**1.0** Big Boulder junction (7,700 feet)

**5.0** Red Ridge Pass (9,600 feet)

**6.5** Frog Lakes (8,800 feet)

**7.3** Willow Lake (8,735 feet)

**9.0** Hourglass Lake (9,500 feet)

**10.0** Windy Devil Pass (10,000 feet)

# 46 Boundary Creek

This hike has fine views of the Sawtooth Mountains to the west. It's also known for subalpine lakes and a chance to see wolves.

**Start:** 55 road miles north of Ketchum and 5.5 road miles south of Stanley
**Type of hike:** Day hike; out-and-back, with overnight or longer backpack options
**Distance:** 5.5 miles to the crest and back; 7.4 miles to Casino Lakes and back
**Approximate hiking time:** 1 to 3 or more days
**Difficulty:** Moderately strenuous due to the climb
**Best season:** July–September
**Trail surface:** Normal dirt and rock
**Land status:** Sawtooth National Recreation Area
**Canine compatibility :** Dogs on leash July 1–Labor Day
**Fees and permits:** Depends on the year. Check with forest service
**Maps:** Casino Lakes and East Basin Creek USGS quadrangles
**Trail contact:** Sawtooth National Recreation Area Headquarters, (208) 727-5000
**Special considerations:** Water is not available on this trail in late summer until you are over the crest. In early summer there is water near the top of the trail on the side that faces the Sawtooth Valley.

**Finding the trailhead:** Take ID 75 north from Ketchum for almost 55 miles or south from Stanley for 5.5 miles to the signed Boundary Creek Trail turnoff road. It is a good dirt road that climbs up into a steep, shallow canyon. It is a mile to the trailhead. GPS: N44 09.40' / W114 52.06'
**Parking and trailhead facilities:** This trailhead has a registration box, hitching post, loading ramp, and bulletin board but no latrine.

## The Hike

This is a steep trail, which quickly climbs to fine views of the Mount Heyburn area of the Sawtooth Range just across the valley. You can hike for just a mile or all the way to Casino Lakes. The trail loses its snow on the west side of the crest fairly early in the year (mid-June). It is open to dirt bikes but not ATVs. I have yet to encounter a dirt bike in my four trips up the trail.

The trail begins in an open forest with grass, sagebrush, and wildflowers, and it climbs gently to moderately. Except for a bridged crossing of the creek at 0.25 mile, the trail stays away from Boundary Creek.

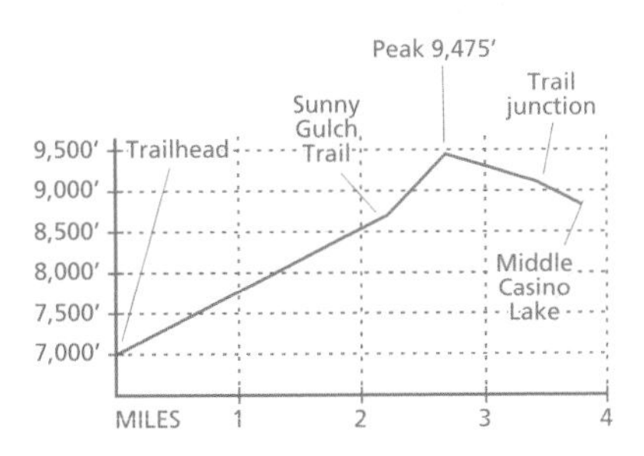


Gradually, the grade increases to steep and, in some places, very steep. You continue to pass through open forest, and you soon gain grand views of the Sawtooth Range and the Redfish Lake moraine in front of

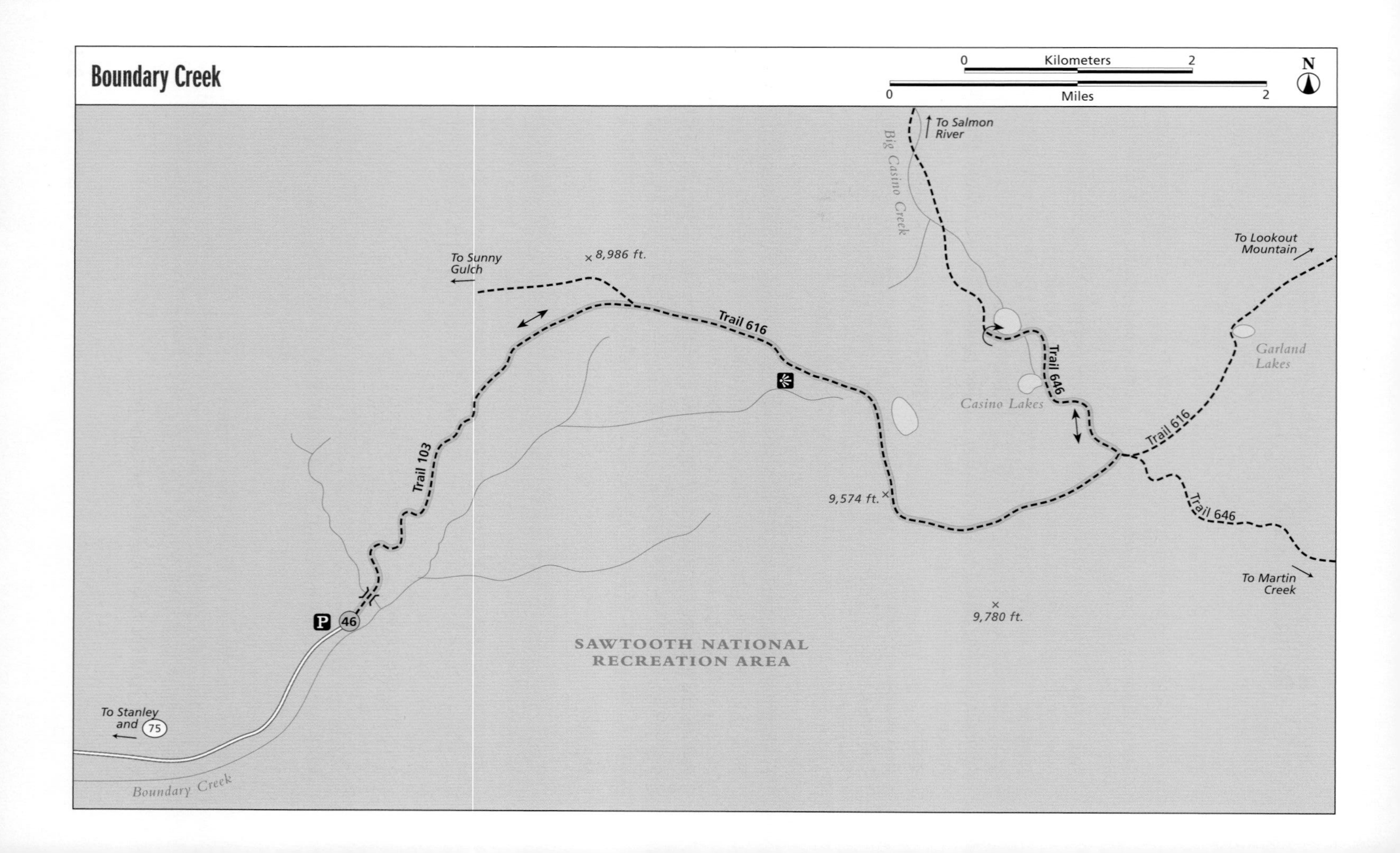
Boundary Creek
0
Kilometers
2
0
Miles
2
N
To Salmon River
Big Casino Creek
To Lookout Mountain
To Sunny Gulch
8,986 ft.
Trail 616
Trail 646
Garland Lakes
Casino Lakes
Trail 616
Trail 103
9,574 ft.
Trail 646
To Martin Creek
P
46
9,780 ft.
SAWTOOTH NATIONAL RECREATION AREA
To Stanley and 75
Boundary Creek

them. The open forest continues until you reach about 8,300 feet. There are some huge Douglas fir trees scattered about.

After the forest, you cross the open top of Boundary Creek Canyon with views of the Sawtooths for about 180 degrees.

At 8,700 feet you suddenly enter a dense ridgetop forest, and the grade of the trail lessens as it reaches a broad ridgetop. Here a very prominent fork to another trail leaves at a ninety-degree angle to the left. This is Sunny Gulch Trail, which comes up from the Salmon River. Stay to the right.

The trail continues to climb through a dense forest, but not steeply. You are now crossing the headwaters of Boundary Creek, and there is often some water in the creek beside, or not far from, the trail. The way is forested, but you pass a nice green meadow.

Slowly, the trail regains the ridgetop. There are views of the Casino Lakes on the other side. Then the trail climbs steeply, gaining 200 feet along the crest, and you go right over Peak 9,475. Just past the peak, the trail curves to the left (east), and you drop down 700 feet to the middle of the three Casino Lakes in the meadowy basin at the head of Big Casino Creek.

**Options:** There is a major trail junction about 0.5 mile above the middle Casino Lake. The left fork goes to middle Casino. The middle trail goes past one of the Garland Lakes and then over a ridge to Rough Lake. The right fork goes past some of the upper Garland Lakes and then turns south and drops into Martin Creek. Martin Creek and the trail go into the wonderful Warm Springs meadow area.

You can exit Casino Lake by going down Big Casino Creek to the Salmon River and a shuttle. There is a bridge across the Salmon River here. This is a densely forested trail, one I found of little interest.

—Ralph Maughan

## Miles and Directions

**0.0** Trailhead (6,950 feet)
**0.2** Bridge (7,020 feet)
**2.3** Sunny Gulch Trail junction (8,700 feet)
**2.7** Peak 9,475 (9,475 feet)
**3.4** Trail junction (9,100 feet)
**3.8** Middle Casino Lake (8,790 feet)

# 47 East Pass Creek

The East Pass Creek trail has some amazing views, a large waterfall, and many resident elk.

**Start:** On the lesser known east side of the Boulder Mountains
**Type of hike:** Backpack; out-and-back or shuttle
**Distance:** 19 miles round-trip
**Approximate hiking time:** 2–4 days
**Difficulty:** Moderate for the out-and-back; strenuous for the near loop into Herd Creek and back to the North Fork of the Big Lost River
**Best season:** July is best
**Trail surface:** Normal dirt and rock
**Land status:** Salmon-Challis National Forest
**Canine compatibility:** On leash
**Fees and permits:** None
**Maps:** Bowery Peak and Meridian Peak USGS quadrangles
**Trail contact:** Lost River Ranger District, (208) 588-3400
**Special considerations:** Bring wading shoes

**Finding the trailhead:** To get to the trailhead, drive to Ketchum and then east through Sun Valley and up to Trail Creek Summit. Another access is from Mackay. Drive northward on US 93, turning west onto the paved county highway near Mount Borah. A third way is to drive southward from Challis on US 93 over Willow Creek Summit and then turn right onto the county road near Mount Borah.

If you came from Ketchum, drive 8 miles beyond Trail Creek Summit down Summit Creek. From the eastern approach (Challis or Mackay), drive 20.7 miles west from the turnoff from US 93, passing by the Copper Basin turnoff. From either direction, you then turn off the main road onto the road up the North Fork of the Big Lost River (FR 444). Head up this broad stream valley on the graveled 10- to 15-mile-per-hour road.

The North Fork of the Big Lost River is a gentle and scenic stream valley, filled with meadows and willows. Lightly timbered mountains, built of the colorful Challis Volcanics, rise to the right. High mountains, with more timber and more typical of the higher parts of the Boulder Mountains, rise across the stream valley on your left as you drive up the North Fork.

As you near the end of North Fork Road, be sure you don't cross the stream. The road to the trailhead (FR 477) leaves to the right just before the main road makes its only crossing of the North Fork on a bridge. At the road junction is a sign that reads Hunter Creek Trailhead. This junction is 10.8 miles from the turnoff onto North Fork Road.

It's a rough mile on this road to where the trail begins. Drive carefully because it may be muddy after storms or early in the year. You could get badly mired. Park at the meadow at the mouth of Hunter Creek, which is the obvious canyon running upward to the north of the head of the North Fork Valley. GPS: N43 55.83' / W114 20.59'

**Parking and trailhead facilities:** The trailhead is undeveloped and mostly in the sun. There is room for about six vehicles. The trail (Trail 050) goes up the steep hill to the north. A sign indicates that it is closed to all motor vehicles. There is a splendid view from the trailhead of the big peaks at the head of the North Fork.

## The Hike

Follow the steep trail up the hill into Hunter Creek Canyon. The trail is easy to follow as it climbs 1,300 feet in less than 3 miles to Hunter Creek Summit at 9,410 feet. You cross Hunter Creek a couple of times (no problem) as you climb the pleasant, mostly forested canyon to the summit, which is a fairly broad clearing.

At the pass, don't be misled and follow the trail that goes along the ridge crest (see Options at the end of this description). Instead, go straight down into East Pass Creek, dropping steeply for 700 feet in less than a mile on a trail that usually has several eroding side routes. You end the descent at a pleasant grassy meadow where the headwaters of East Pass Creek splash by and unnamed peaks, over 10,500 feet, rise around you.

At the meadow's lower end, a mountain with rugged pinnacles and cliffs comes into view downcanyon. For the next 3 miles, its intriguing form looms closer and closer. This mountain is the north end of a high disjunct ridge of the Boulder Mountains topped by Sheep Mountain at 10,910 feet (unseen from this vantage point). The unnamed peaks in sight are higher than 10,700 feet.

The canyon deepens as you walk down East Pass Creek. Two miles below the meadow, East Pass Creek leaps off a ledge, forming a major waterfall.

Below the waterfall, the canyon gets deeper still and begins to dry out. Sagebrush begins to appear in the meadows, and clumps of aspen appear among the conifers. The trail passes directly under the pinnacled mountain, and the canyon bends toward the east. However, at the bend a trail leaves to your left and climbs out of East Pass Creek into Bowery Creek (see Options).

After about 2 more miles, the trail peters out as it approaches a gorge. Although this is the end of the trail, you can choose to continue (see Options).

**Options:** One option starts at Hunter Creek Summit. Follow the ridgeline trail to the right for a 0.7-mile climb to a very fine view on a bare, but scenic, ridgetop. Here at Point 9,923, you have a grand 180-degree view of the Boulder Mountains.

A second option is to take Bowery Creek Trail out of East Pass Creek and down Bowery Creek to ford the East Fork of the Salmon River (requires a major ford early in season), where you will need to have a (50-mile) shuttle. This trail climbs to an 8,600-foot pass and a relatively easy walk down Bowery Creek. You will have a dramatic view of 11,800-foot Castle Peak in the White Cloud Mountains as you descend Bowery Creek. It is about 5 miles from the summit to the East Fork of the Salmon River. The only downside is that this drainage has been subjected at times to very abusive cattle grazing. When we did the hike, the views into the distance were heavenly, but the streamside was cow hell.

A final option is to climb out of East Pass Creek up onto the Bowery Peak–Sheep Mountain ridge to an alpine lake, descend into Herd Creek, and then make a big circle up Herd Creek to Herd Peak and down to North Fork Road for a short shuttle or a walk of about 4 miles to the Hunter Creek Trailhead.

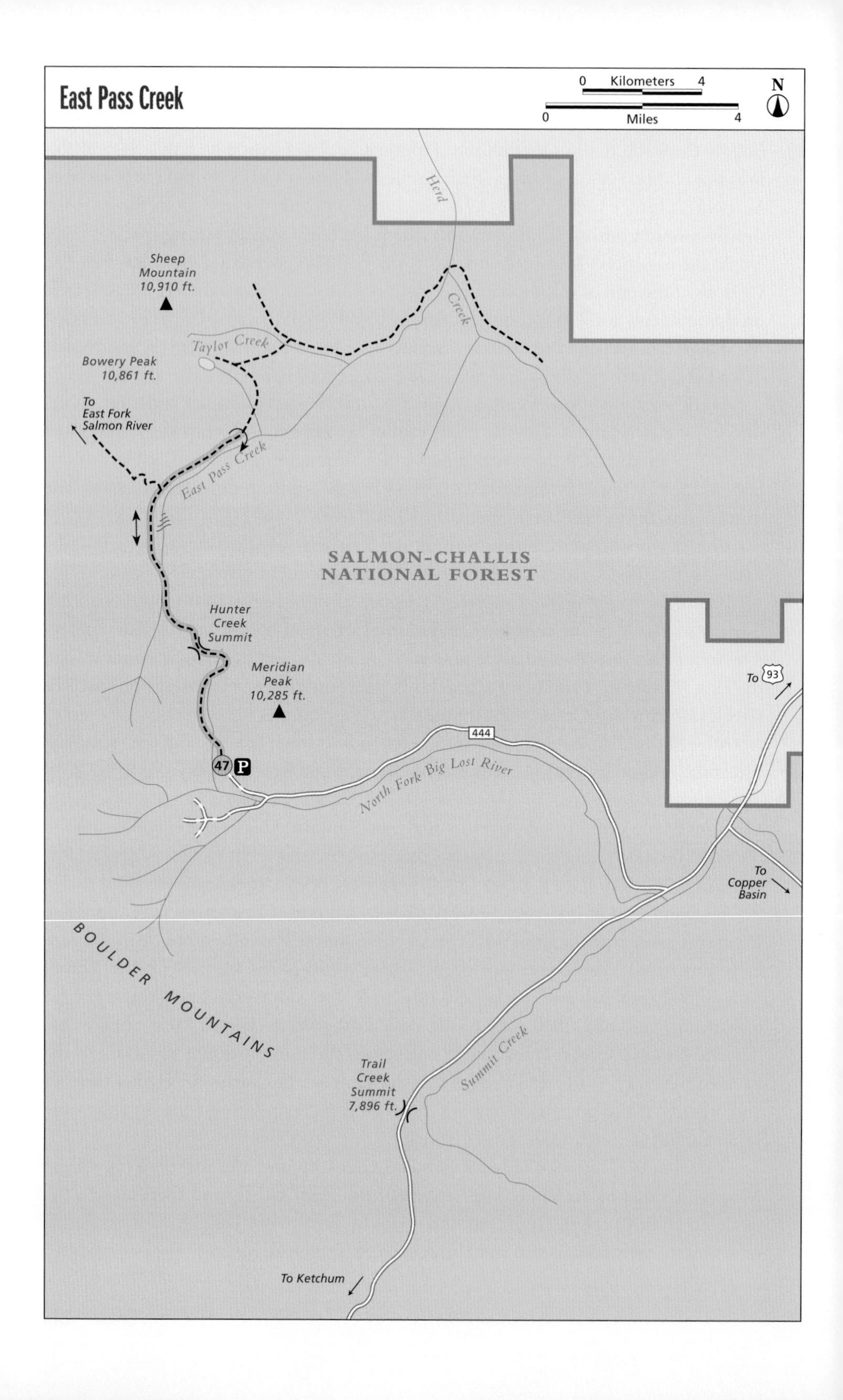
East Pass Creek
0 Kilometers 4
0 Miles 4
N
Herd Creek
Sheep Mountain 10,910 ft.
Taylor Creek
Bowery Peak 10,861 ft.
To East Fork Salmon River
East Pass Creek
SALMON-CHALLIS NATIONAL FOREST
Hunter Creek Summit
Meridian Peak 10,285 ft.
444
47
P
North Fork Big Lost River
To 93
To Copper Basin
BOULDER MOUNTAINS
Summit Creek
Trail Creek Summit 7,896 ft.
To Ketchum

To do the final option, make the difficult climb out of East Pass Creek at the end of the trail to barren Lake 9,436. From the lake, you can climb to the ridgeline that includes Bowery Peak and Sheep Mountain and various unnamed summits of this high northerly extension of the Boulder Mountains. From the ridge, you gain a rare viewpoint of the White Cloud Peaks that lie to the west across the East Fork of the Salmon River. The high southern portion of the Boulder Mountains sweeps around to the southwest. To the east is a tall, treeless ridge that encloses Herd Creek and, rising beyond, the peaks of the Lost River Mountains.

From the lake, you can get into the Herd Creek country by descending from the lake into Taylor Creek until you come upon the trail down Taylor Creek to East Pass Creek, below the gorge that blocked your passage. When you come to East Pass Creek's confluence with Herd Creek, head up the trail along Herd Creek, and then East Herd Creek, into the high and open Challis Volcanic country. A good route is to follow East Herd and then climb up into Lake Basin. From there, attain the ridgeline and follow it all the way to Herd Peak. This is a relatively easy, 8,800- to 9,800-foot ridgeline for 6 miles. By following it you can almost close a loop back to the North Fork of the Big Lost River. A trail exists in places, but the route is always obvious if you use your topographic map. From 9,820-foot Herd Peak, follow the ridge southwestward until it drops down Toolbox Creek to the North Fork of the Big Lost River Road. The Hunter Creek Trailhead is 4 miles up North Fork Road from Toolbox Creek. You will need to walk the road.

This cross-country loop is about 20 miles long. This area of bare mountains, wildflower meadows, hundreds of elk, and views into forever has no official name, but it is increasingly referred to as the Herd Peak Highlands.

—Ralph Maughan

## Miles and Directions

**0.0** Trailhead (8,100 feet)

**2.5** Hunter Creek Summit (9,410 feet)

**3.3** Meadow (8,600 feet)

**5.5** East Pass Creek falls (8,070 feet)

**7.7** Bowery Creek Trail junction (7,770 feet)

**9.5** End of trail (7,400 feet)

# 48 Fourth of July Creek to Born Lakes

Stunning views of the White Cloud Peaks abound with numerous subalpine lakes.

**Start:** On the west side of the White Cloud Mountains, 25 miles northwest of Ketchum
**Type of hike:** Long day hike or backpack; out-and-back
**Distance:** 4 miles (one way) to the Born Lakes
**Approximate hiking time:** 2–4 days
**Difficulty:** Moderate, unless early in the season when snowfields must be crossed on the last leg of the hike to the Born Lakes
**Best season:** Mid-July–early September
**Trail surface:** Normal dirt and rock
**Land status:** Sawtooth National Recreation Area
**Canine compatibility:** Dogs on leash July 1–Labor Day
**Fees and permits:** No fees; self-issued permits
**Maps:** Boulder Chain Lakes and Washington Peak USGS quadrangles; Fairfield and Ketchum Ranger Districts–Sawtooth National Forest map
**Trail contacts:** Sawtooth National Recreation Area Headquarters, (208) 727-5000
**Special considerations:** About a mile of this trail is near the top of a ridge or a high treeless basin, making lightning a threat.

**Finding the trailhead:** Finding the trailhead is easy. Turn off ID 75 in the middle of the Sawtooth Valley 15 miles south of Stanley. Follow this gravel side road directly up into the White Cloud Mountains. You reach the trailhead in 11 miles. The road narrows to one lane, but it is gravel all the way, suitable for a sedan. There are no side roads that would cause you confusion. GPS: N44 02.82' / W114 39.46'
**Parking and trailhead facilities:** The trailhead is a large gravel parking lot with loading ramps, a restroom, and room for about thirty vehicles. It has partial shade but no water except the nearby creek.

## The Hike

This is a busy hike, especially the first 1.4 miles to beautiful Fourth of July Lake.

The trail to Fourth of July Lake is open to all but ATVs and full-size vehicles. The trail from there to the Born Lakes is closed to motor vehicles. The first leg of the trail to Fourth of July Lake has modest scenery, but many use it because the trailhead gives high elevation and deep access into the White Cloud Mountains. The lake itself is very pretty with meadows all around it, and big, bold Patterson Peak (10,872 feet) rises just to the lake's east.

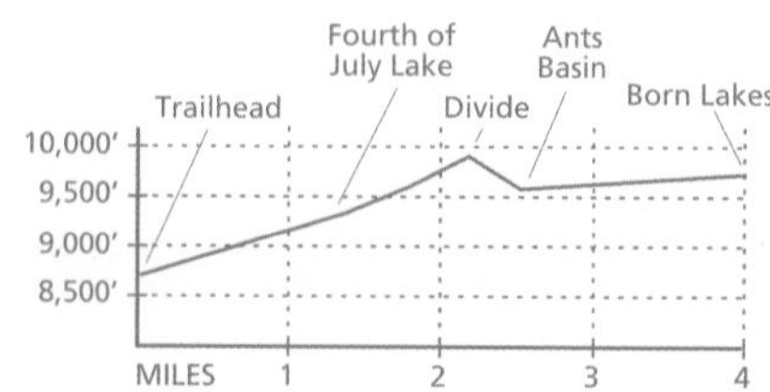


The wide trail is easy to find and leaves directly east of the trailhead. You quickly cross a good bridge over Fourth of July Creek and then come to the Phyllis Lake jeep road, which the trail crosses at a right angle.

*Fourth of July Lake.* PHOTO BY LUKE KRATZ

The trail climbs at a moderate pace all the way to Fourth of July Lake. The first third of the route is a pleasant, willowy meadow to the left of the trail. You get glimpses of the high peaks but cannot really see any of them unless you hike off the trail and search for a viewpoint. Most of this short hike is through forest.

Just before the lake, you encounter a signed trail junction. The fork to the Born Lakes is to the left, but before you take it, continue another 100 yards to the right (on what is now the trail to the Washington Lakes) and walk to the outlet of Fourth of July Lake. It is a beautiful scene with the lake framing Patterson Peak. Otherwise, you will miss seeing the lake until you are high above it.

On Born Lakes Trail, you quickly come to a sign indicating that no motor vehicles are allowed. The trail quickly narrows but is readily evident and easy to follow. Now you'll begin to climb more steeply, rapidly gaining more than 300 feet in 0.3 mile. The trail levels out, and you pass an unnamed, pretty lake with a view of all of the west-facing ramparts of Patterson Peak.

Now the trail climbs to the ridgetop, slanting to the northwest, without switchbacks. This climb through open forest gains just over 200 feet in 0.5 mile. Through the trees, you get excellent views of Fourth of July Lake, Fourth of July Creek Canyon, Patterson Peak, and an unnamed, triangular-shaped, light brown mountain across the canyon to the south (elevation 10,713 feet), and—off to the southwestern distance—Washington Peak (elevation 10,519 feet) and surrounding summits. The summits around Washington Peak are gray and stand in sharp contrast with brownish Peak 10,713 before you.

The trail attains the ridgetop divide and follows it briefly. It does not cross at a pass. On the divide, you get a splendid view in three directions. To the south are the peaks just described. To the west, the high point on your ridge is Blackman Peak (10,300 feet). In the far west rises the jagged Sawtooth Range. Directly below you to the north is meadowy Ants Basin, with a few trees and a pond. All around this side of the ridgetop rise the summits that were originally named the White Cloud Peaks in the years before the entire mountain range between the Salmon River on the north and Pole Creek on the south had that name affixed. Each of the peaks you see has a different shape and color. One in particular, Peak 11,314, can be described as light silver, almost white in some lighting conditions. Other peaks are shades of pink, gray, and brown, all of which change as the sun makes its daily transit across the sky.

These peaks are built mostly of granite, although some of the white peaks are formed of a kind of marble (metamorphosed limestone). I found it difficult to describe what color the granite really was. For example, it may appear pinkish at 100 feet. When you examine the rock closely, you find it is made of many crystals of differing colors: neutral transparent, white, orange-red, black, pink. These are combinations of quartz, feldspar, mica, hornblende, and other minerals. The color your eye perceives is the product of the balance of all of these as illuminated by the color of the sunlight at a given time of day.

Geology lesson over, you drop quickly off the ridge, switchbacking down to Ants Basin. If you attempt this hike too early, this is where you will encounter your greatest problem. Early in the season (for example, late June), this slope will be covered with a steeply inclined snowfield.

As you reach the sod of Ants Basin, the well-worn tread of the trail vanishes. To find it again, walk east-by-northeast and you will soon see the tread leading up into some trees at the basin's edge. From here it drops into the headwaters of Warm Springs Creek, which is the big canyon between Ants Basin and the White Cloud Peaks.

The trail is not shown on the Washington Peak topographic quadrangle. It is shown on the adjacent Boulder Chain Lakes quad, but in the wrong place. Trail traffic has changed a great deal since these maps were compiled in the 1960s.

Soon the trail passes high above the first of the Born Lakes, a pond in a grassy meadow. Keeping high, just above the timber, the trail leads to the other lakes. It is hard to say when you have arrived because there are many Born Lakes (they were named after Boren, a prospector) scattered about in the timber just below the rock line. They are of varying shapes and sizes and number perhaps ten in all. I estimate the distance to the last and highest of the lakes to be about 4 miles from the trailhead.

The entire area is very scenic, situated as it is beneath the north flank of Patterson Peak and other rugged peaks—nameless and with no exact elevation recorded, but all well over 10,000 feet.

If you wish, you can locate an old trail down Warm Springs Creek. You are at its very head. It is the longest canyon in the White Cloud Mountains. In recent years, this has been summer range of a large wolf pack.

**Options:** Back at Fourth of July Lake, if you take the right fork of the trail, it leads over a low divide (9,560 feet) to large, scenic Washington Lake in just 1 mile. This is a busy trail, even more so than the one to Born Lakes.

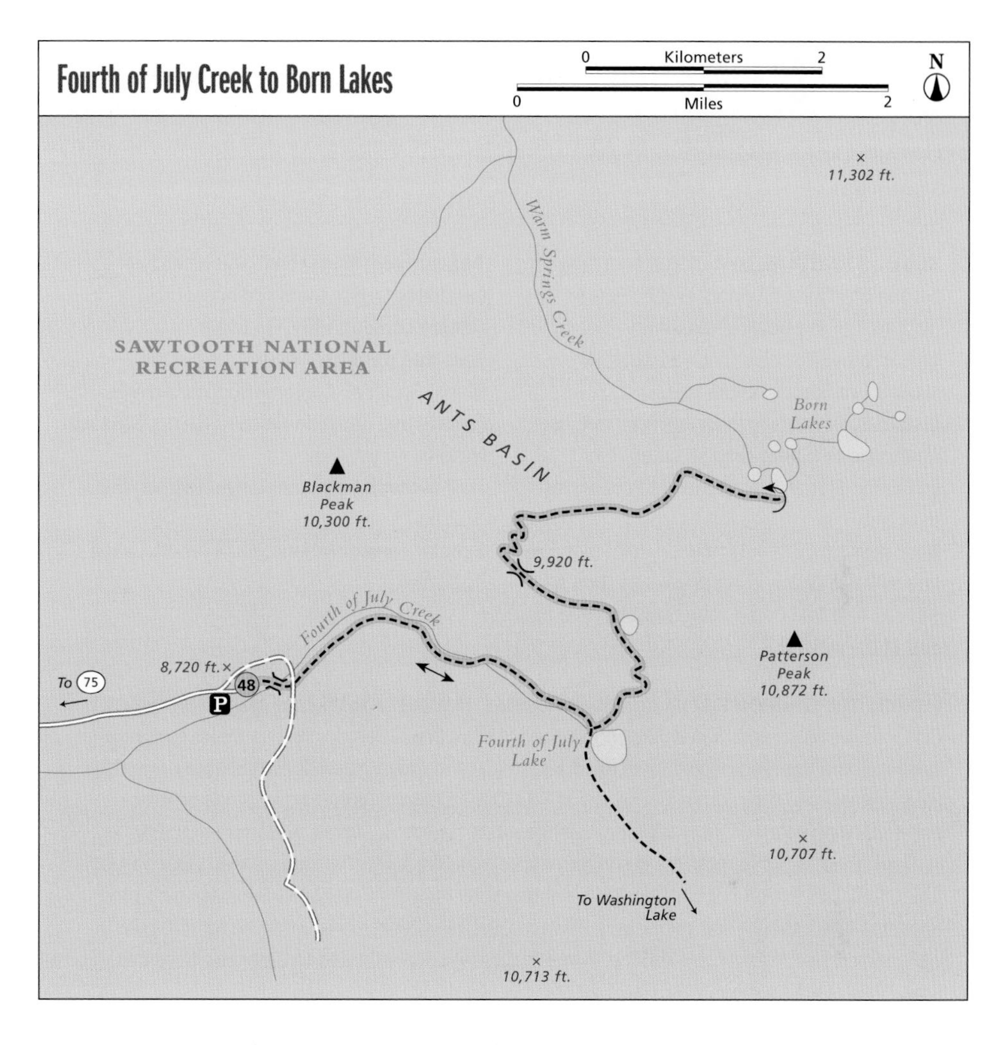


From Born Lakes, you can also scramble over the crest to the east to Four Lakes Basin. This is rugged off-trail hiking, not for those with unsteady balance.

—Ralph Maughan

## Miles and Directions

**0.0** Trailhead (8,720 feet)

**0.2** Phyllis Lake jeep road crossing

**1.4** Fourth of July Lake (9,365 feet)

**1.7** Unnamed lake (9,660 feet)

**2.2** Ridgetop divide; great view (9,920 feet)

**2.5** Ants Basin (9,580 feet)

**4.0** Highest of the Born Lakes (9,700 feet)

# 49 High Ridge Trail

Here are some magnificent views of the glaciated Pioneer Mountains, the Boulder Mountains, and Trail Creek Gorge.

**Start:** 13 road miles east of Ketchum, just beyond Trail Creek Summit, in the southernmost part of the Boulder Mountains
**Type of hike:** Day hike; out-and-back, or shuttle if you do the entire trail
**Distance:** 6.4 miles to Rock Roll Point and back
**Approximate hiking time:** 4 hours
**Difficulty:** Moderately strenuous because of the climb
**Best season:** Early July to Rock Roll Point. The trail to Basin Gulch is accessible as soon as you can ford Trail Creek. Late September is the end of the season.
**Trail surface:** Normal dirt and rock
**Land status:** Sawtooth National Forest
**Canine compatibility:** On leash
**Fees and permits:** None
**Maps:** Rock Roll Canyon USGS quadrangle; Fairfield and Ketchum Ranger Districts–Sawtooth National Forest map
**Trail contact:** Ketchum Ranger District, (208) 622-5371
**Special considerations:** You'll have to wade Trail Creek.

**Finding the trailhead:** From downtown Ketchum, turn east and take the road to Sun Valley. Continue eastward past Sun Valley on this road up Trail Creek Canyon. Just as the canyon begins to narrow and the road begins to climb, the road turns to rough gravel. It climbs on a precipitous ledge above Trail Creek Gorge all the way to Trail Creek Summit. Although hundreds of vehicles travel this road every day, it is winding, washboarded, narrow in places, and without guardrails.

Drive about 0.5 mile past the summit to Park Creek Road, which accesses the upper part of Trail Creek. Turn left onto this dirt road. It climbs gently through a meadow (through which runs ephemeral Park Creek) and then drops down toward Trail Creek. A mile after the turnoff, take the well-marked side road on the left. The road travels down a short grade to a bench above Trail Creek. This is the trailhead. GPS: N43 49.99' / W114 16.90'
**Parking and trailhead facilities:** The trailhead has room for five or six vehicles. It is partially shaded by lodgepole pine. The trail's beginning is obvious and is well posted as closed to all vehicles.

## The Hike

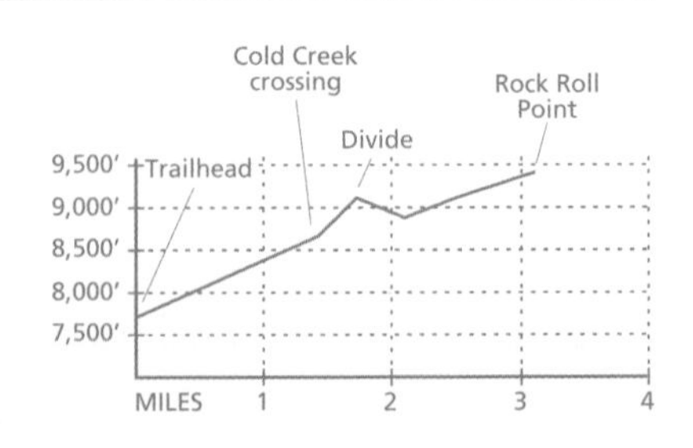


The trail, formerly an old logging road, drops down a short grade to Trail Creek, where the stream meanders through a meadow just before plunging into its famous gorge.

The ford of Trail Creek is in this meadow. It is an easy wade after snowmelt but a torrent earlier in the season. On the other side, the trail is obvious. You walk along it on a

*En route to High Ridge.* PHOTO BY LUKE KRATZ

lodgepole-covered flat near the mouth of Cold Canyon. The old track ends after about 0.25 mile, and you climb very steeply on the trail, gaining about 200 feet, into Cold Creek Canyon. The trailside forest changes to spruce and fir because a moister microclimate prevails in the canyon.

The trail continues to climb at brief intervals interspersed with lengths of relatively level terrain until it breaks out of the forest at about 8,300 feet. Here in the open, the trail immediately becomes fainter. Keeping to it is aided by the rock cairns along the pathway. Here you have a view of the steep cirque headwall at the canyon's top and, downstream, of that part of the Boulder Mountains that rises just north of Summit Creek. (Summit Creek is the geographic divide between the Pioneer and Boulder Mountains.)

The trail crosses Cold Creek exactly at contour 8,600 feet on the map. Look for cairns on the other side. They direct you into, and through, small conifers (struggling back after an avalanche) and up the south side of Cold Creek Canyon for a climb to Basin Gulch. This steep climb is through the timber, reaching the divide of 9,120 feet in about a third of a mile. Then you drop about 200 feet, descending mostly through limber pine, to the relatively flat floor (flat compared with Cold Canyon) of the North Fork of Basin Gulch. Rock Roll Peak (10,458 feet), the southernmost

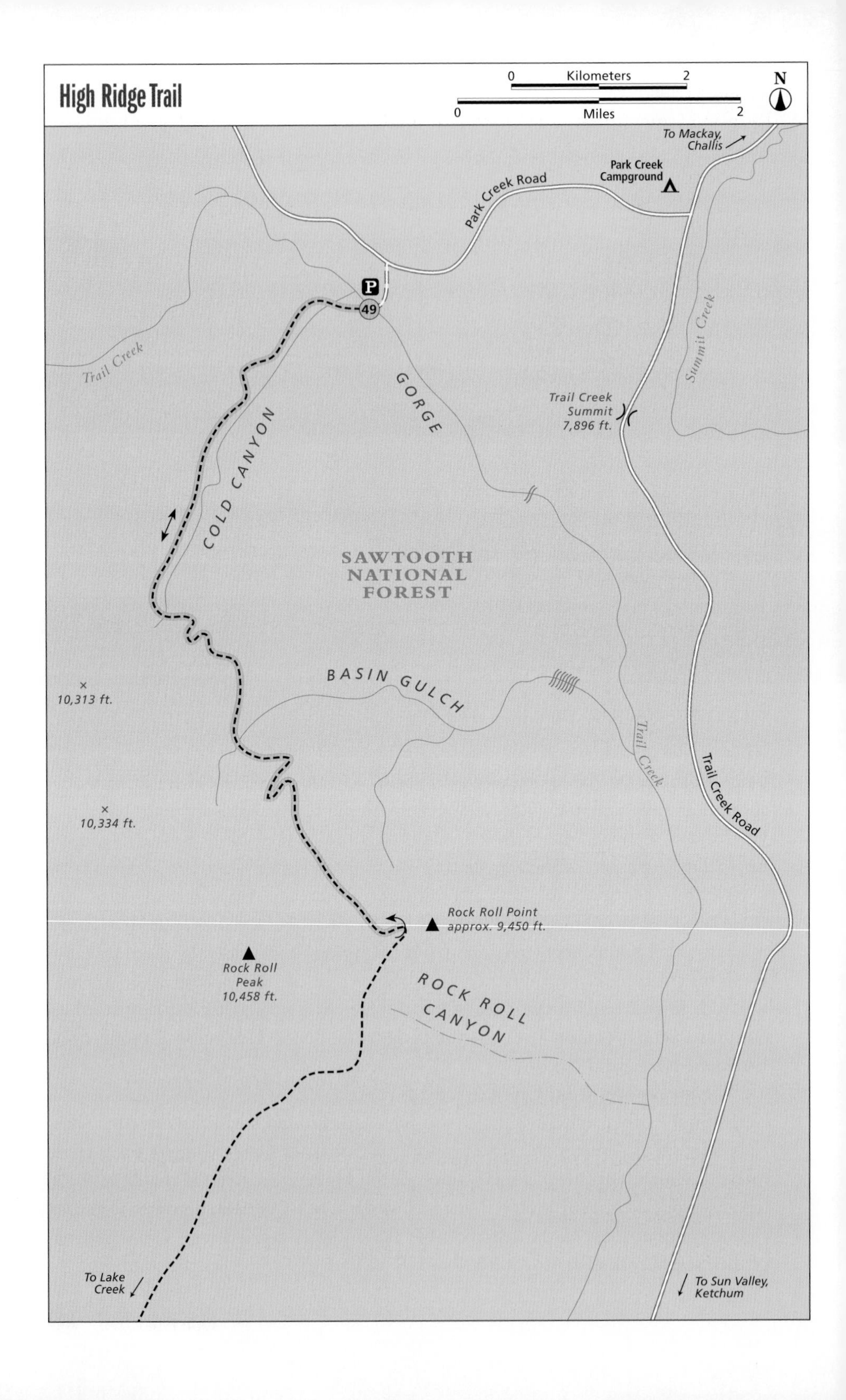
High Ridge Trail
0 Kilometers 2
0 Miles 2
N
To Mackay, Challis
Park Creek Campground
Park Creek Road
P
49
Trail Creek
GORGE
COLD CANYON
Summit Creek
Trail Creek Summit 7,896 ft.
SAWTOOTH NATIONAL FOREST
10,313 ft.
BASIN GULCH
Trail Creek
Trail Creek Road
10,334 ft.
Rock Roll Point approx. 9,450 ft.
Rock Roll Peak 10,458 ft.
ROCK ROLL CANYON
To Lake Creek
To Sun Valley, Ketchum

of the Boulders, rises grandly above the basin. There are some nice flat places in the basin and some springs as well as the stream. The Sawtooth National Forest has designated Basin Gulch a Research Natural Area for limber pine. You may want to check whether camping is allowed.

Looking down the "gulch," you can see part of Trail Creek Gorge, but a much better view comes as you climb over into Basin Gulch's other fork. To do this, follow cairns that lead you into the timber for another brief, but steep, climb over the divide between the two forks of Basin Gulch (a 360-foot climb this time and not quite as steep as that out of Cold Canyon).

Just beyond this 9,200-foot-high divide between the two forks of Basin Gulch, the trail breaks out into the open, high above the gulch's south fork. Here is an awesome view down into Trail Creek Gorge, in which the road clings to the very steep, avalanche-scored slope that rises from the gorge's depths all the way to the peaks of the Pioneer Mountains. Basin Gulch, as seen from the road, is one of the scenic highlights of Trail Creek Road. Each year, tens of thousands of people admire it from below as its stream cascades down the salmon-pink mountainside into the abyss. Of course, only an infinitesimal percentage ever view the scene from the opposite direction.

The trail is narrow across the top of this fork of Basin Gulch, but it seems gripped to the side of Rock Roll Peak, and the going is fairly easy as you traverse to Rock Roll Point, climbing gently most of the way.

The point is obvious. Its elevation is about 9,450 feet. The trail reaches it and swings around for about a 110-degree turn across the top of Rock Roll, a canyon that plunges about 2,600 feet in just 0.75 mile into Trail Creek. Most people stop here, where they can admire the tremendous view of the gorge and the high peaks of the Pioneers that rise immediately to the southwest.

**Options:** You can continue on the trail along the top of Trail Creek Gorge to the ridgeline and eventually down into Lake Creek if you have a second vehicle for a shuttle. It can all be done in one long day.

—Ralph Maughan

## Miles and Directions

**0.0** Trailhead (7,720 feet)

**0.1** Trail Creek ford (7,690 feet)

**1.4** Cold Creek crossing (8,600 feet)

**1.8** Cold Creek/Basin Gulch divide (9,120 feet)

**2.1** Head of north fork of Basin Gulch (8,840 feet)

**2.5** Two forks of Basin Gulch divide (9,200 feet)

**3.2** Rock Roll Point (9,450 feet)

# Pioneer Mountains

East of Ketchum and Hailey, south of the Boulder Mountains, west of the Lost River Range, and immediately north of the Snake River Plain rise the Pioneer Mountains, the second highest range in Idaho. Part of this range consists of the widespread and colorful Challis Volcanics we have mentioned so frequently. The core of the range consists, however, of intruded granitic rocks on the eastern side and a great variety of metamorphic rocks on the western side. The core of the range then consists of very hard rocks polished to perfection by glaciers.

This is a complicated mountain range, roughly oval in shape and very mixed in composition.

On the south, it consists of tall hills, or low mountains, that are almost bare save for groves of aspen overlooking the basaltic Snake River Plain. On the east these mountains are obscured by the somewhat lesser White Knob Range. To the north, they merge imperceptibly with the Boulder Mountains. On their west, they present a large area of ever-rising ridges that top out along a big north–south trending crest of eye-opening peaks, arêtes, and pinnacles. The crest is somewhat similar to the Sawtooth Range but higher (topping 12,000 feet at Hyndman Peak). However, the glaciated peak zone is less extensive than in the Sawtooths.

The Pioneers have almost no commercial timber. The major objection to protecting them as wilderness in their roadless heights has been from the sheep and cattle industry. These livestock are increasingly well controlled on the western (or Hailey-Ketchum) side of the range, but on the east, save for a few drainages like Fall Creek, you will find cattle or sheep to timberline and beyond, such as standing beside Idaho's highest lake—Goat Lake—and defecating in its icy waters. Because of livestock overuse, we have ignored some popular hikes, such as Broad Canyon, Bellas Lakes, Bear Canyon, and others. These mountains are a real favorite of hikers, backpackers, climbers, and mountain bikers.

Where the livestock are under control, wildlife is abundant, including pronghorn antelope, deer, elk, black bear, mountain goats, and an occasional moose. In the spring of 2000, the first wolf pack formed in the heights of the Fall Creek–Wildhorse Creek–Summit Creek area.

There are a score of subalpine and alpine lakes, including Idaho's highest—Goat Lake.

—Ralph Maughan

# 50 East Fork of the Big Wood River

This trail starts off with immediate access to the big peaks of the Pioneer Mountain crest.

**Start:** 25 miles northeast of Hailey
**Type of hike:** Day hike; out-and-back
**Distance:** 1.8 miles (2.3 to Johnstone Pass)
**Approximate hiking time:** At least 2 hours for time to explore
**Difficulty:** Moderately easy, but very difficult to Johnstone Pass
**Best season:** July–mid-September
**Trail surface:** Normal dirt and rock
**Land status:** Sawtooth National Forest
**Canine compatibility:** On leash
**Fees and permits:** None
**Maps:** Gray's Peak USGS quadrangle
**Trail contact:** Ketchum Ranger District, (208) 622-5371
**Special considerations:** The access road requires high clearance. If you try Johnstone Pass, have a hiking stick and boots with good-friction soles.

**Finding the trailhead:** To reach the East Fork Trailhead, turn off ID 75 onto the East Fork (of the Big Wood River) Road about 5.5 miles north of Hailey. Drive about 6 miles up the East Fork on a paved road past many houses to the junction of Hyndman Creek Road and East Fork Road. Keep to the right. About 100 yards past the junction, the oiled road ends to become gravel (often very washboarded). In just over a mile, you reach a Y intersection. Keep to the left. The Sawtooth National Forest boundary is another 1.5 miles ahead. As you cross the boundary, the road narrows to just about a lane and a half. In about a mile, you reach Federal Gulch. Again keep left. Now the road quickly deteriorates to become rocky (with embedded rocks), gradually steeper, and with places where spring water or meltwater runs down the road all year. The road doesn't wash out because it is so rocky.

You bump your way 5 miles to reach the small, unmaintained trailhead. GPS: N43 42.20' / W114 05.39'

**Parking and trailhead facilities:** There is room for about three vehicles, with more (shaded) places to park just before the trailhead. No water is available, not even in the stream, because the road ends at a landslide that absorbs the stream. There are no unloading ramps; visitors are urged to unload horses several miles downcanyon.

## The Hike

The forest service seems to have stopped maintaining this trail. There are no signs, but the trail is obvious, not very steep, and easy to follow most of the time. The canyon is kept well cleared by avalanches. These sometimes bring debris over the trail, but a new trail soon develops a few yards away. You cross through just one grove of mature conifers the entire hike.

The trail climbs briefly up the side of a landslide from the trailhead. You come to a small meadow, where you will find the small headwaters of the East Fork meandering. The Gray's Peak quadrangle shows the trail quickly crossing to the right side of the creek, but in fact it stays to the left side for about a mile. You have almost continuous

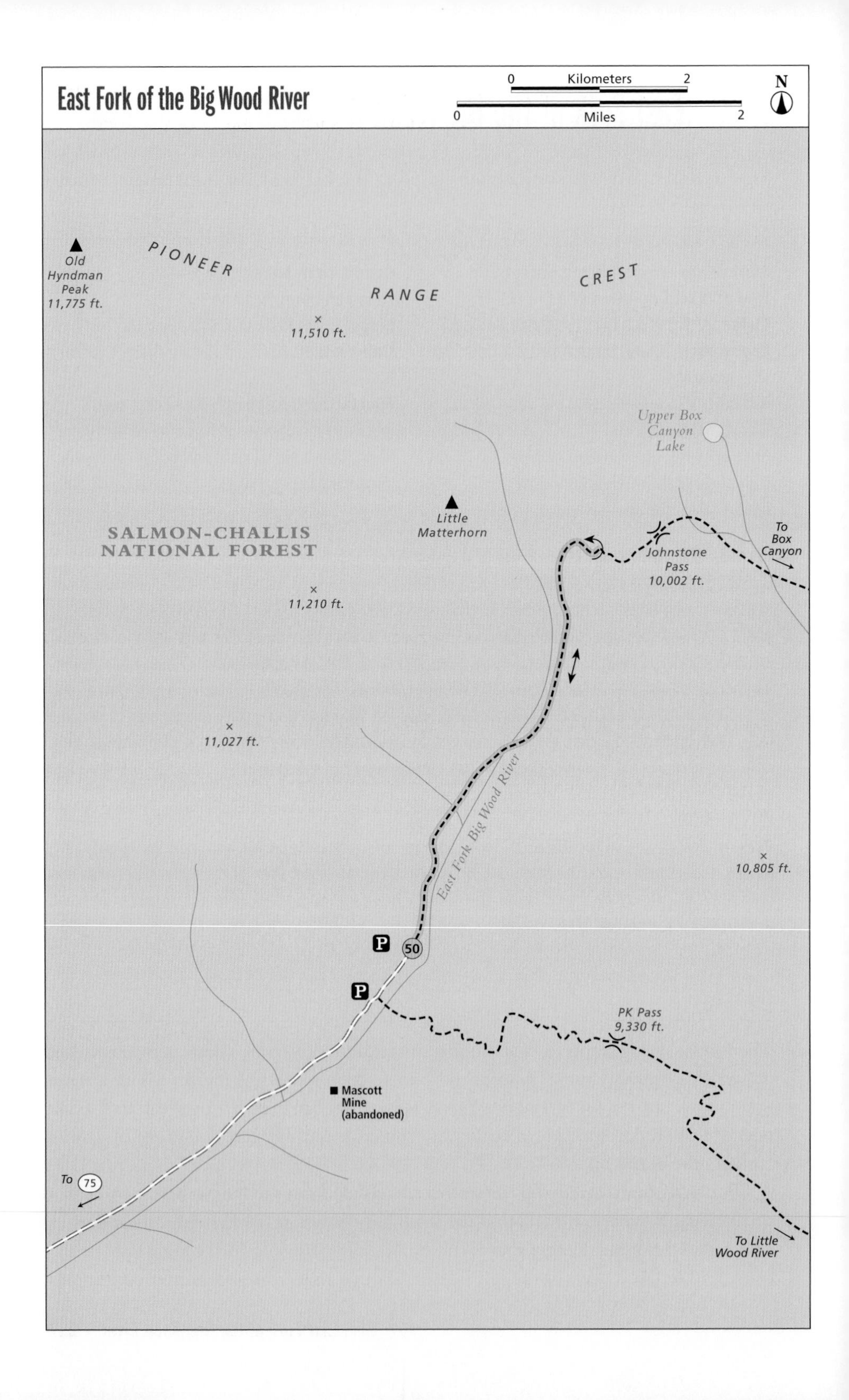

East Fork of the Big Wood River
0 Kilometers 2
0 Miles 2
N
Old Hyndman Peak 11,775 ft.
PIONEER
RANGE
CREST
11,510 ft.
Upper Box Canyon Lake
Little Matterhorn
SALMON-CHALLIS NATIONAL FOREST
To Box Canyon
Johnstone Pass 10,002 ft.
11,210 ft.
11,027 ft.
East Fork Big Wood River
10,805 ft.
50
P
P
PK Pass 9,330 ft.
Mascott Mine (abandoned)
To 75
To Little Wood River

views of the big mountains. Especially prominent from the start is unnamed Peak 11,305 with its soft white granite and red-brown streaks of metamorphic rock.

As the canyon begins to bend just a little to left, suddenly an impressive horn comes into view on the canyon's left side. This is called the Little Matterhorn. It is the most prominent feature of the canyon. A waterfall pours from a couloir just to the left (downstream) from the Little Matterhorn. In wet years and early in the season, the view of the waterfall is very impressive.

Soon after you see the horn, you cross to the creek's right side. The small stream clearly does not fit in such a big gully, but this is the result of a 1984 flood. The crossing is easy unless the snowmelt is still well under way.

Now the trail climbs a bit more steeply, and the tread becomes much more obvious as its base becomes white, decomposed granite (coarse sand). As you reach the base of Johnstone Pass, the trail abruptly makes a 90-degree turn and begins to climb steeply. The trail is good until you reach the big gully washed out by the flood. The trail crosses it on a narrow path that is not really a problem. Then it switchbacks more steeply up the right (west) side of the gully. Although it's steep, you should have no problem until about halfway to the pass. The trail once crossed the then much smaller gully here, but now it is washed out. Instead the trail now climbs a very steep scramble route through rocks and granite sand to the base of cliffs below Point 10,211. Here, the hardy move laterally and cross the steep top of the gully two-thirds of the way and then scramble on all fours to the top of the pass, which is a notch.

The other side of the pass may be washed out, too, but after some brief talus sliding you do reach the trail that goes to Upper Box Canyon Lake and eventually down Box Canyon into the Little Wood River.

The hike halfway up Johnstone Pass is worthwhile for the view. As you look north across the head of the canyon, the Little Matterhorn shrinks to just bump under Peaks 11,210 and 11,020 towering above it.

**Options:** Half a mile before the East Fork Trailhead is the trailhead (alongside the road) to PK Pass (elevation 9,330 feet). The trailhead is well marked, though small, and the trail is maintained for the quick 1-mile, 1,400-foot climb to the pass. The trail is named Iron Mine Trail (Trail 174). From PK Pass, the trail drops 3,000 feet to the Little Wood River, all in just 4 miles from the trailhead.

—Ralph Maughan

## Miles and Directions

**0.0** Trailhead (8,040 feet)

**0.2** Meadow with water (8,200 feet)

**1.0** Crossing of the East Fork (8,600 feet)

**1.8** Base of Johnstone Pass (9,040 feet)

**2.3** Johnstone Pass (10,002 feet)

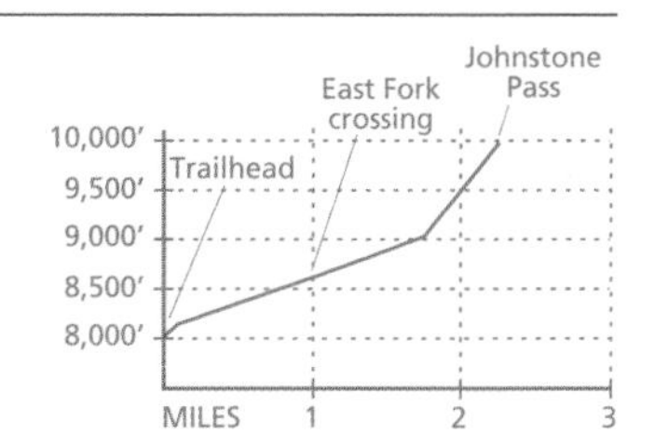

# 51 Fall Creek

Hike through glaciated mountain scenery with access to alpine lakes and impressive erosion scars from a great flood in 1984. Several waterfalls are also available to explore.

**Start:** 20 miles northeast of Ketchum
**Type of hike:** Day hike, overnight backpack, or longer; out-and-back
**Distance:** 1.8 miles to the Left Fork of Fall Creek; 7 miles to the head of Fall Creek
**Approximate hiking time:** At least 3–4 days.
**Difficulty:** Moderately easy to the Left Fork; difficult to the head of Fall Creek
**Best seasons:** Mid-June–mid-July to Left Fork; August–mid-September to head of canyon
**Trail surface:** Normal dirt and rock
**Land status:** Salmon-Challis National Forest
**Canine compatibility:** On leash
**Fees and permits:** None
**Maps:** Standhope Peak USGS quadrangle; Middle Fork, Challis, Yankee Fork, and Lost River Ranger Districts–Challis National Forest map
**Trail contact:** Lost River Ranger District, (208) 588-3400
**Special considerations:** Hiking beyond the maintained trail's end requires strong boots.

**Finding the trailhead:** From downtown Ketchum, turn east and take the road to Sun Valley. Continue eastward past Sun Valley on this road up Trail Creek Canyon. Just as the canyon begins to narrow and the road begins to climb, the road turns to rough gravel. It climbs on a precipitous ledge above Trail Creek Gorge all the way to Trail Creek Summit. Although hundreds of vehicles travel this road every day, it is winding, washboarded, narrow in places, and without guardrails.

Safely past Trail Creek Summit, continue on down gentle Summit Creek until you are 22 miles from Ketchum. Then turn right onto Copper Basin Road.

From Mackay or Challis, turn west off US 93 near the base of Mount Borah onto the paved county highway. Take this road due west across the valley, reaching the Big Lost River as the road enters low, bare, red-rocked mountains. At this point the pavement ends, but the road is good gravel. Turn left onto Copper Basin Road 18.5 miles from U.S. 93.

Follow the gravel Copper Basin Road for 2.5 miles; then turn right and go up Wildhorse Creek. Lower Wildhorse Creek is typical Challis Volcanic terrain: steep, low, reddish mountains fronted by sagebrush bottoms. But upcanyon, toward the head of Wildhorse Creek, stand pointed peaks that stun most tourists. These giants are not your destination, however. Instead, 3.5 miles up Wildhorse Creek, turn off Wildhorse Creek Road onto the gravel Fall Creek Road. Drive 0.3 mile to the obvious trailhead at the mouth of Fall Creek Canyon. GPS: N43 51.15' / W114 04.68'

**Parking and trailhead facilities:** The developed site offers access for people with disabilities to Fall Creek Falls Nature Trail and the trail described here, which goes up Fall Creek Canyon. The trailhead has parking for many vehicles, loading ramps for horses, and an outhouse but no water or shade.

## The Hike

This hike can be a relatively easy day hike to the edge of beautiful, rugged scenery or a two- or three-day rugged trip to the seldom-visited head of Fall Creek Canyon, with its granite walls and alpine meadows harboring elk, mountain goats, bears, and wolves. The trail also provides access to three other splendid trails—the Left Fork (Hike 52), the Right Fork (Hike 53), and Surprise Valley.

Although the mouth of Fall Creek is not impressive, this modest entrance is deceptive. After about 1.5 miles, the trail enters big mountain country. Here, glacier-sculpted peaks, horns, and arêtes rise around the hiker. Some peaks are almost 12,000 feet high. The three forks of Fall Creek are textbook examples of hanging valleys.

Almost half the trailhead traffic is for the wheelchair access trail to the lowest of Fall Creek's several waterfalls. This trail is self-evident and so is not described here.

Cross the pack bridge, and you quickly come to a buck-and-pole fence with a gate to keep out the cattle. The trail sign indicates HORSES AND FOOT TRAFFIC ONLY. The welcome closure of Fall Creek to livestock came in 1998 and has reaped great rewards in improved aesthetics and an increase in wildlife.

The trail follows an old jeep two-track that has now largely faded, but that actually had vehicles on it in the 1970s when I first visited Fall Creek. The trail is always obvious as it climbs moderately about 480 feet in 1.5 miles and then drops a bit as it reaches the Left Fork of Fall Creek. Here, it crosses on a makeshift log bridge. At this point you can see a giant horn that guards the Right Fork, another that guards the entrance to Surprise Valley, and pyramidal, 11,878-foot Standhope Peak. The confluence area is also the largest flat spot in Fall Creek and its forks. On the way to the Left Fork junction, Fall Creek courses 100 feet below the trail. You do not see the waterfall, but the creek is visible from time to time.

The faint Left Fork Trail leaves at a ninety-degree angle immediately after crossing Left Fork Creek. The main trail continues up Fall Creek Canyon with very little grade until you approach some of the erosion from the great 1984 thunderstorm flood. Although the scars have softened, they are still obvious when their origin is known. A black cloud settled over the heads of Fall Creek, Wildhorse Creek, and the East Fork of the Big Wood River on August 9, 1984. In just a few hours, it dropped 10 inches of rain on this uplift of jagged granite peaks. The volume of Fall and Wildhorse Creeks grew to rival that of the Snake River in flood, uprooting trees, washing away meadows, cutting out streamside cliffs, and accomplishing several hundred years of erosion in a few hours.

About 0.4 mile past the Left Fork, the trail crosses (and also splits and goes above) a huge cutbank from the flood. From here on, it climbs gently until you reach the junction with Right Fork Trail. Right Fork Trail is actually the wider of the two, and

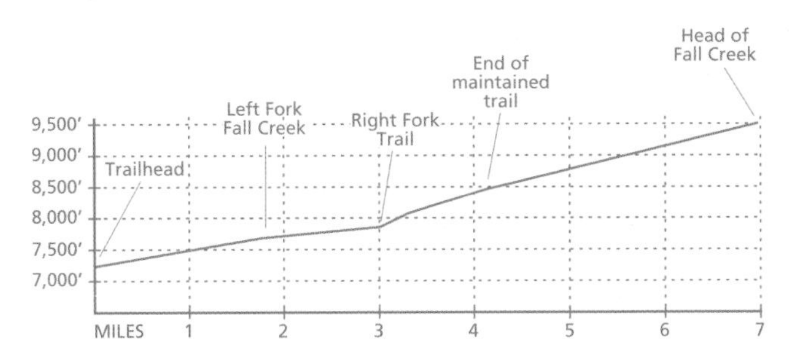

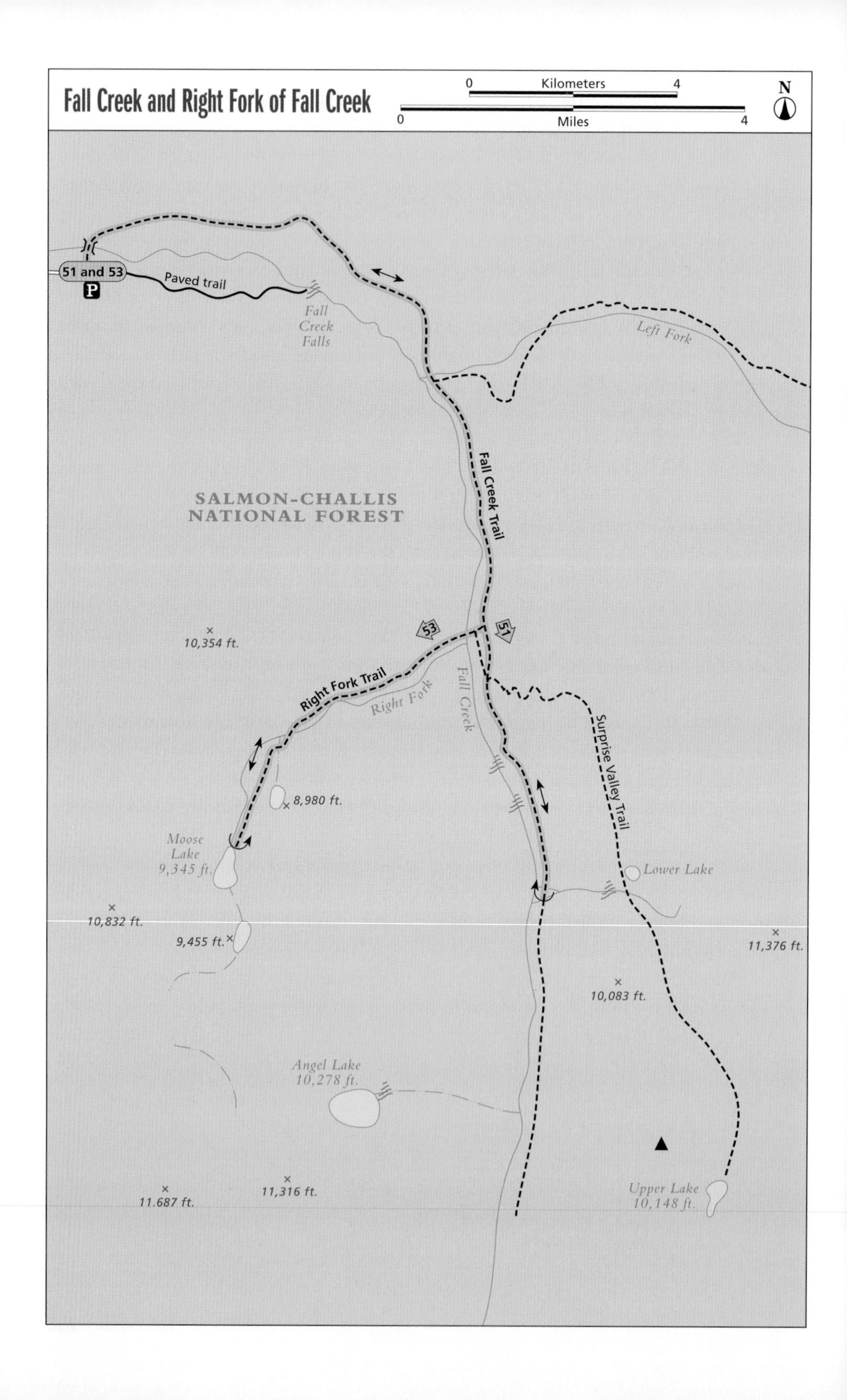
Fall Creek and Right Fork of Fall Creek
0
Kilometers
4
0
Miles
4
N
51 and 53
P
Paved trail
Fall
Creek
Falls
Left Fork
Fall Creek Trail
SALMON-CHALLIS
NATIONAL FOREST
10,354 ft.
53
51
Right Fork Trail
Right Fork
Fall Creek
Surprise Valley Trail
8,980 ft.
Moose
Lake
9,345 ft.
Lower Lake
10,832 ft.
9,455 ft.
11,376 ft.
10,083 ft.
Angel Lake
10,278 ft.
11.687 ft.
11,316 ft.
Upper Lake
10,148 ft.

for years a sign on a large conifer has pointed to it, reading TRAIL, as if the trail up the main fork were some improper route.

Ignore the sign and keep left. The trail now climbs through a dense forest growing amid incredible boulders and dead fallen timber, much of both the result of the great flood. It took a long time to recut the trail through this stretch of the canyon. The area has a very wild, untamed atmosphere. After about 0.3 mile, you reach the junction with Surprise Valley Trail, which is usually signed. This time, stay to the right.

The trail continues to climb through the wild forest and boulders. The horn that guards the Right Fork now appears as what it really is—the beginning of the rugged west wall of Fall Creek Canyon. Early in the season, you can see a number of waterfalls on the west wall, one from Angel Lake. A number of small waterfalls and many cascades rumble just out of sight on Fall Creek itself.

You reach the end of the maintained trail 4.2 miles from the trailhead, where you cross the outlet stream from Surprise Valley, but the trail continues on.

From here on, the trail is maintained mostly by elk. It goes through forest but soon breaks out above a willow patch for your first view of the great headwall of Fall Creek, all of it well above 11,000 feet, with a number of peaks, all of them nameless. A large patch of snow lingers most of the summer beneath the headwall.

The trail continues to the head of the canyon. In places it is easy, but it crosses a number of boggy springs, willow meadows that hold plenty of water in June and July, rockslides, and some deadfall. If you lose the trail, you can soon pick it up again by heading upslope or downslope a bit.

While the beauty of the stream itself is somewhat marred by the erosion scars from the flood, the scenery is tremendous and you will be alone except for the wildlife. In August, the wildlife especially favor the head of the canyon.

—Ralph Maughan

**Options:** Surprise Valley is a great trail used in previous editions and removed only to make space for trails in other areas. The junction is well-defined at 3.3 miles from the main trailhead. The trail climbs through meadows and high pine forests for 3 miles visiting two small lakes and a gorgeous outflow gushing down the mountainside.

—Luke Kratz

## Miles and Directions

**0.0** Trailhead (7,240 feet) then, shortly, pack bridge over Fall Creek

**0.1** Buck-and-pole fence and gate

**1.8** Left Fork of Fall Creek (7,683 feet)

**3.0** Right Fork Trail junction (7,820 feet)

**3.3** Surprise Valley Trail junction (8,100 feet)

**4.2** End of maintained trail (8,480 feet)

**7.0** Head of Fall Creek (9,500 feet)

# 52 Left Fork of Fall Creek

The Left Fork holds rugged mountain scenery with more wildlife and geological variety than most Pioneer Mountain areas.

**Start:** 20 miles northeast of Ketchum
**Type of hike:** Overnight backpack; out-and-back
**Distance:** 4.2 miles (from the junction with the main Fall Creek Trail)
**Approximate hiking time:** 2–3 days
**Difficulty:** Moderate due to elevation gain and some route finding
**Best season:** July–mid-September
**Trail surface:** Normal dirt and rock
**Land status:** Salmon-Challis National Forest
**Canine compatibility:** On leash
**Fees and permits:** None
**Maps:** Big Black Butte and Standhope Peak USGS quadrangles; Middle Fork, Challis, and Lost River Ranger Districts–Challis National Forest map
**Trail contact:** Lost River Ranger District, (208) 588-3400

**Finding the trailhead:** From downtown Ketchum, turn east and take the road to Sun Valley. Continue eastward past Sun Valley on this road up Trail Creek Canyon. Just as the canyon begins to narrow and the road begins to climb, the road turns to rough gravel. It climbs on a precipitous ledge above Trail Creek Gorge all the way to Trail Creek Summit. Although hundreds of vehicles travel this road every day, it is winding, washboarded, narrow in places, and without guardrails.

Safely past Trail Creek Summit, continue on down gentle Summit Creek until you are 22 miles from Ketchum. Then turn right onto Copper Basin Road.

From Mackay or Challis, turn west off US 93 near the base of Mount Borah onto the paved county highway. Take this road due west across the valley, reaching the Big Lost River as the road enters low, bare, red-rocked mountains. At this point the pavement ends, but the road is good gravel. Turn left onto Copper Basin Road 18.5 miles from U.S. 93.

Follow the gravel Copper Basin Road for 2.5 miles; then turn right and go up Wildhorse Creek. Lower Wildhorse Creek is typical Challis Volcanic terrain: steep, low, reddish mountains fronted by sagebrush bottoms. But upcanyon, toward the head of Wildhorse Creek, stand pointed peaks that stun most tourists. These giants are not your destination, however. Instead, 3.5 miles up Wildhorse Creek, turn off Wildhorse Creek Road onto the gravel Fall Creek Road. Drive 0.3 mile to the obvious trailhead at the mouth of Fall Creek Canyon. This trail begins immediately where Fall Creek Trail crosses the Left Fork of Fall Creek. Look for it at a 90-degree angle to the Fall Creek Trail. It is a bit faint at first. GPS: N43 50.73' / W114 02.88'

**Parking and trailhead facilities:** The developed site offers access for people with disabilities to Fall Creek Falls Nature Trail and the trail described here, which goes up Fall Creek Canyon. The trailhead has parking for many vehicles, loading ramps for horses, and an outhouse but no water or shade.

## The Hike

Of the three splendid forks of Fall Creek located in the jagged Pioneer Mountains, the Left Fork is the least often seen. This is probably because, from the start of the trail, the

*View near the junction to the wild Left Fork of Fall Creek.* PHOTO BY LUKE KRATZ

country ahead is not nearly as scenic as the view up the Fall Creek Valley or the horn-guarded Right Fork. In reality, the Left Fork of Fall Creek is very similar to the main Fall Creek in its form, with an unimpressive entrance that eventually turns to the south to head into beautifully ice-sculpted granite. However, the Left Fork is more varied geologically and has more wildlife than the rest of Fall Creek and its tributaries.

The faint but very easy-to-follow trail leaves Fall Creek where Fall Creek Trail crosses the Left Fork. Just past the Left Fork, find the trail at a ninety-degree angle from the main trail. You'll climb steeply, switchbacking several times into the hanging valley of the Left Fork. As you climb in the open, you have a good view across the main canyon toward the Right Fork's hanging valley. The trail does not follow the creek for this first steep section. The creek instead cascades in a minor gorge below to the left. After climbing 500 feet in just 0.6 mile, the grade lessens, and a welcome spring runs across the trail out of the willows. The trail then fords the Left Fork to climb to the left (north) bank. This ford is easy in mid- to late summer but can be

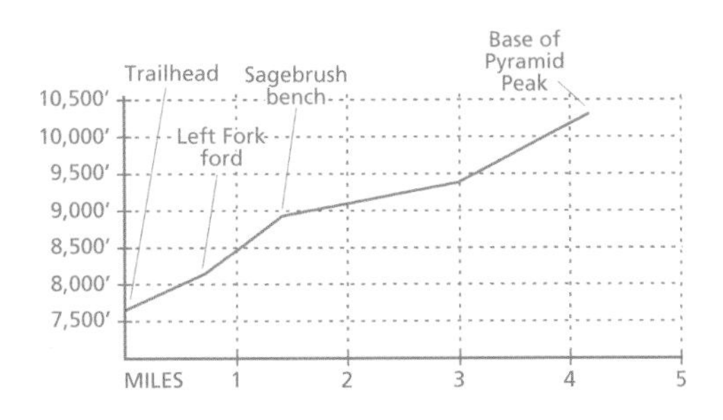

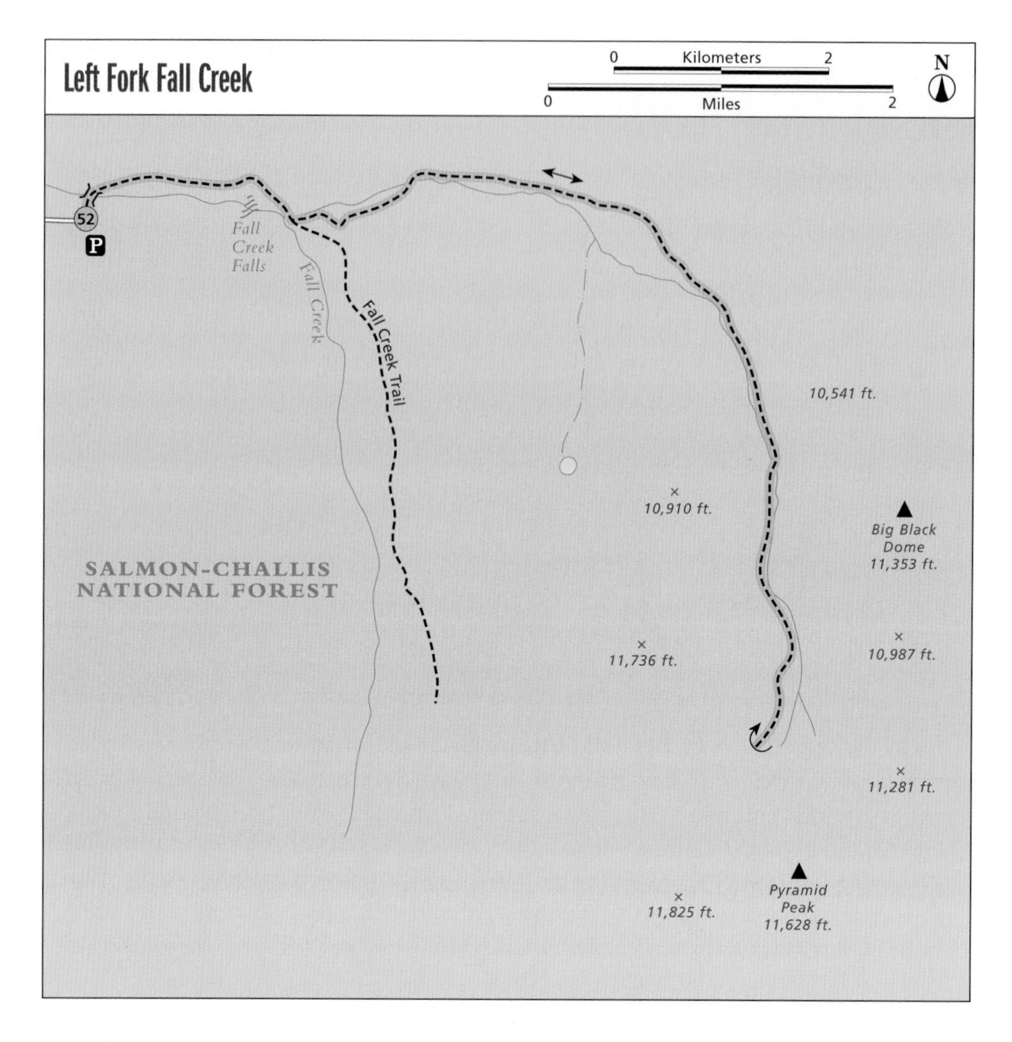


swift when the creek is higher (late June). Now you are in the stream valley, and the creek moves lazily below the trail through a maze of short willows.

The trail wanders through open hillside and patches of silvery quaking aspen and sagebrush that adorn the slope made of reddish brown volcanic rock. Flowers wink at you here early in the summer. A few small springs run across the trail throughout most summers. Across the stream valley, the opposite slope is covered with a dense forest of conifers.

Bare crags of volcanic rock made of the widespread Challis Volcanic Formation poke into the sky above the trail. Soon, the trail contours along a steep sidehill just above a willowy meadow. Be careful here because the tread is narrow for about 0.2 mile.

At 1.5 miles from the trail's beginning, you begin to climb up the mountainside and away from the stream valley. The topographic maps show the trail continuing directly over the mountain and down the other side to Copper Basin, but this trail no longer exists. Instead, the trail leads out over a broad sage- and grass-covered platform and up the Left Fork Valley. Here, the valley begins its big bend toward the south. At first you see, on your left, the talus slopes that form the backside of the Big Black Dome (11,353 feet), a chunk of sedimentary rock lodged between the volcanics to the north and the hard, crystalline, intruded rock to the south. Ironically, this side of the mountain is neither black nor domelike. The rock is light brown, dark brown, and pinkish brown, depending on the angle of the sun. Just below these amazingly smooth talus slopes grow flowers, short willows, and photogenic patches of spruce, fir, and whitebark pine. There are a number of springs, and you often find pronghorn antelope and elk here in the heat of the day.

As you complete the turn to the south, you'll see the rugged, gray, mostly unnamed granite peaks at the head of the canyon. The most prominent is Peak 11,281. The topo map shows 11,628-foot Pyramid Peak, but you can't really see this peak well unless you leave the trail and climb up onto the talus of the Big Black Dome.

Once you turn the corner of the canyon, the trail becomes intermittent, showing up alternately on both sides of the valley. Numerous small springs feed the dense low willows next to the creek. Low flow makes these springs poor sources of water. However, as you continue and enter the land underlain by the hard quartz monzonite of the Pioneer Core area, the streamside becomes less mushy and the springs, though fewer, have a better flow.

In the upper canyon, there are increasingly alpine meadows. Game trails are so numerous and well used they appear to have been constructed. You can follow them right up to the hard rock of the peaks. Although this has always been a good canyon for wildlife, since the cows have been booted out the wildlife has exploded. There are many elk, mule deer, pronghorn antelope, and even some moose, black bear, cougar, and mountain goats; beginning in 2000 a wolf pack began to inhabit the area. I heard them howl for five minutes.

Despite a plentitude of moisture and perfect altitude, the trees grow only in isolated clumps in this canyon. Almost all of the hike is in the sun unless you seek out a tree. My hypothesis is that avalanches from the Big Black Dome keep continuous forest from growing.

—Ralph Maughan

**Options:** See Hikes 51 and 53.

## Miles and Directions

**0.0** Trail begins where Fall Creek Trail crosses the Left Fork (7,683 feet)

**0.7** Left Fork ford (8,210 feet)

**1.3** Narrow contour above meadow (8,600 feet)

**1.5** Trail climbs to sagebrush bench and begins to follow bend of canyon (8,900 feet)

**3.0** Canyon begins to climb much more steeply (9,380 feet)

**4.2** Meadow ends and rock begins at base of Pyramid Peak (10,240 feet)

# 53 Right Fork of Fall Creek

This popular trail heads into rugged mountain scenery with two alpine lakes.

**See map on page 262.**
**Start:** 20 miles northeast of Sun Valley
**Type of hike:** Day hike or overnight backpack; out-and-back
**Distance:** 2 miles to Moose Lake (from the junction with the main Fall Creek Trail)
**Approximate hiking time:** Plan 3–4 hours from the trailhead, or at least 2 days for a backpack
**Difficulty:** Moderately difficult due to a steep climb, but the distance is not great
**Best season:** July–mid-September
**Trail surface:** Normal dirt and rock
**Land status:** Salmon-Challis National Forest
**Canine compatibility:** On leash
**Fees and permits:** None
**Maps:** Standhope Peak USGS quadrangle; Middle Fork, Challis, Yankee Fork, and Lost River Ranger Districts–Challis National Forest map
**Trail contact:** Lost River Ranger District, (208) 588-3400
**Special considerations:** None

**Finding the trailhead:** From downtown Ketchum, turn east and take the road to Sun Valley. Continue eastward past Sun Valley on this road up Trail Creek Canyon. Just as the canyon begins to narrow and the road begins to climb, the road turns to rough gravel. It climbs on a precipitous ledge above Trail Creek Gorge all the way to Trail Creek Summit. Although hundreds of vehicles travel this road every day, it is winding, washboarded, narrow in places, and without guardrails.

Safely past Trail Creek Summit, continue on down gentle Summit Creek until you are 22 miles from Ketchum. Then turn right onto Copper Basin Road.

From Mackay or Challis, turn west off US 93 near the base of Mount Borah onto the paved county highway. Take this road due west across the valley, reaching the Big Lost River as the road enters low, bare, red-rocked mountains. At this point the pavement ends, but the road is good gravel. Turn left onto Copper Basin Road 18.5 miles from U.S. 93.

Follow the gravel Copper Basin Road for 2.5 miles; then turn right and go up Wildhorse Creek. Lower Wildhorse Creek is typical Challis Volcanic terrain: steep, low, reddish mountains fronted by sagebrush bottoms. But upcanyon, toward the head of Wildhorse Creek, stand pointed peaks that stun most tourists. These giants are not your destination, however. Instead, 3.5 miles up Wildhorse Creek, turn off Wildhorse Creek Road onto the gravel Fall Creek Road. Drive 0.3 mile to the obvious trailhead at the mouth of Fall Creek Canyon. GPS: N43 49.95' / W114 02.64' (Right Fork turnoff)

**Parking and trailhead facilities:** The developed site offers access for people with disabilities to Fall Creek Falls Nature Trail and the trail described here, which goes up Fall Creek Canyon. The trailhead has parking for many vehicles, loading ramps for horses, and an outhouse but no water or shade.

## The Hike

The Right Fork of Fall Creek is yet another hanging valley that drops, along with the Left Fork and Surprise Valley, into Fall Creek. The Right Fork is the only one of these three valleys that has a lake with fish—Moose Lake. Therefore, it is by far the busiest of the four hikes in Fall Creek described in this book, and the lake area can look a bit beaten out.

The hike is short from where the trail leaves the Fall Creek Valley to Moose Lake, but the elevation gain is considerable, 1,545 feet. The trail is well constructed, however, and easy to follow.

PHOTO BY LUKE KRATZ

*Moose Lake.*

Begin at a junction in the trail up the main fork canyon, about 1.2 miles above the mouth of the Left Fork of Fall Creek. You merely stay on the most heavily used trail, and it soon leads down to Fall Creek, which you will probably ford, although a rather tricky log has been in place across the creek for some time. The ford is no problem in late summer, but it is rather deep earlier on.

On the other side, you begin the steep climb, making several long switchbacks that are not shown on the topographic map.

A big horn guards the entrance to the canyon on the left, and a less rugged big mountain stands to its right. Once you arrive at the cirque, you'll find the horn is really the end of a mile-long spiny ridge. As you climb through forest and rock, you'll get occasional glimpses of the view back down across Fall Creek to the cream-colored, ribbed wall of the canyon's east side.

As you enter the hanging valley, the grade diminishes but the trail is still anything but level. The two sides of the valley contrast sharply: The left side is made of the rugged igneous rock of the Pioneer Window, while the right is softer sedimentary rock called the Copper Basin Formation.

Just before you reach the lake, you'll wander through meadows near the lake's outlet. Above the lake, a smaller, shallow lake nestles in the rocks. All of this is set in a large high basin, dominated by nameless Peak 11,667 at its head. The only route out of the cirque, besides the way you came, is a rough cross-country hike to Angel Lake, a large, scenic gem that barely hangs on to the side of Fall Creek Canyon. You can spend a day exploring the cirque or drop over to Angel Lake. Otherwise, side hikes are limited.

Moose Lake is overly full of brook trout and some rainbows, too.

**Options:** You can scramble to Angel Lake from the Right Fork Lakes.

—Ralph Maughan

## Miles and Directions

**0.0** Trail begins where Fall Creek Trail splits (7,820 feet)

**0.1** Ford of Fall Creek (7,800 feet)

**2.0** Moose Lake (9,345 feet)

**2.2** Unnamed upper lake (9,455 feet)

# 54 Hyndman Creek

Enjoy wildflowers and good views of the Pioneer Mountains; tremendous views if you do the steep upper portion of the trail.

**Start:** 10 miles northeast of Hailey
**Type of hike:** A long day hike or overnight backpack, both out-and- back. Because the trail is scenic from the start, it can also be a short day hike.
**Distance:** 4 miles to the base of Hyndman Peak
**Approximate hiking time:** At least 3 hours
**Difficulty:** Moderately easy to the base of Cobb Peak. The last 2 miles to the base of Hyndman Peak are strenuous.
**Best season:** July–mid-September
**Trail surface:** Normal dirt and rock
**Land status:** Sawtooth National Forest
**Canine compatibility:** On leash
**Fees and permits:** None
**Maps:** Hyndman Peak USGS quadrangle
**Trail contact:** Ketchum Ranger District, (208) 622-5371
**Special considerations:** You need boots with good friction for the steep parts of the trail.

**Finding the trailhead:** To reach the Hyndman Creek Trailhead (which is also the trailhead for the North Fork of Hyndman Creek), turn off ID 75 onto East Fork (of the Big Wood River) Road about 5.5 miles north of Hailey. Drive about 6 miles up the East Fork on a paved road past many houses to the junction of Hyndman Creek Road and East Fork Road. The road is paved or oiled all the way. The junction may not be signed, but it is an obvious major junction. Hyndman Creek Road is to the left and leaves the junction through a cut. The road is oiled for 2.3 miles (to a private road leading to a house on a hilltop). After this point, the gravel road now drops and crosses Hyndman Creek. It is 0.8 mile to the Bear/Parker Trailhead (Trail 159) and 0.3 mile more to Johnstone Creek Trail (Trail 206).

Now the road narrows. It is just slightly wider than one lane, and it climbs above Hyndman Creek. You might have to back up if you encounter a vehicle. After 1 mile of this, you reach the trailhead. GPS: N43 41.97' / W114 11.30'
**Parking and trailhead facilities:** Ample parking area; fee required.

## The Hike

The trail (Trail 166) leaves to the right from the trailhead at a ROAD CLOSED barrier. The trail immediately drops down and crosses the North Fork of Hyndman Creek on a good, but narrow, footbridge. The trail is closed to all motor vehicles. The trail follows an old road, but the fact that it was a road is now barely discernible.

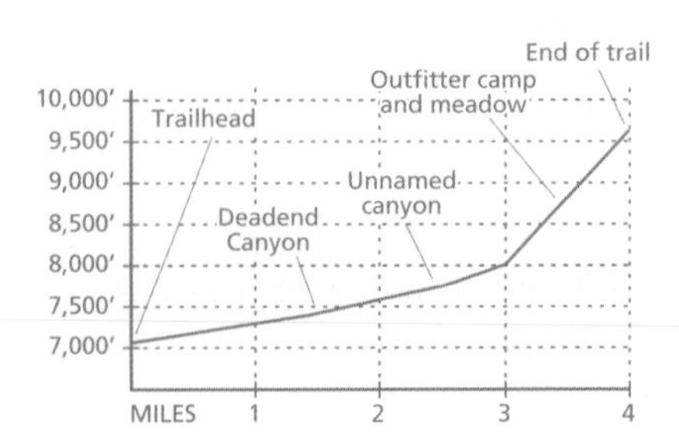


The trail climbs a moderate 380 feet the first mile through aspen groves and meadows with brilliant floral displays from mid-July until mid-August. As you pass

*12,008 foot Hyndman Peak.* PHOTO BY RALPH MAUGHAN

the second avalanche chute, at its base notice several lovely beaver ponds perched across and above Hyndman Creek.

After the first mile, the grade lessens and you pass through some stands of conifers as well as aspens. There is another beautiful perched group of beaver ponds at the mouth of Deadend Canyon across Hyndman Creek. At about this location, you get your first really good view of the southwest face of massive 11,650-foot Cobb Peak.

In 2.5 more miles you pass a minor side canyon to your right. An old jeep road leaves from here, but its beginning is hard to find. The road crosses Hyndman Creek and climbs into the upper reaches of Hyndman Creek, leading to wonderful alpine scenery. In the first edition of *Hiking Idaho,* this was the main trail, and while it is still present and easy to follow once you have found it, few do.

Past this unnamed side canyon, the trail climbs more steeply, and after 0.4 mile it reaches a major but unnamed tributary of Hyndman Creek that tumbles down a steep canyon from the high peaks above. Here the trail turns ninety degrees and begins a very steep climb to the scenic basin where the tumbling creek originates. In 0.3 mile the trail climbs 600 feet as steeply as a trail can climb; then the grade begins to level off, and in 0.2 mile you reach a meadow with a pond and an outfitter camp with a glorious view of Hyndman Peak and rugged Duncan Ridge to its left.

The trail does not end here. Head just to the right of the outfitter camp, stepping over the creek, and the trail begins another very steep ascent of 900 feet in 0.5 mile to an upper meadow. Here the small creek winds lazily beneath Hyndman Peak (12,005 feet) in the center, with Old Hyndman Peak (11,775 feet) back and at 2 o'clock. The great north wall of Cobb Peak is to your right, and the many summits of Duncan Ridge, ending in Duncan Peak, between 8 o'clock and 11 o'clock.

There are three small tarns above the meadow beneath Hyndman Peak. This west side of these great mountains is a complicated mixture of very hard quartzite and other metamorphic roads, some granite, and a few sedimentary rocks, including even soft sandstone.

There are numerous springs in the meadow.

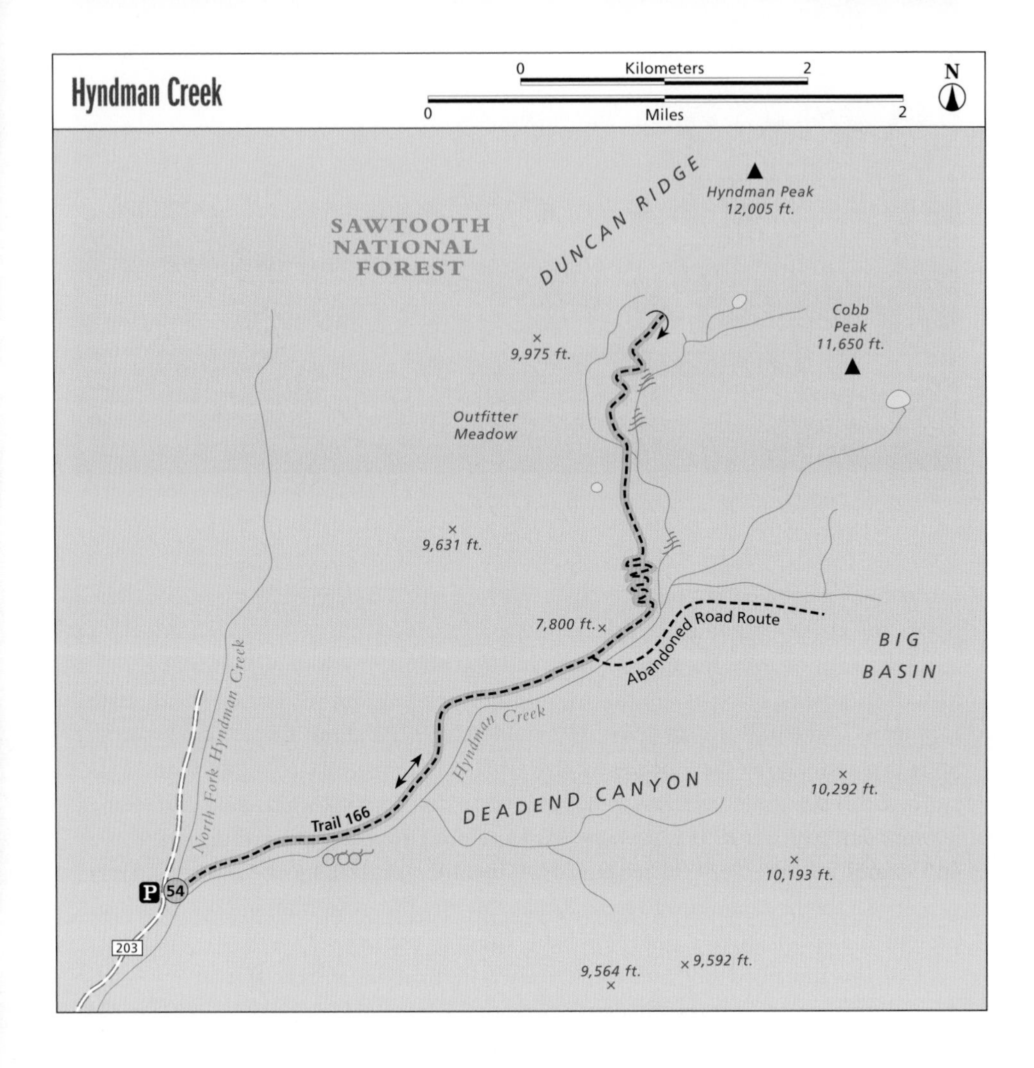


**Options:** Find and follow the old mining road into the upper reaches of Hyndman Creek. From the end of the road, you can scramble to the unnamed and seldom-visited lakes of Big Basin and go to the base of very rugged Old Hyndman Peak.

—Ralph Maughan

## Miles and Directions

- **0.0** Trailhead (7,050 feet)
- **1.5** Deadend Canyon across the creek (7,430 feet)
- **2.5** Unnamed canyon; old road leaves to left and crosses creek (7,760 feet)
- **3.0** Trail begins climb steeply (8,000 feet)
- **3.5** Meadow with pond and outfitter camp (8,724 feet)
- **4.0** Meadow; end of trail (9,610 feet)

# 55 Iron Bog Lake

Several lakes and ponds lie among scenic peaks and uplands.

**Start:** In the southern part of the Pioneer Mountains, about 40 road miles northwest of Arco
**Type of hike:** Day hike or overnight backpack; out-and-back, unless you choose the Muldoon Canyon option, which requires a shuttle
**Distance:** 4.6 miles round-trip
**Approximate hiking time:** At least 2 hours to lakes; 2–3 days for backpacking
**Difficulty:** Moderately easy
**Best season:** July
**Trail surface:** Normal dirt and rock
**Land status:** Salmon-Challis National Forest
**Canine compatibility:** On leash
**Fees and permits:** None
**Maps:** Smiley Mountain USGS quadrangle; Middle Fork, Challis, Yankee Fork, and Lost River Ranger Districts–Challis National Forest map.
**Trail contact:** Lost River Ranger District, (208) 588-3400
**Special considerations:** High-altitude sun with little shade. Make sure you have good sun protection.

**Finding the trailhead:** Drive 10.5 miles north of Arco on US 93, and turn onto Antelope Creek Road. This road is paved for the first 4 miles; then it's 23 miles of gravel and dirt to the trailhead, which is in the Left Fork of Iron Bog Creek. Just after Iron Bog Campground is a fork in the road. Take the left fork, FR 220. The right fork gives access to a trail to Brockie Lake, another nice hike, but the road requires four-wheel drive.

It is about another mile from the turnoff to the trailhead. The road is rough but has recently been improved a bit so that two-wheel-drive access is not difficult. GPS: N43 39.56' / W113 49.19'
**Parking and trailhead facilities:** The undeveloped trailhead has room for about ten vehicles.

## The Hike

The southern portion of the Pioneer Mountains consists of rugged, glaciated peaks with numerous cirques, many with lakes. Despite their height and cool weather, these mountains have very sparse forests. Although this sometimes makes it hard to get out of the high-elevation sun, it does provide for almost constant, scenic views into the distance.

Iron Bog and nearby Fishpole Lakes have a reputation as being among Idaho's prettiest. Iron Bog has a big black mountain (Peak 10,149) rising from its west shore. The hiking distance to the two lakes is not great. These two aspects—scenery and relative ease—make the area a bit crowded sometimes. Fortunately, off-road vehicles have been excluded for the past fifteen years or so, and some of the localized areas of overuse have healed. Nevertheless, violations continue to take place. Please report violations in both Iron Bog and Muldoon Canyon to the Lost River Ranger District in Mackay.

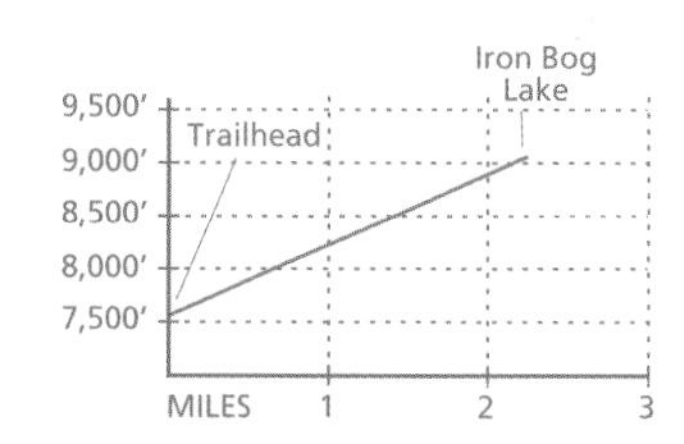

*Iron Bog lake.* PHOTO BY LUKE KRATZ

The well-defined, reconstructed trail climbs the hill slope to the right of the trailhead. There are several springs in the early season along the trail. The trail has fine views of the Left Fork of Iron Bog Creek below.

Due to overuse, please avoid the campsites right on the lake. Less sensitive spots are available just before and beyond the lake. There is a tiny lake above Iron Bog (off the trail) and two small lakes on the way over to the Fishpole cirque (the second being very scenic).

There are fish in Iron Bog and Fishpole Lakes. Mule deer and coyote as well as elk are present in the area, and pronghorn antelope are surprisingly common despite the high elevation. Prior to seeing antelope here, I had been told they do not range at higher than 9,000 feet.

To get to Fishpole Lake, walk to the outlet of Iron Bog Lake, descend about 80 feet along the outlet stream, and you should find the trail. It's about a mile, and a 250-foot climb, to Fishpole Lake. Including Fishpole, the Fishpole cirque contains four lakes.

The country around these lakes is meadow and open forest of whitebark pine and Douglas fir. Wildflowers are abundant before September. Large rugged peaks rise behind the lakes.

The best month for the hike is probably July because domestic sheep begin to graze the area in July, gradually moving higher and reducing the wildlife and camping pleasure. However, the hike is usually accessible from late June through September.

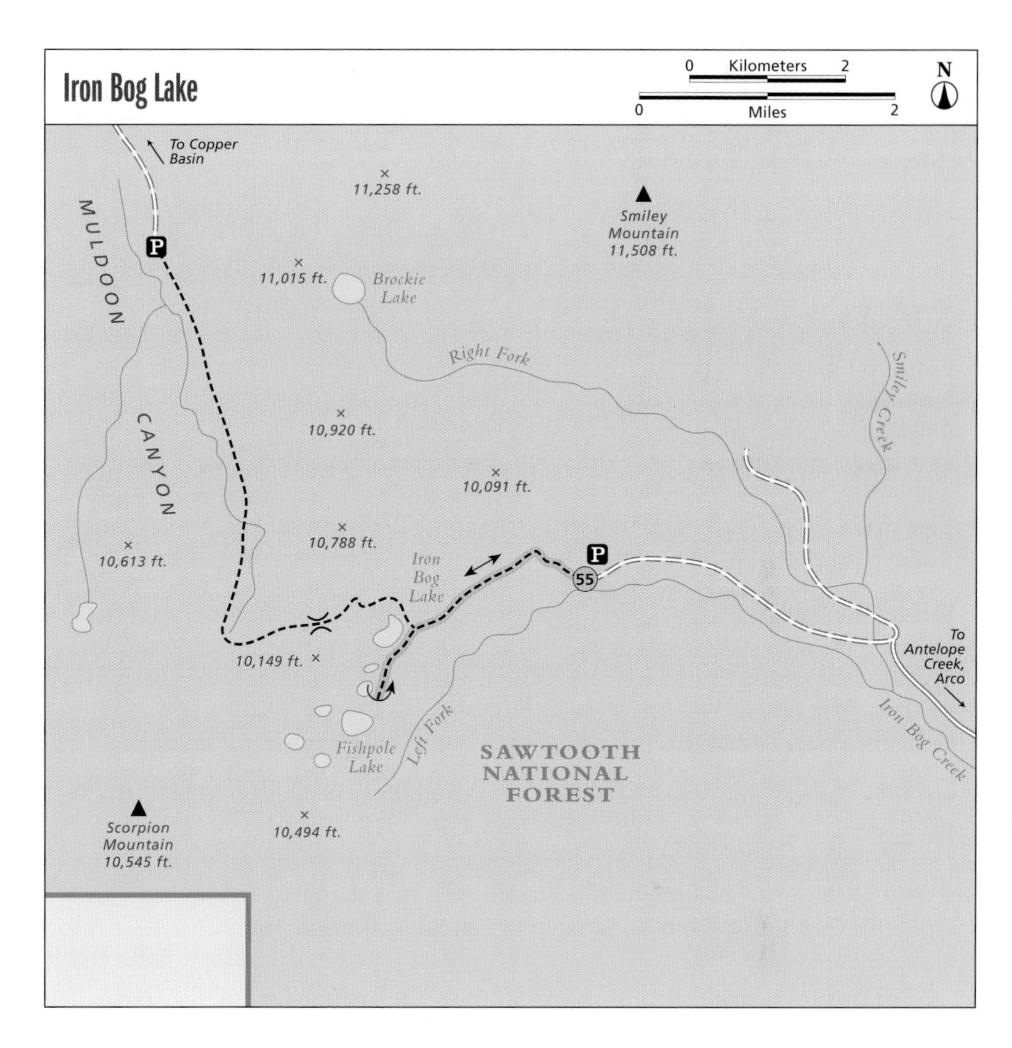


**Options:** A trail climbs from Iron Bog Lake about 400 feet over a pass into the head of Muldoon Canyon, a long, moist-bottomed, but almost nonforested canyon, ringed by scenic peaks. Muldoon Canyon is an alternative route to Iron Bog Lake. You approach it from Copper Basin. However, it involves using four-wheel drive or walking several miles on a jeep road that is mostly in the sun. Even if you don't come up Muldoon Canyon, the short hike to its open and ruggedly scenic head from Iron Bog Lake is very worthwhile for the view and the chances of seeing wildlife.

—Ralph Maughan

## Miles and Directions

**0.0** Trailhead (7,600 feet)

**1.6** Iron Bog Lake (9,067 feet)

**2.5** Fishpole Lake (9,258 feet)

# 56 Summit Creek

Take in the wildflowers and access the Devil's Bedstead West.

**Start:** On top of Trail Creek Summit, 12 road miles from Ketchum
**Type of hike:** Day hike; out-and-back, or shuttle if you descend the Right Fork of Kane Creek
**Distance:** 7 miles round-trip
**Approximate hiking time:** 3–4 hours
**Difficulty:** Moderately easy
**Best season:** July–September
**Trail surface:** Normal dirt and rock
**Land status:** Salmon-Challis National Forest
**Canine compatibility:** On leash
**Fees and permits:** None
**Maps:** Phi Kappa Mountain and Rock Roll Canyon USGS quadrangles; Middle Fork, Challis, Yankee Fork, and Lost River Ranger Districts–Challis National Forest map
**Trail contact:** Lost River Ranger District, (208) 588-3400
**Special considerations:** This trail is closed to motor vehicles and mountain bikes. Although you may see mountain bikes on the trail, their use is not legal here and never has been.

**Finding the trailhead:** Drive east from Ketchum and Sun Valley for 12 miles to the top of Trail Creek Summit. The trailhead is right on the south side of the summit. At the trailhead, you will see an obvious snow-measuring device. Park in its vicinity, and hike leftward across Summit Creek on the obvious trail. GPS: N43 49.51' / W114 15.70'
**Parking and trailhead facilities:** The trailhead has ample parking space and partial shade.

## The Hike

Except for the first 0.25 mile and the last mile, this trail climbs up a gentle mountain valley. The trail is easy to find and in good condition. Water is easy to locate in the creek and in springs.

The canyon is dominated by avalanche runs. Otherwise, it would be mostly a closed forest, but the avalanches keep the forest to about 50 percent.

At the trailhead go left, cross Summit Creek on a log bridge, and then climb steeply for a short distance up a meadowy hillside. There are good views of the Boulder Mountains to the north from this sloping meadow. You will have several more good views of the Boulder Mountains during this hike, but most of the time they are out of sight.

The trail soon levels out and heads through woods, but before long you come to a lovely meadow. In times past, people often lost the trail here as it crossed the meadow, but now the trail's track is fairly visible. After crossing the meadow from left to right, you cross Summit Creek again. It is a ford only in June. From here the trail climbs easily up the canyon, keeping to the

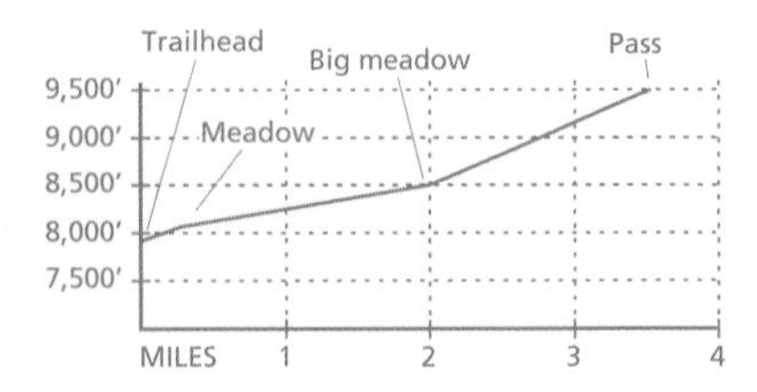

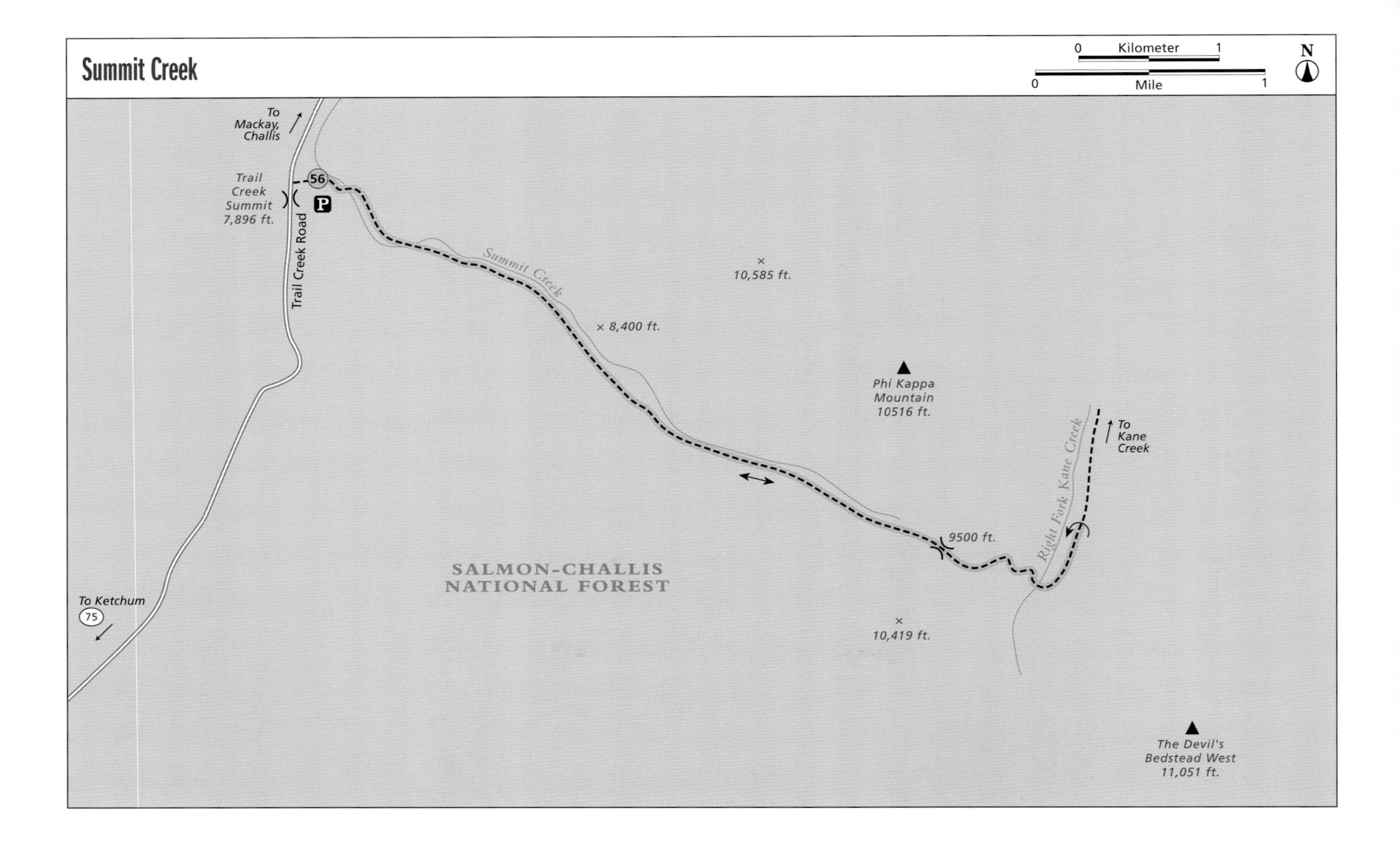
Summit Creek
0 Kilometer 1
0 Mile 1
N
To Mackay, Challis
Trail Creek Summit 7,896 ft.
56
P
Trail Creek Road
Summit Creek
10,585 ft.
8,400 ft.
Phi Kappa Mountain 10516 ft.
To Kane Creek
Right Fork Kane Creek
9500 ft.
SALMON-CHALLIS NATIONAL FOREST
To Ketchum
75
10,419 ft.
The Devil's Bedstead West 11,051 ft.

*Springfed pond along Summit Creek trail.* PHOTO BY LUKE KRATZ

canyon's right side in order to avoid avalanche debris. The trail alternates between subalpine meadow and forest. It is in good condition and easy to follow.

After about 2 miles, the trail begins to climb more steeply, and you emerge from the forest into a large, scenic meadow. Bear left at the meadow's far end. Here you drop down a bit to cross a tributary of Summit Creek that comes from the right. After crossing the tributary, keep going straight to climb a minor ridge between the creek you crossed and Summit Creek. After another mile and on a steeper grade, you reach the pass at about 9,500 feet. The Devil's Bedstead West (incorrectly named simply the "Devil's Bedstead" on the topo) rises near you. You can see it better if you walk just past the summit, and here you can see partway down the Right Fork of Kane Creek.

Wildflowers blaze in the meadows from about mid-July to mid-August.

**Options:** A hike down the Right Fork to Kane Creek is a possible extension of the route. The Right Fork has a fair trail, but you need a good four-wheel-drive vehicle to reach the Kane Creek Trailhead, where you would exit.

—Ralph Maughan

## Miles and Directions

**0.0** Trailhead (7,920 feet)

**0.3** Meadow (8,030 feet)

**2.0** Bottom of a big meadow (8,450 feet)

**3.5** Pass (9,500 feet)

# Lost River Range

Mountains of contorted sedimentary rock, the Lost River Range is by far Idaho's highest. Running southeast to northwest, it parallels the neighboring Lemhi Mountains, separated from them by the broad Little Lost River Valley on the south and the Pahsimeroi Valley on the north.

Borah Peak (12,662 feet) and Leatherman Peak (12,228 feet), Idaho's first and second highest peaks, dominate the middle of the range. Only the nearby Pioneer Mountains and the Lemhi Range have 12,000-footers (and then only one each). Besides Borah and Leatherman, the Lost Rivers count seven others more than 12,000 feet. Only Mount Breitenbach, at 12,140 feet, is officially named. Lost River Mountain (12,078 feet), Mount Idaho (12,065 feet), and Donaldson Peak (12,023 feet) have been surveyed and tentatively named. But Mount Church (12,220 feet plus), although tentatively named, has not been officially surveyed. Finally, Peak 12,010 and Peak 12,003 are not only unnamed but also not officially surveyed—a nice thought in this time when everything seems overexplored and overdeveloped.

The range also hosts scores of peaks that are over 11,800 feet, but when you're standing at the foot of them, 11,800 and 12,000 feet don't look much different.

Although the colorful Challis Volcanics have buried the low northern end of the range and have also washed up on the mountains' east side, the high core of the Lost Rivers is relentlessly limestone—ancient sea deposits compressed into rock and then pushed by innumerable earthquakes until they rose more than 2 miles above sea level. They stand warped, folded, and broken in the dry, cold air of east central Idaho.

The Lost River Range has still fewer hiking trails than its longer neighbor, the Lemhi Range, and—other than climbers seeking the summits of Leatherman and Borah, a few hunters, and stray recreationists—these heights see only cowhands, and too few of those, because overgrazing is a problem. One exception is King Mountain on the range's southern end. It is one of the prime hang-gliding sites in the United States.

The west-facing side of the Lost Rivers rises very abruptly, presenting a bold and austere mountain front towering 5,000 feet above some of the largest alluvial fans in the West. Many people travel US 93, which follows the Big Lost River Valley here, but

*The Lost River front.* PHOTO BY LUKE KRATZ

few reach the mountains, because the access roads are poor and the canyons rough, rugged, and choked with brush.

The east-facing side of the range, on the other hand, contains long canyons, which harbor much more flowing water, some hiking trails and easy routes, and a few lakes near the crest, where the altitude and snowmelt overcome the tendency of water to drain into the limestone. These lakes are rare, but they are among the most beautiful in Idaho.

The Lost Rivers are split into four sections by low passes, unlike the parallel Lemhi Mountains, which have no such passes. The first section begins southeast of Arco near Howe. Often called the Arco Hills, these "hills" rise to 9,045 feet at Jumpoff Peak. With no hiking trails and absolutely no water, this rarely visited area still contains many interesting cliffs and rock formations. To the north, Arco Pass separates the Arco Hills from the next section of the range.

Next comes King Mountain, the first big mountain in the range. At 10,612 feet, King Mountain is one of the few named peaks in what has become known as the 95,000-acre King Mountain Roadless Area. Despite the great height of these mountains, where one would expect water, there is not even a reliable spring. Instead, you'll find little-known country of big mountains, canyons lined with incredible cliffs and rock fins, caves, and other geological oddities.

A good dirt road goes over Pass Creek Summit (only 7,600 feet) and eastward down Wet Creek. This canyon route marks the next division of the Lost Rivers. Here, the really high Lost Rivers begin. This middle portion of the range was proposed for classification as the 115,000-acre Borah Peak Wilderness by the forest service back in the 1970s and again by the Challis National Forest Plan a decade later. Though it contains no commercial timber, no minerals, no dam sites, no proposed ski areas, and the highest mountains in Idaho, anti-wilderness diehards have blocked its classification and protection. Your voice is needed in the campaign to protect this area.

North of the Borah Peak proposed wilderness, a deep trough cuts across the range. Here, at Doublespring Pass (8,318 feet), another good dirt road crosses the mountains. It leads from the upper part of Big Lost River Valley over to the Pahsimeroi Valley. The last and northernmost portion of the range is often called the Pahsimeroi Mountains. It, too, is a little-traveled area of high limestone peaks and little water. Just north of Grouse Creek, the Pahsimeroi Range fades and is buried by the Challis Volcanics, taking on a rolling rather than a rugged appearance. This is a very pretty area in late June, before the livestock trample the area.

From south to north, the major canyons in the Lost Rivers include Ramshorn, Cedarville, Cabin Fork and North Fork of Cedarville, Van Dorn, Basin Creek, Elbow, Pass Creek, Wet Creek, Big Creek, Lower Cedar, Upper Cedar, Long Lost Creek, Dry Creek, East and West Forks of the Pahsimeroi, Mahogany Creek, Willow Creek, Doublespring Creek, Christian Gulch, and Grouse Creek. Roads fill Pass Creek, Willow Creek, and Doublespring Creek, leaving little room for hiking. The rest of the canyons offer good, but sometimes rough, hikes—mostly either on a jeep trail or cross-country. Reliable water can be found in Basin Creek, Big Creek, Bear Creek, Lower and Upper Cedar, Long Lost and Dry Creeks, the forks of the Pahsimeroi, and Mahogany and Grouse Creeks.

By and large, road access to the canyons is plentiful but of poor quality. Drive carefully; carry maps, a shovel, and a spare tire. My truck had to be pulled out of a mud hole in normally waterless Ramshorn Canyon while I was doing research for this edition. A sudden rainstorm turned the road into a quagmire.

Wildlife in the Lost Rivers is varied but not particularly abundant. Most common are antelope, deer, and elk. A reintroduced herd of bighorn sheep is faring well. Cougars are common but rarely seen. As with the Lemhi Mountains, these mountains have been managed for livestock use rather than multiple use, unlike the law dictates. The prevalence of rock, however, keeps the absolute number of cattle down.

On October 28, 1983, the earth at the base of Mount Borah split, leaving a fault scarp 10 miles long from north to south. The scarp is still visible today. The earthquake was the biggest (7.3 on the Richter Scale) in the lower 48 states in 24 years. Those exploring the range found a few rockslides and some rearrangement of the trails. Because the earthquake caused the valley to drop, the Lost River Range's relief may be 15 to 20 feet greater than before the quake. One trail description in this guide (Ramshorn Canyon) was changed by the earthquake.

—Ralph Maughan

# 57 Bear Creek Lake

This is a short hike into a small lake among big, really big mountains.

**Start:** 12 miles northeast of Mackay; 90 miles northwest of Pocatello
**Type of hike:** Day hike or overnight; out-and-back
**Distance:** 5.2 miles round-trip
**Approximate hiking time:** 3 hours
**Difficulty:** Moderate
**Best season:** Late June–October
**Trail surface:** Normal dirt and rock
**Land status:** Salmon-Challis National Forest
**Canine compatibility:** On leash
**Fees and permits:** None
**Maps:** Mackay, Methodist Creek, and Massacre Mountain USGS quadrangles; Middle Fork, Challis, and Lost River Ranger Districts-Challis National Forest map
**Trail contact:** Lost River Ranger District, (208) 588-3400

**Finding the trailhead:** Turn off US 93, 8 miles south of Mackay (19 miles north of Arco) at a clump of houses called Leslie. Here a gravel road travels northward for about 2 miles and then turns northeast heading toward a low spot (an obvious canyon) in the Lost River Mountains. The good gravel road enters this tight canyon, which is called Pass Creek Gorge. The dramatic rugged scenery of the gorge's limestone walls lasts for 2 miles. Suddenly the gorge opens into a broad canyon, where cows graze the pastureland. About 2 more miles brings you to the Bear Creek side road (to the left). This road is 9.5 miles from the US 93 exit at Leslie.

This road heads northward over stream gravel toward a canyon with an impressive walled entrance–Bear Canyon. The portal cliffs rise 600 vertical feet. The road passes through scrubby aspen, past informal campsites, and then into open forest. The trailhead is 1.2 miles from the start of the Bear Creek side road. Don't take a road to the right (it goes right down to the creek) at about the 1-mile mark. I did that my first time in Bear Creek and spent an hour wading through stinging nettle, cow pies, and swamp. Keep left and drive up a short, but steep, hill, navigate a rough road, and park where the road ends in the shade at the trailhead just below the big cliffs. You don't need four-wheel drive, but high clearance helps. Be very cautious if the road is muddy. GPS: N43 59.26' / W113 28.86'

**Parking and trailhead facilities:** The trailhead has room for about four vehicles, although you can park in several other places a few hundred yards back down the road. In fact, this option may be prudent if the road is muddy, even if you have a four-wheel-drive vehicle.

## The Hike

The easy-to-follow trail strikes out straight ahead upcanyon; it begins to climb very steeply, but the climb is brief. It then follows the left side of the canyon for about 0.3 mile and suddenly drops down about 40 feet and crosses Bear Creek, which will probably be dry here by midsummer. The topographic map shows the trail crossing the creek several times, but it is wrong.

Now on the creek's right side, you'll walk through a level, open forest a short distance to the forks of the canyon—Methodist Gulch to the left and Bear Creek to the right. Huge peaks appear up Methodist Gulch, but their full magnitude is frustratingly hidden by nearby trees and a bend in Methodist Gulch.

At the forks ignore a faint (and unmapped) trail to the left, and follow the main trail. It climbs steeply up the mountainside on the right. Climb about 300 feet in 0.25 mile through a Douglas fir forest growing on the dry, rocky mountainside. Next you'll break out into the open. Bear Creek below usually has water year-round at this point, and across Bear Creek you can see the decaying remains of an old horse road once used for logging.

After a climb of about 0.5 mile (and 500 feet) from the forks, you come to a faint sign on a fir that points uphill to the right and reads WET CREEK. Don't follow it. Instead, take the obvious left fork of the trail, which continues up Bear Canyon. Bear Canyon Trail does not appear on the Methodist Creek USGS quadrangle. It is shown on the older 15-minute Mackay quadrangle, however.

Soon you arrive at springs where Bear Creek's waters appear from limestone rubble of the creekbed. After this point the bed is usually dry. Except for one short section, you always stay to the right of the creekbed.

After a waterless 0.5 mile or so, the creek reemerges. Then, just past a small, startlingly green meadow, the trail climbs straight up the hillside to Bear Creek Lake. It's about 0.5 mile, and a tough 300-foot climb, to the lake. The trail twists and winds and can be a bit obscure here, so watch carefully. You may find that it disappears completely, but that's okay. You will find the lake if you keep your eyes on the giant peak ahead and just angle to the right.

Just before you come to the lakeshore, you emerge onto a limestone shelf and are surrounded by glorious peaks, including what I call the "Bear Creek Pinnacles" to your south. This is the south wall of Bear Canyon. These twisted rocks flow toward the sky like taffy from a giant's kitchen. The pinnacles are similar in appearance to the much-photographed, much-climbed Dolomites in the Italian Alps, and they guard a green alpine meadow where Bear Creek begins its tumbling descent in the grass and boulders. If you walk over to the base of the pinnacles (a ten-minute walk on a faint trail), you reach the meadow beneath these crags. Upcanyon from here, you can see lofty and unnamed Peak 11,138 and two other peaks, one about 11,200 feet and the other about 10,900 feet. The various pinnacles are approximately 9,800 to 10,000 feet.

The main trail proceeds to the lakeshore. The shore appears to be rocks and dirt but is really deep mud. Walk carefully as you approach the lake's jade waters. There are no fish in Bear Creek Lake since it loses much of its water by September and therefore is too shallow for fish to winter over.

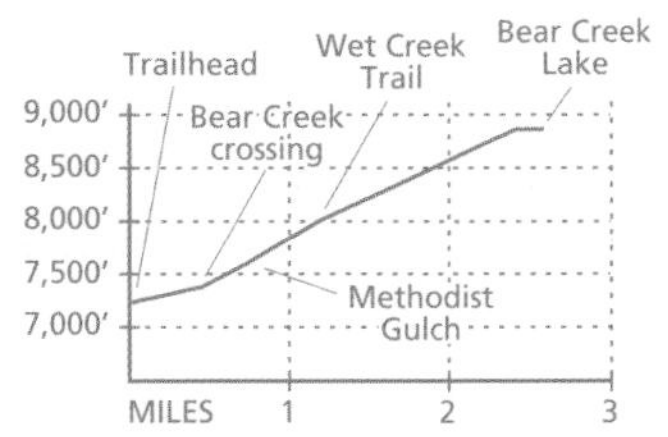


Just a few yards to your right over a minor hill is a beautiful green, flat meadow (it's a pond in early June).

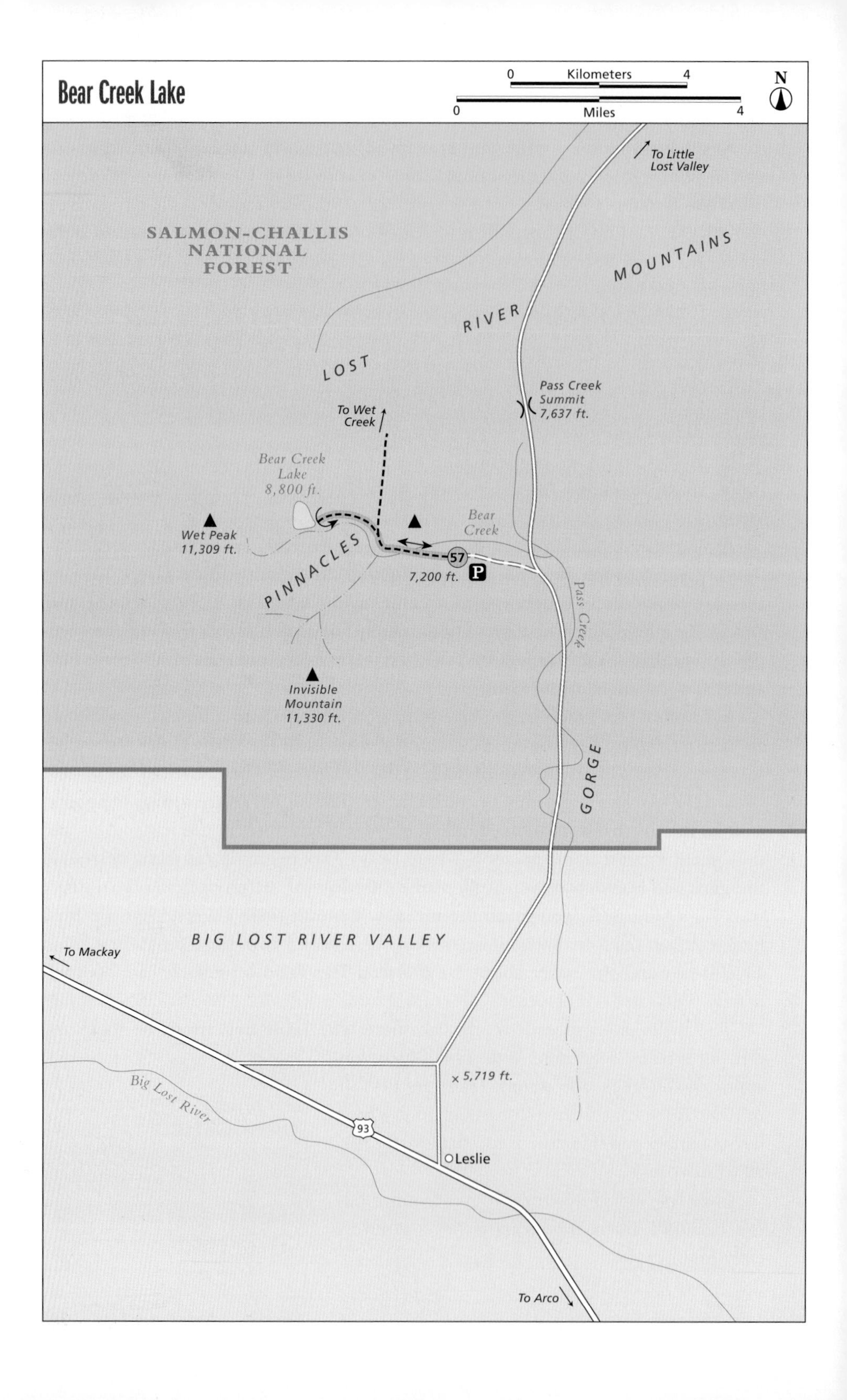
Bear Creek Lake
0
Kilometers
4
0
Miles
4
N
To Little
Lost Valley
SALMON-CHALLIS
NATIONAL
FOREST
MOUNTAINS
RIVER
LOST
Pass Creek
Summit
7,637 ft.
To Wet
Creek
Bear Creek
Lake
8,800 ft.
Wet Peak
11,309 ft.
Bear
Creek
PINNACLES
57
7,200 ft.
P
Pass Creek
Invisible
Mountain
11,330 ft.
GORGE
BIG LOST RIVER VALLEY
To Mackay
5,719 ft.
Big Lost River
93
Leslie
To Arco

*Cliffs of "giant's taffee" overlooking Bear Creek.* PHOTO BY LUKE KRATZ

The giant peak that you have been hiking toward rises as a long wall behind the lake. Northeast of the lake, a long talus gulch slides down from a pass. You can scramble up the gulch for access to Wet Creek (no water!), or you can use it as a scrambling route to the crest of the mountain range. At the pass at the top of the gulch is an interesting area of grassy limestone plateau, complete with wildflowers and ephemeral ponds, all high above timberline.

—Ralph Maughan

## Miles and Directions

**0.0** Trailhead (7,200 feet)
**0.4** Bear Creek crossing (7,420 feet)
**0.7** Methodist Gulch–Bear Creek forks (7,600 feet)
**1.2** Wet Creek–Bear Creek Trail junction (8,000 feet)
**2.5** Shelf above Bear Creek Lake (8,850 feet)
**2.6** Bear Creek Lake (8,800 feet)

# 58 Leatherman Pass

This hike provides astounding views of Idaho's rooftop with ample climbing opportunities.

**Start:** 40 miles north of Arco
**Type of hike:** Day hike or backpack; out-and-back
**Distance:** 3.5–5 miles depending on parking spot
**Approximate hiking time:** 5–8 hours
**Difficulty:** Moderate to strenuous
**Best season:** Summer, fall
**Trail surface:** Dirt and shale
**Land status:** Salmon-Challis National Forest
**Canine compatibility:** Voice command
**Fees and permits:** None
**Maps:** Leatherman Peak USGS quadrangles
**Trail contact:** Lost River Ranger District, (208) 588-3400

**Finding the trailhead:** Take US 93 north for 12 miles past Mackay until you reach a sign on the right indicating SAWMILL GULCH. There is a parking area here, but if you'd like to get a closer start you can mosey farther up the rocky road. I found that 1.5 miles was close enough to begin hiking without killing my truck. There are places to park along the side of the road at this point. Hike up the road as it continues on over rocks and steep shale for another 1.5 miles. You'll hit a junction with jeep road heading left to Coyote Springs, but keep going straight. After you head into the trees another 0.5 mile, the trail to the pass begins. GPS: N44 4.03' / W113 45.78'

## The Hike

The most difficult part of the hike is the long walk up the road through open sagebrush country to get to the trailhead. This is best done in the morning before the sun begins beating down. Once you hit the trailhead at 8,600 feet in elevation, the climb is generally steeper—but so many new sights arise at each bend that it is much more engaging. While you begin the ascent through the forest, water begins trickling down Sawmill Gulch. The trail continues to follow the stream over scree slopes and through forests of pine and aspen. A nice flat bench of forest at 9,600 feet elevation and approximately 1 mile from the pass trailhead has nice places for camping or resting.

The trail leads on through this island of forest, eventually dropping off overlooking Lower Cedar Creek. Continue heading up the ridge until you see the pass to the left of the gigantic face of Leatherman Peak. Trees become more gnarled and scattered until they fizzle out completely. With your end goal is in sight, the trail is more pronounced as it zigzags through the scree to the pass at 10,548 feet. The pass itself is breathtaking, with views of mountains and landscaped valleys on both sides of the crest of the highest mountain range in Idaho.

**Options:** Moving beyond the pass to the other side brings you to a junction with the Pass Lake Trail. Opportunities are available for peak bagging in high Lost River

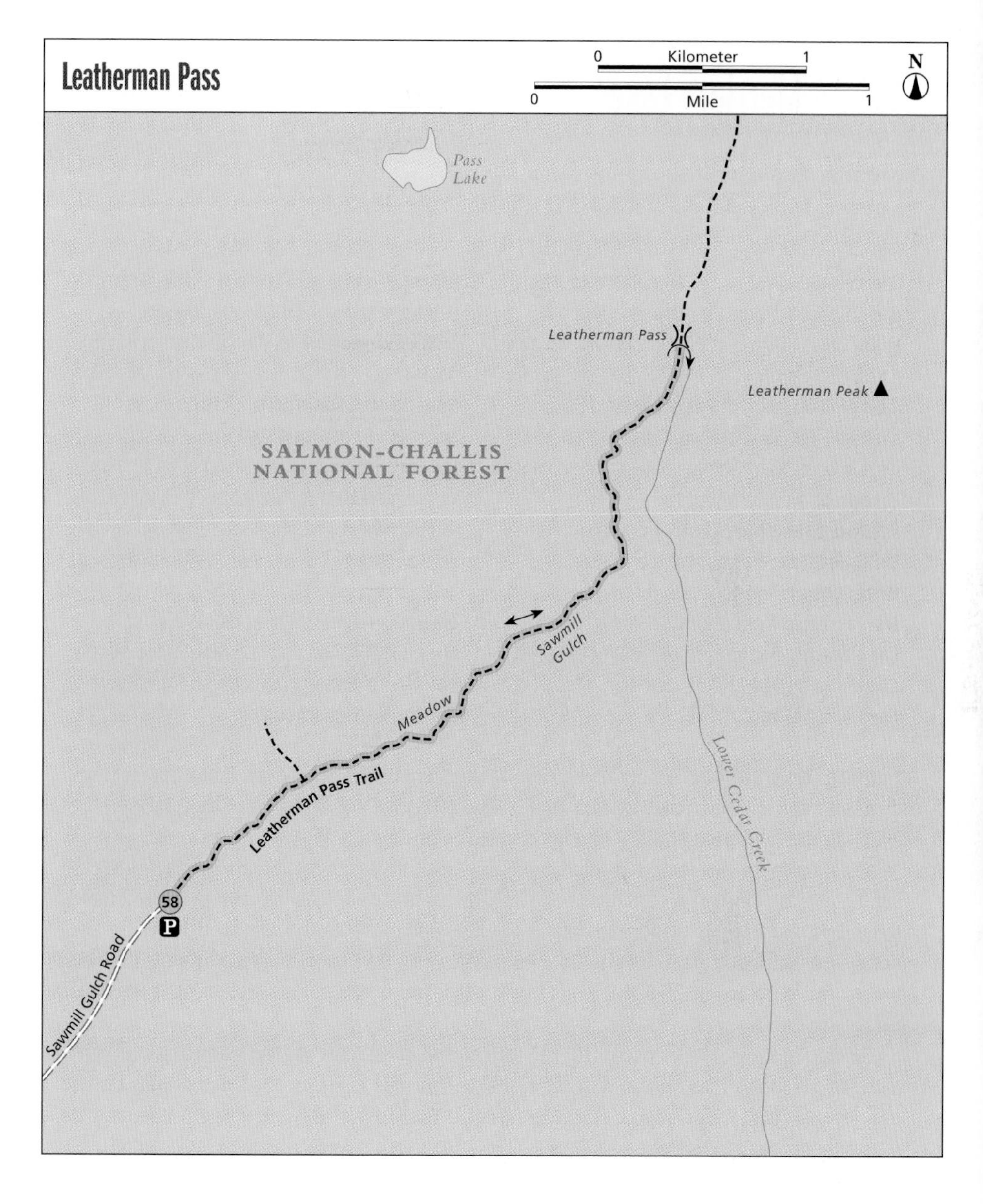


Mountains, including Leatherman (Idaho's second highest summit). Plan ahead to find the most suitable ascents and base camp near the pass with an early start.

## Miles and Directions

**0.0 miles** Trailhead to Leatherman Pass (8,600 feet)
**1.0 miles** Flat forest bench
**1.3 miles** Overlook of Lower Cedar Creek and view of pass
**2.0 miles** Leatherman Pass

# 59 Merriam Lake

Merriam is one of Idaho's most beautiful lakes, set in a large cirque basin and dominated by Mount Idaho, at 12,065 feet, Idaho's seventh tallest.

**Start:** In the crest of the Lost River Range in the proposed Mount Borah Wilderness, 16 linear miles northwest of Mackay and 75 miles south of Salmon
**Type of hike:** A short hike, out-and-back, to a stunning high-mountain lake, a day trip were it not for the time-consuming drive to the trailhead
**Distance:** 4 miles round-trip
**Approximate hiking time:** 3 hours
**Difficulty:** Moderate due to steepness
**Best season:** Mid-July–late September
**Trail surface:** Normal dirt and rock
**Land status:** Salmon-Challis National Forest
**Canine compatibility:** On leash
**Fees and permits:** None
**Maps:** Burnt Creek, Elkhorn Creek, and Leatherman Peak USGS quadrangles
**Trail contact:** Challis Ranger District, (208) 879-4100
**Special considerations:** As with most accesses to the east side of the Lost Rivers, the road to the trailhead is long and harsh. You must take a high-clearance vehicle; four-wheel drive is recommended. The trailhead is approximately 25 miles from US 93. Allow at least an hour and a half for the drive. The road becomes increasingly worse as it approaches the trailhead. The first 0.5 mile of the hike is not very accurately portrayed on the Burnt Creek USGS quadrangle.

**Finding the trailhead:** From Challis, drive south along US 93 over Willow Creek Summit and then 7.8 more miles to May-Patterson (Doublespring Pass) Road to the left of US 93. From Mackay, drive northward on US 93 about 26 miles to this turnoff.

At 2.4 miles on May-Patterson Road, there is a picnic area with interpretive displays describing the effects of the great earthquake of 1983. This area is near Mount Borah, at 12,662 feet the highest mountain in Idaho, and adjacent to a portion of the earthquake scarp. Drive 5 more miles on a fairly good gravel road to Doublespring Pass (8,318 feet). Continue over the pass down broad, dry Doublespring Creek Canyon for 3 more miles. Turn right at the sign indicating HORSEHEAVEN PASS.

For the Pahsimeroi Valley access, drive to the almost ghost town of May; then cross over the valley to the county road that goes up its west side. This road leads up into Doublespring Creek, and 35 miles from May it comes to the Horseheaven Pass turnoff. Drive up a short, steep hill and follow the dirt road to Horseheaven Pass (7,925 feet), which is really a broad rangeland divide between the Lost Rivers and an outlying mountain. This area is frequented by pronghorn antelope.

Seven miles past the turnoff from May-Patterson Road, you reach a junction. The road to the left leads to the Pahsimeroi Valley; keep to the right. In another mile the road comes to a four-way junction just before Mahogany Creek. Continue straight ahead at the junction, and drop down to cross Mahogany Creek. Go up the creek for 0.1 mile; then turn onto the road at the left to go up a steep, short hill. The road then makes a broad 180-degree turn around the hill and enters the broad valley, which contains the headwaters of the Pahsimeroi River.

After about 2.5 miles on an increasingly rocky road, you'll pass a line shack and a corral. Just beyond, the road forks. The left fork follows the East Fork of the Pahsimeroi, in which amazing cliffs and folded rocks are visible. Continue to the right up the valley of the West Fork of the

Pahsimeroi. Another 3 miles on the twisting and rocky road brings you to the trailhead. GPS: N44 07.75' / W113 43.62'

**Parking and trailhead facilities:** Undeveloped and without potable water, the trailhead is often busy because it also serves as the trailhead for Pass Lake as well as Leatherman Pass, which many people use to access Leatherman Peak from the back side.

## The Hike

The permeable limestone core of the Lost River Range is hostile to the formation of lakes, despite the mountains' great height. The few lakes that do exist in these crags are both fertile and scenic. Merriam Lake is possibly the most beautiful. Set in a glacier-carved cirque at 9,600 feet, Merriam reflects the image of picturesque Mount Idaho at the basin's head and is flanked by mountains higher than 11,000 feet on both sides.

The signed trailhead begins on the right (north) bank of the West Fork of the Pahsimeroi. It immediately crosses a smaller tributary stream that runs into the Pahsimeroi at a ninety-degree angle from the hills on the north side of the canyon. This tributary shares the wide gravel trail for a short distance before it meets with the West Fork.

At approximately 0.2 mile the trail forks. This junction is marked by a sign that points left to a trail that crosses the West Fork of the Pahsimeroi and right to Merriam Lake. Stay right.

Just past this trail junction, the West Fork of the Pahsimeroi (which runs from the south from its headwaters near Leatherman Pass) meets with the tributary that drains Merriam Lake to the west. The trail remains adjacent to this tributary for the remainder of the hike.

Merriam Lake Trail is, in general, well trodden and easy to follow with the aid of blazes on trees. Regular trail maintenance is evident by the removal of downed timber, erected erosion control measures, and bridges over wet meadows.

The trail climbs moderately for 1.5 miles, gaining 650 feet in elevation and winding through alpine meadows and conifer forests teeming with deer and elk. Here it nears the tributary that drains Merriam Lake (but it never crosses to the left bank of the tributary). Soon after, the trail crosses a small spring-fed stream before it climbs 800 feet quite steeply, first through forest and then switchbacking up an open slope of quartzite outcrops. On the left side of the trail, the tributary that departs Merriam Lake falls abruptly over staircases of quartzite.

Finally, at 2 miles, you are rewarded for the steep climb with a view of majestic Merriam Lake. The lake sits on a shelf of less erosive quartzite and is surrounded on the north by a spattering of alpine conifers and on the south by a talus slope of sedimentary rock. The huge peak that dominates the view up the basin is the

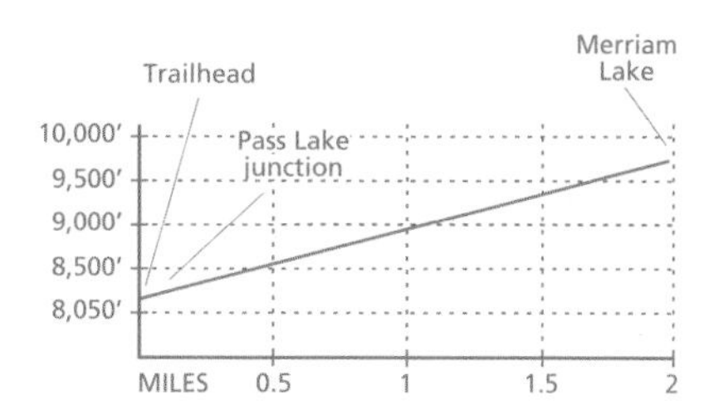

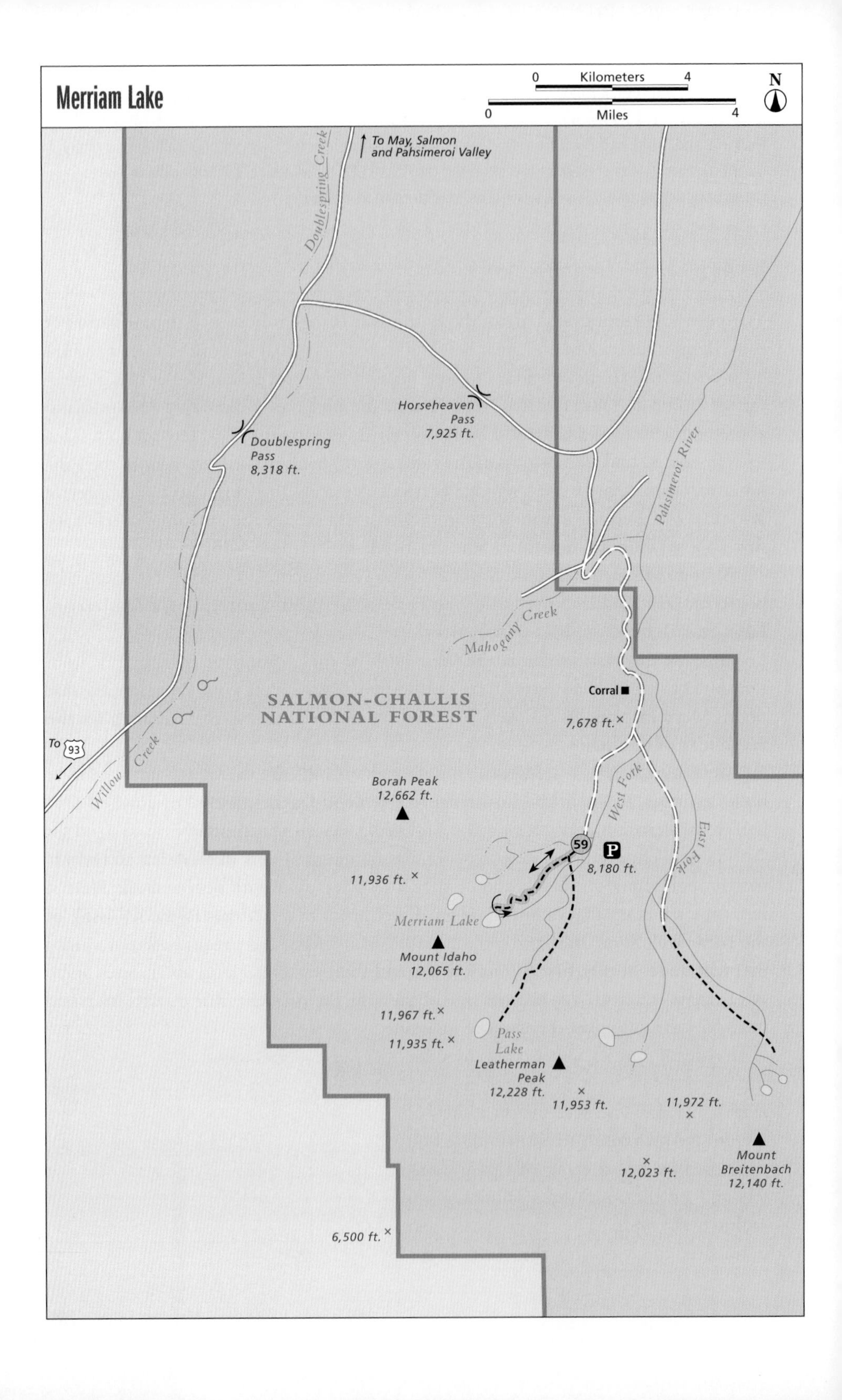

Merriam Lake
0 Kilometers 4
0 Miles 4
N
To May, Salmon and Pahsimeroi Valley
Doublespring Creek
Horseheaven Pass 7,925 ft.
Doublespring Pass 8,318 ft.
Pahsimeroi River
Mahogany Creek
Corral
7,678 ft.
SALMON-CHALLIS NATIONAL FOREST
To 93
Willow Creek
Borah Peak 12,662 ft.
West Fork
East Fork
59
8,180 ft.
11,936 ft.
Merriam Lake
Mount Idaho 12,065 ft.
11,967 ft.
11,935 ft.
Pass Lake
Leatherman Peak 12,228 ft.
11,953 ft.
11,972 ft.
12,023 ft.
Mount Breitenbach 12,140 ft.
6,500 ft.

12,065-foot Idaho Peak. A surprising number of visitors think this peak is Mount Borah. Mount Borah, however, is a good 2 miles to the north and is not visible.

*Merriam Lake among towering giants.*
PHOTO BY RALPH MAUGHAN

Although this trail is hard to access, it is quite popular, so don't be disappointed if you are not alone. There is more solitude above the lake in a rock garden and alpine meadow setting. Please use a stove rather than scavenging the meager woods for a campfire.

For the fly fisher, the banks of the lake on the right (north) and left (south) sides are steep, and fish can be visually tracked. The trail along the north side is moderately wooded, making casting somewhat difficult. Around the west side of the lake, near the inlet, the bank and lake bottom are shallow, and wading is possible. Fish are small, stocked rainbow/cutthroat hybrids and are very plentiful. Their size, on average, is less than 10 inches, with the largest probably no longer than 18 inches.

If you follow the lake's inlet stream upward, you will pass delightful cascades, wildflower-filled meadows, and a few small ponds. Eventually you reach an upper jade-colored lake, set in an alpine rock basin at 10,220 feet. There are no fish here. The sharp peak rising to the lake's northwest is 11,936 feet high and, as is usual for many lofty peaks in these mountains, has no name.

From Merriam Lake, you can also climb the ridge to the lake's northwest. From the top, you look straight down to a no-name lake in a nameless canyon. To the southwest you look across 11,000-foot-high side ridges of bare rock with the high point of Leatherman Peak in the distance. This ridge is a good location for hunting fossils (Paleozoic coral).

**Options:** Because of the long, brutal drive to the trailhead, consider also hiking to Pass Lake on the same trip. Spend a night at each lake. At the Pass Lake Trail junction, take a left and climb 4 miles to Pass Lake at 10,000 feet (use the same topos as for Merriam Lake). This could also be done in conjunction with Leatherman Pass (Hike 58).

—Ralph Maughan, Gwen Gerber, and Doug Gail

## Miles and Directions

**0.0** Trailhead (8,160 feet)

**0.2** Pass Lake junction (8,240 feet)

**2.0** Merriam Lake (9,590 feet)

# 60 Mount Borah

This is quite a mountain, beautiful and bodacious. The peak, Idaho's highest at 12,662 feet, gives an eagle's view of the surrounding high country and high desert valleys. It also harbors Idaho's only glacier.

**Start:** 35 miles southeast of Challis and 45 miles northwest of Arco
**Type of hike:** Day climb; out-and-back
**Distance:** 3.5 miles one way
**Approximate hiking time:** 8–9 hours plus
**Difficulty:** Very strenuous
**Best season:** May and June for the lower slopes; July and August for the summit
**Trail surface:** Normal dirt and rock for first half; shale rock to summit
**Land status:** Salmon-Challis National Forest
**Canine compatibility:** Voice command though the climb is not suitable for dogs due to lack of water and steep inclines on rough surfaces
**Fees and permits:** None
**Map:** Borah Peak USGS quadrangle
**Trail contact:** Lost River Ranger District, (208) 588-3400
**Special considerations:** Very steep and requires excellent physical condition. The climb to the summit, starting at Chicken-Out Ridge, involves a knife ridge, exposure, traversing a small but precipitous snowfield, and scrambling. Keep an eye on the weather since the best summit months are also the best lightning months.

The entire hike can take up to twelve hours, depending on the physical condition of participants. No water is available on the entire route, except possible snowfields. Also, its best to leave early morning to reach the summit by noon, thus avoiding storms.

**Finding the trailhead:** The turnoff is on the east side of US 93 between Challis and MacKay between mileposts 129 and 130. The well-signed Birch Springs–Borah Access Road is gravel and slowly climbs 3.5 miles through the high desert toward the base of the Lost River Range. Here, it turns to the right and runs along the 1983 earthquake fault scarp. (This continuous line of exposed dirt and rock bisects the foothills and is the quake's fracture line.) The road has been improved greatly in recent years. The parking area is 0.5 mile farther. GPS: N44 07.95' / W113 50.07'
**Parking and trailhead facilities:** The trailhead has an outhouse and three developed campsites with picnic tables but no water.

## The Hike

Mount Borah, also called Borah Peak, is primarily a climber's mountain, with one route (described here) accessible to the advanced hiker. This means that to get to and from the summit you must scramble (rock climb using both hands and feet), be tolerant of exposure (vertical drop-offs), ascend and descend small, loose rock, and cross some large boulders.

The hiker's route up Borah has worn its way into becoming an obvious but steep trail. This path ends at about 11,600 feet, and the last mile (and 1,000 feet) of relief is a scramble, partly along the knife-edge Chicken-Out Ridge, then up loose rock, solid inclines, and small cliffs. Hikers with no fondness for vertical exposure can get far enough up the mountain to gain a tremendous view and a sense of accomplishment.

July and August, when the snowfield on the col of the 11,898-foot southern spur is the smallest, are the best months to try the summit. By July most of the grass in the Big Lost River Valley at the base of the Lost Rivers is brown. May and June would be pleasing times to try a partial climb of Borah or nearby mountains.

Until July, you generally can count on melting snow on the mountain during the climb, but this is a poor source of water even in June. Each person should take a gallon of liquid for a one-day round-trip to the top. Avoid carbonated drinks since their containers are likely to leak at altitudes near the summit.

There are several places to bivouac on the mountain, such as on the saddle at 10,632 feet, but all are dry and exposed to wind, rain, snow, and lightning. Users have built small rock windbreaks at several sites for meager protection.

The less steep but slightly longer route described here climbs the open slope to the north of the parking area. It goes northward briefly before starting up the mountain slope. Once on the mountain, you climb, gaining about 800 feet, toward rock Knob 8,714.

Once at Knob 8,714, the trail is obvious.

After Knob 8,714, the trail circles just to its north, then drops to a saddle, losing 100 feet. Here a route from the canyon joins. Just past the saddle, the trail starts a very steep climb through open forest to timberline. After gaining about 1,200 feet, it levels out just before Point 10,632.

As you advance above timberline, the round, gray summit of Borah looms to the left, and the striped, double-peaked spur at 11,898 feet punctures the sky ahead. Between the two is a short, nearly permanent snowslope.

Above timberline the trail continues, growing fainter until about 11,400 feet, where it ends. To your left is a continuous cliff, which drops about 800 feet to a huge basin of a tributary to Rock Creek. To the right, a talus field slopes gradually down into Cedar Canyon, and above Cedar Canyon's south side rises Peak 11,308, a ruggedly beautiful gray with vertical streaks of orange. At Cedar Canyon's head thrusts Mount Idaho (12,065 feet), and as you near the 11,400-foot mark, Leatherman Peak, Idaho's second highest, rises to the left of Mount Idaho. Mount Idaho is the beautiful peak that rises above Merriam Lake (as described in Hike 59).

Look for rock cairns for guidance as the trail fades. Just past about 11,700 feet, you must make a short climb onto Chicken-Out Ridge. After the climb, keep near the ridgetop, which quickly becomes knife-edged with a maximum elevation of 11,898 feet. There is exposure here, and some hikers may want to rope up. Stay on the ridge until you must climb down a short cliff onto the col that harbors the snowslope. Early in the season you will want an ice ax and crampons.

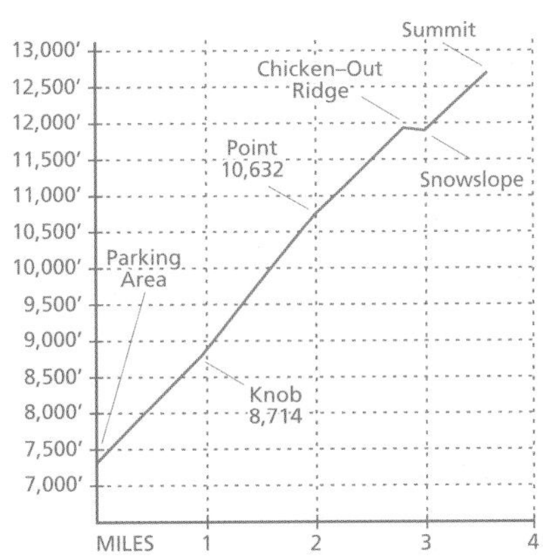

*Heading down from "chicken out ridge".* PHOTO BY JOSH KEELEY

After the snowslope, a faint trail climbs to the left (west) and slightly below another spur. The trail quickly leads to a small flat area between this spur and Borah's summit. The east edge of the flat area provides a startling overlook to unnamed cirque Lake 10,204, which is 2,000 feet below.

Now you begin the last 800 feet up Borah—a scramble. By keeping near the ridgeline, you will avoid more loose rock than if you drift to the left (west). As you approach the summit, you look almost straight down into Lake 10,204, nestled in the seldom-visited east cirque of Mount Borah. There is a pond below Lake 10,204, and in wet years (or early in the season), a third gleams farther downslope on the east.

The summit register was placed by the Mazamas hiking club. Plan for an hour at the top so you can rest and take in the view. The summit is small, with room for perhaps four people. From it, you can see the rest of the 12,000-foot and near-12,000-foot

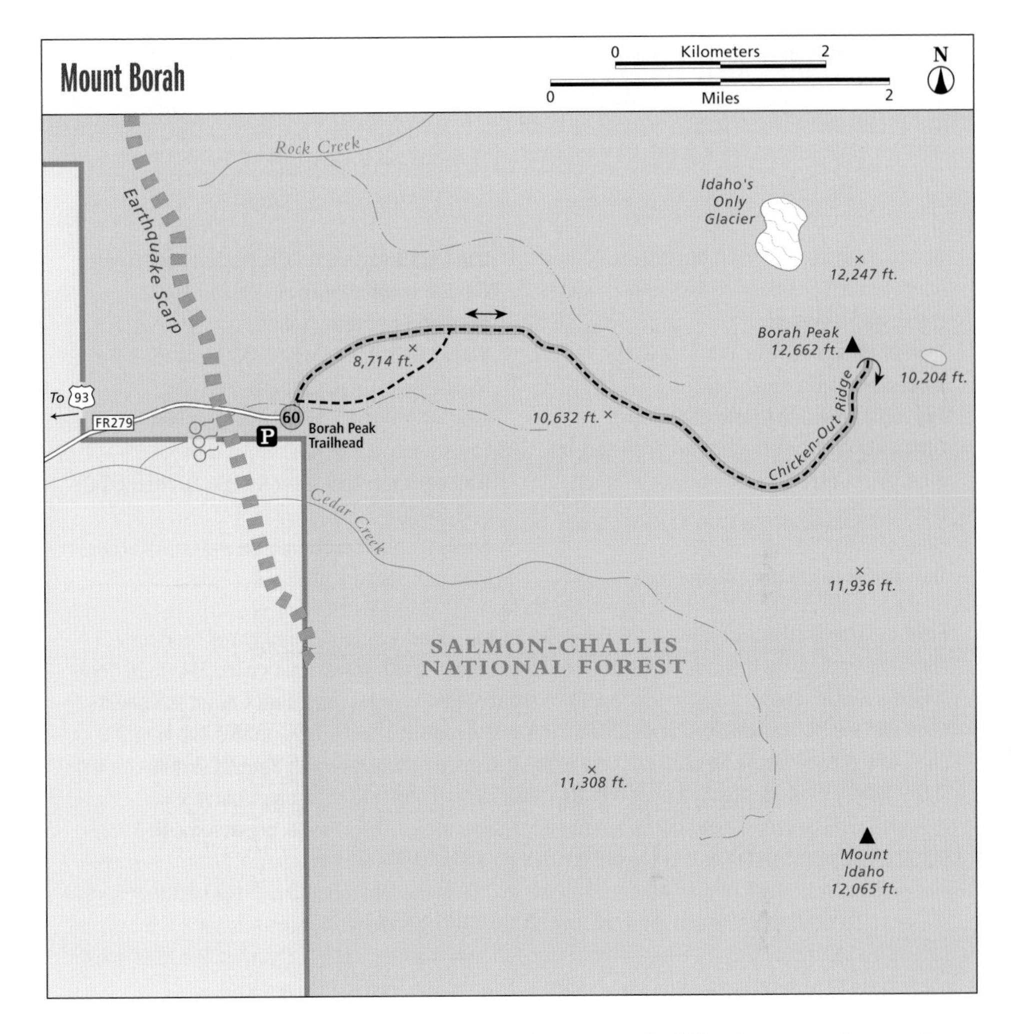


peaks in Idaho. Keep an eye on the weather, however. The hike down requires staying on the ridgetop until you have descended 1,000 feet. The summit is more than 2,000 feet above timberline.

—Ralph Maughan and Jackie Johnson Maughan

## Miles and Directions:

**0.0** Parking area (7,320 feet)

**0.9** Knob (8,714 feet)

**1.1** Alternative route junction

**2.0** Point (10,632 feet)

**2.8** Southern Spur and Chicken-Out Ridge (11,898 feet)

**3.0** Snowslope (11,800 feet)

**3.5** Summit (12,662 feet)

# 61 Ramshorn Canyon

This is a relatively easy hike, with a long season, into very rugged mountains with spectacular rock fins.

**Start:** 20 miles southeast of Mackay, 70 miles northwest of Pocatello, in the southern end of the Lost River Range
**Type of hike:** Day hike; out-and-back
**Distance:** 3 miles round-trip
**Approximate hiking time:** 2–3 hours
**Difficulty:** Easy to the end of the short trail; a cross-country hike of medium difficulty from there
**Best season:** Spring
**Trail surface:** Normal dirt and rock
**Land status:** Salmon-Challis National Forest
**Canine compatibility:** Voice command
**Fees and permits:** None
**Maps:** Ramshorn Canyon USGS quadrangle; Middle Fork, Challis, Yankee Fork, and Lost River Ranger Districts–Challis National Forest map
**Trail contact:** Lost River Ranger District, (208) 588-3400
**Special considerations:** No water. The access road can get very muddy if it rains.

**Finding the trailhead:** Turn off US 93 at Darlington. Head east on a good gravel road for 2.9 miles straight toward the mountains. You come to a north–south gravel road called Hill Road. There is also a fence here with a gate that opens to a dirt road continuing eastward toward the mountains and the big Ramshorn Canyon ahead. This is the road you take. Drive up this dirt road 3.9 miles to the undeveloped trailhead. If the road seems too rutted, go south about 1.5 miles on Hill Road. Here a second, slightly better dirt road goes to the canyon to eventually join the first.

Ramshorn Canyon, though big, is not too impressive at first. It is a wide, dry, steep-sided canyon, the bottom often full of cows and dust, and covered mostly with sagebrush. There are some nice views of 10,612-foot King Mountain, however. This is the first mountain in the Lost Rivers, rising some 5,000 feet above the Big Lost River Valley. Don't get discouraged. At about 3.5 miles, the canyon makes a ninety-degree turn to the north, and the scenery quickly changes. The road ends at the base of a steep slope. This slope marks a dramatic change in the canyon.

This road is not difficult unless muddy, but I got stuck in a late May thunderstorm in which it rained for eight hours. A tow truck pulled my mired truck out four days later. GPS: N43 49.56' / W113 16.84'

**Parking and trailhead facilities:** No formal trailhead.

## The Hike

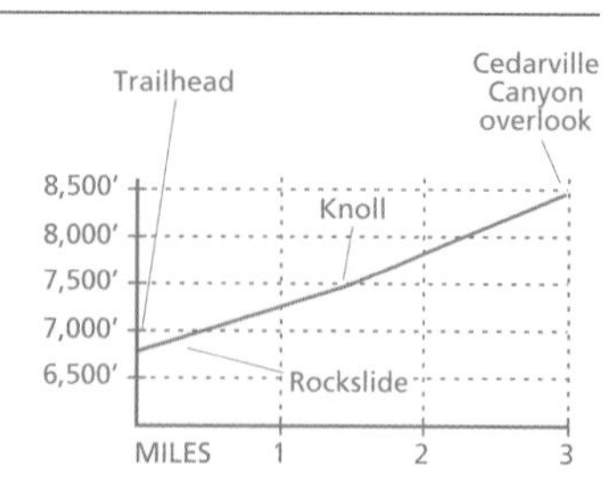


Despite its obvious rugged beauty, the southern end of the Lost River Range, like the northern end, is almost totally overlooked by hikers. South of Pass Creek–Wet Creek Road, which crosses the Lost Rivers, the mountains rise to "only" 10,000 or 11,000 feet, compared with the many peaks over 11,500 or even 12,000 feet in the range's

*Ramshorn Canyon area near the trailhead.* PHOTO BY LUKE KRATZ

middle reaches. Nevertheless, the southern end of the Lost Rivers, most of which is in the King Mountain Roadless Area, looks mighty tall.

Extended hiking in the heights and crags of this part of the mountain range isn't easy due to an almost total lack of surface water and trails. Despite considerable winter snowfall, the limestone that makes up the awesome cliffs and peaks of the Lost River's southern end sucks up water like a sponge. As a result, almost all hiking is day hiking. The best time is late June, when the canyon is still fairly cool and flowers bloom. However, the full season is about May through October. In dry years, the canyon may even be accessible for limited hiking in December or March.

There is a short trail up Ramshorn Canyon, providing an easy, scenic introduction to this part of the mountains. The trail fades and then reappears in places, giving relatively easy access to the higher reaches of the canyon.

Park your vehicle at road's end, and hike up the steep ATV track into a patch of mountain mahogany. The track quickly turns into a good trail. The climb is brief and leads into a pretty defile filled with old-growth Douglas fir. Next, you cross out onto a rockslide, and then the trail descends to a small meadow. This meadow used to be

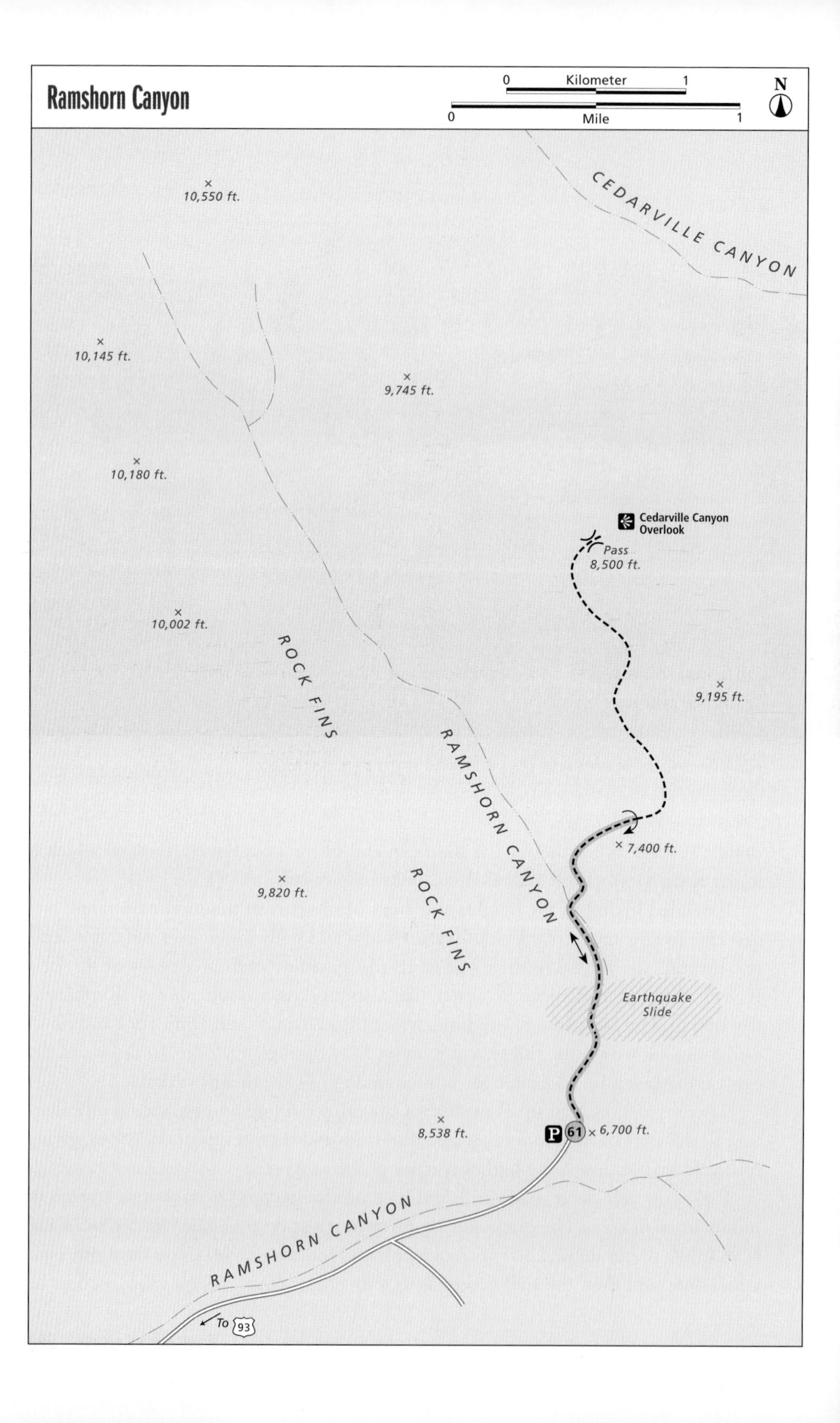

Ramshorn Canyon
0
Kilometer
1
0
Mile
1
N
10,550 ft.
CEDARVILLE CANYON
10,145 ft.
9,745 ft.
10,180 ft.
Cedarville Canyon Overlook
Pass
8,500 ft.
10,002 ft.
ROCK FINS
9,195 ft.
RAMSHORN CANYON
7,400 ft.
9,820 ft.
ROCK FINS
Earthquake Slide
P
61
8,538 ft.
6,700 ft.
RAMSHORN CANYON
To
93

larger, but the Mount Borah earthquake of 1983 shook down much more rock and almost buried the meadow.

The trail crosses the meadow and leads into a shallow canyon, cut into the huge main canyon. The trail climbs up this defile, circles to the right, tops out on a grassy, rolling bench, and seems to end. However, if you continue cross-country to the east and hike up the right side of the canyon, you will find the trail again in places for a considerable distance, though it is essentially a cross-country hike that leads to forested bench, open slope, forested bench, and so on until you reach the ridge crest, where you have a tremendous view not just of Ramshorn Canyon and King Mountain to the south but of rugged Cedarville Canyon over the crest below you to the immediate north.

Once you are on the bench where the trail ends, and more so if you climb higher, you will be overwhelmed by the rows of huge finlike cliffs on the west side of Ramshorn Canyon.

This area is notable for wintering deer, elk, and the cougar that prey on them. In late May I found a partly buried and half-eaten elk in the brush just above the small meadow. There were plenty of cougar tracks in the mud.

Ramshorn looks like a Platonic essence of cougar country—rock ledges, cliffs, shallow caves, brush, and dry meadow everywhere.

**Options:** You can do a number of scrambles along the Ramshorn/Cedarville Divide or up Ramshorn Canyon.

—Ralph Maughan

## Miles and Directions

**0.0** Informal trailhead (6,700 feet)

**0.3** Rockslide (6,800 feet)

**0.4** Small meadow (6,750 feet)

**1.5** End of obvious trail on knoll (7,400 feet)

**3.0** Cedarville Canyon overlook; cross-country (8,500 feet)

# Lemhi Mountains

More than 100 miles long as the crow flies, longer still with the kinks stretched out, the Lemhi Range rises out of the arid lava of the Snake River Plain and advances northwest to central Idaho.

These mountains, which form a high, continuous ridge, are relatively arid in their southern reaches despite the fact that numerous peaks thrust upward above 11,000 feet. Towering Diamond Peak, for example, reaches 12,197 feet, making it the third tallest in Idaho. Nevertheless, you can climb it without an ice ax in late June.

The Lemhi Mountains lie in a rain shadow, and the moisture of Pacific storms is dissipated first by the many mountain ranges of central Idaho. In the southern Lemhis, the precipitation that does fall percolates rapidly through the limestone and dolomite that constitute the mountains' vertebrae, and there is a general absence of lakes and creeks.

One ought not be misled by the arid beauty of the southern Lemhis, however. June storms can dump as much snow as a winter blast, and summer thunderstorms can be violent. In 1987 a tornado even touched down in Sawmill Canyon.

Northward these mountains shrink to a "mere" 10,000 to 11,000 feet but compensate for the lower elevation as their girth spreads to 15 or 20 miles. Here, the sedimentary rock formed under ancient seas gives way to harder rock. As you travel from south to north, dolomite first appears, then changes to an assortment of quartzites through which a number of mineral-bespeckled intrusions have pushed. These quartzites are some of the oldest exposed rocks in Idaho. Adding color, the quartzites of the northern Lemhis are covered in places by the chocolate, red, black, brown, gray, and maroon of the younger Challis Volcanics, the result of a vast outpouring of volcanic activity twenty-five to fifty million years ago. These volcanics washed over and covered large parts of east-central Idaho.

Thanks to the harder rock, water stays on the surface in the northern Lemhis. Cirque lakes huddle beneath peaks, and permanent creeks run down almost every canyon.

Despite years of prospecting, sporadic timber cutting, and little official attention to recreation, almost 500,000 acres of roadless land in these mountains has been identified by the forest service as suitable for congressional wilderness designation. Most of

*The Southern Lemhis in mid-June.* PHOTO BY LUKE KRATZ

the roadless land is in two large blocks: a 187,000-acre roadless area in the southern Lemhis and more than 300,000 acres in the northern Lemhis.

Idaho environmentalists have long proposed that Congress designate 130,000 acres in the south and 180,000 acres in the north of this range as the Lemhi Wilderness. The southern roadless area is sometimes referred to as the proposed Diamond Peak Wilderness in reference to the giant pyramidal peak that rises 5 miles west of Lone Pine. The forest service did propose a small wilderness in the north during the late 1970s but, under pressure, changed its mind. In the early 1990s the Targhee National Forest did finally recommend to Congress that about half of the southern Lemhis, at least the half of the southern half of that forest, be designated wilderness. Meanwhile the proposal has languished because Idaho politicians don't support wilderness protection anymore, and the Targhee has done nothing to protect the area from off-road vehicle abuse. Please come experience this amazing area and show your support!

Four great high desert valleys flank the Lemhi Mountains. To the north are the Pahsimeroi and Lemhi Valleys, lying on the west and the east sides of the Lemhis, respectively. To the south is the Little Lost River Valley on the southwest side and the Birch Creek Valley on the southeast. The streams draining these valleys flow into the volcanic rock of the Snake River Plain and disappear.

These four valleys support the majority of Idaho's pronghorn antelope. You may see them as they speed with seemingly little effort over the desert and open mountain slopes. With massive lungs, they sometimes will race alongside your vehicle and even overtake it on a gravel road to pass in front of you. In addition, it is common to see deer and even elk patrolling the valley floor and foothills. Even black bears are sometimes seen in the valleys. Here truly, the deer and the antelope play.

The typical Lemhi Range hike proceeds like this: A dirt road leaves the highway and gradually deteriorates into a jeep track near the mouth of, or a little way up, a canyon. Intelligence gets the best of inertia, and you park. Wearing your pack now, you follow as the track deteriorates further, and then you set out cross-country. This usually isn't difficult, for in many places these mountains, like the nearby Lost River and Beaverhead Mountains, have little underbrush.

Be sure to take the prescribed USGS topographic maps along. The maps are usually as much for navigating the maze of dirt roads in the valleys as for orienting yourself once you're in the mountains. Shovels will prove a useful accessory since minor washouts are frequent on these unmaintained roads, which cross over the big alluvial fans that have been built by thousands of years of runoff spilling from canyons to desert.

Nights are cold until after July 4. Once spring is past, storms are brief but can be violent: wind with lots of dust, heavy rain, and lightning (remember, much of this is open country). The often numerous mosquitoes of the June rangeland fade to be replaced by biting flies the remainder of the summer.

Motorcycles and ATVs are becoming common, especially on weekends. You will rarely find them far back in the mountains, although they are penetrating the northern Lemhis to a greater distance than in the south. Worse, the Challis-Salmon National Forest even let an ATV trail be built over the crest of the mountains from Patterson Creek. As a result, we have deleted that hike from this edition of *Hiking Idaho*.

Lack of water can be a problem when hiking the Targhee National Forest (southeast) side of these mountains. The South Fork of Pass Creek is the only reliable source, although scenic Rocky Canyon often has a small creek until midsummer. On the other hand, the southwest side has small creeks in most of the major canyons. Water is common in the northern part of the range.

In addition to the deer, elk, and antelope mentioned, there are quite a few black bear, cougar, and bobcat, as well as a growing herd of bighorn sheep from a transplant and a large mountain goat population. Moose were recently transplanted into the Sawmill Canyon area. Occasionally a member of the growing Idaho wolf population may wander through, but there seems to be no reproducing population of wolves yet.

Public interest in the Lemhi Mountains grew throughout the 1980s and 1990s. We hope the day is near when politicians will be required to direct the forest service and the Bureau of Land Management to manage these superlative mountains and valleys for recreation and wilderness rather than for subsidized grazing and logging.

—Ralph Maughan

# 62 Bell Mountain Canyon Loop

Bell Mountain Canyon is an easy hike into a high rangeland canyon with gorgeous eye-popping peaks.

**Start:** On the east side of the Lemhi Range, 65 miles northwest of Idaho Falls, 100 miles north-northwest of Pocatello, and 75 miles southeast of Salmon
**Type of hike:** Day hike; lollipop loop
**Distance:** 4.5 miles
**Approximate hiking time:** 2–3 hours
**Difficulty:** Moderately easy
**Best season:** Late June–early July
**Trail surface:** Normal dirt and rock
**Land status:** Caribou-Targhee National Forest
**Canine compatibility:** On leash recommended
**Fees and permits:** None
**Maps:** Bell Mountain and Coal Kiln Canyon USGS quadrangles; Dubois and Island Park Ranger Districts–Targhee National Forest map
**Trail contact:** Dubois Ranger District, (208) 374-5422
**Special considerations:** No water. You must take two quarts of liquid for each person for a day hike.

**Finding the trailhead:** From Idaho Falls, Pocatello, or Rexburg, follow ID 28 to the town of Mud Lake. Continue on ID 28 at the highway junction just west of town, and drive up into the Birch Creek Valley. Drive past the store and gas station at Lone Pine. Look for an improved, dirt side road to the left of the highway, 13.2 miles past Lone Pine. Here a sign reads CHARCOAL KILNS HISTORICAL SITE, 6 MILES. If you are coming southward from Salmon, this road is 10.3 miles south of Gilmore Summit.

The side road heads almost straight toward the Lemhi Mountains. At 4.8 miles there is a junction. Turn left here onto a primitive dirt road (usually passable to two-wheel-drive vehicles). After 0.4 mile there is another junction. Keep to the right. The dirt road winds around and up toward Bell Mountain and Mammoth Canyons. After about a mile you cross a fence marking the Targhee National Forest, and soon the road forks right, leading steeply downhill. Go down the hill and park (or park on top if it looks too steep). GPS: N44 17.41' / W113 09.99'

**Parking and trailhead facilities:** Unimproved, informal trailhead. Don't follow the road up Mammoth Canyon unless that is your destination (see Options).

## The Hike

At 11,612 feet Bell Mountain is the second highest peak in the Lemhi Mountains. Its most beautiful side faces the east. Bell Mountain Canyon was sculpted to its present form by a glacier that flowed from its northeast slopes.

This hike is a 4.5-mile loop that rambles through meadows, past a spruce-fir forest, and back through meadows. It is exquisitely beautiful from mid-June (when the annual growth is green and wildflowers bloom) until the time cattle are put in (mid-July).

Magnificent Bell Mountain and a similarly shaped unnamed peak in front of it rise before you. You can begin the hike by heading up the faint, grassy four-by-four track in the canyon, or, better, by climbing the end moraine (hill) at the mouth of the

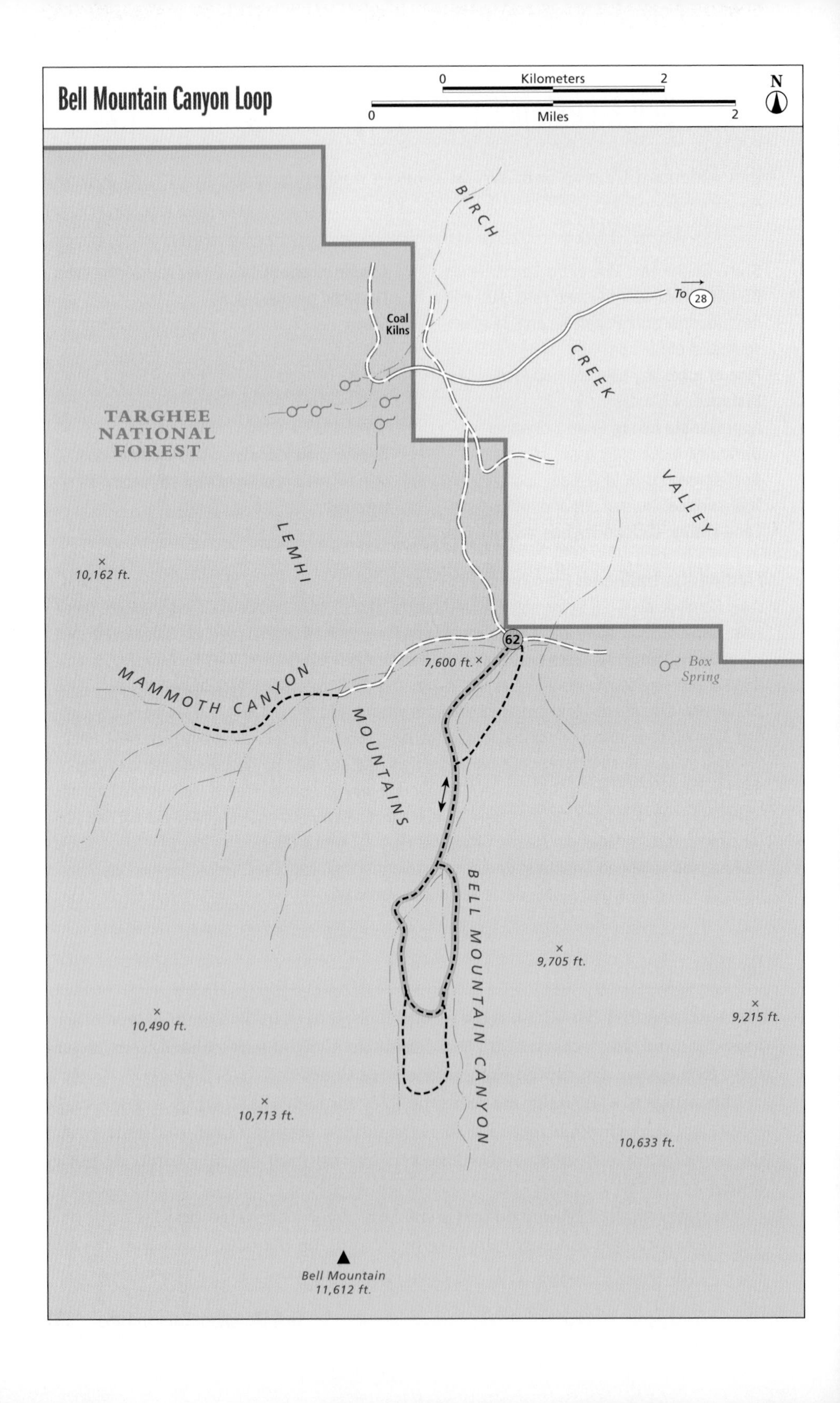
Bell Mountain Canyon Loop
0
Kilometers
2
0
Miles
2
N
BIRCH
CREEK
VALLEY
To
28
Coal
Kilns
TARGHEE
NATIONAL
FOREST
LEMHI
MOUNTAINS
10,162 ft.
62
7,600 ft.
Box
Spring
MAMMOTH CANYON
BELL MOUNTAIN CANYON
9,705 ft.
9,215 ft.
10,490 ft.
10,713 ft.
10,633 ft.
Bell Mountain
11,612 ft.

*Bell Mountain on the left.* Photo by Luke Kratz

canyon and walking along its rolling surface. There are outstanding views from the moraine. After a mile you come to the beginning of the end moraine and drop down into the broad canyon bottom. Here are meadows and patches of trees.

Follow the track up the canyon (or hike cross-country). Eventually you come to the forks, which are separated by a low, timbered hill. Hike up either fork about 0.5 mile, and then cross over into the other fork on a low, unforested pass. If you want to go farther, there is a second low pass after another 0.5 mile.

If you want to go still farther, it is a cross-country hike through forest that obscures the views until you reach the upper canyon, where you emerge onto steeply inclined rock rising up to the summit of Bell Mountain.

This open country could easily be damaged by off-road vehicles. If you find ATVs are tearing up the country, contact the Dubois Ranger District of the Caribou-Targhee National Forest.

Mosquitoes can be bad from mid-June until July unless the previous night saw a hard freeze. Fortunately, hard freezes are common in June. While mid-June to mid-July is the most scenic time of the year, the season is from early June to November (depending on the road condition).

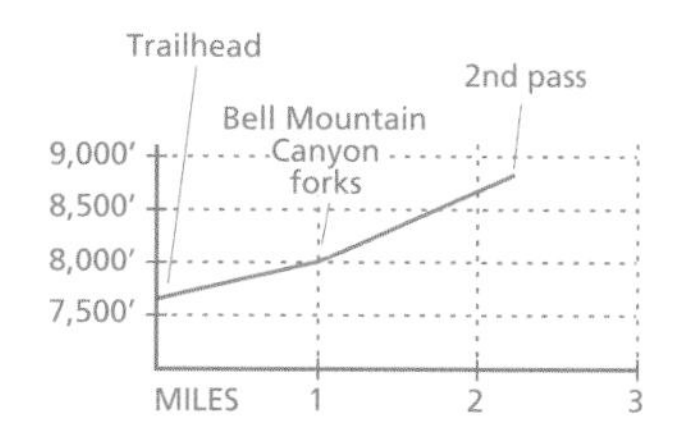


Look for pronghorn antelope and elk. There is also an occasional black bear or cougar.

**Options:** Nearby Mammoth Canyon has a faint trail after the jeep trail ends about a mile upcanyon. The canyon is of moderate scenic interest. It has an impressive, very rugged south-facing canyon wall near the end of the jeep trail.

—Ralph Maughan

## Miles and Directions

**0.0** Informal trailhead (7,600 feet)

**1.0** Bell Mountain Canyon forks (8,000 feet)

**2.2** Second low pass between forks of canyon (8,800 feet)

# 63 Big Creek-Big Timber Creek Loop

There are lofty mountains and high meadows with spacious views on this long loop trail with many additional opportunities.

**Start:** 95 miles northwest of Idaho Falls and 10 miles west of Leadore
**Type of hike:** Backpacking loop
**Distance:** 37.2 miles
**Approximate hiking time:** 5–7 days plus
**Difficulty:** Strenuous
**Best season:** July–September
**Trail surface:** Normal dirt and rock
**Land status:** For the Big Creek and Snowbank Trail portions: Challis Ranger District; for the Big Timber Creek portion: Leadore Ranger District. Both are in the Salmon-Challis National Forest
**Canine compatibility:** On leash recommended
**Fees and permits:** None
**Maps:** Big Creek Peak, Iron Creek Point, Sheephorn Peak, and Yellow Peak USGS quadrangles
**Trail contact:** Challis Ranger District, (208) 879-4100; Leadore Ranger District, (208) 768-2500
**Special considerations:** Early hikers (late June) should be prepared for difficult fords and, on the high passes, a foot or more of snow. There can still be slab avalanches this time of year. Bring wading shoes.

**Finding the trailhead:** Drive 19 miles north from Idaho Falls on I-15. Then turn left (west) onto ID 33. Continue 17 miles to Mud Lake; from here, it is another 28 miles on ID 33 to the small town of Howe. At Howe, turn right (north) off the highway and follow the county road that goes up the Little Lost River Valley all the way to the valley's end at Summit Reservoir. Cross the low divide here, and drop down into the Pahsimeroi Valley. About 57 miles north of Howe, a sign reads BIG CREEK TRAIL. Take a left onto the dirt road here, and drive 3.5 miles to Big Creek. The road ends at the small Big Creek Camp near the forest boundary where Big Creek forms from its north and south forks.

The other access points to the loop are from Iron Creek Trail in Sawmill Canyon and Big Timber Creek Trail with access from Leadore. Iron Creek Road is graveled and located just 2 miles up Sawmill Canyon beyond Mill Creek Road (see Hike 67, Mill Creek Lake). GPS: N44 23.08' / W113 25.71'
**Parking and trailhead facilities:** North Fork Trail leaves from Big Creek Camp, which is a small campsite with a couple of picnic tables at the confluence of the North and South Forks of Big Creek. There is room for only three vehicles. The trail's beginning is signed and obvious.

The South Fork of Big Creek Trailhead is 0.2 mile back up the road and about 70 feet uphill in a wide-open spot with an impressive view of both North and South Big Creek Canyons and Flatiron Mountain, which rises between them. Parking space is ample.

## The Hike

This is a tremendous loop in a mountain range that has few loop trails. If you can't spend most of a week, you will also enjoy hiking portions of the loop. In total it has 12,500 feet of relief. You hike over three divides and through a variety of mountain scenes. You will not encounter many other people, but the area is better known now than when described in the first edition of this book.

Much of the loop is open to off-road vehicles and motorcycles, and you will certainly encounter a few. The South Fork of Big Creek was closed to machines after a big battle. The North Fork of Big Creek is open to them, including ATVs, but gets no ATV use because the trail is too rocky and narrow for them. The Snowbank Trail portion gets the most machine use.

The entire loop is within the area proposed by Idaho conservationists as the Lemhi Range Wilderness.

Commonly seen are deer, elk, mountain goats, antelope, coyotes, and black bears. Moose are occasional. Cougar are abundant, but rarely seen. The profuse whitebark pine in the northern Lemhi would make for outstanding grizzly bear habitat, but there are probably no grizzly bears.

You can begin the hike from either fork. This description describes the loop going clockwise, up the North Fork of Big Creek and ending at the South Fork of Big Creek.

Proceeding up the North Fork of Big Creek, it is 6.6 miles from the trailhead to the Park Fork of Big Creek. The trail leaves the trailhead campground and goes north along the right bank of the North Fork. For a mile, it's rocky, but fairly easy, through conifer, aspen, and cottonwood, with some mountain mahogany present. Near the mouth of trailless West Fork of Big Creek, you reach the first of two fords of the North Fork. The water can be fast and deep, and fortunately, as of the summer of 2000, there was a log bridge upstream for hikers.

Once across, you make a steady, but easy, climb for almost another mile to the second crossing. There will probably be another hiker's log bridge here, too. If no log, this is also a major ford in early season.

There is a small meadow at the second crossing and two more meadows in the next 2 miles. At 4.5 miles you enter the Big Creek burn from the mid-1990s. Upcanyon past the meadows, the trail climbs to what appears to be a large, low glacial moraine, and it stays on this moraine for about a mile. You ford two small tributaries as you cross over talus and glacial cobblestone stretches. Glimpses of large, unnamed peaks upcanyon reward your efforts.

The trail approaches the North Fork closely as you near the Park Fork tributary. You can ford the Park Fork where the trail crosses (it's about 12 feet wide here), or

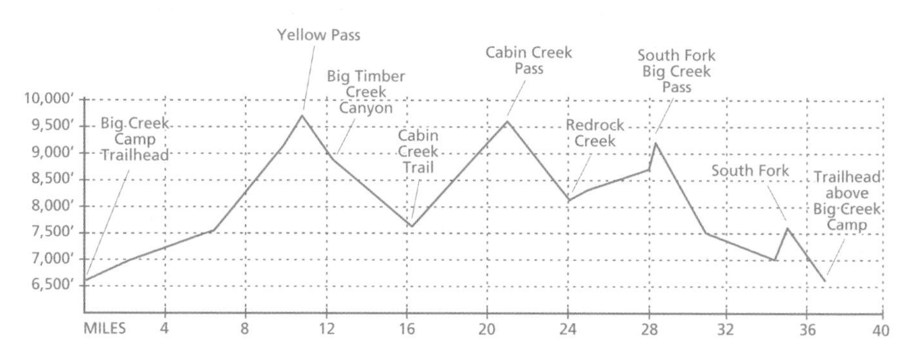

you can search upstream for a log. The Park Fork ford is not bridged, but it is not difficult except in June.

The trail then goes between the Park Fork and the North Fork for about 0.2 mile, leading to their confluence. Here the left fork of the trail continues up the North Fork, giving access to Devils Basin and Big Eightmile Creek (see Options). Take the right fork instead, and head up the Park Fork of Big Creek. It's about 4 miles and 2,000 feet of relief from the bottom of the Park Fork to Yellow Pass (its unofficial name).

The first 0.5 mile of the ascent is a steep, switchbacking, 500-foot climb, paralleling the Park Fork, which thunders down the mountain in June and early July. The gradient then declines. Scout the mountain slopes on the left (north) for mountain goats as you listen to the pikas calling from the talus slides. The trail goes through fir forest interspersed with scenic huge boulders.

The trail keeps to the north side of the creek until you are about a mile below Yellow Pass. After a jump of the Park Fork, the trail to Yellow Pass turns southward at the junction with the trail to the Middle Fork of Little Timber Creek.

Just before reaching this spot, you have the opportunity to make a cross-country hike to Park Fork Lake. Head to the northwest and climb 300 feet to this small lake located at 9,300 feet elevation in a glacier-cut bowl of intruded igneous rock of the Park Fork Stock.

After crossing the Park Fork, you climb quite rapidly toward Yellow Peak (10,968 feet), which probably was named after the slightly yellow quartzite boulders on its slopes. After just 0.25 mile the trail forks. The left fork soon forks again, with one fork leading over to Park Fork Lake and then to Yellow Lake. The second fork goes to the Middle Fork of Little Timber Creek, and the third goes to Rocky Canyon (a tributary of Big Timber Creek). Ignore all this unless your destination is not Yellow Pass. Take the trail to the right. This junction has signs giving destinations. The sign pointing out the trail to Yellow Pass is south and downhill—a bit confusing.

Follow the trail southward to the obvious pass. At Yellow Pass (9,702 feet), you are rewarded with a spectacular view of Flatiron Mountain (11,019 feet) and Big Creek Peak (11,350 feet) to the southwest. An extra hour will allow you to scramble to the top of Yellow Peak for a panorama of mountains grander still.

At Yellow Pass, you cross the crest of the Lemhi Range. The trail drops steeply and is faint in places until, after a descent of 1,000 feet in a distance of 1.3 miles, you reach Big Timber Creek Canyon. From here the trail is good and easy, and you seemingly roll down the canyon for about 4 miles until you reach Cabin Creek, which you will go up to continue the loop. Many elk and mule deer frequent this large drainage. The low whistles and grunts of the elk add to the wilderness atmosphere in this land of striking high mountain scenery and subalpine meadows, which break up the stands of quaking aspen and conifer.

After passing four major side drainages that drop off Flatiron Mountain and Big Creek Peak (11,350 feet), you enter a large meadow that lies directly below Junction

Peak (10,620 feet) and opposite the Cabin Creek and Squirrel Creek side canyons. Signs in the meadow help you locate this important junction. Take Cabin Creek Trail (Trail 127) to continue the loop. Squirrel Creek is a scenic and interesting side option.

The meadow is a large area of hunting and other camps, and it is about 20 miles from here downcanyon to the town of Leadore. The trail that continues down Big Timber Creek from the junction described is a good alternative access trail to and from the Big Creek–Timber Creek Loop. It is 6 miles down Big Timber Creek from Cabin Creek to FR 105, which comes up from Leadore.

The climb to Cabin Creek Pass (its unofficial name) gains 1,600 feet in about 4 miles. The trail stays close to Cabin Creek for the first 1.5 miles; then the grade increases, and the trail follows a fork of Cabin Creek, switchbacking to the pass, which is a small saddle at 9,282 feet. At the pass, walk westwardly along the divide, and you will soon find yourself on Snowbank Trail, where there are likely to be trail machines on weekends. You can hike the trail on this divide either east or west. The route to the east leads to Timber Pass, where you can descend Trail Creek north back to Big Timber Creek or south via Timber Creek in the head of Sawmill Canyon to FR 105. However, to continue the loop, follow the trail to your right.

The ridge on which Cabin Creek Pass sits marks the southern boundary of the wilderness proposed by Idaho environmentalists. Southward, you will see a proliferation of logging roads and the scar of the Little Lost Fire, which burned 9,000 acres in the head of Sawmill Canyon during the drought summer of 1988. Despite this view and possible dirt bikes, the Snowbank Trail is picturesque, especially the first several miles past Cabin Creek Pass.

Snowbank Trail climbs and then contours high above Sawmill Canyon, giving inspiring views of the canyon. As you reach the high point of the trail, you gain excellent views of Bell Mountain and Diamond Peak far to the southeast and also of the unnamed and rarely visited symmetrical peaks and cirque basins to the south of the South Fork of Big Creek. High marshy meadows intermingle with well-weathered conifers as the trail bumps along just below the ridgeline. This ridgeline, unlike the others visited while hiking this loop, is composed of colorful volcanic rocks rather than quartzite, dolomite, or limestone.

You'll follow Snowbank Trail for 7 miles to its junction with Iron Creek Trail (another good access trail onto the loop). There are some high-elevation camping spots about a mile past Cabin Creek Pass.

The trail drops off the ridgeline and rolls through a few small side drainages to Redrock Creek, named for the color of the rock in the area. Past Redrock Creek, the trail climbs and then continues to contour around the upper slopes of Sawmill Canyon. About a mile south of Redrock Creek, you cross an area of clear-cut about 25 years old. A volcanic column looms above you here.

Continue contouring around the upper slopes of Sawmill Canyon and one of its major tributaries, Iron Creek. Massive Bear Mountain (10,744 feet) and pointed Iron Creek Point (10,736 feet) dominate the view as you round a spur and head generally southwest around the top of Iron Creek. From the spur, an easy 1.5 miles brings you to a four-way trail junction, which is signed and obvious. Take the trail that goes upward over the pass to the west. This is the South Fork of Big Creek Trail. Heading down is Iron Creek Trail. Continuing along toward Iron Creek Point is an extension of Snowbank Trail. The climb out of Iron Creek into the South Fork is about 400 feet. If the trail is faint due to the "trail-eating" meadows, just head for the obvious divide above you. The views here of Diamond Peak, Bell Mountain, and the other Lemhi Peaks rival any views in Idaho.

Switchback down into the South Fork of Big Creek Canyon through a mixture of ancient, fire-ravaged ghosts of whitebark pine and new growth. Iron Creek Point rises behind you, and the trail's grade decreases as you come to a place of multiple springs, the birth of the South Fork of Big Creek.

The canyon remains narrow, and you'll cross the creek perhaps ten times in small jumps as the trail descends through thick fir forest. The need to cross talus slopes occasionally slows you down. After crossing a tributary from the north, the trail remains on the right side of the stream.

A major tributary (incorrectly named the South Fork of Big Creek on older maps) flows in from the northeast about 3 miles from the trail junction back at Iron Creek.

Still the canyon remains narrow, and soon another major tributary flows in from the north. Some interesting avalanche chutes spill from the high, unnamed ridge to the south of the creek. The canyon now widens, but the trail traverses talus slides above the marshy, willow- and alder-choked flood plain.

The canyon continues to widen and narrow as you walk downstream, and the trail always stays on the north side of the creek.

About 2.25 miles past the second tributary, you reach a wide green area supported by upslope springs and kept in place by beaver dams. There are good camping sites here. The trail turns left just beyond the beaver dams at a sign that simply says TRAIL. It then fords the South Fork and climbs up around and through the buttresses above the South Fork. Then it contours midway around a steep tributary of the South Fork before reaching the trailhead 2.75 miles from the ford.

**Options:** Here is another possible loop. At the confluence of North Big Creek and the Park Fork, rather than going up the Park Fork, you can continue up the North Fork to Devils Basin and a pass at 9,850 feet into Big Eightmile Creek.

Drop down steeply to the east into the gentle uplands at the head of Big Eightmile Creek. When the grade levels out, head east-by-southeast—that is, contour around the base of Peak 10,601. Eventually turn southeast and climb over obvious Pass 9,892. Drop down toward the Lake Fork, but not into it. Instead contour northeastward to the large cirque that holds Yellow Lake.

From Yellow Lake a trail leads southwest over a pass that is 10,200 feet into the headwaters of the Park Fork. Here you can go back down the Park Fork to complete the loop, or continue over Yellow Pass and down Big Timber Creek.

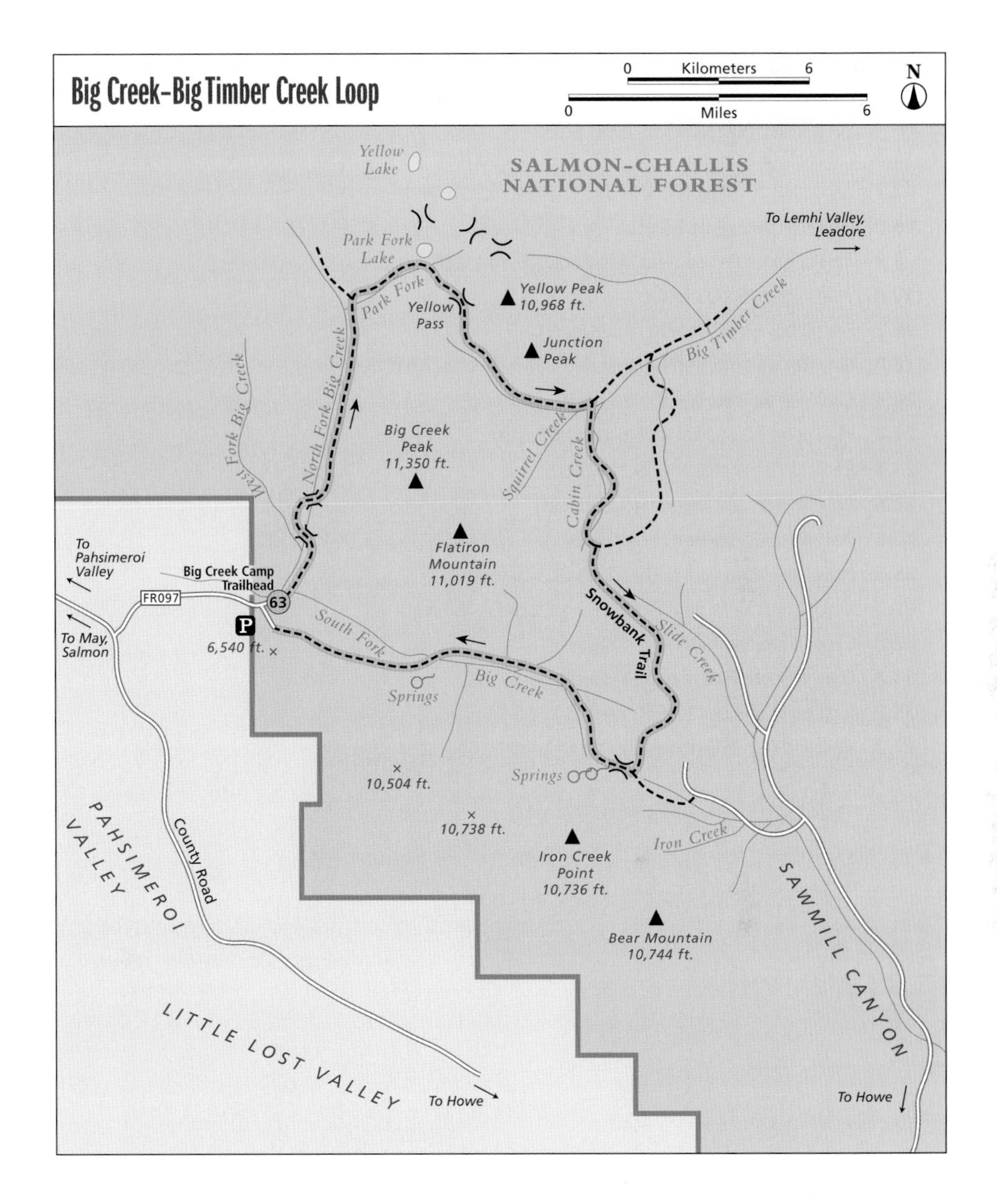


Another option is to make a side loop from Squirrel Creek to Falls Creek and back down to Big Timber Creek (or vice versa). Both the Devils Basin–Yellow Lake Loop and the Squirrel Creek–Falls Creek Loop are very scenic. The Devils Basin Loop should only be attempted after mid-July.

—Ralph Maughan

## Miles and Directions

- **0.0** Big Creek Camp Trailhead (6,590 feet)
- **1.3** First ford/bridge over North Big Creek (6,760 feet)
- **2.2** Second ford/bridge over North Big Creek (6,950 feet)
- **6.6** Park Fork ford (7,581 feet)
- **9.9** Trail junction; go south for Yellow Pass (9,144 feet)
- **10.8** Yellow Pass (9,702 feet)
- **12.2** Big Timber Creek Canyon (8,800 feet)
- **16.4** Meadow with trails up Squirrel and Cabin Creeks (7,610 feet)
- **20.5** Cabin Creek Pass (9,282 feet)
- **21.3** High point on Snowbank Trail (9,680 feet)
- **24.5** Redrock Creek crossing (8,150 feet)
- **25.5** Beneath volcanic column (8,300 feet)
- **28.0** Four-way trail junction (8,700 feet)
- **28.5** Pass into South Fork of Big Creek (9,170 feet)
- **31.7** Major tributary to South Fork of Big Creek (7,460 feet)
- **32.0** Second major tributary (7,405 feet)
- **34.3** Ford of South Fork; begin to climb (7,005 feet)
- **35.2** High point of climb (7,640 feet)
- **37.2** Trailhead 0.2 mile above Big Creek Camp (6,664 feet)

# 64 Buck and Bear Valley Lakes

There are two clusters of cirque basin lakes with excellent fishing amid the grandeur of the northern Lemhi Mountains. This beneath the pyramidal Lem Peak (10,986 feet) an area abundant with wildlife, including mountain goats.

**Start:** About 25 miles south-southeast of Salmon in the proposed Lemhi Wilderness
**Type of hike:** An overnight to several-day backpack with the opportunity to visit several different mountain lakes; out-and-back
**Distance:** 11 miles round-trip
**Approximate hiking time:** 2–5 days
**Difficulty:** Easy to moderate (due to elevation gain) to the trailed Buck and Bear Valley Lakes
**Best season:** July–late September
**Trail surface:** Normal dirt and rock
**Land status:** Salmon-Challis National Forest
**Canine compatibility:** On leash
**Fees and permits:** None
**Maps:** Hayden Creek and Lem Peak USGS quadrangles; Salmon National Forest map
**Trail contact:** Leadore Ranger District, (208) 768-2500
**Special considerations:** The road to the trailhead is easily passable by sedan; however, the condition of the last few miles, which are dirt, is worse in the early summer and after a rain.

**Finding the trailhead:** From the junction of US 93 and ID 28 in Salmon, Idaho, drive 26 miles south on ID 28. Approximately 1 mile north of the unincorporated crossroads of Lemhi, turn to the west (right) onto a paved county road leading up Hayden Creek. The road is signed, indicating the direction of Hayden Creek Road, Basin Creek, and Bear Valley Creek. If you are coming from the south, from Mud Lake, drive north on ID 28 for approximately 95 miles through Lemhi, and turn left on Hayden Creek Road, which is also signed from that direction.

After 3.5 miles on Hayden Creek Road, you reach the Basin Creek intersection, where the road turns into gravel; go left here. The road then gradually narrows, as does the canyon, and remains about 100 feet above the stream on a cut in the steep canyon sideslope. At 8 miles you enter the Salmon-Challis National Forest. Just beyond the forest boundary, you reach another fork in the road. The Hayden Creek Road (FR 008) continues to the left. To reach the trailhead, take the right fork (FR 009). A sign indicates that this is the way to Bear Valley Lake Trail. Remain on FR 009 all the way to the trailhead. It's a generally good dirt road as it climbs and winds tortuously above Bear Valley Creek, crossing several creeks. It finally ends at the well-developed trailhead just past tributary Short Creek. At 12.4 miles you reach the trailhead for pack and saddle horses, and at 13.2 miles you reach the end of the road and the trailhead for hikers. GPS: N44 47.56' / W113 46.77'
**Parking and trailhead facilities:** At the trailhead for pack animals, you'll find a latrine, potable water, and several developed campsites especially equipped for pack animals. At the hiker's trailhead there is also a latrine as well as a water pump, picnic tables, and some minimal camping. The trailhead has a register and is well marked.

## The Hike

Both the Buck and the Bear Valley Lakes nestle in the heart of the proposed Lemhi Range Wilderness. They are situated at the north end of the high Lemhi

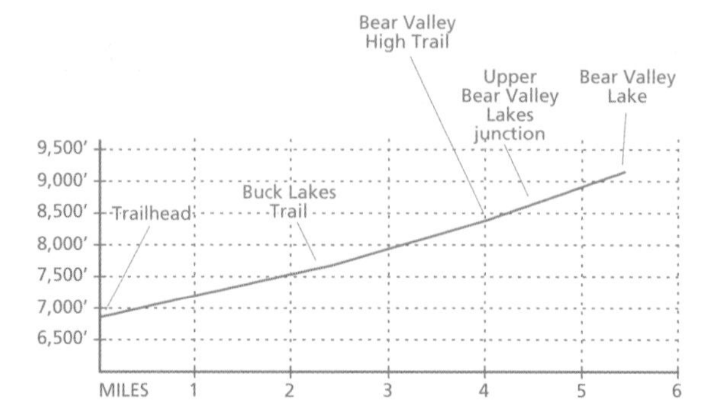


Peaks. This hike describes the trail to Bear Valley Lake, the largest of the lakes. The options describe three alternatives for different hikes along the way, including one to Buck Lakes.

Unfortunately, according to the forest service travel plan, both Buck and Bear Valley Lake Trails are still open to motor vehicles. Fortunately, during my trip to Bear Valley Lake in the autumn of 2000, the trails showed no sign of motor vehicle use.

Bear Valley Trail begins 100 yards below and east of the parking area. Here you cross over Bear Valley Creek on a good bridge and begin to hike westward up Bear Valley Canyon. The trail immediately intersects; a sign indicates BASIN CREEK TRAIL to the right and BEAR VALLEY LAKES—5.5 MILES to the left. Go left. Bear Valley Trail remains along the north side of the creek, near the canyon bottom, and is easy to follow.

The first portion is fairly level and traverses open country but soon enters forest. Here, just inside the forest, in 1989 Ralph surprised a young cougar at close range. After 2.5 miles of gradual uphill, you approach Buck Creek Canyon, visible through the forest to the left. The trail up Buck Creek is marked with a sign on a tree on the right side of the trail. This sign indicates BUCK VALLEY LAKES—2 MILES to the left and BEAR VALLEY LAKES to the right (sometimes these signs are taken down in the winter, and in early summer they might not be back up).

Bear Valley Trail continues to wind through the trees and climbs, rather steeply in places, up Bear Valley. At 4 miles from the trailhead, the trail intersects again. A sign indicates BEAR VALLEY HIGH TRAIL (Trail 178) to the right and BEAR VALLEY LAKES—1.5 MILES to the left; stay left. After another 0.5 mile you reach the signed Upper Bear Valley Lakes junction. The left fork crosses Bear Valley Creek on two consecutive bridges and continues on to Bear Valley Lake. Between this junction and Bear Valley Lake, there are two turnoffs to the left, which are less obvious and unmarked. These trails eventually merge and meet up with a jeep trail that climbs up Allison Creek on the other side of the mountain range.

Bear Valley Lake is a mile, and a 500-foot climb, past the Upper Bear Valley Lakes junction. It leads to the largest of the lakes, which occupies a large cirque at the

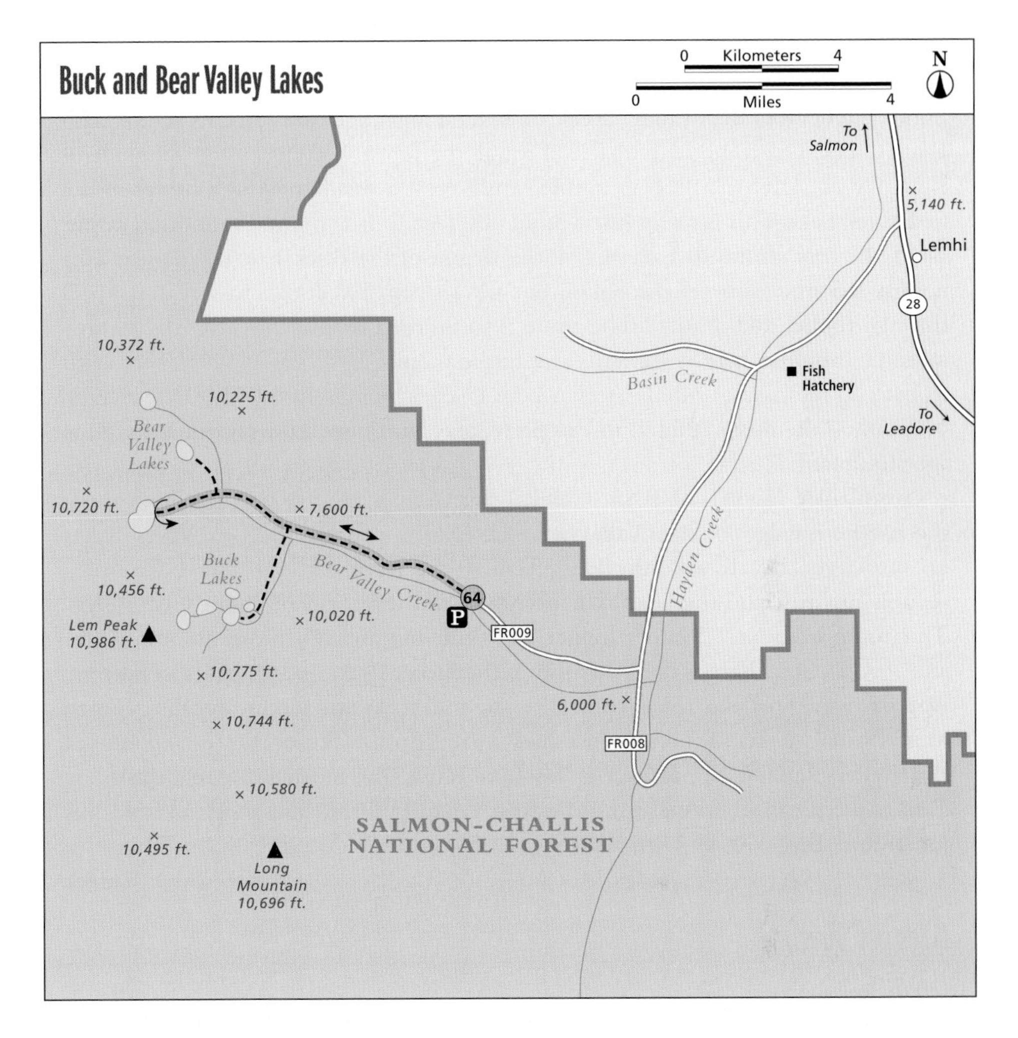


head of Bear Valley Creek, 5.5 miles from the trailhead. The cirque's western bank is splattered with alpine conifers while its other banks jut steeply toward the sky. At 9,135 feet, the translucent waters of Bear Valley Lake reflect the surrounding 600- to 900-foot-high rocky cliffs.

**Options:** Upper Bear Valley Lakes: To visit the Upper Bear Valley Lakes, take a right at the junction 4.5 miles from the trailhead. This junction is signed and points toward the Upper Bear Valley Lakes. It is approximately 1 mile, and a 400-foot climb, to the largest of the upper lakes. The highest Bear Valley Lake lies at 9,240 feet and is another mile, and a 350-foot climb, from the first of the Upper Bear Valley Lakes. There is plenty of room here and a fine view of Lem Peak.

Buck Lakes: Buck Lakes Trail (Trail 081) is not on the USGS topographic map. It leaves Bear Valley Creek Trail at 2.5 miles past the trailhead, at approximately

7,680 feet, after you have begun to climb steeply and have partially passed the mouth of Buck Creek Canyon. Take a right at the signed Buck Lake junction to immediately cross Bear Valley Creek on several logs upstream from its union with Buck Creek. The route switchbacks through the forest, keeping to the west side of Buck Creek. After a little over a mile, you'll cross a small creek, the outlet of the first Buck Lake. This is really just a pond 400 feet above you on the mountainside. Next, the trail climbs to Lake 8,474, the largest of the Buck Lakes. The next lake is only 0.5 mile above Lake 8,474, but it's a steep, 500-foot, cross-country pull through timber and deadfall. The route is to follow the inlet creek up the mountainside; camping here is limited. The highest Buck Lake sits at 9,456 feet with its back to the base of rubble-strewn Lem Peak, which is almost 11,000 feet high. Not only is the route difficult to this prize lake, but there also is just one marginal spot for a tent.

Bear Valley High Trail/Basin Creek Trail: To make a loop trip and hike along the northern ridges of Bear Valley, you can hike to or from the Bear Valley Lakes on the High Trail. To take the High Trail to the lakes, take a right at the intersection just past the trailhead that points in the direction of Basin Creek Trail. This route is about 1.5 miles longer and with significantly more elevation gain and loss. I chose not to take this route; therefore, I am unsure of its condition. Approximately halfway along this route, the trail forks and either continues north to McNutt Creek and then Basin Creek or remains on the northern ridgeline of Bear Valley; stay left at this intersection. The High Trail meets up with Bear Valley Trail at the junction 4 miles from the Bear Valley Trailhead and is signed from this junction as BEAR VALLEY HIGH TRAIL.

—Gwen Gerber

## Miles and Directions

**0.0** Trailhead (6,800 feet)

**2.5** Buck Lakes Trail junction (7,680 feet)

**4.0** Bear Valley High Trail junction (8,400 feet)

**4.5** Upper Bear Valley Lakes junction (8,650 feet)

**5.5** Bear Valley Lake (9,195 feet)

# 65 Bunting Canyon

At the south end of the Lemhis, here is rugged scenery, with a large hole in the mountain. Explore the nearby mining ruins.

**Start:** In the southern end of the Lemhi Mountains, 100 miles north of Pocatello, 60 miles northwest of Idaho Falls, and 25 miles north of Howe, as the crow flies
**Type of hike:** Day hike; out-and-back
**Distance:** 4 miles round-trip
**Approximate hiking time:** 2–3 hours
**Difficulty:** Moderate due to minor route finding
**Best season:** Late June–September
**Trail surface:** Normal dirt and rock
**Land status:** Salmon-Challis National Forest
**Canine compatibility:** Voice command
**Fees and permits:** None
**Maps:** Badger Creek and Fallert Springs USGS quadrangles; Challis National Forest travel plan map
**Trail contact:** Lost River Ranger District, (208) 588-3400
**Special considerations:** None

**Finding the trailhead:** Drive through the hamlet of Howe, and head north up the Little Lost River Valley on the main road. This is a county road that varies yearly in consistency of pavement, chuckholes, new asphalt, and gravel. At 23.5 miles north of Howe, turn right at a small gravel pit. There are two dirt roads leading from the pit. Take the one on the right. It climbs toward the Lemhi Mountains following a fence almost all the way. The road climbs at a gentle grade (but it is bumpy with numerous small rocks) for 5 miles up Badger Creek Bar (a huge alluvial fan) to the mouth of Badger Creek Canyon. You gain 1,000 feet of elevation in the 5 miles. Some old mining scars mark the mountains near the canyon's entrance. Antelope commonly patrol the area from the gravel pit all the way to the rising Lemhi Mountain slopes.

You leave BLM land at the canyon entrance and cross into the Salmon-Challis National Forest. Here you climb briefly on a poor dirt road into what appears to be a narrow, brushy canyon. The road is barely passable by sedans if driven with care. The road is deteriorating, however, and it may soon require four-wheel drive to access the informal trailhead. In just 0.5 mile the scenery changes. You arrive at a pleasant meadowy area of grass and marsh, half encircled by deciduous trees. Badger Creek runs through the meadow, in many places as a deep slot in the sod, although livestock grazing has widened it in spots. The road is easy here, but it crosses Badger Creek twice over creaky old bridges. These bridges are so decrepit that you should park at the first bridge and walk instead. GPS: N44 6.45' / W113 8.4'

**Parking and trailhead facilities:** The informal trailhead at the first bridge has room for perhaps two vehicles.

## The Hike

When you stand in the middle of the semi-arid Little Lost River Valley and look, for the first time, at the jagged, forbidding outline of thirsty, gray rock forming the Diamond Peak massif, you wouldn't expect to find a canyon glen of green softness nestled at its base. Here, however, Badger Creek and its tributary, Bunting Creek, bubble up and flow toward the valley, watering canyon bottoms of meadow, marsh, cottonwood, water birch, and quaking aspen. These riparian zones contrast with the mountain slopes of rock filigreed with grass, sage, mountain mahogany, and a few fir.

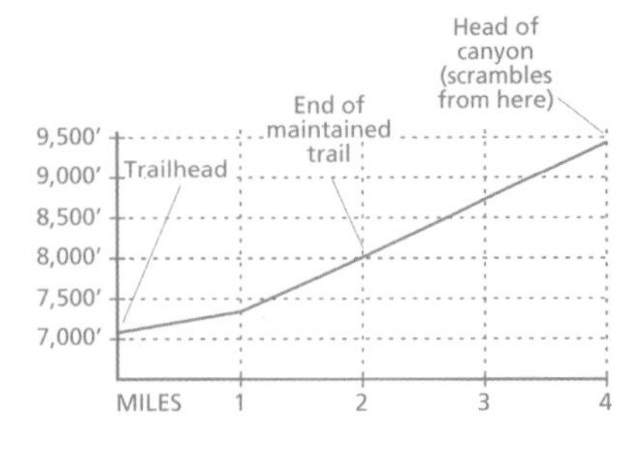


From the old bridge, follow the decaying road on foot. It gets use by dirt bikes and ATVs, but full-size vehicles can't use it. Full-size vehicles were once able to drive about a mile farther, up into Bunting Canyon. This lower section along the old road is very pretty from mid-June to July, with mountain iris in bloom in the meadow along Badger Creek and the new leaves of the quaking aspen bright yellow-green.

Ahead of you lie the forks of the canyon—exactly 1.7 miles from the boundary of the Challis National Forest. To your right is Bunting Canyon, your destination. On the left, a mucky ATV track goes toward an old mining camp. That track soon disappears, but you will find a trail leading to a number of badly deteriorating, bramble-filled log cabins. Badger Creek rises as a large spring just beyond the cabins. Above the spring Badger Creek Canyon widens, and after a walk of about a mile on a good trail, you can gain a view of 12,197-foot Diamond Peak—the third highest summit in Idaho. The walk is dry and not very interesting except for the view of Diamond Peak.

Bunting Canyon, the right fork, has a dying dirt road (and one collapsed bridge) for another 0.5 mile. Just south of the road, clearly visible, are a couple of lovely spring-fed ponds. After the 0.5 mile the road switchbacks up the mountainside. It is impassable to vehicles and leads to some old mining scrapes. Pass this road by, and soon the trail comes to Bunting Creek, which you can probably hop across, and the trail immediately becomes much more intimate. In fact, it isn't marked on the topographic map, although evidence of long-ago horse logging tells us it is at least seventy-five years old.

The path, which gets no motor vehicle use, winds its way through a forest of babbling brook and tall Douglas fir, hemmed in by dark, rugged cliffs of dolomite (calcium magnesium carbonate), a close relative of limestone. You hop across the creek two more times.

Although the trail is somewhat faint, the hike is not strenuous. First-timers are likely to think they are walking up a box canyon because, dead ahead, a continuous ridge of convoluted rock rises very steeply for 3,000 feet to an altitude of over 11,000 feet. It is not a box canyon, however. The canyon turns southward at a right angle when you get to the very base of this ridge. From time to time, you glimpse a huge hole in the side of the ridge ahead. Apparently, this 75-foot-high, 100-foot-deep cavern was formed when a slab of the limestone mountain broke away. The scramble up to it is not easy.

You will probably lose the trail at the canyon bend, near the spring-fed source of Bunting Creek. There is no reliable water beyond this point. There are a few spots to pitch a tent on the right (west) side of the creek just past the canyon bend.

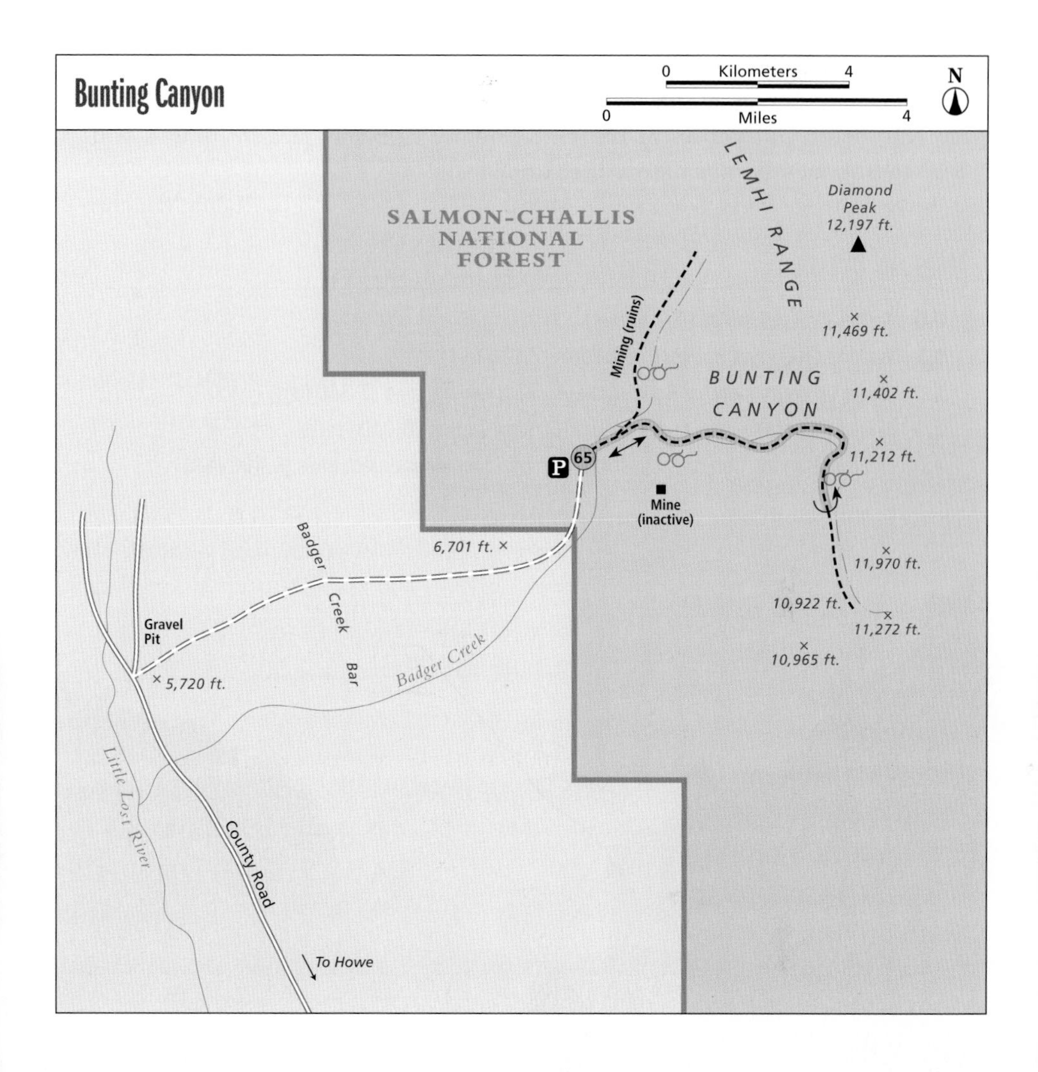


The intermittent and faint trail does continue past the bend. It is located on the right side of the canyon. Here, you walk through open fir and whitebark pine forest to the head of the canyon. Although you climb 1,400 feet in 2 miles before the going becomes really steep, I have never considered this a difficult cross-country hike. Perhaps the sight of the rugged, twisted ridge on the left (east) is so astonishing all the way to the top of Bunting that you forget you are breathing hard. At the head of the canyon, rugged mountains also rise on the canyon's right side, topping out at just over 11,000 feet, but they are not as impressive as the big wall to the east, which has a number of unnamed peaks rising well over 11,500 feet.

There are bull trout in both Bunting and Badger Creeks. These fish are on the threatened species list and must not be caught and killed. After June, the presence of cattle in the lower (roaded) portion of Badger Creek can reduce your pleasure. They mostly use the parcel of private land between the first bridge and the forks. You will not find them very far upcanyon.

This hike is just perfect in late June. Another especially pleasant time is mid-September, when the aspen leaves have turned gold.

—Ralph Maughan

## Miles and Directions

- **0.0** Trailhead at old bridge (7,000 feet)
- **0.5** Bunting Creek and Badger Creek Forks (7,120 feet)
- **1.0** Route up south slope of Bunting Creek to old mining ruins (7,340 feet)
- **2.0** End of trail at the right-angle bend of Bunting Canyon (8,040 feet)
- **4.0** Head of Bunting Canyon, accessible by cross-country and faint trails (9,400 feet)

*Springtime view up Bunting Canyon and southern Lemhis.* PHOTO BY JOSH KEELEY

# 66 Middle Canyon

Come and play among amazing rock formations, cliffs, and unusual vegetation in a very narrow canyon.

**Start:** 5 miles northeast of Howe
**Type of hike:** Day hike; out-and-back
**Distance:** Variable; the maximum is 4 miles out-and-back
**Approximate hiking time:** 3 hours
**Difficulty:** Moderately easy
**Best season:** May–June
**Trail surface:** Normal dirt and rock
**Land status:** Salmon-Challis National Forest
**Canine compatibility:** On leash
**Fees and permits:** None
**Maps:** Tyler Peak USGS quadrangle
**Trail contact:** Lost River Ranger District (208) 588-3400
**Special considerations:** No water. Rattlesnakes. Wood ticks abundant from March to late June.

**Finding the trailhead:** From the hamlet of Howe, drive east on ID 22-33 for 2.5 miles and turn left (north) onto paved CR 1300 West. Take this road through agricultural fields due north for 3 miles to the intersection with CR 3800 North. Continue on 1300 West, which now becomes a gravel road. From here it's 1.1 miles to 3900 North, where you must turn left. Go left for about 100 yards and turn right at the first road junction, which is a primitive road over a canal. Now you are on public (BLM) land, and the ag fields are to your south across the canal. The primitive road follows the canal west for 1.5 miles. Here, turn right onto a primitive road that heads up toward the big mountain (Saddle Mountain, the first of the Lemhi Range).

The road is primitive, but a sedan can follow it up the big alluvial fan (Saddle Mountain Bar) toward some very rugged-looking canyons. There is enough natural gravel base that this road can be driven in rain and even in a couple inches of snow. I have driven up here and hiked in a dry December.

Enter the mouth of Middle Canyon and marvel at the incredible rock formations. The track continues for a mile up the canyon, getting rougher until it ends at the base of a steep slope in the canyon. GPS: N43 53.45' / W112 57.44'

**Parking and trailhead facilities:** The undeveloped trailhead has room for about three vehicles, but you may want to park near the mouth of the canyon and walk the primitive road so you can gawk and marvel at the rock formations—hollowed-out rocks, natural arches, limestone that looks like melted wax running down cliff sides. Bright lichens adorn the rocks everywhere.

## The Hike

From the trailhead, a trail (not on the topographic quadrangle) goes up the steep hillside, contouring through brush and rocks and climbing 200 feet. Suddenly the trail and the canyon flatten out and you are in a flat-bottomed, waterless canyon that is very narrow and deep. The sun shines in the canyon

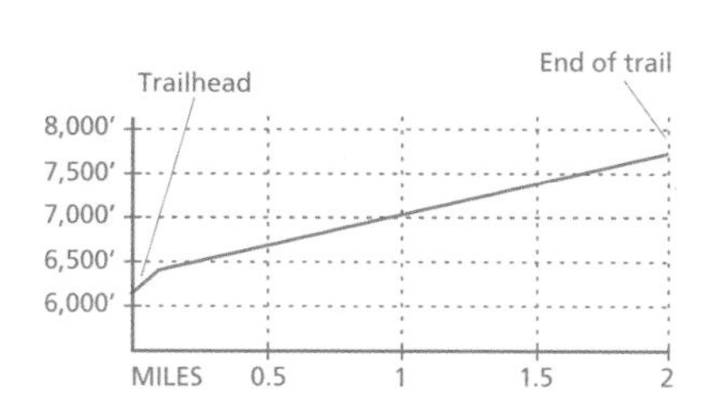

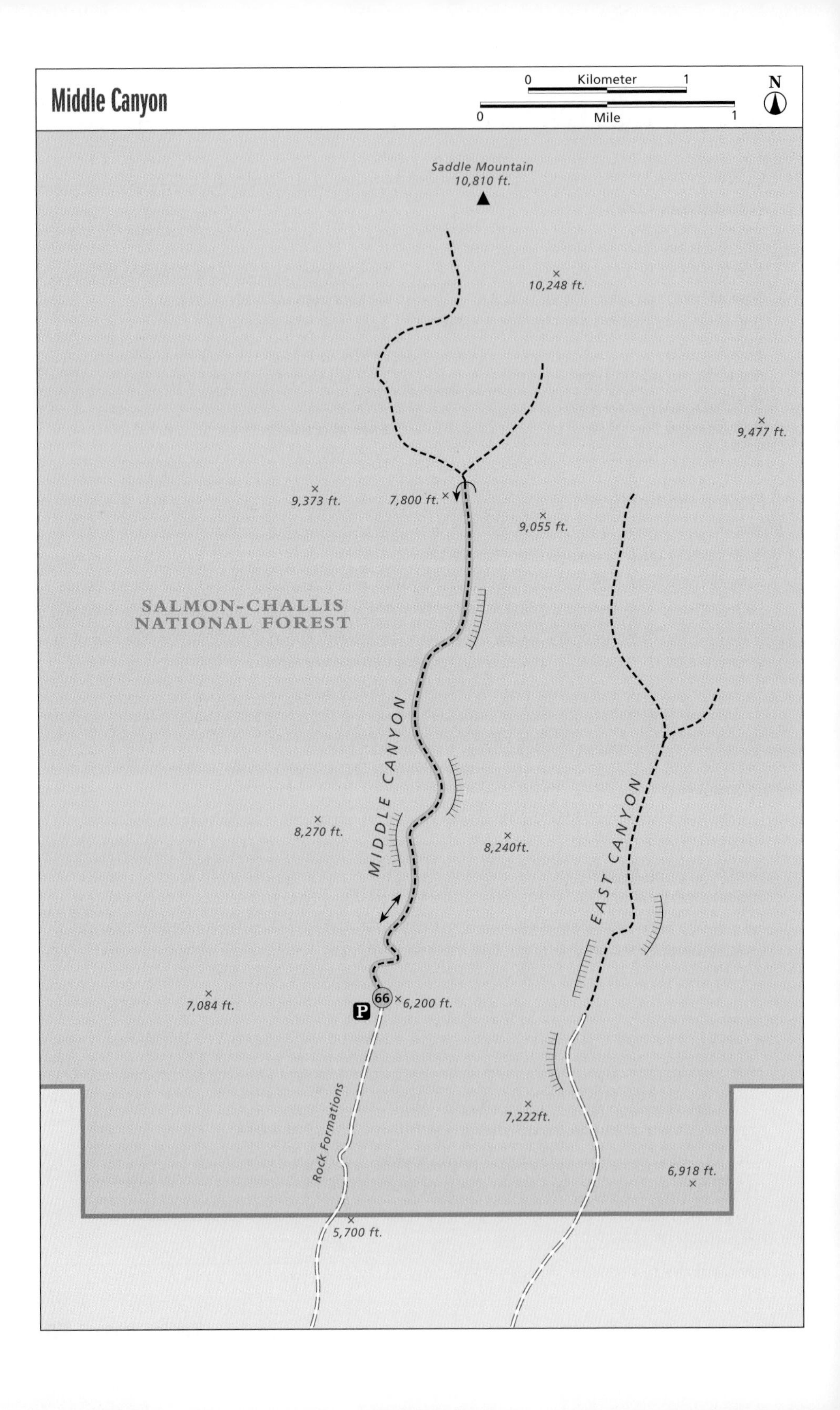
Middle Canyon
0 Kilometer 1
0 Mile 1
N
Saddle Mountain
10,810 ft.
10,248 ft.
9,477 ft.
9,373 ft.
7,800 ft.
9,055 ft.
SALMON-CHALLIS
NATIONAL FOREST
MIDDLE CANYON
EAST CANYON
8,270 ft.
8,240ft.
7,084 ft.
66
6,200 ft.
P
Rock Formations
7,222ft.
6,918 ft.
5,700 ft.

for an average of perhaps one or two hours a day in the summer and hardly at all in the winter, although a few of the south-facing slopes get a lot more. The result is a place with strong vegetation variations within the space of a few feet depending on how much the sun shines. The elevation and location would make this site very hot in full summer sun, but the narrow canyon has nooks and crannies where the sun rarely shines.

You will find sagebrush and mountain mahogany on a dry and hot slope, and 30 feet away under an overhanging cliff, you'll see ferns and moss.

At the top of the steep initial climb, or just a bit before the top, if you look carefully you will see a huge crack to your right. If you enter it—be very careful—it is similar to some of the narrowest slot canyons in southern Utah, but it is limestone and not sandstone.

The trail continues up the canyon for close to 2 miles. In some places the canyon has large old-growth Douglas fir, and in others just brush. Near the end of the trail, you reach the remains of an ancient sawmill. Beyond the mill, the canyon opens up and becomes very rocky; you are on your way to a difficult scramble up the face of Saddle Mountain, which I did one October. The sharp limestone pitted my hands and I ran out of water, but I made it to one of the summits of this tall, double-summit mountain. I was in a dense cloud and could see nothing.

June is probably the nicest month for this hike. The landscape is green and not too hot or too cold. Nevertheless, it is reasonable to consider mid-April though mid-November as the season. I hiked up nearby East Canyon once on New Year's Day in an inch of snow.

**Options:** East Canyon, which is just a mile to the east, is a very similar narrow and rugged canyon. It is not included in this guide because a primitive road goes through most of the really interesting formations.

You can walk along the base of Saddle Mountain from near the mouth of Middle Canyon and hike to East Canyon quite easily. It is cross-county, but you are in the open. Sight alone leads you the correct way. In early June, this gentle foothill area is ablaze with flowers and green bunchgrass. There are a few seeps that provoke dramatic vegetation growth for a month or so.

You can expect to see many antelope on Saddle Mountain Bar and perhaps deer and elk in April. Cougars are common. It is perfect cougar country, but they are rarely seen. Don't worry, they are nearby.

—Ralph Maughan

## Miles and Directions

**0.0** Trailhead (6,200 feet)

**0.3** Top of steep hill (6,400 feet)

**2.0** End of trail (7,800 feet)

# 67 Mill Creek Lake

This scenic lake looks as though it's alpine but opens early in the season.

**Start:** 90 miles northwest of Idaho Falls in the Lemhi Mountains
**Type of hike:** Day hike, overnight, or longer for those who want to explore the Lemhi crest area; out-and-back
**Distance:** 10.5 miles round-trip
**Approximate hiking time:** 4 hours
**Difficulty:** Moderate to the lake; moderately strenuous to Firebox Meadows due to a trail that is faint in some crucial places
**Best season:** July–August
**Trail surface:** Normal dirt and rock
**Land status:** Salmon-Challis National Forest
**Canine compatibility:** On leash
**Fees and permits:** None
**Maps:** Gilmore and Big Windy Peak USGS quadrangles; Middle Fork, Challis, and Lost River Ranger Districts–Challis National Forest map
**Trail contact:** Lost River Ranger District, (208) 588-3400

**Finding the trailhead:** Leaving the hamlet of Howe on the county road, drive north in the Little Lost River Valley for 36 miles. At 36 miles, a generally well-signed and well-maintained gravel road exits to the right (east) for Sawmill Canyon. Follow this road across Mud Flats, and 7 miles from the intersection you will cross Sawmill Creek. Now you drive up into Sawmill Canyon, a large, southward-draining stream valley. After a mile, you enter the Salmon-Challis National Forest. Continue about 3 more miles on the gravel road (which can be very washboarded) to the bridge over Mill Creek. A hundred yards past the bridge, turn right (east) on the dirt road at a meadow that blazes with larkspur and wyethia in June. Go 1.2 miles to the end of the road. GPS: N44 22.07' / W113 21.73'
**Parking and trailhead facilities:** The trailhead has a few picnic tables, with three or four places to camp under a forest canopy. They are right by Mill Creek, the only source of water. There are also several undeveloped campsites downstream but nearby. Unfortunately, in recent years large recreational vehicles have taken to using the shaded trailhead as a camping spot, and hikers find it monopolized by campers who are not interested in using the trail. The forest service plans to eliminate this problem by moving the trailhead downstream.

## The Hike

When winter's ice still grips most high mountain lakes, Mill Creek Lake, in the rugged Lemhi Mountains, is usually suitable for a hike and overnight camping.

Dammed by a landslide, the lake lies in a short, rocky canyon. The rocks and cliffs enclosing the lake may cause you to think the surroundings are more alpine than they really are.

A faint trail above the lake leads to Firebox Meadows and Firebox Summit. This beautiful meadow and forest country, which is important elk range, contrasts sharply with the rocky lake environs below.

You can usually reach the lake by mid-June, although July and August are the best months to visit.

You will easily find the trail. It is obvious, marked with a sign that reads CLOSED TO MOTOR VEHICLES. Set out into the forest for the peaceful, 2.3-mile, 1,200-foot climb to the lake. At first you'll walk easily through a gentle, open forest. There are some small meadows and some large, often leaning, old-growth Douglas fir and an unnamed rivulet of Mill Creek, which you soon cross. Then, after 0.5 mile, you cross Mill Creek on a good bridge.

Across the bridge, the forest becomes denser. The trees have smaller trunks, and the forest floor is rocky with little vegetation. The trail begins to climb a bit, and soon you are in a small canyon. The grade increases, and the trail now keeps about 50 to 75 feet above rushing Mill Creek. After about 0.75 mile, you come to the base of a big rockslide that has filled the canyon. The trees thin out as the trail switchbacks up the slide. Below, Mill Creek pours as a full-blown stream out of the slide's base. The hard rock of the rockslide is quartzite, part of the Kinnikinnick Formation.

A few big, old Douglas fir have struggled to make a living out of the harsh conditions of the slide. These trees are hundreds of years old. Their ancient branches frame the view down the canyon of the Lemhi foothills and, farther to the west, Idaho's highest mountains, the Lost Rivers.

When the switchbacks of this well-maintained trail end, there's a brief reprieve through a level section. Here, in early summer, you pass a small lower lake (not on the map) and a very pretty, small meadow stream that meanders over the top of the slide to feed the lake. These waters are the children of spring and disappear as the season progresses. From this spot, there is one more steep pitch to the lake.

Mill Creek Lake's water level varies. Naturally, it is highest after a winter of heavy snow. The lake supports a good population of fat cutthroat trout. I've been most successful with wet flies and streamers.

You'll find campsites at both ends of the lake, but the north and south sides of the lake are too steep to camp on. Much of the time you'll find a spring flowing just below a rockslide that rests above the lake's east side. The trail around the lake goes around its east (right) side. Although one hiking guide says there is a trail around both sides of the lake, the left side is far too steep for a trail.

To find the trail around the lake, from the lakeside you must climb 30 feet backward on the trail. A marker points to the trail's continuation. It follows the crest of the rockslide and then a cutbank above the lake and into the steeply sloped forest, gradually descending to near the inlet of the lake.

If you wish to hike beyond the lake, a trail climbs at a gradual rate up Mill Creek Canyon through a dense, rocky, and uninteresting forest. The trail remains on the right side of Mill Creek. After 0.5 mile you come to a meadow with springs. Here the canyon bends around to the north.

At the meadow, the trail's tread immediately fades, as is so often the case in such country, but it goes just inside the trees on the right side of the meadow. There are large, but old, blazes on the trees marking the route. The tread does reappear in places, and logs have been sawed. These together help you keep on the trail.

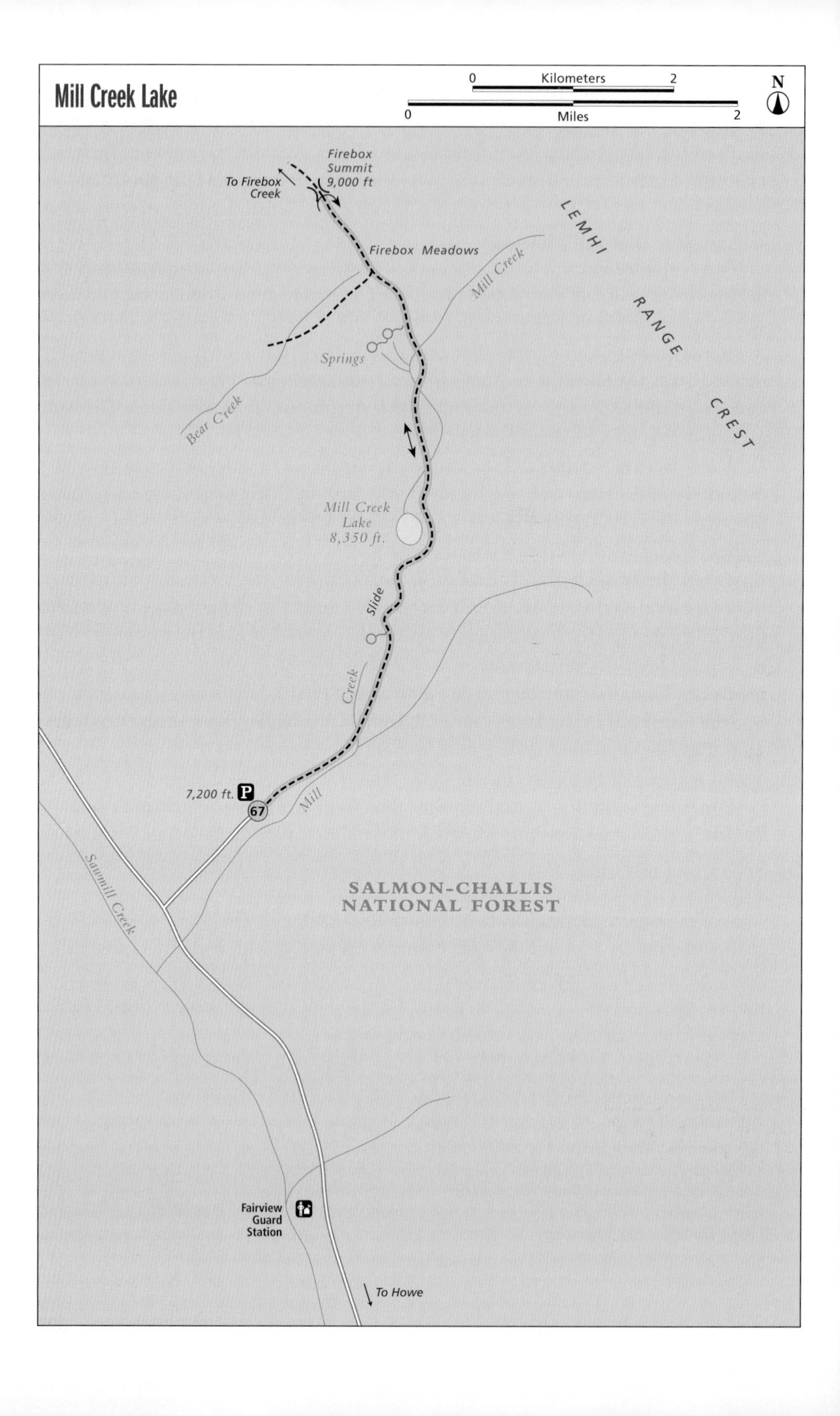

Mill Creek Lake
0
Kilometers
2
0
Miles
2
N
Firebox
Summit
9,000 ft
To Firebox
Creek
LEMHI
RANGE
CREST
Firebox Meadows
Mill Creek
Springs
Bear Creek
Mill Creek
Lake
8,350 ft.
Slide
Creek
7,200 ft.
67
Mill
Sawmill Creek
SALMON-CHALLIS
NATIONAL FOREST
Fairview
Guard
Station
To Howe

At the top of the meadow, it is important that you find the trail if you wish to continue to Firebox Summit at 9,000 feet. Make certain you find the leftmost channel of Mill Creek at the top of the meadow. The trail crosses this channel and heads leftward up into the timber. The tread is obvious once you're in the timber.

From here the trail is easy to follow all the way to pleasant Firebox Meadows. This is a fairly large meadow. It is important for your return trip to note that the meadow drains into Bear Creek, not Mill Creek. You pass over an almost imperceptible divide just before reaching the lower end of Firebox Meadows. Fortunately, at the divide there is a signed trail leading to the left (west). This is Bear Creek Trail, which is on the old 15-minute USGS quadrangle but not the new 7.5-minute Gilmore quad.

The trail keeps just to the right of the meadow and finally passes into a few trees and crosses unheralded Firebox Summit, where a faint trail descends through dry forest into Firebox Creek.

If you walk out onto the meadow, you get a fine view of the Lemhi Crest.

The meadow is surrounded by lodgepole pine, subalpine fir, Engelmann spruce, and whitebark pine. Elk are abundant until the cattle arrive.

When you head back, be very sure you find the trail. Don't just walk down the middle of Firebox Meadows, because you are very likely to reach Bear Creek Trail rather than Mill Creek Trail and find yourself quite a way down Bear Creek before you realize your error.

**Options:** You can follow the trail down Firebox Creek. I did not check its condition, nor the condition of the Bear Creek Trail, which may have been rehabilitated after 30 years of neglect.

—Ralph Maughan

## Miles and Directions

**0.0** Trailhead (7,240 feet)

**2.3** Mill Creek Lake (8,330 feet)

**5.2** Firebox Summit (9,018 feet)

# 68 Nez Perce Lake

Nez Perce Lake is noted for its solitude and the chance to catch Arctic grayling, a rare species in the Rocky Mountains.

**Start:** 7 linear miles southeast of Leadore, beneath 10,465-foot Sheephorn Peak
**Type of hike:** A relatively short, but steep, trail that is ideal for an out-and-back, day or overnight trip
**Distance:** Just under 6 miles round-trip from Nez Perce Spring to Nez Perce Lake
**Approximate hiking time:** 3 hours
**Difficulty:** Moderate day hike with a steep climb
**Best season:** July–late September
**Trail surface:** Normal dirt and rock
**Land status:** Salmon-Challis National Forest
**Canine compatibility:** On leash
**Fees and permits:** None
**Maps:** Purcell Spring and Sheephorn Peak USGS quadrangles
**Trail contact:** Leadore Ranger District, (208) 768-2500
**Special considerations:** Although the road to the trailhead, when dry, is passable with a passenger car, four-wheel drive is recommended.

**Finding the trailhead:** Drive southward on ID 28 from Leadore. After about 6 miles, turn west (right) onto a well-maintained gravel road. The road is marked with a BLM sign indicating the route to Timber Creek and Cold Springs.

Coming north from the town of Mud Lake, take ID 28 for about 69 miles to the gravel road, which is also signed from this direction.

The gravel road crosses Texas Creek (the headwaters of the Lemhi River) and forks at approximately 1 mile. At this intersection, stay left; a sign indicates you are heading in the direction of Cold Springs. At approximately 3.8 miles, the road intersects again just before arriving at a ranch at the base of a butte. Turn right here. This road, in poorer condition, climbs a short distance through a gap between the edge of the mountain range and the small butte. Just short of 5 miles, you pass Purcell Spring on the right. The road soon turns into dirt and its condition deteriorates, especially if it is wet. At approximately 6.2 miles, you reach another intersection; bear right. This fork will soon take you to a gate that leads you into the Salmon National Forest. At approximately 7.5 miles, as you enter a conifer forest, you reach Nez Perce Spring, which may be dry in late summer. The spring, just to the right of the road, bubbles out of the earth here and travels to meet a tributary of Nez Perce Creek. GPS: N44 31.35' / W113 20.99'

**Parking and trailhead facilities:** Informal, unmarked trailhead. It is recommended that you park your vehicle along the road before you enter the forest, because the road becomes exponentially worse. At Nez Perce Spring, a four-wheel-drive road continues through the trees for another 0.5 mile but is very rough.

## The Hike

Seldom-visited Nez Perce Lake is reached by a short hiking trail that is closed to trail machines. The trail is steep but not difficult to follow. It is 2.8 miles, and a climb of about 1,700 feet, to the lake. The hike starts past Nez Perce Spring and is a

*Nez Perce Lake.* Photo by Luke Kratz

four-wheel-drive road for the first 0.5 mile. As the road nears its end, a sign nailed to a tree on the left side of the road indicates the direction of Nez Perce Trail and Nez Perce Lake—2.2 miles ahead. Just past this sign, the four-by-four road ends, and a sign indicates that the area beyond is closed to motor vehicles.

The trail immediately climbs up a steep embankment. An alternative route leaves the trail to the right and switches back to join up with the main trail. Within the first 0.5 mile, you cross a small tributary of Nez Perce Creek (which may be dry in late summer) and switchback to climb a ridge between two tributaries to Nez Perce Creek. Thankfully, 1.2 miles after leaving the road, the trail levels out and actually drops about 100 feet. The remaining mile to the lake is not as steep, and it travels between a high ridge to the south and a major tributary to Nez Perce Creek to the north. You cross this tributary at 0.25 mile from the lake. It has reliable water all year, although the creek in some places runs beneath the sedimentary rocks.

Nez Perce Lake occupies a small cirque basin of Sheephorn Peak (10,465 feet). It is fed by several springs and contains water year-round. Its water level declines slowly over the summer, exposing its rocky banks. There are no fire rings at the lake; please keep it that way and use your stove. Deer and elk are frequently seen in the area, and, if you are fortunate, a mountain goat may be spotted on the flank of Sheephorn Peak. As I was having lunch and relaxing on a warm rock, a billy and a nanny sauntered along the shoreline on the opposite bank.

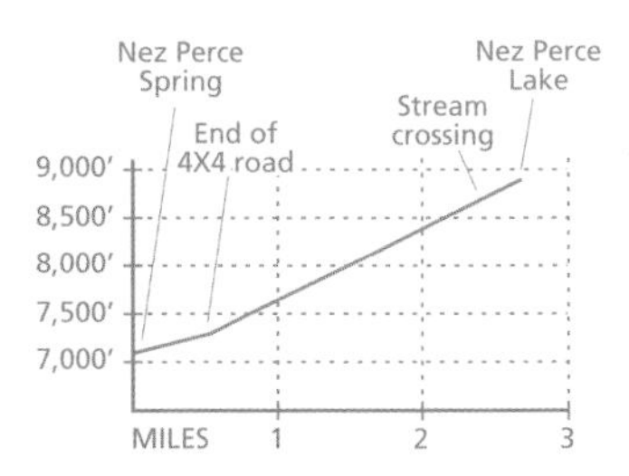

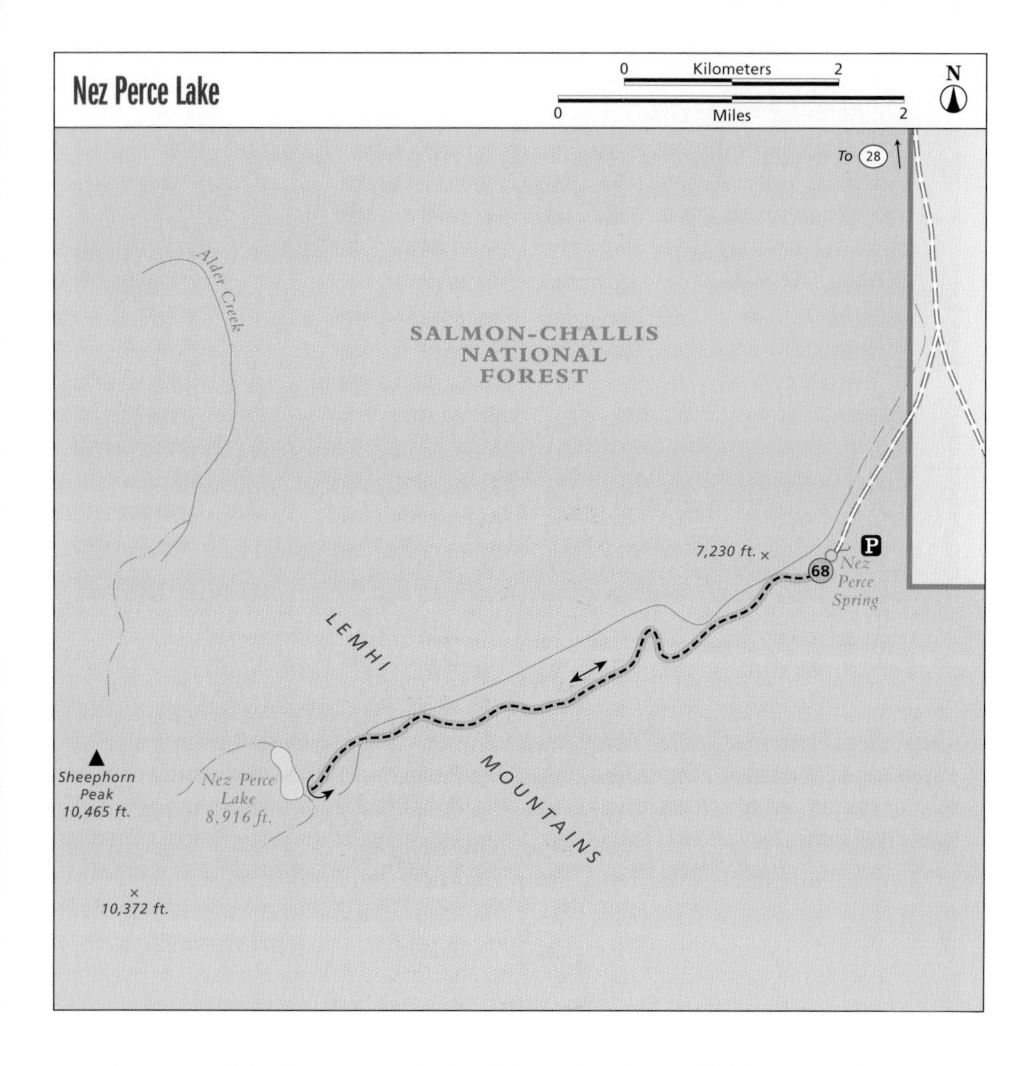


Nez Perce Lake has been stocked with Arctic grayling, which have been known to grow quite large. It is also filled with freshwater shrimp, which are good for growing fat fish but make hooking a grayling more difficult. Trout in this small lake sometimes are winter-killed.

Nez Perce Trail is a good choice if you are looking to stay away from the crowds and enjoy a lake that graciously rewards you with its charm after a steep journey.

—Gwen Gerber

## Miles and Directions

**0.0** Nez Perce Spring (7,120 feet)

**0.5** End of four-wheel-drive road (7,350 feet)

**2.5** Stream crossing (8,600 feet)

**2.8** Nez Perce Lake (8,840 feet)

# 69 Rocky Canyon

Meadowed canyons and interesting cliffs are surrounded by very high semi-arid mountains on this hike into wild Lemhi country.

**Start:** 75 miles northwest of Idaho Falls in the southern Lemhi Range
**Type of hike:** Day hike or overnight; out-and-back. Base camp for further explorations.
**Distance:** 9.6 miles round-trip to the forks of Rocky Canyon
**Approximate hiking time:** 6 hours to 2–3 days
**Difficulty:** Moderate
**Best season:** Late June–mid-July. Cattle are grazed in the big meadow from mid-July–mid-August
**Trail surface:** Normal dirt and rock
**Land status:** Caribou-Targhee National Forest
**Canine compatibility:** On leash
**Fees and permits:** None
**Maps:** Diamond Peak and Nicholia USGS quadrangles; Dubois and Island Park Ranger Districts–Targhee National Forest map
**Trail contact:** Dubois Ranger District, (208) 374-5422
**Special considerations:** Cows come to Rocky Canyon in mid-July, and flowing water becomes unreliable about the same time.

**Finding the trailhead:** From Idaho Falls, drive across the desert on ID 28 through the town of Mud Lake and turn right (still on ID 28) at the highway junction just west of town. From here, drive up into the Birch Creek Valley between the Lemhi Mountains on the left and the Beaverheads on the right. At just over 7 miles north of the unincorporated gas-café spot named Lone Pine, turn left off the highway onto an unimproved road. This road, with a bed of large natural gravel, climbs a hill and leads to a microwave station in 2 miles. Just before the microwave, a road cuts to the right and goes around the station. Take the road to the right for 1.5 miles. Here, there is a fork and probably a sign indicating Rocky Canyon to the left and Meadow Canyon to the right. Take the left. The Rocky Canyon road quickly peters out at a steep hill. Park here. GPS: N44 15.35' / W113 04.47'
**Parking and trailhead facilities:** The informal, undeveloped trailhead sits directly on the rim of the lower part of Rocky Canyon and has ample room for vehicles. The view from the trailhead is beautiful in all directions.

## The Hike

This hike is usually fairly easy, yet it brings you into very spectacular mountain scenery. The only drawbacks are the presence of too many cows in midsummer and increasing damage to the meadows by dirt bikes and ATVs. The best time for this hike is the two-week period from late June to mid-July. Later, you must carry all of your water. The canyon is not closed by snow most years until late October. It may be accessible as early as June 5 or 10.

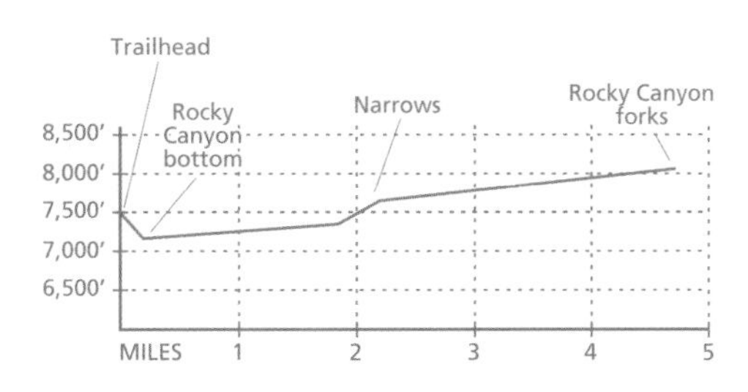

*Rocky Canyon.* Photo by Luke Kratz

The high desert (7,000 to 7,500 feet) around the canyon rim is especially beautiful in the early summer, when wildflowers are abundant and the grass is green. Many large peaks are also visible in the Lemhi Range and as you look to the east across Birch Creek Valley to the high cluster of peaks in the Beaverhead Mountains known as the Italian Peaks (see Hike 75, Webber Creek). The mountain with radiating spurs in the Beaverheads to your northeast is Eighteenmile Peak, the highest mountain on the Idaho-Montana border.

Climb over the hill, and follow a steep trail to the left down into the shallow lower portion of Rocky Canyon. Small cliffs with brilliant lichen-splotched rock line the upper edges of the canyon. The trail leads to a fenced spring. The topographic map shows a jeep trail here, but it is really just a foot trail. Upcanyon from the spring, the trail follows what is usually a brook in June but is dry by midsummer. In heavy snow years, the water can fill the canyon from side to side, making for a difficult hike. In other years, the tiny stream can be almost dry in June. In any case, in early summer this section is quite meadowy, with small, interesting cliffs on the canyon's sides. The scene upcanyon gradually becomes dominated by Peak 10,759.

The path up the canyon is very pleasant until not quite 2 miles, when you reach a gully where ATVs illegally come down from the right. From here on, the trail is wider. The trail next goes through a steep and rocky constriction. This guards the way to the big meadows above, but it doesn't quite guard enough to stop the ATVs. The canyon opens up as you walk into the big meadow. Large mountains stand on all sides. There are usually a spring and a small stream here until mid- to late July. The meadow makes a good base camp for further explorations.

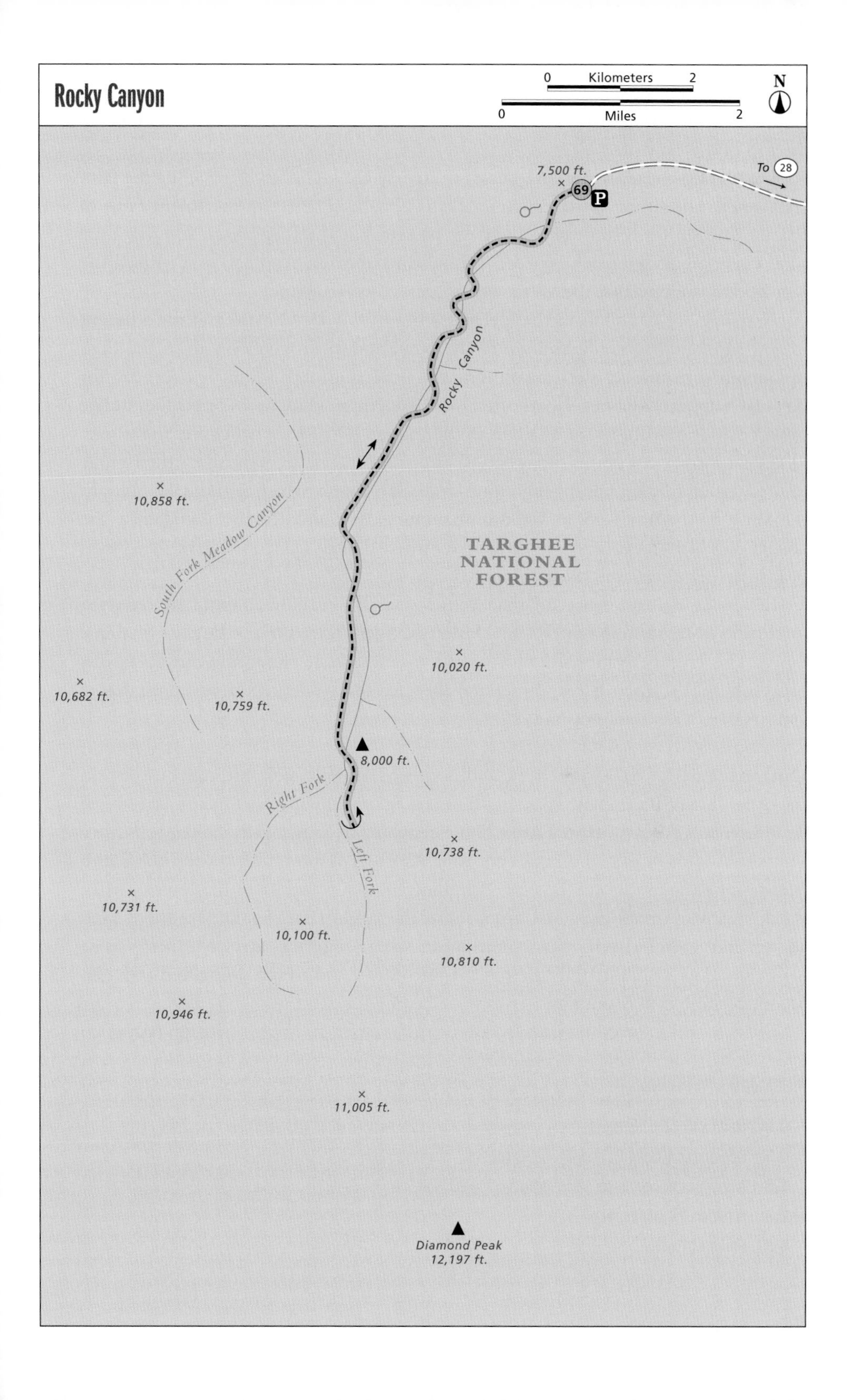
Rocky Canyon
0 Kilometers 2
0 Miles 2
N
7,500 ft.
69
P
To 28
Rocky Canyon
10,858 ft.
South Fork Meadow Canyon
TARGHEE NATIONAL FOREST
10,020 ft.
10,682 ft.
10,759 ft.
8,000 ft.
Right Fork
Left Fork
10,738 ft.
10,731 ft.
10,100 ft.
10,810 ft.
10,946 ft.
11,005 ft.
Diamond Peak
12,197 ft.

The view upcanyon is dominated by Peak 11,005, which some might wrongly conclude is Diamond Peak. But Diamond Peak is visible only briefly at the forks at the top of the canyon.

Once at the meadow, the hike becomes an easy cross-country stroll along the faint ATV track. The route to the canyon forks is obvious. A hike up the Right Fork of Rocky Canyon leads to a very scenic elk pasture, but the year I tried it, a late-June snowstorm precluded reaching a second meadow above it. Another year, I hiked the Left Fork but found that the views were obscured by conifers.

Antelope are common in the lower reaches of Rocky Canyon and the adjacent Lemhi Mountain foothills. You are likely to see mountain goats on all of the high mountains surrounding the canyon. For the novice, a careful look is necessary for what later appears obvious. Goats often look like dingy white rocks or patches of late snow. I saw about fifteen on one trip to the canyon. On a later helicopter flight over Diamond Peak, I saw about fifty goats. Bighorn sheep also are expanding their range in the area after being transplanted into Uncle Ike Creek, which is about 12 miles to the south on the other side of the mountain range. Elk and deer are abundant, as are cougar and black bear. Every time I have visited Rocky Canyon, I have seen black bear sign—diggings, scat, tracks. Hang your food.

Increasing damage from off-road vehicles in the meadows should be reported (preferably with photographs) to the Dubois Ranger District of the Targhee National Forest. The Targhee National Forest was supposed to have closed the canyon to dirt bikes and ATVs when it recommended the area for wilderness designation, but it appears they have done nothing.

**Options:** Parts of Meadow Creek and South Meadow Creek, the canyons just on the other side of prominent Peak 10,759 on Rocky Canyon's north flank, have been designated a Research Natural Area. These canyons are ecologically similar to Rocky Canyon. You may camp and hike here, too, but water is more difficult to find. South Meadow Creek can be reached by scrambling up a low saddle in the lower part of Rocky Canyon or a higher pass from out of the Right Fork. South Meadow Creek has a trail its entire length, with a meadow and some rugged scenery. Meadow Creek is not meadowy. A short trail there leads into rocky and rough going, but provides access to climb Bell Mountain.

—Ralph Maughan

## Miles and Directions

**0.0** Trailhead (7,528 feet)

**0.3** Bottom of Rocky Canyon (7,230 feet)

**1.8** ATV trail descends to canyon floor (7,428 feet)

**2.3** Narrows (7,600 feet)

**4.8** Forks of Rocky

# 70 South Creek

A fairly easy, early-season hike heads up an ungrazed canyon in the southernmost part of the rugged Lemhi Mountains.

**Start:** 55 miles northwest of Idaho Falls
**Type of hike:** Day hike or overnight; out-and-back, although a partially cross-country loop is possible
**Distance:** 7.2 miles round-trip
**Approximate hiking time:** 3–4 hours for a day hike
**Difficulty:** Moderately easy to the sod-roofed cabin, then moderate due to a faint trail
**Best season:** June–July
**Trail surface:** Normal dirt and rock
**Land status:** Salmon-Challis National Forest
**Canine compatibility:** Voice command
**Fees and permits:** None
**Maps:** Howe NE and Tyler Peak USGS quadrangles; Lost River Ranger District–Challis National Forest map
**Trail contact:** Lost River Ranger District, (208) 588-3400

**Finding the trailhead:** From Howe, take the paved county road that goes north up the Little Lost River Valley for about 7.5 miles. Turn right (east) onto the signed, gravel South Creek Road, which heads straight toward the rugged mountains. After about 2.5 miles, there is a junction near some corrals. Take the dirt road to the left. You will soon come to a locked gate. Follow the dirt road as it leads around the private fence line. In about a mile you reach the trailhead and a short section of new trail cut into the mountainside. GPS: N43 54.91' / W113 02.27'
**Parking and trailhead facilities:** The undeveloped, unshaded trailhead has ample room for parking. The obvious trail to the canyon leaves directly from the trailhead.

## The Hike

The stark, rough southern end of the Lemhi Mountains rises abruptly from the Arco Desert just east of the agricultural community of Howe (population about 20). The first peak in the range is 10,810-foot Saddle Mountain—a bold chunk of limestone that rises 5,500 feet (more than a mile) above the floor of the Little Lost River Valley.

South Creek is the only stream that flows from the slopes of Saddle Mountain. It provides a green pathway into the Lemhis as early as May 15. Snow does not close the trail most years until late November, if then. It is also one of the few Lemhi Range canyons that has no livestock grazing. The elimination of a sheep allotment has resulted in a rare high desert riparian zone that is in excellent condition; consequently, there is more wildlife than in nearby canyons.

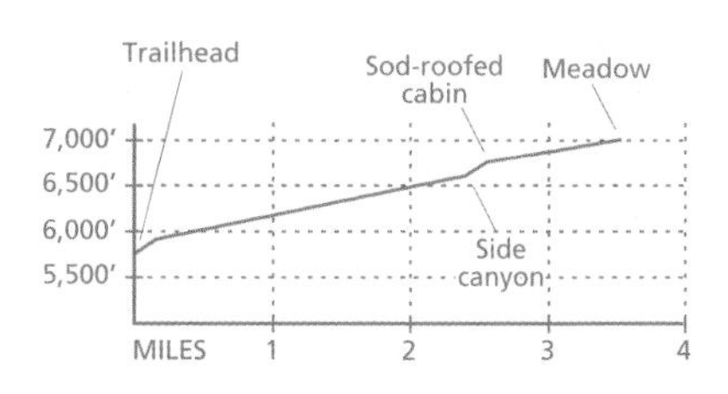


When I first visited South Creek, there was a road up the canyon, but a private land closure at the mouth of the canyon prevented public access for several years, allowing nature

*South Creek Cabin.* Photo by Josh Keeley

to make the road into a trail. The trail was reopened when a new access road and trailhead that avoids private land were built. The trail is open to dirt bikes and ATVs, although it is really too narrow for the latter. They do not use it heavily.

The route of the trail leads to a brief climb up the bare mountainside, but it soon drops into the moist riparian area adjacent to South Creek—a striking contrast. The trail keeps close to this small creek, crossing it a number of times. All the crossings are but a few inches deep. Enjoy the remarkable ungrazed streamside forest of river birch, cottonwood, and quaking aspen.

Small bands of colorful, increasingly rugged cliffs jut from the canyon walls, which are covered with sagebrush and short-growing grass.

After a couple of miles, you reach a dry side canyon. About 100 yards past this fork, up the main canyon, you come to a scenic, abandoned sod-roofed cabin. In this vicinity, the cliffs give their most dramatic display, providing a frame of the Lost River Mountains downcanyon and the first view of craggy Saddle Mountain to the right, near the head of the canyon.

Just past the cabin, the riparian forest begins to include Douglas fir, and the canyon becomes less desert-like, although prickly pear cactus persists on the south-facing slopes to the end of the trail. The trail crosses boggy areas several times, then emerges from the moist canyon bottom and stays on the north side of the canyon to the trail's end at a meadow that begins about a mile above the cabin.

In this meadow the source springs of South Creek bubble up. The meadow has been pristine because vehicles could not reach it. However, with the increasing power of ATVs, they may be able to rip their way through the boggy area and reach the meadow. If you see this, take a photograph and send the photo and report to the Lost River Ranger District. Also try to get the license plate numbers of the perpetrators.

The canyon harbors mule deer, elk, coyote, bear, and mountain lion. The most scenic time is from about the second week of June until early July. During midsummer, expect the lower part of the canyon to be hot.

**Options:** From the very top of the upper meadow, you can climb up a draw on its north side to a saddle above Camp Creek, drop 500 feet into Camp Creek, and then

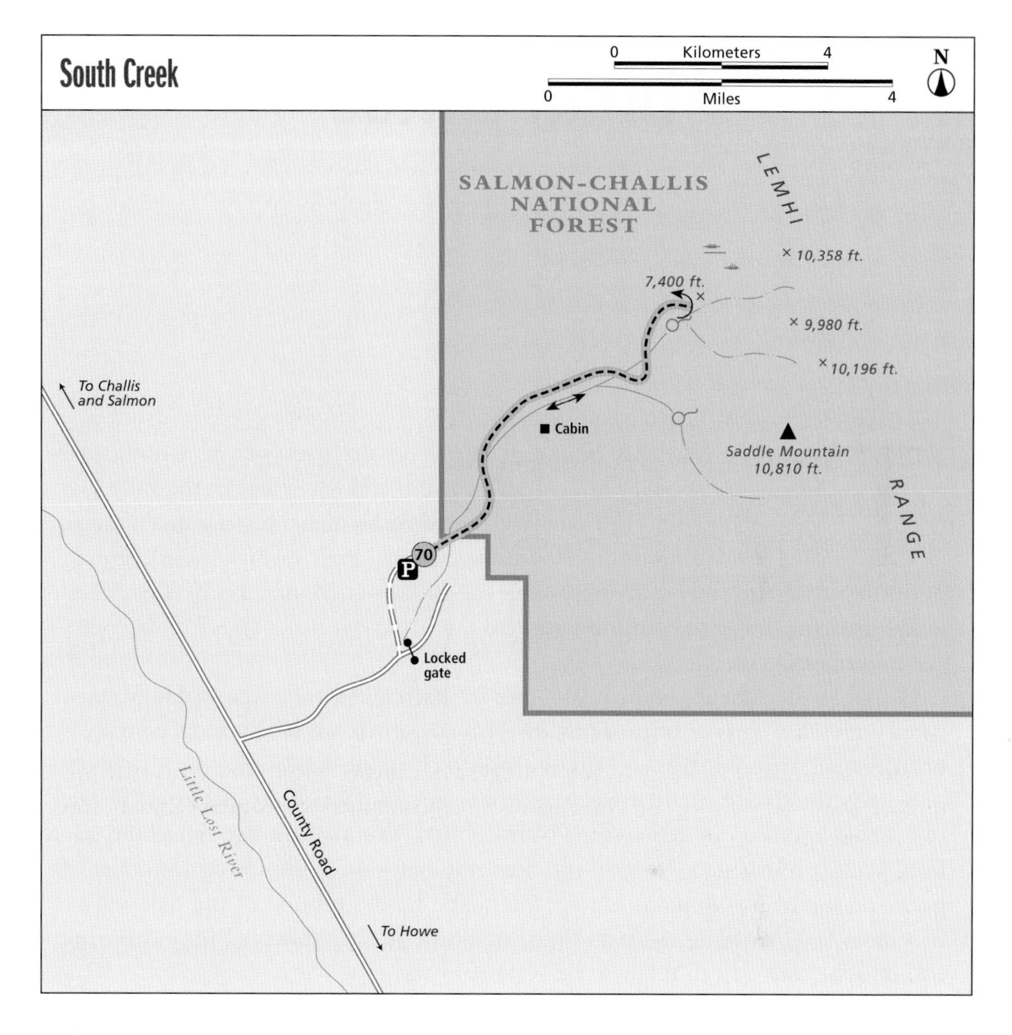


descend this fairly steep canyon. There are springs near its bottom. At the bottom, walk south along the foothills of the Lemhi Range, following old mining roads and game trails, which will lead you to the trailhead. Go south; avoid going southeast. A southeast route will place you on cliffs above South Canyon. This is a nice loop in late June.

—Ralph Maughan

## Miles and Directions

**0.0** Trailhead (5,720 feet)

**0.2** Mouth of South Creek Canyon (5,800 feet)

**2.5** Side canyon (6,650 feet)

**2.6** Sod-roofed cabin (6,720 feet)

**3.6** Meadow, springs, and an upper side canyon (7,020 feet)

# Great Divide

The Idaho-Montana border is borne on the back of the Continental Divide for several hundred miles. Idaho and Montana are the only two states whose mutual boundary is marked by such a big mountain range. The divide runs from Yellowstone National Park northwestward, turning north into Montana only as it approaches the Bitterroot Mountains. Beyond Chief Joseph Pass, the divide stays in Montana and the Idaho-Montana boundary becomes the Bitterroot Divide.

Despite its prominence on maps, this area has been hiked or backpacked little compared with other parts of Idaho. Trails are relatively scarce, but much of the country is open, making trails unnecessary. The situation is changing, however.

In 1989 the Continental Divide National Scenic Trail was dedicated from Canada to the west boundary of Yellowstone National Park. Eventually, it will run all the way from Canada to Mexico. The trail still does not exist on the ground in a number of places on the Idaho-Montana border. The Idaho border portion of the trail will be 253 miles long, entering the state from the north at Chief Joseph Pass and leaving Idaho to the southeast in Yellowstone National Park.

Long neglected by forest service management, the Great Divide has seen little recreation but also only scattered development. Six important roadless areas along the Great Divide are being proposed for wilderness designation by Idaho and Montana conservationists. These six units of the Great Divide Wilderness are—from northwest to southeast—Anderson Mountain, West Big Hole, Italian Peaks, Garfield Mountain, Centennial Mountains, and the Lionhead.

The Great Divide is also divided into three mountain ranges, each separated by a low pass. From Lost Trail Pass north of Salmon southeastward to Monida Pass, where I-15 crosses, the range is called the Beaverhead Mountains. From Monida Pass eastward to Red Rock Pass are the Centennial Mountains, and from Red Rock Pass to Reas Pass, next to Yellowstone, are found the Henrys Lake Mountains.

This chain of mountain ranges is environmentally important because it provides a corridor for wildlife migration from Yellowstone to central and northern Idaho and to western Montana. It is politically significant, too, in the sense that folks in Idaho

*Aldous Lake in Spring.* PHOTO BY LUKE KRATZ

and Montana have been kept socially and economically separated by this range compared with states that have a flat boundary.

Wildlife is abundant in the remote areas of the Great Divide: deer, elk, moose, pronghorn antelope, coyote, eagle, and black bear are common. Grizzly inhabit the Henrys Lake Mountains, and one occasionally may wander all the way from Yellowstone to central Idaho. Wolves have been tracked many times in the area, although no packs seem to exist there as of the year 2001.

The major threats to the area are below-cost logging (particularly in the northern Beaverhead Mountains and on the Idaho side of the Centennials), scattered mining, overgrazing by livestock and, increasingly, off-road vehicles scarring the open grassy slopes so common in these mountains.

The public lands on the Idaho-Montana portion of the Continental Divide are under the jurisdiction of the following agencies: Caribou-Targhee National Forest, Beaverhead National Forest, Salmon-Challis National Forest, Idaho Falls District Bureau of Land Management (BLM), Dillon District BLM, and Salmon District BLM.

—Ralph Maughan

# 71 Aldous and Hancock Lakes

Aldous and Hancock Lakes are two easy-to-reach subalpine lakes that are of quite different character despite their proximity.

**Start:** 65 linear miles north-by-northeast of Idaho Falls, near the Idaho-Montana border
**Type of hike:** Day hike, although camping is possible; out-and-back
**Distance:** 5 miles round-trip
**Approximate hiking time:** 2–3 hours
**Difficulty:** Moderately easy. It's a moderate climb on a well-maintained trail
**Best season:** Mid-June–mid-September
**Trail surface:** Normal dirt and rock
**Land status:** Caribou-Targhee National Forest
**Canine compatibility:** Voice command
**Fees and permits:** None
**Map:** Slide Mountain USGS quadrangle
**Trail contact:** Dubois Ranger District, (208) 374-5422

**Finding the trailhead:** The most trying feature of this hike is finding the trailhead.

Leaving Idaho Falls, drive northward on I-15 for 48 miles to Dubois. Leave the interstate at Dubois. Go through this small town, and head eastward on CR A2. After about 27 miles, a spur from the county road leads a mile north to the crossroads of Kilgore, which used to be a hamlet. As you pass through Kilgore, you come to a T intersection. Turn to the left here, and go west for about 0.3 mile; then turn off to the right to head straight north across Camas Meadows.

After 4.2 miles, there is a junction. Don't take the road to the left (East Camas). Stay to the right. From here, it is 3 miles to the Caribou-Targhee National Forest boundary. The road becomes FR 026. After 0.75 mile you come to a junction; take FR 027 to the right. This junction is just past the bridge over Cottonwood Creek. FR 027 wanders around but goes generally eastward through the foothills of the Centennial Mountains. The quality of its gravel surface is quite variable. After about 5.5 miles the road finally turns north, and at 6 miles reaches the Ching Creek Trailhead.

You can also reach Kilgore by following CR A2 from US 20 in Island Park. This is a more scenic, but much longer, route. GPS: N44 30.46' / W111 50.53'

**Parking and trailhead facilities:** The trailhead is well signed and shady, with room for about ten vehicles, but it is undeveloped. There is a registration box. The eastern continuation of the Continental Divide (CD) Trail leaves from the east side of the trailhead. The trail you follow leads north and is also the CD Trail west until you reach Aldous Lake.

## The Hike

The trail begins by the side of Ching Creek and leads uphill into a diverse conifer forest of lodgepole pine, Douglas fir, subalpine fir, and Engelmann spruce. The trail is very well maintained, with long sections of corduroy spanning a number of perennial areas of seeps and small springs. Interspersed in the forest are patches of small meadows. The trail crosses numerous feeder streams and occasionally approaches roaring Ching Creek. The elevation gain to Aldous Lake is only

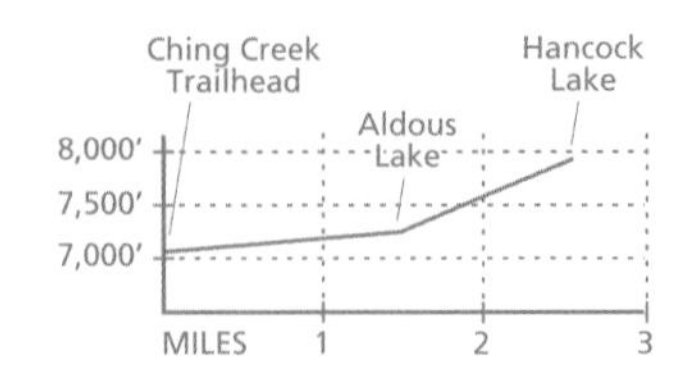

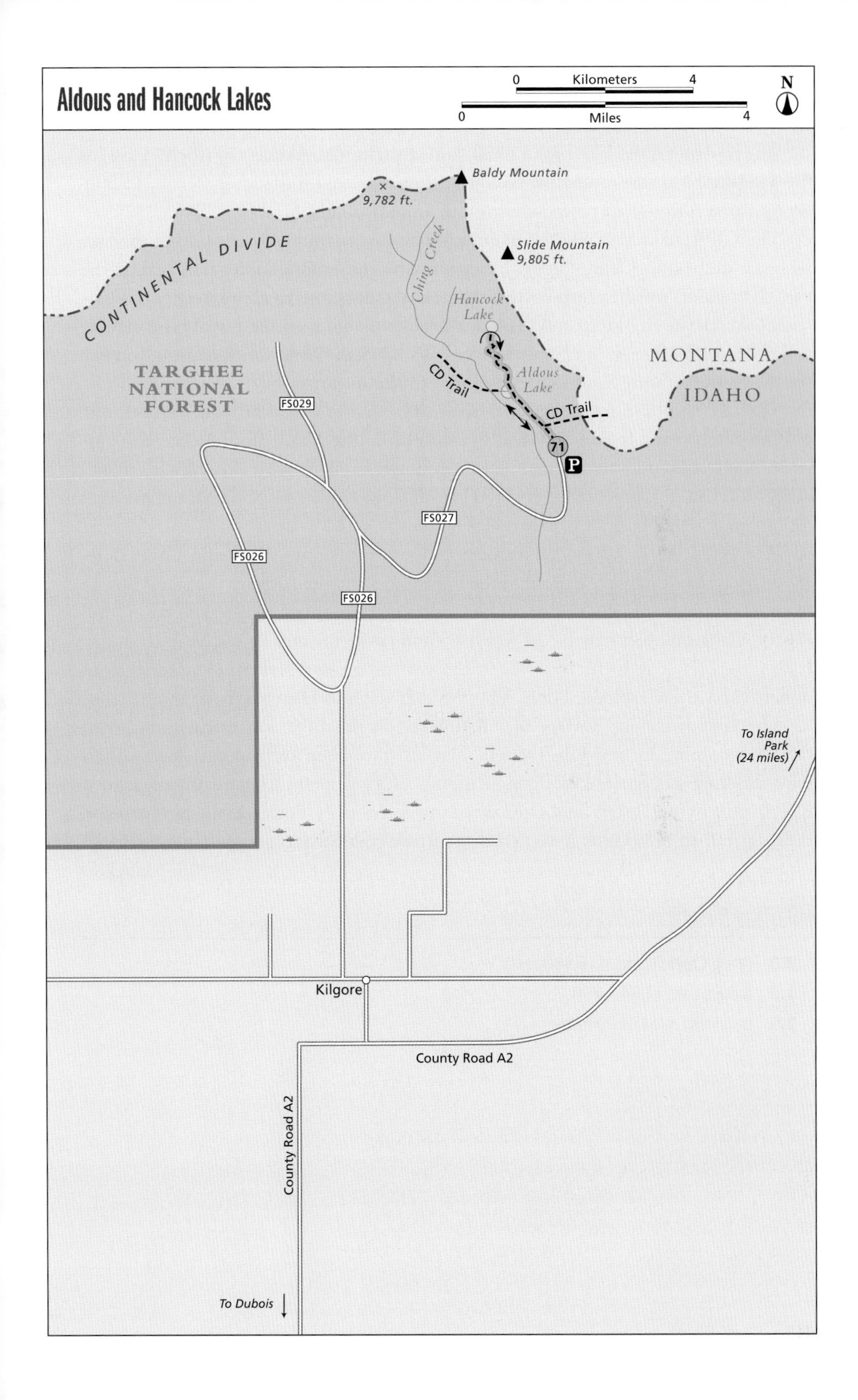
Aldous and Hancock Lakes
0 Kilometers 4
0 Miles 4
N
Baldy Mountain
9,782 ft.
Slide Mountain
9,805 ft.
CONTINENTAL DIVIDE
Ching Creek
Hancock Lake
Aldous Lake
CD Trail
CD Trail
MONTANA
IDAHO
TARGHEE NATIONAL FOREST
FS029
FS027
FS026
FS026
71
P
To Island Park (24 miles)
Kilgore
County Road A2
County Road A2
To Dubois

360 feet, and there isn't much bumping over hill and down dale to get to it. It's a steady, but moderate, climb.

The trail meets the lake near a small dam at the outlet. Aldous or "Micky Lake" as the locals call it is surrounded by stately, healthy trees and is obviously fertile. Fishing is popular at Aldous, but record-setting fish are not caught here.

The CD Trail west leaves the main trail halfway around the west side of the lake where it drops into Ching Creek. Instead, follow the more definite trail around the lake to the lake's northeastern corner, where the trail begins to climb steeply to Hancock Lake. Between Aldous and Hancock Lakes, the trail is covered with pine needles and is steeped in their sweet, pungent scent. With just the right vantage point, you can see the Saint Anthony Sand Dunes 50 miles to the south.

The trail climbs more steeply than the lower section to Aldous; it then levels out, only to climb again. It gains 560 feet in elevation in the 1 mile from Aldous to Hancock. Soon you come over a rim and drop down to Hancock Lake, which sits in a depression in a old, largely tree-covered landslide from adjacent Slide Mountain. That mountain is a landmark from down at Kilgore.

Hancock Lake, at 7,900 feet, is much rockier than Aldous. A lot of driftwood lies about from trees that were caught in the high water and died. Above the lake, you can see the Continental Divide ridge of the Centennial Mountains. The lake's water level is very changeable—it may be 20 feet deep and twice the area in wet years as in dry. It also loses water into the landslide as the year progresses. Nevertheless, small trout usually survive each winter. There is no flowing water at Hancock Lake.

The abundance and variety of wildflowers on this hike is overwhelming, with the peak coming in mid-July. Fifteen varieties have been seen in the space of 0.5 mile: shooting star, fireweed, lodgepole lupine, sticky geranium, heartleaf arnica, great Engelmann (white) aster, field chickweed, dwarf monkey flower, giant-hyssop mint, Indian paintbrush, larkspur, desert parsley, yarrow, cow parsnip, and pearly everlasting!

—Ralph Maughan

## Miles and Directions

**0.0** Ching Creek Trailhead (6,980 feet)

**1.5** Aldous Lake (7,340 feet)

**2.5** Hancock Lake (7,900 feet)

# 72 Salamander Lake Loop

The Salamander Lakes host beautiful meadows flanking the Continental Divide and good wildlife habitat.

**Start:** 76 miles north-northeast of Idaho Falls in the mountains behind the almost ghost town of Kilgore on the Idaho-Montana border
**Type of hike:** The opportunity for various hikes from a base camp. Several possible loops near the Continental Divide in a "low" spot of the Centennial Mountains.
**Distance:** 9-mile loop with shorter options
**Approximate hiking time:** 5 hours to overnight
**Difficulty:** Moderate, with difficulty mostly due to trails whose tread disappears when crossing meadows
**Best season:** Early June–mid-October
**Trail surface:** Normal dirt and rock
**Land status:** Caribou-Targhee National Forest
**Canine compatibility:** On leash
**Fees and permits:** None
**Maps:** Winslow Creek USGS quadrangle; Dubois and Island Park Ranger Districts–Targhee National Forest map
**Trail contact:** Dubois Ranger District, (208) 374-5422

**Finding the trailhead:** From Idaho Falls, drive north on I-15 for 48 miles to Dubois. From Dubois, on the east edge of town, bear left at the flashing yellow light onto CR A2. About 27 miles later turn left (north) on a paved road signed for Kilgore. After you pass through Kilgore, take a left at the T intersection. The road becomes gravel here. At 0.3 mile past the T intersection, take a right and cross Camas Meadows. After 5.8 miles you enter the Targhee National Forest, and 0.5 mile later come to the junction of FR 026 and FR 027; bear to the left onto the good, graveled FR 026. About 0.75 mile past this junction, take Cottonwood Creek Road (FR 029) to the right. This is a decent dirt road when dry but becomes poor after a soaking rain. It is not quite 2 miles from here to the trailhead. GPS: N44 31.16' / W111 55.38'
**Parking and trailhead facilities:** There is parking for about six vehicles 100 yards beyond the undeveloped trailhead, which is obvious and leads up Trail Creek. No potable water or sanitary facilities are available.

## The Hike

There are several broad, low spots in the Centennial Mountains. In these areas, the distance to the Continental Divide is not so strenuous. This hike describes one such spot with the good fortune to have retained an extensive trail system. These trails

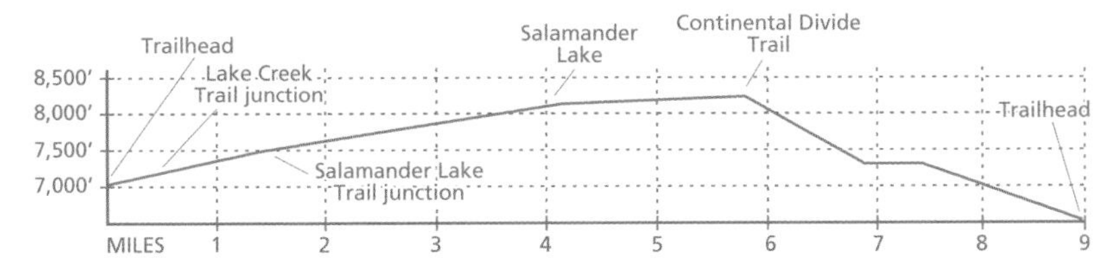

may be used to make a number of loop hikes (a rare situation in the Centennials where, in the past, trail systems have often been neglected or destroyed by logging). So far the area described here has remained intact due to lack of high-value timber combined with topography frequently changed by creeping soil and small landslides.

All of these trails are closed to motor vehicles, and a sign so indicates at the beginning. Trail Creek Trail climbs moderately through small meadows and mixed conifer forest and follows a short distance from the creek for about 0.5 mile to a sign that points to Lake Creek to the left and Trail Creek to the right; take a right. Lake Creek Trail is the trail you will return on to complete the loop described.

After another mile of moderate uphill, the trail intersects again. A sign indicates SALAMANDER LAKE to the left and Trail Creek to the right; stay right. About 0.25 mile past this junction, the trail descends slightly to cross Trail Creek (just a hop on rocks in mid-July). It then climbs briefly, levels out, and drops to cross a major tributary of Trail Creek.

After this crossing, the trail climbs fairly steeply uphill. As you climb, you begin to enter larger and larger meadows and gain a view of the mountainside ahead. Vegetation in the meadows is typical of the 7,500- to 9,000-foot elevation all along the Continental Divide in this locale: beautiful, tall, and generally fleshy forbs, such as monkshood, western coneflower, sticky geranium, wild carrot, lupine, bluebells, cow parsnip, and tall cinquefoil, but little grass. The midsummer growth rate of the forbs is such that they hide the tread of any trail through a meadow not traveled more frequently than every week or so. Be sure to follow the blazes on the trees.

At about 8,500 feet, you arrive at the highest elevation of the loop when you cross a meadow on a shelf that sits between two tributary drainages of Trail Creek. Off the trail to the left are views of the Trail, Salamander, and Lake Creek Valleys. This meadowland with clumps of subalpine fir and whitebark pine continues until the trail descends sharply to a pond (which is sometimes dry by late summer).

The trail then drops about 200 feet, rather steeply, to Salamander Lake at 4.2 miles. This is a small, shallow lake surrounded on the south by a lush meadow and on the north by a conifer forest. Springs keep this lake full of water year-round. It is a pretty location.

Moose frequent this lake and so do a few fish; however, due to the nature of the shoreline, wading is not an option because of the soft earth.

The trail keeps to the left (south) side of the meadowy lakeshore. Below the lake's outlet is an important trail junction. Here a sign indicates TRAILHEAD straight ahead and DIVIDE and LAKE CREEK to the right. To reach the divide and the large loop hike described here, take the right fork of the trail and quickly reach a bridge over Salamander Creek. From this bridge, follow the blazes across the forbs to the obvious trail that enters the forest and climbs 100 feet to a ridgeline. Here you enter a large meadow, and you can see into Montana.

The trail immediately disappears in the tall forbs of the meadow, but trail markers point in the right direction. There are about half a dozen of these markers, occurring every couple hundred yards, to lead you across the meadow and down into the drainage of Lake Creek. The trail never actually climbs to the Continental Divide; however, at 4.8 miles, there is a sign placed at a ninety-degree angle to the trail indicating the Divide Trail with no arrow and no obvious trail junction. This sign also indicates Salamander Lake in the direction from which you came.

After about 0.3 mile, following the arrow-imprinted trail markers, the route swings down into the headwaters of a creek and a streamside meadow. From this point on, follow the blazed trees whenever the tread becomes faint.

Soon the trail leaves streamside and climbs a short distance to a ridge. Just amble down this pleasant ridge between Lake Creek (to the left) and Cottonwood Creek (to the right). Both canyons remain largely out of sight. At 6.8 miles you drop down and, in quick succession, cross Lake Creek and one of its tributaries. You climb briefly to another ridge. After about 0.3 mile you descend from this ridge to cross Salamander Creek. A sign reading DIVIDE points in the direction you came from and points to Lake Trail to the right. The sign doesn't point to the plainly obvious trail to the left that crosses Salamander Creek on a bridge and goes up a little hill on the other side. This junction is 1.5 miles from your vehicle. The trail is sometimes faint as it climbs over a broad ridge and descends to Trail Creek, completing your loop.

The entire loop is good habitat for moose, elk, deer, and an occasional bear and is gorgeous in late spring and early summer, when the wildflowers are in bloom. This area is an extremely important wildlife corridor between Yellowstone National Park and the wilderness of central Idaho. Let's hope this rare and beautiful area will remain as it is.

**Options:** Quick route: To take a quick route to Salamander Lake, turn left at the trail junction at 1.5 miles. This route is 1.25 miles shorter; however, it does not offer the same views. It is a steady climb up the ridge between Salamander Creek and Trail Creek. You can also choose this route from Salamander Lake by turning left at the trail junction at 4.4 miles (in the direction indicated by the sign pointing toward the TRAILHEAD). This choice will get you back to the trailhead almost 2 miles sooner than the large loop described above.

The Divide Trail: The Divide Trail is directly adjacent to the northern portion of the Salamander Lake Loop and is easy to find. To reach the divide, leave your route at the sign indicating the Divide Trail at 4.8 miles at an angle of between forty-five and ninety degrees. Simply keep walking until you are on the divide (about 1,000 feet due north). Once you are on the Divide Trail, you can walk as far as you wish in either direction; watch where you came from, however, since the divide is fairly gentle here and has a large number of big, similar meadows.

—Gwen Gerber

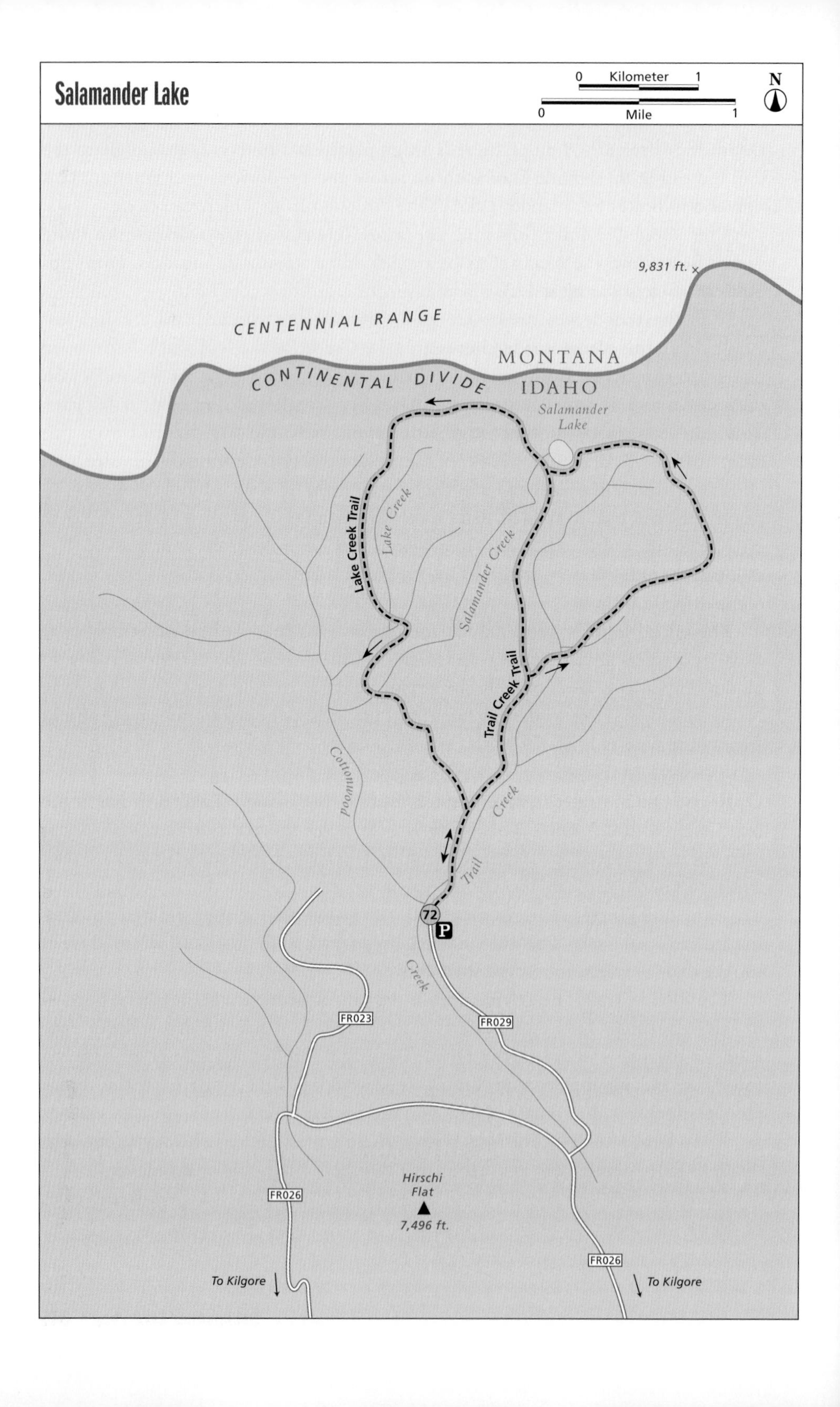
Salamander Lake
0 Kilometer 1
0 Mile 1
N
9,831 ft.
CENTENNIAL RANGE
MONTANA
CONTINENTAL DIVIDE
IDAHO
Salamander Lake
Lake Creek Trail
Lake Creek
Salamander Creek
Trail Creek Trail
Cottonwood
Creek
Trail
72
P
Creek
FR023
FR029
FR026
Hirschi Flat
7,496 ft.
FR026
To Kilgore
To Kilgore

## Miles and Directions

**0.0** Trailhead (7,040 feet)

**0.5** Lake Creek Trail junction (7,240 feet)

**1.5** Salamander Lake Trail junction (7,500 feet)

**4.2** Salamander Lake (8,150 feet)

**4.4** Trailhead/Lake Creek junction (8,120 feet)

**4.8** Continental Divide Trail (8,280 feet)

**6.8** Lake Creek crossing (7,380 feet)

**7.5** Trail Junction/Salamander Creek crossing (7,300 feet)

**9.0** Trailhead

# 73 Sawtell Peak-Rock Creek Basin

This hike offers spectacular views from the Continental Divide into Idaho, Wyoming, and Montana, with such highlights as Henrys Lake, Island Park Reservoir, Red Rock Lakes, and the Teton and Centennial Mountains.

**Start:** About 85 road miles north of Idaho Falls, Idaho, and 35 road miles south of West Yellowstone, Montana, at the eastern end of the Centennial Mountains
**Type of hike:** Day hike or backpack; out-and-back
**Distance:** 8 miles round-trip
**Approximate hiking time:** 4 hours to several days
**Difficulty:** Moderate due to rockslides, snow-covered portions of trail early in the season, and some precipitous passages
**Best season:** Mid-June (mid-July if heavy snowpack)–September
**Trail surface:** Normal dirt and rock
**Land status:** Caribou-Targhee National Forest
**Canine compatibility:** On leash recommended
**Fees and permits:** None
**Maps:** Sawtell Peak USGS quadrangle; Dubois and Island Park Ranger Districts–Targhee National Forest map
**Trail contact:** Island Park Ranger District, (208) 558-7301
**Special considerations:** Popular during hunting season. The first 2 miles are exposed to lightning during thunderstorm season. No water on the trail in midsummer. Scarce wood, so campfires are discouraged. In recent years grizzly bears have sometimes been seen in this area.

**Finding the trailhead:** On US 20, 85 miles north of Idaho Falls or 35 miles south of West Yellowstone, turn west onto the signed Sawtell Peak Road (FR 024). Twelve miles up the mountain on this good gravel road is the signed trailhead. (Driving a little over a mile farther will take you to the top of windy Sawtell Peak, at 9,866 feet, where you'll find great views and can look down into Rock Creek Basin. Located on top is a radar site.) GPS: N44 33.25' / W111 26.72'
**Parking and trailhead facilities:** Small, undeveloped pullout.

## The Hike

More than 90,000 acres of the Centennial Mountains in Idaho and Montana have been studied by the Bureau of Land Management and USDA Forest Service as a possible addition to the National Wilderness Preservation System. This area being truly kept wild could one day become a reality, but united and consistent action must be taken. Despite the high wilderness qualities of the area and the absence of minerals except low-grade coal and phosphate ore, securing wilderness protection is very difficult due to opposition from the timber industry and some snowmobile enthusiasts. In 1996 the

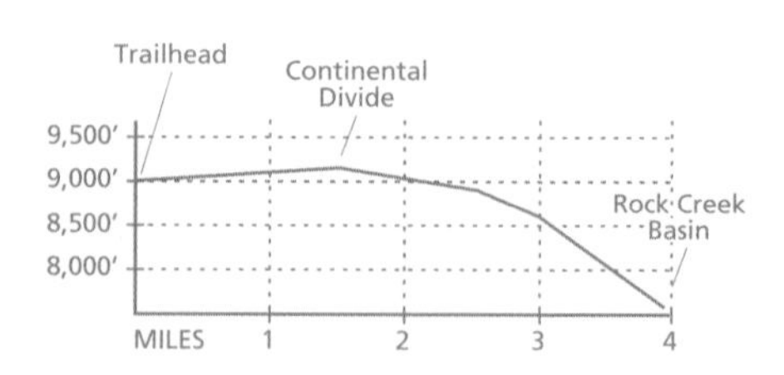

*Mt. Jefferson of the Centennial Range.* Photo by Luke Kratz

Targhee National Forest determined the Centennials to have the greatest biological diversity of the forest. Nevertheless, back in 1990 the forest service officially recommended that none of the Idaho side be protected as designated wilderness.

This route follows an old road that once led to a watershed restoration project. The route is on, or near, the Continental Divide much of the way. Although the overall elevation gain or loss is not great, portions of the trail are steep. The first part of the old road is fairly level with a moderate climb through dead, artistically sculpted whitebark pine. You'll also see lodgepole pine and pointed subalpine fir in the area. Winters are harsh, and a constant wind generally blows year-round. Vegetation is stunted, but wildflowers are prevalent most of the summer, including August. Flowers commonly seen are dogtooth violet, phlox, and buttercup.

As the road dips downward, you cross a rock avalanche field of old lava. The trail then bottoms out and begins to climb and, in 1.5 miles, reaches the Continental Divide. At 2 miles it turns sharply north to begin its descent into Rock Creek Basin.

In the 1960s, after extensive sheep grazing caused soil erosion problems, sheep were banned from the vicinity. In parts of the basin, you can see the artificial terraces that resulted from an experimental attempt to restore vegetation and halt erosion. If you were to come back in another few centuries, you would still see these terraces.

Rock Creek Basin has a perennial stream, appropriately named Rock Creek, that eventually feeds into Henrys Lake. Its roar can be heard miles away. The basin is a rockhound's delight since it abounds with a variety of rock colors and types. You can find low-lying fir and pleasant rest spots anywhere in the basin.

Wildlife is abundant. Bear, elk, moose, and deer scat and tracks are common on and off the trail. Looking into the basin, you can often spot big game. Noise carries a

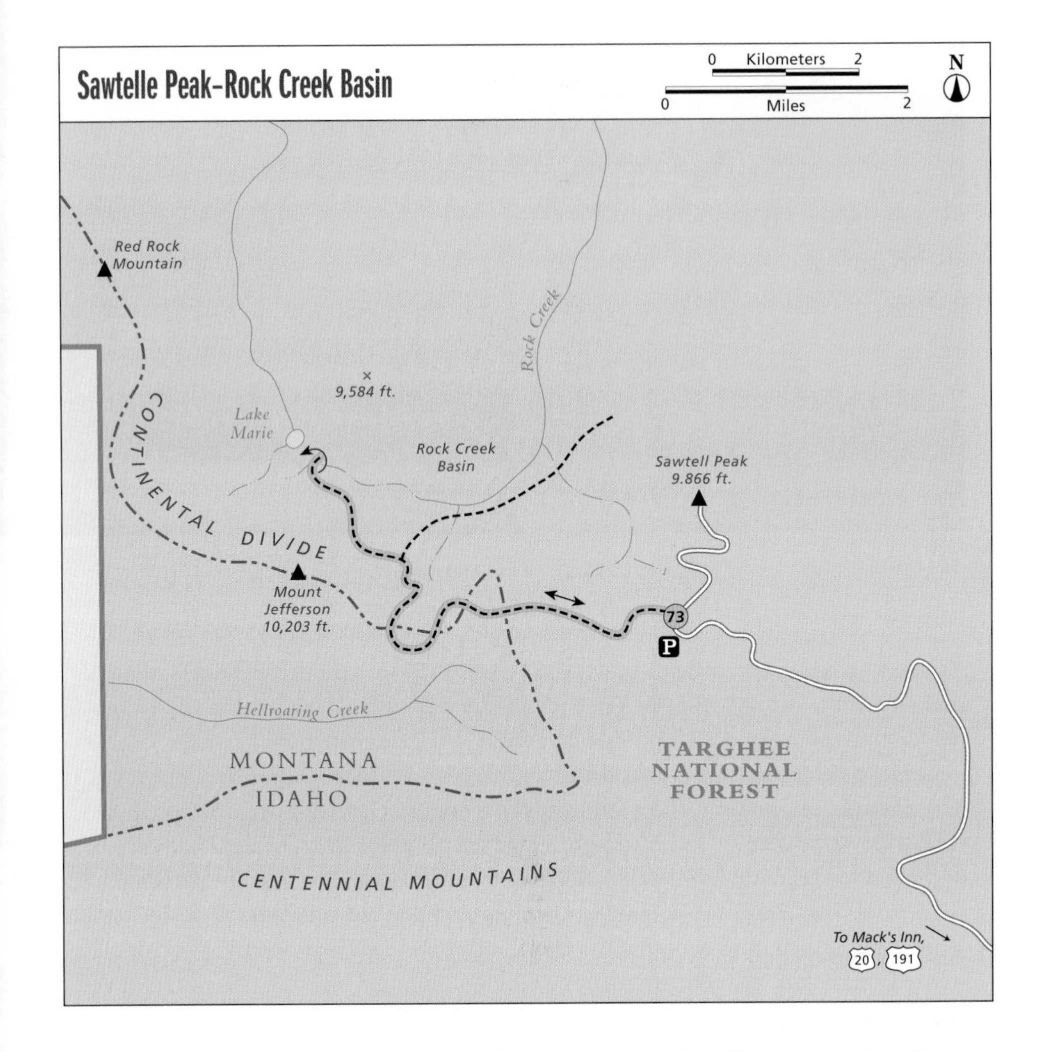


long distance in the area, so chances of seeing game are low if you are noisy. Clark's nutcracker, gray jays, and a variety of hawks frequent the territory. Grizzly bears are sighted almost every year somewhere in the Centennials, although the sighting is usually of a lone bear.

## Miles and Directions

**0.0** Trailhead (9,000 feet)

**1.5** Continental Divide (9,200 feet)

**2.0** Descent into Rock Creek Basin (9,000 feet)

**2.5** Trail leaves old road (8,800 feet)

**3.0** Trail turns east (8,600 feet)

**4.0** Rock Creek Basin (8,000 feet)

# 74 Targhee Creek

Grizzly bears inhabit this country of alpine lakes and meadows along with black bears, moose, elk, and bighorn sheep.

**Start:** In the Henrys Lake Mountains, 40 miles north of Ashton, Idaho, and 10 miles west of West Yellowstone, Montana, inside the proposed Lionhead Wilderness
**Type of hike:** The walk to near the forks of Targhee Creek is a nice day hike, and there also is an option of a backpack loop.
**Distance:** 6.2 miles one way to the first lakes; more to explore the lakes beyond
**Approximate hiking time:** 3 hours to several days
**Difficulty:** Easy to the second crossing of Targhee Creek; moderate beyond due to elevation gain
**Best season:** July and August
**Trail surface:** Normal dirt and rock
**Land status:** Caribou-Targhee National Forest
**Canine compatibility:** On leash
**Fees and permits:** None
**Maps:** Targhee Pass and Targhee Peak USGS quadrangles; Island Park, Ashton, Teton Basin, and Palisades Ranger Districts-Targhee National Forest map
**Trail contact:** Island Park Ranger District, (208) 558-7301
**Special considerations:** This area is serious grizzly country, more so than any other hike in this book. The Henrys Lake Mountains are home to some transplanted bears that were captured in Yellowstone National Park and relocated due to their apparent lack of fear of humans. It is strongly recommended you hike in large groups and carry a pepper spray canister specially designed to repel grizzlies. Grizzlies are most abundant in the lower elevations in late May through June (when the Henrys Lake cutthroat trout spawn in Targhee Creek and grass and forbs are most palatable) and again in September in higher elevations (when the bears feed on whitebark pine nuts). As many as six grizzlies have been spotted in this drainage at one time.

**Finding the trailhead:** From Idaho, drive to Saint Anthony and continue past Ashton on US 20. Drive north into Island Park and the Targhee National Forest. From Island Park, head across scenic Henrys Lake Flat, still on US 20. On the north side of the flat, ignore ID 287, which leaves to the left past Henrys Lake. Drive up into the Henrys Lake Mountains toward the state line at Targhee Pass; 2.2 miles past the junction with ID 287, take the dirt road on the left (west) signed TARGHEE CREEK TRAIL, which turns off US 20 to climb up the obvious cutbank on the left side of the highway.

From Montana, drive over Targhee Pass on US 20. The road to the trailhead is also signed from this direction and is a mile beyond the Targhee Pass.

To reach the trailhead, simply stay straight on the fairly good dirt road for a little over a mile to the obvious, well-signed parking lot and horse-loading ramp. GPS: N44 40.24' / W111 18.78'
**Parking and trailhead facilities:** Parking at the trailhead is spacious, with trees to provide afternoon shade for your vehicle. There are plenty of camping spots along the dirt road, but they are overused so tread lightly. There is no water or toilets. The trailhead is marked with an information board and is signed NO MOTOR VEHICLES.

## The Hike

It's 6.2 miles to Clark Lake and a 2,000-foot climb, with 90 percent of the elevation gain in the last 3 miles. This hike is best done overnight because there are lakes to explore beyond the first one. Every step is a beauty, so you don't need to go clear to the lakes to enjoy it. The 3-mile walk to the forks of Targhee Creek is quite gentle, and many people go just that far.

A jeep road formerly extended all the way to the East Fork of Targhee Creek, but a number of years ago the forest service blocked and ditched the road to prevent vehicle access. This has proven very success action in improving water quality, increasing the abundant wildlife, and greatly increasing the solitude of this splendid stream valley. The forest service deserves praise for its work here.

The plainly evident, but not wide, trail leads gently uphill from the trailhead. It rolls up and down through small meadows and patches of forest. At 0.8 mile a signed trail to the Dry Fork (of Targhee Creek) leaves at a right angle to the left and goes downhill to an immediate ford of Targhee Creek. Continue straight ahead.

The trail soon comes to a larger meadow and approaches Targhee Creek. Moose frequent the creek and nearby willows.

The trail continues through patches of forest, meadows, and willow fields with beaver ponds. Above all this greenery, limestone cliffs line the left side of the canyon.

At 2.3 miles a good footbridge crosses the creek to the left bank and leads through a subalpine meadow with fine views of Bald Peak ahead. As you approach the East Fork of Targhee Creek side canyon (a lesser tributary that the trail does not cross), you enter timber. The trail climbs briefly into the timber, and at 3.2 miles you reach the second crossing of Targhee Creek, presently bridged downstream from the trail by two uneven logs. An actual bridge may be built soon.

The trail now wanders for about 0.5 mile through deep forest that contains small, shaded meadows. It heads upcanyon, climbing moderately toward, but above, the confluence of the main Targhee Creek and West Targhee Creek. This section of trail can be quite muddy, and it smells of the forest primeval with the rank odor of elk and other wild animals. The main fork of Targhee Creek here is really an arbitrary name. West Targhee Creek is just as big, if not bigger.

At 4.2 miles the trail ascends across a meadow that offers views below, up West Targhee Creek, and southward toward a trident of limestone cliffs. West Targhee Creek has a reputation for being exceptionally full of grizzly bears.

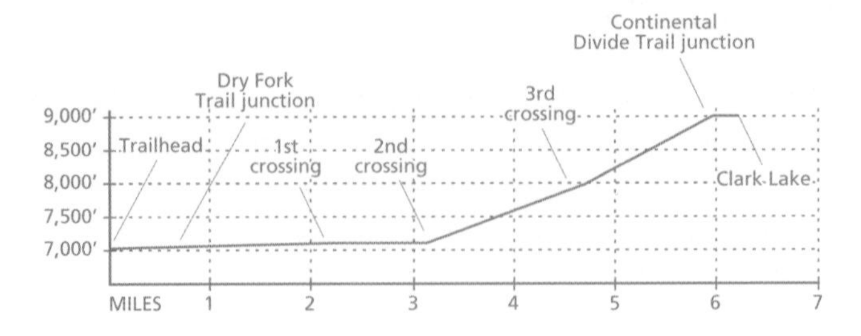

*At the Targhee Creek trailhead in early spring.* PHOTO BY CATHY KRATZ

This is a good place for a lunch stop. If you walk across the sloping meadow to where Targhee Creek thunders downhill on the way to its wedding with the West Fork, you'll find a waterfall. Here, Targhee Creek leaps over a ledge surrounded by columns of brownish black schist studded with gleaming mica.

From here the trail heads upward in earnest through forest and streamside meadows. The right side of the canyon is a nearly continuous cliff. Forest dominates the west side of the steep canyon.

About midway up this section of Targhee Creek, at 4.7 miles, the trail crosses Targhee Creek for the last time. This crossing is a ford early in the season, but there are plans to build a footbridge. The trail continues upward, crossing a number of small trickles that emerge from the flanks of Targhee Peak. A few of these may have washed out the trail for a brief distance, although maintenance of this trail has improved since it was adopted by the Greater Yellowstone Coalition.

Finally, at 5.5 miles, the trail enters a relatively flat meadow above which the canyon forms an obvious constriction. In the meadow, the trail leads you up away from Targhee Creek out of the canyon to the junction with the Continental Divide Trail at 6 miles. This trail, constructed in the late 1990s, is distastefully obvious and is marked with cairns stacked 3 feet high and just as wide. Its location here was rammed through with little public input. This junction is marked with a trail sign pointing toward Watkins Creek Trail to the east (right), Targhee Creek Trail to the west (left), and the Targhee Creek Trailhead 6 miles back in the direction hiked. This trail does not appear on the 1964 USGS quadrangle.

A left at this intersection will take you in the direction of Targhee Peak and the headwaters of the West Fork of Targhee Creek by winding through a majestic forest of mature whitebark pine. The forest is thick with grizzlies in the fall.

To reach the six lakes harbored within Targhee Basin, turn right at this junction. The first (unnamed) lake is just ahead and off to the right of the trail. This lake sits in a little depression, its banks resembling those of a reservoir since it loses water over the summer.

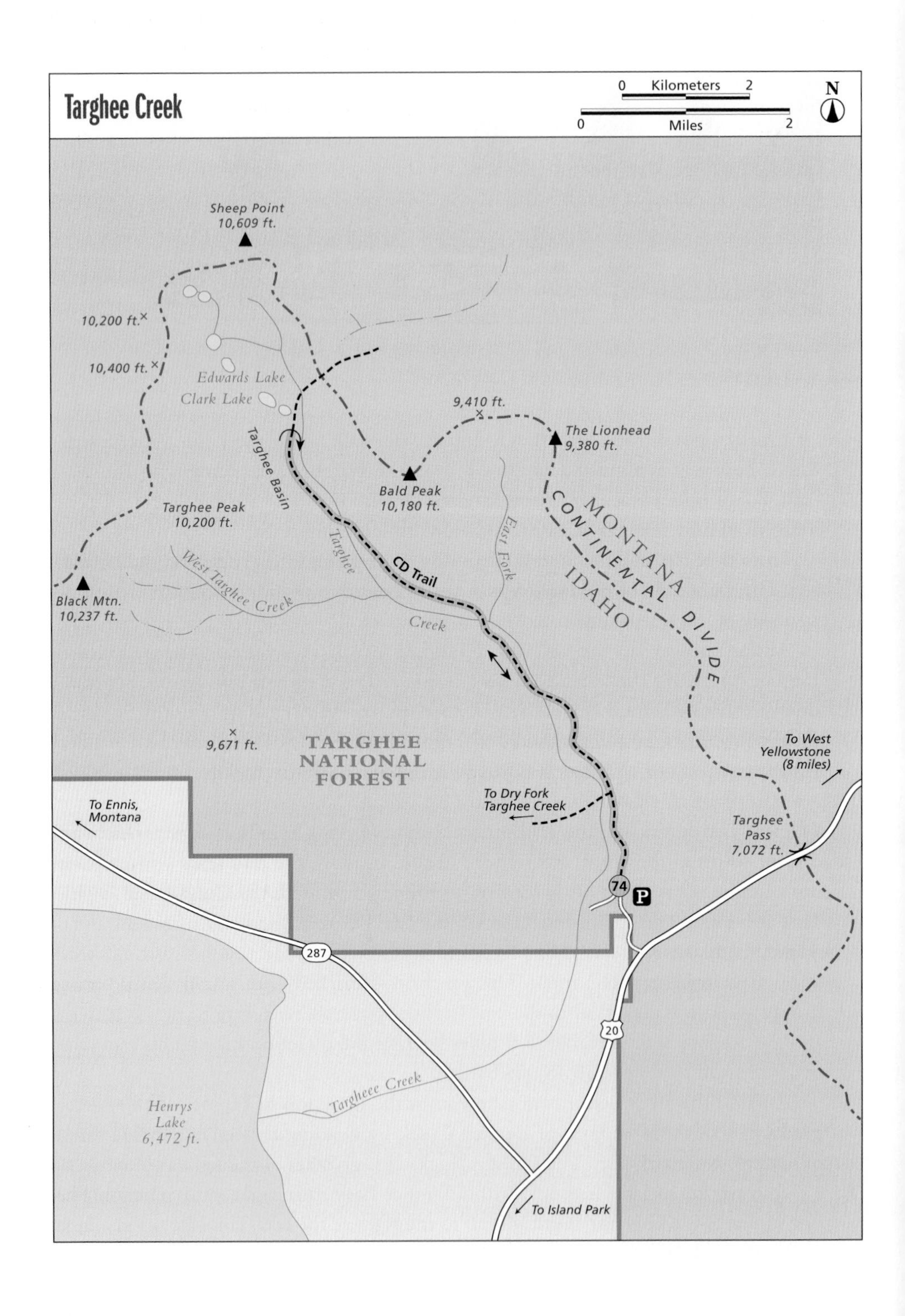

Targhee Creek
0 Kilometers 2
0 Miles 2
N
Sheep Point
10,609 ft.
10,200 ft.
10,400 ft.
Edwards Lake
Clark Lake
Targhee Basin
9,410 ft.
The Lionhead
9,380 ft.
Bald Peak
10,180 ft.
Targhee Peak
10,200 ft.
East Fork
MONTANA
CONTINENTAL DIVIDE
IDAHO
CD Trail
Targhee
West Targhee Creek
Black Mtn.
10,237 ft.
Creek
9,671 ft.
TARGHEE
NATIONAL
FOREST
To West
Yellowstone
(8 miles)
To Dry Fork
Targhee Creek
To Ennis,
Montana
Targhee
Pass
7,072 ft.
74
P
287
20
Targheee Creek
Henrys
Lake
6,472 ft.
To Island Park

From the lake, you look across the upper end of Targhee Creek Canyon to the north side of Bald Mountain—a ridge of cliffs, salmon-colored loose rock, and a smattering of conifers. Just past this lake, the trail leads you to Clark Lake, which is shown as a seasonal lake on the USGS quadrangle. The lakes above are more interesting.

All six lakes tend to lose much of their water as the season progresses. Lakes five and six are very close together and are shown incorrectly on the Targhee Peak quadrangle as one lake.

At the north end of the basin, just inside Montana, is Sheep Point, at 10,609 feet the highest of the Henrys Lake Mountains. To the west and northwest rise several 10,000-foot-plus peaks. Targhee Basin is the northeasternmost point of Idaho.

If you climb any of the mountain slopes above Targhee Basin, you may see bighorn sheep, but the herd is in decline due to the uncontrolled, oversize snowmobiles that power up into this alpine area, overrunning it and greatly stressing the wintering sheep. From these peaks, you gain fine views of the surrounding valleys, including the Madison Valley, which includes Yellowstone National Park, to the east. The Gravelly Range to the west and the Centennial Range to the south are also easily visible. On a clear day the Teton Range is visible. Oddly enough, due to the convoluted state line here, Montana lies to the west and the southwest of Idaho.

Beautiful Targhee Peak to the south rises to almost 10,300 feet and is the tallest Idaho peak in the Henrys Lake Mountains. According to the US Geological Survey, it is a very unstable mountain. An earthquake similar to the massive Hebgen Lake earthquake of 1957 could bring down millions of tons of rock, filling Targhee Creek with rubble, just as happened to the Madison River Canyon 10 miles to the north in 1957. The even larger central Idaho earthquake of 1983, and the numerous small earthquakes that shake the Yellowstone area—including this mountain range—almost daily are constant reminders of what will eventually happen.

**Options:** To do the Targhee Creek–Dry Fork Loop Trail, follow the hike, as described, but take a left at the Continental Divide Trail junction. This trail will eventually lead to the junction with Dry Fork Trail, which loops around and intersects with Targhee Creek Trail just 0.8 mile from the Targhee Creek Trailhead. This loop trail is not shown on the 1964 Targhee Pass and Targhee Peak quadrangles.

—Ralph Maughan and Gwen Gerber

## Miles and Directions

**0.0** Trailhead (6,950 feet)

**0.8** Dry Fork Trail junction (7,050 feet)

**2.3** Targhee Creek crossing (bridge) (7,150 feet)

**3.2** Targhee Creek crossing (logs) (7,200 feet)

**4.7** Targhee Creek crossing (ford) (7,950 feet)

**6.0** Continental Divide Trail junction (9,000 feet)

**6.2** Clark Lake (9,000 feet)

# 75 Webber Creek

A small area of tremendous peaks lies along the Continental Divide. It is also a good area for wildlife observation.

**Start:** 65 miles northwest of Idaho Falls in the Italian Peaks (the highest portion of the Beaverhead Range)
**Type of hike:** Backpack; out-and-back, with the opportunity for longer backpacks requiring a shuttle
**Distance:** 18 miles round-trip
**Approximate hiking time:** 2–5 days
**Difficulty:** Moderate if at least 2 nights are devoted to the trip
**Best season:** July–October. The lower canyon is accessible in mid-June
**Trail surface:** Normal dirt and rock
**Land status:** Caribou-Targhee National Forest
**Canine compatibility:** On leash
**Fees and permits:** None
**Maps:** Heart Mountain and Scott Peak USGS quadrangles; Dubois and Island Park Ranger Districts–Targhee National Forest map.
**Trail contact:** Dubois Ranger District, (208) 374-5422; Island Park Ranger District, (208) 558-7301

**Finding the trailhead:** From Idaho Falls, drive northward on I-15 for 48 miles to Dubois. Leave I-15 at Dubois by turning onto ID 22. Travel west for 6 miles to a paved county road that leaves to the right (north) from ID 22. The road makes three or four right-angle turns. Don't let this lead you to believe you are off track.

You travel through farmland on this road and into the scenic basalt canyon of Medicine Lodge Creek. The yellow flowers covering almost everything in early summer are one of the most noxious weeds known—leafy spurge—and this is one of the worst infestations in Idaho. It began in the early 1990s and is spreading.

The road is paved for about 20 miles, then becomes good gravel. Continue up the gravel road to the signed Webber Creek Road (FR 196) on the left. This is 22.5 miles from ID 22.

It's 5 miles up FR 196 to the Webber Creek Trailhead. The road varies from good gravel at the beginning to two tracks at the trailhead. A sedan can make it if the road is dry or damp, but it does get very slippery in a few spots after substantial rain. GPS: N44 21.81' / W112 41.30'
**Parking and trailhead facilities:** There is a small, unimproved campground at the trailhead with space to park, although it's a squeeze for horse trailers. The trail (Trail 111) is obvious and leaves directly at the upstream end of the campground.

## The Hike

The Italian Peaks, culminating in 11,200-foot-plus Scott and Webber Peaks, are the highest part of the Beaverhead Range, which forms the Idaho-Montana border for about 200 miles.

In the Italian Peaks, mountain goats and bighorn sheep ply the cliffs. Elk graze the high meadows, and deer graze the forest. An occasional moose wanders by. Raptors search the land from the sky. Every so often there are reports of grizzly bear and wolves. This is wild territory.

You begin by hiking from the trailhead into a narrow, densely forested canyon with a damp riparian zone. There are some cliffs near the trail as well as a few sagebrush-dominated meadows. After 3.5 miles the canyon begins to open. Willow and beaver ponds line the stream bottom, and the gray, rugged Italian Peaks appear at the head of the canyon. The massive ice-carved mountain to the left is Webber Peak, nearly 11,300 feet. In the center, partially hidden by a lower pinnacled mountain, is Scott Peak, with a similar elevation. At about 4 miles you reach the confluence of the South and North Forks of Webber Creek. A trail—Meyers Creek Trail—goes up the South Fork, a possible option.

Continue up the North Fork. The peaks draw near and, after about 1.5 miles, you begin the climb into the North Fork's glacial valley. Here you come to a trail junction after climbing 900 feet in 1.5 miles. The right-hand trail (Trail 111) climbs out of the canyon and eventually leads to Divide Creek or Deadman Creek in Montana. This, too, is another hike option.

Up the left fork of the trail (Trail 034), imposing mountains rise on both sides of the canyon in stepped cliffs and awesome fluted pinnacles. In places the strata show in giant folds of limestone. The right wall is the Continental Divide. The trail is gentle, and you actually lose elevation getting to the first lake, which you reach quickly, but then you begin to climb. The uppermost lake is a climb of about 600 feet from the trail junction. It sits tightly against great mountain walls.

These cyan-colored lakes are not for anglers. Because the rock is porous, the lakes lose much of their water by autumn. They are a place to stay overnight and admire the hidden valley sandwiched between a great Idaho ridge and a Montana ridge of the Italian Peaks.

The forest service has long supported designating the core of the Italian Peaks as wilderness. The 1996 Targhee Forest Plan reaffirmed this decision by closing most trails to summertime motor vehicle use, with only a few exceptions. Most of the opposition to protection comes from groups that claim to represent off-road vehicle interests. Report violations of the closures to the Dubois Ranger District. Get a photo and license plate number(s) if possible.

**Options:** Meyers Creek Trail (Trail 113) leads southward up the South Fork of Webber Creek and over the north shoulder (9,220 feet) of rugged Heart Mountain

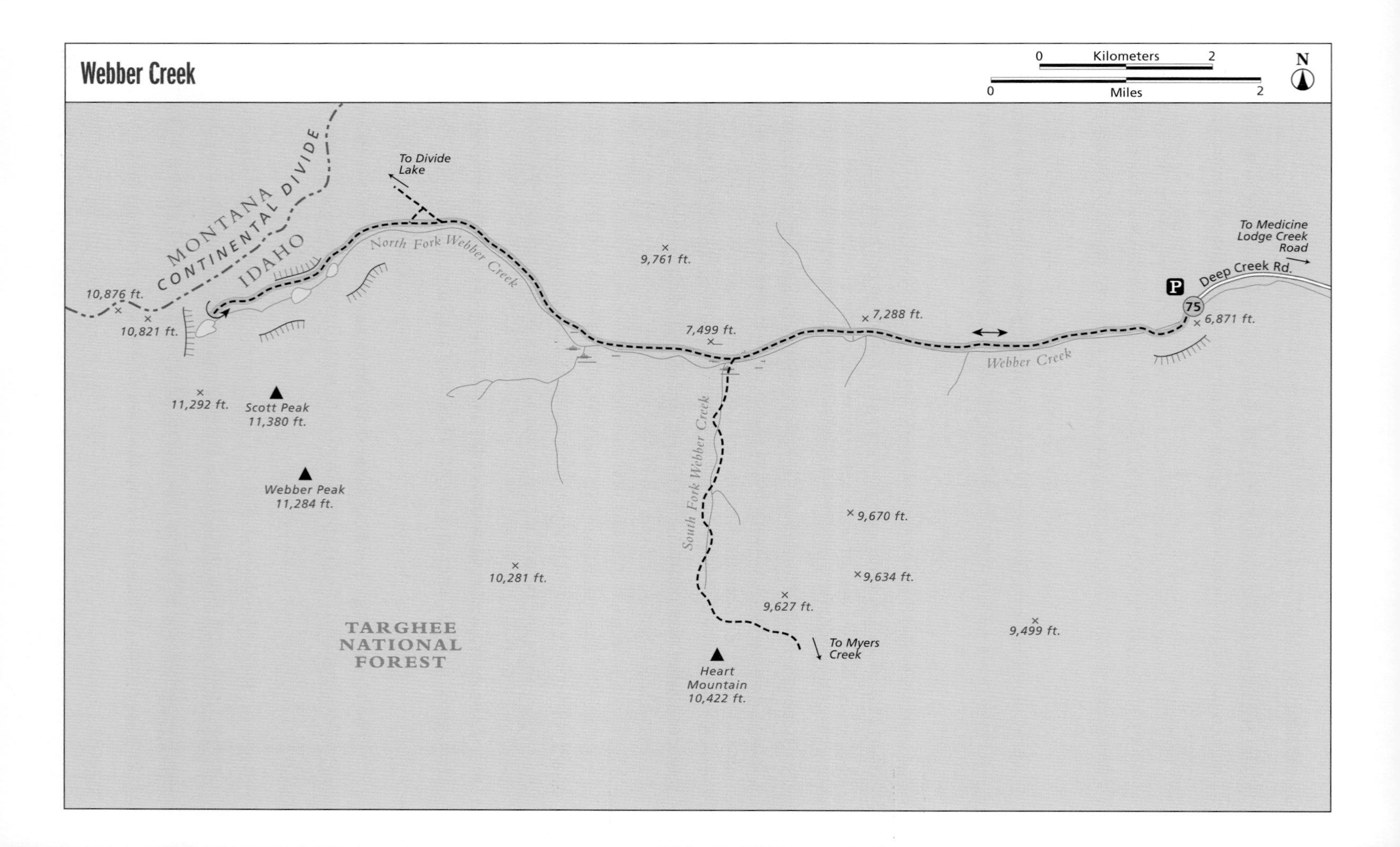
Webber Creek
Kilometers
0
2
Miles
0
2
N
MONTANA
CONTINENTAL DIVIDE
IDAHO
To Divide Lake
North Fork Webber Creek
9,761 ft.
To Medicine Lodge Creek Road
Deep Creek Rd.
P
75
6,871 ft.
7,288 ft.
7,499 ft.
Webber Creek
10,876 ft.
10,821 ft.
11,292 ft.
Scott Peak
11,380 ft.
Webber Peak
11,284 ft.
South Fork Webber Creek
9,670 ft.
9,634 ft.
10,281 ft.
9,627 ft.
9,499 ft.
TARGHEE NATIONAL FOREST
To Myers Creek
Heart Mountain
10,422 ft.

(10,402 feet) before it drops into Meyers Creek and ends at a dirt road (shuttle location). The dirt road is about 10 linear miles from the Webber Creek Trailhead, but the road for a shuttle is longer than that.

Divide Lake is another option. Continue on Trail 111, either bypassing the Webber Lakes or visiting them and then backtracking 2 miles. Trail 111 climbs to a grassy ridge at 9,200 feet, where elk are often seen. Then the trail continues north, drops into timber, and crosses the very head of the canyon of North Fritz Creek. Connecting Trail 112 descends steeply from this point. You could exit here to a shuttle. Continuing, however, complete the traverse of Fritz Creek, and then roll on down a not-very-rugged stretch of the Continental Divide. The trail leads slightly into Montana, then into Idaho, and so on. The large canyon appearing to your left is Deadman Creek in Montana. This is a beautiful side trip. Deadman Creek Trail leads to a 9,700-foot-high pass (between Deadman and Nicholia Creek), a fine place to observe mountain goats and the sheer north face of the Continental Divide at Italian Peak (for more information, see *Hiking Montana,* Globe Pequot Press).

As you walk along the Continental Divide, descending slowly, the character of the land changes rather quickly from rocky peaks and cliffs to open, meadowy mountains and mid-elevation meadows filled with tall, fleshy flowering plants (forbs), such as are visible in Deadman Creek below. As is commonplace in this area, the visible track of the trail fades as you go from rocky forest to meadowy upland. To reach Divide Lake, stay on the divide. Avoid the inclination to drop into Deadman Creek or to climb the hills to your right. Aim for the slot at the base of the mountain that rises on the east (right) side of Deadman Creek. The slot holds Divide Lake.

The lake is barely inside Idaho, being separated from Montana by a 100-foot-high cliff, which is the Continental Divide. Divide Lake is a fertile body of water with a rugged cliff on one side but otherwise surrounded by low, grassy mountains and a ring of conifers, giving an appearance reminiscent of a large meadow pond.

The last leg of this option is all downhill. Follow tiny Divide Creek from where it spills from the lake. It gurgles down the narrow, grassy canyon. The canyon deepens rapidly for a mile but then broadens out. The trail emerges onto a jeep road just above Cow Camp, where you can leave a shuttle.

—Ralph Maughan

## Miles and Directions

**0.0** Trailhead (6,940 feet)

**4.0** South Fork Webber Creek (7,510 feet)

**7.1** Trail 034 junction (8,900 feet)

**7.7** First lake (8,820 feet)

**8.3** Second lake (9,040 feet)

**9.0** Upper lake (9,560 feet)

# Island Park Area

South of the Centennial Divide and north of the Big Hole and Snake River Mountains is the Yellowstone Plateau. This area is predominantly forested with lodgepole pines and has many vast meadows similar to country in Yellowstone Park. Wildlife such as moose, deer, elk, and antelope are commonly seen.

The Island Park caldera is a geothermal hot spot like Yellowstone—but an older version, as in the Snake River Plain lava country. The Henry's Fork caldera contained within the Island Park caldera is much younger and forms a vast circular area like a crater. This is where the community of Island Park is as well as the country most noted to be Island Park.

The Henry's Fork of the Snake River is the life blood of this area. Basalt cliffs to beautiful waterfalls and cascades such as Mesa Falls are popular destinations. Many people also enjoy the Henry's Fork for its world-class fishing. The area has seen development for summer homes and is increasing in popularity, "Caldera National Monument" could become a reality if there is enough local support and politicians perservere in getting it passed. This would potentially preserve 700,000 acres.

The two hikes featured here are fun for the entire family, giving children an opportunity to enjoy hiking in this area.

*Island Park winter scene.* PHOTO BY LINDSEY TUCKER

# 76 Box Canyon

This gentle walk along the Henry's Fork of the Snake River offers chances to view wildlife and beautiful cliffs.

**Start:** In the Island Park vicinity 28 miles north of Ashton
**Type of hike:** Day hike; out-and-back
**Distance:** 6 miles round-trip
**Approximate hiking time:** 2–3 hours
**Difficulty:** Moderate
**Best season:** Mid-May–October
**Trail surface:** Normal dirt and rock
**Land status:** Caribou-Targhee National Forest
**Canine compatibility:** Leash recommended due to popularity of trail
**Fees and permits:** None
**Maps:** Island Park Dam USGS quad; Targhee-National Forest Map
**Trail contact:** Island Park Ranger District, (208) 558-7301
**Special considerations:** Mosquitoes are common after June–August hatches.

**Finding the trailhead:** On I-20, look for Riverside Road just past the Island Park Ranger Station; make a left here. Keep right on this road and park at the Box Canyon Trailhead approximately 0.2 mile farther along. GPS: N44 24.85' / W111 23.52'

*The Henry's Fork with Sawtelle in the background.* Photo by Luke Kratz

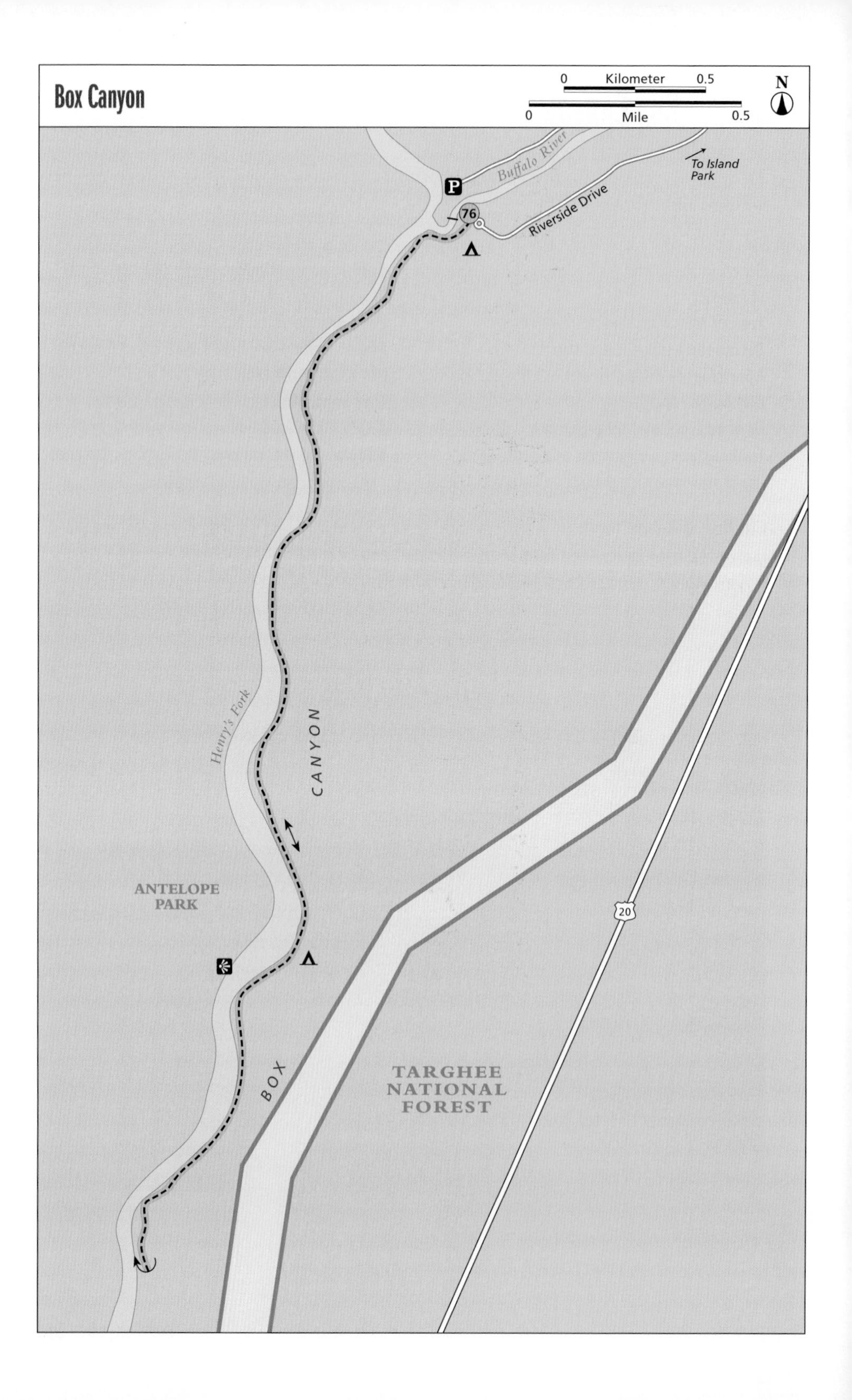

Box Canyon
0 Kilometer 0.5
0 Mile 0.5
N
Buffalo River
To Island Park
Riverside Drive
76
Henry's Fork
CANYON
BOX
ANTELOPE PARK
20
TARGHEE NATIONAL FOREST

## The Hike

The trailhead is next to the hydroelectric dam at the Buffalo River confluence. The trail continues on down the east side of the Henry's Fork. Basalt cliffs drop off between the trail and the river. You can see beautiful views of the river and cliffs on the other side. Watch for ospreys, as their nests are abundant.

After the first 0.5 mile, trails will merge from the Box Creek Campground on the right. There are also two vehicle pullouts merging with the trail. At about 2.5 miles there is a resting bench where you can view a waterfall on the other side of the river. The trail terminates shortly after a residential cabin comes to view. The way back affords views of Sawtell Peak and the Centennial mountains in addition to the river and basalt cliffs.

—Luke Kratz

## Miles and Directions

**0.0** Trailhead

**0.5** Campground entrance

**2.5** Falls

**3.0** End of trail

## DEHYDRATION

**Have you ever hiked in hot weather and had a roaring headache and felt fatigued after only a few miles? More than likely you were dehydrated. Symptoms of dehydration include fatigue, headache, and decreased coordination and judgment. When you are hiking, your body's rate of fluid loss depends on the outside temperature, humidity, altitude, and your activity level. On average, a hiker walking in warm weather will lose four liters of fluid a day. That fluid loss is easily replaced by normal consumption of liquids and food. However, if a hiker is walking briskly in hot, dry weather and hauling a heavy pack, he or she can lose one to three liters of water an hour. It's important to always carry plenty of water and to stop often and drink fluids regularly, even if you aren't thirsty.**

# 77 Coffee Pot Rapids

A pretty and popular area along the Henry's Fork.

**Start:** 35 miles north of Ashton
**Type of hike:** Day hike; out-and-back
**Distance:** 5 miles round-trip
**Approximate hiking time:** 2–3 hours
**Difficulty:** Moderate until the last 0.5 mile climb to Coffee Pot Road which then becomes strenuous
**Best season:** May–November
**Trail surface:** Normal dirt and rocky areas
**Land status:** Caribou-Targhee National Forest
**Canine compatibility:** Voice command
**Fees and permits:** None
**Maps:** Island Park Dam USGS quad; Targhee National Forest map
**Trail contact:** Island Park Ranger District, (208) 558-7301

**Finding the trailhead:** Take I-20 north from Ashton to Island Park. At 31 miles from Ashton, turn left at the Upper Coffee Pot Campground sign onto FSR 130. After 1.8 miles make a right onto FSR 311; follow signs to the campground where the trail begins. GPS: N44 29.44' / W111 22.06'

## The Hike

In 1865 George Rea became the first homesteader in the area. He was canoeing down the calm scenic Henry's Fork one day until he unexpectedly hit a spot of large boulders and gushing white water. His supplies and canoe had all become lost in the rapids except for one small coffee pot giving this trail its name.

The popular hike follows the Henry's Fork, initially heading downstream along calm and tranquil waters. Lodgepole pine and Douglas fir trees dominate the forest growth. Shiras moose are very common here. Also watch for raptors.

After 2 miles the rapids begin cutting through rock and deadfall. The billowing white waters are a sight to behold. Keep to the trail and make sure any canine friends do as well. The rapids go on for less than 0.5 mile until the river returns to a normal flow. The trail surface becomes more rocky and crosses a large rockslide area near the river. This can be a trap for unaware or overconfident ankles! It then veers left up the rocky hillside and joins with Coffee Pot Road. At this point you can walk Coffee Pot Road back nearly 3 miles to the campground or return the way you came.

—Luke Kratz

## Miles and Directions

**0.0** Trailhead
**0.5** ATV trail
**2.0** Ascent to Coffee Pot Road
**2.5** Coffee Pot Road

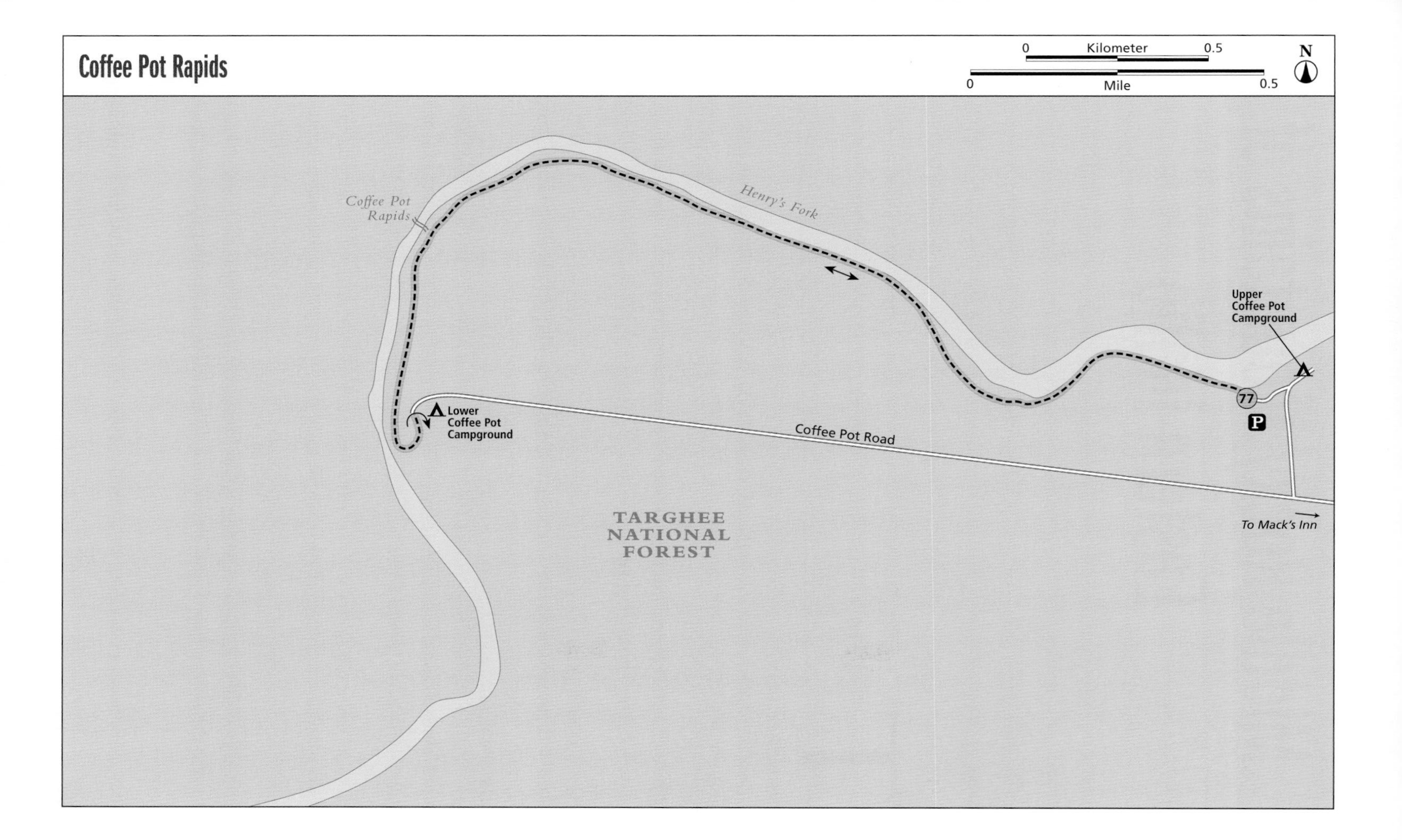
Coffee Pot Rapids
0
Kilometer
0.5
0
Mile
0.5
N
Coffee Pot Rapids
Henry's Fork
Upper Coffee Pot Campground
77
P
Lower Coffee Pot Campground
Coffee Pot Road
TARGHEE NATIONAL FOREST
To Mack's Inn

# Middle Rocky Mountains of Eastern Idaho

The Rocky Mountains include perhaps a hundred mountain ranges, extending from the Yukon Territory on the north to New Mexico on the south. In the lower forty-eight states, they are often broken into three sections, or physiographic provinces (a fancy name for an awful lot of beautiful country).

Northern Colorado to northern New Mexico is the Southern Rockies. The mountains northwest of Yellowstone in Montana and Idaho are the Northern Rockies. In Idaho this includes primarily the Selkirk, Salmon River, Clearwater, Boulder, White Cloud, Pioneer, Smoky, and Soldier Mountains described in this guide.

The Middle Rockies begin with the Wasatch and Uinta Ranges in Utah and bump northward along the Idaho-Wyoming border to just north of Yellowstone National Park. In Wyoming, some of these ranges are very well known: the Wind Rivers, Bighorn, Gros Ventre, Tetons, and Absaroka. The Middle Rockies of eastern Idaho include some fabulous country, and we have spent years enjoying them, but the names will not sound familiar to many: the Big Holes, Snake River Range, Caribou Range, Bear River Range, Aspen Range, Gray's Range, Pruess Range, Gannett Hills, and Webster Range.

Unlike the relentlessly granitic Wind Rivers or the pile of welded volcanic ash that is the Absaroka, all of the Middle Rockies in Idaho consist of soft sedimentary rock in what is known geologically as the Overthrust Belt, a place of amazingly broken and complicated geology. This is where gigantic forces pushed the rock layers eastward, one on top of another, until they overturned, hence the term *overthrust*. The result is that older limestone, shale, dolomite, siltstone, and so forth often rest on top of younger rocks thousands of feet below the older rock. There are many variations among the ranges. This is also earthquake country. The forces that made the mountains are not yet spent.

Throughout much of the area can be found the phosphoria formation from which phosphate fertilizer is made. One result of this is very fertile mountains with large

*Rocky outcroppings along thickly forested slopes in Snake River Mountains.* PHOTO BY LUKE KRATZ

herds of big deer and elk. Were it not for all the livestock, this could be the most productive wildlife area in the West.

The eastern Idaho Middle Rockies range from high, glaciated peaks, such as those found in the Snake River Range, to steep hills with rounded tops, such as the Gannett Hills. Because of the softness of the rock, mountain lakes are fewer in number than in the Northern Rockies. The topography, geology, and climate, however, produce here the largest aspen forests in Idaho. Wildlife includes, as mentioned, elk and deer but also moose, mountain goat, cougar, black bear, bobcat, wolverine, coyote, fox, and an occasional wolf or grizzly bear migrating from Wyoming.

Another feature these mountains have in common is their instability. Mudflows, landslides, and blowouts are common, as are avalanches wherever the topography is steep. Unlike central Idaho, where the forest understory is usually grouse whortleberry, huckleberry, or sagebrush, wherever it lacks enough water for a wet meadow, tall perennial flowers predominate along the Idaho-Wyoming border. Unlike the short flowers of alpine meadows, these are flower fields you can actually get lost in.

—Ralph Maughan

# Big Hole, Snake River, and Caribou Mountains

These ranges hug the border of Idaho and Wyoming. The Big Hole and the Snake River Ranges are really the same mountain range, but an arbitrary division between them was made at Pine Creek Canyon. The Caribou Mountains are the next range to the west, separated from the former by Swan Valley and Palisades Reservoir.

The Big Hole–Snake River Range emerges out of the volcanic rock of the Snake River Plain, just south of Rexburg, Idaho. It begins as a generally forested, semicircular area of steep, but relatively low and intensively dissected mountains. Of course, this makes for many trail possibilities due to the number of canyons and ridges, and these mountains have a lot of trails. Unfortunately, most of them are not well maintained.

Farther to the southeast, the Big Hole–Snake Rivers rise about 1,500 to 2,000 feet higher than the northern section, topping out at more than 10,000 feet at Mount Baird. The general form of the mountains remains the same, however. Even more to the south, this range pushes on into Wyoming, where it is called the Salt River Range, with some peaks that top 11,000 feet. This fine area is described in *Hiking Wyoming,* Globe Pequot Press.

The Caribou Range is a relatively unknown range despite its length, beauty, and abundant wildlife. These mountains parallel the Big Hole–Snake River and Salt River Mountains, which lie across the valley to the east. The topography is rather unique, consisting of numerous ridges interspersed with small, high-elevation stream valleys. They are not as high as the Big Hole–Snake River Range, but they have more forest because fewer avalanches scour it away here.

Both of these mountain ranges are very well watered compared with others in the Middle Rockies to their southwest and especially the Basin and Range Mountains even farther west. As a result, these mountains have many good fishing streams, although the natural instability of the Caribou Range makes fisheries vulnerable if roads are built or timber harvested.

These ranges, like all of the Middle Rockies of Idaho, are mountains built entirely of sedimentary rocks, pushed into complicated jumbles by thrust faulting. The material of these mountains (and of all mountains near the Wyoming border) was once many miles to the west. It was pushed eastward by the forces of continental drift.

This geology allows for hypothetical pockets of oil and natural gas. The oil industry has been exploring the Overthrust Belt of eastern Idaho for almost a generation, but this interest waned in the 1990s. All wells drilled failed to locate commercial quantities of oil or natural gas, but the oil companies used the area's potential to wage a strong campaign against wilderness designation. These mountains are managed much more for wildlife and recreation today than they were in the 1980s, but are still vulnerable to drilling and mining pursuits.

These mountains are full of wildlife. Especially notable are the elk herds of the Caribou Range, but deer, mountain goats, bighorn sheep, and moose are also present. The population of mountain goats, which centers on the Mount Baird area, has shown an impressive increase in numbers. Moose, once relatively rare, have also increased greatly.

The Big Hole and the Snake River Ranges abut a vast area of wild country to their north and northeast in Wyoming—the Greater Yellowstone country. You can hike from US 26 at the south end of the Snake Rivers northward to the Tetons and Yellowstone National Park and only cross one paved highway and one dirt road. The rest is wild. Moreover, the Big Holes, Snakes, and Salt Rivers provide an important corridor for big game to migrate from the Yellowstone country down to southwestern Wyoming, eastern Idaho, and northern Utah. In fact, this is how moose reinhabited Utah.

The entire area is geologically active, and tremors frequently shake the state border. Another large quake is possible at any time.

The Big Hole and Caribou Ranges, due to their relatively low elevation, provide early-summer hiking. The 220,000-acre roadless area in the core of the Snake River Range, which is named the Palisades Backcountry, is large enough to allow you a weeklong backpacking vacation. Several other roadless areas more than 60,000 acres in size are located in these two ranges.

Idaho and Wyoming environmentalists have been trying for years to protect these roadless areas as designated wilderness. They have been successful in keeping them roadless, but unless wilderness designation arrives soon, these pristine areas may fall to the oil companies and the increasingly well-funded dirt bike and all-terrain vehicle lobbies.

—Ralph Maughan

*Beautiful waterfalls.* PHOTO BY RALPH MAUGHAR

# 78 Black Canyon to Big Burns

This is an early-season hike near Idaho Falls. There are low but steep and rugged mountains, cloaked with beautiful mixed forest with some impressive cliffs.

**Start:** 35 miles east of Idaho Falls in the Big Hole Mountains
**Type of hike:** Day hike or overnight near-loop
**Distance:** 10.5 miles one way
**Approximate hiking time:** 5–7 hours or overnight
**Difficulty:** Moderate
**Best season:** Mid-June (or when Big Burns Creek can be forded) through September. Late May is okay for day hikes
**Trail surface:** Normal dirt and rock
**Land status:** Caribou-Targhee National Forest
**Canine compatibility:** Voice command
**Fees and permits:** None
**Maps:** Garns Mountain and Wheaton Mountain USGS quadrangles; Island Park, Ashton, Teton Basin, and Palisades Ranger Districts–Targhee National Forest map
**Trail contact:** Palisades Ranger District, (208) 523-1412, www.fs.usda.gov/ctnf
**Special considerations:** Fishing is prohibited in Big Burns Creek until July to protect the spawning Snake River fine-spotted cutthroat trout. Bring wading shoes if you want to do the Little Burns section of the hike. This hike has a gap of about 0.75 mile that can be made up by walking the road or leaving a shuttle at each trailhead.

**Finding the trailhead:** From Idaho Falls, drive east on US 26 for 11 miles past its junction with ID 43. Here, turn off US 26 to the left onto the paved road at the Kelly Canyon Recreation Area sign. Follow this road north, crossing numerous canals, for about 2 miles until you reach a Y intersection. Bear right onto CR 100 North, and head generally east. The road winds for a mile and crosses the South Fork of the Snake River.

Turn right as you cross the bridge onto the paved Heise Road. In a mile you pass the Heise Hot Springs resort; a mile past the hot springs, the road forks again. The paved road to the left goes to Kelly Canyon ski area. Instead, take the gravel road to the right, which follows the South Fork of the Snake River for 14.2 miles in a very scenic drive to the mouth of Big Burns Canyon. It's another 1.5 miles to the mouth of Black Canyon. The road goes up Black Canyon 0.4 mile and ends at a trailhead. In some places the road is good 40-mile-per-hour, all-weather gravel, while in others you slow to 10 miles per hour to bump over ungraded basalt outcrops or large-diameter gravel. The road varies from two lanes to just a single lane. Seven miles past the junction from Kelly Canyon Road, the gravel county road becomes FR 206.

Traffic is heavy on weekends and holidays. Folks love this stretch of the South Fork, which has fine fishing, abundant wildlife, and the largest cottonwood forest in Idaho. GPS: N43 36.36' / W111 27.98'

**Parking and trailhead facilities:** The Black Canyon Trailhead is unshaded and undeveloped except for a loading ramp. There is room for about five vehicles. The Burns Creek Trailhead is 0.75 mile down a side road that turns left from FR 206. The trailhead is partly shaded and also undeveloped. There is room for about eight vehicles.

## The Hike

The South Fork of the Snake River, particularly in the vicinity of Big Burns Creek and upstream, provides extraordinary wildlife habitat. Moose, elk, deer, bear, bighorn sheep, and all types of waterfowl frequent the area. It's also a nesting area for bald and golden eagles.

Thousands of fishers and hunters boat the South Fork each year. Here, between Big Burns and Black Canyon, dozens of fertile and slightly warm springs emerge just below the dirt road, bursting into riparian ponds brimming with wildlife.

For years, various dams that would destroy this river were promoted. Originally a high dam at the mouth of Big Burns Creek was planned. It would have backed water all the way to Palisades Reservoir, displacing hundreds of people along with wildlife. In recent years plans for dams have faded as the federal government has stopped building dams; now, instead of dams, plans by numerous developers for recreational subdivisions have to be fought.

Assuming you begin at Black Canyon, you follow an obvious trail used by ATVs, trail machines, mountain bikes, horses, and hikers. The trail is pleasant and not especially busy, nor is it eroded.

The path is mostly forested, and the forest is diverse with cottonwood, aspen, chokecherry, Gambel oak, red osier dogwood, wild rose, snowberry, spirea, Douglas fir, juniper, and Engelmann spruce.

After 0.3 mile you come to the first of eight to ten creek crossings. The number may vary over time as the creek changes its course. Most have informal log crossings—but don't count on them. If you must ford, it is easy, and by midsummer you can walk across on rocks.

After the last creek crossing (2.2 miles from the starting point), the trail turns and climbs quickly into a small, steep side canyon. The spring at the bottom of the side canyon is the last water until you reach Little Burns Creek.

Now you march a rousing 1,200-foot climb to the Black Canyon–Little Burns divide (7,800 feet). The trail becomes faint but stays to the bottom of the side canyon, where the shade of the Douglas fir keeps it from becoming a bramble way. Just before the divide, you'll emerge from the forest into a clearing. If you walk out to the point overlooking Black Canyon, you get quite a view downcanyon over green forest to the Snake River at the base of the mountains and to the farmlands beyond. Upcanyon

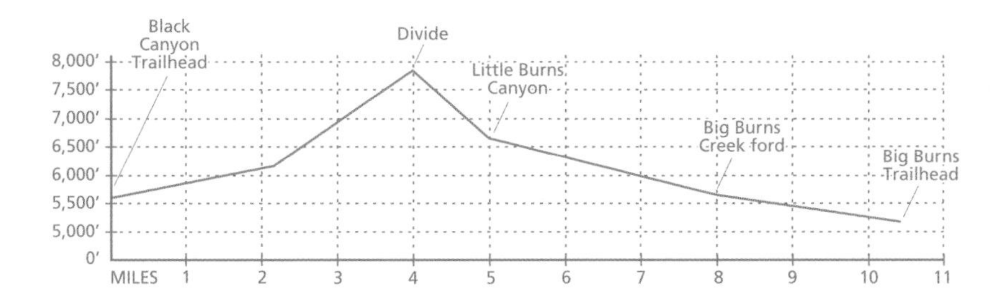

you look right at the face of Black Mountain, its gray, flat-bedded sedimentary slopes scoured by thousands of winters of avalanches.

At the divide, a signed trail continues to climb up the ridge. It leads on to the West Fork of Pine Creek, a nice nonmotorized trail but with about 20 creek crossings. Your trail leads to the left down the ridge. Then, after about 50 yards, it drops steeply into Little Burns Creek for a switchbacking 1,000-foot descent. You pass many forest windows looking across Little Burns to the divide between it and Big Burns Canyon.

After a mile of descent, as the headwater rivulets of Little Burns Creek flow together, you'll reach a trail junction. Here Little Burns Creek Trail splits as it comes toward you. To the right, a well-signed trail fork climbs out of Little Burns and offers access to many trails after crossing the shoulder of Piney Peak. Go to the left here and continue down Little Burns Canyon. Just below this trail junction are some clearings.

Little Burns is a narrow, very scenic, well-vegetated canyon. It is closed to grazing. There are many unimpeded views of the canyon slopes, which are covered with fir, aspen, and brush, with balding spots near the rims.

The trail is not wide, but it's easy to follow because unfortunately some machine riders are gouging their way down into Little Burns.

The trail is well bounded by brush (much of it wild rose and many berries that are ripe in August). The trail fords Little Burns Creek five times in the upper reaches and four in the lower part of the canyon. For 0.75 mile in the middle, there are no crossings. At the bottom of the canyon, you are greeted with a ford of Big Burns Creek. This is cold and swift through June, but only moderately difficult even early in the season. There are three nice big springs in Little Burns; one is exceptionally beautiful.

After wading Big Burns Creek, you step out into a much larger canyon with forested slopes hiding most of the rough limestone cliffs. The canyon bottom is quite meadowy in its middle reaches, and there are many flat places. The trail is easy to find and easy to walk on. Flowers bloom through June.

The creek looks like fine fishing, and it is, but both Big Burns and Little Burns Creeks are closed to fishing until late in the summer. In them spawn the rare Snake River fine-spotted cutthroat trout.

From the confluence of Little Burns Creek, the trail goes down Big Burns for 3 miles to the trailhead. You pass side trails that lead up Jensen Creek and Hell Hole Canyon. Despite what the map shows, you never have to ford Big Burns Creek again. The lower miles of the canyon are an impressive walk below large cliffs, more so than in Black Canyon.

During the weekdays, you will see few people in these canyons. On weekends, expect to see day hikers and a few trail machines in the lower stretches. Motorized vehicles can't make it very far up Big Burns because of a stretch of trail along a narrow cliff.

For years Idaho conservationists have been trying to protect the backcountry and possible future wilderness designation for this area. In the 1970s and 1980s, they were stymied by the oil companies. Now the problem comes from trail bike and ATV enthusiasts who claim "historic use" of the area. I guess history is a lot shorter today than it used to be.

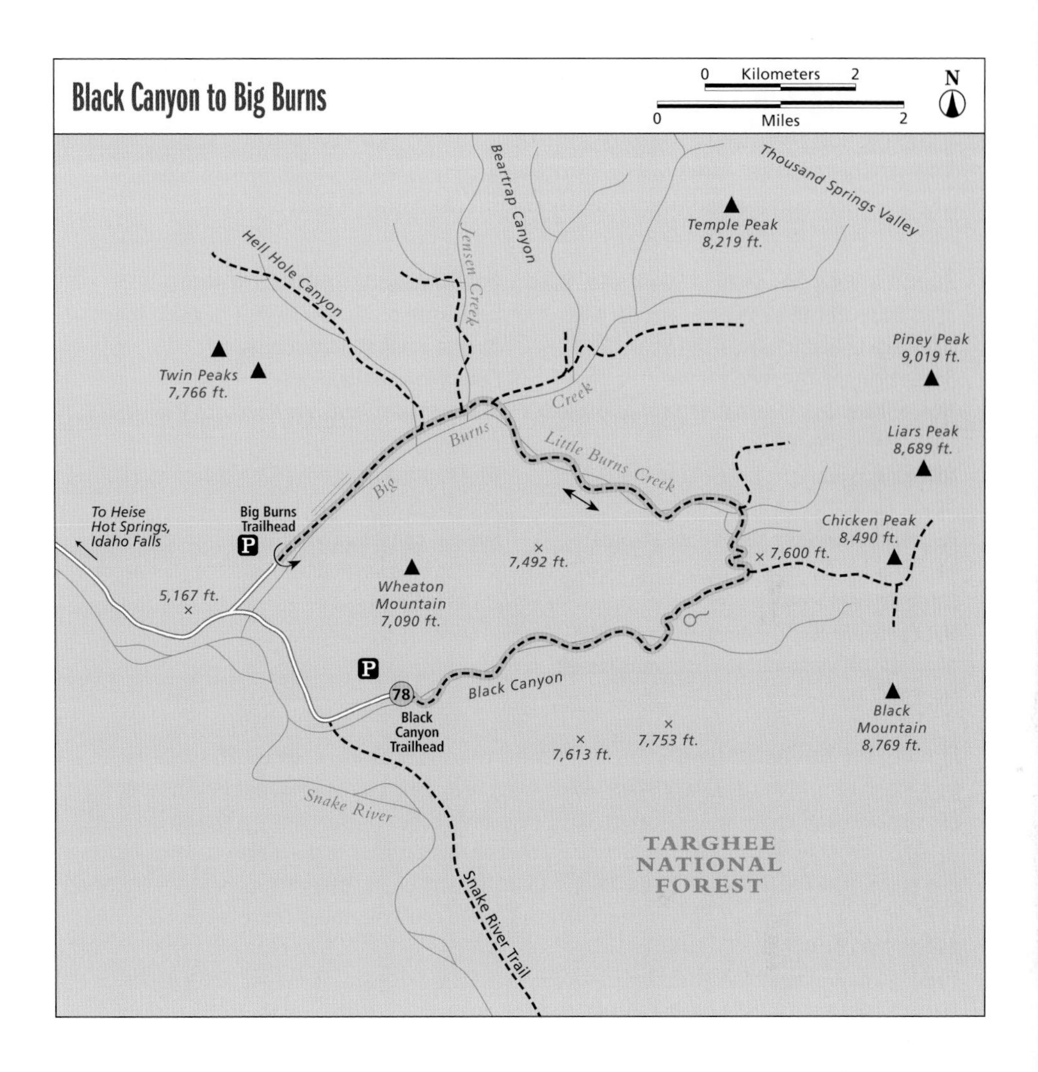


**Options:** Snake River Trail begins at the mouth of Black Canyon and heads south along the base of the Big Hole Mountains. This is a wonderful June hike.

—Ralph Maughan

## Miles and Directions

- **0.0** Black Canyon Trailhead (5,560 feet)
- **2.2** Start of climb out of Black Canyon (6,190 feet)
- **4.0** Black Canyon–Little Burns divide (7,800 feet)
- **5.0** Little Burns Canyon (6,640 feet)
- **8.0** Ford of Big Burns Creek (5,635 feet)
- **10.5** Big Burns Trailhead (5,250 feet)

# 79 Big Elk Creek

This is a big pristine canyon closed to motorized vehicles and livestock. Many avalanche chutes and rugged mountains surround the lushly forested creek area.

**Start:** 17 road miles south of Swan Valley, 3.5 miles south of Palisades Dam, and 50 miles southeast of Idaho Falls, in the Snake River Range near the Wyoming border
**Type of hike:** Day hike, out-and-back, to a long backpack with extended loops
**Distance:** 13 miles round-trip to the Siddoway Fork
**Approximate hiking time:** Plan at least 7 hours for the full hike
**Difficulty:** Moderately easy
**Best season:** July–September (to the Wyoming line); August for the upper reaches of Big Elk Creek
**Trail surface:** Normal dirt and rock
**Land status:** Caribou-Targhee National Forest
**Canine compatibility:** On leash
**Fees and permits:** None
**Maps:** Mount Baird and Palisades Peak USGS quadrangles
**Trail contact:** Palisades Ranger District, (208) 523-1412
**Special considerations:** Wading shoes if you want to hike upstream beyond the confluence of Cabin Creek

**Finding the trailhead:** Drive on US 26 north from Alpine, Wyoming, or on US 26 southeast from Idaho Falls, Idaho, passing through Swan Valley and along part of Palisades Reservoir. At the Big Elk Creek arm of the reservoir, which is 14 road miles south of Swan Valley, a signed dirt road to Big Elk Creek leaves the highway. Drive 2.5 miles on this dirt road to the trailhead, which is the end of the road. The road is on a steep slope above the arm of the reservoir for about a mile. Drive carefully because there are tight curves. Oncoming traffic could put you in the reservoir. GPS: N43 19.55' / W111 06.61'
**Parking and trailhead facilities:** The trailhead is a large parking area in full sun. You'll find a loading ramp and pit toilet nearby and an organization's camp just south of the trailhead. Expect things to be busy.

## The Hike

Less used than Palisades Creek, Big Elk Creek is busy nevertheless. It has an easy trail (Trail 097) leading up a broad, open, scenic canyon. Your hike in this canyon can be as short as a couple of hours, or you can turn it into a four- or five-day exploration

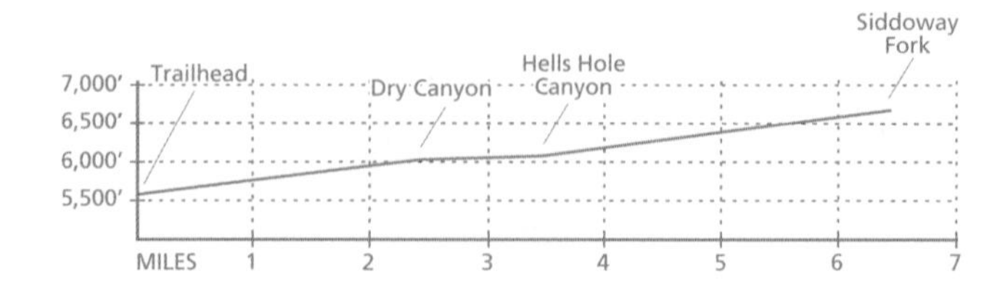

*View up Big Elk Creek from road.* PHOTO BY LUKE KRATZ

of the Snake River Range. Happily, this trail, like the Palisades Creek and the Little Elk Creek Trails, was closed to trail bikes beginning in the mid-1980s. And perhaps best of all, most of it is closed to livestock grazing, which makes wildlife abundant.

Walk from your vehicle up a short sidehill and into the forest, almost immediately crossing a perennial spring. Like Palisades Creek, Big Elk is a substantial stream, running swift and cold into midsummer. The trail does not cross the creek until you are almost to the Siddoway Fork of Big Elk Creek, far upstream (6.5 miles).

For more than 3 miles, the canyon stays wide, offering frequent scenic views of the steep, partially forested slopes of the Snake River Range as you pass in and out of the patchy forest with some big Douglas fir by the trail and cottonwood by the creek. The patchiness is the result of avalanches, to which these mountains are very prone. Most of the chutes run year after year, so they don't fill with trees. Some have carved deep gullies. Occasionally avalanches will run in new places and take out trees,

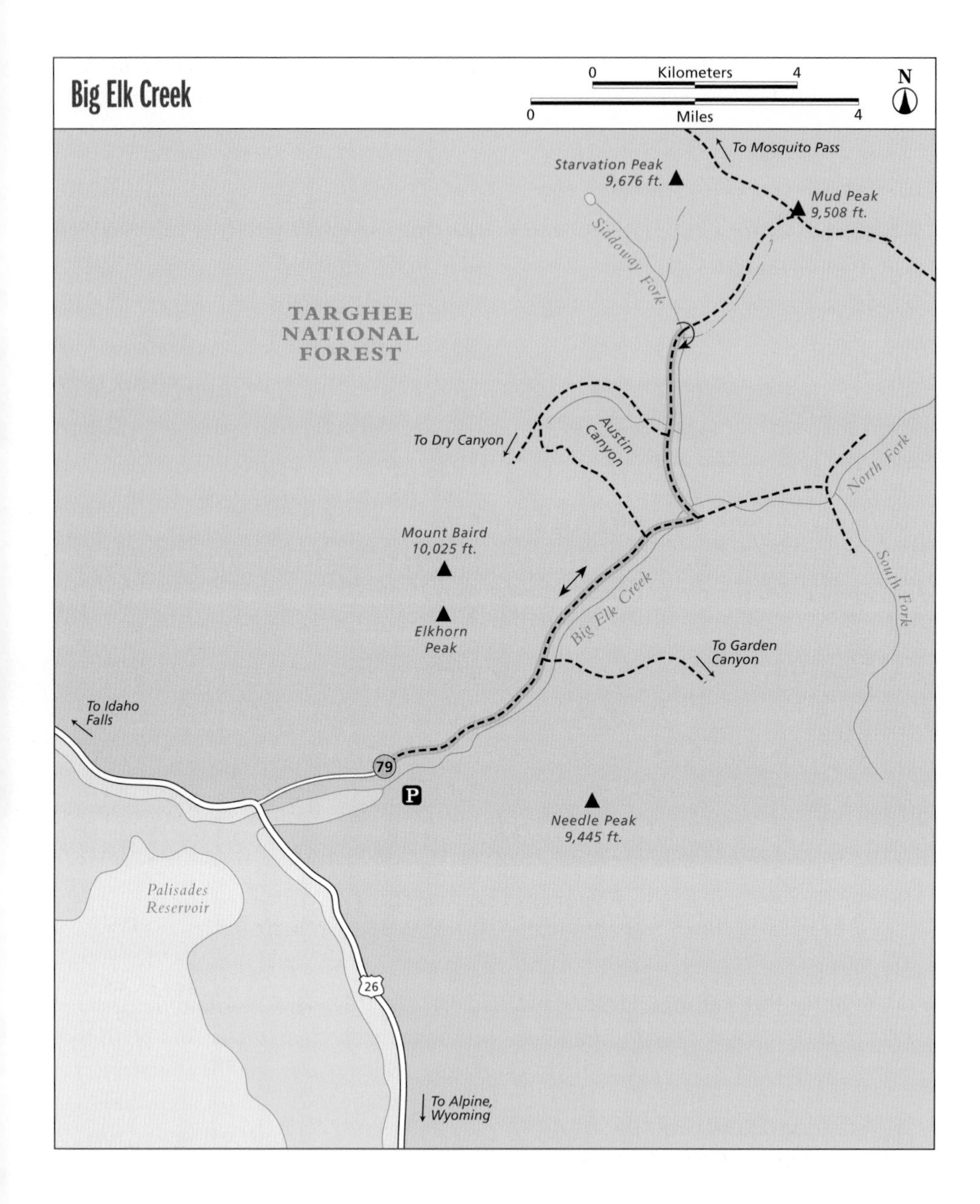


causing huge piles of debris. Although debris piles are uncommon in the Big Elk, there are still perhaps a hundred well-established avalanche chutes in this canyon.

The canyon narrows as you pass Hells Hole Canyon at about 3.5 miles, and the trail follows alongside the stream. Limestone walls rise steeply for 600 feet above you. Just past this gorge, in early summer to midsummer, a falls leaps over an alcove to the left of the trail and onto a bed of grass and tall wildflowers. In this vicinity, you cross into Wyoming.

As you approach the Cabin Creek tributary, the forest thickens. The swamps under the trees look like moose habitat, which indeed they are. The forest service keeps this area ungrazed by domestic livestock.

A very scenic, but faint, trail (Trail 101) in the Cabin Creek drainage leads up over the ridge and onto the meadowy top of Austin Canyon. This, however, involves a difficult 2,100-foot climb. It's easier to do this side hike in the other direction, from Austin Canyon to Cabin Creek.

The main trail crosses Big Elk Creek just below its confluence with the Siddoway Fork (6.5 miles from the trailhead). You can't ford the stream until early July, although a tough 0.25-mile bushwhack and scramble can get you into the Siddoway Fork as much as three weeks before you can wade across the Big Elk. Big Elk Trail crosses the creek and then climbs over a shoulder of a forested ridge to avoid a gorge. Above the gorge, it drops back into the bottom of Big Elk.

The main trail crosses Big Elk Creek several more times in the remaining 1.5 miles from the first ford to the junction of the North Fork and South Fork of Big Elk. This section is best hiked in late July or August to avoid high water.

The forks of Big Elk Creek have beautiful, subalpine elk summer pasture. Unlike lower Big Elk, which is livestock-free, sheep are put in the uplands about August 1. Check with the forest service if you want to avoid the sheep.

**Options:** The Siddoway Fork is a substantial tributary canyon, narrower than Big Elk Creek. Trail 167 winds up this canyon through many delightful little meadows and patches of forest. The canyon runs north to south at a right angle to Big Elk. After 1.5 miles, Siddoway Fork Trail gives you access to pretty Austin Canyon Trail (Trail 105) or to the main crest of the mountain range running north and south between Swan Valley and Jackson Hole.

Three miles up Big Elk Creek, a trail (Trail 125) crosses Big Elk and goes up Dry Canyon. There appears to be a trail, or maybe just a route, from Dry Canyon over into Garden Canyon, a very scenic place that drains into the North Fork of Indian Creek.

—Ralph Maughan

## Miles and Directions

**0.0** Trailhead (5,650 feet)

**2.5** Dry Canyon side hike (6,020 feet)

**3.4** Hells Hole side canyon (6,120 feet)

**4.5** Wyoming state line

**6.5** Siddoway Fork (6,520 feet)

# 80 Little Elk Creek

There are some beautiful views in the highest part of the Snake River Range up this creek. No livestock or motor vehicles are allowed.

**Start:** 2.5 miles south of Palisades Dam; 13 miles south of Swan Valley; about 50 miles southeast of Idaho Falls
**Type of hike:** Long day hike; out-and-back, with options for backpacks (shuttle)
**Distance:** 8 miles round-trip
**Approximate hiking time:** 6–7 hours
**Difficulty:** Strenuous due to the climb
**Best season:** Mid-July–mid-September
**Trail surface:** Normal dirt and rock
**Land status:** Caribou-Targhee National Forest
**Canine compatibility:** On leash
**Fees and permits:** None
**Maps:** Mount Baird and Palisades Dam USGS quadrangles
**Trail contact:** Palisades Ranger District, (208) 523-1412
**Special considerations:** In most years, you will have to carry all your water.

**Finding the trailhead:** To get to Little Elk Creek, drive from Idaho Falls to Palisades Dam on US 26. Once you pass the dam at the reservoir's north end, it's another 2.5 miles to the Little Elk Creek turnoff on your left (east). This is at the scenic Little Elk arm of the reservoir. The gravel road leads in for about a mile to where the creek in Spring Run Canyon forks with Little Elk Creek.

Just before the fork with spring-fed Spring Run Creek, park at the trailhead. Here, trails take off to both the right and the left. Take the trail to the right. GPS: N43 20.28' / W111 08.76'

**Parking and trailhead facilities:** The trailhead is small and has room for three or four vehicles. I found that nonhiking RV campers may take over the trailhead. This is not legal, and I turned them in. The comparatively faint Little Elk trail goes right up the canyon from the trailhead, although the area has become obscured by uncontrolled ATV use.

## The Hike

Little Elk Creek is not a trail for the weak or inexperienced. It's a long, steep 4 miles. From the trail's beginning at 5,960 feet to your destination, a nameless mountain at 9,200 feet, it's a 3,240-foot climb.

The first third of the hike is forested, and the beginning is deceptively gentle, but as soon as you pass by Conglomerate Canyon 1 mile from the trailhead, the route becomes increasingly steep. Sometimes there is water in parts of the stream, such as near Elbow Canyon and in midcanyon, but don't count on it. Carry 4 liters of liquid or more for a day hike.

Begin with a pleasant walk through an open aspen, cottonwood, and conifer forest. The trail climbs gently to where Elbow Canyon joins. There is often water in the creek here in midsummer. Between Elbow and the next side canyon, Conglomerate, the grade steepens. Just downstream from Conglomerate, you come to large swath of outwash gravel from snowmelt or the thunderstorm waters that sometimes run out of Conglomerate.

Once past Conglomerate, you really begin to climb. You climb steeply under trees and soon brush up the left (north) side of the canyon. The brush is due to the great avalanches that scour the canyon. The openness provides very good views of the canyon and the Caribou Range across Palisades Reservoir due west, behind you.

The very steep trail continues until you pass through some small scenic cliffs at elevation 6,800 to 7,200 feet. Here, there may be water in the creek in early summer. Past the cliffs, at about 7,400 feet, the grade lessens and you pass into what is obviously an upper part of the canyon. At 2 miles in and 7,500 feet elevation, you cross the creek (which will probably be dry) to the right side.

Now the trail climbs through a mostly open canyon with patches of conifers. Although you are under Mount Baird, the highest peak in the range, you can't see it. Instead, the view is dominated by the cliffs of Point 9,345 on your left, a point on Sheep Creek Peak.

You continue at a steady rate until you reach the top of the canyon. Then the grade steepens and the trail begins to switchback. This climb begins at 8,200 feet and continues very steeply to about 8,800 feet, where the grade lessens and you break into the open and finally see Mount Baird (10,025 feet).

The grade continues, however, until you top out on a high saddle at about 9,200 feet. From here, the trail quickly drops into the head of Waterfall Canyon (see Hike 84, Waterfall Canyon) and near the many connecting trails in the area.

While you are in the high country, look for mountain goats. This is the core of their range, and the herd is growing.

Once on top, you can enjoy the view of the reservoir behind you (to the west), the unnamed 9,000-foot-plus peaks all about, Palisades Peak (9,778 feet) and Little Palisades Peak (9,707 feet) ahead, and the Tetons in the distance beyond them. Mount Baird dominates the view to the southeast.

**Options:** There are many options, most of which are described in Hike 84, Waterfall Canyon. You can also climb Mount Baird. From the 8,800-foot contour on the Little Elk side of the high saddle, there is a pretty area of basins. Mount Baird rises right at the end of the basin. Walk through the basins, curve east, and gain the ridgeline. It is narrow, but you walk on it almost to the top of Baird. The last 0.25 mile is a scramble.

—Ralph Maughan

## Miles and Directions

**0.0** Trailhead (5,960 feet)

**0.5** Elbow Canyon (6,120 feet)

**1.0** Conglomerate Canyon (6,500 feet)

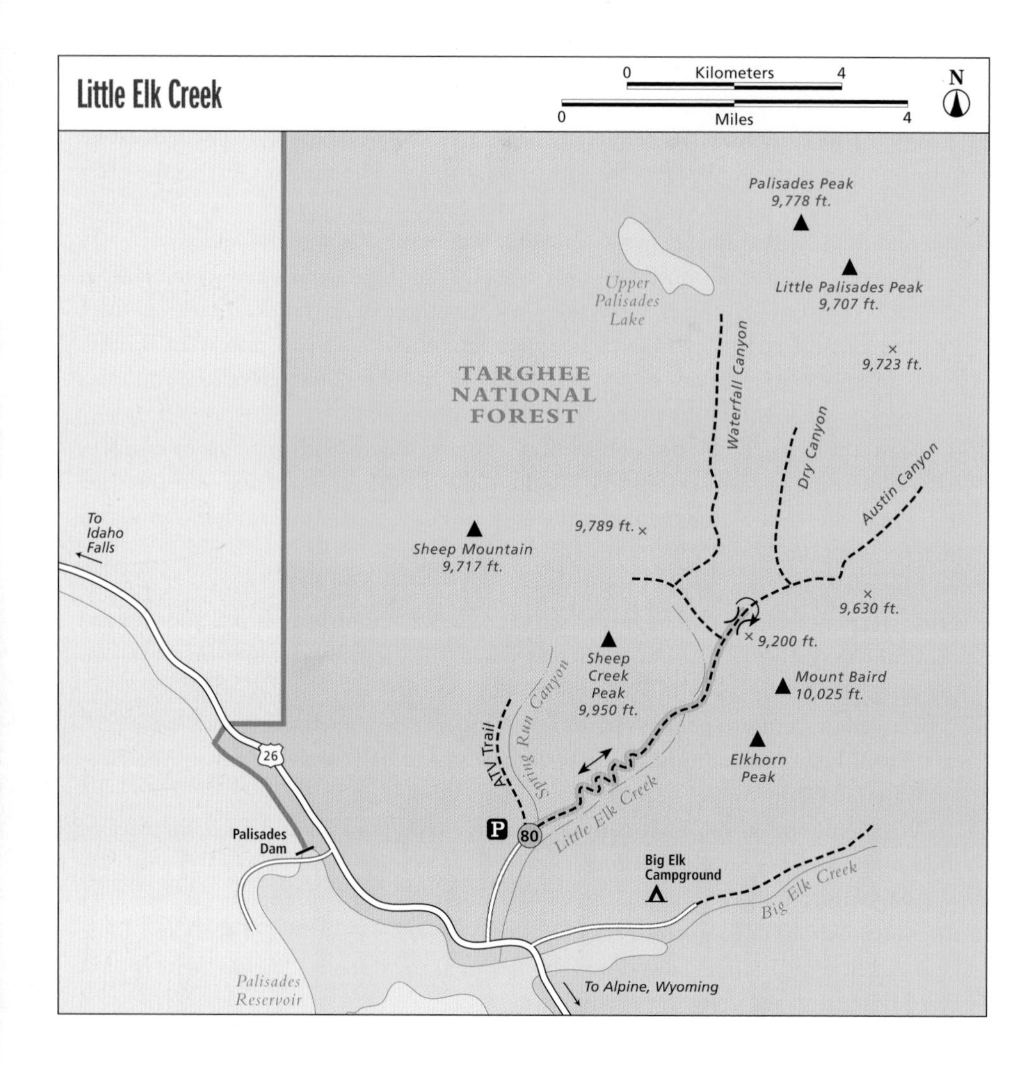


**2.0** Cross Little Elk Creek to right (7,500 feet)

**3.2** Head of canyon; switchbacks begin (8,300 feet)

**4.0** Crest of range on high, broad saddle (9,200 feet)

# 81 Palisades Creek

View the exquisitely beautiful cliffs looming over a large stream as well as wildlife due to no livestock grazing or motorized use.

**Start:** Near the Wyoming border, about 45 miles east of Idaho Falls in the Snake River Range
**Type of hike:** A long day hike or overnight; out-and-back, but with some possible strenuous loops in conjunction with other trails
**Distance:** 12 miles round-trip
**Approximate hiking time:** 5–6 hours
**Difficulty:** Easy
**Best season:** Early June–mid-October
**Trail surface:** Normal dirt and rock
**Land status:** Caribou-Targhee National Forest
**Canine compatibility:** On leash recommended due to popularity of trail
**Fees and permits:** None
**Maps:** Palisades Peak and Thompson Peak USGS quadrangles; Island Park, Ashton, Teton Basin, and Palisades Ranger Districts–Targhee National Forest map
**Trail contact:** Palisades Ranger District, (208) 523-1412
**Special considerations:** There are just two places along this trail where camping is permitted.

**Finding the trailhead:** Drive about 52 miles from Idaho Falls eastward on US 26. Continue through the small towns of Swan Valley and Irwin, and turn left onto a gravel road at the unincorporated community of Palisades. The sign reads PALISADES CREEK, FOREST ROAD 255. After 1.8 miles this gravel road ends at Palisades Campground, set in the mouth of the V-shaped opening to mountain beauty beyond. Parking for hikers is to the left just before the campground entrance and just before the bridge over Palisades Creek. The horse transfer area is on the other side of the bridge and to the right. GPS: N43 23.73' / W111 12.91'
**Parking and trailhead facilities:** Seven campsites, potable water, latrines. The trailhead has room for about ten vehicles at the hiker's parking lot and is often filled to capacity. There are separate trailheads for hikers and horses, although they soon share the same trail. Walk to the east end of the campground (upstream), and you find the beginning of the trail for hikers.

## The Hike

Walk past the forest service information sign and into the narrow mouth of the canyon. Palisades Creek splashes beside the trail (earlier in the season, it thunders). The creek never gets very low because much of its flow comes from year-round springs emerging far up the canyon and up its tributaries. Fortunately, the creek is bridged all the way (except for the remote upper canyon, which is not described in this hike). You cross six bridges.

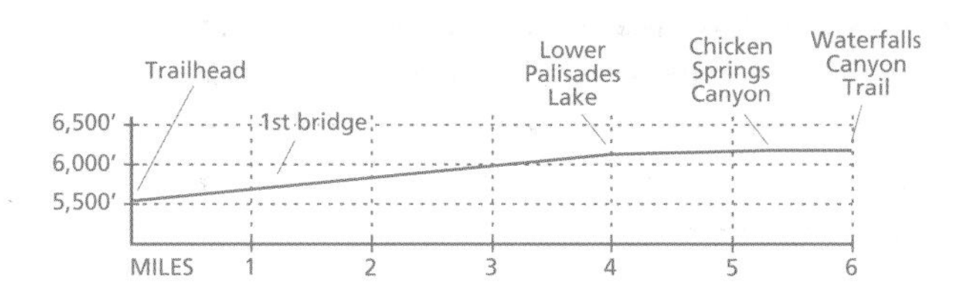

*Upper Palisades Lake.* PHOTO BY LUKE KRATZ

Despite the rugged, steep walls of the canyon, its bottom is forested, shaded by both conifers and deciduous trees. From its beginning at the campground, Palisades Canyon is 2,000 feet deep. Farther upstream it's well over 3,000 feet deep.

The horse trail quickly joins the hiker's trail. The trail follows the creek closely, passing under Douglas fir and towering cottonwoods. After 1.3 miles, near the first bridge, the canyon opens into a large amphitheater. Here, temporarily out of the forest that fills the canyon, you can see the great cliffs lining the side slopes. Look for mountain goats.

After the first bridge, the trail climbs about 75 feet up the north side of the canyon, and the trail proceeds 3 more miles (sometimes following the stream, other times climbing again to about 75 feet above it) up the generally narrow canyon to a landslide that impounds Lower Palisades Lake.

Many people make a day hike to Lower Palisades Lake and back. You can tell when you are approaching the lake because you cross three bridges in fairly close succession and also encounter a corduroy section of the trail over an area of springs just before the last of the three bridges.

A short, switchbacking climb up the slide brings you to the lake. Here you'll find the first of two legal camping areas. The area is nice and flat, but it has no water and appears generally overused. The second campsites are 1.4 more miles farther, at the confluence of Chicken Springs Canyon.

Moose live in the area from the lower lake on. The fertile lake waters have pretty good fishing for cutthroat trout. Better fishing lies ahead at Upper Palisades Lake.

To continue, cross the bridge at the lake's outlet, and walk up the north side of the canyon past the lake and the low willow marsh at its head. Continue to pretty Chicken Springs Canyon, where water splashes over logs at its mouth before flowing into Palisades Creek. There is a sign here, and a bridge leads across Palisades Creek to a pleasant camping area.

A sign at Chicken Springs reads PALISADES CREEK TRAIL 084; UPPER PALISADES LAKE 1.2 MILES; PALISADES CAMPGROUND 5.4 MILES. Another sign reads CHICKEN SPRINGS CANYON TRAIL 092, THOMPSON CREEK TRAIL 1.7 MILES, ATKINSON PEAK 3.9 MILES, RAINEY CREEK 6.5 MILES.

Chicken Springs Canyon is a pleasant walk. The springs rise about 0.75 mile up the canyon. This trail gives access to the other trails mentioned above. They are steep and faint but also very scenic.

Back on Palisades Creek Trail, 0.6 mile past Chicken Springs, our description of Palisades Creek Trail ends at a bridge across Palisades Creek. Here Waterfall Canyon Trail entices hikers, equestrians, and mountain bikers to continue up a side canyon to Upper Palisades Lake.

Probably ninety-nine out of every hundred people who continue go up Waterfalls Canyon Trail, but Trail 084 does continue up Palisades Creek. However, it is faint and wet, and it fords Palisades Creek twenty-two times. Though diminished in size, Palisades Creek is still substantial. It's hard to cross until mid-July. This is important to note, because you quickly come to the first of the twenty-two fords! The upper canyon is full of moose, elk, and black bear. The difficult access makes it a real wilderness experience.

Palisades Creek Trail has a long season due to its relatively low elevation. The forest canopy keeps the heat down in midsummer. Autumn is very beautiful because the cottonwoods turn yellow, and the mountain maple, red. This is probably the most heavily used hiking trail in the Snake River Range. It is closed to motorized vehicles but open to foot, horse, and bicycle traffic.

**Options:** The classic option is to continue up Waterfall Canyon Trail to Upper Palisades Lake and then Waterfalls Canyon (see Hike 84, Waterfall Canyon). You can also take the side trail at Chicken Springs Canyon; walk up Lake Canyon, which is a waterless, but scenic, side canyon at Lower Palisades Lake; or struggle into upper Palisades Creek.

—Ralph Maughan

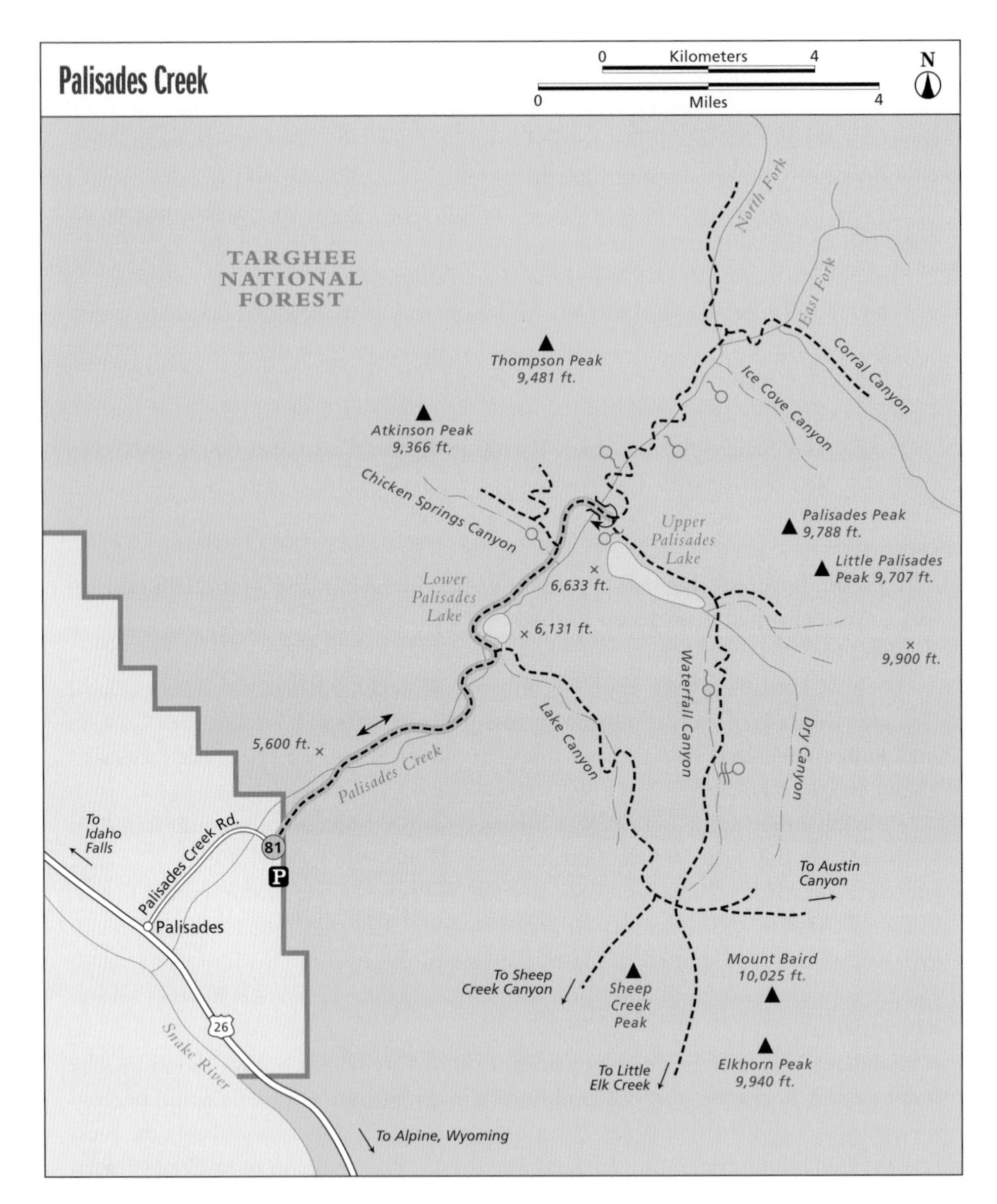


## Miles and Directions

- **0.0** Trailhead parking (5,500 feet)
- **0.1** Hiker's trail begins
- **0.2** Horse trail joins
- **1.3** First bridge (5,720 feet)
- **4.0** Lower Palisades Lake (6,131 feet)
- **5.4** Chicken Springs Canyon camping area (6,200 feet)
- **6.0** Bridge over Palisades Creek to Waterfalls Canyon Trail (6,245 feet)

# 82 South Fork of Tin Cup Creek to Lau Creek

A shuttle hike or loop is available along three different creek drainages and lush meadows. This hike also serves as an entrance point to a wild, roadless area in the Caribou Mountains.

**Start:** 40 miles east of Soda Springs along ID 34
**Type of hike:** Shuttle with options. It is easiest if one group parks at the trailhead while the other parks at the terminus at Pine Bar Campground trailhead.
**Distance:** 6 miles
**Approximate hiking time:** 6–7 hours to 2 or more days
**Difficulty:** Easy to moderate due to route finding
**Best season:** Spring to early fall
**Trail surface:** Normal dirt and rock; can be muddy near crossings
**Land status:** Caribou National Forest
**Canine compatibility:** Voice command
**Fees and permits:** None
**Maps:** Tincup Mountain USGS quadrangle; Montpelier and Soda Springs Ranger Districts-Caribou National Forest map
**Trail contact:** Montpelier Ranger District, (208) 847-0375; Soda Springs Ranger District,(208) 547-4356
**Special considerations:** Mosquito repellent will be needed.

**Finding the trailhead:** Drive east on ID 34 from Soda Springs to Freedom, Wyoming, beyond the towns of Henry and Wayan. After 30 miles you begin to descend along Tin Cup Creek. Look for the sign on the right indicating PINE BAR CAMPGROUND; continue driving another 2.5 miles to the well-marked access to the South Fork of Tin Cup Creek. There is ample parking space. GPS: N42 58.6' / W111 09.95'

## The Hike

The trail begins after you cross the bridge over Tin Cup Creek at its confluence with the South Fork. Continue hiking on the trail along the right side of the South Fork of Tin Cup. This riparian or riverland area is a delicate home to many plant and animal species. Beavers are commonly seen in the creek busy at work. Sheep are grazed periodically in this general area but keep along the drier hillsides. After 2 miles of hiking up and down through forests and clearings parallel to the creek, an easy crossing puts you on the left side. Shortly after this comes the trail junction to Brush Creek. At this point you could return after a nice day hike, continue on the South Fork Trail for more options deep into this roadless area, or make the right up Brush Creek following this trail description.

The trail along Brush Creek can be a bit "flaky." As long as you follow the drainage remaining on the right side and uphill from the creek, the trail will always reappear. Also look for markings on the trees. I've included some GPS points in Miles and Directions to get you back to the trail to avoid any frustration. A mile up Brush

*Gorgeous wildflowers are abundant in the Lav Creek drainage.* PHOTO BY LUKE KRATZ

Creek, nice clearings and level places to camp open up. The trail then weaves in and out of thickly wooded areas and swampy meadows, always adding variety. After 2 miles it begins a slight ascent and moves away from the creek. The trail heads north, climbing into a forested plateau and then a high clearing with patchy dark blue Engelmann spruce groves; you can see that this must be the apex. Begin the descent of Lau Creek.

The trail from here on out is quite good as it drops down through beautiful rolling hills and meadows filled with colorful wildflowers. After 2.5 miles from the top, you can see the drainage opening up into Tin Cup Creek. When the creek gets closer, stay on the main trail by keeping left so you can reach the bridge across Tin Cup without getting scoured by nettles and other cross-country creek hiking hazards. After crossing the bridge to the Pine Bar trailhead, you can rendezvous with the shuttle vehicle or walk/jog 2.5 miles down ID 34 back to the start.

**Options:** The South Fork trail continues on for more than 10 miles and turns into the North Fork of Hyde Creek. Along the way there are many junctions to trails up

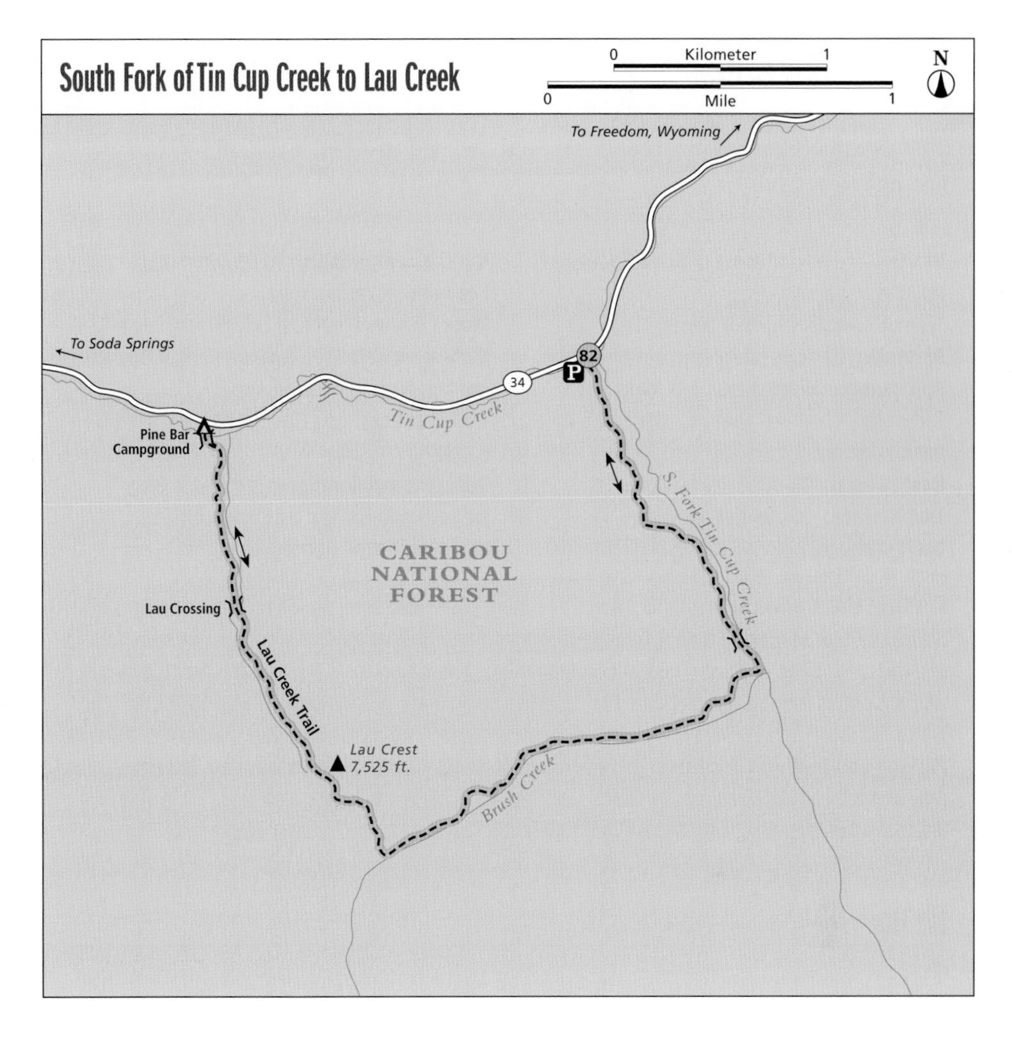


other drainages, including Deer Creek, Crooked Creek, and Stump Creek. These are all nonmotorized trails.

## Miles and Directions (estimates)

**0.0** South Fork Trailhead[ (6,136 ft.)

**2.1** Cross South Fork

**2.3** Turn right at junction up Brush Creek
pick up trail at N42 56.98/W111 9.03, N42 56.9/W111 9.27, N42 56.83/W111 9.98

**3.3** Camping area N42 56.83/W 111 10.32
pick up trail at N42 56.82/W111 10.4

**3.7** Veer north to ascend Brush Creek/Lau Creek saddle

**4.2** Descent into Lau Creek drainage

**6.0** Trail ends at Pine Bar Campground

# 83 Trail Creek

This is a nice long walk through an area burned in 1988 with subsequent good regeneration.

**Start:** 40 miles northeast of Soda Springs in the Caribou Range
**Type of hike:** Day hike or overnight
**Distance:** 10 miles round-trip; out-and-back
**Approximate hiking time:** 7–8 hours
**Difficulty:** Moderately easy for the first 5 miles, then moderate
**Best season:** Mid-June–mid-October
**Trail surface:** Normal dirt and rock
**Land status:** Caribou-Tanghee National Forest
**Canine compatibility:** Voice command
**Fees and permits:** None
**Maps:** Tincup Mountain USGS quadrangle; Montpelier and Soda Springs Ranger Districts–Caribou National Forest map
**Trail contact:** Soda Springs Ranger District, (208) 547-4356
**Special considerations:** The trail is easy except when muddy; then it becomes slippery and sticks to your boots.

**Finding the trailhead:** From ID 34 at its terminus near Freedom, Wyoming, follow the paved Stateline Road northward until you reach Jackknife Road at 2 miles. This is a four-way stop. Turn left. The road leads west into the Caribou Mountains. It is paved for 2.3 miles. It turns to gravel where it enters the Caribou National Forest, and it ends under a mile later. GPS: N43 02.82' / W111 02.04'
**Parking and trailhead facilities:** There is room for about six vehicles at a graveled, but unimproved, trailhead. All parking is in direct sun. The trail is closed to motor vehicles, but no sign indicates this fact. A sign does mark Trail Creek Trail.

## The Hike

This is a very pleasant trail in late June and again in late August through September, although late September is hunting season, and you must wear hunter orange for safety. Because the trail is mostly in the sun and at relatively low elevation, midsummer is perhaps a bit hot.

The trail leaves the parking area and follows the former road along the willow-bottomed Jackknife Creek. Several side trails are available. Watch for moose here and throughout the hike.

After 2.3 miles you enter the Jackknife Creek burn of 1988. This burned the same dry summer as the gigantic Yellowstone fires. The burn has regenerated nicely with aspen, conifers, and many kinds of berry bushes: chokecherries, snowberries, serviceberries, huckleberries. The new forest is neither too thick nor too sparse.

At 2.8 miles you reach a fork in the canyon. To the left is Jackknife Creek and to the right, Trail Creek. The two canyons are equal in size. Trail Creek was burned to a greater degree than Jackknife Creek. There is a sign and a trail up Jackknife Creek, but we found that it soon disappeared in the tall willows due to lack of maintenance.

*New and old growths along Trail Creek.* PHOTO BY LUKE KRATZ

Follow the trail up Trail Creek. The canyon is fairly wide and flat-bottomed. Trail Creek meanders through grassy meadows and patches of willows with occasional patches of lodgepole pine or spruce. The canyon slope to the left was almost completely burned and now has a pleasant small forest. The slope to the right did not burn except in a few places. It is covered with brush, grass, and patches of aspen and conifers.

The trail always stays to the right of Trail Creek, with a minor exception. This is important to remember, because while the first two miles of the trail are easy and almost impossible to lose, the upper part of the trail is a bit confusing: Many game, hunting, and sheep trails leave the main trail. Sometimes they are more apparent than Trail Creek Trail itself.

After about 1.5 more miles, the trail begins to climb up and down a bit more. Sometimes there are parallel trails, created when travelers sought a drier tread during early-season hiking or riding. At about 3 miles from the trailhead comes the first real challenge. This is in the southwest corner of Section 17 on the map (there are no geographic names for reference in this section). The main trail fades at a wide spot in the canyon, and a much more obvious trail crosses the main trail. This is a domestic sheep trail. Do not take it. Continue up the canyon to the right of Trail Creek, and you will quickly find Trail Creek Trail again.

Soon the canyon begins to narrow somewhat and the ridge to the left becomes lower and more intimately dissected. The view ahead suggests you are very close to the pass at the top of Trail Creek. This is deceptive: You still have about 1.5 miles to go.

About 0.3 mile above the sheep driveway, the trail does cross Trail Creek to the left, but just briefly. The reason is that Trail Creek undercut the old trail's route, which was above a cutbank in the hillside. After a couple of crossings of the creek, the trail remains to the right of Trail Creek. If you find yourself climbing up any hill on the left side of Trail Creek, you are going in the wrong direction.

Another 0.5 mile brings you to an unnamed fork in Trail Creek. We found trails in both forks, although the topographic map did not show this. Take the trail up the left fork, but keep to the right of the creek. Be very careful not to take the obvious trail to the left, which crosses the creek and heads up a minor ridge. This ends at a hunting camp.

Beginning in the vicinity of the unnamed upper fork of Trail Creek, small metal signs consisting of a black arrow on a yellow background appear on trees here and there to show the correct route.

The pass always seems just ahead, but this is illusion until surprisingly you reach it. At the pass you have a good view down Taylor Creek and of scenic Bald Mountain to your right. The Taylor Creek Trail is not well maintained and has many ups and downs because the trail traverses the slope above Taylor Creek.

Trail Creek and most of the mountain is grazed by domestic sheep from midsummer until the end of the season. Grazing practices have improved in recent years, and sheep do little obvious damage other than causing a stink in areas they have recently grazed.

Wildlife is abundant, with moose, deer, and elk plentiful. There are also a few bears, cougars, and many coyotes.

Trail Creek and all of the major creeks in the area are slow to clear after snowmelt, and they become cloudy after any substantial rain. You will pass a number of hillside slumps, earthflows, and blowouts. These are not due to the fire or to the grazing but are natural in both Trail Creek and the unburned drainages. The soft sedimentary rocks of this range are covered with clay, and the clays tends to slip over the bedrock when it becomes wet. Because the streams are often cloudy, they are not especially desirable for water, even after filtering.

Fortunately, there are a number of small side creeks and springs in Trail Creek that you can filter and drink without making a face. Be sure to filter all water due to the high density of deer, elk, moose, and domestic sheep.

Late summer is very beautiful in Trail Creek and the other drainages because the ground cover turns red and the aspen gold amid the dark green subalpine fir, Engelmann spruce, and lodgepole pine. Most prominent in the ground cover are grass, cinquefoil, aster, western coneflower, goldenrod, sticky geranium, yarrow, false strawberry, wyethia (mule's ear), and several species of sagebrush.

The only downside is a spreading infestation of Canada thistle, musk thistle, and bull thistle. This probably originated from years of livestock herding and horse travel when hay was carried in containing the seeds of these invasive non-native thistles.

It is notable that we saw a very large number of raptors, including red-tailed hawks, goshawks, rough-legged hawks, and merlins.

**Options:** The burn is not difficult to traverse. Deadfallen snags are not thick in most places, and the regenerated aspen, chokecherry, and kinnikinnick aren't very high. You

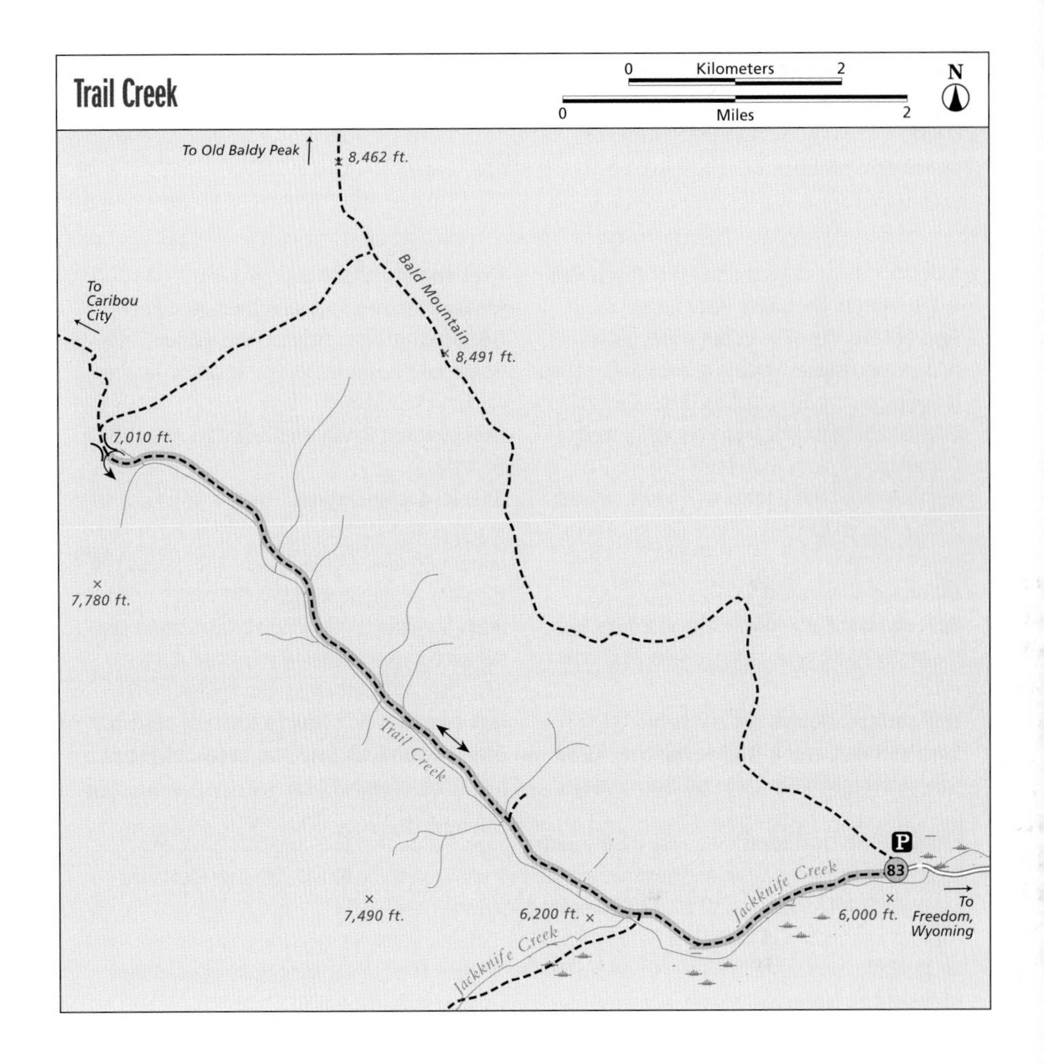


will quickly encounter unmapped game-hunter and sheep trails that lead to all the ridgetops, both major and minor.

A loop from Trail Creek to the top of Bald Mountain (which is actually a long beautiful ridge with a system trail on top) and back to the Jackknife Creek Trailhead is very feasible for those with a little endurance and the ability to find and follow game trails.

—Ralph Maughan and Jackie Johnson Maughan

## Miles and Directions

**0.0** Trailhead (6,200 feet)

**2.8** Jackknife Creek–Trail Creek fork (6,220 feet)

**7.2** Trail Creek–Taylor Creek Divide (7,090 feet)

# 84 Waterfall Canyon

Accessed from the Palisades Creek trail is a scenic canyon with a large, fertile lake and many waterfalls in late June and July, including one cascade more than 900 feet high.

**Start:** 55 linear miles southeast of Idaho Falls in the heart of the Snake River Range
**Type of hike:** Day hike or overnight; out-and-back. Hike assumes you are already 6 miles into the backcountry up Palisades Creek. Several extended backpacking loops are also possible
**Distance:** 24 miles round-trip
**Approximate hiking time:** 6–7 hours. At least 2 days if in conjunction with Palisades Lakes hike.
**Difficulty:** Moderate
**Best season:** Early July for the waterfalls, but the upper basin is usually snow-covered until mid-July
**Trail surface:** Normal dirt and rock
**Land status:** Caribou-Targhee National Forest
**Canine compatibility:** On leash recommended
**Fees and permits:** None
**Maps:** Palisades Peak and Thompson Peak USGS quadrangles; Island Park, Ashton, Teton Basin, and Palisades Ranger Districts-Targhee National Forest map
**Trail contact:** Palisades Ranger District, (208) 523-1412
**Special considerations:** Water is often scarce in upper Waterfall Canyon in late summer. The upper part of Waterfall Canyon and nearby canyons are tremendous avalanche country. Cornices from the winter wind-whipped snow can fall as slab avalanches even in late June and early July. After snowmelt, the flowers in the high meadows can grow so fast they obscure otherwise obvious trails. You absolutely must have a topographic map.

**Finding the trailhead:** See Hike 81, Palisades Creek. Follow that hike to Lower Palisades Lake. Pass Lower Palisades Lake, and continue on the trail until you come to a bridge over Palisades Creek. GPS: N43 26.39' / W111 07.69' (second Palisade Lake)
**Parking and trailhead facilities:** Seven campsites, potable water, latrines. The trailhead has room for about ten vehicles at the hiker's parking lot and is often filled to capacity. There are separate trailheads for hikers and horses, although they soon share the same trail.

## The Hike

This hike begins at the bridge over Palisades Creek at the end of Hike 81, Palisades Creek. The trail immediately begins climbing uphill on a giant landslide that fell off the mountain ages ago, filling the mouth of the canyon that holds Upper Palisades Lake. The trail switchbacks easily up this slide to Upper Palisades Lake, a 375-foot climb. Halfway to the lake, the lake waters emerge from

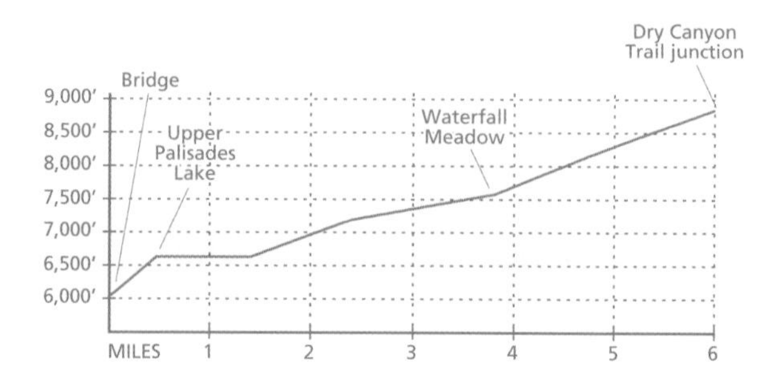

the slide as a beautiful, large spring cascading down into the forest toward Palisades Creek. This spring is a major reason Palisades Creek runs high and clear year-round.

As you approach the lake, notice the bulges of earth in the tops of the avalanche runs in the mountains surrounding the lake. The earth remains unstable in this area.

The lake itself is deep and cool with numerous coves. Abundant cutthroat trout live in the fertile waters that filter down from the limestone and phosphate rock of the mountains. The trail for hikers stays about 50 feet above the east shore of the lake. About 100 yards above this trail is the horse trail. Since the mountain slope plunges steeply into the lake's water, hikers and horse parties won't want to share the same path.

A lightning fire in 1994 burned much of the Upper Palisades Lake area. The trails were rebuilt and are in good condition. As you walk along, see if you can spot the fire scars. The burn has healed very well despite its intensity. The trail contours a steep slope above the east side of the lake until it reaches the lake's inlet, where there are many campsites and the junction of trails from three canyons that rise above the inlet: Vacation, Dry, and Waterfall. It is important that you find the trail up Waterfall Canyon.

A quarter mile above the lake's inlet, you come to the well-marked Vacation Canyon junction. Keep to the right, continue, and cross the creek. Near the creek, the trail to the left goes up Dry Canyon. Continue to the right. The trail is easy to follow. It was substantially rebuilt after the fire, although none of Waterfall Canyon itself burned. It begins to climb, and soon you approach a clear, splashing spring-fed stream in the forest. This is near the unnamed (but marked on the map) Waterfall Canyon spring. Waterfall Canyon recapitulates Upper Palisades Lake and its spring. The trail now climbs 300 feet up a steep slope into Waterfall Canyon.

Waterfall Canyon was left hanging above the lake by a glacier. Its mouth is filled with a moraine, which is also perhaps part landslide. At the end of the 300-foot climb in early July, I found that the trail dropped down and disappeared into a deep snowmelt pond with a snowmelt stream running into it. I skirted the pond going cross-country. Only two days later on my return, the pond was just a puddle inches deep and the snowmelt stream dry. This and other water from the canyon obviously comes out at Waterfall Canyon spring.

The trail climbs gradually now, wandering through patches of forest and meadow. In early summer water still runs in the creek in places but where it is dry, water surely runs underground not far below. The trail is broad and easy to find but strewn with a lot of deadfall at certain points.

As you near the top of the canyon, a spectacular cascade plunges 920 feet down the east wall of the canyon. Its waters flow into a pond. Early in the season, a second waterfall adorns the opposite canyon wall. It has much less volume and is perhaps 200 feet high but very pretty. The roar of the falls was so great I could not camp here at what I will call "Waterfall Meadows." Would it damage my hearing to listen, to feel the roar all night long?

Beyond the falls, the trail soon becomes faint due to annual snowmelt outwash that runs over its tread. Later in the summer it is obscured by tall flowers.

As the canyon narrows, move to the right and cross the creek (or creekbed later in summer). The trail suddenly appears and climbs 300 feet very steeply up a cirque wall carved by ancient glaciers. It is shaded by some giant conifers as you step upward. You then come to ledge overlooking a gorge. In July a side tributary makes a double waterfall down into the awesome gorge, which the creek has carved. Now the trail slowly climbs away from the creek, and you are past the gorge and into a small basin.

The stream, which may not have water in late summer, forks in this small basin. The trail follows the right fork up into a large basin just below the highest peaks of the Snake River Range. From mid-July to late August, this is a vast field of tall flowering perennials. Their growth rate is so rapid that they may obscure the trail, which is plainly obvious just after the snow melts in late June or early July.

At 6 miles from the trail's beginning, you'll reach the junction with Sheep Creek–Lake Canyon Trail. At this junction, the trail fork to the east snakes along the top of Waterfall Canyon. It then passes right over Peak 9,630 and forks into either Dry Canyon or Austin Canyon (if you continue farther eastward). The Dry Canyon route will take you back to Upper Palisades Lake, completing a scenic loop. Note that Dry Canyon lacks water until its very bottom but is quite pretty. Austin Canyon Trail takes you down into Big Elk Creek.

The uplands are exquisitely beautiful.

The Sheep Creek–Lake Canyon fork of the trail heads westward. You climb to a high divide at 9,600 feet and pass south of an unnamed peak that is just over 9,900 feet high. Here you gain a sublime view of the Tetons and all of the other nearby mountains. You can elect to go south, descending into Sheep Creek, or take the trail that goes to the northwest, dropping into Lake Canyon. The latter choice provides a grand loop that takes you down to Lower Palisades Lake. Sheep Creek Canyon is closed until July 15 to protect the mountain goats.

**Options:** The Lake Canyon Trail down to Lower Palisades Lake is faint and overgrown as it descends from the basin just below the high divide. It runs through wet meadow and forest that is kept fairly open by winter's avalanches. In the mid-reaches of Lake Canyon, sheer cliffs arise where mountains goats are commonly seen.

No permanent stream runs down Lake Canyon, but there are snowmelt rivulets in the cliff-walled basin near the high divide. They run until mid-July in average snow years. Hikers who have taken this option since *Hiking Idaho*'s first edition have described Lake Canyon as beautiful to horrible, depending on the year, whether any water was present, and the amount of avalanche debris.

The nice exit hike down Sheep Creek Canyon requires a shuttle.

—Ralph Maughan

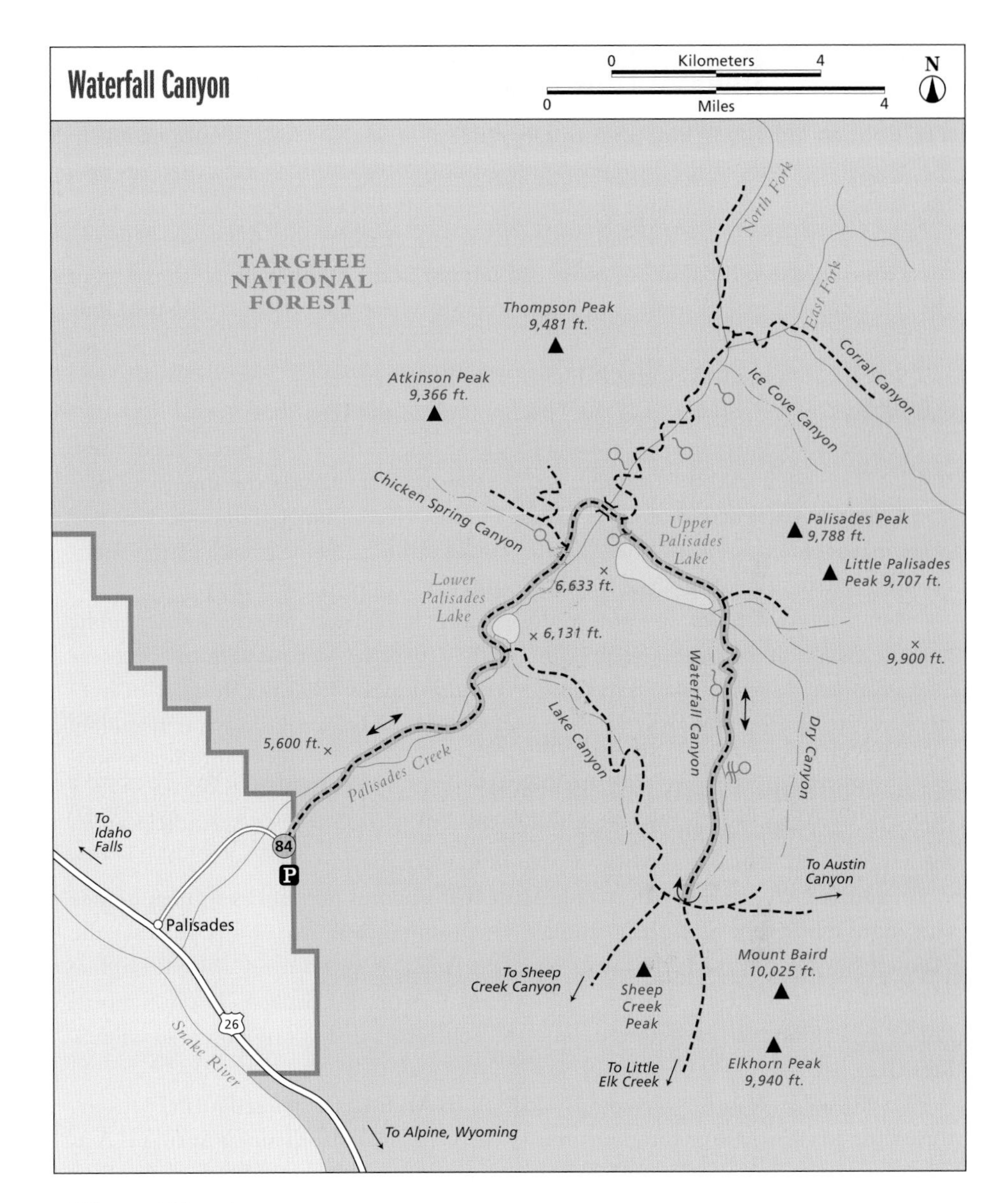


## Miles and Directions

- **0.0** Bridge over Palisades Creek (6,040 feet)
- **0.5** Upper Palisades Lake (6,633 feet)
- **1.5** Upper end of Palisades Lake (6,633 feet)
- **2.3** Top of climb into Waterfall Canyon (7,220 feet)
- **3.8** Waterfall meadow (7,520 feet)
- **4.6** Gorge overlook with double falls in early season (8,240 feet)
- **6.0** Dry Canyon or Little Elk–Sheep Creek–Lake Canyons Trail junction (8,840 feet)

# Gannett Hills Proposed Wilderness

The Gannett Hills are a little-known range of tall, steep hills (or low mountains) of the Middle Rockies in the extreme southeast corner of Idaho. In fact, they lap over into Wyoming. They are unique and important because of their fine elk, moose, antelope, and deer habitat and for their potential as one of the largest wilderness areas in southeastern Idaho. In addition, of special interest is the Bonneville cutthroat trout (BCT), a rare subspecies limited to a few streams where the borders of Idaho, Utah, and Wyoming come together. The BCT is listed by the US Fish and Wildlife Service as a Species of Special Concern. Principal among its critical streams are Dry, Giraffe, and Preuss Creeks, tributaries of the Thomas Fork of the Bear River.

Conservationists raised the fisheries issue in the early 1990s. Since then, these streams have been closed to fishing, and several roads, including the one in Giraffe Creek, have been closed in order to reduce erosion. In addition, the forest service and other management agencies entered into a conservation agreement with cattle ranchers since livestock grazing is the major use and has degraded the fishery.

Many miles of fence to protect the streams have been constructed at public expense. Much of the country, especially Giraffe Creek, has benefited from conservation measures, and the uplands are in good condition. In 1999 the number of livestock was reduced temporarily by 90 percent, and the Gannett Hills were incredibly beautiful. However, fence maintenance is a major problem. Conservationists believe it is the duty of the livestock permittees to fix the fences. The forest service so far has thought otherwise and proposes yet more fence. But what good is more if existing fence is not maintained and cows are able to trample the streams?

In addition to a conservation agreement that requires permittees to mend fence and more effectively herd their animals, environmentalists have proposed that the Gannett-Spring and Red Mountain Roadless Areas (RA) on the Caribou-Targhee National Forest in Idaho and the Gannet Hills RA on the Bridger-Teton National Forest in Wyoming be inventoried, protected, and managed as one potential wilderness area.

The Roadless Area Review and Evaluation (RARE II) completed in 1978 inventoried the Idaho and Wyoming portions of the Gannett Hills–Gannett Spring RA as one unit. Conservationists would like that to continue with the addition of the Red Mountain RA. In addition, they want the Giraffe Creek portion of the Gannett-Spring RA to be included in the most recent inventory. This prime 9,360-acre area appears to have been left out!

Furthermore, they want the unmaintained Boulevard Jeep Road (FR 834) cutting between the Red Mountain RA and Giraffe Creek to be closed. This would make for one continuous wilderness of approximately 70,500 acres. The Boulevard is one of the most difficult and dangerous roads in Idaho.

*Clover Knoll in the Gannett Hills.* PHOTO BY RALPH MAUGHAN

The portion that leads into Dry Creek Road (FR 148) is very steep and has one very severe drop-off that presents the possibility of rolling a vehicle. The road should be closed and decommissioned not only to protect the resource but to protect the public.

Finally, as mentioned earlier, the area is of tremendous importance for big game. Elk, moose, and deer congregate here because of the natural salt licks that occur along the streams. Big game needs big country and that is why, among other reasons, environmentalists propose that the entire 70,500 acres be inventoried as one potential wilderness.

—Jackie Johnson Maughan and Ralph Maughan

# 85 Giraffe Creek Loop

This is a roadless area that includes wetlands, beaver ponds, Bonneville cutthroat trout, wading birds, and big game. It is closed to trail machines and is part of a 70,500-acre proposed wilderness area. (See the Gannett Hills overview.)

**Start:** 90 miles southeast of Pocatello
**Type of hike:** Day hike loop
**Distance:** 4.5-mile loop
**Approximate hiking time:** 2–4 hours
**Difficulty:** Moderate due to some faint places on the trail
**Best season:** Mid-June (if Boulevard Jeep Road is passable)–late September
**Trail surface:** Normal dirt and rock
**Land status:** Caribou-Targhee National Forest
**Canine compatibility:** On leash recommended
**Fees and permits:** None
**Maps:** Giraffe Creek USGS quadrangle for the hike itself; see Montpelier and Soda Springs Ranger Districts-Caribou National Forest map for access roads
**Trail contact:** Montpelier Ranger District, (208) 847-0375
**Special considerations:** The last 1.8 miles on the Boulevard Jeep Trail are accessible to high-clearance four-by-fours only. Do not attempt to drive out southward from the Boulevard to US 89 because of the danger of rolling your vehicle down an 800-foot drop-off!

**Finding the trailhead:** From Montpelier, turn east onto US 89 and continue 7 miles to the Crow Creek Road (FR 111), which skirts Montpelier Reservoir. This road is gravel and continues for 10 miles to where it crosses Preuss Creek. In 3 more miles is a junction where you turn right onto FR 147, which climbs over Red Mountain ridge then drops steeply toward Elk Valley Marsh. Before you reach the marsh, at 3.6 miles you encounter a rough road to the right (south). This unsigned road is the Boulevard, a name that is in the nature of a joke—it's no boulevard. Those without four-wheel-drive, high-clearance vehicles, stop here. Don't be confused by another road to the south at this point. It is just a spur that leads shortly to an informal campsite. The Boulevard continues for 1.8 miles to the trailhead. The trailhead is marked by a sign nailed to a tree on the left (east) side of the road. GPS: N42 28. 53' / W111 05.52'
**Parking and trailhead facilities:** None

## The Hike

This beautiful country has everything the hiker could want, including owls calling at night and wildflowers blooming by day. Public land grazing has been a problem here in the past but steps taken by cattle permittees and management agencies have led to major improvements.

The trail is well maintained as it drops for 1 mile and 400 feet through aspen and conifer forest along the right (northernmost) fork of Giraffe Creek. The trail is not shown on the Giraffe Creek USGS quad but is shown on the forest map.

The country then opens up as you travel along a series of beaver ponds with Table Mountain on the left (north). Here you are likely to see moose, elk, and deer since

*Ponds and meadows along Giraffe Creek.* Photo by Luke Kratz

the high mineral content of the water and natural salt licks seem to attract them and, indeed, makes them particularly healthy. After 0.5 mile the unmapped portion of the trail joins the trail shown on the Giraffe Creek quad. From here it is another 0.75 mile to the lower beaver ponds. Here the forest service has built livestock exclosures in an attempt to protect this Bonneville cutthroat trout habitat from cattle trampling. Look not only for songbirds along all of this hike but also long-legged wading birds in the beaver ponds sections.

Just above the exclosure, you cross the left fork of Giraffe Creek and follow the trail as it follows the creek a little over 0.5 mile then crosses it to veer to the left (west) and steeply uphill through forest. After another 0.25 mile it comes to an aspen slope and then enters forest again to follow along a stream. From here it climbs again through forest and aspen to gain the ridge and the old road at 7,800 feet. From here it is 0.25 mile to the Boulevard and another 0.5-mile walk along the Boulevard back to the trailhead.

**Options:** Elk Valley Marsh is a must-see for bird-watchers. There are also trails into Dry Creek and Preuss Creek. The Giraffe Creek trail continues downstream well into Wyoming, but it is not maintained and it is rough.

—Jackie Johnson Maughan and Ralph Maughan

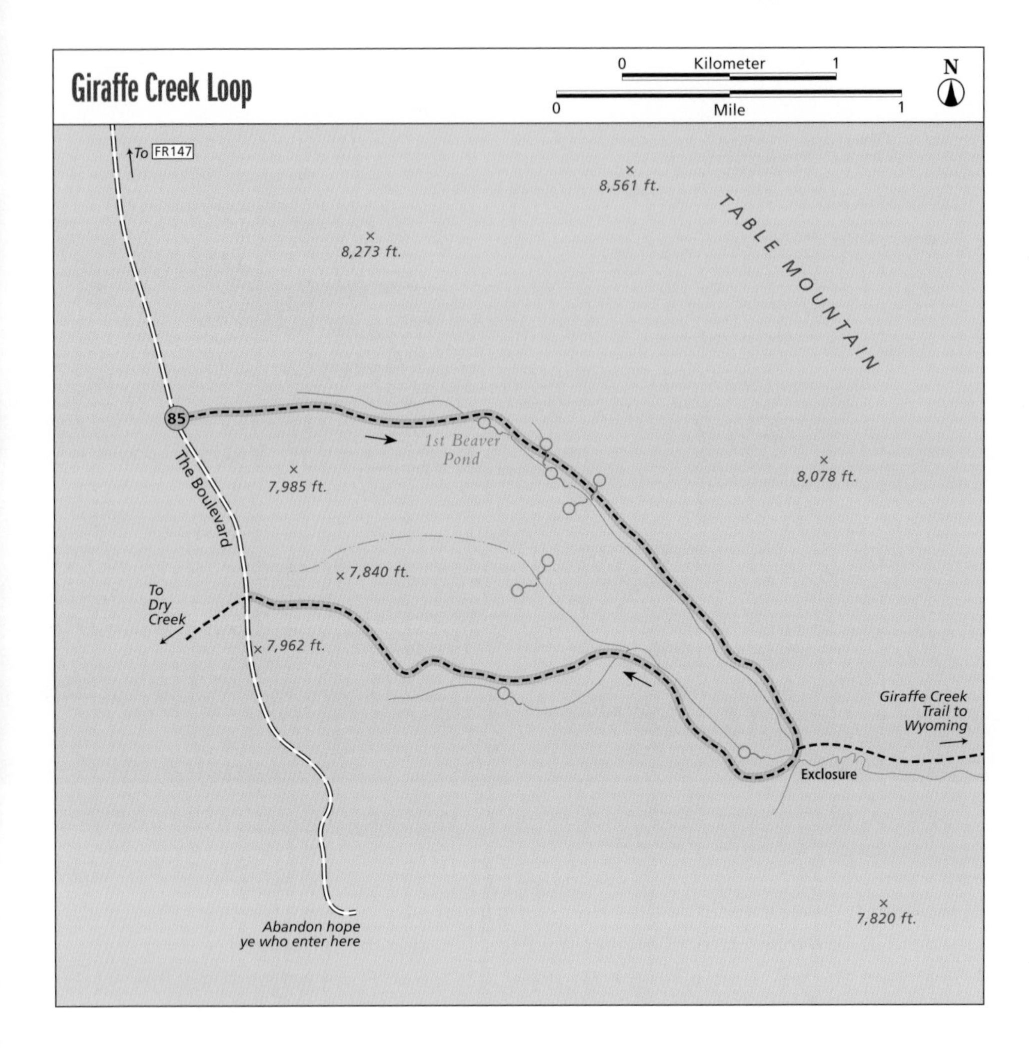


## Miles and Directions

**0.0** Giraffe Creek trailhead (7,840 feet)

**1.0** First of beaver ponds (7,400 feet)

**2.25** Exclosure (7,200 feet)

**2.75** Left fork crossing (7,280 feet)

**4.0** Boulevard (7,840 feet)

**4.5** Trailhead

# Bannock Range

This long, but discontinuous, mountain chain begins at Pocatello and runs southward into Utah, ending on the west side of Cache Valley, where it is often called the Malad Range.

The Bannock is mostly a low ridge, but it boasts a number of exceptions: Scout Mountain, Elkhorn Peak, and Oxford Peak range from 8,700 to more than 9,000 feet high. Small roadless areas partially surround these uplifts, and from the summits you gain fine views of the country where the Middle Rockies merge with the Basin and Range country.

Geologically speaking, the Bannock Range is among the most complex of the many minor ranges of the Idaho–Wyoming border. It looks much like a typical mountain range from the Basin and Range Province, but it has been subjected to much overthrusting, with many of the rocks being pushed to their present location from 30 miles to the west.

The range is brushy with the higher portions having pockets of Douglas fir, some of them very large old growth, at least large by the standards of this semi-arid country. Deer are the most common large mammal, but there are some elk and a few black bears and cougars. Occasionally, moose reinhabit the area, but they tend to get poached out.

The area just south of Pocatello is the part of the Bannock Range used the most for recreation.

—Ralph Maughan

*Fall colors up City Creek trail near Pocatello.* PHOTO BY JOHN KRATZ

# 86 Corral Creek

Pleasantly climb through a mixed forest with some good views of the Bannock Range; savor the brilliant wildflowers in late May and June.

**Start:** 10 miles south of Pocatello
**Type of hike:** Day hike; out-and-back or shuttle
**Distance:** 2 miles one way
**Approximate hiking time:** 1–2 hours
**Difficulty:** Moderately easy with a 400-foot climb at the very top
**Best season:** June and autumn
**Trail surface:** Normal dirt and rock
**Land status:** Caribou-Targhee National Forest
**Canine compatibility:** Voice command
**Fees and permits:** None
**Maps:** Clifton Creek USGS quadrangle; Westside Range District, Caribou-Targhee National Forest map
**Trail contact:** Westside Ranger District, (208) 236-7500
**Special considerations:** Corral Creek spring has a naturally occurring high level of arsenic.

**Finding the trailhead:** Drive south from Pocatello on Bannock Highway up Mink Creek Canyon. From the CARIBOU FOREST BOUNDARY sign, continue 4.1 miles to the junction with South Fork Mink Creek Road (to your left). Continue 50 yards past this junction on Bannock Highway to the fenced trailhead parking lot. GPS: N42 42.71' / W112 25.38'
**Parking and trailhead facilities:** Large, undeveloped, unshaded dirt parking area.

## The Hike

This is a very pleasant late-spring hike near Pocatello that leads up a mostly forested draw and eventually climbs to broad (officially unnamed) "Corral Creek" summit, which has fine views of the crest of the Bannock Range from the summit's east rim. The trail is open to motor vehicles, but use is not heavy.

The trail begins at the parking area. The tread is entrenched and obvious as it winds gently uphill around the toe of the ridge, which is the south side of shallow Corral Creek Canyon or, more aptly, "draw."

You quickly reach tiny Corral Creek. It flows under the trail in a culvert, but the area is often a bit muddy. Here the trail makes a right-angle turn and heads up the canyon, climbing persistently but not steeply. The pleasant burbling of Corral Creek nearby belies the fact that the creek has a high natural level of arsenic.

The trail is mostly shaded by a forest of aspen, chokecherry, willow, and rod osier dogwood (which blooms in late May and early June). To the right of the trail is open meadow, and soon juniper-clad hillslope. This open area blazes with the blooms of arrowleaf and Hooker's balsamroot in late May, and later sticky geranium, lupine, and golden aster, amid the sagebrush and grass.

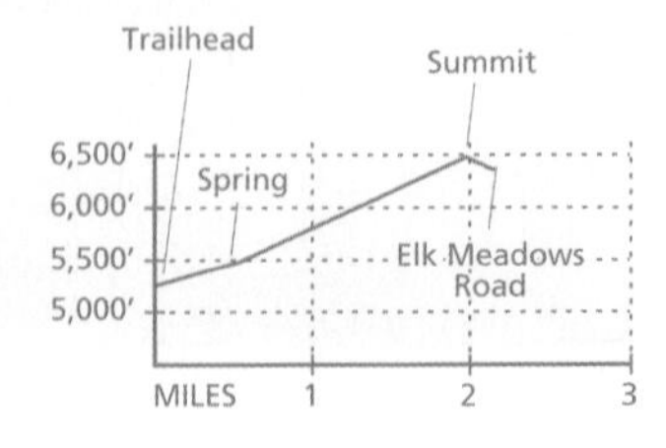

*Views of the Portneuf Range from Corral Creek Trail.* PHOTO BY LUKE KRATZ

After about 0.5 mile you pass the source of Corral Creek and continue up the increasingly shady draw. Douglas fir begin to appear in the forest.

Near the top, the trail begins to climb steeply and makes several switchbacks. At this point it breaks out into the open, with fine views of Scout Mountain to the east, behind you, as well as the lesser summits in the Bannock Mountain range. As you climb to the summit, the trail goes over several gentle ledges of bedrock. A fence with a wooden cattleguard marks the edge of the summit.

Just past the summit, a fading trail to the right (north) follows the unnamed summit ridge. This side path is growing brushy, however, and may fade away unless maintained.

Corral Creek Trail continues across the broad summit, increasingly becoming more and more like a dirt road, until it reaches Elk Meadows Road in about 0.25 mile. After Memorial Day or so, this road is open to the public and could be a place where a shuttle meets you.

The low elevation of the trail makes for a somewhat hot hike, despite the shade, in midsummer. It is once again pleasant during the fall when the leaves of the dogwood, aspen, and chokecherry change color.

—Ralph Maughan

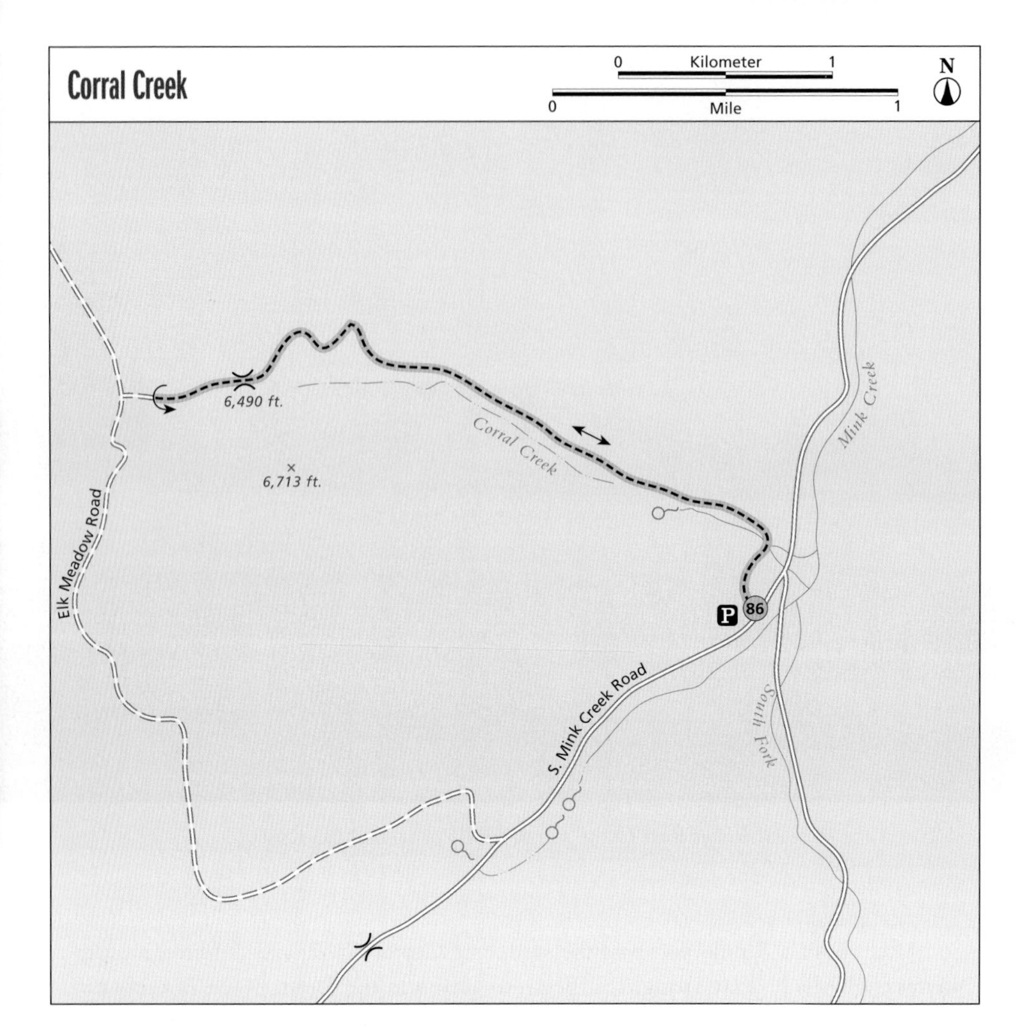


## Miles and Directions

**0.0** Corral Creek Trailhead (5,380 feet)

**0.1** Corral Creek crossing on culvert (5,410 feet)

**0.5** Corral Creek spring (5,500 feet)

**2.0** Summit (6,490 feet)

**2.2** Elk Meadows Road junction (6,400 feet)

# 87 Gibson Mountain Loop

Good views of the city of Pocatello, the Pocatello Range, the Portneuf Range, and beyond are on this mountain outside "Poky."

**Start:** 5 miles south of Pocatello
**Type of hike:** Day hike; loop
**Distance:** 8 miles round-trip
**Approximate hiking time:** 3–4 hours
**Difficulty:** Moderate
**Best season:** June through September, depending on snow
**Trail surface:** Normal dirt and rock
**Land status:** Caribou-Targhee National Forest
**Canine compatibility:** Voice command
**Fees and permits:** None
**Maps:** Pocatello South USGS quad; Westside Range District–Caribou-Targhee National Forest map
**Trail contact:** Westside Ranger District, (208) 236-7500

**Finding the trailhead:** Drive south from the center of downtown Pocatello on South Arthur Street until it becomes Bannock Highway. Turn right (south) onto the signed Gibson Jack Road 4.7 miles south of the center of Pocatello and directly opposite the country club. It is 3.3 miles of good road from the highway to the trailhead. At the trailhead, the Gibson Mountain Trail leaves to the left and immediately crosses a small bridge over Gibson Jack Creek. The more obvious trail that leads straight ahead from the trailhead is the Gibson Jack Trail. GPS: N42 47.58' / W112 25.75'
**Parking and trailhead facilities:** Undeveloped trailhead with partially shaded parking.

## The Hike

Taking the loop counterclockwise, head straight and climb up an open side hill above Gibson Jack Creek to rise about 200 feet in 0.25 mile on the Gibson Jack Trail. The grade then becomes less steep as the trail works its way toward the creek. Because the drainage is not grazed by livestock, this open section is rife with wildflowers from May to mid-June, and many people walk here to admire them.

After 2 miles, having entered into the deep foliage of the creek, the trail comes to a fork. There is a bridge here as you go left up the South Fork of Gibson Jack Creek.

The trail now climbs more steeply to pass through conifer and aspen for the next 1.5 miles to the top of the ridge. There are some very large old-growth Douglas fir here. After 1.5 miles the trail breaks out of the forest, and you can look down into the top of the West Fork of Mink Creek drainage to the west and to the north to see points along the crest of the Bannock Range, including Wild Horse Mountain.

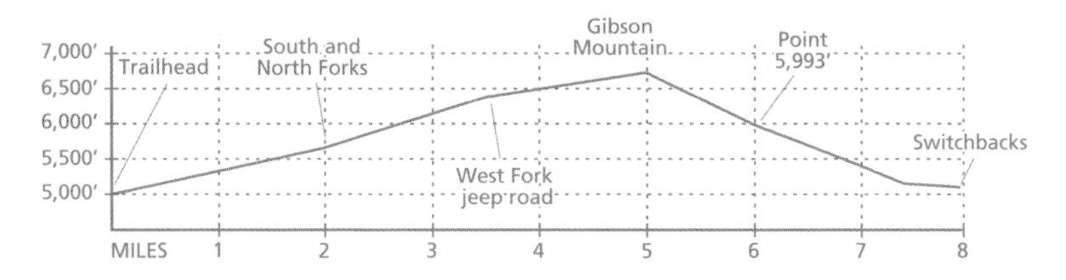

*Dogs enjoy getting "watered" on the Gibson Mountain Trail.* PHOTO BY LUKE KRATZ

The trail circles to the left (southeast) to meet the West Fork jeep road. In less than 0.25 mile, you encounter a trail to the left, which leads up to Gibson Mountain. This trail is not shown on the USGS map because the trail is newer than the map. Your route up Gibson Mountain is visible here, and you will climb 300 feet through open hillside and forest. In about a mile, after reaching the top of the switchbacks, the trail forks. Stay to the left to continue to the top of the mountain. You may find snowfields on top in the middle of summer, and there is only one good viewpoint since the mountain is forested.

The trail then drops rapidly to follow the top of the ridge between Gibson Jack Creek and Dry Creek. (Dry Creek is incorrectly labeled as the South Fork of Gibson Jack on some earlier USGS quads.) The majority of the route back to the trailhead is unshaded except for some large mountain mahogany, and it is rocky until it reaches the toe of the ridge, where it flattens out to pass through sagebrush and, in May and June, numerous wildflowers. You will have dropped 1,300 feet in just under 2 miles. The views are especially good along the way and give an excellent sense of the lay of the Portneuf River Valley, which contains Pocatello, the Pocatello Range, Portneuf Gap, and the Portneuf Range in the distance.

The last 0.25 mile will find you coming to a fence line and a fork in the trail. The trail to the right goes up Dry Creek. Stay to the left (north) to follow two long switchbacks down through chokecherry and dogwood to a bridge over Gibson Jack Creek and back to the trailhead.

—Jackie Johnson Maughan

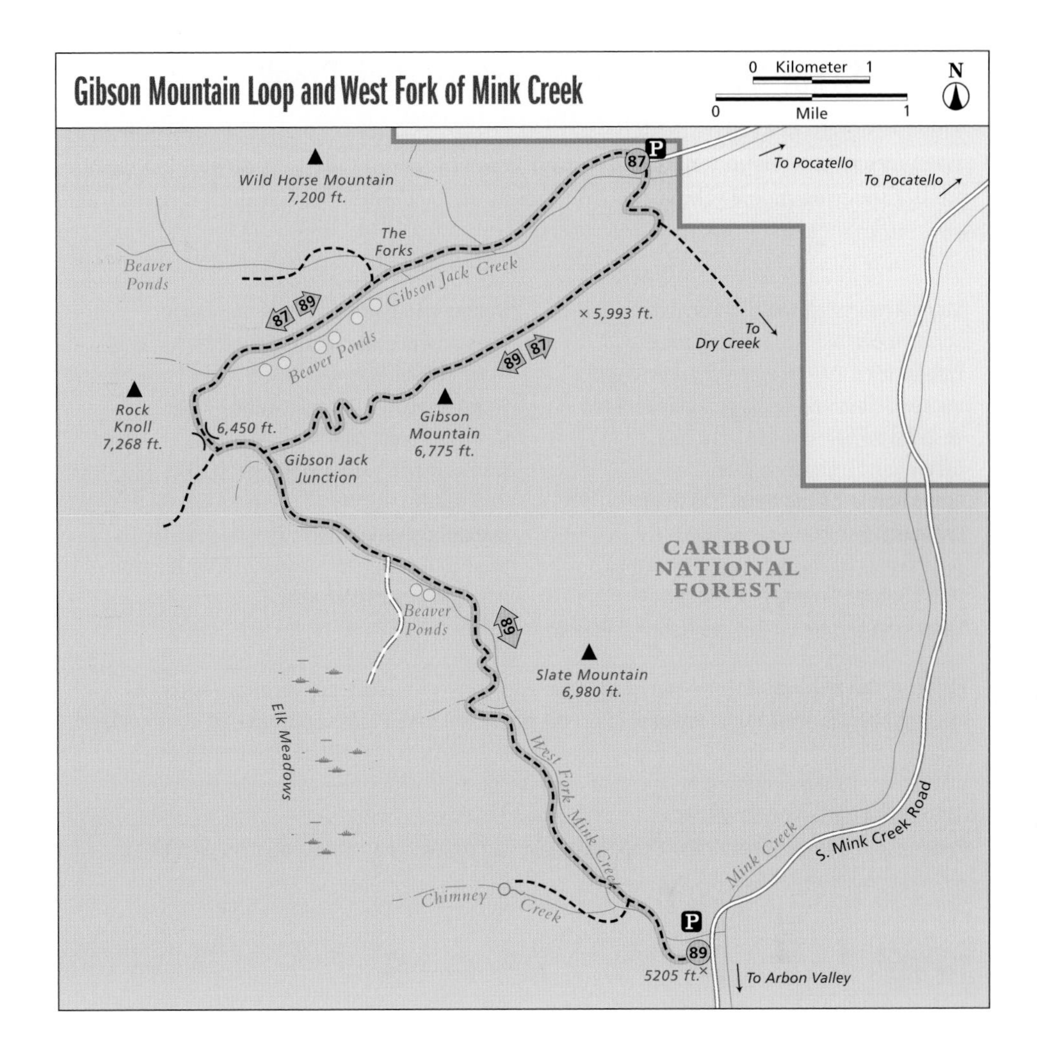


**Options:** You can take Hike 89 down West Mink Creek once you have climbed out of Gibson Jack Creek.

## Miles and Directions

**0.0** Trailhead (5,080 feet)

**2.0** South and North Forks meet (5,700 feet)

**3.5** West Fork jeep road (6,400 feet)

**5.0** Gibson Mountain (6,775 feet)

**6.0** Point 5,993

**7.0** Toe of ridge (5,400 feet)

**7.8** Switchbacks (5,200 feet)

**8.0** Arrive back at the trailhead (5,080 feet)

# 88 Scout Mountain-East Fork of Mink Creek

The pleasant woodland trail leads to good views of Arbon Valley and to an old beaver pond. Especially nice is taking this hike late in the day, when the setting sun lights the forest in orange and gold.

**Start:** A few miles south of Pocatello in the northern end of the Bannock Range
**Type of hike:** Day hike or a short overnight backpack; out-and-back, or a shuttle if you descend on Valve House Draw Trail
**Distance:** 4 miles round-trip
**Approximate hiking time:** 2-3 hours
**Difficulty:** Easy
**Best season:** Late June and September
**Trail surface:** Normal dirt and rock
**Land status:** Caribou-Targhee National Forest
**Canine compatibility:** Voice command
**Fees and permits:** Campground fee
**Maps:** Scout Mountain USGS quadrangle; Westside Range District-Caribou-Targhee National Forest map
**Trail contact:** Westside Ranger District, (208) 236-7500
**Special considerations:** This popular trail is used by hikers, trail machines, ATVs, equestrians, and mountain bikers.

**Finding the trailhead:** Drive southward from Pocatello on the Bannock Highway. Follow this road for about 8 miles to the national forest boundary. The paved road winds up Mink Creek. After about a mile, turn left at the East Fork of Mink Creek-Scout Mountain Road. Continue 6 miles on pavement up the mountain. Turn right, and continue past the picnic area to the signed trailhead. GPS: N42 41.33' / W112 21.58'
**Parking and trailhead facilities:** Scout Mountain Campground has water and thirty-one units, with many suitable for RVs.

## The Hike

People from Pocatello use this area to get out of the summer's heat. This west-facing slope of Scout Mountain is characterized by aspen and conifer. Big-game species are not much present, but songbirds, maybe even an owl, can be seen, especially as you near the old beaver pond.

The trail rises steadily through forest for 600 feet until it reaches a plateau and good views of the Arbon Valley to the west. On the way you will encounter Valve House Draw Trail on the right (west).

The trail then drops a bit and continues gently uphill. Don't take the signed trail to Box Canyon on your left (east). This suggests a good route up to the top of Scout Mountain, but it only leads to thicket and brush. Instead continue to the 2-mile point of the old beaver pond.

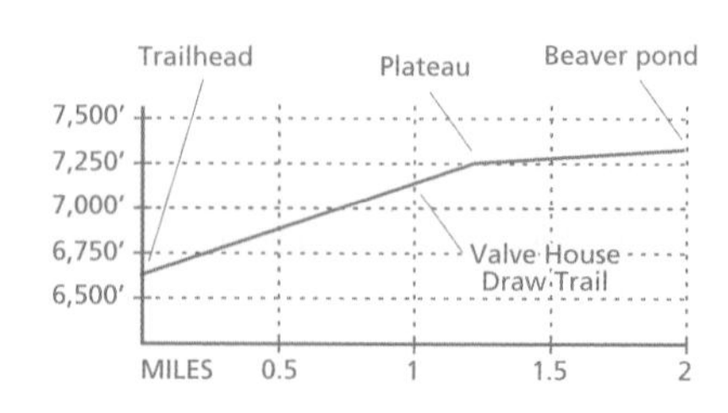

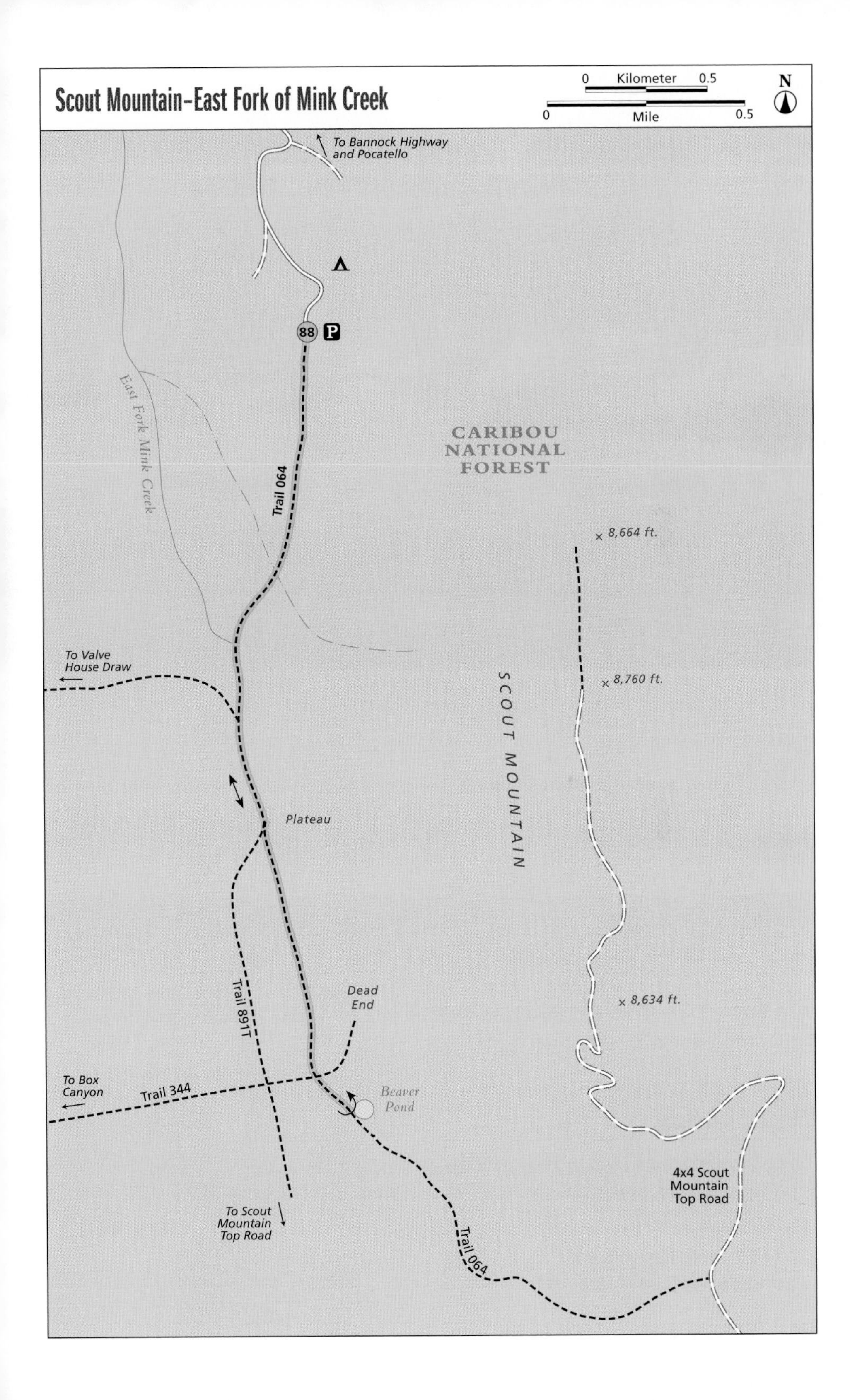
Scout Mountain–East Fork of Mink Creek
0 Kilometer 0.5
0 Mile 0.5
N
To Bannock Highway and Pocatello
88
P
East Fork Mink Creek
CARIBOU NATIONAL FOREST
Trail 064
× 8,664 ft.
To Valve House Draw
× 8,760 ft.
SCOUT MOUNTAIN
Plateau
Trail 891T
Dead End
× 8,634 ft.
To Box Canyon
Trail 344
Beaver Pond
4x4 Scout Mountain Top Road
To Scout Mountain Top Road
Trail 064

*Scout Mountain and its pond in early spring.* PHOTO BY LUKE KRATZ

The beaver pond is a good stopping point. The beavers are long gone, but the pond shimmers in late-afternoon light. It is less compelling in midsummer when cows use it for a stock pond.

**Options:** The trail continues for another mile, and 600 feet elevation gain, to join the primitive, four-wheel-drive Scout Mountain Top Road. From here, it is another 2 miles, and 900 feet elevation gain, to the top.

Taking the 5-mile trail down Valve House Draw requires a 9-mile shuttle to the Valve House Draw Trailhead. (See Hike 89, West Fork of Mink Creek, for directions.) This is also a trail machine route.

—Jackie Johnson Maughan

## Miles and Directions

**0.0** East Fork of Mink Creek Trailhead (6,600 feet)
**1.0** Valve House Draw Trail
**1.25** Plateau (7,200 feet)
**1.75** Box Canyon Trail dead end
**2.0** Old beaver pond (7,320 feet)

# 89 West Fork of Mink Creek

The West Fork of Mink Creek trail is ungrazed by livestock and closed to motorized vehicles. Wildflowers are abundant from mid-May to July.

**See map on page 407.**
**Start:** A few miles south of Pocatello in the northern end of the Bannock Range
**Type of hike:** Day hikes, one requiring a shuttle
**Distance:** 6 miles round-trip to the beaver ponds, very suitable for families; 8 miles point-to-point ending at the Gibson Jack Creek Trailhead
**Approximate hiking time:** 2–4 hours
**Difficulty:** Moderately easy for the 6-mile hike; moderate for the 8-mile hike
**Best season:** Mid-April–mid-November
**Trail surface:** Normal dirt and rock
**Land status:** Caribou-Targhee National Forest
**Canine compatibility:** Voice command
**Fees and permits:** None
**Maps:** Clifton Creek and Pocatello South USGS quadrangles; Westside Ranger District-Caribou-Targhee National Forest map
**Trail contact:** Westside Ranger District, (208) 236-7500
**Special considerations:** No overnight camping.

**Finding the trailhead:** Drive south from the center of downtown Pocatello on South Arthur Street until it becomes Bannock Highway. Follow this road for about 8 miles to the forest boundary. You will pass subdivisions, orchards, and a couple of golf courses, but once the buildings cease, you'll see the low, brushy mountains with patches of aspen and fir and thick vegetation in the bottom of Mink Creek Canyon that are typical of the highlands of southeast Idaho.

The paved road winds up Mink Creek. Ignore the paved road to the left (to the East Fork of Mink Creek, Justice Park, and Scout Mountain) that leaves about a mile past the forest boundary. Continue until you are 3.2 miles past the forest boundary. The trailhead is on the right, just past a Pocatello city water intake structure in the stream on the left.

To reach the Gibson Jack Creek Trailhead, see Hike 87, Gibson Mountain Loop. GPS: N42 43.35' / W112 25.17'

**Parking and trailhead facilities:** The parking area has room for six or seven vehicles.

## The Hike

The West Fork of Mink Creek area presents a long and successful history of environmental restoration. The Bannock Mountains were overgrazed long ago, but grazing in the West Fork of Mink and nearby Gibson Jack Creek ceased in the early 1900s when these canyons were closed to the grazing of domestic livestock in order to protect Pocatello's municipal water supply.

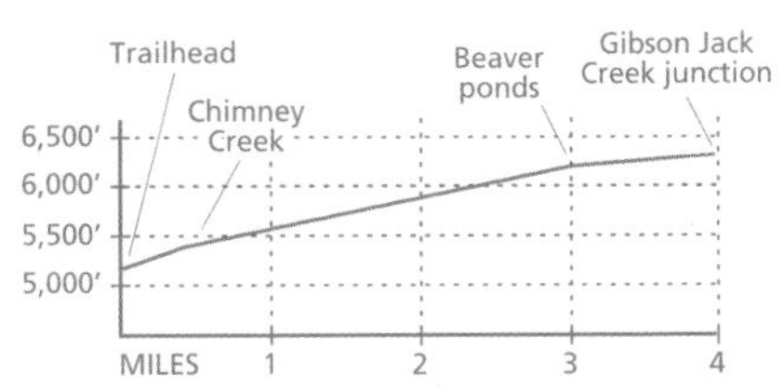


For more than half a century after the livestock closure, however, drainage from a muddy wagon track, and later a jeep track, was allowed to fester into the city water. In the early 1970s this pollution of the city's water was finally stopped when the Caribou National Forest closed the area to four-wheel-drive vehicles. Still, the use of trail motorcycles and ATVs was permitted to continue until the late 1970s, when strong pressure from environmentalists overcame forest service resistance. West Mink Trail was closed to all forms of motorized recreation.

The trail is very popular today as the only trail of substantial length in the area that is closed to motorized vehicles. It receives heavy use from hikers, equestrians, and mountain bikers. The trail is shady from the start and has a large, well-maintained trailhead.

This good trail, no longer recognizable as an old jeep road, leads directly up the canyon, mostly in the shade, climbing moderately past willow, aspen, river birch, chokecherry, and beaver ponds. A few large old-growth Douglas fir tower over the low-growing deciduous forest. After rising 200 feet in about 0.5 mile and crossing the creek once over a bridge, the trail passes a clearing on the left. A side trail descends to the clearing, a common destination for those on a stroll. The side trail crosses the clearing and the creek and climbs up a thickly vegetated side canyon (Chimney Creek). In the 1960s this was a road, but now it is an overgrown, faint trail. You can follow it for 0.5 mile alongside a spring-fed brook that bubbles between numerous beaver ponds. The trail ends at a cool spring covered by a small structure built to protect the water's purity.

The main trail continues up the West Fork Canyon. An open slope of sagebrush (and in late May, many wildflowers) rises steeply to the right, and a more gentle, forested slope is on the left.

You cross the creek on a bridge, and the trailside is enveloped in forest. In about 0.5 mile you enter a Research Natural Area. Here are many large old-growth Douglas firs and many snags. The snags are full of holes, needed by cavity-nesting birds. This protected area extends from the West Fork of Mink Creek over the top of Slate Mountain and down into Gibson Jack Creek. Ungrazed land like this is such a rarity in southeast Idaho as to be of scientific importance, hence the designated natural area. The tall flower stalks you find here in August cannot be found in nearby drainages. Dust and noxious weeds are commonplace instead.

Finally, after about 3 miles and an elevation gain of 900 feet, the grade lessens and you arrive at the beaver ponds. These are at the headwaters of the West Fork. Their number, structure, and size vary from year to year. Visitors occasionally see moose at the beaver ponds. Moose are colonizing the highlands of southeast Idaho and northern Utah, and the ungrazed ponds area is excellent habitat.

Continuing to the top of the ponds, you find a number of small structures originally built to protect Pocatello's water at its spring source. Soon you come to a fence, a gate, and a primitive road. Beyond lies cow and off-road vehicle country. You'll be impressed by the difference. You can follow the road up the hill to the left to Elk Meadows—a place of tall, virgin Douglas fir, aspen, and small meadows, and unfortunately after about June 15, cows.

The undulating topography and forest at Elk Meadows screen views of surrounding mountains and valleys, and every year a few people briefly get lost in this small area.

If you continue straight up the "road" (which is actually a broad trail) instead of climbing to Elk Meadows, you climb gently up the now broad, shallow, streamless, but pleasant canyon for about a mile until you come to a signed trail junction indicating Gibson Jack Creek to the right. You quickly cross over a wooden cattleguard and fence and begin the drop into Gibson Jack Creek Canyon.

Once again, you are in an area closed to grazing. The trail descends through lush meadow with aspen and some large Douglas fir. Here the flowering forbs often stand 6 feet tall in midsummer. You cross a creek several times, but it is usually dry by late summer.

Soon the trail begins to contour down an open, dry hillside. Below the trail in the canyon bottom, however, you view a pretty and moist area along the creek. There are many beaver ponds here, and the opposite side of the canyon has a heavy stand of Douglas-fir.

Before long, you come to a bridge over the creek. This marks the "forks." A sign, NO MOTORIZED VEHICLES, indicates a vehicle closure up the fork to your left. This is a shady canyon with a faint, unmaintained trail.

Continue down Gibson Jack Creek. The excellent trail eventually moves away from the riparian zone into rangeland with views of the Portneuf and Pocatello Mountains in the distance to the east. This rangeland is beautiful in late May and June but hot and dry later in the summer.

Both trails can be very busy on weekends and on late-summer afternoons. The lower portion of Gibson Jack Trail, which has no shade, is very popular in May and early June due to the profusion of wildflowers made possible by the long-standing prohibition on domestic livestock grazing.

**Option:** Off-road vehicles were finally banned from Gibson Jack Creek in 1993. An alternative route for them was provided. It (see Hike 87) begins at the Gibson Jack Trailhead, immediately crosses the creek, and climbs up the hillside to the south. It soon swings to the southwest and climbs the ridge. This trail is a pleasant hiking alternative at times and on days when traffic is low.

—Ralph Maughan

## Miles and Directions

**0.0** Trailhead
**0.5** Chimney Creek and clearing
**3.0** Beaver ponds
**4.0** Junction to Gibson

# Bear River Mountains

The Bear River Mountain—an extension of Utah's famed Wasatch front—dominate the skyline of the Cache Valley. They host a variety of terrain and are one of the most prominent areas for wildflowers in the Rocky Mountains. Many of the limestone and dolomite peaks are over 9,000 feet, providing unique subalpine areas rarely found in southeastern Idaho. Unfortunately, a majority of the trails on the Idaho side are open to off-road vehicles, offering little opportunity for the hiking purist. The majority of the trail to Worm Creek is "hiker only," however; initial segments for motorcycles are rarely used.

*Southeastern Idaho splender.* PHOTO BY LUKE KRATZ

# 90 Worm Creek

Access a remote, scenic area in southeast Idaho.

**Start:** 20 miles west of Montpelier, 100 miles south of Pocatello
**Type of hike:** Day hike or backpack; lollipop
**Distance:** 10.4 miles
**Approximate hiking time:** 6–7 hours
**Difficulty:** Strenuous up to ridge above horse flats; moderate to easy on the loop
**Best season:** Late June–September
**Trail surface:** Normal dirt and rocks; narrow trail
**Land status:** Cache National Forest
**Canine compatibility:** Voice command
**Fees and permits:** None
**Map:** Paris USGS quadrangle
**Trail contact:** Montpelier Ranger District, (208) 847-0375

**Finding the trailhead:** From Montpelier take US 89 through the towns of Ovid and Paris, then on to Bloomington. At the sign reading BLOOMINGTON CANYON, turn west toward the mountains. This road leaves pavement after a little over a mile and enters national forest land at 4.6 miles. It's a good road, but watch for rocks and oncoming traffic—it gets narrow in places. After 7 miles the road forks. Take the left fork, FR 409, up toward Bloomington Lake for less than 0.5 mile, then make a left onto FR 459. Follow this road for 0.5 mile to its end near the South Fork of Bloomington Creek and park at the trailhead. GPS: N42 10.43' / W111 33.05'

## The Hike

For the first 0.5 mile, the trail follows the South Fork of Bloomington Creek. Watch for resident moose lurking through willows and trout darting between pools. This used to be a road but has been blocked off with large boulders. At the junction head through the forest, crossing a small bridge, and begin the ascent up the ridge above Horse Flats. This section of the hike is available for motorcycle use, but the narrow trail would seem too steep and difficult to negotiate through its rocks and tree roots. After an uphill hike of 1 mile (seeming like 5) with two switchbacks, you reach the ridge overlooking Horse Flats to the east. On the other side are beautiful views of Paris Peak and surrounding Bear River Mountains. Here at nearly 8,400 feet, a junction to the right continues along the ridge. Follow this trail instead of descending down into the broad valley of Horse Flats. For 1.6 miles meander along the ridge until you reach Worm Lake, catching occasional distant views of Idaho and Utah's well-visited Bear Lake area.

Worm Lake can be little more than a giant puddle depending on when you visit. It does have a beautiful backdrop of lush pine forests and green-walled alpine cliffs. At the lake, the trails begin to fizzle; keep to the left side to begin the loop. After picking up this trail, head north down to the spring of Worm Creek. Follow this for over a mile until you reach a campsite area near a draw. If you reach large cliffs

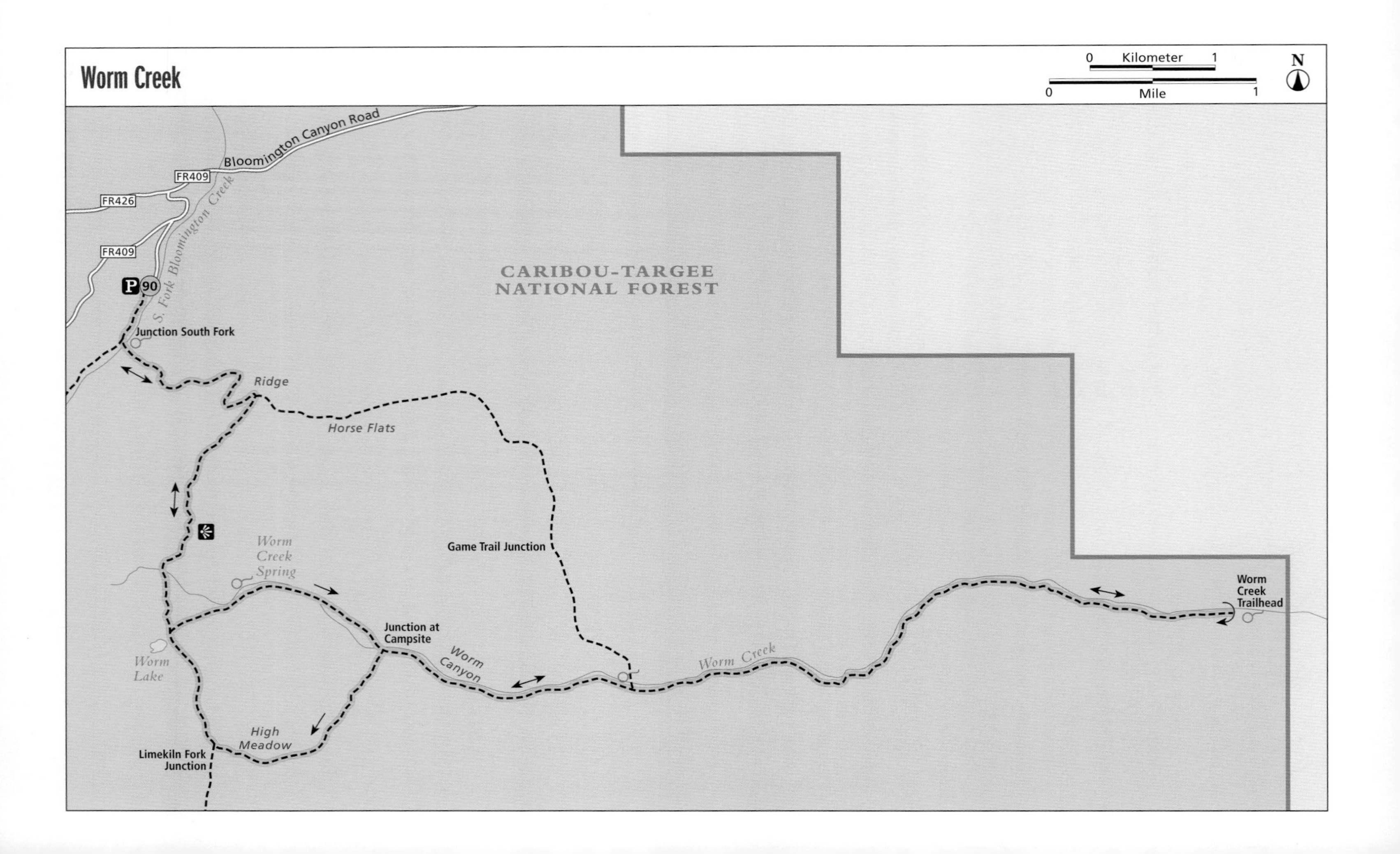
Worm Creek
0 Kilometer 1
0 Mile 1
N
Bloomington Canyon Road
FR409
FR426
FR409
S. Fork Bloomington Creek
P
90
Junction South Fork
CARIBOU-TARGEE
NATIONAL FOREST
Ridge
Horse Flats
Worm
Creek
Spring
Game Trail Junction
Junction at
Campsite
Worm
Canyon
Worm Creek
Worm
Lake
High
Meadow
Limekiln Fork
Junction
Worm
Creek
Trailhead

over Worm Creek Canyon (though they are worth checking out), you've gone too far; you'll need to retrace your steps to the camp area. The trail junction is faint, but turn right up the draw and pick up the trail again. As you continue ascending, to your left you may catch a glimpse of the rock formations above the forest. Deer are very common here.

Finally at the top there is a great open area. The trail disappears here, but you can pick it up again if you remain near the forest edge instead of crossing the open meadow. The rest of the way simply loops you back to southern part of Worm Lake, where you can take the trail back down the mountain to arrive back at the trailhead.

**Options:** Another way to access the loop part of this lollipop hike is to begin at Worm Creek from Worm Creek Road and follow the creek itself for 4 miles until it reaches the junction at the camp area. You cannot be in the area without visiting scenic Bloomington Lake. Continue up FR 409 to the trailhead; it's an easy 0.5-mile hike to this pristine gem of a lake.

## Miles and Directions

**0.0** Trailhead (7,444 feet)
**0.6** Junction with South Fork of Bloomington Creek
**1.5** Ridgetop trail junction
**3.1** Worm Creek and trail heading north to Worm Creek Springs
**4.4** Campsite area
**6.6** Keep right (north) at meadows
**7.2** Return to Worm Lake on south side
**7.3** Head back from Worm Lake 3.1 miles the way you came
**8.9** Ridgetop trail junction
**10.4** Arrive back at the trailhead

# Mount Bennett Hills

The Mount Bennett Hills are located on the northern edge of the Snake River Plain in an area where volcanic rocks overlap the Idaho Batholith. The hills consist of a horst (an uplifted block of the earth's crust) bounded by the Camas Prairie graben (a depression) on the north and the Snake River Plain to the south. The hills rise abruptly out of the Snake River Plain and run from west to east, with their highest points on the west. On the east, they gradually disappear under the basalt of the Snake River Plain.

From the Camas Prairie on their north, they look like hills, and not very interesting ones at that, but from the much lower Snake River Plain, they look like mountains. Their southern flank, which drains into the Snake River Plain, has many miles of little-explored canyons with eroded volcanic rocks, many in fantastic shapes. The best-known portion of this eroded flank is the Big City and the Little City of Rocks areas, where the City of Rocks tuff (welded together volcanic ash) has been sculpted by water and wind into huge clusters of odd shapes, often called "hoodoos."

Much of the land in these hills is private, but the majority is public, managed by the Bureau of Land Management, and mostly used for low-value grazing.

—Ralph Maughan

# 91 Gooding City of Rocks

Enter a world of fantastic volcanic rock "hoodoos" painted with brilliant-colored lichens. Wildflowers flourish in the spring.

**Start:** In the Mount Bennett Hills south of Camas Prairie and Fairfield, about 15 linear miles north of Gooding
**Type of hike:** A short day hike (out-and-back) and a long day hike (loop)
**Distance:** 7.3 miles for the loop
**Approximate hiking time:** 2–4 hours
**Difficulty:** Fourmile Canyon is easy. The Coyote Creek Loop is moderately strenuous due to the lack of a trail and the need to keep track of forks
**Best season:** Mid-May–mid-June
**Trail surface:** Normal dirt and rock
**Land status:** Shoshone District, Bureau of Land Management
**Canine compatibility:** On leash recommended.
**Fees and permits:** None
**Maps:** Fir Grove Mountain and McKinney Butte USGS quadrangles
**Trail contact:** Shoshone Field Office, BLM, (208) 732-7200
**Special considerations:** Rattlesnakes. Also, you could get lost in these hoodoos. The 7.5-minute topographic map is an absolute must. Bring wading shoes for Coyote Creek unless it is midsummer or fall; bring drinking water in summer.

**Finding the trailhead:** To reach the City of Rocks area, one must travel on Idaho Highway 46 for approximately 17.5 miles north from Gooding or for 14 miles south from the Highway 20 junction east of Fairfield. At this point there is a dirt road heading west so turn left on it if coming from the south or turn right if coming from the north. Follow this good dirt road for 7  miles then turn left at the obvious junction, which usually is signed. Follow the signs to the City of Rocks, and park near the rock with the whited-out sign (still legible) City of Rocks. Don't go down this road if it's muddy. You will probably get stuck even in a four-wheel drive. Fortunately, this dirt road is fairly good when dry, and it dries in about twelve hours after a thunderstorm. GPS: N43 08.62' / W114 45.89'
**Parking and trailhead facilities:** The trailhead is undeveloped. It is a flat place on a knoll above and among the rocks. There is room for about five vehicles.

## The Hike

The hoodoos and pinnacles of ancient volcanic ash flows, welded together by time and pressure, are at their most impressive in the Mount Bennett Hills at the Gooding City of Rocks and the nearby Little City of Rocks.

The most scenic parts of the Gooding City of Rocks are the canyon portions. In the canyons, the attraction of the odd rock formations is supplemented by small creeks (in spring and early summer) and intimate streamside meadows. In addition, many of the canyon bottoms are generally not grazed by domestic livestock, a rarity in the public rangelands of the West, where typically all rangeland is under grazing permit and is generally greatly modified from pre-Euro-American conditions. Thus, there are plants you normally do not see and more wildlife, even including elk, deer, and an occasional black bear.

*A playground of basalt.* PHOTO BY LUKE KRATZ

The time to do these hikes is in the late spring. Summer is too hot, and there is no water in the fall.

Following are descriptions of two separate hikes at the City of Rocks—one short and easy, the other a lengthy loop.

### *Fourmile Creek*

This is an easy hike. Most of it is a stroll. From your parking spot near the whited-out sign, walk through the hoodoos off in an easterly direction. You will soon descend into Fourmile Creek (a shallow canyon). The only thing you have to remember is to carefully note where you descended, for finding your way back could be momentarily confusing because of the maze of similar-appearing hoodoos.

The canyon bottom is only from 5 to about 50 feet wide, but it is meadowy with a rivulet gurgling its way along in May and early June. Walking is easy amid the dark brown rocks splotched with bright yellow and orange lichens.

After about a mile, the canyon opens up and dries, and the rocks become less numerous. There are many places to camp as the canyon begins to open up. Return to your vehicle the way you came.

### *Coyote Creek Loop*

This complete hike is a long day hike or a comfortable overnighter. It would probably be considered moderately difficult because of the need for map-reading skills, several narrows, and the lack of a trail. It is not physically strenuous, however. It is mostly walking along meadows beside tiny streams.

If you are not planning to do the entire loop (perhaps you will only want to walk to the narrows and return), make a careful note of where you descended and of the number of several similar-appearing side canyons that you soon pass.

Walk south-by-southwest from the parking area, and the hike immediately leads down a scenic, shallow canyon much like Fourmile Creek. The rocks become more impressive as you continue. Some look like giant chickens, others like toadstools. There are a number of windows or arches in the rock, too.

You are approaching the narrows of "east" Coyote Creek when you come to a narrow pour-off with a pool below it in May and much of June. This barrier is easy should you choose to wade. Downstream from the pour-off, the rock formations soon become higher and take on a very bizarre appearance, and soon you are in the narrows. You may want to wade, and the wading is easy, complicated only by the presence of some brush. If the day is cool, the narrows may be uncomfortably cold since they are in the shade and it's often windy. I saw no poison ivy here (or anywhere in the City of Rocks). You should watch for rattlesnakes, however. They are scattered throughout the Mount Bennett Hills.

After about 0.25 mile, the narrows end abruptly. The canyon widens, and the stream disappears. From here to the junction with Coyote Creek, the canyon is more open but still scenic. The stream rises and disappears several more times. You do pass by two large hoodoo-lined side canyons on your right, but you will know they are not Coyote Creek because they are smaller than the canyon you are following. They do make interesting side hikes.

You reach Coyote Creek about a mile below the narrows when the east fork is joined by a side canyon larger than the one you have been following. In May this canyon has two or three times the flow of its east fork.

Head up Coyote Creek. It is fairly easy walking and is filled with impressive rock formations from the beginning. In addition to hoodoos and pinnacles, there are quite a few natural arches (perhaps better described as "windows" in the rocks). I found the canyon very beautiful.

Coyote Creek has two sets of narrows. The first one you will encounter is easy, although you may have some shallow wading. The second is the more spectacular, but you must climb about 40 feet up the left side of the canyon and go around part of the upper narrows. This is not at all difficult, but exercise caution.

A large side canyon enters at the upper narrows. Its mouth is blocked from easy entry by a 10-foot-high cliff. In spring a waterfall spills over the cliff. Its entrance is guarded by five or six 50-foot pinnacles that look like the upright femur bones of some giant.

Above the upper narrows, the stream disappears briefly and the rocks shrink in size. I spotted a rattlesnake here. They try hard to get out of your way, but you should always walk with care. Use of a walking stick is helpful.

Rattlesnakes like flat, sunny areas near water.

Continue following Coyote Creek to its origin at an ugly grazed-out area and water trough called Coyote Springs. All but the last 0.25 mile is scenic. The only difficulty is choosing the correct fork of the canyon as you head upstream. The rule to follow is this: In every case where the forks are large enough to be confusing, choose the right fork.

From Coyote Springs, follow the dirt road 0.25 mile back to your vehicle.

—Ralph Maughan

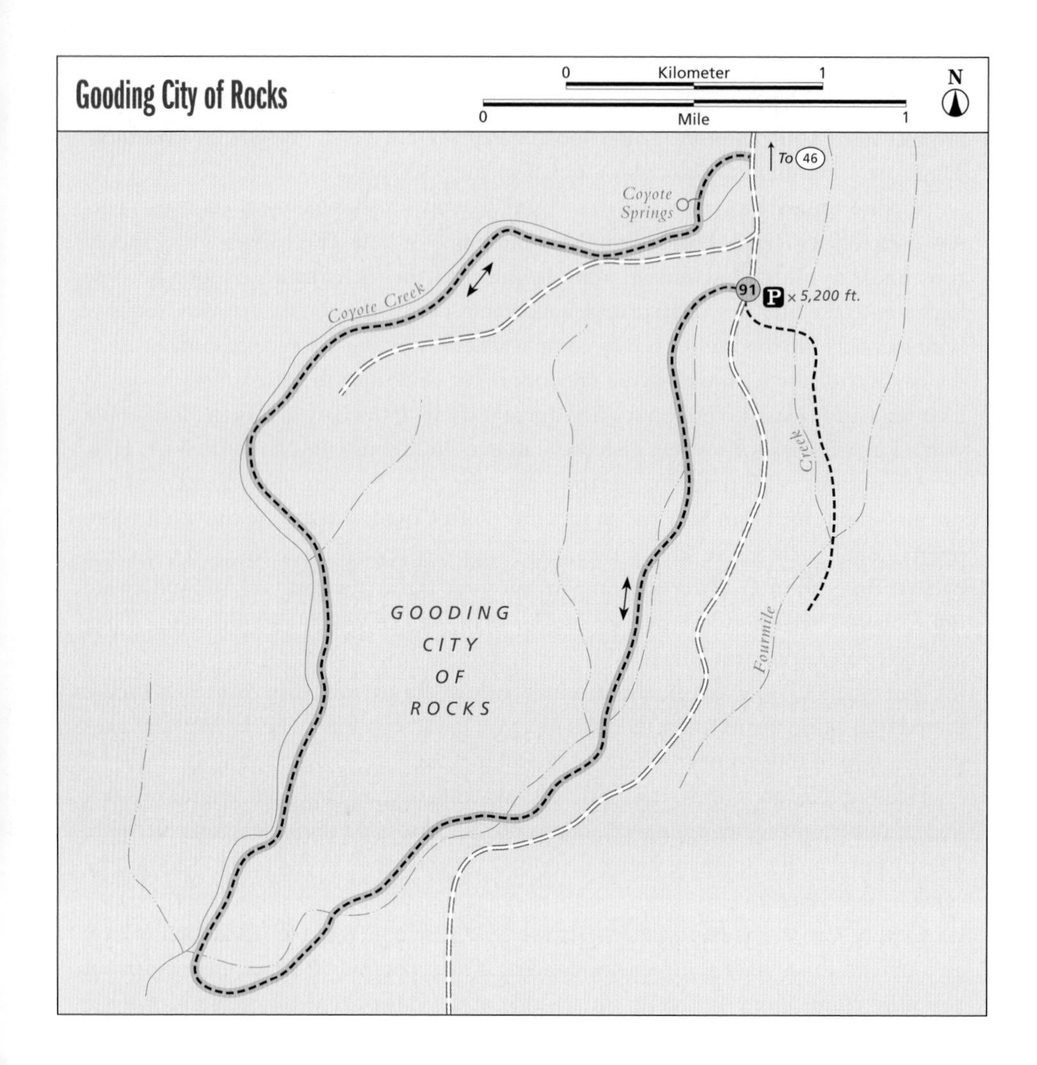


## Miles and Directions

**(Coyote Creek Loop)**

**0.0** Trailhead (5,200 feet)

**2.0** Narrows (4,680 feet)

**3.0** Confluence with Coyote Creek (4,420 feet)

**3.7** Narrows (4,500 feet)

**5.5** Narrows (4,760 feet)

**7.0** Coyote Spring (5,160 feet)

**7.3** Trailhead (5,200 feet)

# Craters of the Moon National Monument and Wilderness

Craters of the Moon National Monument protects the most unusual part of one of the largest lava flows in North America.

In contrast with lava spewed from the summit of a volcano, the molten rock that formed the Snake River Plain flowed from rifts (cracks) miles long. Lava from the Great Rift, as the largest rift is known, formed a series of caves (actually lava tunnels), tree molds, spatter cones, and huge craters—a landscape so unearthly that the NASA astronauts trained for the moon landings here.

The landscape is also remarkable for the tenacious life-forms that eke out an existence in the almost barren lava fields. Scattered here and there inside the flows are pockets of soil that support some grasses, sagebrush, often rare wildflowers, and an occasional limber pine. This is a rare landscape similar to volcanic areas of Hawaii, which is why some of its terminology is Hawaiian in origin. These islands of vegetation in a sea of lava are called *kipukas*, a Hawaiian term meaning "window in the lava." Many of these kipukas have never been grazed by livestock. That in itself makes them unique.

This is a stern, harsh land, very demanding of the plants and animals that live on it and the hikers who visit it. Dense fogs can roll in from the Snake River to the south, making the hard walking even more difficult by obscuring distant reference landmarks. Problems with orientation become even more difficult because a magnetic compass fails to work properly due to the high iron content of the basaltic rocks. GPS units can solve at least that difficulty.

Although the land is harsh, it holds its own special fascination. Late May and early June can reward the hiker with bright lichens on the basalt and wildflowers growing in the black cinders. Summer hiking is very hot. Not many do it. Once again, fall has nice temperatures. While some ski the loop road in the winter, hiking over snow-covered blocks of basalt is pretty much an impossible task, though hiking the modest system of trails is not arduous.

The core of the present monument, that portion beyond the loop road, was classified by Congress as a unit of the National Wilderness Preservation System in the 1970s.

Efforts to protect all of the vast Craters of the Moon Lava Flow, which extends far beyond the monument boundary, and the Wapi Flow to its southeast seem to have reached fruition. At the end of his second term, President Clinton enlarged the national monument twelvefold. The enlarged national monument, now over 715,000 acres, includes all of the Craters of the Moon Lava Flow, the Wapi Lava Flow to its southeast, all of the Great Rift, plus some intervening and surrounding sagebrush steppe.

—Ralph Maughan

# 92 Echo Crater

In Idaho's only national monument, you can witness very uncommon terrain. A moonscape of beautiful, tormented, colorful lava introduces the Great Rift—a huge volcanic fissure in the earth's surface. Unique desert, blooming flowers, and lava landscapes highlight this area for hikes of varied distances.

**Start:** About 75 miles west of Idaho Falls
**Type of hike:** Day hike or overnight; out-and-back
**Distance:** 10 miles round-trip
**Approximate hiking time:** Plan for at least 5 hours for the full round-trip
**Difficulty:** Moderate becoming more difficult
**Best season:** Late May and June; early fall
**Trail surface:** Lava rock and dirt
**Land status:** Craters of the Moon National Monument
**Canine compatibility:** Not allowed
**Fees and permits:** Backcountry permit required for overnight excursions; vehicle entrance fee of $8 and campground fee of $10.
**Maps:** Inferno Cone, The Watchman, and Fissure Butte USGS quadrangles
**Trail contact:** Craters of the Moon National Monument, (208) 527-3257, www.nps.gov/crmo
**Special considerations:** Carry adequate water, sunscreen, and insect repellent. The backcountry seems even larger due to its stark topography. Flashlights are needed for exploring tubes and caves. Don't wander too far off the trail because navigation is extremely difficult in the convoluted buckling of the lavascape. Compass readings don't work because of magnetic reversal in the lava rock.

**Finding the trailhead:** Drive to Craters of the Moon National Monument, 18 miles southwest of Arco on US 20/26. After stocking up on water, drive around the paved loop road and turn onto Tree Molds Road to arrive at the trailhead. GPS: N43 25.70' / W113 32.78'
**Parking and trailhead facilities:** Visitor center, restrooms, fifty-two-site campground, water taps. No hookups. The monument is open year-round, with guided walks and programs in the summer.

## The Hike

After leaving the parking lot, the paved trail quickly becomes dirt and cinders. In a little over 0.25 mile, the Wilderness Trail leaves the main Tree Molds Trail from the right (northeast) and heads down a short steep bank. It circles Broken Top, where the Buffalo Caves are located off trail on the right (west).

It then leads over an iridescent blue pahoehoe lava flow to begin to skirt Big Cinder Butte (6,515 feet), following cairns. In about a mile the trail joins the abandoned Monument Road to continue southeast toward the notch between Big Cinder and Half Cone Buttes, soon entering the Craters Wilderness. Big Cinder is the largest butte in the monument. The hiking is easy on this abandoned road for somewhat over a mile as you cross Trench Mortar Flat. Keep an eye out for the lava trees about 50 yards off the trail to your right, approximately an eighth mile after topping the low rise between Big Cinder and Half Cone. Here the rapidly cooling lava at the front of a flow encased the bases of standing trees, preserving their outlines in rock for posterity.

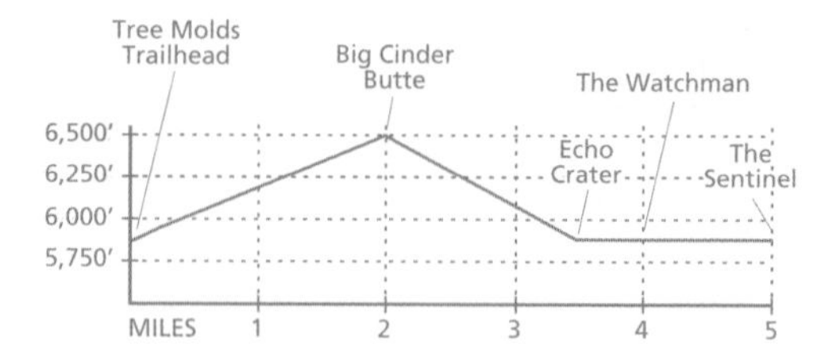


While crossing Trench Mortar Flat, stay to your right at a junction with another old road, which heads toward Crescent Butte. Mule deer can often be observed on the flanks of Coyote Butte. As the road reverts to a trail, it continues to the south, around the west side of Echo Crater (recognizable by the reddish cinders on the upper rim), then swings back toward the southeast, where it fades away completely between the Watchman and the Sentinel. Shortly after beginning the gradual descent from the gap between Coyote Butte and the low cones on the flank of Crescent Butte, you must decide whether to go cross-country to Echo Crater or the Watchman (an easy, obvious route) or to follow the old road around to the Sentinel.

To reach Echo Crater in 0.75 mile, start out soon after leaving Coyote Butte and head across the cinders toward the low lip of the crater on the northeast side. Travel through the sage is relatively easy as you parallel the Great Rift on the left (east). Bobcats are occasionally seen in the vicinity, and mule deer are common in the Craters backcountry. Enter Echo Crater from the low spot on the rim. Here you'll find resting places in limber pine in the lower portion and among juniper/sagebrush in the higher section. A short trip up the southeast ridge of the cone takes you to the red cinder top at 5,850 feet. Fair views of some of the cones and the cairns marking the site of Bearsden Waterhole in the Great Rift can be seen from here.

Bearsden Waterhole is 0.75 mile east of Echo Crater in the most discernible part of the rift. The waterhole is in a small, 20-foot-deep depression, and you must climb down from the northwest edge (an easy route) to reach the small cave. It usually has a few inches of water into the summer, but check with the park service since the water supply fluctuates greatly. Please take only a minimum, since local animals and birds rely on this supply. Little Prairie Waterhole, 0.8 mile farther southeast in the rift from Bearsden, generally holds snow and sometimes water in the spring.

Continuing a mile southeast of Echo Crater along the Great Rift will take you to the Watchman, a relatively old cone with a more recent, darker flow on the northwest face. From here, it is 0.5 mile cross-country to the Sentinel. On the northwest side of the Sentinel, you will find the end of the old road and the route back to the trailhead.

Hiking becomes more difficult beyond the Watchman, primarily because of thick brush. Split, Fissure, and Sheep Trail Buttes are progressively scattered in line with the rift. An intermittent and unreliable waterhole is located in the northwest depression of Sheep Trail Butte. To the southeast of Sheep Trail Butte lies the Vermilion Chasm, nearly at the edge of the designated wilderness. Venturing from the rift area leads you onto the Little Prairie Aa Flow to the north or the Sawtooth Aa Flow to the south. This is rough, boot-eating terrain. Just say the Hawaiian names for the lava—*pahoehoe*

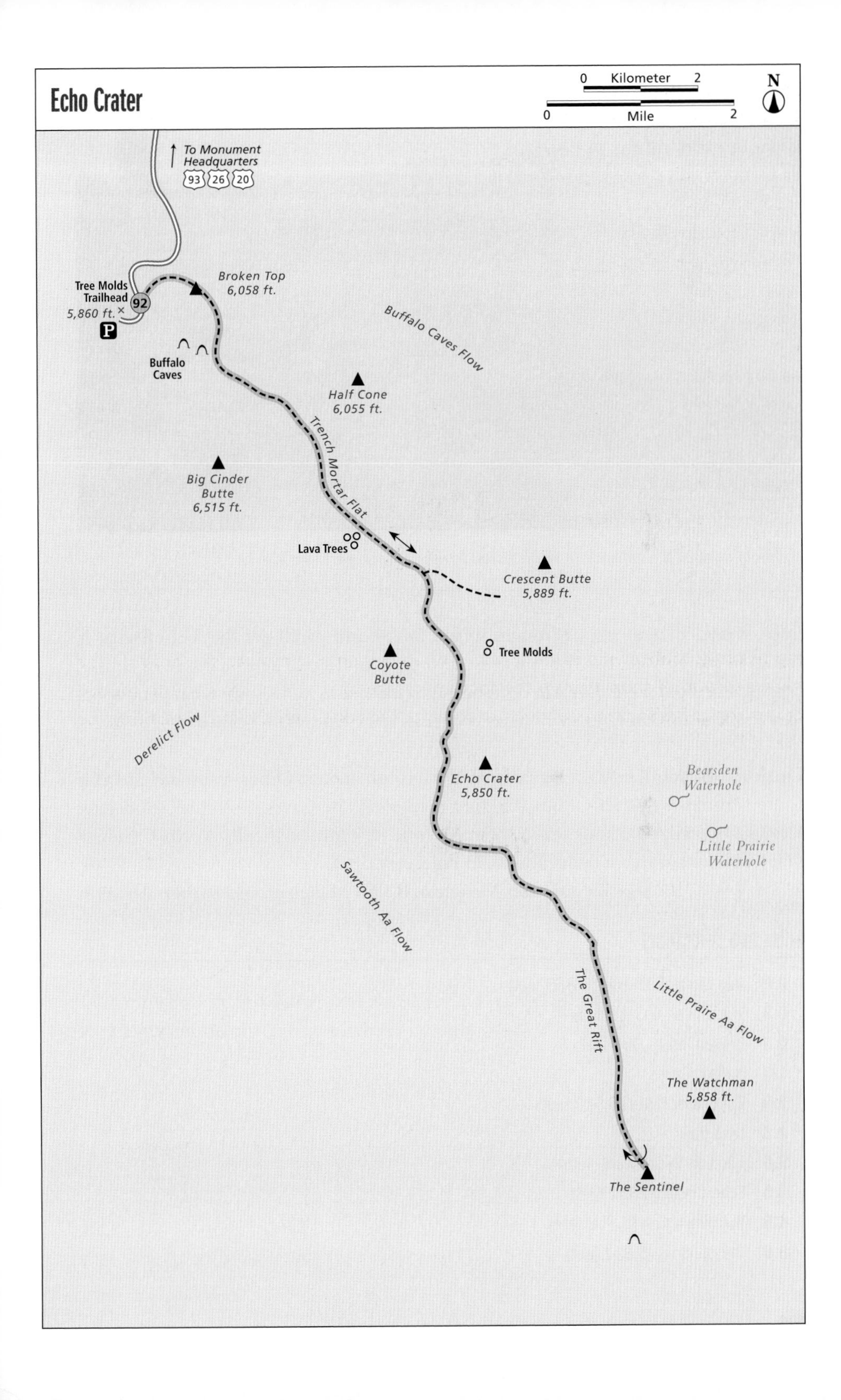

Echo Crater
0 Kilometer 2
0 Mile 2
N
To Monument Headquarters
93 26 20
Tree Molds Trailhead
92
5,860 ft.
P
Broken Top 6,058 ft.
Buffalo Caves
Buffalo Caves Flow
Half Cone 6,055 ft.
Trench Mortar Flat
Big Cinder Butte 6,515 ft.
Lava Trees
Crescent Butte 5,889 ft.
Tree Molds
Coyote Butte
Derelict Flow
Echo Crater 5,850 ft.
Bearsden Waterhole
Little Prairie Waterhole
Sawtooth Aa Flow
The Great Rift
Little Praire Aa Flow
The Watchman 5,858 ft.
The Sentinel

*A lone pine near the gateway to the lava wilderness.* PHOTO BY LUKE KRATZ

(ropy, wrinkled lava) and *aa* (rough, jagged lava)—and you'll get the feel of what it would be like to walk barefoot on these two types of flows. There's a catch, of course, because fractured pahoehoe can be as brutal to traverse as aa. Despite what your boots may think of this hike, you will never forget its stark, unearthly beauty.

**Options:** A good map is available at the visitor center. Other trails include Big Craters from the Spatter Cones, 0.5 mile, moderate; The Caves, 1–2 miles, moderate; Devil's Orchard, 0.33 mile, easy; Inferno Cone, 0.5 mile, difficult; North Crater, 3 miles, difficult; North Crater Flow, 0.25 mile, easy.

—Jackie Johnson Maughan, Ralph Maughan, and Robert N. Jones

## Miles and Directions

**0.0** Tree Molds Trailhead (5,860 feet)
**0.3** Wilderness Trail junction
**0.8** Broken Top (6,058 feet)
**1.5** Buffalo Caves
**2.0** Big Cinder Butte (6,515 feet)
**2.5** Lava trees
**3.0** Junction to Crescent Butte
**3.5** Echo Crater (5,850 feet)
**4.5** The Watchman (5,858 feet)
**5.0** The Sentinel (5,812 feet)

# Hell's Half Acre

Hell's Half Acre is the easternmost lava area on the Snake River Plain and definitely the most accessible. Hell's Half Acre, Craters of the Moon, and the Wapi flow from north of Rupert all are vast expanses of rugged lava territory. If nothing else, they can be possibly one the best places on the planet for playing hide-and-seek!

*Indian Paintbrushes amid the lava.* Photo by Cecile Perez

# 93 20 Mile Rock

Hike and explore a lava/desert playground close to Idaho Falls.

**Start:** 20 miles west of Idaho Falls
**Type of hike:** Loop or out-and-back
**Distance:** 1-mile loop or 4.5 miles (one way) to lava vent
**Approximate hiking time:** 2–8 hours
**Difficulty:** Easy to moderate
**Best season:** March–December
**Trail surface:** Predominantly lava rock
**Land status:** Upper Snake BLM
**Canine compatibility:** Voice command
**Fees and permits:** None
**Maps:** USGS BLM map
**Trail contact:** Upper Snake Field Office BLM, (208) 524-7524
**Special considerations:** Plenty of water and good footwear are both musts.

**Finding the trailhead:** From Idaho Falls drive west on US 20 until you reach Milepost 287. Continue for another 0.3 mile until you see a sign for Lava Trails; turn left on the gravel road. Keep left for less than 0.5 mile until you reach the picnic site and parking area for the trailhead. GPS: N43 33.22' / W112 26.66'

## The Hike

The Hell's Half Acre lava flow is one of several lava flows in Idaho's Snake River Plain that erupted about 4,100 years ago. It's 222 square miles, or 162,000 acres. The loop trail through this unusual terrain is marked by blue-tipped poles. Enjoy the abundant wildflowers such as evening primrose, Indian paintbrush, wild onions, penstemon, geraniums, and prickly pear cactus in May and early June. Since there is no actual trail other than following markers, you can take your time exploring the cracks and crevasses in the lava rock. Halfway through the loop there is an intersection with the trail to the lava vent that is marked with red-tipped poles. It is a slow 4.5 miles to the vent as you travel up and down through the waves and cracks of the flow.

**Options:** A more popular access to Hell's Half Acre is at the rest areas 20 miles south of Idaho Falls on I-15. There is an interpretive nature walk along pavement and a boardwalk. Cross-country exploration on any of the flows is permitted at the hiker's own risk. A handheld GPS can help guide you through miles of this somewhat desolate yet intriguing landscape.

## Miles and Directions

**0.0** Trailhead
**0.5** Intersection to lava vent trail
**5.0** Lava vent

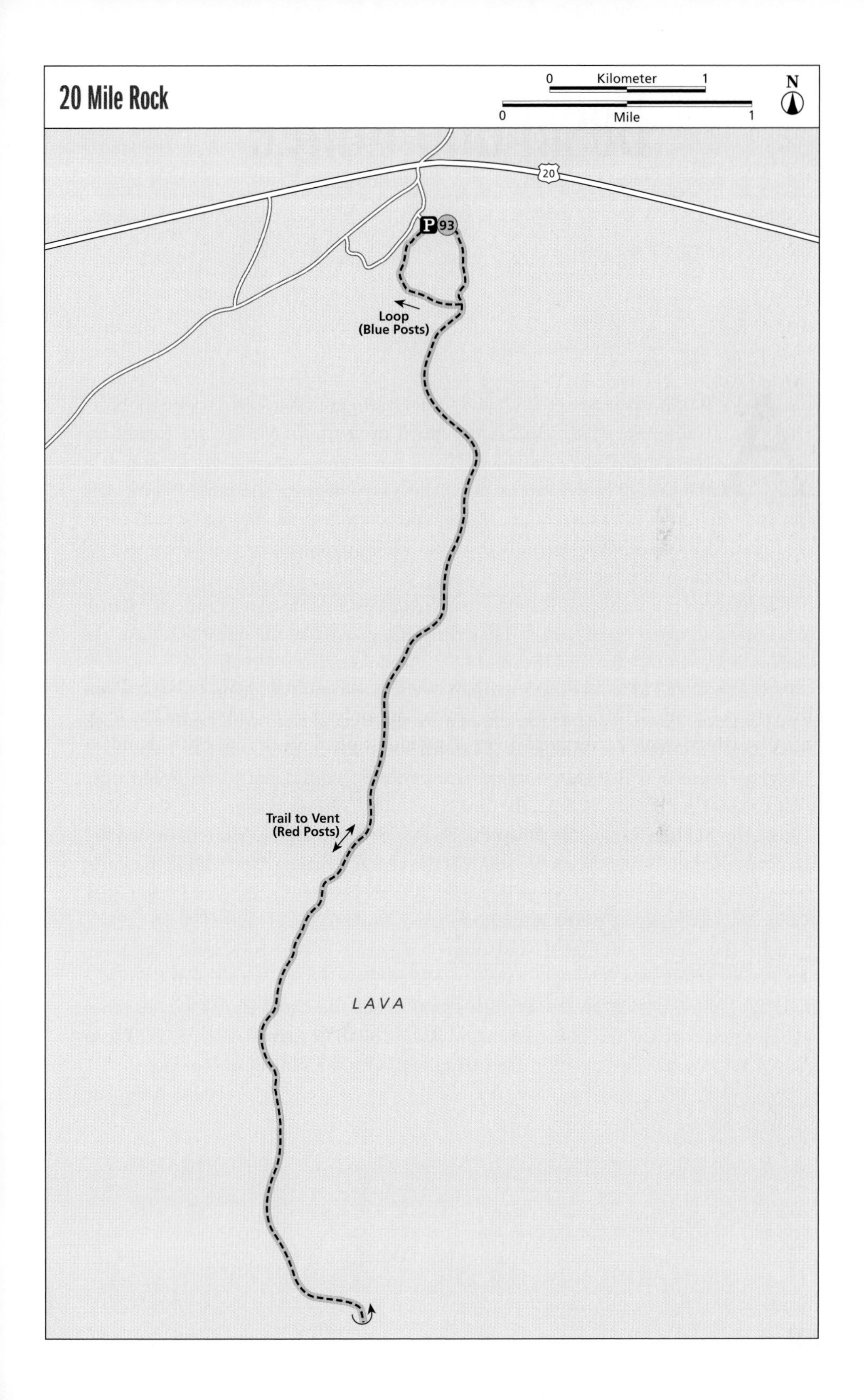
20 Mile Rock
0
Kilometer
1
0
Mile
1
N
20
P
93
Loop
(Blue Posts)
Trail to Vent
(Red Posts)
LAVA

# Basin and Range

All of Nevada, western Utah, southeast Oregon, southern Arizona, a bit of California, a bit of Idaho, and much of northern Mexico are part of the Basin and Range Province. This is not a governmental subdivision. It is the land of broad, mostly arid valleys separated by hundreds of long, narrow, and often high mountain ranges. As one person put it, the map of Nevada looks like hundreds of caterpillars crawling to the south. The caterpillars are the ranges, and between them are the big basins.

The heart of the Basin and Range is the Great Basin—that part of America where rivers flow but never reach the sea. They flow into places like the Great Salt Lake, the Carson Sink, Mono Lake, and Pyramid Lake. All drainage is internal.

Part of southern Idaho is on the margins of the Basin and Range, and a smaller part is in the Great Basin, that portion drained by the Bear River, which oddly enough flows mostly through the Middle Rockies before it dies in the Great Salt Lake.

Idaho's Basin and Range mountains are generally considered to be, going from west to east, the Albion Range, the Jim Sage and Cotterel Range, the Black Pine Range, the Sublett Range, the Deep Creek Range, the Samaria Mountains, and the Clarkston Range. While they share some of the characteristics of the Middle Rockies, most also put the Bannock Range, Pocatello Range, Portneuf Range, and Fish Creek Range into Idaho's part of the Basin and Range Province.

Idaho's tall Lemhi and Lost River Ranges have many of the characteristics of Basin and Range mountains. They are narrow, uplifted fault blocks, with normal faults at their base (none of that tricky overthrust stuff or big old batholiths). However, they are separated from the rest of the Basin and Range by the anomaly of the Snake River Plain. Due to proximity, we list these two ranges with the Northern Rockies.

—Ralph Maughan

# Deep Creek Mountains

As you move westward across southern Idaho, the Deep Creek Mountains are the first obvious substantial range in the Idaho portion of the Basin and Range Province.

Rising out of the Snake River Plain just south of American Falls, Deep Creek is a typically narrow and tall, Basin and Range chain of mountains. The range has a sharp single crest until Deep Creek Peak is reached. Deep Creek Peak is the highest point in the range at 8,748 feet.

Separated from the rest of the crest by the long canyon of Bull Creek, the Deep Creek Peak ridge creates what amounts to a double crest for about 10 miles.

There is a second peak that stands out in the Deep Creeks. In the north third of the range Bannock Peak rises to 8,263 feet and is a landmark visible for a long distance.

The range is made of limestone and, in this semi-arid area, this results in little surface water although there are a number of springs and short segments of perennial creeks. The result of the limestone is also many scenic folds, cliffs, and other interesting rock outcroppings.

The east side of the northern third of the range is on the Fort Hall Indian Reservation and is closed to entry by nontribal members. Part of the northern third also burned in one of the many wildfires of the year 2000.

The range is brushy with quaking aspen and Douglas fir on the moist side of the slopes. This makes cross-country hiking difficult due to the lack of foot trails. However, if you can attain the crest, long crestline hikes are possible in a number of places.

—Ralph Maughan

*The windy Deep Creek Crest.* PHOTO BY LUKE KRATZ

# 94 Deep Creek Crest

Cross-country hike to the crest of a southern Idaho Great Basin mountain range and fine views.

**Start:** 30 miles southwest of Pocatello
**Type of hike:** Day hike, cross-country
**Distance:** Variable, from 0.6 mile to more than 10 miles, depending how far you want to walk along the ridgeline
**Approximate hiking time:** 1–3 hours
**Difficulty:** Moderate cross-country due to elevation gain and loss and some small cliffs
**Best season:** June–September
**Trail surface:** Dirt and brush (cross-country)
**Land status:** Pocatello Field Office or Upper Snake River Field Office of the Bureau of Land Management
**Canine compatibility:** Voice command
**Fees and permits:** None
**Maps:** Deep Creek Peak USGS quadrangle; Pocatello, Idaho, BLM Surface Management Status map
**Trail Contact:** BLM Pocatello Field Office (208) 478-6375; Upper Snake River Field Office, (208) 524-7524
**Special considerations:** We think this is an easy-to-follow route, but some people get confused without a trail. There is no drinking water. Thunderstorms would make the ridge dangerous.

**Finding the trailhead:** From I-86, take exit 52 at Arbon Valley. Drive south from the exit on the paved Arbon Valley Road. After 24 miles, you come to an unincorporated cluster of houses called Pauline and the junction with the Crystal Summit Road (paved) on the left. Continue straight on the Arbon Valley Road for 3 more miles, and turn right on paved, then gravel, Knox Canyon Road. It goes due west toward the Deep Creek Mountains. In about 3 miles there is a cattleguard, and the road narrows greatly as you drop down into Knox Canyon. This canyon stretch of the road is usually in good condition for all kinds of vehicles, but the road is narrow and has many blind curves due to the vegetation. The road climbs to the pass (7,330 feet) in 7 miles. GPS: N42 27.78' / W112 41.98'
**Parking and trailhead facilities:** There is no trailhead. Pull off right at the pass and park by the dirt roadway. There is informal room for several vehicles, but you will likely find none.

## The Hike

This is a rare opportunity to drive to a pass near the summit of a narrow Basin and Range mountain and hike along it without following a motor track.

At the pull-off area, there is an obvious old track that leads steeply uphill through some brush with an old NO MOTOR VEHICLES post in the middle of it. Follow it and climb steeply. The old track quickly fades, and you break out onto a trailless, open slope. Grand views are instantaneous. Your immediate goal, and perhaps the goal of the hike if you want to make it short, is the limestone buttress you see above (Peak 7,814). You reach it in just 0.3 mile but with a 500-foot climb.

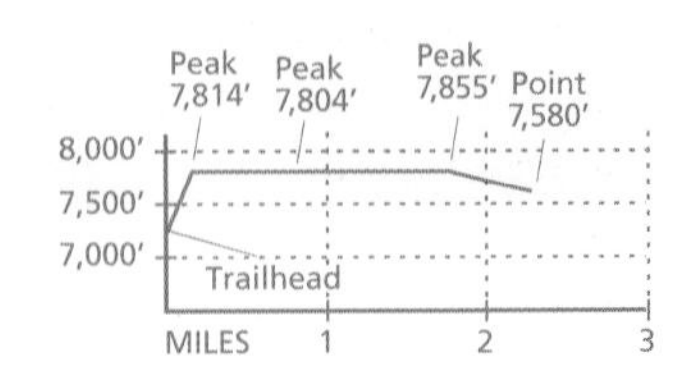

It is easy to walk around the buttress to its right (east). During the flowering season (usually June), you will have already seen many low-growing ridgetop wildflowers. They are especially beautiful where they grow out of the cracks in the limestone, such as on the buttress at 7,814. The limestone is also coated with patches of bright orange lichen at the buttress and many other places.

Past the buttress you can see your farthest possible goal, distant Bannock Peak to the north. Actually, you must stop just before the peak because it is on the Fort Hall Indian Reservation and is closed to the public. Only the most intrepid hikers would make it that far anyway. To your immediate east, across the head of Knox Canyon, is the other grand peak of the range—Deep Creek Peak, elevation 8,748 feet. It is set just to the east of the crest of the Deep Creek Mountains. It actually helps form a double crest for about 5 miles. Its sparsely forested slopes and many lesser summits to the southeast are bedecked by scores of low, but lengthy, limestone benches.

Continuing north, the crest drops 200 feet and then climbs back up almost 200 feet to the top of Peak 7,804. The saddle between the two peaks is interesting because the drop of 200 feet changes the vegetation. From Peak 7,804, there are fine views of Rockland Valley to the west and the Great Basin Sublett Range on the valley's west side.

Now you drop almost 400 feet to the next saddle. Some conifers encroach on the ridgeline. There are more small, but interesting, limestone cliffs and rock formations, many with a lot of quartz in them. Across the head of the small canyon (Porter Canyon) that begins at the saddle and drops into Rockland Valley is a peak, elevation approximately 7,800 feet, with a number of interestingly shaped cliffs on its flanks. You hike on the crest just to the east (right) of this peak and eventually gain Peak 7,855.

Past 7,855, the ridgetop becomes broader and gains sagebrush as you walk to Point 7,580 to the northeast. You may have a tendency to head north-by-northwest instead to Point 7,601, but this takes you out onto a lesser side ridge.

Most people won't go beyond Point 7,580 because of another 400-foot drop, and this description will end at 7,580. But the adventurous can continue about as far as they wish. Each peak is a little different, and so is each saddle.

You may not see much wildlife, but the Deep Creek Range is notable for its large mule deer population and the substantial number of cougar that prey on them. There are many ledges and small overhangs providing good cougar resting, denning, and observation spots.

As is often the case with high desert mountain ranges managed by the Bureau of Land Management, there is little recreation and cows are overabundant, but only a few will be found on the crest of the range. In late September, the golden leaves of the quaking aspen groves in the canyons below add to this hike. In the spring enjoy a good run through the snowfields along the slopes.

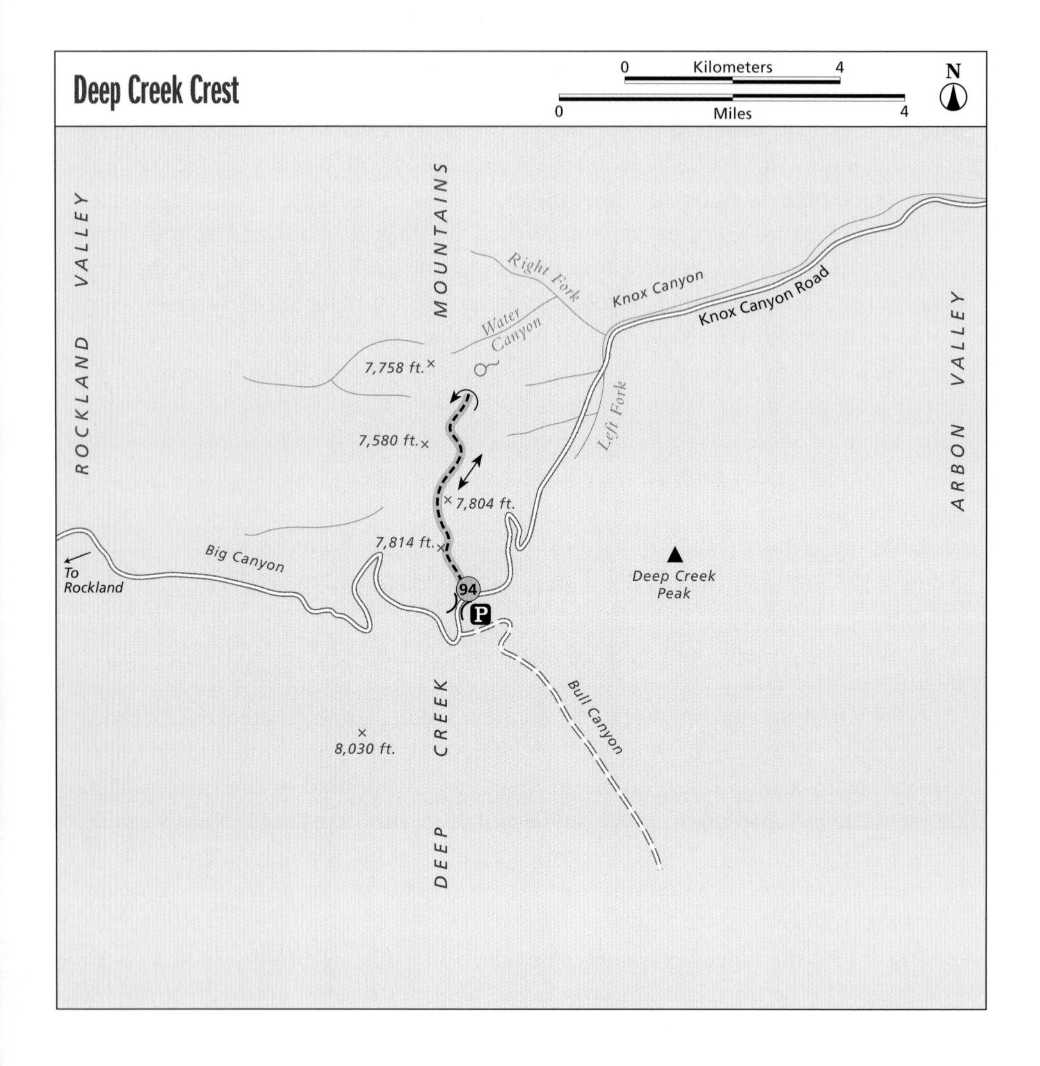


**Options:** From the informal trailhead, you could also climb Deep Creep Peak and walk a long way along its ridgeline southward, gradually losing altitude. A climb of the ridge to the immediate south of the summit road does not look desirable due to thick brush and heavy timber on the slope that faces you (the north slope).

—Ralph Maughan

## Miles and Directions

**0.0** Informal trailhead
**0.3** Summit of Peak (7,814 feet)
**0.8** Summit of Peak 7,804 feet)
**1.7** Summit of Peak (7,855 feet)
**2.2** Point (7,580 feet)

# Albion Range

The Albion Range is the westernmost of Idaho's slice of the Basin and Range Province. The Goose Creek Mountains (South Hills) to the west are part of the Columbia River Plateau and are geologically much different from the Basin and Range Province or the Rocky Mountains.

The Albion Range rises southeast of the town of Burley and due east of Oakley. It is the highest mountain range south of the Snake River, culminating at 10,339-foot Cache Peak. The range consists of two big mountains connected by a lower ridge (crossed at Elba Pass). On the north is Mount Harrison and, to its south, massive Independence Mountain, of which Cache Peak is the highest point.

An impressive cirque was carved by glaciers into the northeast side of Mount Independence. Here are four lovely lakes, accessible only by trail. This hike is described in this section.

Mount Harrison has a road-accessible subalpine lake as well as a fire lookout and the Pomerelle Ski Area, which is notable for having plenty of snow even when other resorts lack snowpack.

At the southern end of the range, soft granite has been exposed to the elements and eroded into numerous odd-shaped monolithic domes, pinnacles, and huge boulders. This area, called the Silent City of Rocks, is a national reserve created by Congress. This designation gives the area protection from vandalism and promotes the development of hiking trails, sanitation facilities, and camping and picnicking facilities. The Silent City of Rocks National Reserve is a splendid area for rock climbing or an easy family outing in the fall or late spring. We describe this fascinating rock garden in this section.

—Ralph Maughan

*The Albion Mountains.* Photo by John Kratz

# 95 Independence Lakes

Here are four scenic subalpine lakes high on Independence Mountain. Grand views are available of Mount Harrison, Elba Basin, Cache Peak, and the Jim Sage Mountains.

**Start:** 35 road miles southeast of Burley
**Type of hike:** Day hike or overnight backpack; out-and-back
**Distance:** 4.4 mile
**Approximate hiking time:** 2 hours to the lakes
**Difficulty:** Moderate
**Best season:** Mid-July–August
**Trail surface:** Normal dirt and rock
**Land status:** Sawtooth National Forest
**Canine compatibility:** On leash recommended
**Fees and permits:** None
**Maps:** Cache Peak USGS quadrangle; Twin Falls and Burley Ranger Districts–Sawtooth National Forest Map
**Trail contact:** Burley Ranger District, (208) 678-0430
**Special considerations:** Water is scarce below the lakes

**Finding the trailhead:** Drive about 20 miles south of Burley on ID 27 to the small town of Oakley. Turn left onto 2000 South from Oakley's Main Street (which is also ID 27). Take this paved county road directly east toward Independence Mountain. The road is paved for 6 miles. As the pavement ends, a sign indicates that the rough gravel road ahead leads to Independence Lakes. The road, which seems to have been covered with inordinately rough gravel, climbs more than 2,000 feet steeply. It switchbacks 5 miles up to Elba Pass (7,106 feet). The road surface improves after 2 miles, when you enter the Sawtooth National Forest.

At Elba Pass there is a fine view of the South Hills to your west as well as part of Mount Harrison to the left and massive Independence Mountain at two o'clock.

The road forks at the pass. Do not continue across the pass, but take the road to the right. A sign indicates that the Independence Lakes Trailhead is 4 miles. Head over a rise and down the other side and you come to a fork after about a mile. Keep to the right. After about 1 more mile, you come to Potholes Junction. Here take the fork to the left. Now continue to the trailhead. The road climbs through some aspen with good views of Mount Harrison to the north. About 0.3 mile from the trailhead, you come to the horse transfer trailhead. Pass it by, and follow the road as it swings downhill to end at Dry Creek (which has water).

Elba Pass can also be accessed from the east by turning onto CR 1950 South at Elba. This road eventually becomes FR 548. The pass is 10 miles of gravel, then dirt road from Elba. GPS: N42 13.11' / W113 40.39'

**Parking and trailhead facilities:** There is a spacious trailhead with an outhouse, bulletin board, stock-loading ramp, and walk-in picnic area surrounded by a fence to keep the omnipresent cattle at bay. Park and open the gate to the campground (close it to keep the cows out), cross Dry Creek on a good bridge, and walk through the campground to the broad trail. You are now on your way.

## The Hike

The broad and easy trail, which is closed to motorized vehicles, climbs gently across the forested north face of Independence Mountain toward Green Creek, staying far above Dry Creek. There are breaks and meadows in the fir, spruce, and aspen forest with outstanding views to the north and northeast.

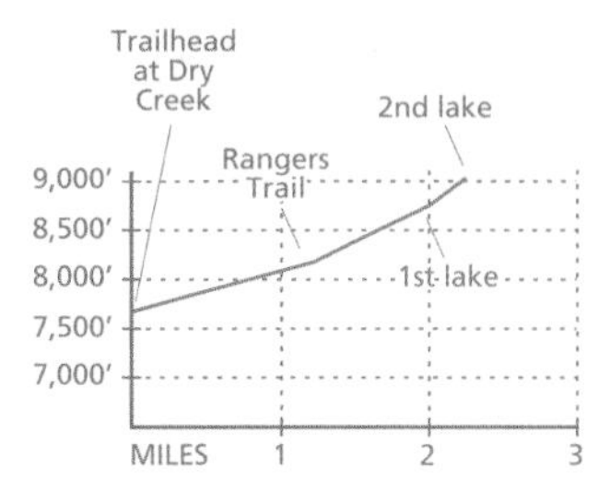


I approached the trail with trepidation because of all the cattle gathered at the fence around the picnic area. I thought this perhaps would be a trek through environmental degradation, but there were few cows on the mountain itself, perhaps because the sparse understory consists mostly of inedible or toxic native plants like penstemon, lupine, western coneflower, and astragalus (the locoweed genus).

Shortly before you begin the climb up into the cirque that holds the lakes, the trail passes just above a small forest fire burn and there is a trail junction. To the left is the Ranger Trail (not on the map), which drops into Green Creek. Keep to the right, and begin to climb steeply toward the lakes.

The trail never drops into Green Creek but keeps on a shelf just to its right (west). There are many forks in this broad trail, but they are all switchback cutoffs. After climbing 900 feet, you suddenly come upon the first lake, which is large, shallow, and partially filled with marsh grass. It has plenty of small fish, however. Behind the lake is the steep cirque wall just below Independence Peak. This impressive wall continues up the entire west side of the cirque.

The cirque is very rocky with boulders of granitic rock and beautiful white quartzite of the Eureka Formation (metamorphosed white sandstone).

The trail continues to the second lake, which appears to be by far the largest on the topo but in fact is not by the end of the summer. This lake is deep, however, and has large trout.

There is no trail to the upper two lakes. The route is over and through many granitic gray boulders. Although the lakes are fishless, this hike over the rocks is worthwhile because the upper two lakes are beautiful, especially the very last, which is large, but shallow, with very clear water. Sunlight through the clear water does beautiful things to the moderately large, flat, submerged rocks.

Cache Peak, which is the highest point on Mount Independence, rises just east of the lakes, but that side of the cirque wall is not as impressive as the west side. Cache Peak, which tops out at 10,339 feet, is also the highest mountain in Idaho south of the Snake River.

The only downside is the fact that a few cows do make it to the lakes. Complain to the Sawtooth National Forest, for this mountain has no real food for them, and it shows bad public priorities, given the popularity of this trail and these lakes.

**Options:** You can scramble to the top of the mountain from the head of the cirque, although this is not easy. From the top, you have a wonderful 360-degree view of all the mountains and valleys of southern Idaho and of the Silent City of Rocks

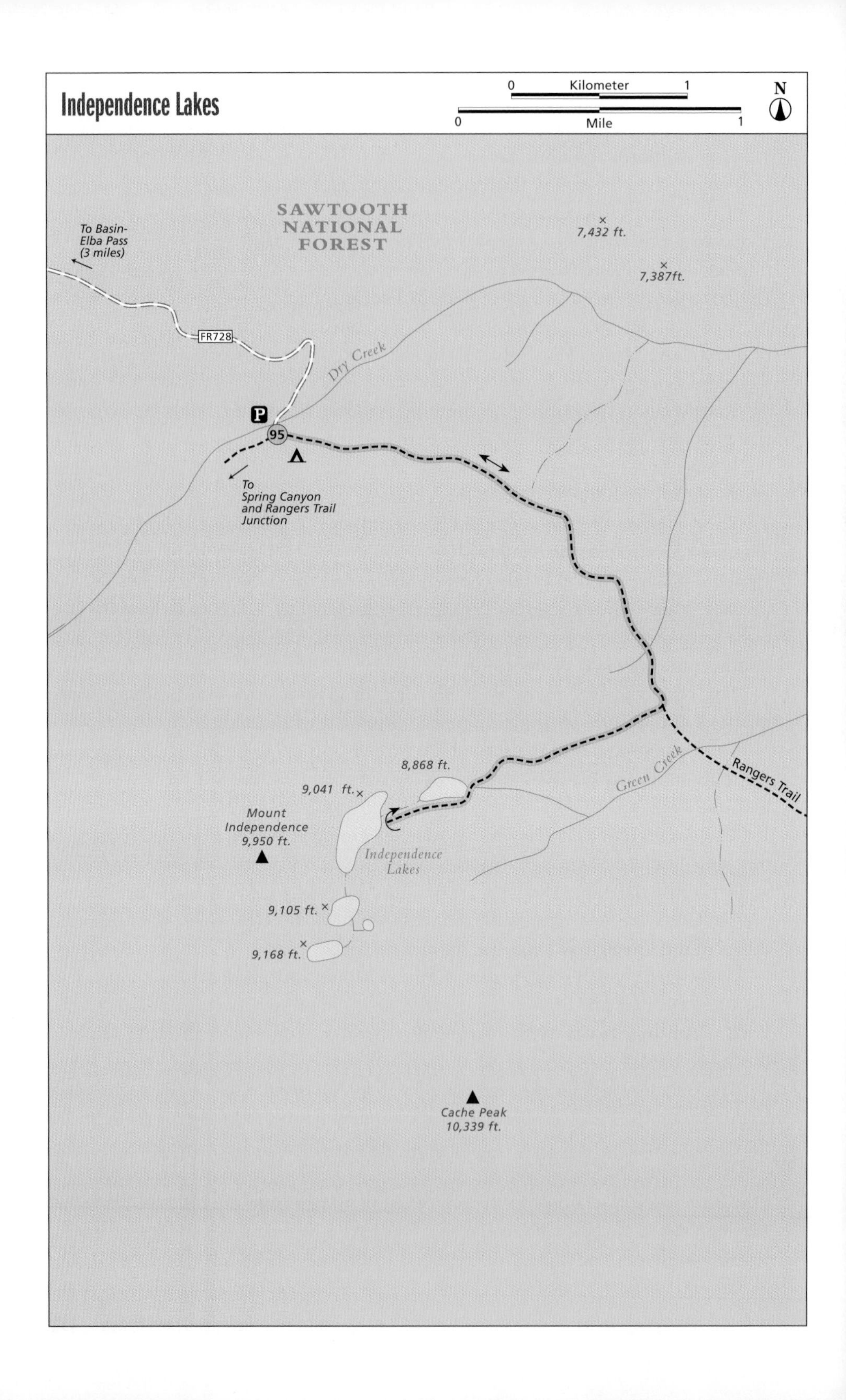
Independence Lakes
0
Kilometer
1
0
Mile
1
N
SAWTOOTH NATIONAL FOREST
To Basin-Elba Pass (3 miles)
7,432 ft.
7,387ft.
FR728
Dry Creek
P
95
To Spring Canyon and Rangers Trail Junction
8,868 ft.
9,041 ft.
Mount Independence 9,950 ft.
Independence Lakes
Green Creek
Rangers Trail
9,105 ft.
9,168 ft.
Cache Peak 10,339 ft.

*The first Independence Lake.* Photo by Luke Kratz

National Reserve just to the south, plus the bold Raft River Range just inside Utah. Walk around the ridge to climb either Cache Peak or the somewhat lower Independence Mountain (9,950 feet).

—Ralph Maughan

## Miles and Directions

**0.0** Trailhead at Dry Creek (7,720 feet)

**1.2** Junction with Rangers Trail (8,100 feet)

**2.0** Lower lake (8,868 feet)

**2.2** Second lake (9,041 feet)

# 96 Silent City of Rocks

The City of Rocks—as it is most commonly called—is an area with a tremendous number of granite monoliths. It is popular for hiking, but more especially rock climbing.

**Start:** About 25 linear miles southeast of Burley and about 40 road miles south from the I-86/84 exchange. It is 5 miles by road southwest of Almo at the end of the Albion Range.
**Type of hike:** Day hikes
**Distance:** There are a number of short hikes and loops of up to 1.5 miles.
**Approximate hiking time:** Allow 2–6 hours for hiking and climbing.
**Difficulty:** Easy to moderate
**Best season:** Late May–June, and September
**Trail surface:** Dirt and granite rock
**Land status:** Silent City of Rocks National Reserve
**Canine compatibility:** On leash
**Fees and permits:** None
**Maps:** Almo and Cache Peak USGS quadrangles. The best is the map of short hikes provided by the national reserve. Even the most detailed topographic quadrangle fails to show many of the individual rocks.
**Trail contact:** Silent City of Rocks National Reserve, (208) 824-5910
**Special considerations:** The Silent City of Rocks National Reserve is open April 1–October 31.

**Finding the trailhead:** The most common access to the area is from I-84, then to the small town of Malta. From Malta, take ID 77 toward the mountains, and then turn left at Conner Junction (to the south on a paved county road). Drive to the tiny, beautiful hamlet of Almo. Here is the headquarters office for the City of Rocks National Reserve. Follow the road south out of town, and follow the signs directing you to the City of Rocks. Turn right at the road junction to the Twin Sisters—that is, don't drive to the Twin Sisters. The junction is 4.6 road miles from Almo. Drive 1.3 miles to Bath Rock, which is on the left side of the road. Trails also leave from a number of other places along this road.

Access to the City of Rocks is also available going south from Burley to Oakley on ID 27, then south up the paved, then gravel, forest service road to the rocks. This road goes up Emery Canyon and takes you over a pass, but snow blocks this higher-elevation access road until about late May. Tea Kettle GPS: N42 4.11' / W113 42.53'; Bumble Trail GPS: N42 5.33' / W113 43.70'
**Parking and trailhead facilities:** A number of short trails including Tea Kettle and Bumble Trail lead from the campgrounds along the road or at parking places beside large rocks, such as Bath Rock.

## The Hike

After many years of effort by local residents to protect this small but unique area of oddly eroded granite, Congress established the Silent City of Rocks National Reserve in 1988.

The national reserve status (which is weaker than a national park, monument, or wilderness area) put an end to spray-painting of rocks and off-road vehicle abuse. It also provided for maintenance and construction of trails, interpretation, picnicking, and campgrounds. The grazing of domestic livestock may also be reduced eventually.

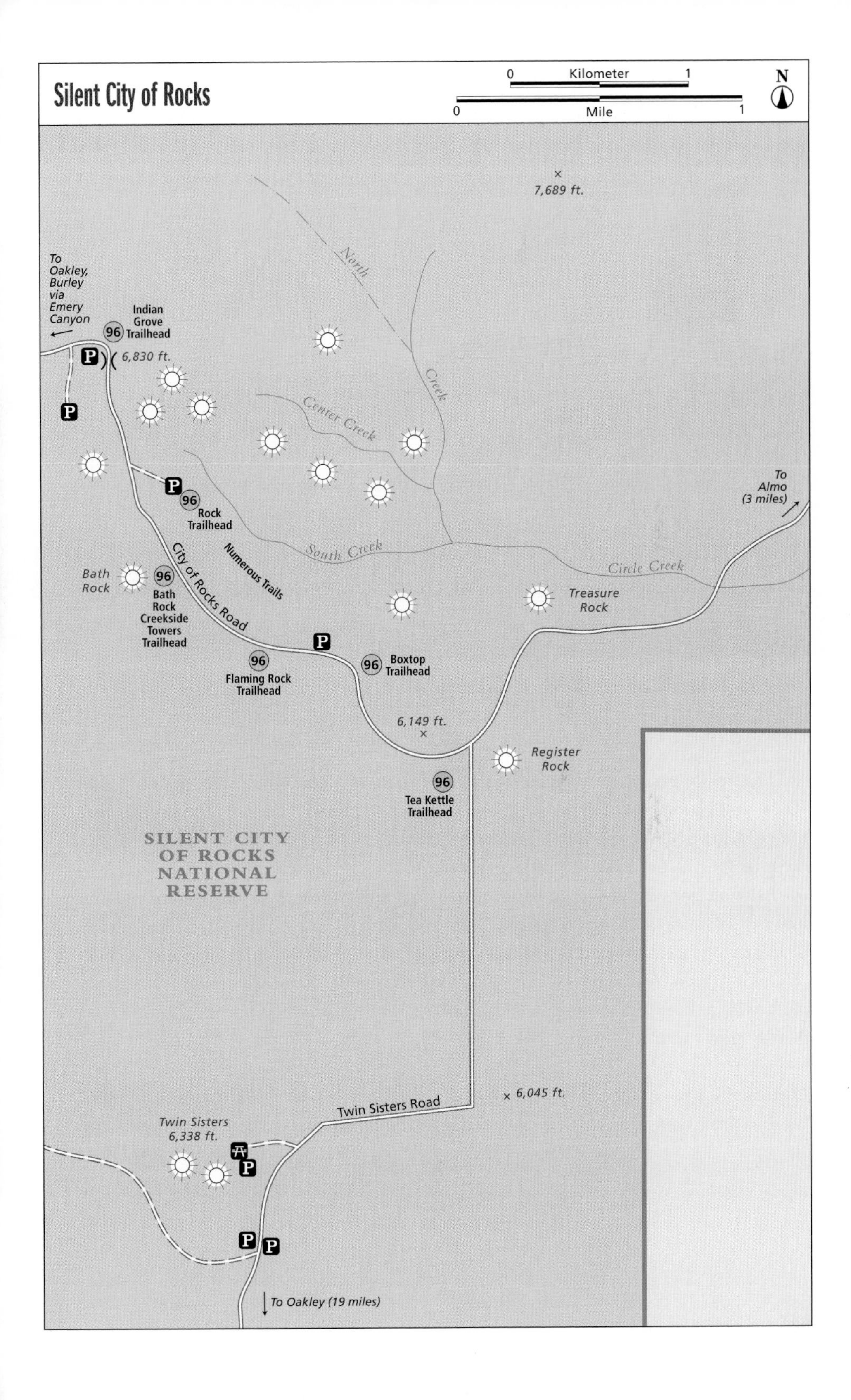

Silent City of Rocks
0
Kilometer
1
0
Mile
1
N
7,689 ft.
North
Creek
To
Oakley,
Burley
via
Emery
Canyon
Indian
Grove
Trailhead
96
6,830 ft.
Center Creek
96
Rock
Trailhead
To
Almo
(3 miles)
South Creek
Numerous Trails
City of Rocks Road
Circle Creek
Bath
Rock
96
Bath
Rock
Creekside
Towers
Trailhead
Treasure
Rock
96
Flaming Rock
Trailhead
96
Boxtop
Trailhead
6,149 ft.
Register
Rock
96
Tea Kettle
Trailhead
SILENT CITY
OF ROCKS
NATIONAL
RESERVE
6,045 ft.
Twin Sisters Road
Twin Sisters
6,338 ft.
To Oakley (19 miles)

*The Lost Arrow and all other rock monoliths.* PHOTO BY LUKE KRATZ

The rocks (many of which have names such as Bath Rock, the Arrow, Turtle Rock, and Flaming Rock) are popular destinations for rock climbers. I still remember the cold, gray March day in 1973 at the City of Rocks when I first roped up under the guidance of the Idaho State University Outdoor Program.

As time goes by, more and more rocks get official or informal names and the number of trails increases, so make sure you get the latest map from the reserve headquarters. A number of trails lead past big rocks and through the various forks of Circle Creek. You will find not only huge rocks but also small creeks with quaking aspen, red osier dogwood, small meadows, sand (from decomposed granite), and prickly pear cactus.

**Options:** There are too many options to describe here, but as a final option you might want to drive down to the Twin Sisters and scramble around on these huge monoliths.

—Ralph Maughan

# South Hills

The South Hills, also known as the Twin Falls Hills, Goose Creek Mountains, and Cassia Mountains, don't look like much from the interstate near Twin Falls, just some small, dome-shaped rises to the south. Most hikers turn north toward Sun Valley and the Sawtooth National Recreation Area. But get down in them, and you will find lovely nooks of desert streams, cliffs, volcanic formations, and mountain vistas well worth your time. In late spring and early summer, there are numerous species of birds, and the 25-acre Shoshone Wildlife Pond supports nesting waterfowl and wading birds.

The paved Rock Creek Road is the main entry to the South Hills and leads to the Magic Mountain Ski Area. Along the way are seven developed campgrounds plus the beautiful Harrington Fork Picnic Area, a perfect stopping-off point in early or late season. In addition, there are another eleven campgrounds and two more picnic areas beyond Magic Mountain or requiring different access.

These hills are the playground for Twin Falls, and most folks consider a gas-powered vehicle the equipment of choice. Consequently, trails good for hikers are hard to find, and the Twin Falls–Burley District of the Sawtooth National Forest has put 99.9 percent of its emphasis on off-road-vehicle trail development. There are signs that this is starting to change with increased use by mountain bikers and cross-country skiers. Hikers, too, should weigh in and let the district know that more of this handsome country should be devoted to self-propelled traffic. The district recently constructed Rim View Trail, which is open to foot and horse traffic only. We give access information to this trail in the options portion of Hike 99, Third Fork Rock Creek–Wahlstrom Hollow Loop.

—Jackie Johnson Maughan

*Aspen forests are common along slopes in the south.* Photo by Luke Kratz

# 97 Eagle Loop

This pleasant woodland loop is closed to horses and off-road vehicles. It is an excellent novice hike, suitable for children, especially the first mile.

**Start:** 36 miles south of Twin Falls
**Type of hike:** Day hike; loop
**Distance:** 2.5 miles
**Approximate hiking time:** 1 hour
**Difficulty:** Easy
**Best season:** May–June, and September
**Trail surface:** Normal dirt and rock
**Land status:** Sawtooth National Forest
**Canine compatibility:** On leash
**Fees and permits:** None
**Maps:** Pike Mountain USGS quadrangle; Twin Falls and Burley Ranger Districts–Sawtooth National Forest map
**Trail contact:** Twin Falls Ranger District, (208) 737-3200, www.fs.usda.gov/sawtooth
**Special considerations:** Flying and biting insects can make this a poor July or August hike.

**Finding the trailhead:** From the south end of Twin Falls, turn left (east) onto Kimberly Road. After 5 miles, jog to the right (south) to enter Kimberly. (Do not take ID 50, which is to the left.) Then, shortly, a sign directs you onto US 30. After 3 miles you will see a sign marking ROCK CREEK CANYON, COUNTY ROAD G3. Continue for a very short way to reach the turnoff to Rock Creek, which is marked by a sign and a filling station and is just on the outskirts of Hansen. As you drive due south up the paved Rock Creek Road, the South Hills rise directly in front of you. This is open range country, and there might be livestock on the road. After about 18 miles, you will reach the first of four campgrounds preceding the Third Fork Trailhead; continue for 5 miles more to the Pettit Campground, close to the top of the range, on the right, just after you pass Rock Creek Ranger Station and the Magic Mountain Ski Area. GPS: N42 10.95' / W114 16.93'
**Parking and trailhead facilities:** The trailhead is at the south end of the campground and is signed. Pettit Campground has eight individual units and one group unit. Its elevation of 6,800 feet makes for cold nights.

## The Hike

This hike rises gently through open forest to contour south to the end of a low, open ridge. It then loops north and drops around the west side of the ridge into thicker forest and a less maintained trail, and then back to the campground. In season there are lots of birds, including juncos, tree swallows, western bluebirds, and flickers. None of this trail is shown on the 1978 Pike Mountain quadrangle, but it is shown on the forest map.

The first part of the hike is right next to Rock Creek Road so it's pretty hard to get lost. Benches are positioned along the way, but the interpretive signs have not been maintained. You will make your way for 0.75 mile through aspen, subalpine fir, and lodgepole. Keep to the right (uphill) as the trail begins to swing west. If you go left and downhill, you will find yourself on an ATV trail that does a small circle and leads to Diamondfield Jack Campground. (Diamondfield Jack, a large dirt

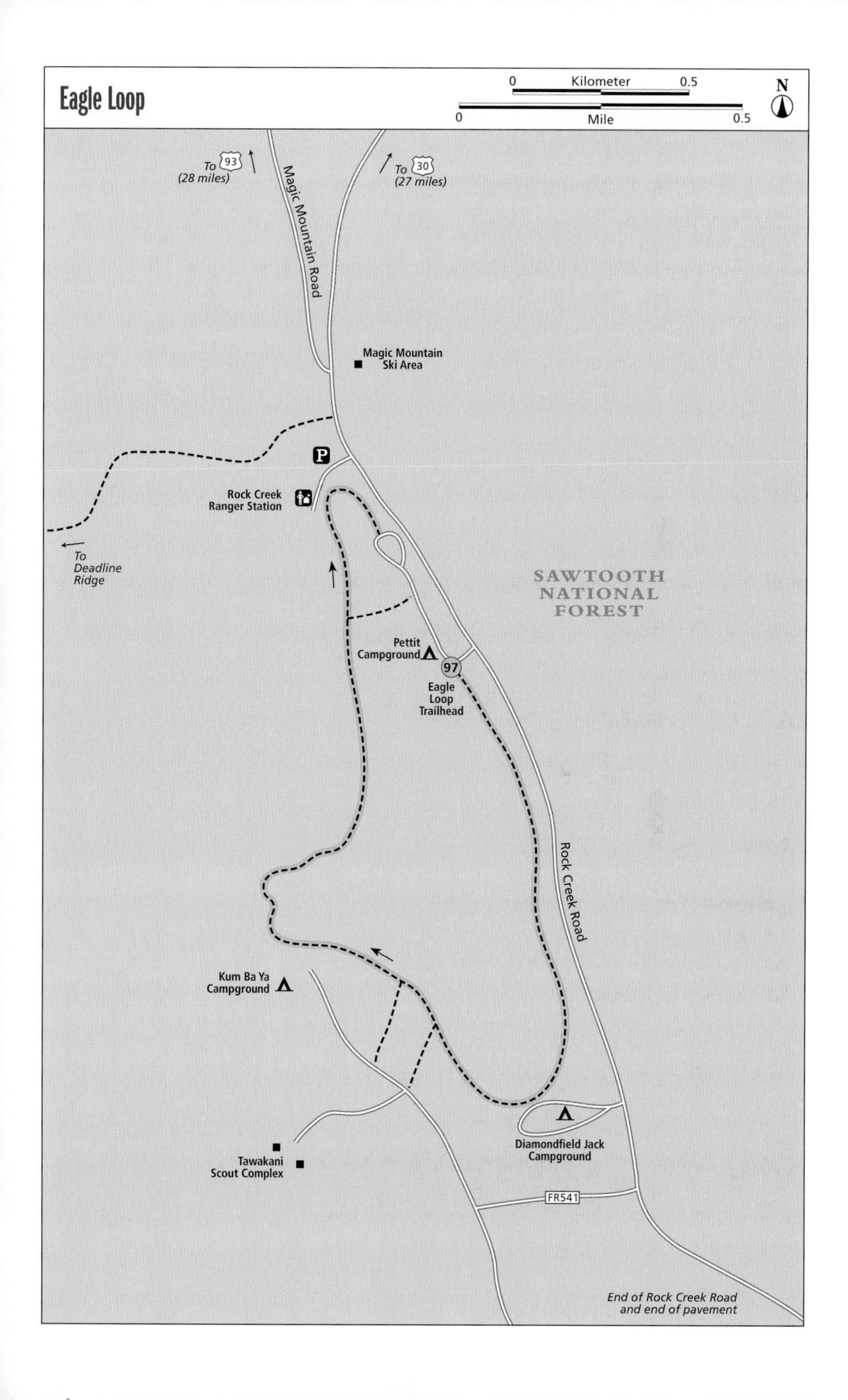
Eagle Loop
0
Kilometer
0.5
0
Mile
0.5
N
To 93
(28 miles)
To 30
(27 miles)
Magic Mountain Road
Magic Mountain
Ski Area
Rock Creek
Ranger Station
To
Deadline
Ridge
SAWTOOTH
NATIONAL
FOREST
Pettit
Campground
97
Eagle
Loop
Trailhead
Rock Creek Road
Kum Ba Ya
Campground
Diamondfield Jack
Campground
Tawakani
Scout Complex
FR541
End of Rock Creek Road
and end of pavement

opening in the lodgepole, is frequented by numerous gas-powered vehicles of all descriptions, particularly on weekends.)

Staying to the right, you will do a small, steep section and find yourself on top of the ridge. Here, the country is rocky and open with sagebrush, bitterbrush, and arrowleaf balsam root. You will have now reached the southern end of the loop. This vantage point offers views of Trapper Peak to the southeast, and to the southwest you can see a well-developed dirt road and the Tawakani Scout complex. This is the 1-mile point. From here you travel right (north) along the west side of the ridge. There are a couple of trails coming up from your left (west), but don't follow them. You will also encounter a large campfire area with benches and an old, wooden cross. Keep to the right and follow the well-defined trail on the uphill side. The trail continues along the western side of the ridge. It then begins to drop, and as you enter the forest you have reached mile 1.5.

From here, the going is easy until you reach a junction. Keep to the middle route. The one to the right (east) is a steep shortcut down and then up over the ridge. The one to the left (west) is the road that leads to the ski area. As you continue for the next 0.75 mile and back to the campground, the going can be a bit confusing since roads cross the trail a couple of times. But you won't go wrong if you stick to the trail and don't follow any roads. Keeping to the trail, which becomes somewhat faint through the thick aspen, you then begin to ascend and cross the northern portion of the loop through dense, conifer forest at mile 2.3. Once you stop going uphill, you have reached the northern point of the ridge; from here the trail is an easy downhill of less than 0.25 mile to the campground.

—Jackie Johnson Maughan

## Miles and Directions

**0.0** Eagle Loop Trailhead (6,800 feet)

**0.8** Trail leaves forest

**1.0** Southern point of loop; south end of ridge (7,080 feet)

**1.5** Trail drops back into forest

**2.3** Northern point of loop; north end of ridge (6,900 feet)

**2.5** Trailhead (6,800 feet)

# 98 Third Fork Rock Creek-Wahlstrom Hollow Loop

Extraordinary desert stream to mountain habitat with volcanic rock formations and beaver ponds are present in this area of the South Hills.

**Start:** 31 miles south of Twin Falls
**Type of hike:** Day hike or backpack; loop
**Distance:** 9 miles round-trip
**Approximate hiking time:** 3–5 hours
**Difficulty:** Moderate for first half; moderately difficult for second
**Best season:** May–June, and September
**Trail surface:** Normal dirt and rock
**Land status:** Sawtooth National Forest
**Canine compatibility:** On leash
**Fees and permits:** None
**Maps:** Pike Mountain, Rams Horn Ridge, and Trapper Peak USGS quadrangles; Twin Falls and Burley Ranger Districts–Sawtooth National Forest map
**Trail contact:** Twin Falls Ranger District, (208) 737-3200, www.fs.usda.gov/sawtooth
**Special considerations:** Desert to mountain weather, bull snakes (common), rattlesnakes (uncommon). There is an elevation gain of 2,000 feet if you do both sides of the loop. Flying and biting insects plus heat make this a poor midsummer hike.

**Finding the trailhead:** From the south end of Twin Falls, turn left (east) onto Kimberly Road. After 5 miles, jog to the right (south) to enter Kimberly. (Do not take ID 50, which is to the left.) Then, shortly, a sign directs you onto US 30. After 3 miles you will see a sign marking Rock Creek Canyon, County Road G3. Continue for a very short way to reach the turnoff to Rock Creek, which is marked by a sign and a filling station and is just on the outskirts of Hansen. As you drive due south up the paved Rock Creek Road, the South Hills rise directly in front of you. This is open range country, and there might be livestock on the road. After about 18 miles, you will reach the first of four campgrounds preceding the Third Fork Trailhead, which is at mile 23. GPS: N42 15.12' / W114 14.85'
**Parking and trailhead facilities:** The trailhead is easy to miss. It is on the left (east) side of the road, but the only sign reads trailers. The trailhead has ample parking and a latrine.

Third Fork is not a good place to camp, and there are a number of better developed sites within easy driving distance. Among these are Steer Basin, Lower and Upper Penstemon, and Pettit.

## The Hike

This lovely piece of terrain has been dismissed by some because of use by off-road vehicles. However, on a busy Memorial Day weekend, we found only a few

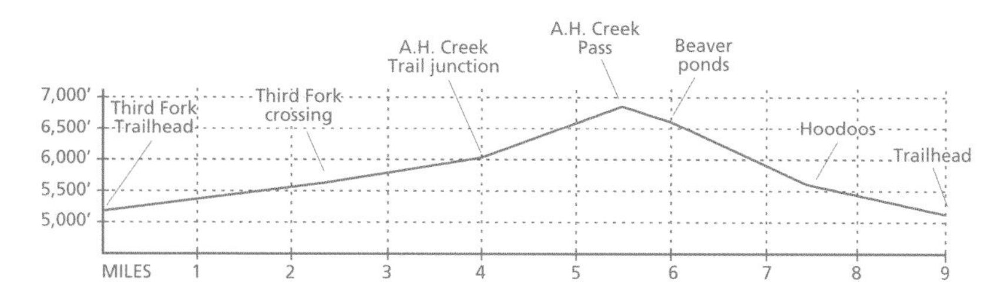

motorized bikers and a few mountain bikers on the Third Fork portion of the loop. We saw many, many ATVs and motorcycles going up the Rock Creek Road, but this trail doesn't appear to be a favorite. After the marshes on the Wahlstrom Hollow portion, we saw no one except a couple of equestrians. There has been a rumor that the Third Fork portion of this hike is slated for ATV development. Please contact the ranger district to protest the ruining of this one of only three or four trails not already devoted to mechanized use.

The South Hills were created by volcanic action, and this hike takes you through welded volcanic ash deposit formations (tuff) that have eroded into hoodoos and pinnacles. These ash deposits are capped with black basalt cliffs at the top of the loop. Consequently, there is not only interesting geology but a variety of flora and fauna as you start out in willows and sage, top out in subalpine fir, descend through aspen and beaver ponds, then drop back to the trailhead through red rock and hoodoos.

Going clockwise, cross a bridge over Third Fork and start out on a sagebrush bench close to the creek. The rise is gentle as you travel through aspen and willow and, in season, a riot of birdcalls, including those of lazuli buntings and yellow warblers. There are bridges over Second Fork and where the trail crosses Third Fork near Cotton Creek, 2.5 miles in. Here, you will have climbed 400 feet from the 5,200-foot trailhead. Ahead is unnamed Peak 7,068, and to your left is Cotton Ridge.

Now the canyon begins to narrow, and the elevation gain becomes more pronounced as you swing gradually to the west and climb 240 feet in 0.75 mile. Lupine and penstemon are abundant in June, as is the sound of hummingbirds. From here, the trail continues to curve west along a 200-foot basalt cliff face to reach the A. H. Creek Trail junction in 0.75 mile. Now will come the most difficult portion of the hike as you leave this meadowy junction to continue to your right (northwest), climbing up the aspen-covered hill some 800 feet to the pass. The trail, rather than going straight up A. H. Creek as shown on the Trapper Peak and Pike Mountain USGS quads, has been rebuilt into three long switchbacks. The upper portion here is open and unshaded.

Once on top, it's easy to lose the trail because it isn't shown on the Pike Mountain quad and it is intersected by a road and Trail Canyon Spring Trail. To keep your bearings, do not turn left onto the road or the other trail or right onto the road. Instead bear straight ahead and north-northwest to find the trail as it drops slowly off the top to descend on the right (east) side of the creek in Wahlstrom Hollow. You will descend 260 feet in slightly less than a mile. Off to your west is a series of marshy beaver ponds.

If you do get sidetracked and onto the road, it's okay. Simply follow it to the west (left) for 0.75 mile. From there, it will intersect with the road down (to your right and going north) to the Wahlstrom Hollow beaver ponds. Just past the ponds, the road peters out, crosses the stream, and joins the trail.

Once the trail meets the stream, it drops steeply 800 feet in just over a mile. The country changes dramatically as it enters red rock formations and the canyon. The

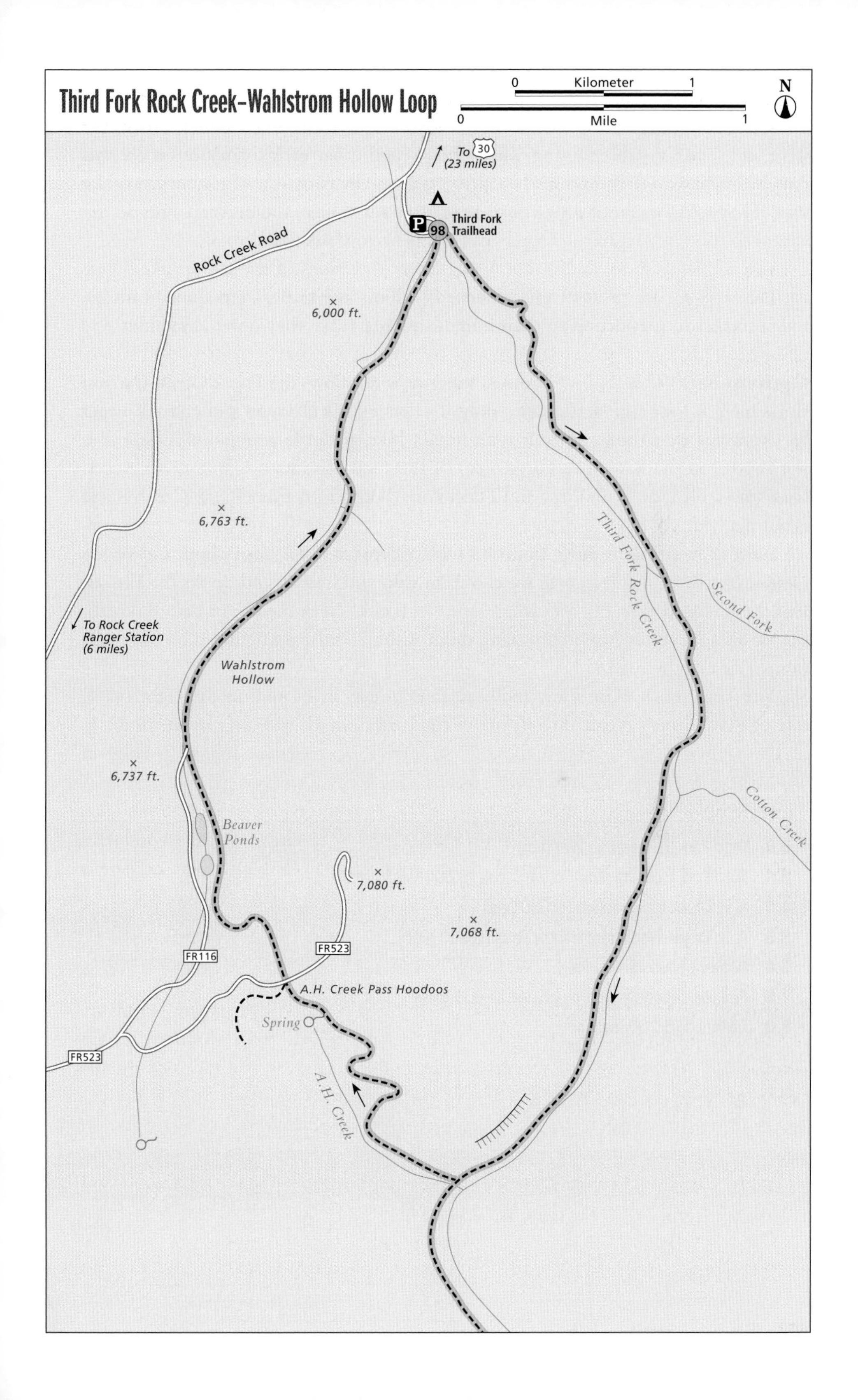
Third Fork Rock Creek–Wahlstrom Hollow Loop
0
Kilometer
1
0
Mile
1
N
To 30
(23 miles)
Third Fork
Trailhead
98
Rock Creek Road
6,000 ft.
6,763 ft.
To Rock Creek
Ranger Station
(6 miles)
Wahlstrom
Hollow
6,737 ft.
Beaver
Ponds
7,080 ft.
7,068 ft.
Third Fork Rock Creek
Second Fork
Cotton Creek
FR116
FR523
A.H. Creek Pass Hoodoos
Spring
FR523
A.H. Creek

two stream crossings are not bridged but are small enough not to require wading. In the last 2 miles, the trail continues its downward drop, and you will also encounter scree and some unstable footing. The hoodoos and other rock formations make this part of the hike quite stunning. The canyon is generally narrow, and getting out of the way of horse traffic can present a challenge. Mountain bikers and motorcyclists do not appear to use this part of the loop because it is narrow, steep, and rocky.

You are likely to see bullsnakes in the lower elevations of the entire hike. These harmless reptiles are protectively patterned to look like rattlers, but their heads are much smaller in proportion to their bodies and, of course, they don't have a rattle.

**Options:** Rim View Trail is 9.5 miles one way as it follows the Rock Creek Canyon rim. Open to foot and horse traffic only, it offers excellent views and enough water for overnight excursions. Since it is a through hike, a shuttle is required. This trail is not shown on the Sawtooth Forest map or the Pike Mountain USGS quad. Access to its two trailheads (Rim View and Third Fork–Rim View) from Rock Creek Road is not marked.

Starting at the Rim View Trailhead will save you a 2,000-foot climb out of the canyon, but there is still significant elevation gain and loss up and down the rim. To find the trailhead, take FR 500 where it leaves Rock Creek Road just before (north) the ski area. In about 3 switchbacking miles is the 7,200-foot trailhead on the right (north) side of the road.

The Third Fork–Rim View trailhead (5,200 feet) is located on the right (west) side of Rock Creek Road, directly across the road from Third Fork Campground.

—Jackie Johnson Maughan

## Miles and Directions

**0.0** Third Fork trailhead (5,200 feet)

**2.5** Third Fork crossing near Cotton Creek (5,600 feet)

**4.0** A. H. Creek trail junction (6,000 feet)

**5.5** A. H. Creek-Wahlstrom Hollow Pass (6,800 feet)

**6.0** Beaver ponds (6,400 feet)

**7.5** Red rock hoodoos and pinnacles (5,600 feet)

**9.0** Trailhead (5,200 feet)

# Owyhee-Canyonlands Wilderness

Where the corners of Idaho, Oregon, and Nevada transect lies one of the largest blank spaces on the map. Always drawn to such places, I undertook to explore it over two summers. What I found on the eastern (Bruneau) side were bad roads and rattlesnakes plus classic overgrazing western-style. The western (Owyhee) side is more visited, and we've included hikes accordingly. But mostly this harsh and rugged country is unexplored, and this is precisely what protects the largest herd of California bighorn sheep in the world, the 6,000 pronghorn antelope, the hawks and eagles, the redband trout, the seven species of bats, the sage grouse, and the songbirds.

River runners have discovered the Bruneau and Owyhee Rivers, but hikers are rare. In fact, when my friend and I finally found a way down to the Bruneau (via the Roberson east trail), these kayakers did a double take and wanted to know how we'd gotten there.

This is Big West country, as Mike Medberry of the American Lands Alliance puts it.

—Jackie Johnson Maughan, 2001

The name Owyhee may sound native, but it originally was attributed to Hawaiian explorers who ended up missing in this rugged and desolate area.

On March 2009 the Omnibus Public Land Management Act was signed by President Barack Obama to protect 517,000 acres of basalt canyons and wild river country in southwestern Idaho, restricting all motorized and mechanized access. This area was designated the Owyhee-Canyonlands Wilderness. It is divided into seven areas: Big Jacks Creek Wilderness, Bruneau-Jarbridge Rivers Wilderness, Little Jacks Creek Wilderness, North Fork Owyhee Wilderness, Owyhee River Wilderness, and Pole Creek Wilderness. These are truly wild areas of deep river canyons that attract whitewater rafters as well as havens for many animal species, such as desert bighorn sheep and Great Basin collared lizards. Most exploration is done by way of the rivers. Hiking trails are rare in this pristine area, and good access roads are seemingly even rarer.

Luke Kratz, 2014

# 99 Big Jacks Creek

This is a spectacular hike into a remote canyon in the Owyhee Wilderness. There is extensive rhyolite and the opportunity to observe raptors, bighorn sheep, and pronghorn antelope.

**Start:** 36 miles south-southwest of Bruneau
**Type of hike:** Day hike; out-and-back
**Distance:** 1.5 miles one way; much more if desired
**Approximate hiking time:** 1 or more hours
**Difficulty:** Easy for 1.5 miles
**Best season:** May–June and October
**Trail surface:** Normal dirt and rock
**Land status:** Owyhee Field Office, Bureau of Land Management
**Canine compatibility:** Not allowed
**Fees and permits:** None
**Maps:** Wickahoney Crossing USGS quadrangle; Glenn's Ferry, Bureau of Land Management map
**Trail contact:** Owyhee Field Office BLM, (208) 896-5933

**Finding the trailhead:** Two miles west of Bruneau, turn off ID 78 and south onto ID 51. Continue 25 miles south on ID 51 to a junction with a good gravel road that heads both east and west. This is just beyond Milepost 45 and is the Wickahoney Road. Turn right (west), and follow this road 5 miles to a junction with a rough dirt road but one that low-clearance rigs can pass carefully. Turn right (north), and follow this road 3 miles to a Y intersection. Bear left and go around a small knoll on the left to a dead end. This is the trailhead. GPS: N42 35.58' / W115 58.64'
**Parking and trailhead facilities:** Unimproved.

## The Hike

The Parker Grade descends about 1.5 miles, and 600 feet in elevation, to Big Jacks Creek. Big Jacks is a very scenic canyon and one of the most accessible in the Owyhees. Rhyolitic hoodoos, needles, and pinnacles tower above, and nighthawk guano festoons the walls. Bighorn sheep ply the rugged canyon rims while raptors soar overhead.

Cattle have pioneered trails up- and downstream. Downstream travel brings you to the terminus of the canyon and a cowed-out grazing allotment, while upstream travel takes you into the deep, dark canyon of Big Jacks Creek.

**Options:** A rugged hiker and desert rat can proceed up- or downcanyon looking for exits from Big Jacks. A variety of routes are attainable by those with map-reading skills and sure feet, since scrambling in and out of the canyons is necessary. It is important to carefully choose your route in and out of the canyons because falls here often prove fatal. No water is available on the sagebrush steppes above the canyons. Nights spent out on these steppes are filled with stars. On some nights in some years, the northern lights are visible.

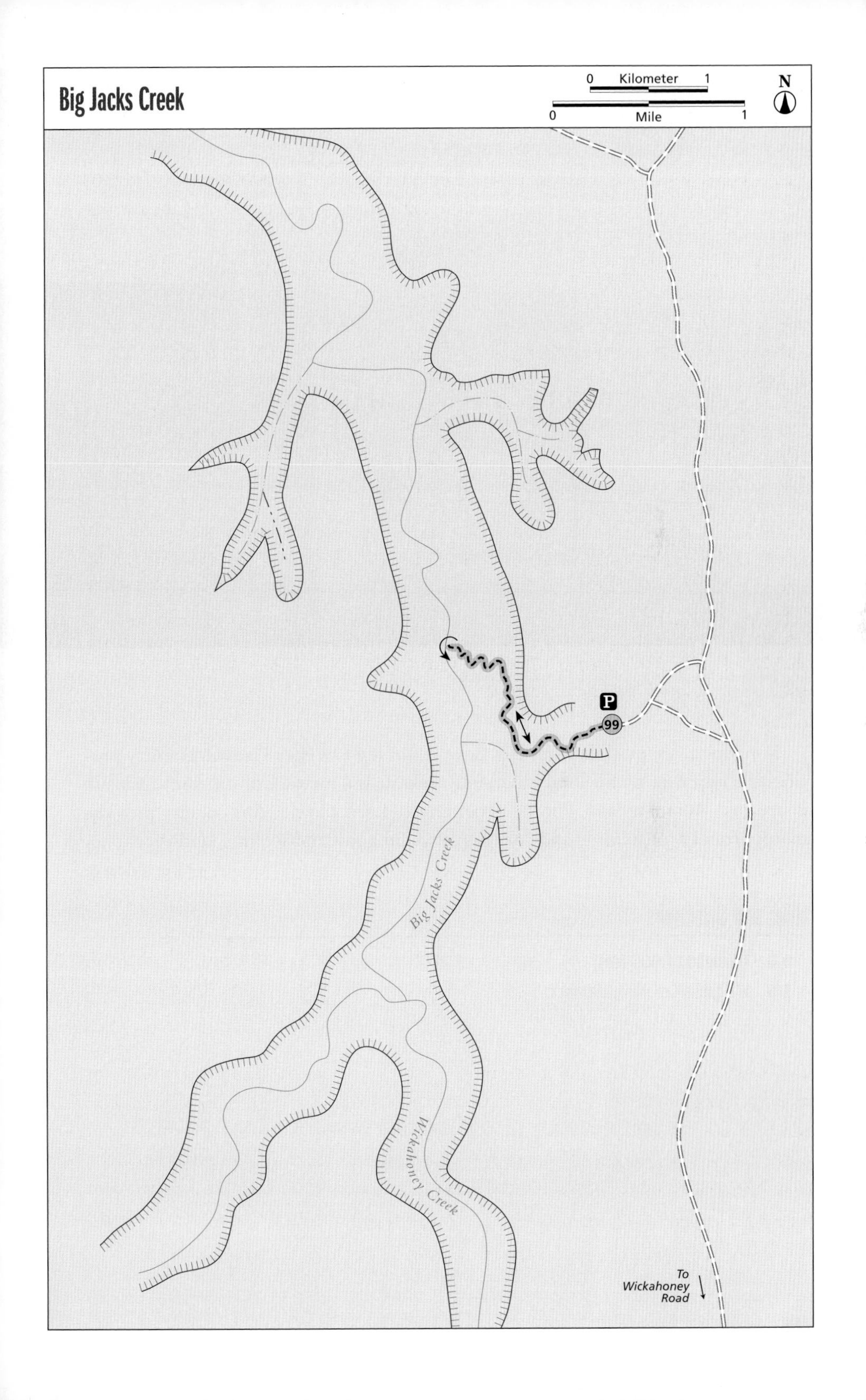
Big Jacks Creek
0 Kilometer 1
0 Mile 1
N
P
99
Big Jacks Creek
Wickahoney Creek
To Wickahoney Road

*Big Jacks in the distance.* PHOTO BY LUKE KRATZ

Long loops are possible from Big Jacks. All of the Owyhee Canyon country provides the opportunity for long wilderness treks. It is a mixture of canyon, sagebrush steppe, and juniper upland. For the experienced desert traveler, this country provides an opportunity for solitude and contemplation in a vast and sublime landscape.

—Lee Mercer

## Miles and Directions

**0.0** Trailhead (4,600 feet)

**1.5** Big Jacks Creek (4,000 feet)

# 100 Shoofly Overlook

This trail offers both spectacular canyon scenery and the opportunity to observe wildlife.

**Start:** 30 miles southwest of Grand View
**Type of hike:** Day hike; out-and-back
**Distance:** 0.5 mile round-trip to saddle; 3.5 miles round-trip to Bald Mountain summit; 5.5 miles round-trip to West Fork Shoofly Canyon overlook
**Approximate hiking time:** 1–5 hours
**Difficulty:** Moderate; requires cross-country navigation
**Best season:** April–May, and October
**Trail surface:** Normal dirt and rock
**Land status:** Owyhee Field Office, Bureau of Land Management
**Canine compatibility:** On leash but not allowed in any of the wilderness areas
**Fees and permits:** None
**Maps:** Snow Creek USGS quadrangle; Triangle Bureau of Land Management map
**Trail contact:** Owyhee Field Office BLM, (208) 896-5933

**Finding the trailhead:** The Owyhee Uplands National Backcountry Byway, also known as Mud Flat Road, is the access route. Just south of Grand View, head east on ID 78 for approximately 1.5 miles; turn south onto the well-signed byway. The byway makes a 99-mile loop to Jordan Valley, Oregon, and is the jumping-off point for many Owyhee hikes. Late-spring wildflower displays along this road are often breathtaking. The road is paved for the first 4 miles and then turns to gravel. It passes several side roads, including, at mile 15.3, the signed Oreana cutoff intersection on the right (north). You pass the Poison Creek picnic area, also signed. At the 22.2-mile point (2.4 miles beyond the Poison Creek picnic site), park on the relatively broad flat area on the east side of the road across from Fall Creek. GPS: N42 43.65' / W116 20.28'
**Parking and trailhead facilities:** Unimproved.

## The Hike

Proceed south, ascending the north-facing slope to a high ridgeline between the Poison Creek and Shoofly Creek watersheds. The western part of this ridgeline is known as Bald Mountain. Poison Creek, which usually has little water, flows at the side of the flat parking site. Cross the creek and begin a moderately steep hike up the north-facing slope. Follow the sagebrush along the eastern edge of a patch of colorful, taller vegetation: an aromatic jumble of mountain mahogany, rose, bitterbrush, currant, and serviceberry. A small 1-acre enclosure here excludes cattle. Note the vivid contrast between lush grass growth inside the enclosure and heavily grazed areas outside.

Proceed uphill along the band of vegetation. It becomes easier to walk in low sagebrush. Climb 0.5 mile to a large bench midway to the high Bald Mountain ridgeline. There is a small wetland and pond on this bench, hidden from the road below. The pond is shown on the Snow Creek USGS quad. Skirt the eastern edge of the wetland and continue toward the high ridgeline. Scrutiny of this ridge reveals two

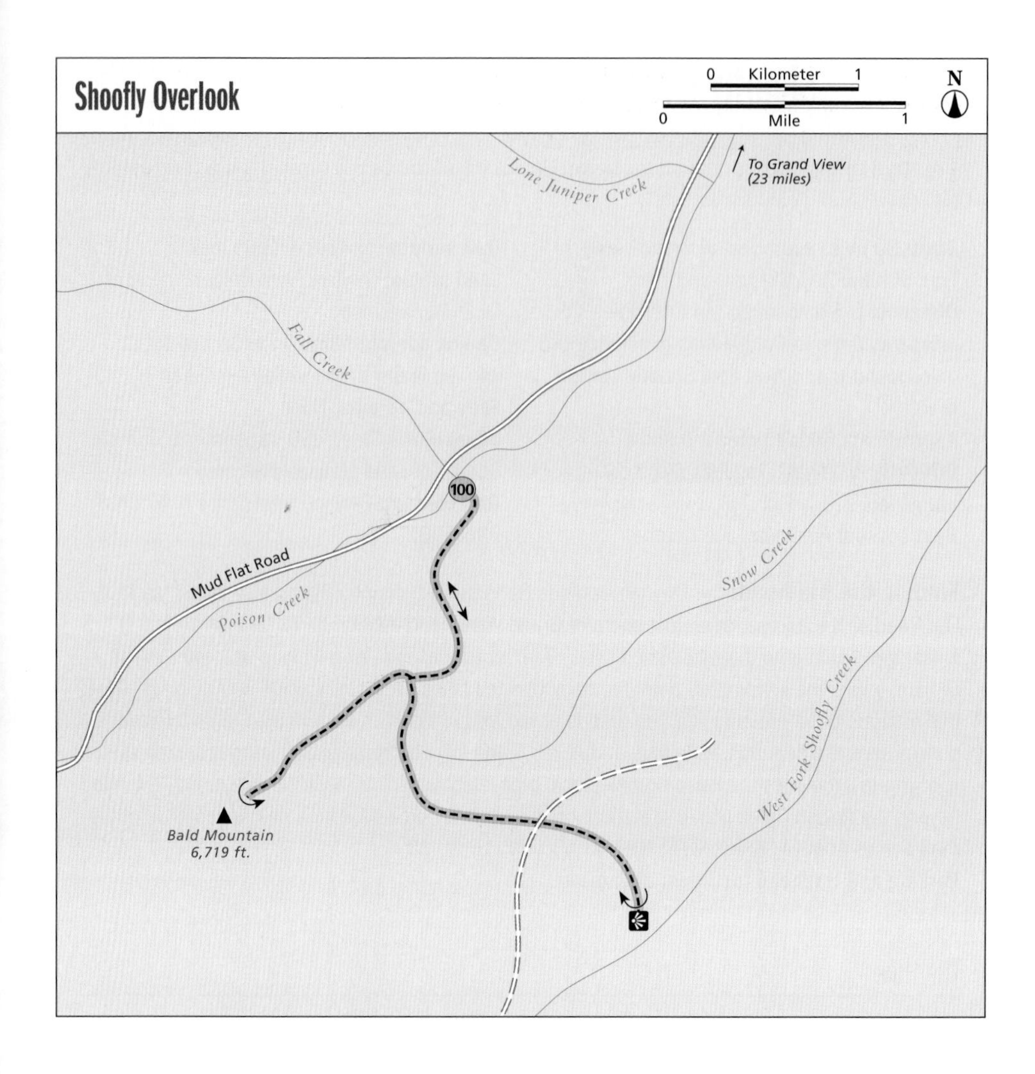


saddle areas. Head toward the eastern saddle. A hint of an actual trail, the easiest route to the ridge, climbs to this saddle.

Once you're on the main ridge (1 mile and 800 feet above the road), enjoy the panoramic view of the north–south trending Shoofly Canyon complex, home to redband trout and some California bighorn sheep. Much of the Shoofly complex is located in the BLM Little Jacks Creek Wilderness Study Area. To the northwest lies the rugged broken Rough Mountain country between Poison and Birch Creeks. The Snake River Plain is visible to the north. Inexplicably, the BLM's flawed wilderness inventory omitted much of the Bald Mountain ridgeline from wilderness consideration.

**Options:** From the saddle, proceed southeast toward the West Fork of Shoofly Creek. Red rhyolite cliffs and platy talus stripes give a taste of Owyhee Canyon hiking. The distance to the canyon from the ridge is 1.5 miles.

Another option is to continue west and south on the main ridge toward Bald Mountain for 1.5 miles. Farther along this ridge, a panoramic view unfolds that on a clear day includes the Jarbidge, Independence, and Santa Rosa Mountains in the distance. Closer in lie Juniper Mountain, South Mountain, and the main Owyhee Mountains: millions of acres of fine high desert country.

—Katie Fite

## Miles and Directions

**0.0** Trailhead (5,000 feet)

**0.5** Bench (5,440 feet)

**0.75** Bald Mountain ridge saddle (5,800 feet)

**1.75** Bald Mountain summit option (6,719 feet)

**2.75** West Fork Shoofly Canyon overlook option (5,700 feet)

# Additional Hikes

*Lower Snake River topography.* PHOTO BY LUKE KRATZ

# 101 Bruneau Dunes State Park

These are the tallest sand dunes in North America. The trail winds through two small lakes where fishing and bird-watching opportunities abound. It's a unique mix of desert, dune, prairie, marsh, and lake habitats.

**Start:** About 16 miles south of Mountain Home and 76 miles west of Twin Falls
**Type of hike:** Day hikes, loops. Scrambles to top of sand dunes
**Distance:** 5-mile loop; 2-mile loop; 1-mile loop
**Approximate hiking time:** 1–3 hours
**Difficulty:** Easy for short loops; moderately easy for long loop
**Best season:** March–May, and September–November
**Trail surface:** Normal dirt and rock
**Land status:** Bruneau Dunes State Park
**Canine compatibility:** Not allowed. Do not bring dogs on hikes; sand can burn their feet.
**Fees and permits:** $5 motor vehicle entrance fee; camping fee $10
**Maps:** Bruneau Dunes USGS quadrangle; Glenns Ferry USGS Surface Management Status map
**Trail contact:** Bruneau Dunes State Park, (208) 366-7919
**Special considerations:** Desert hiking conditions, hot, sandy, mosquitoes, possible rattlesnakes (uncommon) and scorpions. Carry water, sunscreen, and insect repellent. Swimming and nonmotorized boating is allowed, but beware of swimmer's itch caused by flatworm larvae: A brisk, soapy shower is suggested. The visitor center is open February through the middle of October, 8 a.m. to 4:30 p.m. weekdays and 9 a.m. to 5:30 p.m. weekends.

**Finding the trailhead:** From Mountain Home drive south on ID 51 for 15.6 miles. Turn east onto ID 78 and travel for 1.8 miles to the signed and paved Bruneau Dunes State Park road. From points east, take the Hammett exit of I-84. From Hammett, turn west onto ID 78 and drive 16 miles to the signed park turnoff. One mile south from the turnoff is the visitor center.

Park at the visitor center instead of the picnic areas to locate the 5-mile loop trailhead. From the northwest corner of the visitor center, you will see a sign reading SAND DUNES HIKING TRAIL. Access to the 1-mile loop is from the Observatory Picnic Area. GPS: N42 53.73' / W115 41.85'
**Parking and trailhead facilities:** Visitor center, flush toilets, parking, two picnic areas, boat launch; forty-eight campsites, thirty-two with hookups, 35-foot length; dump station, showers. Group campsite area.

## The Hike

The sand dunes are a remarkable and entertaining piece of topography. There are two major dunes, the tallest being 470 feet, and several smaller dunes. Climbing the tallest dune is a popular destination, but requires a good level of fitness. Climbing the smaller dunes is fun for children and adults alike, provided the day is not too hot. Remember, the sand itself can become scorching, and travel in the deep sand is two steps forward, one step back.

*Bruneau sand dunes.* PHOTO BY LUKE KRATZ

This 4,640-acre state park is located at an elevation of 2,500 feet and sits in an old meander scar of the Snake River. The dunes are still active, and on windy days a plume forms on top of the largest dune. The lakes are surrounded by Russian olive trees, tamarisk, and rushes—good habitat for a variety of birds. Among the birds identified in late May were barn and tree swallows, belted kingfisher, killdeer, long-billed curlew, meadowlark, mourning dove, nighthawk, pheasant, yellow-headed blackbird, yellow warbler, and western tanager. Also spotted, on the western portion of the 5-mile loop, were black-tailed jackrabbits.

Five-mile loop: From the visitor center, the trail strikes out south across the prairie. If it has been recently mowed, the way is obvious. If not, you will have to navigate from trail-post to trail-post. They can be difficult to locate. Some are painted red on top, and others are white. You'll count three by the time you reach the edge of the marsh. Here in the sand the trail becomes indistinct and additional trail-posts could not be located, but the way is obvious since you're circling the marsh and in the general direction of the tallest dune. The going is easy on this first third of the loop. As you approach the Big Dune, the sand becomes deeper and the walking more difficult. But you will encounter an obvious trail, worn by all the folks who climb the tallest dune.

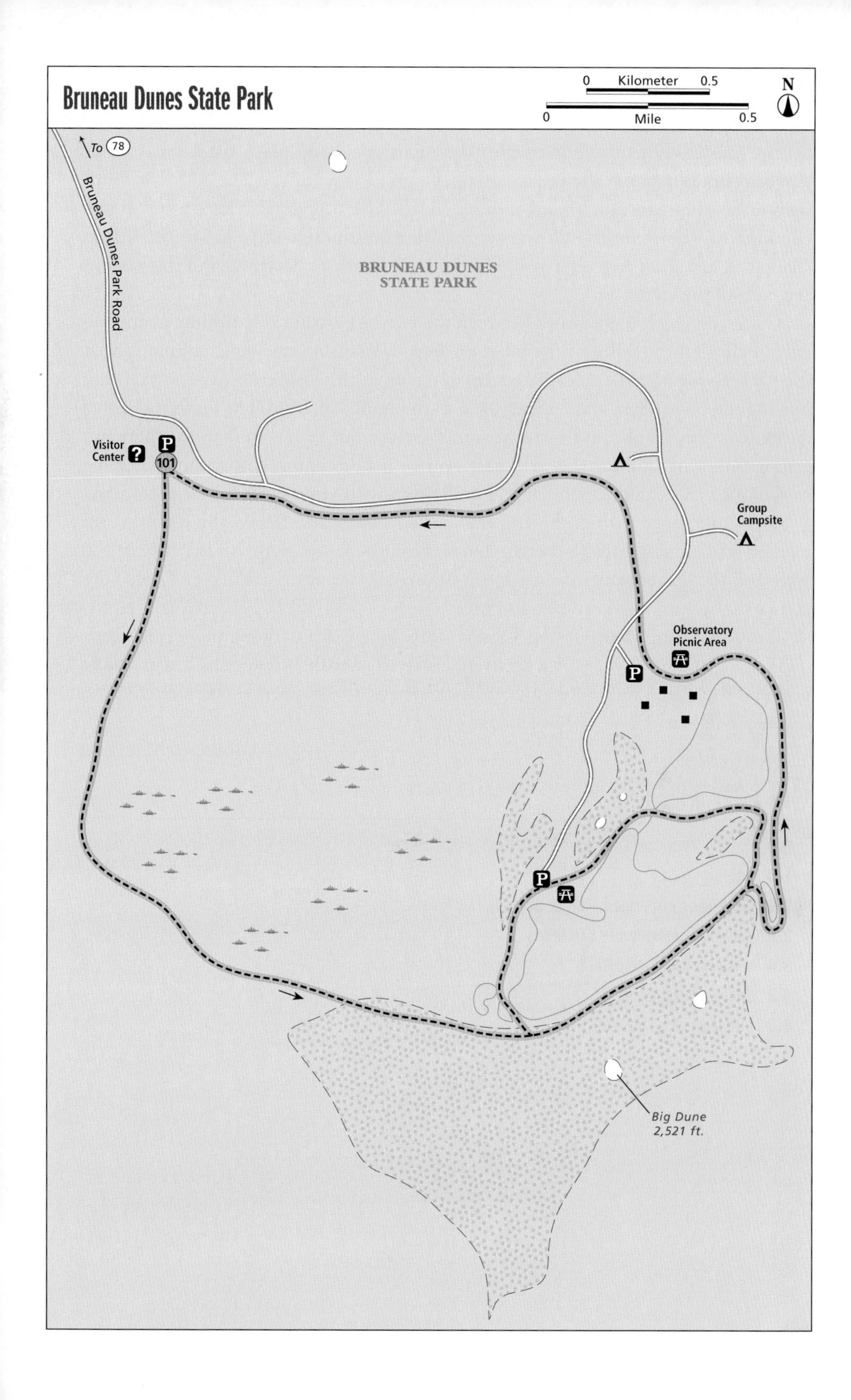
Bruneau Dunes State Park
0 Kilometer 0.5
0 Mile 0.5
N
To 78
Bruneau Dunes Park Road
BRUNEAU DUNES
STATE PARK
Visitor
Center
101
Group
Campsite
Observatory
Picnic Area
Big Dune
2,521 ft.

Once you're past the Big Dune, keep between the dunes and the lake. Expect more people in this section—although not many actually make the full trek from here to the eastern terminus of the lakes. This is a good place for a break since you can thrash through the foliage and get a good view of the lake and waterbirds without getting too much sand in your lunch. The topography rises a bit as you continue east between the dunes and the lakes and mount the edge of the dunes. The going is harder here, but you'll be rewarded with good views and the swoops and calls of the swallows.

Once you reach the isthmus between the two lakes, you can continue north and circle behind the smaller of the lakes or drop down and cross here, coming out at the Observatory Picnic Area. The map available at the visitor center shows a trail skirting the picnic area and leading back to the trailhead. Although some trail-posts do exist in this section, it's easier to simply strike out cross-country for the main campground then follow the road back to the visitor center. This seems preferable to walking across a hot open flat and ending up with your socks full of cheatgrass.

Two-mile loop: Park at the Big Dune Picnic Area and follow the obvious and marked trail, which leads to the Big Dune. From here you must circle between the lakes and the dunes until you reach the isthmus between the two lakes. Cross here and circle back to Big Dune Picnic Area.

One-mile loop: Park at the Observatory Picnic Area. From the observatory itself, walk northeast across the grass and into the brush, where you'll see a trail-post and the trail. From here you can walk around the smaller lake and circle back to the picnic area.

—Jackie Johnson Maughan

## Miles and Directions

**0.0** 5-mile loop trailhead, located behind visitor center

**1.0** Marshy area

**2.1** Southwestern edge of larger Sand Dunes Lake

**2.9** Isthmus between the two lakes

**3.4** Observatory Picnic Area

**4.2** Main campground

**5.0** Arrive back at trailhead

# 102 Malad Gorge State Park

Enjoy scenic overlooks into 250-foot Malad Gorge and Hagerman Valley, along with a 60-foot waterfall, springs, and raptor-watching.

**Start:** 30 miles northwest of Twin Falls
**Type of hike:** Day hike or shuttle; out-and-back
**Distance:** 2 miles one way
**Approximate hiking time:** 1–3 hours
**Difficulty:** Moderate. The walking itself is easy, but the trail is right along the gorge rim, and there is the danger of the unwary or clumsy falling into the gorge.
**Best season:** Year-round
**Trail surface:** Normal dirt path
**Land status:** Malad Gorge State Park
**Canine compatibility:** On leash
**Fees and permits:** $4 per car
**Maps:** Tuttle and Hagerman USGS quadrangles
**Trail contact:** Malad Gorge State Park, (208) 837-4505
**Special considerations:** Although Malad Gorge State Park is open year-round from 7 a.m. to 10 p.m., this is a desert and therefore hot in the summer. The hike described here, the South Rim, is not recommended for children due to steep drop-offs. On the other hand, the nearby 3-mile Devil's Washbowl loop is fenced on the precipitous portions near the gorge.

**Finding the trailhead:** From I-84, turn left (south) at exit 147 and follow the signs leading about 1 mile to the park entrance. After the entrance, keep right at the two-way junction and continue 0.25 mile to the historic stone house and interpretative area. GPS: N42 52.05' / W114 51.26'
**Parking and trailhead facilities:** Two picnic areas, restrooms; interpretive area and trailhead. No overnight camping.

## The Hike

This 652-acre state park is located at an elevation of 3,270 feet, making for a good early- or late-season excursion. The basalt of the Malad Gorge was formed by lava flows and the canyon itself by melting glacier runoff. The waterfall at Devil's Washbowl has retreated 2.5 miles over the millennia, carving the canyon you see. The side canyons at Alcove Lake and Woody's Cove were created by two similar waterfalls. The Big Wood River flows through the Malad Gorge to meet the Snake River just north of Hagerman Valley.

Among birds present in the gorge are canyon wrens, swallows, doves, kestrels, red-tailed hawks, and golden eagles. Mammals in the park include cottontails, jackrabbits, coyotes, and mule deer.

The Malad Gorge State Park handout, available at the interpretive area, shows the route of the 3-mile Devil's Washbowl loop. This loop is also shown on the park's website along with two other short hikes that take off from Woody's Cove. These last two hikes are not shown on the handout.

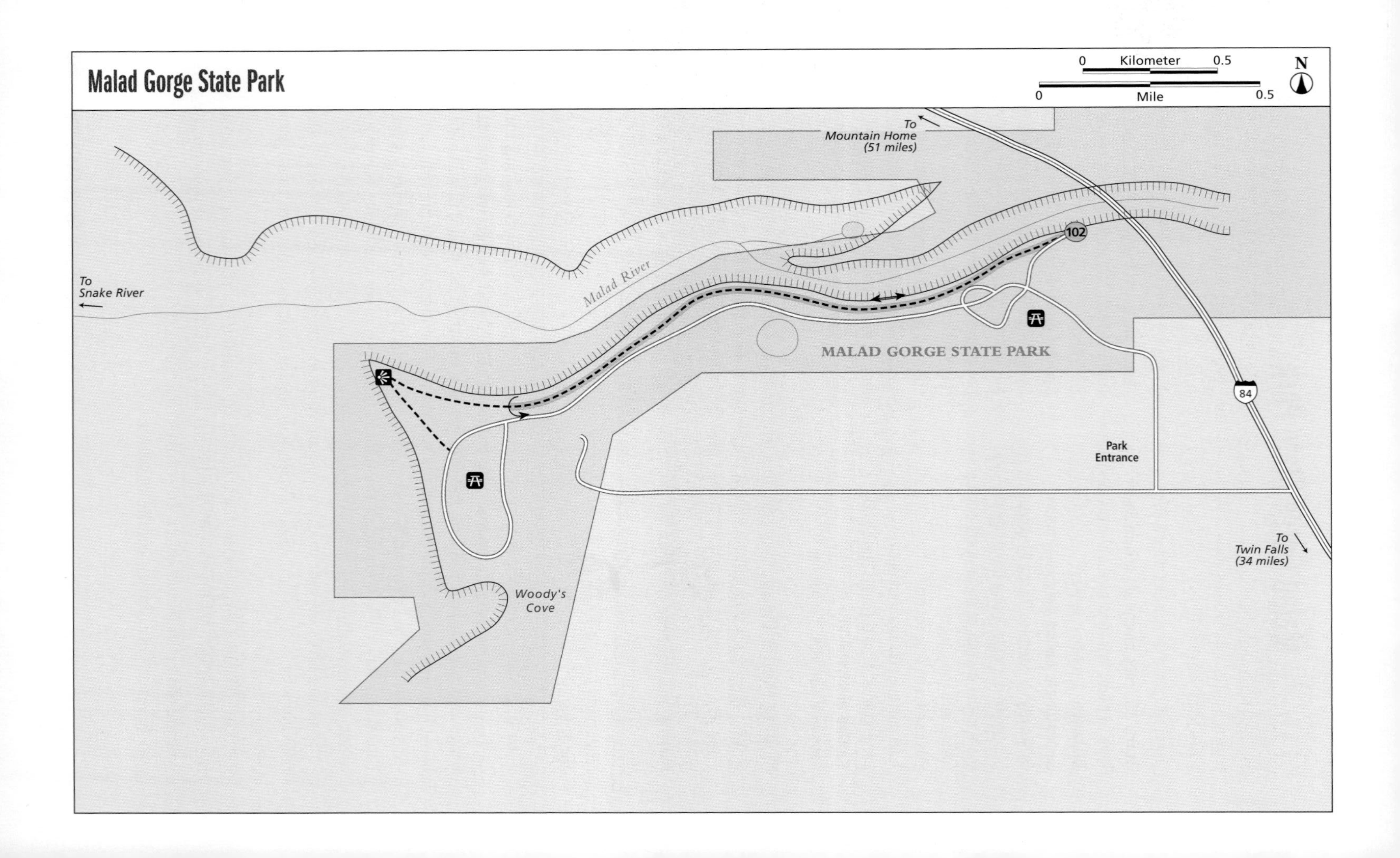
Malad Gorge State Park
0 Kilometer 0.5
0 Mile 0.5
N
To Mountain Home (51 miles)
To Snake River
Malad River
102
MALAD GORGE STATE PARK
84
Park Entrance
Woody's Cove
To Twin Falls (34 miles)

**South Rim:** This route looked more interesting and less dusty than the Devil's Washboard loop. Access to South Rim is via an informal trail that starts just behind (west of) the historic stone house. There is a somewhat intermittent trail along the south rim of the Malad Gorge, between the park scenic loop road and the rim, sometimes dangerously close to the rim.

During the first third of the hike, the canyon is narrow and abrupt. The scenery downstream is enhanced by a waterfall where an agricultural canal discharges over the rim. Just before the waterfall, beautiful springs emerge from near the base of the canyon, providing clear water, in marked contrast with the rest of the river.

*Malad George.* Photo by Ralph Maughan

Downstream from the springs, the middle third of the hike, the trail routes away from the rim, blocked by a long, deep crack where the canyon wall is slowly collapsing. This pristine canyon bottomland is occupied by a hydropowered diversion canal. The canyon then widens with a vast, basalt boulder field between the rim and the river.

The trail fades in the final third of the hike near the point where the Big Wood River flows out into the Hagerman Valley. The end is a rugged point with a fine view of the pastoral valley and Snake River below. From this point it is just over 0.25 mile cross-country and south through sagebrush to the road and Woody's Cove.

—Jackie Johnson Maughan and Ralph Maughan

## Miles and Directions

**0.0** Interpretative area and trailhead

**0.4** Springs

**1.0** Diversion flume

**1.8** Overlook into Hagerman Valley

**2.0** Woody's Cove

# Appendix A: Conservation Organizations and Resources

Boise Office
PO Box 844
Boise, ID 83701
(208) 345-6933
(208) 344-0344 (fax)
Street address: 710 North 6th Street
Boise, ID 83702

Committee for Idaho's High Desert
PO Box 2863
Boise, ID 83701
(208) 384-1715

For Wolves
www.forwolves.org

Friends of the Clearwater
PO Box 9241
Moscow, ID 83843
(208) 882-9755
www.friendsoftheclearwater.org

Greater Yellowstone Coalition
13 South Wilson, Suite 2
Bozeman, MT 59715-4610
(406) 586-1593
www.greateryellowstonecoalition.org

Hells Canyon Preservation Council
PO Box 2768
La Grande, OR 97850
(541) 963-3950
hellscanyon.org

Idaho Conservation League
www.idahconservation.org

Idaho Office
162 North Woodruff Avenue
Idaho Falls, ID 83401
(208) 522-7927

Idaho Rivers United
PO Box 633
Boise, ID 83701
(208) 343-7481
(800) 574-7481 (toll-free)
www.idahorivers.org

Ketchum Office
PO Box 2671
Ketchum, ID 83340
(208) 726-7485
(208) 726-1821 (fax)
Street address: 110 West 5th Street, Suite 201
Ketchum, ID 83340

The Nature Conservancy
www.nature.org

Roadless Land
www.roadlessland.org

Sandpoint Office
PO Box 2308
Sandpoint, ID 83864
(208) 265-9565
(208) 265-9650 (fax)
Street address: 102 South Euclid, Suite 207
Sandpoint, ID 83864

Sierra Club Idaho Chapter
PO Box 552
Boise, ID 83701
(208) 384-1023
www.idaho.sierraclub.org

Sierra Club Outing Department
85 2nd Street, 2nd Floor
San Francisco, CA 94105-3441
(415) 977-5630 (24-hour voice mail)
www.sierraclub.org/outing

The Lands Council
517 South Division Street
Spokane, WA 99202
(509) 838-4912
www.landscouncil.org

Western Watersheds Project
PO Box 1602
Hailey, ID 83333
(208) 788-2290
www.westernwatersheds.org

Wild Rockies
www.wildrockies.org
Wilderness Society, Idaho Office
710 North 6th Street, Suite 102
Boise, ID 83702-5544
(208) 343-8153
www.wilderness.org/idaho

Wildlands CPR is the only national conservation group in the United States that specifically targets off-road vehicle abuse of public lands and actively promotes wildland restoration, road removal, and the prevention of wildland road construction.
www.wildlandscpr.org

Wolf Recovery Foundation
PO Box 44236
Boise, ID 83711-0236
(208) 363-0203
www.wolfrecoveryfoundation.com

# Appendix B: Addresses, Land Management Agencies for Hike Information

*Boise National Forest*

Cascade Ranger District
PO Box 696
540 North Main
Cascade, ID 83611
(208) 382-7400

Emmett Ranger District
1805 Highway 16, #5
Emmett, ID 83617
(208) 365-7000

Idaho City Ranger District
PO Box 129
3833 Highway 21
Idaho City, ID 83631
(208) 392-6681

Lowman Ranger District
7359 Highway 21
Lowman, ID 83637
(208) 259-3361

Mountain Home Ranger District
2180 American Legion Boulevard
Mountain Home, ID 83647
(208) 587–7961

*Caribou-Targhee National Forest*

Ashton Ranger District
PO Box 858
46 Highway 20
Ashton, ID 83420
(208) 652-7442

Dubois Ranger District
PO Box 46
Dubois, ID 83423
(208) 374-5422

Island Park Ranger District
PO Box 220
3726 Highway 20
Island Park, ID 83429
(208) 558-7301

Montpelier Ranger District
322 North 4th Street
Montpelier, ID 83254
(208) 847-0375

Palisades Ranger District
3659 East Ririe Highway
Idaho Falls, ID 83401
(208) 523-1412

Soda Springs Ranger District
410 East Hooper Avenue
Soda Springs, ID 83276
(208) 547-4356

Teton Basin Ranger District
PO Box 777
Driggs, ID 83422
(208) 354-2312

Westside Ranger District
4350 Cliffs Drive
Pocatello, ID 83204
(208) 236-7500

*Clearwater National Forest*

Clearwater National Forest Supervisor's Office
12730 Highway 13
Orofino, ID 83544
(208) 476-4541

Lochsa Ranger District
502 Lowry Street
Kooskia, ID 83539
(208) 926-4275

North Fork Ranger District
12730 Highway 13
Orofino, ID 83544
(208) 476-4541

Palouse Ranger District
1700 Highway 6
Potlatch, ID 83855
(208) 875-1131

*Nez Perce National Forests*

Nez Perce National Forest Supervisor's Office
104 Airport Road
Grangeville, ID 83530
(208) 983-1950

Clearwater Ranger District
Route 2, PO Box 475
Grangeville, ID 83530
(208) 983-1963

Red River (Elk City) Ranger District
300 American River Road
Elk City, ID 83525
(208) 842-2245

Moose Creek Ranger District
Fenn Ranger Station
831 Selway Road
Kooskia, ID 83539
(208) 926-4258

Salmon River Ranger District
Slate Creek Ranger Station
304 Slate Creek Road
White Bird, ID 83554
(208) 839-2211

Powell Ranger District
192 Powell Road
Lolo, MT 59847
(208) 942-3113

*Hells Canyon National Recreation Area*

Riggins Office
PO Box 832
Highway 93
Riggins, ID 83549
(208) 628-3916

*Idaho Panhandle National Forests*

Idaho Panhandle National Forest Headquarters
3815 Schreiber Way
Coeur d'Alene, ID 83815
(208) 765-7223
www.fs.usda.gov/ipnf

Bonners Ferry Ranger District
Route 4, PO Box 4860
Bonners Ferry, ID 83805-9764
(208) 267-5561

Priest Lake Ranger District
32203 Highway 57
Priest River, ID 83856-9612
(208) 443-2512

Sandpoint Ranger District
1500 Highway 2, Suite 110
Sandpoint, ID 83864-9509
(208) 263-5111

St. Joe Ranger District
St. Maries Office
PO Box 407
St. Maries, ID 83861-0407
St. Maries Office (208) 245–2531
Avery Office (208) 245-4517
Clarkia Office (208) 245-1134

Coeur d'Alene River Ranger District
Fernan Office (208) 664-2318
Silver Valley Office (208) 783-2363

*Payette National Forest*

Payette National Forest
800 West Lakeside Avenue
McCall, ID 83638-3602
(208) 634-0700

Council Ranger District
PO Box 567
2092 Highway 95
Council, ID 83612
(208) 253-0100

Krassel Ranger District
500 North Mission Street
McCall, ID 83638
(208) 634-0600

McCall Ranger District
102 West Lake Street
McCall, ID 83638
(208) 634-0400

New Meadows Ranger District
PO Box J
3674 Highway 95
New Meadows, ID 83654
(208) 347-0300

Weiser Ranger District
851 East 9th Street
Weiser, ID 83672
(208) 549-4200

*Salmon-Challis National Forest*

Salmon-Challis National Forest Supervisor's Office
1206 South Challis Street
Salmon, ID 83467
(208) 756-5100

Challis–Yankee Fork Ranger District
HC 63, Box 1669
Highway 93
Challis, ID 83226
(208) 879-4100

Leadore Ranger District
103 Ranger Street
PO Box 180, Highway 28
Leadore, ID 83464
(208) 768-2500

Lost River Ranger District
716 West Custer
PO Box 507
Mackay, ID 83251
(208) 588-3400

Middle Fork Ranger District
HC 63 Box 1669, Highway 93
Challis, ID 83226
(208) 879-4101

North Fork Ranger District
11 Casey Road
PO Box 180
North Fork, ID 83466
(208) 865-2700

Salmon-Cobalt Ranger District
311 McPherson Street
Salmon, ID 83467
(208) 756-5200

Yankee Fork Ranger District
HC 67, Box 650
Highway 75
Clayton, ID 83227
(208) 838-2201

### *Sawtooth National Forest*

Sawtooth National Forest Supervisor's Office
2647 Kimberly Road East
Twin Falls, ID 83301-7976
(208) 737-3200

Burley Ranger District
3650 South Overland Avenue
Burley, ID 83318
(208) 678-0430

Fairfield Ranger District
PO Box 189
102 1st Street East
Fairfield, ID 83327
(208) 764-3202

Ketchum Ranger District
PO Box 2356
206 Sun Valley Road
Ketchum, ID 83340
(208) 622-5371

Twin Falls Ranger District
2647 Kimberly Road East
Twin Falls, ID 83301
(208) 737-3200

Minidoka Ranger District
2306 Hiland Avenue
Burley, ID 83318
(208) 678-0430

### *Sawtooth National Recreation Area*

Sawtooth National Recreation Area Headquarters (Sawtooth NRA)
5 North Fork Canyon Road
Ketchum, ID 83340
(208) 727-5000
(800) 260-5970 (toll-free)

Sawtooth National Recreation Area—Stanley Office
HC 64, Box 9900
Stanley, ID 83278
(208) 774-3000

### *Other Offices*

Bruneau Dunes State Park
27608 Sand Dunes Road
Mountain Home, ID 83647
(208) 366-7919

Craters of the Moon National Monument
PO Box 29
Highway 93 (18 miles west of Arco)
Arco, ID 83213
(208) 527-3257

Malad Gorge State Park
1074 East 2350 South
Hagerman, ID 83332
(208) 837-4505

Silent City of Rocks National Reserve
PO Box 169
Almo, ID 83312
(208) 824-5910

Bureau of Land Management (BLM)
Idaho State Office
1387 South Vinnell Way
Boise, ID 83709
(208) 373-4000

Owyhee BLM Field Office
20 1st Avenue West
Marsing, ID 83639
(208) 896-5933

Pocatello BLM Field Office
4350 Cliffs Drive
Pocatello, ID 83204
(208) 478-6375

Shoshone BLM Field Office
400 West F Street
Shoshone, ID 83352
(208) 732-7200

Upper Snake BLM Field Office
1405 Hollipark Drive
Idaho Falls, ID 83401
(208) 524-7524

Bruneau BLM Field Office
3948 Development Avenue
Boise, ID 83705
(208) 384-3344

Jarbidge BLM Field Office
2536 Kimberly Road
Twin Falls, ID 83301
(208) 736-2358

Four Rivers BLM Field Office
3948 Development Avenue
Boise, ID 83705
(208) 384-3347

Challis BLM Field Office
1151 Blue Mountain Road
Challis, ID 83226
(208) 879-6217

Cottonwood BLM Field Office
1 Butte Drive
Cottonwood, ID 83522
(208) 962-3782

Burley BLM Field Office
15 East 200 South
Burley, ID 83318

Salmon BLM Field Office
1206 South Challis Street
Salmon, ID 83467
(208) 756-5474

# About the Authors

Luke Kratz grew up in Pocatello and has been hiking in Idaho since he was very young. When he got his copy of the *Hiker's Guide to Idaho,* it was a new trail every weekend to explore and enjoy! He has degrees from Missouri State University and Idaho State University and has always been involved in environmental protection organizations. In addition to hiking and traveling he enjoys writing, recording, and performing music on piano and guitar. He currently lives near the Idaho border in Star Valley Ranch, Wyoming, where he has been teaching music for Lincoln County School District for the last eight years.

Ralph Maughan is a professor of political science and coauthor of the FalconGuide *Hiking Wyoming's Teton and Washakie Wilderness Areas*. He draws on thirty years of wilderness experience and leadership in such groups as the Greater Yellowstone Coalition, of which he was a founder.

Jackie Johnson Maughan is a writer and a university instructor of English. She has published two outdoor recreation books related to women and has compiled and edited *Go Tell It on the Mountain* (Stackpole Books), a book of essays by fire lookouts. Jackie was a fire lookout for four summers.